Performance and Fault Management

Paul L. Della Maggiora
Christopher E. Elliott
Robert L. Pavone, Jr.
Kent J. Phelps
James M. Thompson

CISCO SYSTEMS

CISCO PRESS

Cisco Press
201 West 103rd Street
Indianapolis, IN 46290 USA

Performance and Fault Management

Paul L. Della Maggiora
Christopher E. Elliott
Robert L. Pavone, Jr.
Kent J. Phelps
James M. Thompson

Copyright© 2000 Cisco Press

Cisco Press logo is a trademark of Cisco Systems, Inc.

Published by:
Cisco Press
201 West 103rd Street
Indianapolis, IN 46290 USA

Printed in the United States of America 1 2 3 4 5 6 7 8 9 0

Library of Congress Cataloging-in-Publication Number: 99-64089

ISBN: 1-57870-180-5

Warning and Disclaimer

This book is designed to provide information about **performance and fault management**. Every effort has been made to make this book as complete and as accurate as possible, but no warranty or fitness is implied.

The information is provided on an "as is" basis. The author, Cisco Press, and Cisco Systems, Inc., shall have neither liability nor responsibility to any person or entity with respect to any loss or damages arising from the information contained in this book or from the use of the discs or programs that may accompany it.

The opinions expressed in this book belong to the author and are not necessarily those of Cisco Systems, Inc.

Trademark Acknowledgments

All terms mentioned in this book that are known to be trademarks or service marks have been appropriately capitalized. Cisco Systems, Inc., cannot attest to the accuracy of this information. Use of a term in this book should not be regarded as affecting the validity of any trademark or service mark.

Feedback Information

At Cisco Press, our goal is to create in-depth technical books of the highest quality and value. Each book is crafted with care and precision, undergoing rigorous development that involves the unique expertise of members from the professional technical community.

Readers' feedback is a natural continuation of this process. If you have any comments regarding how we could improve the quality of this book, or otherwise alter it to better suit your needs, you can contact us through email at ciscopress@mcp.com. Please make sure to include the book title and ISBN in your message.

We greatly appreciate your assistance.

Publisher	John Wait
Executive Editor	John Kane
Cisco Systems Program Manager	Jim LeValley
Managing Editor	Patrick Kanouse
Acquisitions Editor	Kathy Trace
Development Editor	Laurie McGuire
Project Editor	Nancy Sixsmith
Technical Editors	Mark Basinski
	Bobby Krupczak
	Jim O'Shea
	Peter Welcher
Team Coordinator	Amy Lewis
Book Designer	Gina Rexrode
Cover Designer	Louisa Klucznik
Compositor	Steve Gifford
Indexer	Tim Wright

CISCO SYSTEMS

CISCO PRESS

Corporate Headquarters
Cisco Systems, Inc.
170 West Tasman Drive
San Jose, CA 95134-1706
USA
http://www.cisco.com
Tel: 408 526-4000
       800 553-NETS (6387)
Fax: 408 526-4100

European Headquarters
Cisco Systems Europe s.a.r.l.
Parc Evolic, Batiment L1/L2
16 Avenue du Quebec
Villebon, BP 706
91961 Courtaboeuf Cedex
France
http://www-europe.cisco.com
Tel: 33 1 69 18 61 00
Fax: 33 1 69 28 83 26

Americas
Headquarters
Cisco Systems, Inc.
170 West Tasman Drive
San Jose, CA 95134-1706
USA
http://www.cisco.com
Tel: 408 526-7660
Fax: 408 527-0883

Asia Headquarters
Nihon Cisco Systems K.K.
Fuji Building, 9th Floor
3-2-3 Marunouchi
Chiyoda-ku, Tokyo 100
Japan
http://www.cisco.com
Tel: 81 3 5219 6250
Fax: 81 3 5219 6001

Cisco Systems has more than 200 offices in the following countries. Addresses, phone numbers, and fax numbers are listed on the Cisco Connection Online Web site at http://www.cisco.com/offices.

Argentina • Australia • Austria • Belgium • Brazil • Canada • Chile • China • Colombia • Costa Rica • Croatia • Czech Republic • Denmark • Dubai, UAE Finland • France • Germany • Greece • Hong Kong • Hungary • India • Indonesia • Ireland • Israel • Italy • Japan • Korea • Luxembourg • Malaysia Mexico • The Netherlands • New Zealand • Norway • Peru • Philippines • Poland • Portugal • Puerto Rico • Romania • Russia • Saudi Arabia • Singapore Slovakia • Slovenia • South Africa • Spain • Sweden • Switzerland • Taiwan • Thailand • Turkey • Ukraine • United Kingdom • United States • Venezuela

About the Authors

Paul L. Della Maggiora, CCIE #1522, is a Technical Marketing Engineer for Cisco's Performance Design and Verification Center. He has also served as Escalation Engineer and NMS team lead for the TAC and Product Marketing Engineer since joining Cisco in 1994. For the past 10 years, he has worked as a network manager, network engineer, and network designer. Paul has a BS in Computer Science from the University of South Carolina.

Christopher E. Elliott, CCIE #2018, has 25 years experience in the networking industry, starting on the ARPANET. He currently works for the Cisco Systems TAC. For the last eight years he has concentrated on network management, including designing and managing a large network; writing network management applications, including a distributed SNMP polling system; and supporting users of network management applications. He is CCIE re-certified in ATM and LAN switching.

Robert L. Pavone, Jr., CCIE #1265, is a Network Auditor and Tools Consultant in the Net Tools Team at Cisco within the Customer Advocacy organization. He has been in the communications industry for the past 10 years, spending the last 6 years with Cisco. He has dealt with everything from configuring analog modems to troubleshooting complex customer IP networks. He is CCIE re-certified in ATM and LAN switching.

Kent J. Phelps, CCIE #2149, has over 15 years experience with information systems and communication networks. With Cisco Systems since 1996, he has concentrated for the past six years in network management and analysis. Kent has a BS in electrical engineering from the University of Florida.

James M. Thompson, CCIE #1758, has over 20 years experience in data and communications networking from working with the ARPANET and MILNET through support of customer networks with more than 10,000 routers. He is currently a High Availability Network Consultant with Network Supported Accounts at Cisco Systems.

About the Technical Reviewers

Mark Basinski, CCIE #4422, is a senior support engineer for Cisco Systems' Technical Assistance Center, specializing in network management products and issues since 1997. His previous experience includes stints as a software developer for telecommunications products and as a senior member of the Network Operations staff at the University of Arizona.

Bobby Krupczak was a co-founder of Empire Technologies and is a principal architect and developer of Empire's system and application management products. In addition to those duties, he also performed sales, marketing, and business development at Empire. Bobby has a Ph.D. in computer science with a focus on systems, networking, and telecommunications. Prior to Empire and graduate school, Bobby worked at NCR where he worked on network management and communication protocol development. He can be reached at rdk@empire.com.

Jim O'Shea, CCIE #1541, has been with Hewlett-Packard in a variety of network- and security-related positions for nearly 13 years. He currently is Operations Services Division R&D engineer and focuses on creating better tools to manage networks and enhance the overall security of the entire management environment. Previously, he was a Consultant in the Operations Services Centers, responsible for analysis of network data and aiding customers in decision making and investment allocation within their enterprise networks. Jim received a BS engineering in 1982 from Wayne State University.

Peter Welcher received his Ph.D. in mathematics from MIT in 1978 and then taught math at the U.S. Naval Academy. After 15 years he realized he liked computers and programming more. He switched to Chesapeake Network Solutions (then CCCI) in 1993 worked on some of the router CLI code that Chesapeake developed for Cisco Systems, Inc., and became a CCSI in 1994, a CCIE #1773 in 1996, and has taught a number of classes, including ones on the network management products CiscoWorks, CiscoWorks 2000, Netsys, and HP OpenView. Peter authors courses for CNS and Cisco Systems, Inc., and writes a monthly column for *CiscoWorld* magazine (back issues can be found at www.ccci.com).

Acknowledgments

No book is the sole effort its authors. This book is certainly no exception. We all would like to start by thanking our co-authors for helping us stick with the project.

The authors of this book would like to thank the following people (in no particular order) and places for their parts in helping to make this book happen:

Reviewers:

Mark Basinski, Cisco Systems

Bobbie Krupczak, Empire Technologies

Jim O'Shea, HP

Peter Welcher, CCCI

Anthony Edwards, Tavve Software

Technical contributors from Cisco Systems: Billie Ansell, Joel Dinkin, Srinivas Narayan, Anand Narwani, Dean Rogers, and Kris Thompson.

Cisco Systems contributors to the switch management paper, out of which this book and team of authors grew: Gerard Berthet, Mark Marsula, Dean McDaniel, Barbara Retzlaff, Johnnie Salim, and David Stiff.

We'd also like to thank:

Don Bowman, Cisco Systems, for showing us how to take it to the next level

Peter Fritz and Brad Kintner, Cisco Systems, for the use of the PDVC lab

Chris Mcgugan, Cisco Systems, for the use of his digital camera

Priscilla Oppenheimer, for use of her figures originally published in *Top-Down Network Design*

Places:

Cisco Systems, which provided many of the resources used to produce this book and without which this book would not have been possible—or necessary!

Indy 500 conference room—home away from home

China Garden, RTP, NC

Rudino's, RTP, NC

The pizza guy that we stiffed, without whom we wouldn't have found Rudino's

Finally, last, but not least, we'd like to acknowledge our Cisco Press editing team for their patience and not so gentle, but beneficial prodding: Alicia Buckley, Laurie McGuire, and Kathy Trace.

Personal Acknowledgments

Paul—First, to my beautiful wife Christine and kids, Max and Adam: thanks for your loving support and patience. To Mom, Dad, Bob, Marian, Jeff, Nick, Gladys, Nick III, Jeanette, Louise, Gina, and Suzie: thanks for encouraging me. To Bart, Tank, Eric, and Dean: thanks for being great friends and for your advise on this book. To Barry, Gabrielle, Gary, and Andy: thanks for helping me understand the book business and your support. Finally, thanks to Chris, Kent, Rob, and Jim for their extreme efforts and perseverance. We did it!

Chris—I would like to acknowledge, first and foremost, my wife, Carolyn Maynard. Both of my kids, Jeremy and Emily Ellison, showed amazing amount of patience throughout this endeavor. I'd also like to thank Jerry Saunders, US Library of Congress, for teaching me the joy of programming; and Vint Cerf, MCI, for taking me under his wing in the early days of TCP/IP. I would like to dedicate this book to my parents, who always encouraged me to explore.

Rob—I'd personally like to thank first and foremost my family: my wife Terri, and my children Lauren and Evan. They were very supportive of me and gave me the time, especially on weekends, to work on this book and to achieve this personal goal of mine. I'd also like to thank my manager at Cisco, Drew Powell, for giving me the time during the week to work on my chapters, especially as deadlines approached. He has continued to motivate and challenge me technically as well as personally.

Kent—I want to give my heartfelt thanks to my family—my wife Catherine and my two sons Julian and Samuel—for putting up with me while I spent all too many hours plinking away my laptop. Without their support my contribution to this book would not have been possible.

Jim—I want to thank my family from the bottom of my heart for the sacrifices they made on behalf of this book. My wife, Sarah, particularly deserves special thanks for putting up with my frequent absence from our life and my daughter Jamie who put off her scuba diving with me while I worked on the book.

Contents at a Glance

Contents

Preface

The server guys just came in the room and said it's your problem: the network is slow. People have been calling the help desk since early this morning (it's now lunch) complaining that the sales order application has been extremely slow or unreachable. You looked at your Network Management Station earlier on and noticed nothing particularly wrong. Yet, the server guys claim it's the network, not their servers.

Also seated in the room are your boss, her boss, and the boss's boss. Orders aren't being placed and everyone now seems to think the fault lies in the network; it's your problem now.

This is a common situation with people who design and manage networks. When something goes wrong, no matter what it is, the first reaction is to blame the network. Maybe the network is to blame for the problem, maybe it is not. To know for sure, you will need to have implemented some level of performance and fault management techniques that help you isolate the cause of a particular performance related problem.

The Meaning of Performance and Fault Management

Performance and fault management encompasses a wide array of tools and topics.

Traditionally, network management tools provided logs of network systems messages (traps, syslog) and colored statuses of each device and interface (green means up, red means down). While these systems were valuable for network troubleshooting, they did not report on or inform an engineer of the health of a network system until it actually went down.

Understanding the activities of a router or switch requires more than knowing whether the device is up or down. You probably want to know some of the following types of information:

- How much traffic is passing through the interfaces? Is it too much? How much is too much?
- Is the device CPU busy? How busy? How much is too much?
- Is the device running out of memory?

Aside from general device health, you probably also want to understand how characteristics of the network devices affect the reliability of the network. For instance, are too many people trying to dial into your ISDN router? Are too many collisions occurring on the Ethernet segments?

How much traffic is too much? How much is normal for the network? These are essential questions that network engineers and managers ask. Questions about how much is too much come into the Cisco TAC, and the answer, much to customer dismay, is "it depends."

Performance and fault management encompasses issues such as the following:

- You need to implement performance and fault management, but don't know where to begin.
- You find people are either ignoring the current network management tools or that the tools are providing useless information.
- Problem resolution times are taking considerably longer then they should
- Cisco publishes bunches of MIBs. Where do you begin?
- You need to select network management tools but aren't quite sure how to do so.

- You've been told to manage the Frame Relay connections for your 17,000 site network, but you aren't sure what characteristics to look at to determine whether the connections are working right.
- You want to make sure the network devices are healthy, but don't know what to measure or what is considered acceptable in making a determination.
- You don't know what traps are available or how to configure your NMS trap receiver to print the trap information in a human readable format.

This book addresses these issues. In addition, it teaches you how to navigate Cisco's documentation, MIBs, and management in order to keep up with the constantly changing pace of managing Cisco devices.

Approach and Objectives

This is not your typical network management book. Most network management books in the market provide an exhaustive explanation of SNMP and its protocols and reprint publicly available MIB documents. While the information is helpful for MIB developers and to some extent practitioners, these types of books tend not to be useful for someone needing to get their management up in a quick and useful manner.

Our experience, both from cases we received in the Cisco TAC and from consulting with customers, has revealed that these books are useful in academic and engineering settings. However, they provide little practical value for those who have to implement the concepts in their networks. The concepts are too general, and the authors typically do not offer experience based recommendations.

Performance and Fault Management departs from the pattern of generic SNMP reprint books. It is a detailed primer on setting up and reporting fault and performance management and a reference that helps Cisco customers cut through the complex management of Cisco devices. Each chapter provides explanations and data only for those things that we feel are important based on our experiences in implementing network management and our know-ledge of Cisco devices.

The objectives of this book are to

- Provide an overview of router and LAN switch operations in order to help the reader better understand how to manage the devices
- Provide guidance on the essential MIBs, traps, syslog messages, and show commands critical for managing Cisco routers and LAN switches, including undocumented IOS commands
- Describe techniques for implementing fault and performance management based on the authors' experiences
- Help Cisco customers understand and navigate the many MIBs and management interfaces of Cisco devices

After completing this book, you will be able to

- Design and implement fault and performance monitoring that will measure and report the effectiveness of your Cisco network investment.

- Generate reports and alerts that report network information and status to management and operations staff.
- Navigate Cisco's documentation and MIBs in order to determine what elements to manage for a given technology

Audience

Whether you are new to Cisco equipment or are a seasoned Cisco router jockey, this book will help you develop an effective network management strategy. It will also help you identify key MIB values, SNMP traps, syslog messages, and show commands that will assist you with analyzing faults and performance.

This book is intended primarily for network engineers and network management engineers who are responsible for the operation and timely resolution of problems in their corporate network. While this book applies generally to the management of Cisco networks, it was specifically written with medium to large enterprise networks (more than a hundred Cisco devices) in mind.

Specifically, the following people will benefit from this book:

- **Network operations managers** can develop an understanding of the process of crafting an effective network management strategy.
- **Network engineers** can obtain a detailed understanding of device and technology operations from a management perspective.
- **Network management teams** can use this book as a reference when crafting a network management strategy.
- **New Cisco customers** will learn about the management capabilities of Cisco devices and have a reference for quickly establishing management of the devices.
- **Customers of other network device vendors** can learn how to implement effective performance and fault management. Although some of the MIB references are Cisco specific, the concepts apply to all types of network routers and switches.
- **Network equipment sales engineers, consultants, and developers of commercial network management software** will find this book useful for identifying characteristics that must be monitored by or for their products.

The book assumes a working knowledge of network management and thus does not discuss basic network management methodologies. The references at the end of each chapter refer to useful publications that will assist readers who want to learn more about prerequisite topics.

Organization

The book is divided into four parts.

Part I: Foundations, Approaches, and Tools

Part I describes how to learn, document, and implement network management on your network. It is mainly for people who are getting started with their network management strategy and would like guidelines on how to assess the current state of the network and its management. It then explains how network managers can effectively implement monitoring and reporting to assist their teams.

The approach we take with Part I is to assume that you have inherited the network, its processes, and its policies in a certain state. You must first learn and document the network in its current state, and then you can investigate the policies and procedures.

This part of the book also helps existing network management teams determine how they can more efficiently work with the processes and tools they already have. Many engineers simply throw tools at the problem of network management only to find out that the tools alone do not improve their organization to understand network performance and react to network faults.

Please note that some of the techniques and approaches recommended in Part I are ideals that network managers should aim for but that may be difficult to attain. The difficulties arise because some of the concepts require customization with different tools and because some are resource-intensive to implement. A discussion of customization is beyond the scope of this book. However, we've provided sufficient detail for you to learn the necessary concepts and to work with your network management tool vendors or experienced network management implementor.

Part II: Managing Devices and Technologies

Part II is for all audiences and provides concise, detailed information on managing routers and switches. It includes coverage of device and system management, LAN management, and WAN management.

Each chapter provides information on how each of the technologies works, detailed explanations on what the authors consider the most important aspects to manage, and helpful reference to other data that may be useful to network management.

The authors feel that the objectives can be accomplished through conversational instruction using the following method:

1   Provide brief explanations of each of the manageable technologies. How can you determine what to monitor and set thresholds against if you do not understand the technologies you are trying to manage?

2   Recommend the top data variables to manage for a technology, providing all of the information that a network engineer will find useful when setting up fault and performance management. No ad-nausea reprints here; we provide you with the top items to watch for and point you to the MIBs posted on the web for more information.

Although some background and context is provided about devices and technologies, it is not the goal of these chapters to provide exhaustive architectural details. Rather, each chapter provides enough example/context information to support the discussion of SNMP MIB objects, SNMP traps, show commands, and syslog messages.

Throughout Part II there are many output Examples from show commands. The relevant lines of output have been annotated and cross-referenced to explanations that follow the Example. This includes the association of relevant SNMP MIB objects to show command output.

Part III: Optimal Management

With this part of the book, you will learn how to optimally configure your Cisco devices for management. Part III also provides a concise listing of frequently asked questions (and answers) that are addressed by this book.

- Chapter 18, "Best Practices for Device Configuration," explains how to enable network management capabilities in Cisco devices through the configuration of telnet access, loopback interfaces, NTP, SNMP, RMON, and syslog logging. For each of these technologies, real life configuration examples are given as well as explanations on how the techniques will help you manage your Cisco devices more effectively.

- Chapter 19, "Frequently Asked Questions," provides a list of questions and answers to the most commonly asked performance and fault management questions that are addressed by this book. All question/answer pairs refer back to the chapters and sections that provide more details on the topic. The inside front cover of the book provides a list of the questions addressed in this chapter.

Part IV: Appendixes

The appendixes provide additional information not found in the rest of the book, including

- Detailed information on how to find, understand, and select from among the Cisco MIBs and traps published on Cisco's website.

- Details on how to decode an ATM accounting file.

How to Use This Book

This book has been written to provide both instructional and reference information for the performance and fault management of Cisco devices.

Depending on your level of expertise with the management of Cisco devices, we recommend the following reading order:

- Look at the inside front cover for a summary of issues addressed by the book, and Chapter 19 for quick answers to frequently asked questions.

- If you are relatively new to network management or inexperienced with Cisco devices you should begin with Part I, which explains general techniques for auditing your existing network and implementing performance and fault management. Then, read Part III, which explains how to configure management on Cisco devices. Finally, look through Part II at the chapters that discuss the technologies found in your network.

- If you have expert-level knowledge of Cisco devices, read Chapters 4–7 to ensure that you are familiar with general fault and performance management techniques. Then read Chapter 18 to ensure your understanding of management configuration on Cisco devices. Finally, use Part II as a reference when determining which MIBs, traps, syslog messages, and show commands to use for your network.

- Sales engineers, consultants, and developers should read Chapter 18 to understand how to configure Cisco devices and then use Part II as a reference for which MIBs, traps, and show commands to use when managing fault and performance.

PART I

Foundations, Approaches, and Tools

Filled with tips and advice on designing and deploying effective fault and performance network management, Part I provides you with the background to understand the techniques and data presented in Part II. The tips and techniques were gathered from the authors' individual experiences as network managers, developers, network engineers, Cisco TAC engineers, and network management product managers.

Chapters 1–3 discuss techniques that should be considered and in place before implementing performance and fault management. These chapters describe the steps necessary to build a sound network management infrastructure, including:

- Auditing and documenting the existing network
- Baselining and reporting the performance of the existing network
- Creating a knowledge base for the storage of the elements that make up rules, policies, and service level agreements

Chapters 4–7 describe techniques useful for defining, collecting, and reporting network and network device performance and fault data.

- Chapter 4 discusses four areas of network performance: Availability, Response time, Accuracy, and Utilization.
- Chapter 5 introduces thresholding in which collected data can initiate events based on preset threshold values.
- Chapter 6 discusses events and how to integrate them into a fault environment. Once an event occurs, what do you do about it?
- Chapter 7 discusses network statistics and data manipulation. This chapter introduces the statistical methods and techniques typically used with network performance and fault related data.

Chapters 8 and 9 highlight the general protocols and tools that apply to the concepts in earlier chapters.

- Chapter 8 provides a brief overview of the technologies described and used in Part II. This includes SNMP, RMON, syslog, and Netflow.
- Chapter 9 highlights various fault and performance tools discussed in the book. Use this chapter to learn helpful criteria to consider when purchasing network management tools.

CHAPTER 1

Conducting a Network Audit

You bought this book to find out which management data to collect from the network, so why is the first chapter about audits and documentation? Simply put: You can't measure performance and watch for faults effectively without understanding where everything is and how it's connected. No matter how sophisticated the tools you purchase or build may be, the measures and alerts mean nothing without understanding how the network works.

Effective network management begins with a well-designed network. Unfortunately, most people do not have this luxury; if they do have network access, they usually cannot redesign the network to improve their ability to manage the infrastructure. Aside from simplifying the management, starting with good network design or improving existing network design facilitates simpler and quicker resolution of network problems.

In order to implement effective network management, you must begin by learning and documenting the network as it currently exists. This includes documenting the physical and logical makeup of the network and its components, the people involved and their responsibilities, and the processes in place (if any) to enhance and maintain the network. These are the steps that make up a network audit. This chapter describes the primary tasks that are useful for learning and documenting how the servers, network devices, and users are connected. By learning and documenting the physical connectivity and logical configuration of your network, you will simplify the troubleshooting process when problems arise. The resultant information provides the foundation and integrity necessary to proceed with the creation and seeding of the knowledge base described in Chapter 3, "Developing the Network Knowledge Base."

Although not an exhaustive study, this chapter covers the following topics:

- The purpose of network audits
- Why documentation is important
- Conducting a physical inventory audit
- Conducting a connectivity audit
- Conducting a process and personnel audit

The Importance of Network Audits

The purpose of a *network audit* is to accurately assess and document the current state of the network, its components, the people involved, and the human processes used. The audit, in effect, documents the purpose and priorities of the network. Without the audit, you must rely on people's memory, hearsay, and possibly out-of-date or inaccurately documented maps and databases.

Without proper documentation and understanding of how things change in the network, you cannot reliably deploy performance and fault network management. You must determine how all devices are connected to each other—both physically and logically—and where the network components are located. From this information, you can determine which devices, ports, and connections are important for the development of your performance and fault management strategy.

NOTE   When you are working with outside consultants for network design or management issues, the network audit should be the first action they initiate. Without understanding the components, people, and processes, an outside consultant cannot accurately determine the state of the network and develop a plan of action. Regardless of your company's level of documentation, the consultant must still verify that the information matches the physical reality.

Without a proper understanding of physical connectivity and the location of network components, it will take longer to isolate network problems and you stand a greater chance of mistakenly introducing faults into the network during moves, adds, and changes.

Although commercial auto-discovery and mapping tools do a good job of drawing logically connected networks, they cannot discover on which floor, building, desk, or closet the devices are located. Trace a cable under the floor or between closets at 3 a.m. and you'll never underestimate the importance of a physical map again!

When a portion of a network goes down or becomes unstable, troubleshooting the source of the outage is done through a process of fault isolation. During an outage or fault, network administrators work as quickly as possible to search out and isolate the source of the problem. In order to do so, they typically begin somewhere in the middle or at the edge of the affected area, and work to reduce the fault domain or area of affected devices. The goal is to get as much of the network operating around the fault domain as possible. With proper documentation, this goal is much easier to achieve. In addition, in a well-documented network, the network manager knows which applications and users are affected by a problem, and can proactively notify the user community.

In a poorly documented network, fault isolation becomes a game of finding a needle in the haystack. The goal of fault isolation is to reduce the affected area; how can you do so if there is no documentation? Some administrators resort to brute force by splitting networks in half or randomly plugging and unplugging connections until they narrow down the affected areas. This prolongs the time to resolution and increases the chance of introducing additional faults. It also frustrates and angers users (and your boss) as they witness flaky, intermittent service.

All in all, the inconvenience of maintaining useful network documentation will be most appreciated during outages.

If you have not previously documented your network as described in this chapter, you will need to begin the process by auditing the physical network and its connectivity. Through the audit, you will learn and document which devices are in your network, where they are located, how they are connected, and who is responsible for the device. This will be the starting point for your network documentation.

As part of the audit, you will identify those ports that are critical to the successful operation of the network. Critical ports tend to be those with routers, switches, hubs, servers, channel service unit/data service units (CSU/DSUs), and the key users (such as the CEO) connected to them.

Monitoring all ports and connections in a network can be overkill and cause over-management of the network. Monitoring generates traffic load on the network and sucks up network device resources (memory, CPU). Is it really necessary to monitor user ports? Probably not, although you may want to monitor the traffic performance on key user ports in order to use them as a baseline for their floor or workgroup.

TIP   If a device or port goes down and nobody cares, don't manage the port any longer. Manage only those devices and ports that are critical to the operation of the network.

In order to select which ports to monitor, you must know how your network is connected, both physically and logically. Without this information, the importance of a port cannot be determined. The network management infrastructure can become crippled with information from devices (such as user PCs) that have no impact on the operation of the network. You must determine where network devices and servers are located, how they are connected, and who is affected if they become slow or unavailable.

The Importance of Documentation

Unless you were lucky enough to build your network from the start, chances are that you inherited an "organically grown" network. Perhaps different independent networks were built years ago and subsequently connected to the corporate net, or different organizations have had control over parts of the network and turned over their control to your organization. Or perhaps your group has grown the network over the years but has not documented the changes. However your network has grown, trying to manage it without understanding where devices are and how they're connected can be extremely difficult.

Documenting and tracking the physical inventory and logical connectivity will not only simplify the task of implementing effective network management, but it will also greatly enhance the timeliness of problem resolution. With the network being the backbone of corporate data exchange, your group's timeliness in resolving network problems has the ability to affect the enterprise's bottom line.

If a financial firm loses the capability to trade stocks due to a network outage, not knowing where network devices are located and how they are connected ultimately translates into lost revenue for the company. Do you know how much money per hour of downtime your company loses with unplanned outages?

Documentation can be maintained on anything from scraps of papers and napkins to intricate database systems. Ultimately, however it's maintained, the documentation should communicate its contents clearly and should easily be shared by those who need the information. It must also be easy to update and modify by those who need to.

The ultimate test is at 3 a.m. when you are paged out of bed to determine why several buildings dropped off of the network. If you find yourself tracing cables and wondering whether a router is connected to the right switch despite your documentation, perhaps it is time to reconsider your documentation practices.

Please see Chapter 9, "Selecting the Tools," for more details on criteria for tools that can help you with documentation.

TIP	Effective and reliable documentation must contain the following traits:

- A consistent and integrated method for storing information, such as a database or spreadsheet.

- Non-intrusive processes surrounding the maintenance of the documentation. If the docs are too difficult to keep up-to-date, the documentation will be rendered useless.

- Easy online access to the documentation for those who need it. This includes viewing as well as updating the documentation.

- Automation (self-documenting) whenever possible. Automated data collection helps you keep your documentation up-to-date.

- Port standardization and interface description usage (discussed later in this chapter).

It is important to determine the usefulness of each form of documentation and compare it to the organizational cost (that is, the difficulty in maintaining it). Sometimes, organizations can get documentation paralysis in which the maintenance of a particular piece of documentation overweighs its usefulness. It tends to be a matter of trust with documents because after the users of a particular document or knowledge base find that the information is out-of-date or wrong, they lose trust for the information. And after a couple of attempts that result in the discovery of out-of-date information, the documentation will no longer be used.

Ultimately, there is a natural balance. Too much documentation is difficult to maintain and becomes useless. Not enough documentation results in not having information when you need it.

Part of maintaining accurate documentation is implementing automated methods for updating the information. For instance, in a network made up of Cisco devices, you can automatically discover and track physical connectivity between routers and switches by using the Cisco Discovery Protocol (CDP). Or, the location of Media Access Control (MAC) addresses can be tracked by querying the Content-Addressable Memory (CAM) tables from the LAN switches.

Unfortunately, there are preciously few tools that take advantage of this information to produce a Layer 2 topology. The CDP and CAM tables are available via SNMP, enabling you to build your own applications.

Some things cannot be automated, such as physical wiring termination. For those that cannot be automated, you should work to integrate the documentation of a change into the overall process of making the change.

Take the running of new cables between wiring closets as an example. As part of running the cables, labels that identify the source and the destination of the run should be created and attached to the wiring racks. In addition, labels that identify either end should be attached to the cables themselves.

Whenever a connection is physically modified, the change should be indicated in a knowledge base, which is discussed in Chapter 3, "Developing the Network Knowledge Base." Thus, the database becomes the source of connection information.

TIP   Following are some tips on tracking and documenting moves, adds, and changes. Although these tips describe the best possible tool scenario, they should be used as goals when building and buying software:

- Make changes electronically in a method that allows the change to be automatically documented when the change occurs. Examples include activating a previously unused switch port or switching a user to a different VLAN, and capturing the changes through syslog messages and SNMP traps.

- Integrate the change tools so they populate the knowledge base automatically.

- Integrate the change tools with a change management tool so overlapping or competitive changes are regulated and documented appropriately.

- Make sure that configuration changes can be tracked and logged. Using tools that track user configuration changes and enforce configuration policies will help you prevent and/or track unauthorized and mistaken changes.

Conduct a Physical Inventory Audit

The first step in a network audit is to identify physical network assets. The audit provides a nice side benefit because you can collect the device asset information. If your company requires the collection and reporting of asset information, you'll be able to do both with the same effort.

A physical inventory audit consists of the following:

- Documenting the wiring closet locations
- Documenting the wiring
- Documenting the network devices
- Documenting the servers
- Documenting the key users

Where Are Your Wiring Closets?

It's 2 a.m. and the network is down; do you know where your wiring closets are? Surprisingly, some enterprises would have to answer "no" to this question.

You must document the location of each wiring closet, lab, and raised floor area in which cabling terminates and network devices are located. This is an important step in documenting the network because knowing where the wiring closets are helps you determine where connections terminate. The documentation of wiring closets will become invaluable when fighting network problems and trying to isolate the source of a problem.

You should document the location of each wiring closet in two ways. First, develop and maintain a list of wiring closets that contains the following information about each location:

- Building, floor, and location
- Name of wiring closet
- Key or badge type of access
- Description of purpose (for example, server room, floor 2 wiring, or development test lab)

Second, obtain building engineering documents and mark up the wiring closet locations. By visually representing the wiring closets, such documents aid you in understanding the relationship of the wiring closets to each other.

TIP   Scan the plans or save them with a CAD system as JPEG files and put them on a secured website. Link them together so that a person can drill down. Starting with a map of the various corporate sites, drill down to a location, then a building, then a floor—and up pops the appropriate floor plans with the wiring closets highlighted. This procedure can help your operators or anyone else needing access to the wiring closets to quickly drill down and determine the location.

If you are not sure where each of the wiring closets are, this is a perfect opportunity to hunt them down and understand what state of disrepair they may be in. If you end up visiting each of the wiring closets in order to verify their location and purpose, use the opportunity to answer the question raised in the following section.

NOTE   While you're out inventorying the wiring closet, make sure you lock them down. It becomes an impossible task to maintain good documentation and integrity with the network when multiple groups of people with possible conflicts of interest have access to the wiring closet.

If someone walks in and moves cables around or switches off a device, you may be ultimately held responsible for their actions.

Where Are Your Wires?

You've got wiring closets spread all over the campus, perhaps all over the world. Fiber between floors, service provider demarcations, cables running under a bridge, copper running between wiring closets—all of these become indistinguishable when you are sitting in a wiring closet or computer center trying to isolate a problem. You must have and maintain accurate schematics of wiring termination and purpose.

The main purpose of a cabling audit is to ensure that connections run where you think they run. This is important when documenting the logical connections.

The easiest method to track connections is by implementing an organized labeling system in the wiring closet by labeling both ends of a cable with the same label. The label should clearly identify the source, destination, and purpose of the cable. Thus, when looking at a cable or a wiring rack, you can clearly understand the purpose and termination of the cable.

Select a Wiring System that Fits with Your Organizational Needs

There are plenty of vendors who offer organized wiring systems. The goal is to purchase racks that make it easy to snake wires to their connection points and contain labels identifying the wire's purpose or destination at the other end.

Rack systems provide multiple color labeling and connectors, allowing you to color-code the type of connection. For example, you may designate blue to represent servers, red to represent wiring closet connections, yellow to represent user connections, and so on. Using the colored wires that match the colored connectors allows for easy identification of a wiring mistake.

A poorly maintained wiring closet makes troubleshooting become more complicated than it need be. In Figure 1-1, cables are going everywhere (including on the floor), making it very easy to introduce more problems during troubleshooting.

Figure 1-1   *An Example of a Bad Wiring Closet*

Too frequently, network administrators have been shocked to find out that a connection is not what it seems. For example, what they thought was a connection to a new server was actually a redundant link to a switch that happens to have spanning tree turned off. The result: a bridging loop that may cripple the network.

There are standards for organizing wiring and wiring closets, such as structured tested cabling and wiring closet locations. You should review these standards and stick with those that work with you.

Finally, be sure to keep your wiring closets organized. The identification systems in place (such as color-coding) do no good if patch cables are hanging all over the place. Motivate the operators to keep clean wiring closets with cables tucked away properly and everything labeled appropriately. This will greatly simplify the identification of connections while troubleshooting problems.

If you haven't tracked physical connections or feel that the current documentation method is out-of-date, you will need to audit each wiring closet and trace where the wiring goes. This can be a tedious process, especially if you have no idea of the state of the cabling.

TIP   If you have a third party managing your cable for you, be sure that they maintain the labeling as they make changes. Build incentives into their contract, which are based on the cleanliness and accuracy of the wiring closet.

In addition to cleanly running and maintaining cabling, they should remove cables that run nowhere—that is, cables that once connected network devices that have been removed.

Figure 1-2 is an example of a typical floor wiring diagram.

Figure 1-2   *Example of a Floor Wiring Diagram*

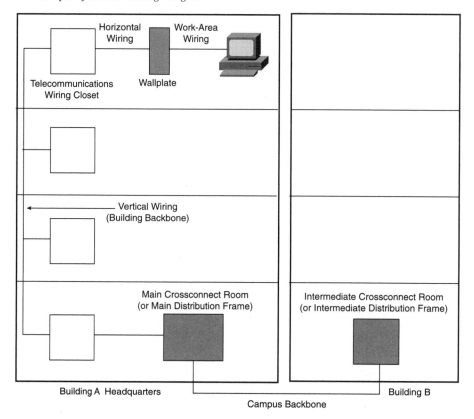

This example represents a typical floor wiring diagram in which the source and destination of wiring is documented. Table 1-1 is used to document the wiring locations and terminations.

Table 1-1   *Example of a Wiring Documentation Table*

Building Name:
Location of telecommunications closets:
Location of cross-connect rooms and demarcations to external networks:
Logical wiring topology (structured, star, bus, ring, centralized, distributed, mesh, tree, or whatever fits):

Table 1-1   *Example of a Wiring Documentation Table (Continued)*

Vertical Wiring:						
	Coaxial	**Fiber**	**STP**	**Category 3 UTP**	**Category 5 UTP**	**Other**
Vertical Shaft 1						
Vertical Shaft 2						
Vertical Shaft *n*						

Horizontal Wiring:						
	Coaxial	**Fiber**	**STP**	**Category 3 UTP**	**Category 5 UTP**	**Other**
Floor 1						
Floor 2						
Floor 3						
Floor *n*						

Work-Area Wiring:						
	Coaxial	**Fiber**	**STP**	**Category 3 UTP**	**Category 5 UTP**	**Other**
Floor 1						
Floor 2						
Floor 3						
Floor *n*						

Where Are Your Network Devices?

You've found and documented all of the wiring closets worldwide and implemented a well-documented wiring system with labels. Now, it's time to physically learn and document the location of the routers, switches, hubs, firewalls, and other network-related equipment that make up your network.

You should start by collecting and recording an inventory of the devices and their locations. At a minimum, you should track the following:

- Device name
- Device location

- Device IP address (the IP address to manage the device by)
- Person or group responsible for the device

Note that although manual tracking of information is quite common, you should consider automating the collection of device information and the association of that information with contact information. For instance, use a Layer 3 auto-discovery routine to generate the device list. Then, have a routine query each of the devices to obtain the MIB II sysContact and sysName variables to correlate the device name and contact name. The routine can then use the contact name to look up contact information (phone number, pager).

The final report would then include all information listed previously, but would be generated in an automated fashion. This will save time compared to the manual method as well as increase the chances that the documentation is up-to-date and accurate.

Table 1-2 is an example of a spreadsheet used to track network devices.

Table 1-2   *Example of a Spreadsheet for Tracking Inventory*

Device Name	Device IP Address	Device Location	Contact Information
bb-rtr-01	10.50.50.1	Building 4	Adam Smith
		Floor 2	999-999-9999
			800 page-me1
		Rack 3	afrog@fake.edu
bb-rtr-02	10.50.50.2	Building 4	Adam Smith
		Floor 2	999-999-9999
			800-page-me1
		Rack 4	afrog@fake.edu
bb-sw-11	10.50.50.102	Building 4	Gina Jones
		Floor 2	999-999-8888
			800-page-me1
		Rack 4	jedi@fake.edu

In Table 1-2, the network manager chose to track the minimum amount of device information, as well as the device contact. Typically, the contact is the person who should be called when an incident involves the owned device.

Collecting Other Inventory Information

Inventory information, such as serial number, firmware revs, hardware revs, software and configuration, is extremely useful for the network management process.

Serial numbers are particularly relevant for tracking your assets and working with Cisco support. Unfortunately, some devices do not provide their serial numbers via SNMP (this is mainly because of the way the devices are manufactured). When this is the case, you can set the serial number via SNMP by entering the **snmp-server chassis-id** command and providing the serial number.

Some companies have to march through their wiring closets and server rooms every couple of years to document devices for asset tracking purposes. This usually involves verifying that each device has an asset tracking "brass tag" on it and that the equipment is where it was thought to be.

If this is your experience, you should consider purchasing or developing software that automates the collection of this information. Cisco and other vendors provide software that performs this function.

Where Are Your Servers?

Tracking the location of shared servers and how they are connected into the network is just as important as tracking network devices. Too often, when a user complains of slow response time, the server support teams point the finger at the network support team. By knowing how servers and key applications connect into the network, you will be able to determine definitively whether the source of a slow response problem, for example, is the network or a device connected to it.

Using the methods described in the previous sections, you should document where the servers are physically located and how they connect back to their associated switches or hubs. Server types include the following:

- File and print servers
- Mainframes
- Network infrastructure servers such as DNS/DHCP servers
- Corporate web servers
- Any other shared devices that are considered critical to a particular operation

Table 1-3 illustrates a server tracking spreadsheet.

Table 1-3 *Example of a Server Tracking Table*

Device Name	Device IP Address	Device Location	Switch	Switch Port	Contact Information
mail-02	10.29.30.2	Building 4 Floor 2 Rack 3	Ser-sw-01	4/2	Adam Smith 999-999-9999 800-page-me1 afrog@fake.edu
mail-03	10.29.30.3	Building 3 Floor 2 Rack 1	Ser-sw-01	5/2	Suzie Q 999-999-8888 800-page-me1 suzieq@fake.edu
dns-02	10.40.44.2	Building 3 Floor 2 Rack 1	ny-sw-07	2/7	Adam Smith 999-999-9999 800-page-me1 afrog@fake.edu

Documenting the servers, as shown in Table 1-3, is important when troubleshooting. It also makes a handy reference when performing administrative tasks on the servers.

You may consider working with the server administrators to develop a questionnaire that identifies relevant information concerning each server that would help to understand the server and its application's availability. Examples include the documentation of the following:

- How the server is configured
- What applications run on the server
- What group or business unit owns the server
- Preventive maintenance and backup schedules.

By documenting and keeping accurate the server information, your operations staff will be able to distinguish between planned maintenance and unplanned outages. The server administrators may never offer thanks, but you will impress them when your network documentation actually helps them do their job.

Where Are Your Key Users?

For larger organizations, it can become burdensome to track every network connection for every user. Each managed connection requires a bit more hard disk space and network bandwidth. Only those ports that are considered business-critical should be monitored. This avoids filling event logs with link-down messages when users turn their PCs off for the day. Additionally, monitoring that many ports will generate reams of data that will probably not be used and can complicate the reporting process.

Network performance and server access for a user or group of users can be inferred by measuring the availability and performance of the connecting network devices and servers involved. This conserves the amount of polling to the network devices (because information for every hub or switch port will not be generated) and considerably cuts down the amount of stored data to process.

However, from a management perspective, monitoring certain key users may still be important. It can be helpful to identify a single user out of a group in order to measure their network connectivity and performance. The information from the single user can then be used to infer performance for the rest of the group. For instance, you may choose to monitor the network port for named users from individual groups in order to use the port as a gauge for the availability of the network for the entire group.

It may also make political sense to monitor the ports of certain executives (or "mahogany row") to ensure that you catch performance problems before they occur. With both fault and performance monitoring, it is usually in the network manager's best interest to ensure that the boss's connection is running smoothly. This may seem sneaky or underhanded (it is), but it generally ensures that the executive's view of the network (and, therefore, your company's investment in the network) is as fast and clean as the network infrastructure. You do not want the VP of Sales who is responsible for your network's funding to call in a network down or performance problem with their connection.

You should never sacrifice the performance and availability of network services for a group of people in order to provide greater-than-ordinary access to an executive. Or as Spock once said, "The needs of the many outweigh the needs of the few or the one."

NOTE   Sometimes, catering too much to the executive level can backfire. It may be advantageous to have certain executives experience network problems, as felt by the majority users, in order to gain budget. If this is the case, let them feel your pain!

Conducting a Connectivity Audit

Understanding how devices are logically and physically associated with each other is the next step of a network audit. Without tracking this information, you can never be sure what the true source of traffic to a device can be. It makes a huge difference whether traffic coming into a switch is from a server, user, or another switch. When deciding which ports to monitor in the network, you may mistakenly choose not to monitor a particular port because you thought it was a user port, when in fact it was the mainframe connection.

Unfortunately, after the audit is complete, you must maintain the currency of the documentation. The nature of business is that people move (and so do their connections), devices move, and networks undergo change. As a result, the documentation will be good as long as it is accurate. As soon as its accuracy declines, people will learn not to trust the information and eventually find other methods to keep track of network connectivity. Most of the time, the alternative method is guesswork, which leads to unnecessary outages due to mistakes.

Connectivity maps tend to be the most-used pieces of documentation with network operations. Therefore, it is important to integrate appropriate maintenance of the information within the framework of work. Don't let the information get out-of-date.

Documenting network connectivity consists of the following:

- Standardization
- Layer 2 Automation
- Layer 3 Automation

Standardization

Standardization involves setting up standard methods for naming, connecting devices, and locating equipment. Develop a naming scheme that will allow people (and automated tools) to quickly identify the type and use of a device. Use DNS names, hostnames, and interface descriptions to implement the naming. Interface description usage is especially helpful because the description can be obtained both from the device configuration file as well as SNMP.

Another form of standardization involves consistently using physical ports on devices to identify the type of device connected. For instance, the first port of the first card on a Catalyst 5000 could be used exclusively for connecting building routers.

Figure 1-3 provides an example of port standardization. In this case, port 1/1 is used for connection back to the backbone router, whereas port 1/2 is always used to connect to a redundant switch.

Figure 1-3   *Example of Port Standardization*

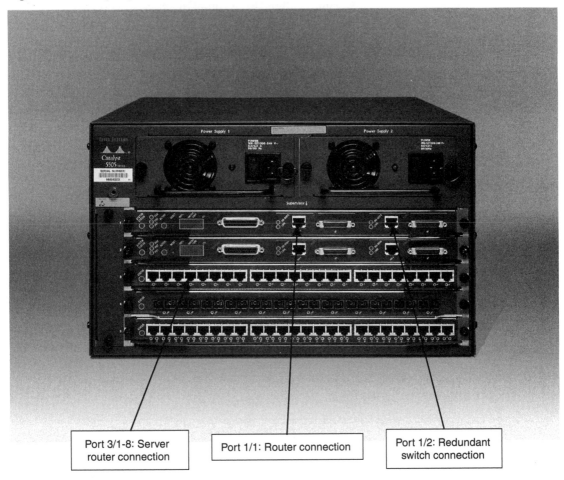

Port 3/1-8: Server router connection

Port 1/1: Router connection

Port 1/2: Redundant switch connection

You should also indicate the purpose of the port in the configuration of the port name or interface description. For example, the switch in Figure 1-3 might have port names such as *bb-rtr-2* for port 1/1 and *redun-flr1-sw-2* for port 1/2.

Finally, you can standardize on IP address assignment. For instance, for each subnet, the following host portions would be reserved:

- .1–.9 are reserved for routers, switches, and RMON probes
- .10–.20 are server addresses

So, if you see a problem with an address such as 172.26.10.6, you would know that it is a router, switch, or RMON probe, as opposed to a user workstation or server.

Documentation Using Data Exchange

Network administrators typically begin documenting physical network and connection information using spreadsheets. With spreadsheets, it's quite easy to quickly create something for tracking IP address assignments, wiring schemes, and just about anything else. Spreadsheets are quick and easy to set up, but do not work well when trying to build an interconnected and automated knowledge database.

If you determine the need to move beyond spreadsheets, you should consider software built upon a relational database that will allow the tracking of assets and how they're connected. Chapter 3, "Developing the Network Knowledge Base," describes the selection and building of a knowledge database.

Regardless of your approach, you should strive to implement a software solution that can integrate with other database systems such as your network monitoring, element management, and HR database systems (for contact information). Data exchange among various systems will allow the presentation of a more unified system to its users.

Layer 2 Connectivity

The next stage of a connectivity audit involves learning and documenting the physical relationships between devices. In this context, the physical relationships include the following:

- The physical locations of the devices
- How the devices are connected together
- The name of one device's port that connects to the name of its neighbor's port (for example, switch 1 port 2/1 connects to switch 2 port 1/1)
- Redundant paths (for example, HSRP router peers and redundant bridged paths, port channels)

Network management software from Cisco and other vendors provides Layer 2 discovery in which given a particular switch, Layer 2 and physical relationships between switches and routers can be discovered. The software can be used to seed your documentation with the current connectivity of devices, which generally requires the use of proprietary protocols. This is because there is no standard method for network devices to learn and report their Layer 2 neighbor relationships.

With Cisco devices, the Cisco Discovery Protocol (CDP) is used. CDP runs on each Cisco device and allows it to track those Cisco devices connected off of each of its ports. CDP works well in an all-Cisco network for documentation and troubleshooting, but becomes less useful in a multi-vendor network because non-Cisco devices do not participate in CDP, and thus will not be known by their neighbor.

Figure 1-4 compares the CDP discovery of Cisco devices with a Cisco and a non-Cisco device in-between. If a Catalyst 5000 connects two Cisco routers, a CDP discovered map would display the proper relationship. However, if two Cisco routers are connected by a hub or switch from another vendor who does not participate in CDP, the map will simply display the routers as directly connected without a switch in-between.

Figure 1-4   *CDP Discovery with a Cisco Switch and a Non-Cisco Switch*

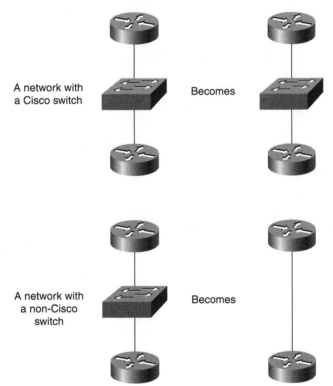

A CDP discovery application generally requires the specification of a starting, or seed device. The seeding involves manually entering a device name or IP address, community strings, and possibly Telnet passwords for each device of interest. This provides the auto-discovery routine with enough information to be able to interrogate the device for more information. The downside of this approach is that if devices are swapped out, moved around, or reconfigured, the changes must manually be tracked.

Given the seed device, the application queries the device's CDP neighbor table. Once discovered, the application can continue to track the changes that occur in the network. The discovered network can then be displayed or printed in map form.

The map displays the physical connectivity relationship between network devices. For each device, there is a line that connects to each of its physically adjacent network device peers.

Figure 1-5 provides an example of a map that was discovered using CDP. Notice that the map is able to display the Layer 2 and Layer 3 relationships of Cisco devices.

Figure 1-5 *Example of a Hypothetical Map Discovered Using CDP*

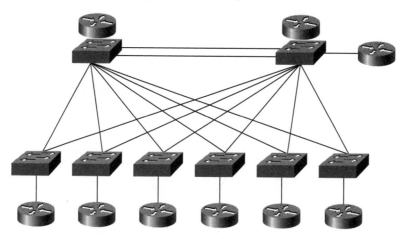

By using CDP, the application can determine how each device is physically connected, down to the port/interface number. Unfortunately, auto-discovering the physical relationships among multi-vendor networks is considerably more difficult because of the complete lack of standard neighbor discovery protocols.

Cisco has submitted the CDP standard to the IETF.

Layer 3 Connectivity

Unlike physical connectivity, Layer 3 connectivity is easier to auto-discover and map. This is mainly due to public domain methods and MIBs to collect the necessary information.

Logical connectivity maps demonstrate the distribution and relationship of network layer addresses. There are multiple methods for documenting logical connectivity (as mentioned for physical connectivity), including auto-discovering network management software, spreadsheets, and databases.

The data/reports should then be made available to those who need it. You could generate reports or capture screen shots and place them on an internal web server. Or you could simply print them out and distribute. (Don't forget to date them so people know whether they've got the latest version.)

In addition, DNS and DHCP servers can be used to capture and enforce the distribution of addressing. Network management products that auto-discover logical networks can also be used as reference documentation.

TIP

Never allow network devices to dynamically learn their network addresses. You should always assign a static address so that the device is definitively known by that address.

Automatic discovery of logical connectivity is relatively commonplace in today's network management tools. By parsing through each router's routing table, an auto-discovery routine can determine the neighbor router for each learned route. The routine then can query the routing table from the neighbor and discover the neighbor's neighbors.

TIP

You can take certain preventive steps to help auto-discovery routines more accurately discover your network and in general provide you with a cleaner network to manage:

- Ensure that the network management software is installed with the latest patches. This will help prevent bugs that may exist with the base release of the software.

- Ensure that the IP addresses for each network device are consistently and appropriately named across your DNS servers. Problems can arise when two DNS servers refer to the same IP address with different names. Also, problems can arise when an IP address has multiple names associated with it, the reverse lookup name doesn't match the forward lookup name, or finally two IP addresses are associated with the same name. Ensure that there are no duplicate IP addresses in the network. This situation, aside from causing more general connectivity issues, causes difficulty for network management software. Software vendors must take special cases into consideration when writing their software (for example, fault-tolerant features such as HSRP).

- Use consistent SNMP community strings across all devices and network management software. When the strings vary from device to device, some network management software might not be capable of handling the differences. Some network management software might have to wait for the use of the first incorrect community string to time out before trying the second correct community string. This causes unnecessary delays. Inconsistent community strings occur frequently when different groups in an organization manage different types of devices.

There are third-party tools available that allow you to draw the network connectivity as it makes sense to your organization. One method for mapping the logical network is to draw maps that display the physical network and identify the IP addresses and networks between network devices. You may also choose to incorporate connecting port and server information as well. You may also choose to store MAC addresses in the system.

Typically, hybrid maps will evolve in which logical and physical information is displayed together. This is the kind of information that people will print out and store in their notebooks or pin up on the wall. Figure 1-6 provides an example of a hybrid map.

Figure 1-6   *Example of a Hybrid Connectivity Map*

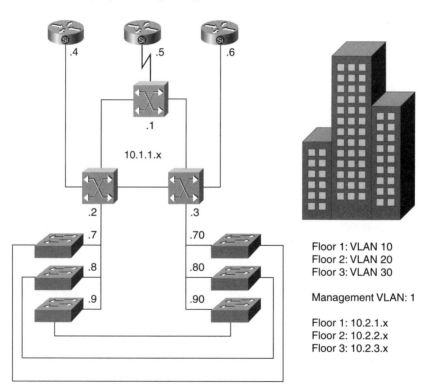

In this map, notice how physical connectivity, physical device traits, logical addressing, and VLAN information are displayed on the same map. Notice the following:

- The IP addressing is indicated for each of the network interface.

- A picture of a building provides a quick visual cue that we are talking about the building network infrastructure versus a floor or campus.

- The pictures of the devices themselves provide visual cues as to the type of device.
- VLANs are indicated by color, thereby weaving in the Layer 2 element of the topology.

Who Is Responsible for the Devices?

For larger organizations, tracking-device responsibility is the next step in a network audit. Typically, this type of tracking involves matching a device name or device type with a particular person or group. Some companies take this to the next step by linking the person or group with an HR database, and thus being able to associate a device with the location, phone, and beeper of responsible parties.

Tracking device responsibility becomes important when determining what types of performance reporting to produce and who should have access to the reporting.

Process Analysis

The final step of conducting your audit is process analysis. Process analysis means learning the various processes used to design, maintain, and troubleshoot the network. By understanding how things get done in your organization, you will be able to more effectively make process changes to help document your network.

Specifically relevant to this chapter, the following will help determine how effectively you can maintain the information gathering:

- Is there a change control process? If so, is it adhered to?
- How does each form of documentation get updated?
- How does a fault get created and tracked?
- How are the causes of outages determined and documented?
- How is customer satisfaction tracked?

The study of organizational processes is not for the faint of heart. There are plenty of resources and consultants available to assist you with this process. Kornel Terplan provides an excellent discussion on process analysis for a network management organization in *Benchmarking for Effective Network Management* (see "References").

Summary

You must first learn and document your network before introducing performance and fault management. Tracking and documenting network devices and their connectivity is vital when analyzing performance data, as well as during fault isolation.

When determining what and how to document, be sure to track the information in a timely and correct manner. Otherwise, the documentation will become less reliable over time, and it will cause operators to look elsewhere for their information.

Understanding device ownership and processes in place to manage leads to the effective implementation of low-impact and maintainable documentation.

After you have documented the network as described in this chapter, you will be prepared for the next chapter, "Policy-Based Network Management," in which you conduct a baseline analysis of the network.

References

Books

Leinwand, A. and K. Fang Conroy. *Network Management: A Practical Perspective.* Reading, MA: Addison-Wesley, 1996.

Stallings, W. *SNMP, SNMPv2, and RMON: Second Edition.* Reading, MA: Addison-Wesley, 1996.

Terplan, Kornel. *Benchmarking for Effective Management.* New York, NY: McGraw-Hill, 1995.

Terplan, Kornel. *Communication Networks Management.* Upper Saddle River, NJ: Prentice Hall, 1992.

Paper

Berthet, Gerard and Paul Della Maggiora. "Cisco Network Monitoring And Event Correlation Guidelines." *Cisco White Paper*, 1998.

Internet Resource

Cisco Discovery Protocol MIB

http://www.cisco.com/public/mibs/v2/CISCO-CDP-MIB.my

CHAPTER 2

Policy-Based Network Management

Routers have become quite complex when compared to their original task of simply routing. To name a few features: routers now provide QoS, firewall, packet-encryption, tunneling, filtering and web-caching capabilities. These features require that multiple routers be configured similarly in order to be able to deliver a consistent level of capabilities. If QoS packet coloring and queuing features, for example, are not implemented consistently through your network, packets will not be colored and queued similarly as they travel through the network.

Likewise, Layer 2 LAN switches have become more complex since their original bridging intentions. Some Catalyst switches now make forwarding decisions based on Layer 3 network and Layer 4 transport portions of a packet. Consistent implementation across your network of features, such as portfast/uplinkfast/backbonefast, dynamic port VLAN membership, Layer 3 protocol filtering, and QoS becomes increasingly difficult.

What these router and switch features provide, though, is the capability to control how traffic is passed through the network. Time-sensitive applications such as voice over IP and video require that packets make it to their destination on time. Additionally, network managers want to limit bandwidth for some applications (such as file transfers and backups) in order to let other traffic through.

Unfortunately, configuring these features and determining whether they actually do what you configured them to do can be difficult. Also, as configuration changes take place in the network and new applications are introduced, previous network device configurations may no longer meet their original objectives.

Traditionally, the configuration of router or switch features has been done on a device-by-device basis. If you wanted to restrict access to various parts of a network to a particular group, you had to configure the access lists from the device command line for each device that the group's traffic may traverse.

More recently, network management tools have shifted (or attempted to shift) their focus away from device-centered management to *network-centered management* (also called *policy-based management*). This chapter discusses three areas of policy-based management that pertain to the fault and performance management of your network:

- Defining network policies

- Baselining the network to determine network policy suitability
- Using service level agreements to measure and report on the effectiveness of policies

The chapter concludes with an example scenario in which these aspects of policy-based management are applied to a network.

An Overview of Policy-based Management

Policy-based management involves the following:

- Developing a set of policies (rules) that describe the desired network configuration.
- Baselining your current network. The baseline data is used to confirm that the network is capable of handling a particular policy, and for other tasks such as long-term planning.
- Using tools that translate policies into individual device-configuration changes. These configuration changes can then be applied to the affected devices.
- Reporting on whether the policy is being met. Whether the policy was not implemented correctly or a subsequent change undoes a previously implemented policy, you need a method to validate that things work as you expected. This validation is achieved with service level agreements (SLAs).

Although the practice of defining computing policies has been around for decades, the idea is relatively new with distributed networks. Not until recently have networking technologies become sophisticated enough to implement, enforce, and report on policy-related functionality.

Voice and video over packet networks have driven the need for QoS, which in turn has driven the need for policy-based management tools. QoS can be difficult to implement and maintain across large numbers of switches and routers. Policy-based management tools can simplify the consistent implementation and management of QoS-related features.

NOTE	Policy-based management does not necessarily simplify the task of network-wide device configuration and validation. The configuration changes that policy software make to network devices can be quite complex and possibly destructive to the normal operation of the network. Before using policy-based configuration tools, you should learn the underlying technologies the tool configures on the devices.
	At the time of this writing, few policy-based tools have been released, partly due to the complexity of developing such tools and partly due to their potentially destructive nature to networks.

Defining Network Policies

Policy-based networking is a recent approach to network configuration that transcends the traditional command line by converting business-related policies into network-configurable commands. The technology underlying the policies is generally nothing new: access lists, queuing mechanisms, and network protocols.

However, policy-based networking adds a level of abstraction to the typical command-line approach to configuration. It involves describing a policy in a human-readable form and using network management software to translate the policy into router and switch commands.

The strength of this approach is the capability to define a central set of policies and distribute them to affected routers and switches. It eliminates some of the complexity and chance of error involved in managing configurations on a device-by-device basis. Policy-based networking also hides implementation differences between different devices.

As an example, let's say you want to implement QoS in your network. For all user switch ports, you want to set the IP type of service (ToS) field to equal zero by default. Zero is the lowest ToS value and thus will be treated with the least priority in a QoS enabled network. This is to protect against users that try to increase the ToS field for traffic coming from their workstation.

So the written policy may read as follows:

For all switched user ports, assign lowest priority to traffic by default.

However, to implement this policy, different commands must be given, depending on what type of Catalyst switch is to be configured. It means setting the ToS equal to zero for all IP packets. Also, you will need to know which ports are considered "user ports." What applications will cause the ToS to be set to something other than zero?

Understanding the components that make up a policy is the key to writing clear, configurable policies. A policy describes an expectation from a part of the business. You must learn the business needs that drive the success of the network.

Communication and Network Policies

When articulating policies, you should do so from the user or network consumer's point of view. Latency, utilization, and response times mean very little to non-network personnel. From their perspective, an application must be available when they need it and at a speed that does not hinder their ability to do their work.

For most companies, business requirements are vague or unspecified. The expectation may simply be that the network "runs" whenever somebody wants it. In this case, you should determine what you feel accurately reflects their needs. Doing so will help lead toward stronger policies that can then be reflected in service level agreements, which will be discussed later in this chapter.

Importance of Open Communication with Users

When you set expectations honestly and in layman's terms, your user community will better understand what to expect from the network and any limitations that may occur due to the current network design.

For instance, suppose that your user community considers a particular application business-critical and requires that it be available 24 hours a day, seven days a week. However, when conducting a network audit (as described in Chapter 1, "Conducting a Network Audit"), you discover that certain key connectivity points to the application's server contain no redundancy. You feel that with the current design you cannot reliably deliver around-the-clock availability.

Rather than hoping that the network doesn't break, it is better to communicate the network vulnerability and present alternatives. This communication enables you to argue effectively that better service requires a larger budget and empowers your users by helping them understand the very real business issues.

Converting Policies into Technologies

After you collect the user community needs, you must convert them into distinct policies that together describe the network portion of the business requirement. Although the policies should be written in layman's terms, the actual elements that make up the policy should be written as concrete, measurable data that can be collected.

Part of the policy is to identify the configuration changes that must take place in order to condition the network to implement the policy. Although outside the scope of this book, configuration changes include the commands that must be run to implement a particular technology, such as QoS or encryption. The value of policy-based configuration software is its capability to let you define a policy that translates into configuration changes on affected devices.

The other part of defining policies is identifying the data that can be used to verify successful and effective policy implementation. This is the process of identifying the collectable data that will reflect your policy, such as SNMP variables and **show** commands. What can you measure and report on that reflects the success or failure of the business requirements? What data can you observe that will allow you to spot a policy-violating problem before or as it happens? How do you know that a newly configured policy actually does the job?

The network management must be designed to report on the appropriate information that allows the detection of policy violations or failures when they occur. Configuring, enforcing, and reporting network-related information in terms of business policies is the art of the network manager, and, frankly, what makes network management interesting.

Suggesting policies that don't reflect the true nature of what the network can deliver will only result in improperly set expectations. A baseline analysis of your current network will help you determine how to draft effective policies, given your current network performance.

Network Baselining

To determine whether a network can deliver a particular policy, you should measure the network's current performance. This process is called *baselining*, whereas the process of interpreting the data is called *baseline analysis*. Baselining allows you to discover the true performance and operation of the network in terms of the policies that you've defined. It is an attempt to determine what is "normal" so that you know when an event is abnormal.

After identifying data of interest for a policy, baselining allows you to take a snapshot of the current state of those variables throughout the network. Baseline analysis leads to an understanding of what service levels can actually be achieved.

How does the network perform day to day? Where are the under- and over-utilized areas? Where are you seeing the most errors? What thresholds should you set for the devices you plan to monitor? Can the network deliver the identified policies? Conducting a baseline analysis of your network also allows you to measure and answer these types of questions.

The purpose of conducting a network baseline is to measure the performance and availability of critical network devices and links, and compare them over time. The baseline allows a network manager to determine the difference between abnormal behavior and "business as usual." It also provides insight into whether the current network design can deliver required policies and SLAs.

NOTE   There is a plethora of tools to choose for your baseline analysis. Chapter 9, "Selecting the Tools," identifies the criteria to use for selecting tools and discusses whether to build a tool yourself or buy it.

Generally, the tool that you plan to use for your day-to-day performance monitoring will suffice as a baseline tool. Be sure that you can segregate the baseline data from the day-to-day monitored data and that you have the ability to store the baseline data over long periods of time.

The collected data will reveal the true nature of congestion or potential congestion in the network. It may also reveal areas in the network that are underutilized. Analysis after an initial baseline tends to reveal hidden problems and quite often leads to network redesign efforts based on quality and capacity observations.

Another reason for conducting a baseline is that no two networks operate or behave the same way, so books such as this one cannot provide concrete threshold or "worry" values. Part II of this book provides suggested thresholds based on real-life experience, but the values are meant to be used as starting points rather than definitive settings. Your baseline will reveal appropriate thresholds for your network.

Analysis of the collected data will also serve to populate the knowledge base, as described in Chapter 3, "Developing the Network Knowledge Base."

Without a baseline, you can only guess the nature of network traffic and congestion. Network engineers glean this information, either when they put a network analyzer on the network for troubleshooting or when they happen to be logged into a router or switch and run a **show** command. This technique can be problematic because a single view at a single time does not capture the true performance of the network over the hours and days of its operation.

Following sections describe the general methodology for defining, collecting, and reporting a network performance baseline. The study entails the collection of key performance data from the ports and devices considered to be mission-critical. The baseline is a vital preliminary step in determining the network's personality. It also simplifies the creation of effective service level agreements and thresholds.

The following are steps to building a baseline:

- Planning for the first baseline
- Identifying devices and ports of interest
- Determining the duration of the baseline

Planning the First Baseline

When conducting your first baseline, start out simply—select a few variables that represent your defined policies well. If you begin by collecting many data-points, the amount of data can be overwhelming, and determining how to make sense of the collection can be difficult. Hence, start out simply and fine tune along the way.

Generally, some good starting measures are interface and CPU utilization. Please see Part II for recommended variables and usage.

Collect the data for a day or two before starting the actual baseline study to determine whether you are getting the right data from the right devices. After you collect a couple of days' worth of data, play with it. Graph the findings in different ways until you find something that makes sense to you. Slicing through the data in different ways can reveal interesting and sometimes surprising observations.

Pick the top couple of reports that have meaning and study them to determine whether there is more information you need in order to understand a particular pattern or trend. Then, fine-tune the data to be collected and begin the actual baseline study.

TIP   You should plan on conducting a baseline analysis of your network on a regular basis. Whether you conduct an annual analysis of your entire worldwide network or baseline different sections of the network on a rotating quarterly basis, you must conduct a baseline regularly in order to understand how the network grows and changes.

Gathering the information in a consistent manner and analyzing the data will keep you on top of your network and allow you to make informed design decisions as well as hasten your fault isolation. You'll also get better at it with practice.

Identifying Devices and Ports of Interest

As part of planning the baseline, you must identify the ports of interest. Ports of interest include those network device ports that connect to other network devices, servers, key users, and anything else considered critical to the operation. By narrowing the ports you plan to poll, your reports will be clearer and you will minimize network and device management load. The sections "Where Are Your Network Devices?", "Where Are Your Servers?", and "Where Are Your Key Users?" in Chapter 1 provide more detail on ways to select critical ports.

After the ports have been identified, you must ensure that processes are in place to either keep that connection from being changed or to inform you if the connection gets changed. Without this assurance, your reports will become inaccurate.

For example, a report may indicate that a backbone port on a particular port is performing fine, when in fact the device connected to that port is no longer a router—but a user's PC. You've been monitoring the wrong port!

TIP   One method to track the ports of interest is to use the port description fields on devices to indicate what is connected. For instance, if backbone router A is connected to switch port 1/1 on the main campus, you should configure the port descriptions for each of the devices to describe the device connected at the other end.

The port description can then be used for adding clarity to the reports you will be creating from the baseline and performance monitoring.

Determining the Duration of the Baseline

How long should the baseline collection last? The duration should last as long as it takes to gather a "typical" picture of the network.

The collection needs to last at least seven days in order to capture any daily or weekly trends. Unless you are looking for specific long-term trends, the baseline needs to last no more than six weeks. Generally, a two-to-four-week baseline is adequate.

Do not perform the collection during times of extraordinary traffic patterns. For example, do not conduct the baseline over a holiday or during December if most of the company is on vacation.

When conducting the baseline, you should set the duration in seven-day increments. Weekly trends are just as important as daily or hourly trends.

For example, suppose that on Sundays at 2 a.m., the engineers in Building 7 run a massive backup and software refresh (which you didn't know about) on all 200 of their workstations. Because the backup server happens to be in Building 9, the push and backup saturate the corporate backbone. If you chose to run your baseline from Monday through Friday, you would have missed the saturation.

However long you decide to conduct your initial baseline, plan to try different durations on subsequent baselines. This will allow you to discover the optimal analysis collection for your network.

Using the Baseline Data

This is where your efforts pay off. You have defined the policies that drive your efforts, you have identified those variables that measure the policies, and you have collected the data from critical devices and connections for a period of time. By baselining your network, you should be able to gain a clearer understanding of the true nature of the capacity and quality of service your network delivers. You must now analyze the snapshot.

You can use the data in the following ways to learn more about your network:

- Identify undesired network behavior
- Identify thresholds for fault and performance monitoring
- Analyze long-term performance and capacity trends
- Verify policies

Identifying Undesired Network Behavior

An immediate benefit of baselining your network is the objective identification of undesired network behavior. By generating reports that identify the most utilized lines, for example, you can objectively pinpoint those areas of the network that are either experiencing problems or are prime for failure.

At the same time, you can identify under-utilized areas of the network. Where redundancy is involved, you may discover that traffic is routing almost entirely over one link of redundant connections and not the other. This may be undesirable because you can almost double the bandwidth available in normal operating network with load sharing.

The identification of undesired network behavior may lead to a network redesign or a change in network policy. Or you may simply find a device that is misconfigured.

Identifying Thresholds

Efficient fault management requires the setting of thresholds that reflect different levels of warning. Arriving at the appropriate thresholds for each of your network policies requires a baseline analysis.

Initially, most network managers consult their network device documentation or vendor technical support for a set of recommended or default thresholds. Generally, the answer they receive is "It depends—the thresholds vary according to your network."

Unfortunately, the nature of distributed networking forces the process of identifying or predicting a fault to be an art. Vendors who develop performance and fault tools can provide you with a set of defaults. More often than not, however, you must fine-tune the settings to meet your particular network activity.

The baseline analysis provides you with the data to study performance and fault patterns over a period of time. From the data, you can derive the appropriate thresholding as it applies to your network policies.

Predicting Long-Term Performance and Capacity Trends

As part of the planning cycle for your network, you can benefit from studying network growth over time. You can begin to understand how the network may continue to grow in the future, and more reliably provide concrete data when trying to obtain funding for network expansion.

As stated earlier, you should plan to conduct baseline studies on a regular basis—usually anywhere from annually to quarterly. By comparing the data from each baseline, you can isolate long-term growth tends.

These types of reports tend to be reported in terms of total bandwidth or total capacity for each link, device, and perhaps for the network as a whole.

Network growth tends to occur in large bursts. Hopefully, you can anticipate new application growth by working with application owners and then grow the network accordingly.

Verifying Policies

Determining whether a policy can be achieved in your network is a good use of a network baseline. By reporting the data in terms of the defined policies, you can determine whether the network is adhering to or violating a policy, and to what degree adherence or violation is occurring.

If the data reflects a policy violation, you must consider how to resolve the issue. First, how serious is the violation? How often does it occur and how long does it last? Is the source of the violation a misconfiguration? Either you must redefine the policy based on what the network currently delivers or you will need to redesign the network.

If the study reveals the need for a network redesign, data from a good baseline analysis can be used objectively to justify the need for new equipment or service purchases.

Using Service Level Agreements

Depending on your organization, service level agreements (SLAs) may be necessary. An SLA is an agreement between the network provider and the customer that guarantees a level of service and calls out damages if a service level is not met. For internal customers, damages may be in the form of losing a quarterly bonus for not meeting the SLA. The agreement can be between you and your Frame Relay service provider (where you are the customer) or between you and your company's accounting department (where you are the network provider). SLAs center around a set of policies and must be realistically achievable.

SLAs are business agreements that define a set of policies and business objectives that must be met and the consequences if they are not met. The SLA must translate into concrete data that is measurable and can be reported.

Traditionally, service levels were measured in terms of services being delivered: response time, availability, and mean time to repair. In today's distributed networks, however, service levels are really more like "technical performance levels" because the measurements are based on concrete variables available from the devices, such as interface utilization or ping response times. The advantage of measuring technical performance levels is that the data is more easily collected and reported. The disadvantage is that technical performance is more difficult to associate with business objectives.

In reality, measuring traditional service levels is difficult to do in today's distributed networks, and using technical performance measures is a good solution in place of doing nothing at all.

Part of the SLA is specifying the cost that will be required in order to make the network capable of delivering the requested level of service. Although this can become politically sticky, it tends to be a great method to have another part of the business validate and justify any network modifications you may put forward.

Using the Baseline to Define SLAs

When drafting SLAs between your IT group and other internal business units, the baseline plays an important role in drafting achievable SLAs. The baseline allows you to proactively measure and monitor the factors that contribute to the service level. That is, it allows you to set realistic service goals, which is an important consideration because there will be consequences for not meeting an agreement.

For instance, suppose that you specify a service level of response time less then 250ms across each of your remote office's WAN links. However, your baseline analysis reveals that the average response time is slightly higher than 250ms with peaks greater than 500. In this case, the original service level suggestion is unrealistic and should be revised.

Sometimes, an SLA can be measured with concrete data and reporting adherence is achievable. For example, response time can be measured using ICMP pings, and quantitative reports can demonstrate whether the response time service level was met.

Using Operational Concepts to Define SLAs

Whereas baseline data focuses narrowly on network performance, your network's *operational concept* is a document that broadly defines the network's role and goals in relation to the overall success of the organization. Both resources are important in defining SLAs.

Network management is a complex business operation that is an essential support function for the entire business organization. Thus, it is essential that the network demonstrate network management's importance to the organization, both tactically and strategically. Today, managing network environments requires a well-defined operational concept that includes detailed performance and capacity goals. This up-front definition of network performance and capacity goals helps you to address the problem of measuring the actual service levels that the network is delivering to the user's desktop.

The key requirement of the network management operational concept is that it will provide a business foundation upon which you can build precise definitions of the variables needed or the features desired in your network. It is, therefore, through the development of this document that you can enhance the overall effectiveness of your organization. Not going through the process of developing an operational concept for network management can lead to a lack of goals or to goals that are constantly shifting due to customer demands.

The focus of this document is to form the long-range operational planning activities for network management and operation. It will also provide guidance for the development of all subsequent definition documentation, such as service level agreements. Obviously, this initial set of definitions cannot focus too narrowly on managing specific network problems. Rather, it should focus on those issues that emphasize the network's importance to the overall organization and the network costs (such as monthly WAN service fees) that must be managed. Some of the objectives that can be included in an operational concept document are as follows:

- Identify those characteristics essential to efficient use of the network infrastructure
- Identify the services/applications that the network supports
- Initiate end-to-end service management
- Initiate performance-based metrics to improve overall service
- Collect and distribute performance management information
- Support strategic evaluation of the network with feedback from users

In other words, the network management operational concept should focus on the overall organizational goals and your philosophy to meet those goals. The document therefore consists of the higher-level definitions of the network's missions, mission objectives, system goals, organizational involvement, and overall operational philosophy.

As a network manager, you are often in the position of trying to unify the inconsistent performance expectations of your users. For instance, if the primary requirement for the network is the transfer of large files from one location to another, you will want to focus more on high throughput and less on the response times of interactive users.

One of the things that you must be careful of during the creation of the network management operational concept is not to limit your view of performance without careful thought. For instance, look at the load levels that are being used when testing a network. Often, the load is based on very small packets and the throughput on very large packets. Although either of these performance tests may produce a very positive picture, traffic load may not present a true picture of performance for your network (depending on your network). Your network's performance should be studied under as many workload conditions as possible, and the performance should be documented.

Finally, ensure that you are not making unrealistic expectations of your network performance. This usually comes from misunderstanding the details of networking protocols or of the applications. Often, if you are experiencing poor performance, the fault may not be in the network but rather in poor application design. The baseline analysis should help you isolate the cause.

The following six steps are used in developing and documenting the network management operational concept:

Step 1   Define the network management goals in general business terms.

Step 2   Identify appropriate variables needed to further refine the network management goals in technical terms.

Step 3   Define the variables in terms of data type.

Step 4   Define the types of statistical and data manipulation valid against the defined data types.

Step 5   Define a process for the performance evaluation lifecycle.

Step 6   Redefine the goals based on the metrics defined previously.

Using Policy-Based Management: An Example

This section uses an example network scenario to illustrate the components of defining network policies and conducting a network baseline.

In this example, you are responsible for a 600-site network that connects all of your company's sales and customer service offices to the corporate backbone. You grew weary of various business heads knocking on your door every time they perceive what they think is a network problem. To address the problem, you decided to talk with different parts of the company and identify networking requirements.

You begin by talking to the various business heads that have an interest in how the network operates for the remote sales locations. They include the following:

- Marketing—Who depends on the network for distributing product materials and pricing in a timely manner.

- Accounting—Who must have up-to-the-minute access to sales data.

- Sales—Who require speedy and guaranteed access to the order entry system. Because delays in booking orders affect the corporation's bottom line, they must be minimized.

- Manufacturing—Who forecasts its production based on booked sales and thus needs timely access to the numbers.

- IS telecom—Who roll out IP telephones to the remote sites over the traditional data network. Delays over 150ms are unacceptable for voice over IP.

- IS applications development—Who is responsible for the home grown applications that the sales force uses.

Drafting the Policies

After talking with all of the interested parties, you draft policies that capture the expected requirements. Examples include the following:

- The sales order application must be available 24 hours a day, seven days a week.

- The Ethernet phones require that voice traffic experience no more than 150ms latency across the WAN.

- The network must be up and available 99.98 percent of the time, according to your CIO. (You are not sure how she arrived at that number, but for political reasons you must adhere to it.)

- Non-critical traffic must be restricted during normal business hours at each sales office in order to keep the lines clear for voice and data transactions. This includes any game-playing, data backups, file transfers, or database syncs.

When collecting requirements, you also must attach costs to improving the network in order to deliver the levels of service people ask for. Non-IT executives tend to forget that there is a cost associated with guarantees.

Consider the first list item as an example: The sales order application must be available 24 hours a day, seven days a week. The network is a key component to the execution of this policy. The phrase "the network is the computer" holds more truth than ever.

In order to provide 24×7 access, the server that the application runs on must be accessible all the time. You walk over and talk to the group that administers the server and they have decided to run two machines redundantly; the second takes over if the first fails. This means that there must be two network connections and the devices must run HSRP. Notice that the discussion of service-level guarantees leads toward network design issues.

Next question: Which users use the application and where are they located? The sales people use the application and they are located all over the world. Some will use the application from their sales office, which is connected back to corporate via Frame Relay. Others dial in from home to run the application.

The VP of sales has sent a note to the CIO (your boss's boss) indicating that the sales order application is business-critical, and that the company loses $20 million in unbooked revenue for every hour this application is unavailable. In her words, this application is absolutely critical to the bottom-line success of the company and its stock. Usually, this type of statement is grandstanding, but you will need to present the cost of achieving the desired level so that the VP can make an informed business decision.

Your boss has come to you and asked that you put together some monthly reports that can be viewed by the interested business leaders across the company. These reports must demonstrate that the network is doing what you have promised. And, oh, by the way, you must identify network criteria by which your boss can evaluate you when determining your annual bonus.

All in all, there will need to be a meeting of the minds to agree on a final set of policies and SLAs. Some of what is asked for is unachievable. You will need to be prepared to defend a budget that you consider necessary for implementing what they ask.

Conducting the Baseline Analysis

First, you must conduct the baseline you've been avoiding since you took this job. Based on the policies you crafted, you determine that the baseline should last four weeks and will be conducted against all remote sites.

You also decide that the following data should be collected:

- Router availability
- WAN interface utilization
- WAN response time

You install and configure a set of baseline collection and reporting tools. In this case, MRTG will do the job nicely (see the References at the end of this chapter for more information on MRTG). Initially, you try a dry run for a couple of days to make sure that the collection is configured correctly and the data is useful, and then finally kick off the actual baseline.

During the collection period, you look at some of the data and play with the reporting. This allows you to set up reports that provide the information needed to document the baseline. It also allows you to identify troublespots that may get in the way of delivering your policies.

After the baseline is complete, you look at the "Top 10" reports that identify the worst response times, worst availability, and worst utilization. The response times look pretty good, but the availability looks terrible. On average, the availability of WAN links was 96.6 percent, a far cry from the expected 99.8 percent expectation. You plan to look deeper into the causes of these outages.

Also, the "Top 10" interface utilization reports reveal that more than 15 percent of the sites are experiencing heavy load in excess of 90 percent most of the business day. You will need to study the interfaces closer in order to determine whether traffic is being dropped and if customers are noticing delays.

For the sake of this example, after subsequent analysis, you determine that a network redesign is necessary in order to meet the corporate requirements. In this case, you decide to run redundant Frame Relay connections back to each remote office to form a dual regional star topology. In addition, you plan to review the SLAs you have with your telco providers. If there are no SLAs, you need to get one.

You make a business case for the additional cost using the baseline study data, and hopefully the sales organization agrees to fund the effort.

Meanwhile, it's time to empower your customers. You determine that the best way to please your customers month after month is to clearly articulate the service levels they can receive from the network. You must negotiate levels of service and consequences when they are not met, have your customers agree to the service levels, and provide reports that demonstrate the network's actual delivery of the service levels. In addition, rewards in the form of quarterly bonuses are given to the IT staff for meeting or exceeding the SLAs.

Charting the SLA

By setting expectations up front and communicating how well the network meets those expectations, you eliminate finger pointing and instead shift the focus to a cooperative, measurable agreement.

You draft an SLA that specifies the following:

- A restatement of customer expectations in non-networking terms
- An explanation of how the expectations translate into the data that will be used for reporting the service level adherence
- Details of the types of reports that will be used, how they will be distributed, and how frequently they will be updated
- Agreed-upon terms that identify the penalties and resolution to unmet service levels

You decide to publish the reports on the Web, thereby making the service level reporting accessible all the time and by whomever needs to view the reports. Business heads can view the data whenever they want, and you have clearly documented and agreed-upon service levels that drive your design.

Although this is a simplified example, you can see how communication and agreement on operating levels make your job easier and raise the satisfaction of your customers.

Summary

This chapter described how to do the following:

- Identify business policies that dictate network operation
- Conduct a baseline analysis of the network to understand its current operating levels
- Negotiate SLAs based on what the network can deliver and what your customers expect

The key to successfully delivering the network services that your customers expect is communication. You must understand what your network is capable of and then communicate these findings to your fellow IT groups and the business groups that fund its operation.

In the next chapter, you will learn how to take the data retrieved from the baseline and SLA data collection and implement a knowledge base.

References

Books

Oppenheimer, Priscilla. *Top-Down Network Design*. Indianapolis, IN: Cisco Press, 1999.

Terplan, Kornel. *Benchmarking for Effective Network Management*. New York, NY: McGraw-Hill, 1995.

Internet Resource

MRTG (Multi Router Graphing Tool), programmed by Tobias Oetiker and Dave Rand and a number of other people from the Global Village

http://www.mrtg.org

CHAPTER 3

Developing the Network Knowledge Base

A *knowledge base* is a collection of information about your network that you use in the process of managing your network. This information can be anything from a collection of flat files to a full-blown DBMS. The knowledge base should be stored in a way that makes it easy to use and update.

Although collecting and maintaining the information can be quite time-consuming, the time spent gathering the information will be well spent when your first network crisis arrives. Having this information will enhance the management of your network and improve your ability to respond in a timely manner. The resulting knowledge base will make managing your network easier. It will allow you to quickly determine the key areas in your network that need attention and reduce the number of times your network management station "cries wolf" or reports excessive or false faults to an acceptable level.

This chapter discusses the following:

- Why develop a knowledge base?
- Defining the knowledge base structure
- Understanding data sources
- Keeping the knowledge base current

Why Develop a Knowledge Base?

Network administrators will typically start managing their network by purchasing a management package that supports auto-discovery. After they turn the package on, it discovers every device in their network. It then starts generating events as PCs come and go on the network, equipment is tested in labs, and a myriad other reasons. Some events may point to legitimate faults in your network. However, the signal-to-noise ratio is excessively high to be useful. A knowledge base will help your network management system to reduce that signal-to-noise ratio to an acceptable ratio via a variety of methods, including indicating which devices and ports should be managed.

For example, suppose an SNMP trap comes in that indicates that port 2/3 on device Switch1 has gone down. With no knowledge of this network, it is impossible to determine whether this event is reporting a fault in the network, much less the severity of the possible fault. For example, this port may be the connection from your company to the Internet. Loss of this link may affect access to external critical resources for all your company if it is the only connection, and fixing it quickly is critical. On the other hand, if there is a redundant link, fixing the connection may be a lower priority. Alternatively, this port may be connected to one end user's PC and they may have turned their PC off for a plethora of reasons. In this case, you probably don't even want to know it happened, or you want it logged to a file that will only be looked at if some other issue in the network requires re-evaluating your events. You can't tell which of these scenarios applies without knowledge of the topology of the network.

Without knowledge about the performance of this network, it is unlikely that you can set thresholds for performance analyses that don't result in too many or too few events. Thus, the information gained from baselining the network needs to be placed in your knowledge base so it can be used for generating useful thresholds for your network.

You also need knowledge about how important this network and specific pieces of this network are to the operation of the company. This is often stored as a set of rules that are derived from your established network and communications policies. These policies collectively implement the service level agreements (SLAs) that you have with your users. Chapter 2, "Policy-Based Network Management," covers policies, SLAs, and rules. You can choose to store only the rules in your network knowledge base and/or store the information the rules are derived from. As network management becomes more advanced, you will be able to specify this type of information at an increasingly higher level.

An example of using this information is a trading house that may have several networks in-house and places the highest priority on the trading network during trading hours because the core business of the company is impacted. A network tying remote offices may be assigned a medium priority because an outage may affect only a few customers. In addition, a network primarily used to connect PCs to printers may be assigned the lowest priority—the company may be willing to accept longer outages on such a network in trade for lower equipment or support costs.

Another level of knowledge that may be reflected in SLAs or may be more an oral tradition in your company is the financial, political, or religious level. The network connection that deserves more attention than others is an important piece of information. Obviously, the CEO's connection is important, but what may be less obvious is the connection of a particular bright and rising star who has the ear of the CEO. To properly process faults, this information is important.

There may be tactical ways of managing this information that fits in the existing structure of your knowledge base, such as treating these devices as in the same class as critical servers.

Another example would be verifying connectivity to an important group of top executives, all of whom use laptops that are often connected to and disconnected from the network.

Your knowledge base may have information about other devices on the same portion of the network, such as a printer, that could be monitored to verify connectivity to this portion of the network, thus acting as a proxy for the availability of these laptops.

Defining the Knowledge Base Structure

In the process of baselining your network, you have started to accumulate information for your knowledge base. As you expand the types and extent of network management you implement, you can develop a more extensive knowledge base. Use this chapter as a reference to start out collecting the data you need and expand it as you go along.

After you select the tool(s) you plan on using to implement your knowledge base (see Chapter 9, "Selecting the Tools"), you will want to spend some time designing the structure or schema of this information. Carefully read this chapter and use the guidelines contained here, combined with your knowledge of your network, to define this structure. Here are some tips that may help you to structure your network's knowledge base successfully:

- Administering your knowledge base will be much simpler if you implement a method of grouping similar objects. You will probably find large groups of devices or objects such as interfaces that you want to monitor and to which you want to assign similar characteristics, such as importance, priority, or what information you want to collect. For example, you might want to put all ports on your switches that are connected to file servers in a group.

- You may want to be able to relate different views of your network to each other, such as logical views versus physical views. You may want to store information about applications and services as well as devices and ports. Keeping a flexible structure will be important as you go forward with network management because networks are dynamic and changing, and the technology they are based upon is also dynamic and rapidly changing.

- After you've defined a structure to hold your data, it's time to look into how you will be able to get the information in and out of your knowledge base. The current trend is to make everything available through a Web interface, and it is a trend that we heartily endorse. Web access and the ability to make updates through the Web will allow your network engineers to document changes using lightweight laptops or pretty much any desktop that happens to be close at hand. So, select a tool that allows Web access and build screens that allow users to both view and modify the information in your knowledge base.

Understanding Data Sources

This section breaks out each network management task you'll want to implement and discusses the knowledge you'll want to have in your knowledge base to support these tasks.

The order in which these tasks are discussed is in general the optimal order for performing them, but you may need to modify the sequence for your network.

Network Inventory

The first task you need to do to manage your network is to perform a network audit. Out of this audit, you will obtain the information required to create an inventory of your network. Performing this audit is covered in Chapter 1, "Conducting a Network Audit." The information collected should include the following:

- Device name
- Device IP address(es)
- Device location
- Contact information

If the device is connected to a switch, you may want to include information about this connection, as follows:

- Switch
- Switch port

You may want to include the following information about these devices in your knowledge base. This information may be useful in automating your performance and fault management functions:

- Device function
- Logical access methods such as passwords or community strings
- Physical access methods such as keys or badges

To keep track of your network's layer 2 connectivity, you'll need to add the following information to your knowledge base:

- The device's MAC address(es)
- The name of one device's port that connects to the name of its neighbor's port (for example, switch 1 port 2/1 connects to switch 2 port 1/1)—this is a more detailed and bi-directional form of the switch and switch port information listed previously
- Information on layer 2 redundant paths (for example, redundant bridged paths, or port channels)

You may also want to track your layer 3 connectivity. You'll want to add the following information to your knowledge base:

- Layer 3 connectivity information such as default routes and routing tables
- VLAN information
- Information on layer 3 redundant paths (for example, HSRP or VRRP router peers)

Policy-based Network Management

The knowledge required to support policy-based network management consists of the following:

- Service level agreements
- Policies
- Rules that are required to implement these agreements and policies

Policy-based network management is covered in Chapter 2.

You may want to implement a two-tier structure that allows you to describe the rules in a device-independent way and a set of commands that implement a particular type of rule on the type of devices in your network. For example, you may have a rule that states:

> For all switched user ports, set ToS equal to zero

You would then add to your knowledge base the commands required to change the ToS on each device that this rule might be applied to.

A key part of policy-based network management is verifying that the policies are being met. The information collected during the baselining of your network will provide the base values to compare to the current state of your network and allow you to determine your network's rate of compliance with those policies. This information will be stored in the performance monitoring section of your knowledge base, which is covered next.

Performance Measurement and Reporting

Performance measurement and reporting entails several types of tasks and, therefore, several types of information:

- Availability
- Response time
- Accuracy
- Utilization
- Reporting

Performance measurement and reporting is covered in detail in Chapter 4, "Performance Measurement and Reporting."

We suggest that you implement availability monitoring first. Your knowledge base should contain information to support this, and if kept flexible, it will support additional performance measurements as well. Keep this in mind when designing your knowledge base.

You'll want to add which devices are considered "interesting" or important to your knowledge base to support performance measurement and reporting. Note that most network managers select to ignore most end user devices such as PCs. Monitoring the availability of hubs, switches, routers, servers, and possibly key users will be important. The easiest way of supporting this in your knowledge base may be by supporting groups or classes of devices that you want to monitor at the same service level. Examples of classes of devices are WAN devices, backbone network devices, and server farms.

Let's look at what knowledge is required in your knowledge base to support each component of performance measurement and reporting.

Availability Monitoring

The information your knowledge base will require to support availability monitoring includes the following:

- The address to use for availability monitoring
- The protocol or protocols to use, such as PING or SNMP
- The frequency to monitor, such as every five minutes
- The number of attempts to reach the device to make
- The length of time to wait for a response

Portions of your network may be "interesting" only during certain times of the day. For example, an office environment that is staffed from 8 a.m. to 5 p.m. may be interesting during these hours and not monitored other hours of the day. Note that you may need to modify these hours to account for things such as network-based backups or automated report generation.

Response Time Monitoring

To implement response time measurements, you need knowledge of your network at the applications level. You need to know where the users of the applications you want to instrument are located in your network and where the servers are located for those same applications.

Just as you did for availability monitoring, you need to define what your expectations are for response time. You should have information about the response time performance of your network from the baseline. This information should be in your knowledge base and can be used to determine significant variances from this baseline. If you have SLAs or policies, these can be translated into rules that detail the times and expectations for responses expected in your network.

To support response time monitoring, your knowledge base will need to include the following information:

- Key source and destination points for measuring response time
- Response time expectations for each source/destination pair

You may also want to include the following:

- Protocol to use to measure response time

Accuracy Monitoring

Evaluating the accuracy with which data is transmitted in your network requires much the same information you've accumulated for availability monitoring. For a thorough discussion of accuracy, please see the "Accuracy" section in Chapter 4.

You probably want to monitor the same interfaces for accuracy that you monitor for availability. Only a little more information will be required to support accuracy monitoring, including the following:

- The objects to monitor for accuracy for each interface type
- The level of accuracy you expect for each object and interface type

Utilization Monitoring

For utilization, you may be able to use the same list of interfaces you use for availability and accuracy monitoring because most network managers don't monitor utilization on links going to individual PCs.

The information you'll need to add to your knowledge base for utilization monitoring includes the following:

- The utilization limit, or rising threshold, for each interface type
- If your utilization-monitoring software supports hysteresis (see the "Hysteresis" section in Chapter 5, "Configuring Events"), the falling threshold for each interface type

Performance Reporting

Many network managers and network management stations start out with hard-coding the available reports. However, if you design your reporting tool to be flexible, and take definitions of the reports and the groups of devices and interfaces you want to report on from your knowledge base, you will have much more flexibility in producing the desired reports.

You'll want to add the following to you knowledge base:

- Report definitions
- Groups of devices and interfaces to use for each report type

Configuring Events

Your next step in implementing network management is configuring events (this is covered in detail in Chapter 5). You should have collected the data you need to add during baselining. This information will build and expand upon the data you put in your knowledge base to support performance measurements.

The specific information required include what objects are interesting to monitor for specific interfaces or groups of interfaces and what thresholds seem appropriate for these interfaces. Note that you will want to include both rising and falling thresholds for each object to allow you to implement hysteresis to reduce the volume of events received. You may consider implementing thresholds based on network technology. For example, acceptable error thresholds for LANs may be significantly lower than for WAN links.

The information to add to your knowledge base include the following:

- Objects to configure events against
- Devices and, if applicable, interfaces to configure events on
- Values for each object and device or interface type

Prioritizing Faults

The information needed to process events and faults is an extension of the information you have already collected, as outlined thus far. The difference is the focus. Although you need to know what ports are interesting in order to start availability management, you need to supplement this information with prioritization information. That is, for each port that you might receive an event about, you need some information about whether the port is interesting (already in the knowledge base) and what priority of fault an outage on this port generates.

There are several ways to determine the priority of a fault. You could keep it simple and assign a priority to each port or group, or you could try to derive this information from your knowledge of the network. A good example of where prioritizing faults gets ugly is to look at redundant links. If you lose one link, there is no outage on your network, but fixing the problem is still important because your network now lacks redundancy. You may decide to wait until a scheduled outage period to fix the problem if fixing it requires you to bring down production services. However, if the only other link goes down while the first link is down, the priority of this outage becomes very high. Your fault management system could determine priority by information on each port or from a more generalized view of the topology of the network.

Another use for topology information is event correlation. One issue with availability monitoring is that it is usually done from one place in the network. This can give a radically skewed view of the priority of an outage if, for example, the port that the monitoring system is connected to goes down. The network-management station would perceive this as the whole network being down.

If topology information about the network is available, the fault management system can use event correlation techniques to determine that the directly connected link is down and, therefore, is the place to start determining the actual source of the fault. Placing a high priority on a fault of this type is probably desirable because there may be other faults that you cannot detect during the period in which your network management application cannot contact the network.

The priority of a fault can vary, depending on influences outside of the network itself. These outside influences include the following:

- SLAs and associated policies
- Users impacted by the outage (for example, the CEO, your boss, etc.)
- The time of day the outage occurs (3 p.m. may have higher weight than 3 a.m.)
- The type of traffic flow (for example, ERP applications)
- The criticality of the segment(s) involved (for example, Sales receipt)

If you defined an SLA, you may have specified criteria that you need to take into consideration, such as an agreement that a certain category of fault will be fixed within a certain period of time. As that time approaches, the priority of the fault may need to be increased to ensure that proper attention is given to it, considering your SLA.

Other considerations that may influence the priority of a given fault include who specifically is affected by the fault. For example, if the CEO of the company is affected by a fault the priority should probably be increased. This is the *mahogany row effect*.

Another consideration that could modify the priority of a fault is the time of day it occurs. The previous example covered in the availability monitoring section, in which an office network is very important during business hours but is much less important during other hours, is one example of time modifying the priority of the fault. Another example is a trading floor, in which it is desirable to have the network up at all times, but it is critical to have the network up during trading hours.

You could also determine the priority of a fault by periodically examining the traffic statistics on the link affected by a fault, determining how much traffic and what type of traffic will be affected, and storing this information in your knowledge base. Obviously, this requires knowledge about traffic flow on your network.

Another way of evaluating fault priority is by looking at the financial consequences of a fault. In this case, you need information about what the financial contribution portions of your network make to your company's bottom line.

We recommend that you start out with a simple priority scheme and enhance it where and when required. If you start with a simple yet flexible scheme, you'll be able to add capabilities as you expand your network management.

So, the items you'll want to add to your knowledge base to support prioritizing faults will include the following:

- Priority of interfaces and ports
- How time of day affects priorities

Keeping the Knowledge Base Current

If a knowledge base is not accurate, its usefulness quickly degrades. Several techniques can help keep the information current.

The first technique is to establish procedures for documenting network changes in your knowledge base. To make this work, you probably want to allow the engineers and technicians in your network access to change the knowledge base. There should be an easy way to change the data and some way of logging what was changed and by whom. The procedure to enter these changes should enhance the likelihood that it will be used. These changes should be recorded during or right after the change to the network is made. Web-based interfaces may enhance the ability to record changes quickly, easily, and from any point in the network.

You will also want to implement a procedure to verify changes. Even with change-tracking procedures in place, your knowledge base will be subject to the "creeping crud syndrome." Errors will be introduced, either through incorrect data entry or through changes that were not documented. Therefore, it is important to periodically survey the network in order to correct any errors in your knowledge base. Some things can be checked using automatic procedures; other things will require someone to physically inventory your network. The following sections cover aspects for which you can automate checking.

Layer 2 and Layer 3 Connectivity

With some types of layer 2 topology discovery, such as the Cisco Discovery Protocol (CDP) or other techniques, you can determine the layer 2 topology of your network. Using this information, you can verify connections between any two devices. Note that CDP will show only Cisco devices and will not show intervening non-Cisco devices.

If you are keeping topology information in your database, you can utilize some sort of automated discovery to track changes to this topology. This will allow you to verify topology information independently of your network engineers or technicians updating the network documentation and knowledge base.

Device Connectivity

Using information collected from the bridge table combined with ARP and reverse name resolution (DNS, etc.) allows you to determine which devices are attached to which ports on your switches. This information is referred to by some network management packages as user tracking data. If you have standardized on some type of naming convention, it may be possible to determine which types of devices are connected to which ports and then verify or correct information in your knowledge base.

Another way to determine ports that may be interesting is to watch for ports that have more than one MAC address associated. In all probability, these ports support more than one user and should probably be monitored for availability.

Verifying Interesting Ports

If you consistently find ports that are up and have a high level of traffic passing, yet your knowledge base declares these ports as "uninteresting," it may be time to re-evaluate those ports.

Detecting Redundancy

If ports are discovered to be in the spanning tree blocking status, they are redundant links. This information can be obtained from the bridge MIB. If your knowledge base does not reflect this information, it will not be able to correctly associate the priority of outages on this port and the port or ports it is redundant with.

If you are using a protocol such as HSRP, you may be able to verify that your knowledge base contains information about this redundancy by parsing the configuration files from your routers.

Name Resolution

With the information provided by a name resolution system such as DNS, you can verify that the devices and associated IP addresses in your knowledge base match the information returned by name resolution, with both forward and reverse lookups.

Verification of Device and Port Configuration

You can verify the information in your knowledge base by polling devices for the protocols supported, or associated interfaces or ports. For example, it is possible that devices that did not have SNMP capabilities have been upgraded to support SNMP or have had SNMP enabled.

Polling for the speed of an interface (MIB II ifSpeed) and comparing to the thresholds stored in your knowledge base may allow you to detect unreasonable threshold values. Typically, the volume of events generated will detect values that are too low, but hysteresis may suppress most of these. This method should be effective in detecting high thresholds or misconfigured bandwidth statements in the configurations of network devices.

As performance reports are analyzed, inaccuracies may be detected in your network knowledge base. It could be that changes have been made to your network and not recorded, or the way the network is being used has changed. It should be easy for network administrators to update the knowledge base when such inaccuracies are detected.

The most accurate way of keeping your knowledge base up-to-date is to make critical functions rely on the information in your knowledge base. For example, if the list of devices in your knowledge base is used to create your Domain Name System (DNS) tables, it is likely that someone will attempt to contact a new device through its name and, if the knowledge base doesn't have this information, they will report the deficiency. Any technique that you can use to link operational procedures to your knowledge base will significantly increase the accuracy of your knowledge base.

Summary

The previous sections covered many kinds of information you will want to include in your knowledge base. This summary brings this information together.

Taken together, all the information that you desire to store in your knowledge base will define its schema. Collecting this information as you define your needs for your network will allow you to define a custom schema for your knowledge base. Table 3-1 compiles the information from the preceding sections into an example schema.

Table 3-1 *Network Knowledge Base Schema*

Knowledge Base Section	Subsection	Object	Required?
Network inventory	Device	Name	Yes
		IP address(es)	Yes
		Location	Yes
		Contact information	Yes
		Switch	No
		Switch port	No

Table 3-1   *Network Knowledge Base Schema (Continued)*

Knowledge Base Section	Subsection	Object	Required?
		Function	No
		Usernames/passwords	No
		Community strings	Yes
		Physical key or badge requirements	No
		MAC address(es)	No
		Layer 2 connectivity	No
		Layer 3 connectivity	No
		VLAN	No
Policy management		Service level agreements	No
		Policies	For policy management
		Rules	For policy management
Performance measurement and reporting		Interesting devices	Yes
		Device groups	No
	Availability	Device name or address	Yes
		Protocols to use	Yes, unless only one
		Frequency to poll	Yes
		Number of attempts	Yes
		Timeout value	Yes
	Response time	Source/destination pairs	Yes
		Response thresholds	Yes
		Protocol to measure	Yes, unless only one
	Accuracy	Objects for each interface type	Yes
		Accuracy thresholds	Yes
	Utilization	Rising thresholds	Yes

continues

Table 3-1   *Network Knowledge Base Schema (Continued)*

Knowledge Base Section	Subsection	Object	Required?
		Falling thresholds	If hysteresis is supported
	Reporting	Report definitions	Yes
		Devices or groups to report on	Yes
Configuring events		Objects to set thresholds on	Yes
		Devices and interfaces	Yes
		Trigger values	Yes
Prioritizing faults		Port or interface priority	Yes
		How time of day affects priorities	Desirable

Choose a method of implementing your knowledge base that starts out simply, yet can expand as you expand the amount and type of network management activities. Keep things simple and only implement the items that are more difficult if they are truly required in your network.

The bottom line for all this information is use it or lose it. If you are not actively using this information, it will quickly become out-of-date and useless. So, rely on this information and you will keep it accurate.

Now that you have a storage vehicle for information about your network, you can use it. The next chapter discusses performance management of your network, and will rely on the knowledge base to determine what to collect and to store the collected data.

CHAPTER 4

Performance Measurement and Reporting

As companies have migrated from centralized mainframe-based networks with strong performance-related tools to distributed networks, they have discovered the increased complexity of trying to monitor and analyze performance data gathered from varying vendors' devices.

For example, mainframe availability is a key performance measurement for traditional SNA networks. IT groups measure the availability of their mainframe, its applications, and its network connections and controllers. They then roll these numbers into a single availability number. This is the coveted "five nines," or 99.999 percent, which some IT groups try to achieve.

Upon moving to a distributed networking model, data and applications are distributed across multiple file servers and the network is segmented into multitudes of routers, switches, and concentrators. The determination, collection, and reporting of performance-related data have become considerably more difficult. The capability to roll up performance analysis into reports that can be consumed by upper management is equally difficult.

Fortunately, as methods and equipment for distributed networks mature, methodologies and tools that collect and report on performance data have become more accessible.

This chapter covers the following aspects of performance measurement and reporting:

- What performance management is
- Performance data collection
- Performance data reporting
- Measuring network performance

What Is Performance Management?

In terms of networking, *performance management* is the configuration and measurement of network traffic for the purpose of providing a consistent and predictable level of service. Performance management involves monitoring the network activity and adjusting network design and/or configuration in order to improve its performance and traffic handling. Performance measurement can help identify the following:

- Normal baseline network performance (for comparing to perceived "bad" network behavior)
- Current or potential utilization problems
- Slow response time
- Application, server, and network availability
- Optimum data transfer times

Performance measurement can be broken into two categories: performance monitoring and performance reporting. *Performance monitoring* is the collection of performance-related data from network devices. *Performance reporting* is the presentation of the collected data. With performance reporting, the collected data can be used to analyze faults, growth, and capacity of the network.

The following sections discuss performance data collection and reporting in more detail.

Performance Data Collection

Performance data collection is the process of collecting performance-related management data from network devices and storing them in a database or data file. The following issues should be considered when implementing performance data collection:

- Polling versus event-based collection
- Data aggregation and reduction
- Differences when measuring QoS networks

Polling Versus Event-based Collection

There are two methods for collecting performance data: active polling and event reporting. Each has its own strengths and weaknesses.

The first method, *active polling*, involves a management station actively obtaining specific management data from network devices. A single management station may do the collection or multiple distributed data collectors may be used. If data collectors are used, the data is temporarily stored and then forwarded onto a central data repository.

The collected data is then stored in a database and used later for reporting. The advantage of active polling is that as long as a managed device is accessible, data is collected and stored in regular intervals. Disadvantages include the following:

- Collecting large amounts of data from devices can impact the performance of the managed device, the data collector, or the network.
- Keeping large amounts of data over time can fill up hard disks and cause reports to take a long time to generate.

TIP

Care must be taken when an SNMP counter wraps back to zero or a device reboots—this causes the value of a counter to start over at zero. Both of these events are natural occurrences and your data collection application should be able to handle the events.

In most cases, it is best to throw out the data from a poll cycle in which the collected value is less than the previously collected value. Having a lesser value should never happen with a counter type of SNMP variable because, by definition, a counter always increases.

The second method is *event reporting*, or polling by exception. With this model, active polling does not occur; instead, the managed device or agent generates a trap or event that is then received and logged by the manager. Because this method requires that events be generated based only on thresholds, the manager can assume that the lack of an event indicates that the particular item being measured is performing within acceptable ranges. The advantage of event reporting is that traffic is generated only if an exception occurs or is corrected. The impact to the network and network management station is potentially lessened.

The disadvantages to event reporting are as follows:

- It is more difficult to determine the duration and frequency of an event.

- Traps are unreliable (although the use of informs is not—see Chapter 8, "Understanding Network Management Protocols," to compare traps and informs). Losing an event trap means you may not be able to determine the start or stop of an event.

Active versus passive polling becomes a trade-off between active polling actually affecting the performance numbers you are collecting and events potentially getting lost in the network.

Generally, you should employ a combination of polling and event-based reporting. Have the devices monitor themselves and notify the manager of critical items such as interface utilization exceeding 90 percent. Regular polling can be reduced when you also conduct exception polling because you no longer need to poll for the events at the same frequency. The polled traffic becomes less necessary for real-time fault identification and more useful for long-term analysis of the network's performance.

Data Aggregation and Reduction

Collecting performance-related data from large distributed networks presents challenges for storing the collected data. Consider collecting 50 variables from 500 devices every 15 minutes. Additionally, suppose that each of the objects collected is, on average, 5 bytes in size. When storing the data, add an additional 40–100 bytes for timestamps, devices, and interface instances for each collected object. For this example, assume an average total size of 50 bytes per object.

After one hour, you will have stored 5 MB of data. After one day, the number would grow to 120 MB of data. After one year, you will have stored slightly over 40 GB of data. The data can become overwhelming to store and manipulate.

There are methods for efficiently storing and reducing the collected data. Specifically, statistical methods and aggregating data as it becomes old can reduce the amount of data stored. Aggregation provides a useful method for reducing stored data over time. However, you lose detail as you aggregate. Also, your reporting applications must take into consideration the aggregated data when reporting. Some commercial applications perform aggregation automatically and are able to report seamlessly across reduced data. Chapter 7, "Understanding and Using Basic Network Statistics," provides more detail on data reduction and aggregation techniques. Chapter 9, "Selecting the Tools," provides more detail on selecting tools for this purpose.

Differences When Measuring QoS Networks

Part of performance management is the actual configuration of queuing mechanisms and traffic prioritization that enforce different levels of service. After you have designed and implemented Quality of Service (QoS) mechanisms in your network, the natural next step is to see whether traffic is moving as you expect it to: Is it being marked, shaped, or queued appropriately? Unfortunately, this can be difficult to measure and verify.

Some show commands on routers, for instance, allow you to view how different traffic flows are handled within a particular router. With show commands, however, there is no easy method for verifying that all of the routers in a path are successfully and correctly handling your desired QoS.

In response to increased customer use of QoS mechanisms, vendors are providing tools that allow you to model, configure, measure, and report on network-wide QoS. For the case of measuring and reporting, these tools tend to involve placing devices on either end of a path that can emulate the stream of traffic generated by a particular application. Thus, the two devices can conduct their appropriate operations and measure how reliably the network reacts to the conversation.

As QoS deployment continues to grow, the configuration and reporting tools will mature as well. Please refer to Chapter 2, "Policy-Based Network Management," for more details on how policy-based networking will help, and see Chapter 9 for details of the types of tools that are available.

Performance Data Reporting

A natural next step of collecting performance data is generating reports. Reports are useful only if properly correlated data is presented in a useful manner to its intended audience. For example, upper management tends to want reports that report the network's performance in simple measurable terms, such as a network availability summary report. As a network engineer, you need both a single at-a-glance indication of the network's health and detailed reports of relatively raw data. You need an alarm mechanism that tells you when something is wrong and where the problem occurred. And you need to be able to drill down and obtain more detail to isolate the problem.

For example, the network engineer comes to work in the morning and looks at the at-a-glance health rating for the network. The at-a-glance reports provide quick information on any fault or failing events in the network. Additionally, she runs reports whenever she needs to understand how traffic flows change over time. Finally, she runs reports during and after faults in order to understand any anomalies that may have occurred before or during a fault. Fortunately, the different reports can be built from the same set of collected data. Each of the report types varies, based on the intended audience and use. When implementing performance management, it is important to determine the types of reports needed for your operation. Don't produce reports that no one uses. The following are examples of performance reporting:

- Network and device health
- Fault
- Capacity planning

Network and Device Health Reporting

Network and device health reports provide "dashboard" or at-a-glance reporting about the relative health of the network and its components. Health reporting summarizes the relative healthy states of devices and the network—for example, device availability and interface utilization. This type of reporting is extremely valuable for help desk, operations, engineering, and management.

Implementing health reporting provides the quickest benefit when you initially implement performance monitoring and reporting tools. The collected data can be processed, analyzed, and displayed quickly. Thus, when a user calls the help desk, the help desk technician can bring up the present state of the user's network through health reporting, rather than having to Telnet directly to devices or ask the network guru what the status is.

Third-party health reporting systems are reaching a very useful maturity. Traditional reporting for distributed networks tended to look at a device level, whereas newer commercial systems provide reporting at a more comprehensive network level that encompasses the member devices. For examples of the type of health reporting tools, please see Chapter 9. Health reports become even more valuable when they incorporate knowledge of devices and device types. This may involve using proprietary MIBs from devices in order to report on specific health factors. The following sections describe several specific types of health reporting.

Device-Level Health Reporting

The simplest form of health reporting involves reporting device-level performance information. The information is reported by using graphs or graphical elements to indicate each collected variable for each device. Graphic elements include gauges, speedometers, level meters, and on/off switches.

The information is reported in real-time that permits an engineer to monitor the information while troubleshooting, as opposed to sifting through archived data. The disadvantage of this type of reporting is that it doesn't scale past a single device very well. However, this type of reporting is useful for troubleshooting.

Figure 4-1 shows an example of a real-time health report using speedometers to indicate CPU and interface utilization. Elements such as speedometers and gauges are effective in quickly communicating the state of the variable.

Figure 4-1   *Example of Simple Real-Time Health Reporting Using Speedometer Graphic Elements*

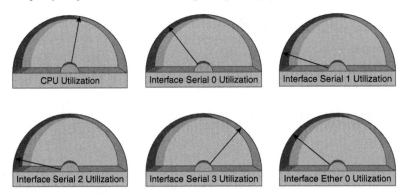

Tabular Health Reporting

A more sophisticated method for health reporting involves the use of tables to indicate the best and worst elements for a particular collected variable. The advantage of this type of report is that you can present the best and worst for a given element across the whole network. Being able to look at the macro view through these reports helps a network engineer or operations person quickly understand where trouble spots exist or are about to occur.

Reporting is usually done in a top 10 and bottom 10 type of format. Top 10 generally reflects the highest values across devices, whereas the bottom 10 reflects the lowest values. Bottom 10 reports can be just as useful as top 10 reports. For example, looking at the least-utilized WAN links in a network may identify redundant links that are not in use, even if they should be.

Table 4-1 demonstrates a literal "top 10" list in which the top 10 routers exhibiting the highest CPU utilization are listed, starting with the worst of the bunch.

Table 4-1 *Example of a Top 10 Health Report for Router CPU Utilization*

Rank	Device Name	CPU %
1.	Comfy-home1	98
2.	Outback-r4	97
3.	Eng-rr-3	85
4.	Eng-rr-5	84
5.	Eng-rr-1	67
6.	172.26.11.13	66
7.	Fw-1	66
8.	Old-router	63
9.	bb-rr-2	62
10.	Du-mr	57

A variation on this type of report is listing only the devices that exhibit a certain CPU threshold or greater. This is called an exception report. For instance, if the threshold of concern for router CPU utilization is 60 percent and none of the routers have utilization greater than 50 percent, the report will simply list that there are no entries.

Correlated Predictive Reports

The final example of health reporting is called correlated predictive reports. Predictive reports apply rules and knowledge of specific device characteristics against collected data in order to attempt to predict trends or potential faults that may result. Predictive reports typically look at collected data, gather more if needed, and make some sort of conclusion based on sets of rules.

For instance, suppose that a router's CPU utilization is extremely high (98 percent). Rather than simply reporting high CPU, a predictive analysis may dig deeper by obtaining a **show proc cpu** command. Example 4-1 shows sample output from this command.

Example 4-1 *Partial output from router **show proc cpu** indicating high CPU utilization with CDP as the cause.*

```
CPU utilization for five seconds: 98%/99%; one minute: 99%; five minutes: 99%
 PID Runtime(ms) Invoked uSecs  5Sec  1Min  5Min TTY Process
   1        628   490033     1  0.00% 0.00% 0.00%   0 Load Meter
   2       4008     2692  1488  0.00% 0.00% 0.00%   0 PPP auth
```

continues

Example 4-1 *Partial output from router **show proc cpu** indicating high CPU utilization with CDP as the cause. (Continued)*

```
  3  1800432   289902  6210   0.00%   0.05%   0.05%  0 Check heaps
  4        0        1     0   0.00%   0.00%   0.00%  0 Pool Manager
  5        0        2     0   0.00%   0.00%   0.00%  0 Timers
  6     3876    44111    87   0.00%   0.00%   0.00%  0 ARP Input
  7     7304   273357    26   0.00%   0.00%   0.00%  0 DDR Timers
  8        0        1     0   0.00%   0.00%   0.00%  0 Entity MIB API
  9        0        2     0   0.00%   0.00%   0.00%  0 Serial Backgroun
 10        0        1     0   0.00%   0.00%   0.00%  0 SERIAL A'detect
 11     2240  1281395     1   0.00%   0.00%   0.00%  0 LED Timers
 12        0        3     0   0.00%   0.00%   0.00%  0 CSM timer proces
 13      324     1568   206   0.00%   0.00%   0.00%  0 POTS
 14    40124 2447944247863 99.00%  99.00%  99.00%  0 CDP Protocol
 15   785576   772809  1016   0.16%   0.02%   0.09%  0 IP Input
```

From the output in Example 4-1, you can see that something other than normal behavior is causing the high CPU: CDP. You can assume that something is wrong with this router: All of the other processes are running extremely low.

- CDP should not be running so high.

- After running a show interface, packets are being dropped seemingly because of CDP dominating the processor.

So, rather than simply reporting high CPU, the tools could instead report anomalous behavior with high CDP Protocol utilization as the root cause.

Additionally, if this is a known condition, the predictive report could recommend a suggested resolution. By first providing a tactical solution and then searching for a long-term remedy, the software can help quickly solve the problem and suggest ways to permanently avoid it. In this example, you can assume that CDP should never run this way, so predictive software might suggest doing a bug search on Cisco's bug navigator Web site (www.cisco.com).

Predictive analysis for network devices is still in the early stages of maturity as vendors continue to learn more about available devices and devise rule sets around their behavior.

Fault Reporting

A nice side benefit of collecting performance-related data is that the data can be used for multiple purposes. Not only can you use the data for reporting, but you can also set thresholds on the collected data. The thresholds can be used to generate alarms to an event-handling network management station. Thresholds and fault management are discussed in Chapter 5, "Configuring Events," and Chapter 6, "Event and Fault Management."

Faults can be reported in several ways. For catastrophic or severe events such as a device disappearing or an interface becoming non-operational, you must have real-time status reports. These reports may be in the form of topological maps that indicate device and interface status by color, such as turning a port red when it dies. Or they may be tabular reports that list faults in order of severity and duration.

Fault reports are useful for help desks. A person taking trouble calls can refer to the report when determining whether a user's problem may be related to a network outage.

Most, if not all fault-reporting software will do its job out of the box, but require customization for a smooth fit into your organization. Every network needs to be managed differently, so you must fine-tune and customize the reports. The risk in not customizing these types of systems is rendering the tool useless as people learn not to trust the severity or messages associated with events.

Depending on your budget, you can purchase different levels of sophistication with these types of tools. However, any tool you purchase will require some level of customization in order to reflect your organization's politics and policies.

Capacity Reporting

When drafting a budget or considering network redesigns, you need solid, real-life data in order to understand the current network's capacity. Armed with good data, you can identify congestion and trouble areas in the network that need to be relieved, either through additional equipment or network reconfiguration. You can also identify devices that are being underutilized or have available chassis slots.

The data collected can be reported to reveal available capacity or lack of capacity in the network. The result is accurate and real-life data that helps you understand and plan for network capacity.

Measuring Network Performance

Performance management is an umbrella term that actually incorporates the configuration and measurement of distinct areas. This section discusses four areas of performance that are useful for measurement in distributed networks:

- Availability
- Response time
- Accuracy
- Utilization

Availability

Availability is the measure of time for which a network system or application is available to a user. From a network perspective, availability represents the reliability of the individual components in a network. Different events can interrupt the reliability of network devices:

- Faulty hardware or components
- Bugs
- Human error
- Backhoes chopping up fiber
- Electrical interference
- Planned outages

Unlike the mainframe world, accurately measuring the availability of a distributed network is extremely difficult and not very practical. This would require measuring the availability of services from every point in the network to every other point in the network, or measuring from the perspective of one or more polling stations. If a polling station fails or becomes disconnected, data will become missing and lead to skewed availability reporting.

Measuring availability requires coordinating real-life measures (phone calls from the help desk) with the statistics collected from the managed devices. The availability tools cannot capture all occurrences that may keep a packet from getting to its destination.

For instance, perhaps a network operator erroneously modifies an access list by entering the wrong TCP port number and filtering SMTP (email) instead of another protocol. As a result, all email to a particular set of servers is no longer accessible and users are affected. However, the availability tools report that the affected router and its interfaces are up and passing packets.

This example demonstrates the difference between network device availability and service availability. Even if measurements may indicate a certain level of network availability, the reality may indicate something different. In this case, the network device and routes are available, but the particular service (email) is not.

Another factor to consider when measuring availability is network redundancy. The failure of a particular port may not be as important if a redundant path is available—the traffic routes around the failure. However, with certain technologies, redundant paths can be used for traffic load balancing, as opposed to having one link operational and one link in standby (doing nothing).

As a result, if one of the links fails, the traffic still has a route to take, but the overall capacity of the path may be diminished, perhaps in half.

Rather than being down, the loss of redundancy indicates a decrease in service. The result, depending on the technology and traffic load, may be slower response time and perhaps loss of data due to dropped packets. These results will show up in the other areas of performance measurement such as utilization and response time.

Different methods exist to measure availability in a distributed network that can provide approximate representation without the complexity. Each method varies in implementation difficulty, and thus varies in the reported results. The key is to implement one method and use it consistently across your network. Implementation is discussed next.

Measuring Availability

According to Stallings (Stallings 1996), availability is expressed by the mean time between failures with the following formula:

Availability = MTBF/(MTBF + MTTR)

where MTTR is Mean Time To Repair. Please refer to Stallings (Stallings 1996) for mathematical examples that use this approach for measuring availability in both redundant and non-redundant connections.

We recommend the following practical approach to begin monitoring availability in your network. This method is similar to those methods used by network management stations that indicate device availability through GUI maps.

ICMP pings are the easiest to use and report on when measuring availability. Equation 4-1 shows the relevant formula:

Equation 4-1

AVAIL = ((Total # of PINGS received) / (Total # PINGS sent)) × 100

Here's how to implement availability measuring in your network using ICMP pings:

1. Select an IP address from each device you want to monitor availability for. Typically, this is the configured loopback address for the device (if configured) or the IP address of the interface closest to the network management station. You may also choose to ping the IP addresses of additional interfaces in a device in order to check that particular interface's availability. Please see the section "Setting Up a Loopback Interface" in Chapter 18, "Best Practices for Device Configuration," for details on managing devices with loopback interfaces.

2. Ping each device at a frequency that will allow you to detect the outage of a device in an acceptable amount of time for your organization. Typically, this is between one and 15 minutes.

3. Send multiple pings for each attempt (up to four). If at least half of the pings are responded to, consider the device available.

4. Keep track of the inconsistency of responses and report that information separately in a way that allows the tracking of the most inconsistent responses. Loss of ping responses tends to indicate congestion or errors in the network. If fewer than half of the responses are replied to, consider the device as not available.

5 If no responses are received, you may want to conduct additional testing (such as send out additional pings or conduct other protocol connectivity-related tests). You can then place the results in a log or generate events based on the tests.

6 Your application should then indicate the fault (or the correction of fault) through the generation of an event. See Chapter 6, "Event and Fault Management," for more details.

7 Store the availability data in a database or flat file. The data can then be used for fault reports (at-a-glance, which devices are down) and longer-term performance reports.

NOTE   If you are held responsible for meeting a Service Level Agreement, it may be important to take scheduled outages into account. These outages could be the result of moves, adds and changes, plant shutdowns, or other events that you may not want reported. Typically, accurately measuring outages is not an easy task and may actually be manual in nature.

Response Time

Network *response time* is the time required for traffic to travel between two points, and is typically measured for a round trip—the time it takes a packet to reach its destination and a response to return to the source. Slower than normal response time can indicate congestion or a network fault, for instance if a redundant network connection goes down.

Response time is the best measure to gauge how users perceive the network's performance. Users get frustrated as a result of delayed traffic. No matter what the source of the slow response is, user reaction is usually "the network is slow."

With distributed networks, many factors affect the response time. Some examples include the following:

- Network congestion
- Less than desirable route or lack of route to destination
- Underpowered network devices
- Network faults such as a broadcast storm
- Noise or CRC errors

For networks employing QoS-related queuing (such as priority or custom queuing), response-time measurement is important for determining whether types of traffic are moving through the network as expected. For instance, when implementing voice traffic over IP networks, voice packets must be delivered on time and at a constant rate in order to keep the call from sounding horrible. By generating traffic classified as voice traffic, you can measure the response time of the traffic as it appears to users.

Measuring response time helps resolve the battles between server and network folks. Network administrators find themselves in the position of being presumed guilty rather than innocent when an application or server appears to be slow. The network administrator is then in the position of having to prove that the network is NOT the problem. Response time data collection provides an indisputable means for proving or disproving that the network is the source of application troubles.

You should measure response time as it appears to users. A user perceives response as the elapsed time from when they press Enter or click a button until the resultant screen displays. This elapsed time includes the time required for each network device, the user workstation, and the destination server to process the traffic.

Unfortunately, measuring at this level is nearly impossible due to the number of users and lack of tools. Further, incorporating user and server response time provides little value when determining future network growth or troubleshooting network problems.

You can use the network devices and servers to measure response time. Through the use of ICMP or related mechanisms, you can measure the time a transaction takes; this approach provides a usable approximation of response time for an IP packet. It does not take into effect (nor is it designed to) the delays introduced in a system as the packet gets processed by the upper layers. This approach solves the problem of understanding how the network is performing.

Chapter 9 describes the types of tools that will measure response time.

Measuring Response Time

At a simplistic level, you can measure response time by timing the response to pings from the network management station to key points in the network, such as a mainframe interface, end point of a service provider connection, or key user IP addresses.

The problem with this method is that it does not accurately reflect the user's perception of response time between their machine and whatever destination they try to connect with. It simply collects information and reports response time from the network management station's perspective. Figure 4-2 demonstrates this.

Figure 4-2 *The Two Possible Paths in the Network*

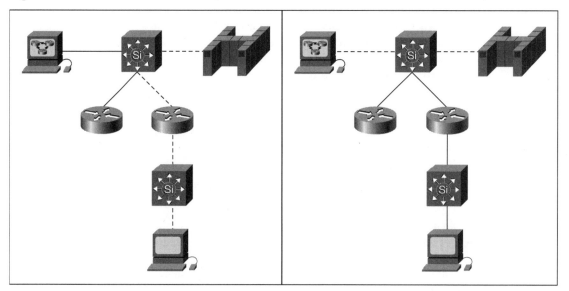

The dashed lines in this figure represent the pathways traveled by data. On the left, data travels from the user PC to the host with a round-trip response time of 75ms. On the right, the data travels from the network management station to the host with a round-trip response time of 55ms.

This method also masks response time issues on a hop-by-hop basis throughout the network.

For instance, if you measure ping responses at the far end of a Frame Relay connection (see Figure 4-3), the measure reflects the time required for the packet to make its way through the various elements (the two switches, three routers, and various switches in the Frame Relay cloud). If you detect a slower response time than usual, there is no indication in the measure where the actual delay occurs. Your first reaction may be to blame the Frame Relay service provider, when the delay may be occurring at one of the local routers.

Figure 4-3   *Example of How End-to-End Response Time Can Mask Hop-by-Hop Response Time Issues*

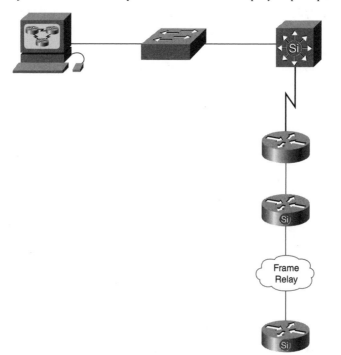

However, there are advantages to this method as well. It is a relatively easy method of collecting a consistent measure of response time trends. A noticeable increase in response time may indicate congestion or errors somewhere and can be used to initiate troubleshooting. Or you can track the response time to various points over time for trending purposes.

An alternative to server-centric polling is to distribute the effort closer to the source and destination you want to simulate for measure. This can be achieved through the use of distributed network management pollers, as well as implementing Cisco IOS Response Time Reporter (RTR) functionality.

Enabling RTR on routers allows you to measure response time between a router and a destination device such as a server or another router. You can also specify a TCP or UDP port, thus forcing traffic to be forwarded and directed in the same manner as the traffic it is simulating.

With the integration of voice, video, and data on multi-service networks, customers are implementing QoS prioritization in their network. Simple ICMP or UDP measurement will not accurately reflect response time because different applications will receive different priorities.

Also, with tag switching, the routing of traffic may vary, based on the application type contained in a specific packet. Thus, an ICMP ping may receive a different priority in the way each router handles it and may receive different, less efficient routes (refer to Figure 4-3).

In Figure 4-4, notice how different traffic types come into the router, and the queuing mechanisms ensure that high priority traffic gets the bandwidth or time slices needed.

Figure 4-4   *Example of Router Priority Queuing Mechanisms*

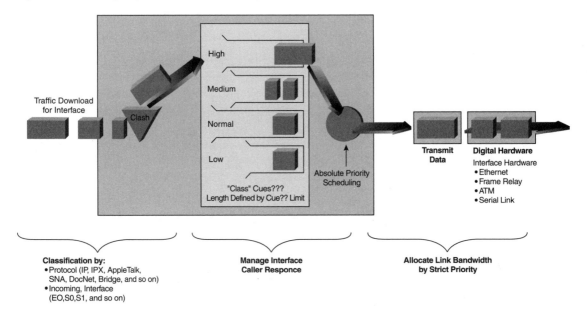

This image was lifted from http://www.cisco.com/warp/public/cc/cisco/mkt/ios/tech/tch/qosio_wp/qosio_w2.gif.

In this case, the only way to measure response time is to generate traffic that resembles the particular application or technology of interest. This forces the network devices to handle the traffic as they would for the real stuff. You may be able to achieve this level with RTR or through the use of other application-aware probes. For more details, see Chapter 9.

Accuracy

Accuracy is the measure of interface traffic that does not result in error. Accuracy can be expressed in terms of a percentage that compares the success rate to total packet rate over a period of time. You must first measure the error rate. For instance, if two out of every 100 packets result in error, the error rate would be 2 percent and the accuracy rate would be 98 percent.

With earlier network technologies, especially in the wide area, a certain level of errors was acceptable. However, with high-speed networks and present day WAN services, transmission is considerably more accurate and error rates are close to zero unless there is an actual problem.

Some common causes of interface errors include the following:

* Out-of-specification wiring
* Electrical interference
* Faulty hardware or software

A decreased accuracy rate should be used to trigger a closer investigation. You may discover that a particular interface is exhibiting problems and decide that the errors are acceptable. In that case, you should adjust the accuracy threshold for this interface in order to reflect where the error rate is unacceptable. The unacceptable error rate may have been reported in an earlier baseline.

If you see a steady increase of errors on an interface, it usually indicates some sort of physical problem and should probably be checked out. On the other hand, you may decide that for some segments, higher error rates are okay. From the baseline, you will be able to determine where in the network you should allow higher rates of errors.

Measuring Accuracy

To measure accuracy, collect the error rates regularly from a given interface and compare the rate with overall traffic for that interface. Determine what you will consider an acceptable error rate for that type of interface: this will determine your threshold.

Table 4-2 describes the variables used in accuracy and error rate formulas.

Table 4-2   *Accuracy and Error Formula Variables*

Notation	Explanation
ΔifInErrors	The delta (or difference) between two poll cycles of collecting the snmp ifInErrors object, which represents the count of inbound packets with an error.
ΔifInUcastPkts	The delta between two poll cycles of collecting the snmp ifInUcastPkts object, which represents the count of inbound unicast packets.
ΔifInNUcastPkts	The delta between two poll cycles of collecting the snmp ifInNUcastPkts object, which represents the count of inbound non-unicast packets (multicast and broadcast).

The formula for error rate is usually expressed as a percentage, as shown in Equation 4-2:

Equation 4-2

$$\text{Error Rate} = \frac{(\Delta \text{ifInErrors}) \times 100}{(\Delta \text{ifInUcastPkts} + \Delta \text{ifInNUcastPkts})}$$

NOTE   Please notice that outbound errors are not considered in the error rate (see Equation 4-2) and accuracy (see Equation 4-3) formulas. That is because a device should never knowingly place a packet with errors on the network, and the outbound interface error rates should never increase. Hence, inbound traffic and errors are the only measures of interest for interface errors and accuracy.

The formula for accuracy takes the error rate and subtracts it from 100 (again, in the form of a percentage):

Equation 4-3

$$\text{Accuracy} = \frac{100 - (\Delta \text{ifInErrors}) \times 100}{(\Delta \text{ifInUcastPkts} + \Delta \text{ifInNUcastPkts})}$$

These formulas reflect error and accuracy in terms of MIB II interface (RFC 2233) generic counters. The result is expressed in terms of a percentage that compares errors to total packets seen and sent. The resultant error rate is subtracted from 100, which produces the accuracy rate. An accuracy rate of 100 percent is perfect, whereas less than 100 percent might be less than optimal.

Because the MIB II variables are stored as counters, you must take two poll cycles and figure the difference between the two. Hence, the delta (Δ) used in the equation.

For example, assuming that the cabling is within specification and that you've conducted a baseline analysis, you decide to use 2^{-5} (0.00002 or 0.002 percent) as an acceptable rate threshold for your fast Ethernet connections.

As you measure, you find the following: Out of 234,000 packets transferred and received over a 15-minute interval, 110 resulted in error. This generates an error ratio of 0.00004700854 (approximately 0.005 percent), which translates into an accuracy measurement of 99.995 percent. This exceeds the threshold of anything less than 99.998 percent and thus raises a cause for concern.

Different protocols have different types of errors. For instance, with Ethernet there are runts, giants, alignment, and FCS errors. The ifInErrors variable used in the previous formula reflects all of these errors. If you need to break down errors by specific types, there generally are additional MIBs that measure the different error types. For instance, with Ethernet, RFC 1757 defines variables that handle each of the error types (etherStatsCRCAlignErrors, etherStatsUndersizePkts, etherStatsOversizePkts, etherStatsFragments, and etherStatsJabbers). These and other variables are examined in more detail throughout Part II of this book.

A final note: Some protocol features are misconstrued as errors. For example, with half-duplex Ethernet, collisions are a natural and expected part of the protocol. The presence of collisions is not necessarily a bad thing. But collisions above a certain threshold do interfere with the capability for devices to put traffic on the network. In this case, measuring collision rates using the error rate formula makes sense, although the thresholds for collisions will be set higher than thresholds for errors. For more details about how to handle Ethernet collisions, see Chapter 13, "Monitoring Ethernet Interfaces."

Utilization

Utilization measures the use of a particular resource over time. The measure is usually expressed in the form of a percentage in which the usage of a resource is compared with its maximum operational capacity.

Through utilization measures, you can identify congestion (or potential congestion) throughout the network. You can also identify under-utilized resources.

Utilization is a handy measure in determining how full the network pipes are. Measuring CPU, interface, queuing, and other system-related capacity measurements allows you to determine the extent at which network system resources are being consumed.

High utilization is not necessarily a bad thing. Low utilization may indicate that traffic is flowing in the wrong place. As lines become over-utilized, the effects can become huge. Over-utilization occurs when there is more traffic queued to pass over an interface than it can handle. Sudden jumps in resource utilization can indicate a fault condition.

As an interface becomes congested, the network device must either store the packet in a queue or discard it. If a router attempts to store a packet in a full queue, the packet will be dropped. Forwarding traffic from a fast interface to a slower interface can result in dropped packets.

When a packet gets dropped, the higher layer protocol may force a retransmit of the packet. If lots of packets get dropped, the result could be that of excessive retry traffic. This type of reaction can again result in backups on devices further on down the line.

You should consider setting varying degrees of thresholds, as described in Chapter 5.

Measuring Utilization

Calculating utilization depends on how the data is presented for the particular thing you want to measure. For instance, when calculating CPU utilization for a router, the busyPer object from http://www.cisco.com/public/mibs/v1/OLD-CISCO-CPU-MIB.my is reported as a percentage value.

However, when calculating interface utilization for a half-duplex 10BaseT interface, you have a choice—using MIB II (RFC 2233) variables or vendor-specific variables. In the case of MIB II variables, your application must calculate the percentage manually by doing the following:

1 Calculating the delta (difference) between two collections of ifInOctets and ifOutOctets each

2 Adding the deltas together

3 Converting the combined value to bits per seconds ($\times$ 8 / (num of seconds in Δ))

4 Dividing the bits by ifSpeed (interface speed in bits)

5 Multiplying the result by 100 to form a percentage

There are also Cisco-specific variables in http://www.cisco.com/public/mibs/v1/OLD-CISCO-INTERFACES-MIB.my called locIfInBitsSec and locIfOutBitsSec, which eliminate the need for step 1 in the previous example. Please note that sub-interfaces are not supported consistently by this MIB. Please see the section "Special Considerations for Sub-Interfaces" in Chapter 12 for details.

Guidelines for Selecting Utilization Variables

Because there are multiple methods for collecting utilization, we recommend using the following rules when selecting which variable type to use:

1. Select public domain MIB objects before turning to enterprise-specific MIBS. If you stick with public domain MIBS, there is a high probability that these MIB objects

will be implemented across vendor platforms; you can reuse your code for other device types with similar functionality

2. Use raw data rather than device-generated or NMS calculated averages when storing collected data. For long-term trending, it is important that the data be as raw as possible—aggregating or summarizing previously calculated or smoothed data produces less accurate results. Please refer to Chapter 7, "Understanding and Using Basic Network Statistics," for further details.

In addition, please note that these variables report only the traffic seen by the particular interface. This means that the router can report only on traffic that is either addressed directly to or passing through the router.

Concerning utilization, a rule of thumb is that you should not assume that 0 percent is necessarily good and 100 percent is necessarily bad. Theoretical maximum utilization does not always reflect problem thresholds. You must use your baseline analysis to determine which thresholds are of concern for your organization.

For example, a router CPU utilization that peaks at 100 percent occasionally is not necessarily a bad thing. This just indicates that the device has very little idle time. However, if a CPU remains at 100 percent for periods of time, it may indicate that packets are being dropped, in which case you should check other information, such as packet drops.

A converse example is half-duplex, shared media 10BaseT Ethernet utilization. Even if the theoretical maximum capacity of 10BaseT is 10 MB, reaching half its capacity can render the medium unusable in some cases. In this particular case, the reason is that as utilization rises, so does the Ethernet collision rate. Based on your baseline analysis, you may determine that a particular shared Ethernet segment should threshold an event at 30 percent in order to indicate a high water mark.

Interface utilization is the primary measure used for network utilization. The following formulas should be used, based on whether the connection you measure is half-duplex or full-duplex. Shared LAN connections tend to be half-duplex, mainly because contention detection requires that a device listen before transmitting. WAN connections typically are full-duplex because the connection is point-to-point; both devices can transmit and receive at the same time because they know there is only one other device sharing the connection.

Because the MIB II variables are stored as counters, you must take two poll cycles and figure the difference between the two (hence, the delta (Δ) used in the equation). Table 4-3 explains the variables used in the formulas.

Table 4-3   *Utilization Formula Variables*

Notation	Explanation
ΔifInOctets	The delta (or difference) between two poll cycles of collecting the snmp ifInOctets object, which represents the count of inbound octets of traffic.
ΔifOutOctets	The delta between two poll cycles of collecting the snmp ifOutOctets object, which represents the count of outbound octets of traffic.
IfSpeed	The speed of the interface, as reported in the snmp ifSpeed object. Please note that ifSpeed may not accurately reflect the speed of a WAN interface. Please see "Performance Monitoring for System Interfaces," in Chapter 12, "Monitoring System Interfaces," for more details on utilization on half-duplex versus full-duplex interfaces.

For half-duplex media, use Equation 4-4 for interface utilization:

Equation 4-4

$$\frac{(\Delta \text{ifInOctets} + \Delta \text{ifOutOctets}) \times 8 \times 100}{(\text{number of seconds in } \Delta) \times \text{ifSpeed}}$$

For full-duplex media, calculating the utilization is trickier. For example, with a full T-1 serial connection, the line speed is 1.544 Mbps. What this means is that a T-1 interface can both receive and transmit 1.544 Mbps for a combined possible bandwidth of 3.088 Mbps!

When calculating interface bandwidth for full-duplex connections, you could use Equation 4-5, in which you take the larger of the in and out values and generate a utilization percentage:

Equation 4-5

$$\frac{\max(\Delta \text{ifInOctets}, \Delta \text{ifOutOctets}) \times 8 \times 100}{(\text{number of seconds in } \Delta) \times \text{ifSpeed}}$$

However, this method hides the utilization of the direction that has the lesser value and provides less accurate results.

A more accurate method is to measure the input utilization and output utilization separately, such as the following:

Equation 4-6

$$\text{Input Utilization} = \frac{\Delta \text{ifInOctets} \times 8 \times 100}{(\text{number of seconds in } \Delta) \times \text{ifSpeed}}$$

and

$$\text{Output Utilization} = \frac{\Delta\text{ifOutOctets} \times 8 \times 100}{(\text{number of seconds in } \Delta) \times \text{ifSpeed}}$$

As a final note, these formulas are somewhat simplified because they do not take into consideration any overhead associated with the particular protocol. Although more precise formulas exist to handle the unique aspects of each protocol, for most cases, the general formulas presented in this chapter can be used reliably across all LAN and WAN interface types. As an example, please refer to RFC 1757 for Ethernet-utilization formulas that take into consideration packet overhead.

Summary

Performance management involves the collection and reporting of performance-related data. This chapter described four areas of performance measurement:

- Availability
- Response Time/Latency
- Accuracy and Errors
- Utilization

Performance reporting is a hot area in network management as vendors help customers make sense of the distributed networks they must manage. Managers and engineers alike want to know how their investment performs and where congestion, bottlenecks, and faults occur.

A nice benefit of performance data collection is that the collected data is useful for more than simply reporting. One vital use of the data is thresholding, in which you set high and low water marks against collected data to alert you if there are problems or a problem has been corrected. The next chapter discusses thresholding.

References

Books

Leinwand, Allan and Karen Fang Conroy. *Network Management: A Practical Perspective*. Reading, MA: Addison-Wesley, 1996.

Stallings, William. *SNMP, SNMPv2, and RMON*, Second Edition. Reading, MA: Addison-Wesley, 1996.

Terplan, Kornel. *Benchmarking for Effective Network Management*. New York, NY: McGraw-Hill, 1995.

Terplan, Kornel. *Communication Networks Management*. Upper Saddle River, NJ: Prentice Hall, 1992.

Internet Resources

http://www.cisco.com/public/mibs/v1/CISCO-RTTMON-MIB-V1SMI.my

ftp://ftp.isi.edu/in-notes/rfc1757.txt (RMON) (page 16)

ftp://ftp.isi.edu/in-notes/rfc2021.txt (RMON)

ftp://ftp.isi.edu/in-notes/rfc2233.txt (Interfaces group)

Cisco IOS documentation

RFC 2275 http://info.internet.isi.edu:80/in-notes/rfc/files/rfc2275.txt

CHAPTER 5

Configuring Events

As network administrators, we all want our network to be as reliable as possible. If the network develops a problem or is reaching capacity in some area, we want to know about it as soon as possible—preferably before users begin complaining.

Your network devices will report symptoms of problems by generating events. An event in this context is a message indicating that a device or application in your network has discovered something of note. Your network devices will generate many types of events automatically. In addition, you can use triggers to define or modify the conditions under which events are generated. Triggers are points of interest in specific data objects that generate events when these points are satisfied. A threshold is a type of trigger set on continuous data streams.

Now that you've baselined your network and started collecting performance data on that network, you have enough information to make sure that your network alerts you when things become abnormal. The steps you'll need to do this include the following:

- Determine what information is interesting and what states or levels are normal for your network.
- Evaluate the events your devices will automatically generate and make sure that the desired events are turned on and the undesired ones are turned off or filtered out.
- Define and configure methods to generate events that are not built-in.

The events generated need to be analyzed to determine whether they represent a fault condition or diagnosis of a problem in your network. This analysis is done by an event management system. This system then takes action on faults, such as notifying network operators about the fault, paging you, or just logging the fault to a file for later analysis. The process of analyzing events and processing faults is the subject of the next chapter, "Event and Fault Management."

This chapter covers the following topics:

- Types of generated events
- Controlling event generation
- Using built-in events

- Determining when you want events to be triggered
- Generating events using RMON by programming devices and collecting and analyzing data.

Understanding Event Types

A *data stream* is any collection of data from one data source. The source determines the type of data stream and, therefore, what type of threshold is applicable. Data sources can be either continuous or discrete:

- In *continuous data* (also known as *time series data*), each data value represents a point in a continuous curve of information.
- In *discrete data*, each possible data value represents a change of state for the data source.

NOTE   In this chapter, we are not using the terms continuous and discrete in a strict mathematical way. We are using the terms to distinguish data that changes on a relatively continuous basis (no digital computer-based data is truly continuous) from data that has a discrete set of possible values.

One way to distinguish one class of data from the other is to consider graphing the data over time. Lines or curves can validly connect the values for continuous objects as the data represents change over time. Discrete objects cannot be plotted in the same way because their values are distinct and should be represented as the state of the object at a given time.

Continuous data can be represented using two methods:

- Each new sample is added to the sum of the previous data points. The value of the object is the sum of all points since this object was initialized, cleared, or wrapped. SNMP uses the Counter object type for these objects.
- Each new sample is averaged with the previous values or is used to calculate a rate over a given time interval. SNMP uses the Gauge object type for these objects.

NOTE   Averages or rates are sometimes calculated as moving averages. There are several different types and methods of calculating moving averages. The type of moving average that Cisco IOS uses is known as a five-minute, exponentially decaying, weighted moving average. The method for calculating this form of a moving average is explained on Cisco's Web site: http://www.cisco.com/warp/customer/66/3.html.

There are two different algorithms for checking thresholds on continuous data. The simplest algorithm checks the threshold against the value of the object. This algorithm is useful for objects such as gauges or anywhere you are interested in the actual value of the object. Since these thresholds operate against the absolute value of continuous objects, we call these *absolute continuous thresholds*.

The other algorithm involves calculating the delta value of an object over a given time period by sampling the object twice and subtracting the second sample from the first. This algorithm is useful for counter-type objects or when you are interested in how much the object changed over a time period. We call these thresholds *delta continuous thresholds*.

Discrete data can be represented as different text messages or as a series of values, each with a defined meaning, also known as an enumerated object. A *boolean object* is a special case of an enumerated object where the possible values are limited to two, one representing true and another representing false.

An overview of SNMP data types, including counters and gauges, is covered in the "SNMP Object Types" section of Chapter 8, "Understanding Network Management Protocols."

Table 5-1 shows the relationships between the different data sources and the trigger types that can be applied against them. The next two sections cover each of these types of data sources and their associated trigger types in detail.

Table 5-1   *Trigger Types Applicable to Data Source Types*

Data Source Types		Threshold Types		
		Continuous		Discrete
		Relative	Absolute	
Continuous	Counter	X		
	Gauge		X	
Discrete	Enumerated Values		[1]	X
	Boolean		[1]	X

[1] Absolute continuous thresholds can be applied to discrete data sources only under certain situations—see "Setting Continuous Thresholds on Discrete Objects."

Configuring Events for Continuous Data Sources

Continuous data sources present a continuously changing curve of values. Examples of continuous data sources include

- The number of packets received on a network interface

- The CPU utilization on a device
- The number of calls completed on an ISDN interface

These data sources are sampled at some rate to produce a data stream.

The type of trigger applicable to continuous data sources is a continuous threshold. This threshold type generates an event when the most recent value in a continuous data stream becomes interesting, such as when a device's CPU utilization exceeds 90 percent or the temperature of your tropical fish aquarium goes below 72 degrees Fahrenheit. You probably want to know when things are back to normal as well as when they exceed your threshold. Thus, you need to trigger events both when the data stream rises across your threshold values and when it falls across your threshold values. The values of 90 percent for CPU utilization and 72 degrees for the aquarium are the points at which the data stream becomes interesting and, therefore, are the values you assign to the threshold. The values are known as the *threshold set points*.

Another example of the use of a continuous threshold is detecting when the utilization on an interface exceeds a reasonable limit. Let's use an example of monitoring one of your WAN links for high utilization. As described in Chapter 12, "Monitoring System Interfaces," you can choose the object ifInOctets to monitor the incoming utilization on that link. This object, ifInOctets, is from the ifTable in MIB II, where it is defined as a counter, so you will need to use a relative threshold. If you set a threshold at 80 percent, an event will be generated every time the data stream crosses this threshold in either direction.

Configuring Events for Discrete Data Sources

Discrete data sources present data that can have several discrete states. Examples of discrete data sources include

- The state of a network interface (up, down, testing)
- The operational state of a device (operational, faulty, reloading)
- The environmental status (normal, warning, critical, shutdown, notPresent)

Discrete data streams are derived from discrete data sources by recording the time at which the source changes state.

Examples of discrete data streams include the time(s) when

- A network interface went down
- A device rebooted
- A power supply failed and the environmental status changed to warning

Discrete data can be represented by data types, including enumerated data, Boolean data, or text data fields with a fixed range of text values or states. Chapter 8 goes into detail about these data types.

Often, discrete data is collected as the state of the source at a particular time. Because the interesting information in this data stream is when the state changes, this data stream can be reduced to the times at which the state changed and the new state of the source. These state changes can be treated directly as faults, but they usually should be filtered to determine which are interesting.

To set a discrete event, you specify one or more states and whether an event is to be triggered if the object equals one of the states or if it does not equal any of the states.

It is sometimes possible to use a continuous threshold on discrete data. An example of using a continuous threshold on a discrete event is detecting PVC status on an ATM network. "Setting Continuous Thresholds On Discrete Objects" (later in this chapter) discusses this in detail.

Controlling Event Generation

It is obviously very important to generate events when there is some sort of problem. It is also important to limit the number of events generated to prevent an excessive load on your network and your event management system.

For example, if your utilization on a link rapidly changes, it may cross a threshold many times and generate lots of events. Similarly, if a WAN link is changing from up to down and back rapidly (flapping), many events will be generated by a threshold on this interface.

You can control the rate at which events are generated in the following ways:

- Throttling events
- Lengthening the sample rate
- Hysteresis

The following three sections cover these techniques in detail.

Throttling Events

Throttling events means that a device throws away events generated over a certain rate. Often, the device will throttle events system-wide. This means that if one event is often being repeated, the system will indiscriminately throw away events to keep the event rate below the set rate. This technique is very useful for preventing a device from flooding a network or system with events. However, it also underscores the fact that events may not be received by the event management system for many reasons.

Lengthening the Sample Rate

Lengthening the sample rate ensures that events are generated less often. If your data stream is highly variable so that every sample period generates an event, if you sample once per second, you will generate one event a second, which is probably many more events than you or your event management system can handle. Reducing the sample rate to once every five minutes may produce useful events at a more reasonable rate. It also significantly reduces the load on the system processing the threshold. Longer sample rates also have the effect of smoothing the data stream, which probably will reduce the number of events generated at the cost of missing some peaks. You, as the network administrator, must determine what sample rate is best for your network. Many network administrators start with very aggressive rates and then are overwhelmed with the amount of data generated.

If you are polling and then processing the data to generate events, high sample rates will also increase the load that network management adds to your network. If you are using the Remote Management MIB (RMON) or another method to have the device check for events, the sample rate will affect the traffic on the network only if events are triggered very often.

Hysteresis

Hysteresis is a mechanism to reduce the volume of events generated by thresholds on rapidly varying continuous or time-series data.

For example, take a network segment going to a server that you are monitoring for utilization with a 70 percent threshold without hysteresis. A large project is coming to an end and the engineers are pushing out lots of large drawing files to this file server in a mad rush to finish their parts of the project. During this time, this segment goes from an average utilization of 10 to 20 percent to averaging between 60 and 80 percent. Every time the utilization rises above 70 percent, an event is generated. What would be more useful is information about the time at which the threshold is first crossed and how long this abnormally high utilization lasts. Hysteresis will allow you to get this information without lots of redundant events.

This mechanism works as follows:

1 A threshold is set up to track the value of an object.

2 Different rising and falling set points are assigned to this threshold, with the rising set point exceeding the falling set point.

3 An event is triggered when the rising set point is crossed.

4 Once this threshold is crossed, an event is not generated again until the falling threshold is crossed. The same mechanism prevents falling thresholds from being generated until the rising threshold is crossed again.

Figure 5-1 presents an example of how the hysteresis mechanism operates.

Figure 5-1   *The Hysteresis Mechanism*

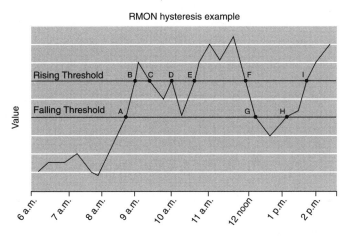

Notice in Figure 5-1 that because the initial state was set to trigger on a rising threshold, no alarm is generated at point A. As the value of the object increases to above the rising threshold, an alarm is generated at point B. No alarms are generated at points C, D, E, or F until a falling alarm is generated when the falling threshold is crossed at point G. Once again, no additional alarms are generated at point H until one is triggered by crossing the rising threshold at point I. This mechanism can drastically reduce the volume of events without eliminating the information required to determine whether a fault exists. Without hysteresis, nine alarms would have been generated; with hysteresis, only three are generated. Often, the reduction is more dramatic.

Determining When You Want Events to Be Triggered

You will need to take the following steps to determine the events you want to have triggered:

- Select the objects or variables.
- Select the devices and interfaces.
- Determine the trigger values for each object or object/interface type.
- Determine the severity for the event.

Determining what triggers to use on which objects and for which devices and interfaces requires an assessment of the baseline data gathered. If you've been doing what we recommend in this book, you have done a fair amount of the work already. Chapter 2 helped you understand how to gather and analyze the baseline data. In Part II of this book, we provide recommendations for what objects to set trigger points on and what range of settings might make sense. You will need to tailor these recommendations for your particular network.

You need to establish trigger points or thresholds (possibly rising and falling) for each object of interest on every device of interest in your network and, for each interesting interface if the object has instances for each interface on the device. If you've taken our advice from Chapter 3, you grouped the devices in your knowledge base. You'll probably only need to determine triggers for each media type and each category of device you defined, instead of for each device and object on that device you are interested in.

An example is CPU utilization on your routers. You will want to set different thresholds for routers processing lots of packets through the CPU (process switching), such as your dial access routers versus your core routers that are able to switch most packets through hardware. If you group all your dial access routers (such as Cisco AS5x00) together, you will be able to select a single threshold that makes sense for all of them. Likewise, one threshold setting will do for all of your core routers (such as Cisco 7xxx).

As another example, you'll probably want to set different utilization thresholds for LAN and WAN networks. Most network administrators set fairly conservative thresholds for utilization on LANs because keeping the LAN performance crisp is usually important and cost-effective. However, WAN bandwidth is an expensive recurring charge and administrators will often choose to allow higher utilization percentages across these more expensive links. See the recommendations in Part II of this book for what thresholds make sense for each media type.

You can use a combination of the importance of the interface or category and the severity of the particular trigger to set the priority of the event and, therefore, what attention the event should receive.

The more you can group and categorize your devices and interfaces, the easier it will be to automate the configuration of events. Use your knowledge base as the resource for this information.

Now that you know what events you want to configure in your network, it is important to understand what events are already built into your network devices. You can then determine which ones you can use. The next section covers this in detail.

Using Built-in Events

Most network devices and host computers have a variety of triggers already set or programmed into them to generate events. Before you start configuring events, you should understand what is already set up on the devices you are interested in.

Built-in events are reported using a variety of techniques, including the following:

- Devices write messages to their console. Some of these messages may be the result of thresholds being crossed, for example,when the temperature of the device exceeds a set point.

- Many systems log messages to files. Windows NT has an event log that records system events. Many UNIX systems use the syslog protocol to log system events. Network devices such as routers and switches can record system events on a syslog server. Applications may also log messages to files. Some of these messages are the result of applications finding that a threshold has been crossed, such as a database management system noticing that a database partition is within 90 percent of capacity.

- Devices supporting SNMP generate notifications (traps or informs) when a variety of things happens. These notifications are defined as part of MIB supported by these devices.

All of these events or messages are generated from built-in triggers on these devices. Some of these events will be useful; others won't. Some can be disabled to prevent them from generating undesired events. Others can't be disabled, so if they are not useful, you'll still need to process and discard the events. One of the most important functions of an event management system is to filter events and only generate faults when an action needs to be taken. Avoiding generating useless events makes the work of an event management system that much easier.

A good example is that devices supporting SNMP generate link up and link down notifications if the link status of an interface changes state. It would seem that you want to know if a link in your network goes down. However, do you really want to know when someone reboots their PC? On the other hand, if the link to a large office in New York goes down, you'll want to be notified as soon as possible. Here, you have the same trigger, same object type, different interface, but vastly different priorities.

The next three sections cover each of the built-in event types in detail.

Console Messages

Many devices print messages to a console port. Sometimes, these messages are extremely important to capture and process. For example, a device that crashes may be able to write a key message explaining the nature of the crash or the problem leading up to the crash to the console port, but not be able to send the message anywhere else. Several techniques allow you to capture these messages and process them.

You can configure Cisco routers and switches to send the majority of their console messages as syslog messages, thus making it less essential to take special action to capture the console messages. However, even with these devices, some console messages will be produced that are not available any other way that can be highly beneficial in troubleshooting problems. For example, sometimes messages are printed just before a crash that can help diagnose the nature and cause of a crash. The device is unlikely to be able to generate a syslog message and send it out if it is in the midst of crashing. Also, devices that are failing to boot usually are able to print messages only to the console.

Usually, the devices that need to have the messages printed to their console ports monitored are clustered in computer rooms and equipment closets. A recommended way of logging these messages for processing is to connect the console ports of these devices to terminal servers. Then, one or more centralized systems can run a process that keeps Telnet sessions open to these devices and logs the output. This output can be processed as explained in Chapter 7's section "Collecting and Normalizing Log Files."

An additional benefit of connecting your network devices to terminal servers is that it is fairly easy to get to the console port of any device from any other point in the network. This can greatly speed up troubleshooting and problem resolution.

However, terminal servers normally allow only one session to a given port. So, you will need some method to allow you to log messages to the console port and still gain access for troubleshooting. One way is to terminate the logging Telnet sessions attached to the terminal server ports going to each console port before you start an interactive Telnet session. A much more elegant way is to enhance the process managing the Telnet sessions to allow a mechanism to remotely tap into that Telnet session and provide two-way communications and logging of both sides of the conversation. This approach has the added benefit of giving you a log of changes made through the console port on all your network devices.

System Event Logs, Syslog Messages, and Applications Logs

Cisco IOS devices can be configured, starting in IOS version 11.2, to send syslog messages above a configurable level as SNMP notifications to a management station.

Scripts can be written, and probably some exist to process UNIX syslog messages and to\ forward messages on to an event management system. The same holds true for the Windows NT event log or applications logs. Although processing these logs falls more in the domain of systems management, the borders between system management and network management continue to blur. The network manager increasingly needs information about the health of systems and applications to be able to answer the age-old question: "The network is down, can you fix it?"

SNMP Notifications

Most network devices support SNMP and send SNMP notifications. Many notifications are preconfigured and others can be enabled. MIB II defines several notifications that are mandatory for all SNMP devices to support:

- coldStart: The device fully rebooted

- warmStart: The device soft or warm reinitialized
- authenticationFailure: SNMP community string incorrect
- linkDown: An interface changed state to linkDown
- linkUp: An interface changed state from linkDown to one of several other states
- egpNeighborLoss: The device lost an EGP neighbor

The authenticationFailure notification and the two link state notifications can generate lots of messages. We recommend that the authenticationFailure notifications be counted and discarded. If excessive notifications of this type are seen on a device or across the network, further steps could be taken to determine the source of the SNMP queries with invalid community strings.

As we discussed before, you should only enable link state notifications on "interesting" interfaces. Otherwise, you'll be buried in notifications, especially if you have hyperactive PC users or flapping WAN links.

See the second part of this book for more details on notifications applicable to specific devices and management areas.

Configuring Events

There are two ways to configure events. The easiest way and the least costly to your network is to have the network device check the trigger points and generate the event. It is easier because you don't have to collect the data you need to analyze. The data you want to query already exists in the device on which you are configuring the event. It is less costly to your network because the only traffic that traverses your network is when an event is generated. However, if you rely solely on this method, you risk missing events that can't be delivered for a variety of reasons.

The other method is to collect data at a management station and analyze that data against thresholds there. This method is discussed in more detail in "Setting Triggers by Collecting and Analyzing Data" later in this chapter.

Thresholds on devices, also known as *agent-based thresholds*, allow your network devices to directly generate events when something interesting happens on your network. One way to set thresholds on devices is with SNMP and the RMON MIB.

RMON supports continuous thresholds on counters and gauges. Although RMON can occasionally be used on discrete objects, see "Setting Continuous Thresholds On Discrete Objects" for details on the limitations of doing this.

Setting an RMON threshold usually means using SNMP to configure devices. Some devices also support setting RMON thresholds through other methods such as a command-line interface (CLI). Cisco IOS devices have supported the alarms and events RMON groups since IOS 11.1 in selected feature sets. Cisco Catalyst devices have supported mini-RMON (the etherStats, history, alarms, and events groups) since version 2.1.

You can set RMON thresholds through SNMP by using a utility that can create SNMP sets or by using a management station that can configure RMON events. Both of these methods require software. Refer to the "Configuring Events" section in Chapter 9 for advice on selecting your tools.

The next three sections cover how to set up RMON thresholds using SNMP, RMON-aware management applications, and the command-line interface on Cisco IOS devices.

Setting RMON Thresholds Using SNMP

To set a threshold using RMON, you need to create a row in two RMON tables: the eventTable and alarmTable. By setting up a row in the alarmTable, you are telling the agent to analyze a specific SNMP MIB object according to your criteria and create an RMON event if the criteria are met. RMON events are not communicated outside of the agent and do not create SNMP notifications. You must set up an entry in the eventTable to take action on the RMON event generated by the alarmTable, such as creating and sending a SNMP notification. If the device you are configuring supports RMON2 and you want to control the destination of any SNMP notifications, you will also want to configure the trapDestTable.

Setting RMON Thresholds Using RMON Managers

In most cases, using a RMON manager to set RMON thresholds is much easier than setting them manually. From reading the previous section, you should understand what information you need to fill in to get the results you want.

Typically, the RMON manager discovers the attributes of the device for you, including the type and speed of all interfaces. Then, it presents you with a list of objects, including interface-specific and other SNMP objects, and allows you to set up the rising and falling thresholds. If you are using an object that refers to an interface, typically the manager computes the number needed, given the speed of the interface and the interval from the percentage value. For other objects, you often can specify the rising and falling rates and have the manager compute the number to set in the rising and falling threshold objects.

A RMON manager can replicate the same settings across all similar interfaces on a device or even across your network. You should have the information about what you want to configure in your knowledge base. Unfortunately, you probably will find it difficult to integrate this information with a RMON manager. If the RMON manager has a command-line utility or API to set thresholds, you may be able to write a simple glue script to implement thresholds to the specifications in your knowledge base.

Setting RMON Thresholds Using the Cisco IOS CLI

The Cisco IOS allows you to set up RMON events and alarms from the command-line utility (CLI.) The following discussion provides the syntax of the commands required, using the same names used for the eventTable and alarmTable. First, here's the syntax for setting up an event:

```
rmon event eventIndex [log] [trap eventCommunity] [description eventDescription]
[owner eventOwner]
```

If neither the log nor the trap options are specified, then alarmTable object eventType is set to none. If only log is specified, then eventType is set to log. If only trap is specified, then eventType is set to snmp-trap. If both are specified, then eventType is set to log-and-trap.

To set up an event to send a trap when triggered, you would enter this command:

```
rmon event 3 log trap public description 'Event to create log entry and SNMP
notification' owner 'RMONman 171.68.118.103 2643'
```

And here's the syntax for setting up an alarm:

```
rmon alarm alarmIndex alarmVariable alarmInterval alarmSampleType rising-threshold
alarmRisingThreshold [alarmRisingEventIndex] falling-threshold
alarmFallingThreshold [alarmFallingEventIndex] [owner alarmOwner]
```

The alarmVariable is specified as either the entire dotted decimal ASN.1 OID for the object or with the table entry name followed by the table object number and the instance. For example, to specify ifInOctects for the first interface, you would enter ifEntry.10.1.

To set up an alarm to trigger the event we just configured, you would enter the following command:

```
rmon alarm 2 ifEntry.10.12 30 delta rising-threshold 2400000 3 falling-threshold
1800000 3 owner 'RMONman 171.68.118.103 2643'
```

Setting Continuous Thresholds on Discrete Objects

RMON only supports continuous thresholds. However, sometimes you will want to use RMON to set thresholds on discrete objects. In some cases, you will be able to get the results you want, depending on the object and the thresholds.

A good example of using RMON to set a threshold on a discrete object is detecting PVC status on ATM networks. The object atmVclOperStatus from the ATM-MIB (RFC 2515) is the one you need to monitor (see "Monitoring PVC Status" in Chapter 14). The object atmVclOperStatus is an enumerated variable that should have a state of up, or 1. Any other state indicates a problem with the PVC.

Because up is the first enumerated variable, you can set a continuous-type absolute threshold against this enumerated variable and get the kind of alarms you want. Just set the rising threshold to 2 and the falling threshold to 1. Be sure to attach the rising threshold to an event because this is the alarm that tells you when your PVC has an abnormal status. You may also want to attach the falling threshold to an event that alerts you to a restoration of the normal state.

This will work only with enumerated variables that have the desired state or states as the first possible value or as the last possible value or values, where you would set the falling threshold to one less than the desired value and the rising threshold to the desired value. In this case, you would attach the falling threshold to an event to alert you to this abnormal condition and the rising threshold to an event to alert you that the normal state has been restored.

Programming Devices to Configure Events

Using RMON is not the only way to configure events. Devices that have facilities to allow administrators to run programs can be programmed to check triggers and generate events. These type of devices include

- UNIX- and NT-based servers
- Routers based on open operating systems
- Specialized networking equipment that has auxiliary processors running open operating systems
- Specialized networking equipment that supports a programming or script language with sufficient flexibility to check thresholds and generate events

These devices give you the most flexibility in determining what you want to check for triggers, what type of thresholds you want to implement, and the type of events to generate from the triggering of these settings.

There are two major techniques you can use to take advantage of these facilities. The first is to program the checking of triggers and generation of events yourself. The second is to take advantage of the work of others and obtain an application that is designed to perform these functions. Check out the configuring events section in Chapter 9, "Selecting the Tools," for more information on tools available for this purpose.

Programming Triggers

You may find it useful to program your own triggers for specialized or unique data objects that your network depends upon to supply services. An example might be instrumenting client/server applications to verify a load on the server and setting thresholds on that load. Other examples might include

- Monitoring space used in a database

- Monitoring translations per second in a protocol gateway
- Monitoring the state of ATM PVCs

You can use any suitable programming language to check thresholds and generate alerts.

Using Applications to Check Triggers

Several types of applications support configuring events, including the following:

- Network management systems
- Extensible SNMP agents
- System management applications
- SNMP proxies

You will need to determine what objects you want to monitor and choose the application that allows you the most flexibility in monitoring those objects and generating events.

Chapter 9 provides more details on selecting these applications in the section Configuring events.

Setting Triggers by Collecting and Analyzing Data

Triggers set by collecting and analyzing data are also known as network management system-based triggers. This method of setting triggers and generating events is more flexible than having network devices check triggers and generate events. But it also is more costly to your network and requires more maintenance.

In the previous chapter, we explained how to collect performance data on your network. Although this technique of configuring events has the most flexibility, it can have the highest impact on your network because, instead of transferring data only when an event is triggered, you will be transferring data at your sample rate for each object being monitored. You may also find that polling your devices through SNMP may cost more on those devices in CPU load than setting RMON thresholds directly on the devices.

How you choose to collect this data may help you determine how best to check thresholds and generate events. Many of the techniques listed earlier in this chapter can be used to check thresholds against collected data.

NOTE	A common belief is that if the threshold requires a calculation, you usually must collect the data and calculate the value at the management station. However, a MIB, known as the *expression MIB*, allows you to form composite SNMP objects for calculations on other objects. So it is sometimes possible to avoid collecting the data and analyzing the threshold on a management station if you use this MIB.

Summary

In this chapter, you learned what configuring events is all about. Then, we discussed why you would want to configure events and what types of triggers are used to generate events. Then, we discussed how to determine what events you want to have configured on your network. Next, we talked about what events your devices may already have configured. Finally, we discussed how to configure the events you need in addition to the events built-in to your devices.

Next, we are going to have to process all these events and determine what to do with them. Chapter 6, "Event and Fault Management," covers this topic in detail.

References

Standards

RFC 1213, "Management Information Base for Network Management of TCP/IP-based Internets: MIB-II"

RFC 1757, "Remote Network Monitoring Management Information Base"

RFC 1903, "Textual Conventions for Version 2 of the Simple Network Management Protocol (SNMPv2)"

RFC 2021, "Remote Network Monitoring Management Information Base Version 2"

RFC 2233, "The Interfaces Group MIB Using SMIv2"

RFC 2515, "Definitions of Managed Objects for ATM Management"

RFC 2579, "Textual Conventions for SMIv2"

CHAPTER 6

Event and Fault Management

Your event management system (EMS) is the place where everything comes together and where the network lets you know when it needs attention. If your EMS is configured and working properly and if your thresholds are properly set, you can relax and wait for the system to report problems to you. If you don't want to spend your days analyzing reports or listening to complaints from network users, you'll want to invest the time required to configure this system properly for your network.

The problem is that the network will produce many more events than you'll want to deal with directly. So your EMS needs to process all these events and somehow just report to you when there's a problem that needs your attention. To do so, your EMS must have the knowledge to determine what events require what type of action, if any. This chapter will assist you in ensuring that your EMS can perform this function successfully.

Your EMS should be the point to which all events are delivered and the point to which everything interested in faults should go to find them. So, for example, when your availability monitor discovers devices it can't contact or regains contact with devices, it should deliver this information as events to your EMS. The network devices will discover issues that you'll want to process through your EMS. Your EMS is responsible for determining when there are faults and distributing these faults to your team to repair and to your network health displays. The EMS also is responsible for logging low-priority faults. And finally, it needs to record faults and time to resolution and deliver the faults to reporting systems to enable you to determine your network reliability or uptime. These relationships are shown in Figure 6-1.

Figure 6-1   *Event and Fault Management System*

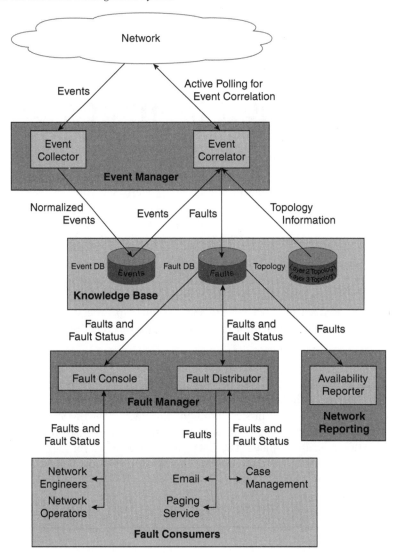

For clarity of discussion, this chapter treats your EMS as if it were separate and distinct from your NMS. We are distinguishing your EMS from the rest of your NMS, regardless of whether your EMS is a separate product or set of scripts, or an integrated part of a commercial NMS.

This chapter covers the following:

- An overview of events, including event producers, event types, and event delivery protocols and methods
- Event-processing to determine faults—including collection, normalization, correlation, and fault determination
- Fault management, including fault tracking, fault delivery, and network self-repair

Event Overview

In order to successfully process all events, you need to be able to understand the different event producers, types of events, and the methods used to deliver them.

Events can be divided into two broad categories: state change and performance. *State change events* are triggered when something in the network changes state. *Performance events* are generated when a possible performance issue is noticed by some component of your network. Most performance events are generated by thresholds that are defined by you on your network devices or NMS stations.

Table 6-1 summarizes these items, and the next three sections discuss them in detail.

Table 6-1   *Methods Used by Event Producers to Deliver Events*

Methods		Event Producers			
		Network Device	Server	Network Management System polling	Trouble Ticketing System
Event Type	State Change	SNMP notification Syslog message\	SNMP notification Syslog message Log file entry	SNMP notification NMS event Log file entry	NMS event Log file entry
	Performance	SNMP notification	SNMP notification Syslog message Log file entry	SNMP notification NMS event Syslog message Log file entry	NMS event Syslog message Log file entry

Event Producers

Any device on the network can produce an event. In addition, events can be produced by your network-management systems or call-tracking systems. Network engineers can identify issues and directly enter them as events.

Some examples of components that produce events and the types of events they might generate are as follows:

- Devices that provide network connectivity such as hubs, switches, and routers can generate events such as the loss or re-establishment of connectivity between two devices.

- Computers providing services can generate events such as a database or print server becoming available or unavailable.

- Network-management systems can generate events such as an event that is triggered if, after calculating the number of collisions versus the network load, a sample falls outside the expected curve.

- An event could be produced by an end user of the network calling the help desk and reporting a problem such as the inability to reach a particular printer. The help desk technician may generate an incident report that would trigger an event describing the incident reported.

State Change Event Types

Examples of state change events include the following:

- A network device loses power and the NMS notices it via availability polling and generates an event.

- A WAN link goes down and the network devices attached to it generate link-down events.

- A device using spanning tree becomes the root bridge and reports this event as a newRoot SNMP notification.

One of the first types of network monitoring that companies typically implement is availability monitoring. Typically, an application or system will send pings or SNMP requests to devices to determine whether they still have network connectivity. If devices change state, an event is generated.

Performance Event Types

Examples of performance events are the following:

- An NMS is polling for interface utilization and triggers an event when utilization exceeds 80 percent.

- A network device triggers an event when an RMON alarm determines that the number of errors on a WAN link exceeds 10 per second.

- A database on a network server reports that it only has 10 percent free space for new data.

Performance events may represent high-priority faults on your network. For example, the number of errors on the WAN link may represent all data on that link and, therefore, a total loss of connectivity on that link.

On the other hand, many performance events represent a capacity issue on a link or device. You may have used most or all of your bandwidth on a link, or the CPU on a device may be very busy for a significant amount of time. Both of these situations represent degradation of the network. If the degradation is severe enough it may represent a high-priority fault. If not, the faults can be logged for viewing at a convenient time.

Protocols

Many protocols or methods can be used to save or deliver events. You'll have to deal with several of them to handle all your network devices. Many network devices send your EMS some events via SNMP and others through the syslog protocol. To make matters more complicated, some events are sent by only one protocol or the other, whereas other events are sent via both protocols. Your EMS will have to deal with duplicate events, in some cases. The following sections discuss the commonly used delivery protocols. For more details, see Chapter 8, "Understanding Network Management Protocols."

Log Files

Log files are used by many event producers to record the events they generate. Sometimes, the only way to determine that these events occurred is to parse the log files and extract the event information. Some log files only have event information. Others have a variety of data mixed in with the event information. Your EMS must extract the event information and then process the events. In addition, it must keep track of how much it has processed so that it can continue to process the file in the correct place, even if the system has been rebooted. Also, your EMS must understand how to manage your log files so it can keep track of its place.

Some examples of log files that might have event information include the following:

- syslog log files
- system console log files
- application message files

Syslog log files have some degree of structure, unlike most other log files. Log files are the most difficult source of events that your EMS has to deal with. The section "Collecting and Normalizing Log Files" provides some tips on how best to handle them.

Syslog Messages

The syslog protocol usually is associated with UNIX environments. Syslog was developed to manage console messages for the UNIX OS. It is now used for many different applications. It is suited to free-form text messages and allows the sender of the messages to associate a facility or category and a priority to each message. Typically, a syslog server collects these messages into a log file. An event management system needs a process to watch this file and process the messages as events. For more information on syslog, see the "Syslog" section of Chapter 8. We'll cover details on how to handle syslog files in the section "Collecting and Normalizing Syslog Messages" later in this chapter. At least syslog log files have some semblance of structure!

Cisco devices send messages to the console. These messages are the same messages that are delivered via the syslog protocol, with the exception of boot and crash messages.

SNMP Notifications

The Simple Network Management Protocol has a facility for agents (typically implemented as a process running on each device on the network) to send asynchronous messages to a trap receiver. These messages are much more rigidly formatted than syslog messages and, therefore, are more complex to define and administer. This same rigidity, however, facilitates the normalization of these messages into a common event format. These notifications, sent as either SNMP traps or informs, are defined in the SNMP Management Information Base supported by the agent. For more information about SNMP notifications please see the "Notifications" section of Chapter 8.

Traps Versus Informs

The first version of SNMP that was standardized, typically referred to as SNMPv1, defined *traps* as the mechanism to deliver asynchronous messages. When SNMP was being redesigned, a new delivery mechanism was defined in the SNMPv2 proposals. Although SNMPv2 never was ratified as a standard, the same mechanism was carried over to the SNMPv2c protocol, which is now an Internet standard. This mechanism, *informs*, is similar to traps and adds a reply mechanism so the SNMP agent can better ensure that a message is delivered. Although this mechanism provides an acknowledgment, it can't ensure that every notification gets to its destination. If there is no network connectivity to a destination, the agent eventually stops trying to send the notification. If the agent is reset, usually all notifications and states are lost. Informs use more resources in the agent than traps. If connectivity is lost to the management station for awhile, some of the notifications delivered after connectivity is restored may no longer be relevant.

Agents that implement SNMPv2c or SNMPv3 can deliver all SNMP notifications to a given destination via either the traps or informs method. Thus, the agent can choose to send informs for all SNMP notifications, including those defined before the informs mechanism was defined.

RMON Alarms/Events

RMON defines a generalized alarm mechanism, whereby an alarm can be defined as an SNMP object crossing a threshold. A hysteresis algorithm is built-in through the definition of rising and falling thresholds (see "Hysteresis" in Chapter 5, "Configuring Events"). RMON alarms trigger RMON events. RMON events can be defined that cause the SNMP agent to send a SNMP notification.

Syslog Events Delivered as SNMP Notifications

Certain devices can trigger an SNMP notification every time a syslog message is generated. This mechanism provides a unified delivery mechanism for all syslog messages and SNMP traps or informs. However, the details of the message are still contained in text and must be parsed out as if the event were a syslog message.

Cisco IOS devices allow you to deliver syslog messages as SNMP notifications with the **syslog** keyword on either the **snmp-server enable** or the **snmp-server host** commands.

NMS Events

NMS generate events for a variety of reasons, including thresholds set on polling objects. Your EMS needs these events delivered to it for processing, along with all other events. If your NMS includes the functions of your EMS, the delivery will be built-in. If not, you will have to choose a method to deliver these events. The method you choose will depend on both your NMS and your EMS. Often, your NMS will support sending SNMP notifications and your EMS should be able to receive them.

Event Processing to Determine Faults

The goal of event management is to collect all event information and determine what, if any, actions need to be taken as a result of each event. The art to event management is learning what events not to display or react to.

There are several steps that must be taken on receipt of an event:

1 Events must be collected. Usually, events will come in from a variety of sources through several different methods or protocols, as described in the previous sections of this chapter.

2 Upon receipt, the events should be normalized to facilitate their processing. *Normalizing* means to format the events in a consistent way.

3 Next, you must determine whether this event can be filtered or deleted. Because the volume of events to be processed can be very high, it is important to eliminate undesired events as early as possible. *Filtering* means to eliminate undesirable events by comparing them to some pattern and eliminating those events that match the pattern.

4 Next, the management system should correlate events and determine the faults that exist in the network. *Correlate* in this context means to examine events to determine the root cause of a problem.

5 Finally, the event and fault management system must take some sort of action on each of these faults.

The following sections go through these steps in more detail.

Event Collection, Normalization, and Filtering

Events need to be collected in a variety of ways. Each protocol will require a different technique and these techniques will be covered in the following sections on each protocol.

You need to normalize the events so that they can be processed in the same way, regardless of the delivery mechanism. The EMS you choose may do much or all of the normalization for you. Or it may require you to supply scripts to do some of the normalization—for example, for delivering events to it that are delivered via protocols not supported by that EMS.

Filtering these events is important to do as early as possible to reduce the processing load on your EMS. You may choose to filter events before they are normalized or normalize your events and then filter them all at the same time.

The EMS you use determines the format you use to normalize your events. We are proposing a list of information that needs to be included in the normalized events so that we can discuss the steps to normalize events delivered by the different protocols or methods. This information includes the following:

- Source
- Time
- Priority
- Type
- Variables

You must choose how to represent each of these in the normalized event format.

First, the source of the event often comes in as an IP address. You may want to convert it to the hostname of the device or a specific IP address such as a loopback address. Also, because some devices have many IP addresses, you may want to control which IP address is used when these devices produce events. This is covered in detail in "Setting Up a Loopback Interface" in Chapter 18, "Best Practices for Device Configuration." Selecting what to use as the time of the event depends on several things. The time of the event is often best set by the event producer. Some protocols provide the capability to supply the time the event occurred, or at least the time the event was sent from the event producer. If you are using Network Time Protocol (NTP) or another way of setting the time throughout your network, the time from your event producers will be the most accurate time. Otherwise, you are better off using the time that the event was delivered to your EMS. More detail on time and NTP is covered in "Setting Up NTP" in Chapter 18, "Best Practices for Device Configuration."

One other decision is how to represent and store time. In most cases, your EMS will make this decision for you. But you'll still need to be aware of the issues and make sure that your EMS handles time sufficiently well for your environment.

If all of your network is in one time zone, you won't have to deal with time zone issues. But if your network is spread across time zones, you should pick a standard way to represent time, either in universal time or in the time zone of your network operations center. You still need to preserve the zone that the device is in so that you can do thresholding and report performance data on a business-hours basis.

Often, the easiest way is to store time in the native format for the platform your EMS is running on. A standard UNIX-format time is stored as a four-byte integer that represents the seconds elapsed since January 1, 1970. You probably also want to store the time zone of the source device.

The priority of the event itself (as distinct from the event producer's priority) is sometimes supplied with the event. Alternatively, you need to get it from your knowledge base. Even if the event supplies a priority, you may choose to override it with information from your knowledge base. In fact, because the device has no concept of the relative importance of different interfaces or ports, you will usually have to adjust or override the priority of the event.

You should always be able to deduce the event type from the event; otherwise, the event will be just so much scrap. Details on how to do this are included in the following sections.

The variables or variable bindings sometimes are supplied by the event. Sometimes, they need to be parsed out of a text field. Even if they are supplied, they often need to be translated in some fashion. For example, SNMP will supply ifIndex for many traps associated with interfaces. However, you will probably want to represent your interfaces with names or functional labels such as **T1toBombay** or names such as **Ethernet0**.

After the events are normalized, they need to be saved into a central repository so they can be processed. Depending on the size and topology of your network, you may choose to have several repositories in different locations. The important thing is to collect all events for a given part of your network in the appropriate repository. If an event affects multiple parts of the network, it may need to be delivered to multiple repositories.

A repository can be a database, a formatted file, or a pipe between the event collector and normalizer and the event correlator—whatever works for your EMS.

The following sections go through each type of delivery mechanism and what needs to be done to collect and normalize these events.

Collecting and Normalizing Log Files

Many delivery mechanisms place the information into files, usually text files. Basically, the steps your EMS needs to take in order to extract the events contained in log files are as follows:

1 Lock the file. If a lock can't be obtained immediately, wait until one is available.

2 Read a line.

3 Filter, if required, to extract just the events or desired events.

4 Send events on for processing.

5 Mark the location in the file in a stateful way.

6 Unlock the file.

When you manage your log files, whether that means truncating them or archiving them, you'll need to take the following steps:

1 Lock the file. If a lock can't be obtained immediately, wait until one is available.

2 Determine the marked location.

3 Truncate or archive the data before the marked location.

4 Re-mark the location.

5 Unlock the file.

Many administrators schedule log-file maintenance once a night or once a week. Another choice is to set a threshold on how large the log file is allowed to grow.

To make a robust system, you need to take a few more steps. One important step is to track the rate at which events are added to the file and the rate at which they are being processed to determine whether your EMS can handle the rate at which events are being generated. You also want your processes to be able to be stopped at the right point when the system is shut down or the EMS system needs maintenance. You need a reliable mechanism for starting automatic processes.

Collecting and Normalizing Syslog Messages

Syslog is normally used to collect information about the system it is running on, as well as to collect messages from other systems. Syslog messages are sent to a particular *facility* and also have a particular priority. The syslog server can be configured to send messages with certain facilities and/or priorities to certain log files. See the "Syslog" section of Chapter 8 for more information on syslog facilities. Cisco routers and switches, by default, send their syslog messages to the facility "local7." Therefore, it is easy to configure the syslog server to log all messages from Cisco devices to one file. Then, you can process this log file following the steps in the previous section.

Normalization of syslog messages can be fairly easy. However, extracting the type of message and the variables embedded in it requires knowledge of each possible syslog message. For example, consider a syslog message that indicates that an interface went down:

```
Sep 19 16:51:07 10.29.2.1 79: Sep 19 16:50:24: %LINEPROTO-5-UPDOWN: Line protocol
on Interface Ethernet0, changed state to down
```

The first three strings show the date and time when the message was received at the syslog server. The next field shows the address or name of the event producer. The next field is the process ID of the process on the event producer that sent the message. All the rest is the text of the message. So, here are the standard fields, as shown in the example:

- Date/time from the syslog server = Sep 19 16:51:07
- Event producer IP address = 10.29.2.1
- Process ID on the event producer = 79

Cisco IOS devices format the text field as follows:

- The first field or fields is a representation of the date and/or time on the device if you have "service timestamps" configured on the device. This can make it a bit interesting to parse this file if you don't have your devices configured the same way.
- The next field is formatted into three subfields: facility, severity, and mnemonic. Note that the facility is not the same as the facility that's part of the syslog protocol. This facility documents what part of the Cisco IOS generated the message.
- The final field is the freeform text message. Often important information, such as which interface this message applies to (as in the previous message), is included in this field.

Cisco IOS syslog messages are documented in the "Cisco IOS Software System Error Messages" manual. This document can be used to help normalize syslog messages. The facility, severity, and mnemonic fields can be used to look up messages in this manual.

Once again, here is the Cisco-specific part of the example message:

- Date/time from the Cisco event producer = Sep 19 16:50:24
- Cisco facility that generated the message = LINEPROTO

- Severity = 5
- Mnemonic of the error = UPDOWN
- Text = `Line protocol on Interface Ethernet0, changed state to down`

Note that two date/time entries appear in the syslog message, one recorded by the syslog server and one by the device sending the message. The entry you should use depends on how you manage time on your network. The most accurate time for the event will be the one supplied by the device, provided you've used something such as NTP to set the time accurately for your entire network.

The event producer is sent to the syslog server as an IP address. Most syslog servers attempt to resolve the address to a hostname and, if successful, put the name in the log. By default, Cisco IOS devices use the address of the interface that sends the packet out as the source address. You can specify a different address with the **logging source-interface** command. It is a good idea to specify a loopback interface as the chosen interface for this command. Then, you can rely on all syslog messages having the same address or name from this device.

Interpreting the text part of the example message, you can see that the type of this event is a link-down message and the interface that went down is Ethernet0. As just discussed, you can choose to track interfaces by name or by a functional label.

The event shows the severity or priority of this message as 5. You can choose to override this priority with information from your knowledge base. To summarize, the example trap would be normalized to the following:

- Source = `10.29.2.1`
- Time = `Sep 19 16:50:24` (may want to convert to UTC)
- Priority = 5
- Type = `linkDown`
- Variables = `Interface Ethernet0`

Collecting and Normalizing SNMP Notifications

SNMP notifications are somewhat easier to deal with than the preceding event types because they usually are delivered directly to your EMS from the event producer and they come formatted, not as an unformatted text string.

With the definition of SNMPv2, you can choose to send SNMP notifications as either traps or informs. For the purpose of collection and normalization, it doesn't matter which mechanism delivered the event.

Consider the example event from the previous discussion of syslog messages, but this time delivered via SNMP. We show how it's delivered as a SNMPv1 trap as that is the most obscure to decode. A linkDown notification that is equivalent to the previous syslog message would have the following interesting fields:

> Source = `10.29.2.1`
> Generic trap ID = `linkDown` (3)
> Specific trap ID = `0` (not applicable because this is a generic trap)
> SysUpTime = `203137`
> Trap OID = `snmpTraps` (1.3.6.1.6.3.1.1.4)
> Varbinds =
> ifIndex = `1`
> ifAdminStatus = `Up`
> ifOperStatus = `Down`

First, how do you know what trap this is? The generic trap ID tells you this is a linkDown trap and the trap OID tells you that it is the standard MIB-II version of this generic trap.

Before getting into details of normalizing it, it is helpful to look at the definition of a linkDown trap, from MIB-II as defined in RFC 2233:

```
linkDown NOTIFICATION-TYPE
        OBJECTS { ifIndex, ifAdminStatus, ifOperStatus }
        STATUS  current
        DESCRIPTION
                "A linkDown trap signifies that the SNMPv2 entity,
                acting in an agent role, has detected that the
                ifOperStatus object for one of its communication links
                is about to transition into the down state."
        ::= { snmpTraps 3 }
```

The source address of the notification identifies the event producer. Similar to syslog messages, Cisco IOS devices use the address of the interface that the message goes out unless told otherwise. Once again, the easiest way to control the address is to choose a loopback interface and select that interface through the **snmp-server trap-source** global configuration command. See the section "Setting Up a Loopback Interface" in Chapter 18 for more information about using loopback interfaces.

The time for this event must be the time that the event is received at the EMS because SNMP provides only sysUpTime, but doesn't provide a way to correlate sysUpTime to the actual time that an event occurred.

SNMP doesn't provide any hints about the priority of this event, so you have to rely on your knowledge base to supply the priority of a link-down event. For this example, assume that the knowledge base supplies a priority of 5.

Next, the variable bindings for this notification provide some useful information about this event. The first tells you the ifIndex of the interface. Of course, you need to translate this to some sort of meaningful term. You can choose to use the interface name or a description of the function of this interface.

The ifAdminStatus and ifOperStatus may help you determine what happened to shut down the interface, so you will want to preserve these variable bindings. There are times when the interface status changes so quickly on the device that it shows the interface up even though the event is link-down. What is happening in this case is that the event is queued for delivery, but the objects for the variable bindings are not sampled until the packet is being generated. This situation can lead to what looks like inaccuracies in the data.

Here's the event after normalization:

- Source = 10.29.2.1
- Time = <Sep 19 16:51:07> (from the local EMS system time)
- Priority = 5 (from the knowledge base)
- Type = linkDown
- Variables = Interface Ethernet0
  - AdminStatus 'up'
  - OperStatus 'down'

RMON events are always delivered as SNMP notifications. Syslog messages can be delivered as SNMP notifications. The following two sections discuss briefly how to collect and normalize these events.

Normalizing RMON Alarms/Events Delivered as SNMP Notifications

RMON alarms can trigger RMON events. RMON events can be delivered to your EMS as a SNMP notification. Take a look at the definition of these SNMP notifications:

```
risingAlarm TRAP-TYPE
    ENTERPRISE rmon
    VARIABLES { alarmIndex, alarmVariable, alarmSampleType,
                alarmValue, alarmRisingThreshold }
    DESCRIPTION
        "The SNMP trap that is generated when an alarm
        entry crosses its rising threshold and generates
        an event that is configured for sending SNMP
        traps."
    ::= 1

fallingAlarm TRAP-TYPE
    ENTERPRISE rmon
    VARIABLES { alarmIndex, alarmVariable, alarmSampleType,
                alarmValue, alarmFallingThreshold }
    DESCRIPTION
        "The SNMP trap that is generated when an alarm
        entry crosses its falling threshold and generates
```

```
                        an event that is configured for sending SNMP
                        traps."
                ::= 2
```

RMON alarms are triggered by an object's value crossing a threshold, so most RMON alarms are set on performance-related objects and, therefore, generate performance events. Because these events are delivered using a standard definition, there will be very little information about the specific object. To fill out the variable bindings for this event, or even the specific event type, you'll first have to determine what the alarmVariable is. You may need to query the event producer for additional information.

Other than these small differences, RMON events can be treated as standard SNMP notifications.

Normalizing Syslog Events Delivered as SNMP Notifications

Syslog messages can be delivered as SNMP notifications by Cisco IOS devices. This relieves the EMS from dealing with log files and can improve the reliability of delivery through the informs mechanism defined in SNMPv2. So, processing these events is a combination of receiving the event through SNMP and processing the event as if it were a syslog message. See the previous sections on syslog messages and SNMP notifications to review how to process these events. Just remember that even if the event is delivered as a SNMP notification, the information is contained in the text portion of the message, just like a syslog message.

You may decide to use this mechanism to deliver all syslog messages from Cisco IOS devices. This will mean that you have one fewer log file to track and manage. Managing SNMP notifications should be much less costly for your EMS.

Collecting and Normalizing NMS Events

Your NMS will usually have a built-in event system. Both your NMS and associated applications use this event system to deliver and consolidate events. Your NMS may receive an event of one type and this may trigger the creation of another event. You may want to deliver some or all of these events to your EMS. For example, your NMS may collect all SNMP notifications. It will be important that your EMS receive these events.

There may be several mechanisms to deliver these events to your EMS. The mechanisms may log the events to a file, which can be processed as outlined previously for log files.

Most NMS systems have a mechanism to take an action upon receipt of an event. The NMS could deliver the event through this mechanism to your EMS. The EMS would then normalize the event and continue to process it in the same way as any other message.

The details on normalizing messages depend on the NMS used and the format of its events.

Correlating Events to Determine Faults

After you have all your events in the same format, you can start to correlate them and determine whether they represent faults in your network. The steps required to process your events are discussed in following sections. We introduce the concept of correlation and discuss some specific correlations that can be performed. More correlations are covered throughout Part II of this book.

Correlating Duplicate Events

When you receive an event, an obvious correlation is to look for a duplicate event that has been processed with a timestamp close to the timestamp of the first event. Duplicate events may be found because the device delivers the same event through two different protocols. Or duplicate events may indicate that there is a repeating problem. In the first case, one event can be deleted. In the second case, the EMS should store only one event and extend the information about this event to include the timeframe over which it is occurring and how many instances of this event have occurred.

The time frame in which to look for duplicate events should be short, on the order of just a few seconds in most cases. It is important to not conceal instances when, for example, interfaces may be flapping. At the same time, it is important to reduce the many events produced by the flapping down to one fault that reports the flapping interface and the duration of the problem.

The events left after the elimination of duplicate events should be correlated using the techniques in the following sections.

Passive and Active Correlation

Correlation engines can work in two ways, either operating with the knowledge of network state as delivered by events, or using events as a starting point and actively polling network devices in response to events received. The first method is known as *passive correlation*; the second method is known as *active correlation*. Both are valid ways to determine faults and have their advantages and disadvantages.

Passive correlation may take more time to determine the root cause of one or a group of events. However, it doesn't put any additional load on your network.

Active correlation can sometimes significantly reduce the time to determine root cause and, therefore, network faults. But it does so by increasing the amount of traffic on your network. In most cases, this traffic will be small, but the application must be designed carefully to ensure that it does not cause more issues than it resolves.

Both techniques can be applied to the correlations in the following sections.

Correlating Network and Segment Events

This section discusses the kind of network and segment correlations that can be performed without prior knowledge of the topology of the network. Many more correlations can be done with knowledge of the Layer 2 or Layer 3 topology of the network; some of them are discussed in the section "Correlating Events on the Basis of Topology."

Certain things can be correlated easily across a network or subnet. For example, Layer 3 broadcast and multicast traffic is seen by all nodes on the same logical network segment or VLAN. If thresholds for the amount of non-unicast traffic are in place around the network, many events may be generated by high amounts of this traffic. Instead of creating new faults for each event, your EMS could update the first fault with the number of instances seen and the timeframe over which it is occurring. The only Layer 3 knowledge required is the IP address and subnet mask to be able to correlate these events. Note that if a switch supports VLANs, you can't assume that all ports can be correlated.

Correlating information on a point-to-point link is easy also, given that both sides share a common IP subnet. Utilization should be the same and should trigger the same events. Networks utilizing IP unnumbered links require Layer 2 topology knowledge to correlate these links. The Cisco Discovery Protocol (CDP) enables you to correlate these links.

Correlating Events on the Basis of Technology

Often, you can correlate events based upon the technology to verify whether a fault exists. Part II of this book goes into technology correlation in detail. A couple of examples are discussed here.

If you have thresholds on both utilization and collisions on an Ethernet interface and if both thresholds are triggered at nearly the same time, the fault is almost always the utilization. Collisions on Ethernet are a product of the high utilization. A possible way of avoiding the need to do this correlation is to have a more complex threshold for collisions that takes into account the network utilization and only triggers an event if the number of collisions increases without a corresponding increase in network utilization.

Excessive collisions, although indicative of a problem with the network, can also cause many other symptoms on the same interface. For example, you will often see output queue drops on this interface as the packets back up because they can't be sent. If you have thresholds set on queue drops, you may find correlations there also.

Very high utilization on an interface also correlates with output queue drops, so it's important to look at the interface as a whole and determine the root of the problem. So, if you see high collisions and high utilization, as well as output queue drops, you can correlate all of these events to high utilization on this physical Ethernet segment. However, if you see high collisions and high output queue drops, but not high utilization, there is probably a physical problem on that segment.

Correlating Events on the Basis of Topology

When you know the topology of the network, you can make many more correlations, thus allowing you to eliminate many events and report just the underlying fault. The tradeoff is that maintaining accurate knowledge of the network topology can be quite difficult and applying that knowledge to event correlation can be equally difficult. The next two sections review some of the benefits of applying these types of correlations.

Layer 2 Correlation

With knowledge of where the network management station is in relation to the Layer 2 topology of a network, your EMS can determine whether many events are due to one fault.

For example, suppose you have a switch in your datacenter connected to switches on each floor of your building. You may have multiple switches feeding parts of the fifth floor off the main floor switch. You may also have departmental servers on the fifth floor. Suppose you lose the trunk port going from the datacenter to the fifth floor switch. It may be a cabling issue or a board or port failure on one of the switches. In any case, you lose connectivity to all networked devices on the fifth floor. You will very soon receive many events.

Probably the first event to arrive is the link-down event from the datacenter switch, indicating that the trunk port is down. Your availability monitor will also report many events over the next few minutes, indicating that all the devices on the fifth floor are down. However, your EMS can generate a fault from the link-down event, based on knowledge base information that this port is a critical port. If your EMS incorrectly reported faults from any availability events, these incorrectly reported faults will need to be suppressed or retracted. Any availability events for these devices that arrive after the root cause fault has been determined can be directly suppressed as being symptoms of the same fault.

It is important that your EMS have knowledge of when the fault is resolved because while this fault was being resolved, other faults may have occurred that your EMS didn't have visibility to because they occurred on the other side of this fault. So, after this fault is resolved, your EMS should make certain to check the status of the devices on the other side of the fault and create new faults, if necessary.

Another example is correlating CRC and frame alignment errors with duplex mismatches on twisted-pair Ethernet technology connections. If autonegotiation fails to negotiate both sides correctly or if the devices on either side of the link are configured incorrectly, there may be a duplex mismatch. This will result in CRC and/or frame-alignment errors on the receiving side of one or both sides. With knowledge of Layer 2, your EMS can correlate the duplex settings of both sides and determine whether these errors and associated threshold events are due to this duplex mismatch. Your NMS could check the whole network for duplex mismatches or your EMS could check for duplex mismatches only when a CRC or frame-alignment threshold is triggered.

Layer 3 Correlation

Layer 3 correlation can do many of the same kinds of things that Layer 2 correlation can, only for things such as IP networks and subnets instead of segments and LANs.

Consider an example of network failure that affects the Layer 3 topology of the network. Say you have a routed topology that has a connection from a router in your home office in Chicago, Illinois to a regional office in Denver, Colorado. You have some servers in the regional office and the router in Denver also provides connectivity to smaller offices around the southwest. The link from Chicago to Denver goes down. So, just as in the previous example, you'll get a linkDown trap from the home office router.

Your knowledge base should indicate that this link is critical to your southwest operations and that a high-priority fault has occurred. Without correlation, this issue would soon be buried in all the availability events that start coming in soon after. With correlation, it becomes obvious that these availability events are due to the link-down fault and should be suppressed until this issue is resolved.

As in the Layer 2 correlation example, it is important for the EMS to notice when repairs are affected and start processing the suppressed events again so that any more minor faults that may have occurred can be noticed and reported.

Another Layer 3 correlation that may be a bit more interesting is a network where OSPF is used as the routing protocol. Availability polling is reporting intermittent connectivity issues in the network. CPU load on the routers in Area 1 is quite high, as noticed by events generated by thresholds on the avgBusy5 object from the OLD-CISCO-CPU-MIB or (preferred) the cpmCPUTotal5min from the CISCO-PROCESS-MIB. And a high rate of ospfOriginateLsa events is coming from one of the same routers. Lots of ospfIfStateChange events are coming from the same router. Link-down events are also coming from the same router and the same interface. The EMS can correlate all of these events and determine that a flapping interface is causing a high rate of change in the OSPF routing table, enough to cause the CPU load on the routers to stay high. There is intermittent connectivity loss due to routes dropping as the routers fail to keep up with the high rate of change.

All these events can be suppressed until the issue with this interface is cleared up. Your EMS should maintain a careful watch to ensure that it suppresses only the events that can reasonably be expected to be the result of this issue. Then, after the fault is resolved your EMS can review the suppressed events to determine whether there are any other faults hiding behind the resolved fault.

Fault Delivery, Notification, Reporting, and Repair

Now that faults have occurred, you need to do something with them. You uncovered a problem with the network. Of course, not all problems are as important as others are. The next few sections will discuss the following:

- Methods of fault delivery
- Notifying key personnel of critical faults
- Reporting faults
- Effecting fault repair

Methods of Fault Delivery

The first step to processing faults is delivering them to the correct recipients. Faults need to be delivered to a repository so that they can be processed easily and in a manner that reflects their priority. The lowest-priority faults should be logged to a file for processing when time allows. Higher priority faults should be delivered to a system for tracking faults.

Logging Faults

The only faults that should be logged are low-priority faults. Issues such as performance faults representing utilization thresholds exceeded on links on your network should be logged and processed for planning increased capacity in those areas of your network.

Low-priority faults do not include those that represent either a loss of connectivity on your network or a reduction of redundancy in the network so another fault could cause a loss of connectivity.

Delivering Faults to a Tracking Application

Faults that require attention should be delivered to a tracking application to assure that these faults receive the attention they deserve.

Two possibilities for tracking faults are a fault console—a lightweight mechanism for tracking and distributing faults—and a trouble-ticketing system. Trouble-ticketing may be overkill for smaller networks, but for larger ones it may be very appropriate. Both of these options are discussed in the following two sections.

Fault Consoles

Faults on a fault console should be sorted and viewable by priority and the time the fault occurred so network engineers can determine easily where to start on all of the issues being tracked. It should be possible to view all faults of a particular type so that an engineer working on capacity issues, for example, can easily view the relevant faults. If the network is large and complex and there are many network operators and engineers, a checkout procedure is desirable so it is clear which faults are being worked on by and by whom.

Trouble-Ticketing Systems

For a trouble-ticketing system to work as a tracking system for your network faults, it must do all that a fault console does and more. For example, your trouble-ticketing system should have the capability to add detailed notes on the status of the processing of the events and the resolution of the event. Trouble-ticketing systems will often be able to track the time to repair a fault. Also, they may be able to track how a fault was resolved. If this includes the replacement of equipment, it may be able to communicate this information to your inventory system so your inventory stays current.

Although a fault console may allow a fault or a group of faults to be closed with just a couple of clicks of the mouse, most trouble-ticketing systems require more time from your operators and engineers. It may be possible to get enough data from the type and nature of faults and their resolution to make this time worthwhile. However, you must convince your operators and engineers of this. Otherwise, much of the information in your expensive trouble ticketing system may consist of lots of "not-applicables."

Notifying Key Personnel of Critical Faults

Some faults represent critical issues in your network that need immediate attention. After delivering these faults to a tracking application, you may wish to notify key personnel that these faults have occurred. First, you must determine which group to deliver the fault to. Normally, most network support organizations will have two groups to deliver faults to: network operators and network engineers.

Some faults, such as WAN link outages, require an operator to contact your service provider with the circuit ID that appears to be down. Other issues when the problem is not so well-defined, such as late or excessive collisions on a network segment that will require analysis of the issue to determine the component at fault and therefore will have to be sent to a network engineer.

Your knowledge base should have details on how you want your faults delivered. Issues that are not well-defined or not in your knowledge base should be delivered to your network engineers for further analysis.

What is to be done with different priority faults, such as paging network engineers for high-priority faults, should be set as a policy on your network and be part of your knowledge base.

Because network engineers and technicians need to be mobile to be able to deal with faults, your EMS needs to be able to determine how best to contact them for different priorities of faults. Some of the alternatives are discussed in the following sections.

Popup Fault Notifications

Some faults should be forwarded to network engineers or technicians via online notification such as a popup window.

Often, operator notifications are handled through pop-up windows on the operator console. This only works for a low rate of notifications because a screen covered with lots of pop-up windows is annoying in the least and can require acknowledgment of each screen before you can use the system, which can take lots of time. For a very low rate, some sort of audible or visual alarm should be added. No one is going to stare at a screen for hours at a time.

Email

It is often useful to email notice of a fault and its associated ID or number to the assigned engineer or technician. Including the priority and nature of the fault allows the engineer to treat the fault with the proper urgency.

Pager and Phone

If your network engineers or technicians carry pagers or portable phones, you'll probably want to notify them about faults assigned to them that are high-priority. Some organizations choose to have a dispatcher or network operator take the fault and notify the appropriate person by page or phone. Other organizations choose to have the EMS do this directly. Once again, it is important to give as much information as possible, but to keep it very short.

Reporting Faults

Faults can be reported many ways. The next two sections discuss the following methods:

- Reporting network status
- Reporting network health

If you've done a quality job up until now, the active faults on the network should accurately map the problems with your network. In each of these two reporting methods, you will be using the active faults on your network to determine the state of the network.

Reporting Network Status

If you have a network map as part of your NMS, it should be possible to have faults change the color of the affected devices as a way of tracking your network's status. The problem with the highest priority that isn't being currently worked on should generate the reddest color. If you have an escalation policy for faults, such as all Priority 2 faults not resolved within three hours are automatically promoted to the next level or receive additional attention, the color of the affected devices should also reflect this escalation. This can be done as part of your fault console or as an action triggered by your trouble-ticketing system.

Reporting Network Health

A report of network health is the inverse of reporting the fault status of your network. There are many ways of reporting the health of your network. Network health reporting is discussed at length in the "Network and Device Health Reporting" section of Chapter 4, "Performance Measurement and Reporting."

Effecting Fault Repair

You've come a long way from where you started. Instead of having to wait for users to tell you when things are broken, you have the network intelligently reporting problems. The next step is to have your network attempt to repair itself. This capability isn't going to put you out of business by any stretch of the imagination. In fact, designing and implementing such a system for your network require your imagination and experience. The benefit can be a possibly dramatically decreased mean time to repair your network and, therefore, happier users.

Levels of Autonomy

In some cases, it might be possible for your EMS to determine the source of the fault and to effect a method of bypassing or repairing it. There are several levels of autonomy that you might give to your EMS in this area:

- Recommend action.
- Ask, then repair.
- Just do it.

The lowest level of autonomy is for your EMS to recommend a course of action to repair or bypass the fault. At times, this is the only course of action available to your EMS because many faults require human intervention, at least until robotics becomes much more advanced and inexpensive.

The next level of autonomy is for your EMS to ask permission to take an action. The small amount of time required for someone to examine the suggested repair and ensure that it makes sense probably is worthwhile, at least the first couple of times. After an engineer approves the repair, the EMS can implement it. As your confidence grows regarding your EMS' reliability in recommending certain types of repairs, you can consider increasing its autonomy.

The highest level of autonomy is for your network to detect a fault and repair it without any human intervention. You already use this level of autonomy if you use spanning tree, HSRP, or a dynamic routing protocol in your network. What we are talking about here is doing things that the view that your NMS has of your network makes possible. Now, let's look at some examples of what might be possible in your network.

Examples of Fault Repair

Your knowledge base can enable your EMS to determine what actions to take to repair the network. One of the simpler things that your EMS can do is to watch for devices that are misbehaving in ways that affect other devices on the network.

For example, consider a device that is connected to a switch and that continually links to the network and then drops that link. The device's behavior could cause the switch to continuously recalculate its spanning tree—possibly enough that the reliability of the network is affected. The signs of this issue are a port on the switch that is reporting a high rate of link down and up events and a high CPU load on that switch. With the high rate of transitions, it's unlikely that anything useful is being done on that port. Therefore, the EMS could safely recommend that the errant port be shut down. An easy next step would be for the EMS to report the problem for followup later.

Another example involves solving an issue with IP multicast traffic sourced from a switch using CGMP to limit the traffic to only ports that find the traffic "interesting." As CGMP is only able to limit multicast traffic coming from a router, it is possible for one port to flood other ports on the same VLAN on the same switch with a high rate of multicast traffic. If there are ports of varying speeds in that VLAN, it is especially easy for the higher-speed ports to saturate the lower-speed ports with multicast traffic.

Knowing these things about the nature of multicast traffic, you easily can establish a policy for the maximum amount of multicast traffic that is allowed to be sourced from any port. Setting a threshold on the amount of multicast traffic sent on all ports (ifOutMulticastPkts in the IF-MIB from RFC 2233) to the chosen limit will alert you when this policy is violated.

You probably also want to set a separate policy on the maximum amount of broadcast traffic that can be sourced across all ports on that VLAN. In both cases, you can set thresholds. First, you need to select a port that should always be operational and for which the connected devices do not subscribe to any multicast groups. Setting thresholds on the selected port for the amount of multicast traffic received (ifInMulticastPkts) will generate a fault if this VLAN is exceeding this threshold.

Your EMS can report misbehaving ports and shut down ports if the issue is a serious enough problem.

Other possibilities for network self-healing include the EMS understanding recent changes in the network, such as configuration changes on devices or software-image changes, and being able to roll back the changes if problems occur on the network that could be attributed to those changes.

Summary

The process of managing faults and errors can be summarized as follows:

- First, events must be collected. Usually, faults come in from a variety of sources through several different methods or protocols, such as SNMP notifications, syslog messages, entries in log files, or NMS events.

- Next, the events should be normalized to facilitate their processing. Normalizing means to format the events in a consistent way.

- Next, you must decide if the event can be filtered. Filtering means to identify events that don't need to be processed immediately, or ever. Because the volume of events to be processed can be very high, it is important to filter undesired events as early as possible.

- Next, the management system should correlate events and determine the faults that exist in the network. To correlate events means to look for relationships between them to help determine the root cause of a problem. Correlations can exist between duplicate events or between network and segment events; they can occur on the basis of technology or topology.

- Finally, the event and fault management system must take some sort of action on each of the faults. Possibilities include logging the fault, delivering it to the appropriate tracking application, immediately alerting key personnel of a critical fault, or implementing a repair of the network fault.

The next chapter discusses the statistics that a network manager may need to understand in the course of managing a network.

CHAPTER 7

Understanding and Using Basic Network Statistics

Before beginning this chapter, please make sure that you understand the material in Chapter 2, "Policy-Based Network Management." The operational objectives for network management from Chapter 2, in conjunction with the material presented here, will assist you in defining measurable policies and agreements.

Why does a network manager need to have basic statistical knowledge? And what probability and statistical knowledge is needed to understand networking data? This chapter addresses these questions. In particular, it will focus on presenting the level of statistical knowledge that we feel is needed to understand network management and performance, especially with regard to service level objectives/agreements. The only mathematics needed to understand this chapter is algebra.

This chapter discusses the following:

- Reasons for understanding some very basic statistics for network management and analysis
- Some basic statistics needed for network management and performance analysis
- Using these statistics to analyze or understand performance data

We will first concentrate on some basic statistics that should help you understand the data being collected. Second, we will go over some preliminaries to assist you in choosing the variables needed to analyze the performance and capacity on your network.

| NOTE | Most of the equations and figures in this chapter were created using a "mathematical scratchpad" called Mathcad from Mathsoft, Inc., 101 Main Street, Cambridge, MA 02142-1521. Mathcad has a scratchpad-like interface and the software uses real mathematical notation, which makes it easy to learn and deploy by network managers and analysts. |

The Need to Understand Network Statistics

In this section, the need to understand statistics will be shown through the following:

- Availability data

- Random nature of the variables collected for baselines and trending
- The need to aggregate data
- The use of simulation modeling for networking new solution deployment and design

Availability Statistics

One reason that network managers need an understanding of basic statistics is so they can apply availability data effectively in monitoring the network and service-level agreements. To amplify on the availability discussion in Chapter 4, availability can be defined as the probability that a product or service will operate when needed. In data network environments, this can be defined as the average fraction of connection time that the product or service is expected to be in operating condition. For a network that can have partial as well as total system outages, availability is typically expressed as network availability.

Equation 7-1

$$\text{Availability} = \frac{1-(\text{total connection outage time})}{(\text{total in-service connection time})}$$

Equation 7-2

$$\text{Availability} = \frac{1-[\Sigma \, (\text{number of connections affected in outage i} \times \text{duration of outage i})]}{(\text{number of connections in service} \times \text{operating time})}$$

NOTE   In discussions of availability, the term *unavailability* is often required within some of the different types of availability calculations. For instance, see Equation 7-3:

Equation 7-3

Unavailability = 1 – availability

Two key statistical metrics provide more detail for the analysis of availability: mean time between failures (MTBF)and mean time to repair (MTTR).

The time between when the device broke and when it was brought back into service is called the *mean time to repair* (MTTR). In real networks, MTTR can be controlled by using good processes, using a well-developed sparing plan, or paying for high-end service contracts. For example, if you have a device that breaks and you have Cisco's onsite service (with a four hour guaranteed response), the probability is a higher that the device will be down for four hours rather than twenty-four hours. It should be noted that the MTTR includes response time (both Network Operations Center (NOC) and dispatch to the site if necessary), isolation of the fault, time to fix the fault, and verification that the fix did indeed correct the original problem. A trouble ticket can help you measure MTTR by including the times for failure detection, craft dispatch, (if any), fault diagnosis, fault isolation, the actual repair, and any software resynchronization time needed to restore the entire service.

Obviously, a device that breaks down four hours per year is more desirable than a device that is down for twenty-four hours per year. What may not be as obvious and is certainly not easy is the methodology and procedures an organization needs in place to accurately gather this metric.

Mean time between failures (MTBF) is calculated by measuring the average time between failures of a device. In the preceding example, the assumption is that the device fails once each year. This would indicate an MTBF of 8,760 hours (365 days $\times$ 24 hours) less the MTTR of 24 hours, which together equal the number of hours between failures for a year. In fact, if we have MTBF and MTTR, we can then go immediately to solution for availability by using the following mathematics:

Equation 7-4

MTBF = Availability / Number of Failures

Equation 7-5

MTTR = (1 – Availability) / (Number of Failures)

Equation 7-6

MTTR/MTBF = (1 – Availability)/Availability

Equation 7-7

Device Availability = MTBF / (MTBF+MTTR)

NOTE   Equation 7-7 applies to an individual component and its hardware MTBF and MTTR.

In the networking community today, it is somewhat common to hear a requirement for a server to have a 99.999 (or five nines) percent availability. How much time does that translate into? Assume that the time frame is a seven-day by 24-hour operational year. One year = 32,000,000 seconds or 32×10^6 seconds. Looking initially at a yearly availability of 99.9999 would mean that a failure can occur only 1/(1–0.999999) = 0.000001 times per year. Using scientific notation, this works out to a failure rate of $32 \times 10^6 \times 10^{-6} = 32$ seconds for a single device or component. For five nines of availability, this number would be multiplied by 10 for 320 seconds. In a computer network, there are dependencies and redundancies that will impact the aggregate system availability. All of the previous discussion concerns device availability.

Chapter 4's discussion of availability included several different types. In order to show a broader picture of the issues with availability, these areas of path availability, application availability, and reachability will be expanded on and briefly discussed.

Path Availability

Path availability refers to availability from one point in the network to another. Availability from point A to point B in the network can be defined as shown in Equation 7-8, where X is equal to a failure due to software, hardware, power, human error and path convergence time in redundant systems.

Equation 7-8

$$\text{Path availability} = \text{MTBF}_{(x)} / (\text{MTBF}_{(x)} + \text{MTTR}_{(x)})$$

This definition is very useful in predicting the availability of new network systems where the network has a well-defined hierarchy and connectivity from any end point to any other is similar. However, predicting the availability of new software systems and power and the likelihood of human error. Cisco currently has a tool that can predict path availability where X is equal to hardware failures.

Application Availability

Application availability is defined as the probability that an application service will operate when needed. In data network environments, this is defined as the average fraction of application connection time for which an application is expected to be in operating condition for all users of that application (see Equation 7-9). Application availability can then be expressed as the sum of network availability and server/application availability for the users of that service (see Equation 7-10).

Equation 7-9

Application availability = 1 − (total application user connection outage time + total server-application outage time) ÷ (total in-service connection time)

Equation 7-10

Application availability = 1 − [Σ(num application users affected in outage^i × duration of outage^i)] ÷ (operating time × number of application users)

In general, application availability takes into account network availability and server/application availability. The definition of application availability does not include individual user or client workstation issues. This definition is useful for enterprise organizations where application availability is the ultimate goal or requirement.

Server application availability is typically measured by accessing the individual application over time, but may not take into account other network problems that affect connectivity to that application. Comparing the general definition of availability and device availability given earlier, you can see that application availability is a special case of device availability.

Reachability

Another measurement of availability is *reachability*. It can be defined simply as the capability to successfully ping a device B in the network from another device A in the network. An ICMP echo packet is sent to the destination IP address; if the device is reachable, it returns an ICMP echo response to the originating device. If device A receives the ICMP echo response, device B is said to be reachable from that location. Reachability can be used to determine network availability from certain points in the network to other points in the network using the Layer 3 IP protocol. This does not guarantee network availability from all points in the network to all other points and does not guarantee the delivery of upper-layer protocols or other Layer 3 protocols. Reachability can be a useful method, however, of estimating network availability in IP environments.

Other Availability Measurement Methods

Other availability measurement methodologies include the following:

- *Impacted user minutes (IUMs)* can be defined for an organization by the total amount of unproductive user time due to network or server downtime and performance issues.

- *Link & device status* is the cumulative "up" time and "down" time of both the devices and links being measured.

- *ICMP reachability* is the "ping" test on whether a device responds to a ping or not.

- *Application reachability* is a modified "ping" test. It usually uses a udp or tcp form of a ping that goes to the application port or socket. If the application then responds, it is "reachable."

- *Response Time Reporter (RTR)* is a feature set on Cisco routers that allows them to send ICMP pings and other types of packets that devices may respond to. RTR has the additional advantage of being RMON-like in setting thresholds, using events and alarms.

- *Defects per million (DPM)* is the number of calls lost per million calls processed. DPM is particularly useful for measuring the availability of switched virtual circuit (SVC) services in a multiservice switch, where connections are constantly made, sustained, and torn down.

- *Combined methods* could be any or all of these. It usually includes some type of correlation and often heuristics.

Measuring availability is a complicated problem. There are a variety of techniques that can only approximate availability for a given environment. Several major problems exist with measuring availability accurately for a given environment. See the sections "Availability" and "Measuring Availability" in Chapter 4 for more discussion of major inhibitors to accurate availability measurement and the resulting measurement dilemma.

The practical result of the measurement dilemma is that availability numbers themselves have become less meaningful. Both vendors and service providers quickly announce five nines solutions or even 100 percent availability, yet the reality is that the majority of these solutions cannot achieve this level of availability over time (as you saw in the previous five nines example).

Although many end users have become confused about and wary of high availability, they continue to ask for high availability solutions. Customers, vendors, and service providers are all trying to understand what it takes to achieve high availability from a technology, people, expertise, and process perspective.

What the industry needs is a fairly accurate and useful definition of availability that can be applied to most networks and situations. Organizations need to better understand their network availability and what it takes to achieve a higher availability environment. As you can see, an understanding of your network's availability requires some level of knowledge of mathematics and statistics.

Availability Example

Following is a short example of computing the MTBF and availability numbers for the Cisco IOS 11.x software version.

Figure 7-1 shows 472 inter-failure times observed for Cisco's 11.x IOS series software in a "scatter graph." This group includes all minor versions running in a network from the 11.0, 11.1, 11.2, and 11.3 releases. Figure 7-2 shows a histogram of these data plotted under a normal curve.

Figure 7-1   *Scatter Graph of 472 Inter-failure Times Observed for Cisco's 11.x IOS Series Software*

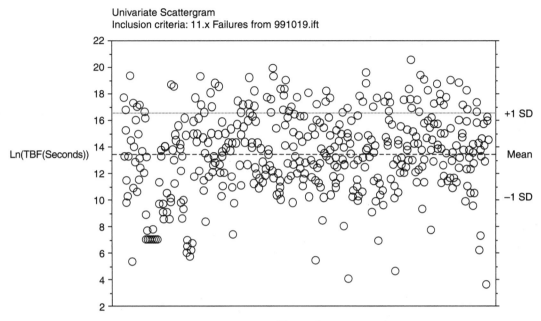

The two figures are the data collection and distributions for the IOS failure rates. The collection of 472 data points can provide a more accurate MTBF.

It's common to assume an exponential distribution for hardware failure rates. However, both theory and experience indicate that a lognormal distribution is more appropriate for software failure rates. Looking closely at the scatter graph in Figure 7-1, the experience with this type of data indicates that the data from this report will fit the lognormal distribution. As you can see in Figure 7-2, the use of the lognormal distribution does in fact closely match the data histogram. This provides you with the proper statistical measurements that can be used. In this case, the mean, standard deviation, and variance are calculated by using scaled parameters in Equation 7-11.

The use of mean, standard deviation, and variance will be explained in the section "Basic Statistical Measures and Applications" later in this chapter. They are used here as an example of determining MTBF and system availability.

Figure 7-2   *Histogram of the Data Plotted Under a Normal Curve*

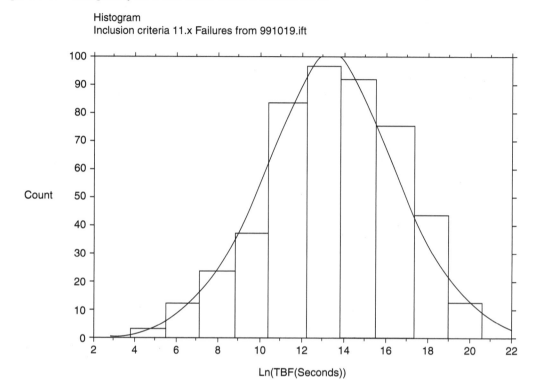

Table 7-1 gives summary statistics for the 11.x series observations.

Table 7-1   *Descriptive Statistics for 11.x Failures*

Statistics	Ln(TBF(Seconds))
Mean	13.395
Standard Deviation	3.143
Count	472
Minimum	3.689
Maximum	20.646
Variance	9.878

Ln(TBF(Seconds) is read as lognormal(Time between failure(in seconds)). Using the equations given by Kececioglu (see Equation 7-11), you can calculate the MTBF using the Mean of the log inter-failure times in conjunction with the Variance.

Equation 7-11

$$MTBF = \exp(Mean + 1/2(Variance))$$
$$= \exp(13.395 + 1/2(9.879))$$
$$= 91742839.7 \text{ seconds}$$
$$= 25484.1221 \text{ hours}$$

The availability of the Cisco IOS 11.x software is given by equation 7-12. We are using a MTTR for IOS software as approximately 6 minutes (.1 hrs) in this calculation. This approximation is based on observation of the average router reload times for the 472 data points recorded.

Equation 7-12

$$Availability = MTBF / (MTBF + MTTR)$$
$$= 25484.1/25484.2$$
$$= .999996076$$
$$= 99.9996076\%$$

Using the data for the Cisco IOS software availability, we are now ready to place the data into system availability equations. Equation 7-13 provides the overall system availability.

Equation 7-13

$$\text{System availability} = a_1 \times a_2 \times a_3 \times \ldots \times a_n$$
where "a_i" is component or device availability.

From Equation 7-12, we will use 25484.1 from the previous IOS MTBF in the Availability of IOS equation following. We still need MTBF and MTTR for the other components of a router. The MTTR is 24 hours for everything except the IOS reload. The following MTBF numbers are provided for the example:

Chassis MTBF: 250,000

Circuit board MTBF: 250,000

Power supply MTBF: 500,000

Availability of Cisco chassis (a_1) = (250,000/250,000+24) = .999904

Availability of circuit board (a_2) = (250,000/250,000 +24) = .999904

Availability of power supply (a_3) = (500,000/500,000+24) = .999952

Availability of IOS software (a_4) = (25484.1/(25484.1+0.1)) = .999996076

System Availability =
$(.999904) \times (.999904) \times (.999952) \times (.999996076) = .999756 = 99.9756\%$

Equation 7-13 describes system availability as simply the product of all the component availabilities. Depending on the network topology and the redundancy built within your network, more complex equations would be needed. Kececioglu provides several examples of calculations with both redundant and non-redundant networks, as does Stallings (see end-of-chapter references).

NOTE   As you can see in the preceding equations where 24 is used for the MTTR, one way to increase availability is through a reduction of the MTTR. The development of a formal sparing plan for the network's major geographic locations and the training of personnel doing the hardware replacement can provide tremendous dividends in the reduction of the MTTR.

Random Nature of Network Performance Variables

Another reason that a network analyst needs to have some knowledge about probability and statistics is the concept of randomness. *Randomness* refers to the unpredictability of certain data or events.

Randomness is a major characteristic for all computer networks. At a basic level, all the data carried by networks has random properties. For example, both response time and utilization can be defined as random processes. Therefore, virtually every performance measurement made on a network is a sample of a random process.

Performance factors are not the only random processes in the network. Other random variables that the network manager must be aware of are errors and overhead. *Overhead* includes such things as SNMP polling, routing protocol updates, and those packets that are not application-related. The pervasiveness of random properties makes it essential for a network manager or a performance analyst to understand the basics about probability and statistics.

Although some recent literature refers to the non-random nature of ethernets and self-correlation due to packet trains and burstiness, randomness works as a first approximation and is generally found to be applicable in practice.

Simulations

Network managers need a tool to collapse the data that they have collected. Sampling and statistical techniques are needed to analyze and condense the data collected from the computer network for utilization reports, performance reports, availability reports, and reliability/stability reports.

For network planning and design of very large networks, it can be important to define the data traffic streams as mathematical distributions and network processes as additional distributions, and then build a statistical model. Such modeling can reveal bandwidth and latency issues, which are the essence of capacity planning. Statistical modeling now can be accomplished through relatively inexpensive computer systems.

NOTE	Although some may disagree, an informal survey of several simulation vendors indicates that there is an increased use of computer network simulations in the area of capacity planning and network design. As will be shown in the use of network statistics section, capacity planning and network design require statistical knowledge.

The drawback of statistical modeling and simulation is that the mathematical sophistication needed by the user to develop a verifiable statistical model or simulation can initially be quite high. For that reason, modeling is not covered in this book. The rest of this chapter concentrates not on mathematical modeling but on using the data that you gather in ways that allow you to glean the most practical information from it. The understanding required for performance reports and capacity planning is in fact the same needed for analysis of the output from simulations and mathematical modeling. So, even if simulation will not be explicitly covered in this chapter, it is of growing importance and is covered implicitly.

Baselining requires some understanding of statistics. Also, many of today's larger enterprise networks, as well as most Internet Service Providers (ISPs), collect basic statistics on their network's performance and traffic flows. Usually, this measurement includes metrics on throughput, delay, and availability. Again, an understanding of statistics is necessary in order to do the basic analysis on this data.

Often, the statistics and mathematics needed for understanding your network are presented in a formal manner. These usually include proofs of each of the formulas and concepts. In this chapter, we present the statistics and mathematics in as practical and empirical a manner as possible. The emphasis is on practical application of the techniques and how to determine the correct variables to collect for your network. Although proofs and mathematically correct presentation are not part of this chapter, a bibliography has been provided with several references that do present the material in this way.

Basic Statistical Measures and Applications

This section defines some basic statistical values and gives simple examples of how they apply to network management. The following indexes are considered:

- Average
- Mode

- Median
- Range
- Variance
- Standard deviation

Before defining and looking at examples of these values, a bit of background is in order.

At its most basic, data analysis provides us with ways of organizing information. Descriptive measures such as averages and standard deviations—combined with graphing techniques such as histograms, pie charts, and line diagrams—can provide us with an overall picture of the data characteristics.

Because data from a network represents random samples, you can form confidence intervals to make inferences about the network itself. From these confidence intervals, you can define confidence levels that you want to see in your data. Confidence levels are estimates of your uncertainty about your parameters and thus indicate numerically your confidence in the results. Often, the standard deviation is chosen as the 68 percent confidence level. That is, you are 68 percent sure that the conclusions that you make from the data are what you will see in reality. The wider the interval, the more confident you are that it contains the parameter. The 95 percent confidence interval is therefore higher than the 68 percent confidence interval.

Another term that you may see for confidence interval is *margin of error.* You can think of the margin of error at the 95 percent confidence interval as being equal to two standard deviations in your polling sample.

This is probably a good place to touch on sampling size and its statistical significance. Perhaps the easiest way to figure this out is to think about it backwards. Let's say you decided to collect a network value during seven half-hour intervals over the course of a week. What is the chance that the times you picked do not accurately represent your network as a whole? For example, what is the chance that the percentage of low values received during your seven sampling periods does not match the percentage of low values over an entire week?

Common sense suggests that the chance that your sample is off the mark decreases as you add more time marks to your sample. In other words, the more times that you sample the data, the more likely you are to get a representative sample. This is easy so far, right?

The formula that describes this relationship is basically as follows:

The margin of error in a sample = 1 divided by the square root of the number of variables in the sample. Or as expressed in Equation 7-14:

Equation 7-14

$$m := \frac{1}{\sqrt{s}}$$

The formula is also derived from the standard deviation of the proportion of times that a researcher gets a sample "right," given a large number of samples. Both the standard deviation and variance formulas are discussed in detail after we have gone through a few other statistics.

Polling Interval Versus Sampling Size

There is often some confusion about the difference between polling interval and the sampling size. *Polling* is a mechanism to collect data over time. *Sampling* is a statistical methodology that uses the data gathered through the polling process. For instance, you might want to poll an interface for the ifInOctets variable every 15 minutes. This would mean that over a period of 24 hours you would have a sample size of 96 (4×24) data points, or 672 data points in a week.

This would give a margin of error = $1/\sqrt{672} = 0.039$. As you continue to gather data, the margin of error will continue to decrease. For instance, in a four-week period, you would have 2,688 data points, which would give you a margin of error of 0.019. As your margin of error decreases, the more confidence you can have in your sample size and in the decisions that you make based on this data.

For instance, by polling the different variables that you have identified through the process described in Chapter 3, "Developing the Network Knowledge Base," and logging that data to a server, you have created a database of historical values. This database can be used in a number of different ways:

- To understand network performance during a certain time period in the past
- To analyze network problems
- To plan for capacity requirements for your network
- To verify network designs and changes that are made on the network

However, in each of these cases, the raw data can be overwhelming. So, you use statistical techniques to aggregate the data to a more manageable form. Besides reduction of the data, statistical analysis often can derive additional meaning from the data. One way that you accomplish this analysis is through the use of standardized reports on the network health. For instance, in the area of performance analysis and capacity planning, the use of the averages can be a major factor in planning for future capacity.

For example in Tables 7-2 and 7-3, average utilization has been calculated for the serial line and CPU of several routers. The data indicates that the serial line utilization on Rtr001 and Rtr002 is very high, but that the CPU for both routers remains at a manageable state. Now, by looking closer at the actual traffic on the two serial lines, a decision can be made on whether an upgrade is needed or not.

Table 7-2   *Serial Line Utilization*

Resource	Address	Speed	Average Util (%)	Peak Util (%)
Rtr001	10.101.2.2	1.544 Mbps	87.3	97.9
Rtr002	10.101.2.1	1.544 Mbps	88.5	98.2
Rtr003	10.102.2.1	64 Kbps	69.2	89.5
Rtr004	10.102.2.2	64 Kbps	69	89.7

Table 7-3   *CPU Utilization*

Resource	Address	Average Utilization (%)	Peak Utilization (%)
Rtr001	10.101.2.2	52.4	95
Rtr002	10.101.2.1	48	81
Rtr003	10.102.2.1	35.2	98
Rtr004	10.102.2.2	34.7	93

Aggregation of data refers to the replacement of data values on a number of time intervals by some function of the values over the union of the intervals (RFC1857). Although this may sound complex, it is important to understand that the raw data will have to be reduced through aggregation in almost every network. Also, the shorter-term aggregates may be re-aggregated.

Data aggregation not only reduces the amount of data; it also reduces the available information. Depending on the use of the data (for instance, troubleshooting), this reduction can hinder problem resolution. However, for trending of the data over a three-month or longer period of time, this reduction is very useful. The data reduction model from RFC 1404 and 1857 will be discussed later in the chapter.

Particularly in the area of problem determination and troubleshooting, it is important that the historical data stored be highly granular.

Performance polling gathers data over time that can be analyzed to determine trends and to aid in capacity planning. First, determine what MIB variables to poll for. Chapter 3 describes how you can make a list of variables for data collection, and Part II of this book recommends specific variables for specific technologies.

For performance polling, individual data points are stored intermittently on the polling machine. Depending on the polling mechanism you are using, the data could be in either a raw format (the default for HP's Openview) or a relational database.

As stated earlier, to keep the data manageable, aggregate the raw data periodically, and store it in another database or data file for future reporting. The norm is to keep the raw data some specified period of time for backups, but eventually purge this data and keep only the aggregate data. Use the aggregate data to produce reports to determine trends and patterns. Depending on what you are planning, you can use the raw collected data to determine minimum, maximum, and average values for each variable; and then delete the raw data. Or, you can use a plan that summarizes the data and enables you to do more accurate statistical analysis on a larger historical sample.

The suggested aggregation periods from RFC 1857 are as follows:

- Over a 24 hour period, aggregate to 15 minutes
- Over a 1-month period, aggregate to 1 hour
- Over a 1-year period, aggregate to 1 day

Setting up this type of data reduction is not an easy task. However, all of the current commercial network performance-reporting applications provide an aggregation mechanism for you. Understanding what is going on "behind the veil" of such applications enables you to use the data gathered in the most efficient and effective ways.

Average, Mode, and Median

Measurements in network performance are rarely exact or repeatable because of the random nature of network traffic. It often cannot be predicted with certainty and usually contains a time-dependent nature as well. This randomness forces network managers to consider statistical values, specifically average response times.

An average, also known as an arithmetic mean, is calculated by adding up all the sample data (x_i) and then dividing the result by the number of samples (N). Equations 7-15 and 7-16 show alternative representations of the average.

Equation 7-15

$$ave = \frac{x_1 + x_2 + x_3 + \ldots + x_N}{N}$$

Or

Equation 7-16

$$ave := \frac{\displaystyle\sum_{i=1}^{N} x_i}{N}$$

The average is one measure of how data points tend to cluster around the center of a distribution. This clustering is sometimes referred to as the central tendency of the data. Besides the average, there are two other indexes of the central tendency of data: mode and median. Very simply, the mode is the most frequently reported data point in a distribution. The median is the midpoint within the distribution. Of the three statistics, the average is the most sensitive to data changes to all scores in a distribution.

If the average is more sensitive to all scores in a distribution, why bother with the mode or median? One of the most practical arguments is that they are easy to obtain. After the data points are grouped, the mode is obtained by simple inspection. If the data points are ranked, the median is also easy to obtain.

Another reason for obtaining the median is to look for a significant value discrepancy between it and the average. Normally, the two values should be fairly close. But if the distribution contains extremely high or low scores, the average may skew significantly from the median. For a more accurate average, statisticians often omit the highest and lowest values in the distribution as anomalies, and you may need to consider doing the same. For instance, consider gathering data by pinging a device across the wide area network (see Table 7-4). The normal round-trip time may be 120ms, but due to a backup that takes place early in the morning, the time increases to 2400ms for several data-collection points. These anomalous high values can cause the average to be higher than it would be normally. Both the mode and median help to point out the discrepancy

Table 7-4   *Example of the Use of Mode and Median with Average*

Ping (ms) collected on an hourly basis											
120	119	121	110	120	100	128	2400	2390	2405	120	121
100	110	119	120	120	120	121	121	128	2390	2400	2405

Sum of all (24) data points: 8254

Average: 687.833

Mode: 120

Median: 120

Range, Variance, and Standard Deviation

Just as there are indexes to describe how data cluster around the center of a distribution, there are those that describe the dispersion or scatter across the measurement scale. The most common of the dispersion indexes are the range, variance, and standard deviation.

The range is the highest "score" in a distribution, minus the lowest score. The range is a very crude measurement. Just as the mode and median are insensitive to all but a few data points, so is the range. In the example in Table 7-4, the range would be 2405 minus 100 or 2305. Although this information is not very useful by itself, if you were expecting a range of about 100ms, it would indicate a network issue that needs to be explored.

Variance is basically the average of the squared deviation scores about the average of the distribution. Variance, which is also known as "the first moment about the mean," is calculated by subtracting each x value from the average, squaring the difference, summing the squares of the differences, and dividing everything by the number of samples minus 1 or $(N - 1)$. See equations 7-17 and 7-18.

Equation 7-17

$$var = \frac{(ave - x_1)^2 + (ave - x_2)^2 + \ldots + (ave - x_N)^2}{N - 1}$$

Or

Equation 7-18

$$\text{var} := \frac{\displaystyle\sum_{i=1}^{N} (\text{ave} - x_i)^2}{N - 1}$$

NOTE The variance could almost be the average squared deviation around the mean if the expression were divided by N rather than N–1. It is divided by N–1, called the degrees of freedom (df), for theoretical reasons. If the mean is known, as it must be to compute the numerator of the expression, then only N–1 scores are free to vary. That is, if the mean and N–1 scores are known, it is possible to figure out the Nth score.

Variance, like the mean (arithmetic average), is sensitive to all data points in a distribution. By comparing the average, standard deviation, and variance, you can develop an expected value range. If the variance or standard deviation is much greater than expected, you must look at the data more closely or discard it altogether. Thus, the standard deviation and variance are similar to the earlier statistics considered with the average as a balance point about the distribution.

The first column of Table 7-5 includes the ping data from Table 7-4. The second column is the square of the average minus the data point, or $(\text{avg} - n_1)^2$. Summing the values in the second column gives the "sum of the squares"—in this case, 11703875.67. Dividing the sum of the squares by N–1 produces the variance. Table 7-6 shows the variance for the original data, 1063988.697, and for a second data set in which the three high data points (>2300ms) have been replaced with the median value (120ms). The variance for the second set of data is 48.20454545. This example shows why other statistical values are needed beyond the simple arithmetic average.

Table 7-5 *Sample Data for Calculating Variance*

Data	Power(Avg – n_i)^2
120	322434.6944
119	323571.3611
121	321300.0277
110	333891.3611
120	322434.6944
100	345548.0277
128	313413.3611

Table 7-5   *Sample Data for Calculating Variance (Continued)*

2400	2931514.695
2390	2897371.361
2405	2948661.361
120	322434.6944
121	321300.0277

Table 7-6   *Comparison of Example Data, With and Without Three High Data Points*

Value	Original Data Statistics	Statistics without Three High Data Points
Sum	8254	1419
Avg	687.8333333	118.25
Max	2405	128
Min	100	100
Variance	1063988.697	48.20454545
Variance (population)	975322.9722	44.1875
Standard Deviation	1031.498278	6.942949334
Standard Deviation (population)	987.5844127	6.6473679

Note that Table 7-6 also contains the standard deviations for the original and revised example data. The standard deviation is the square root of the variance (see Equation 7-19).

Equation 7-19

$$ \text{dev} := \sqrt{\text{var}} $$

A practical advantage of using the standard deviation rather than the variance as the index of dispersion is that its values are easier to use because of its natural relationship to the mean. The standard deviation gives us the basis for estimating the probability of how frequently certain data points can be expected to occur based on the sampling rate (or the margin of error discussed earlier).

The variance and standard deviation both calculate how much variation the samples have around the mean value. Therefore, small variations indicate a strong central tendency of the samples. This also indicates that the sample set has little statistical randomness. Larger variations indicate very little central tendency, and show large statistical randomness. Central tendency is a typical or representative score. The three measures of central tendency that have been discussed in this chapter are the mode, median, and mean.

The variance and standard deviation are important statistics for understanding traffic distributions for a link or network. They are the initial metrics used in defining the type of statistical distribution that may be of use to the analyst.

Deviations from the mean and the concepts of variance and standard deviation are crucial for understanding statistical models. It is important to be able to conceptualize their interrelationships. One method of doing this is through the use of graphing techniques. Figure 7-3 shows graphically the data from Table 7-4.

Figure 7-3   *The Cumulative Distribution Function for the Data in Table 7-4*

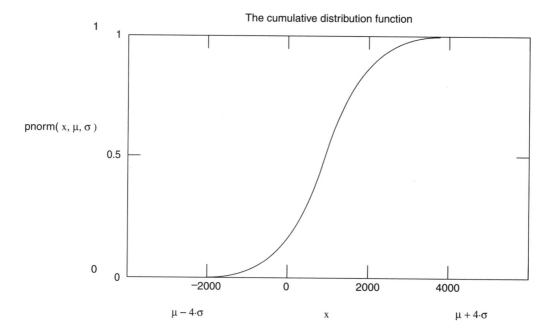

Although this enables you to get a certain feel for the data using the mean and standard deviation, the use of a normal distribution as in Figure 7-4 is usually more helpful.

Figure 7-4   *The Normal Distribution for the Data in Table 7-4*

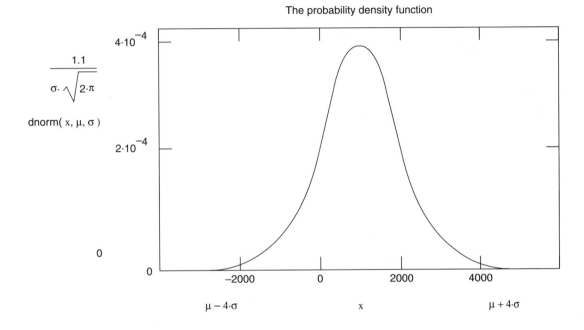

The data in Figure 7-4 was generated using the following statistics from Table 7-4:

The normal distribution is also known as the bell curve, due to its symmetry about the mean. This figure has a mean (μ) = 687.8333 and a standard deviation (σ) = 1008.825. This shows in a clearer fashion than Figure 7-3 the use of standard deviation. In Figure 7-5, the long ping times (>2000 ms) were removed. So Figure 7-5 has a mean (μ) = 118.7083 and a standard deviation (σ) = 7.055551, which is more in line with what was expected for this interface.

Figure 7-5 *Normal Distribution of Ping Data Without Points > 2000ms*

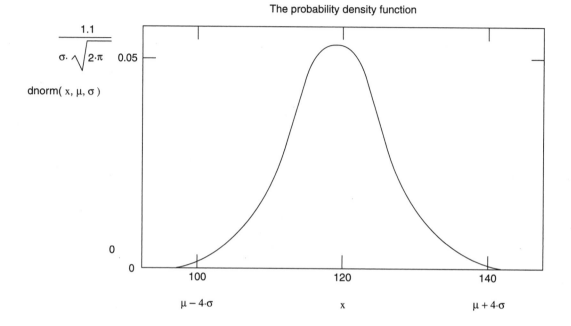

There are many other distributions that can be useful in the analysis of performance data. The distributions that can be useful in network management are the poisson, exponential, uniform, lognormal, and fixed. Many examples of these can be found in the sources listed in the References at the end of this chapter. One of the easiest ways to use these distributions is with a mathematical scratchpad. It allows you to import data from a spreadsheet and, by using the correct statistical values for the distribution, graph your sample data.

Weighted Mean

Another context in which statistics can be of help to you is when applying a single requirement to multiple applications. For instance, if you have three applications (Voice over IP, Database transactions, and Web video) that have different response time requirements, how do you make a decision on the most affordable network design?

One way is to use a *weighted mean*. In this case, you weight each application based on how critical it is to the enterprise, giving the most critical the highest weight. It is important that you understand that this weight is an arbitrary value that you have subjectively chosen, but the relationship between the various weights is significant. By setting a high weight on the critical applications, you ensure that their needs are met.

The weighted mean can be used as a decision analysis tool. It allows you to analyze the critical applications within your organization, assign a weight to them, and then use the new value in calculations. In the following example, each step will be explained.

To find the weighted mean, do the following:

1   Find the average response time required for each of the applications.

2   Select weights for each application based on how crucial it is to the enterprise.

3   Multiply the required average response time for each application by its assigned weight and sum the products.

4   Divide the sum of the products by the sum of the weights.

Here is an example:

- Voice over IP = 150ms average response time; assigned weight = 4.

  Voice over IP is an application that is currently being placed in several areas on the network and is therefore quite important. This is indicated with a moderately high weighting of 4.

- DBMS transactions = 300ms average response time; assigned weight = 6

  The database transactions are the most critical application for this customer and therefore have gotten the highest weighting (6).

- Web video = 500ms average response time; assigned weight = 2

  In Web video, you have an application that is just being looked at by the customer and is not of critical importance. However, because this organization is actively making some tests of the application, we give the Web video a relatively low weight or 2 rather than a very low weight (1) for our calculations.

For this example, the weighted average works out to be the following:

$(150 \times 4) + (300 \times 6) + (500 \times 2)/16 = 3400/16 = 212.5$ms

The non-weighted average is as follows:

$(150) + (300) + (500) = 316.6$ms

Note that the weighted average is still less than the non-weighted average. Because you are looking for the lowest response time, the weighted mean can be seen as more favorable to your goals. Comparing the weighted versus the non-weighted averages is usually a good sanity check of you weighting scheme and the results.

Application of the Statistical Methods

This section includes an example of how the statistical principles can be used in network management. It begins with some preliminary information about response times and simulation models that you need to understand for the example. If you already are familiar with these topics, you may wish to skip these sections. Response time was chosen as an example because it is an issue that interests most users. The section concludes with a discussion of the moving exponential average for calculation of Cisco routers' CPU, another application of statistical measures.

Response Times

Intranets have several delay components and are generally more complex than campus networks. An intranet will usually have multiple Wide Area Network (WAN) links as well as many distributed Local Area Networks (LANs). A WAN is made up of full-duplex links between two end-points, usually between routers. Because full-duplex means that there are two independent simplex links, it is possible to have a link congested in only one direction while lightly utilized in the other.

Network delay components include propagation delay, transmission delay, queuing delay, and router latency.

Propagation delay is the time it takes for an electrical or optical signal to travel from one point to another. Delay is defined as a function of the speed of light through copper or fiber. Essentially, data signals will travel through telecommunications networks at approximately 2/3 the speed of light in a vacuum, or 192,000 kilometers per second. Obviously, this is not instantaneous. In fact, as networks grow nationally and internationally, propagation delay becomes the largest component of total delay and cannot be reduced. Propagation delay is the main reason that WANs can never have the performance of LANs. The larger the distance between sites or nodes, the slower a WAN is.

Transmission delay is the time it takes to send a given amount of data at a given transmission speed. The mathematics for this are straightforward. For example, a line with a speed of 100 kbps will take ten seconds to transmit 1000 kilobits of data (one million bits of data) and a line at 500 kbps will take only two seconds. You can create a table for the transmission rates within your network. As you will see, transmission delay becomes particularly significant when large amounts of data are sent.

NOTE   Increasing the bandwidth of a WAN link does reduce transmission delay, but not propagation delay. If you use the analogy of a pipe that has both width and length, increasing the width of the pipe is similar to a bandwidth increase, but it doesn't reduce the length. Therefore, if an application is bandwidth-constrained, increasing the bandwidth will improve performance. However, our experience shows that most interactive client/server applications send relatively small amounts of data and therefore are more affected by the propagation delay.

Queuing delay in a network occurs when many devices (including clients and servers) are trying to send data over the intranet at the same time. In the case of media access delay, each network device holds onto its own data packets until it gets an opportunity to transmit. In the case of queuing delay, all the data packets are sent to a device (usually a router), which has the access to the WAN. Transmission bandwidth is one of the main factors in determining the time that it takes for a router to transmit all the queued packets. For instance, if a router had a backlog of 10 KB, it would take more than a second to drain the queue over a 56-kbps link. On the other hand it would take less than 1/10 of a second over a T-1 line that transmits 1544 kbps. Router latency is a measurement of the time it takes the router to move a data packet from one interface to another. This is normally a small constant. Router latency can be reduced on Cisco routers through the use of different switching paths. Although the delay is small in itself, end-to-end router latency can become a significant factor if there are many hops. Minimizing router latency can be a significant design challenge on large networks. Router latency is usually more of an issue on a campus network than on a corporate intranet.

The time for a transaction is spent in three ways: by packets traversing the network, by the server retrieving data, and by the client accepting data and asking for more data. The network component is referred to as *network delay*, discussed previously. The server and client delays are sometimes referred to as *think times*. The delays can be measured for the whole transaction or per-packet. The important point is to determine the fraction of the transaction delay attributed to network, server, and client.

Our primary assumption is that the client is requesting data from the server. Therefore at least two points of measurement are needed: the client local network and the server local network. On the client side, you will measure client delay. At the packet level, this is the delay between the time the client receives a frame of data until it requests the next frame. Also on the client network, you measure the combined (network + server) delay. The second measurement is on the server network and measures the server delay.

Given all the delay components, the response time for an application is given by Equation 7-20:

Equation 7-20

ApplicationDelay = ClientTime (t_1) + 2 × NetworkDelay (t_n)) × NumberOfTurnarounds + ServerTime (t_3)

where NetworkDelay is a combination of propagation delay, transmission delay, queuing delay, and router latency.

In order to perform this calculation, you would need to collect packet-arrival times for each packet in a transaction. The transaction of interest should be easily determined through your knowledge of the critical applications for your organization or through discussions with your users. This type of analysis cannot be made for every link or, in most organizations, for every application. It is essential to identify the critical applications based on your network's operational objectives, as discussed in Chapter 2.

The determination of the number of turnaround times often can be accomplished through the software within the analyzer being used. It involves comparing packets, comparing window sizes, and calculating the differences (delta) for the transaction.

The following are typical client/server applications:

- A character-echo application (such as Telnet) requires that for each character typed, a packet is sent from the client to the server and echoed back.

- A database application requiring a client to read multiple records located on a server usually retrieves the records in blocks. These blocks may range from a few kilobytes to 512 bytes in size.

- Graphical user interfaces (GUIs) may need to send small packets back and forth to the server to determine status of different widgets. Also, a GUI may require updates to follow the mouse movements.

The more interaction between the client and server, the more packets go back and forth, and the more sensitive the application is to network delay. This sensitivity is in part because there is a turnaround time associated with each exchange. For example, the client sends and waits for the server to respond before it sends again. Thus, for any increase in network delay, the turnaround time increases by a factor of two; first for the network delay going from the client to server, and then for the return.

In a campus LAN, this turnaround time can be a few milliseconds. However, on a corporate WAN that spans a country or the globe, the turnaround time can be factors of ten or hundreds of milliseconds. Obviously, the effect of this increased turnaround time for an application can be dramatic. This delay is one of the primary reasons that many application deployment projects fail. For instance, a 50ms network delay (100ms turnaround delay, which is a fairly typical delay between Raleigh, NC and San Jose, CA) will add two seconds to an application response time.

Some of the questions that need to be asked in analyzing response-time performance are the following:

- How many turnarounds does the application require? This examination of the application's traffic can be accomplished with a protocol analyzer or network probe. It is the first step for understanding the application's traffic pattern, and may show tens or hundreds of network turnarounds for a single application transaction.

- What is the network delay of the production network? As already shown, this delay metric is fundamental to the performance of an application's response time. Knowing the network delay also assists you in making the design decisions for the network. For instance, the delay on a 1000-mile-long T-1 is less than the satellite delay of a similar connection.

- Does the sum of the numbers t_1, t_n, and t_3 fall within the response time required by the service level agreement or operational objectives? If the answer is "no," there may be an opportunity to tune the application to reduce the number of turnarounds and improve performance. It is also possible that the application will not function within the user's expectations.

Another way to look at it is that when you are evaluating an application for use across a WAN, the more data it sends is bad; less data is good. This is particularly true with larger and slower WANs. They will be much less tolerant of applications sending a lot of data and requiring multiple transactions. Therefore, in looking at application response time, it is necessary to examine the application protocol behavior, network performance, and the client/server performance and scalability.

Using Network Simulations to Analyze Response Time

The entire process just described is complicated and takes a great amount of time. Most network managers find themselves facing very short deadlines and the demand to roll out new client-server applications, or just to improve current network performance. Simulation of the new application or of the current environment can help ensure that network changes meet user needs. As discussed in Chapters 2 and 3, one of the first and most critical steps is to baseline your network. You have a grasp of the critical applications from the operational concept. Now, it is important to understand how those applications perform within the network.

One way to gain this understanding is to choose a small group of users to be monitored. They should not necessarily be from the engineering group in the NOC, but they do need to be fairly savvy users. Gather data from this group, taking into account the statistics of the source and including such parameters as peak and average bytes per second, peak and average frames per second, and the time intervals between peaks. In this case, the sampling of the data needs to be relatively high and a time resolution for these measurements should be one second.

At this point, you have the data needed to create and run a simulation model. The model should incorporate the network topology and the background traffic that you have collected from your sample users. With your knowledge of your end users' needs, your network's operational objectives, and the baseline data, you have the information needed to evaluate how the simulation runs. This evaluation is called a *test of simulation validity* and is essential to successfully running a simulation of your network.

The aim of simulations is to exactly duplicate the packet conditions on the network. One simulation method used is a *probability distribution*. In order to use a simulation that uses statistical processes, you need to understand what statistical parameters are needed. For instance, each of the distributions mentioned previously—poisson, exponential, uniform, lognormal, and fixed—have specific statistical parameters and equations. So, given the data that you have collected, you must now "fit" it into a distribution. An example of this was shown in Figure 7-1 and 7-2. It is imperative that you understand the statistical calculations that are valid for the distribution chosen. Again, in the earlier example, Table 7-1 and Equation 7-11 show the use of the statistics for a lognormal distribution.

Although simulation may sound too difficult to possibly apply, it is not. By following the development of the statistics discussed in this chapter and using off-the-shelf, curve-fitting software for a PC, most of the work that initially deters people is done. Further, after you have created a simulation model of your current network (and validated that the simulation runs are within your expected parameters), you can use the model for many different tasks. For instance, simulation models can be used to evaluate WAN link capacity, LAN technologies, and server performance.

The simulation run takes from minutes to hours, depending on the complexity of the model and the speed of the computer systems running the simulation. However, in a matter of only a few days, it is possible to generate a series of simulations that can help to definitively evaluate a network or application issue (new solution deployment or problem resolution). Quantitative results are generated for network utilization, router buffer utilization, dropped packets, serial line utilization, statistical distribution of application response times, effects of prioritization (or precedence) on response times, and effects of window size on throughput, as well as many other variables that you can select.

The quantitative results of a simulation can be compared to the baseline data and statistics that you have collected. This comparison can be initially used to validate the simulation model, but it also provides the data needed to actively provide the capacity planning that will keep your network performance at its peak.

Applying Statistical Analysis to Response Time in an Example Network

Most corporate intranets are provisioned with sufficient bandwidth. However, without adequate data, you may not be able to rule out network congestion as a contributor to poor application performance. One of the clues for congestion or errors is if the poor performance is intermittent or dependent on time of day, like the network in Figure 7-6. The graph shows that performance is adequate late in the evening, but very slow in the morning and during peak business hours.

Figure 7-6   *Response Time in a Case Study Network*

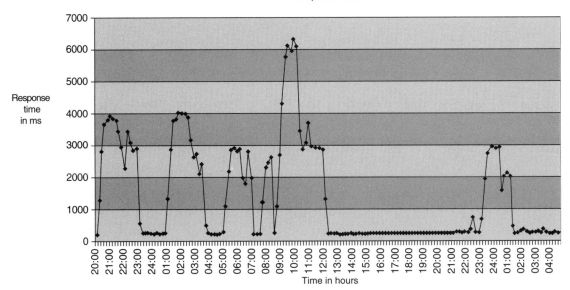

Figure 7-6 is based on an actual troubleshooting problem that we dealt with. On the graph, the round-trip ping times are displayed in milliseconds on the vertical axis. The average round-trip ping time is 1460ms, with a maximum round-trip time of 6420ms and a minimum of 232ms. Looking at the performance of this link, we found that the highest response times were from 8 p.m. to 9 a.m. Eliminating those hours, the average was reduced to about 500ms, with a peak of 2837ms.

Investigation revealed that the cause of the abnormally high ping times was due to a number of application backups that started at 8 p.m. We could talk with the local site system administrator and work out a better backup strategy. After these backups were dealt with locally, the response time to the site fell to relatively reasonable levels.

This example shows the need to view the data by at least average, minimum, and maximum data. When we looked at just the average (1460ms) it provided a very skewed view of the data. As we began viewing the average, maximum, and minimum values for several weeks worth of data, we obtained the data in Table 7-7.

Table 7-7   *Descriptive Statistics*

Site	Average (ms)	Maximum (ms)	Minimum (ms)	Standard Deviation	Variance
Test_rtr01	1460	6420	232	1564.115	2446456.062

The value of the variance and the fact that the standard deviation is larger than the mean were indications that the data needed to be examined in detail.

Moving Exponential Average for Cisco Routers CPU Calculation

Another application of statistical methods is being able to understand the differences between the 5sec/1min/5min averages used on Cisco devices. This section discusses the use of the moving exponential average, as used by Cisco.

A *moving average* is basically a smoothing mechanism. Trying to make sense of data is often difficult if the data contains wild spikes in one direction or the other. It is often useful to apply a tool such as a moving average to smooth the data so it is easier to spot trends.

There are five basic types of moving averages:

- Simple (or arithmetic)
- Exponential
- Triangular
- Variable
- Weighted

The basic difference between these types is the weight assigned to the most recent data.

Cisco IOS uses the exponential moving average to give a five-minute average to following statistics (among others):

- The five-minute bit-per-second average in the local interfaces table or the **show interface** command
- The interface load in the **show interface** command
- The interface reliability in the **show interface** command
- The CPU load in the **show process CPU** command

The five-minute average is calculated by taking difference every 5 seconds. Here is the algorithm for the five-minute moving average:

Equation 7-21

$$\text{newaverage} = ((\text{average} - \text{interval}) \times \exp(-t/C)) + \text{interval}$$

The values in Equation 7-21 are as follows:

- newaverage = the value you are trying to compute
- t is five seconds and C is 5 minutes.
- average = newaverage value calculated from the previous sample
- interval = value of the current sample
- $\exp(-5/(60 \times 5)) == .983$ (the weighting factor)

The equation takes the average from the last sample less the quantity gathered in the current sample, and weights that down by the decay factor. The result is a variable that changes more slowly than the actual data. Therefore, it is smoothed out and not subject to the wild spikes that are inherent in LAN traffic and CPU load.

If the value of the quantity being measured (that is, CPU utilization) is increasing, the average value in the previous calculation will be a negative number and will cause the "newaverage" value to rise less quickly on traffic spikes. And if the value of the quantity being measured is decreasing, the average value in the calculation will be a positive number and will make sure that the "newaverage" value falls less rapidly if there is a sudden stoppage of traffic.

For example, if utilization were at 100 percent for some time and then instantaneously went to 0 percent, the exponential moving average would show a different picture. Over five-second intervals, the exponentially weighted utilization would go from

$1.0 - .983 - .983^2 - .983^3 - \ldots .983^n$

Or

$1.0 - .983 - .95 - 0.9 - 0.86 -$ and so on.

In this example, utilization drops from 100 percent to 1 percent in 90 intervals, or 450 seconds or 7.5 minutes.

The exponential moving average is a good example of how to utilize statistical methods to massage the data to make it easier to interpret.

Summary

This chapter presented several statistics that can be important for network management: mean, mode, median, range, standard deviation, and variance. Although the amount of work needed to analyze a single MIB variable may seem intimidating, please note that it is not necessary to analyze every variable that you have in your network baseline. Although the application of the correct statistic will assist you in the analysis of data and variables, it is more important to use the knowledge of your business operations to define critical applications and how their successful performance is measured. After you have accomplished this, you can use the statistical methods in this chapter to translate "how successful performance is measured" into what needs to be measured.

References

Books

Buchanan, Robert. *The Art of Testing Network Systems*. New York, NY: Wiley, 1996.

Evans, Merran, Nicholas Hastings, and Brian Peacock. *Statistical Distributions*. New York, NY: Wiley, 1993.

Ferrari, D. *Computer Systems Performance Evaluation*. Upper Saddle River, NJ: Prentice Hall, 1978.

Gilchrist ,W. *Statistical Forecasting*. New York, NY: Wiley, 1976.

Jain, Raj. *The Art of Computer Systems Performance Analysis*. New York, NY: Wiley, 1991.

Kececioglu, Dimitri. *Reliability Engineering Handbook*. Upper Saddle River, NJ, Prentice-Hall, 1991.

Naugle, Matthew. *Network Protocols*. New York, NY: McGraw-Hill, 1994.

Robertazzi, Thomas G. *Computer Networks and Systems: Queueing Theory and Performance Evaluation*, 2nd ed. Springer, 1994.

Spohn, Darren L. *Data Network Design*. New York, NY: McGraw-Hill, 1993.

Stallings, William. *SNMP, SNMPv2, and RMON*, 2nd ed. Reading, MA: Addison-Wesley, 1996.

Terplan, Kornel. *Benchmarking for Effective Network Management*. New York, NY: McGraw-Hill, 1995.

Periodical

Foster, K. "Math on the Internet." *IEEE Spectrum*, Volume 36, Number 4, April, 1999.

Standards

RFC 1757, "Remote Network Monitoring Management Information Base," Steven Waldbusser, February 1995.

RFC 1857, "A Model for Common Operational Statistics," M. Lambert, October 1995.

RFC 1902, "Structure of Management Information for version 2 of the Simple Network Managemenet Protocol," Case J., McCloghrie K., Rose M., and Waldbusser S., April 1993.

RFC 2063, "Traffic Flow Measurement: Architecture," Brownlee, N., Mills, C., and G. Ruth, January 1997.

RFC 2064, "Traffic Flow Measurement: Meter MIB," Brownlee, N., January 1997.

CHAPTER 8

Understanding Network Management Protocols

Network managers need to have a base level of knowledge about the protocols used to do network management. This chapter will help you acquire this knowledge or review the protocols if you already are familiar with them. The chapter is designed to give you an overview of the most-used protocols and to discuss Cisco-specific information concerning them.

The protocols that are covered in this chapter are as follows:

- Ping
- Traceroute
- Terminal emulators
- SNMP
- RMON MIB
- Syslog
- Cisco Discovery Protocol
- Name service

Ping

Ping is commonly used to check connectivity between devices. It's the most common protocol used for availability polling. It can also used for troubleshooting more complex problems in the network.

Ping uses Internet Control Message Protocol (ICMP) Echo and Echo Reply packets to determine whether one IP device can talk to another. Most implementations of ping allow you to vary the size of the packet. Table 8-1 shows packet size statistics for Cisco IOS and Catalyst devices.

Table 8-1 *Ping Packet Sizes for Cisco Devices*

Device	Minimum Packet Size	Maximum Packet Size	Default Packet Size
Cisco IOS	36 bytes	18024 bytes	100 bytes
Cisco Catalyst	56 bytes	472 bytes	64 bytes

Most host-based implementations of ping send one packet per second. Cisco IOS allows you to send packets as fast as the CPU and the network device can generate them and the network can take them. Of course, such stress testing should be done with discretion on production networks.

There are several issues that you should be aware of when using ping. Pings are generated and answered by using the CPU on Cisco devices. Although pings do not usually take a huge amount of CPU time, you should be cautious about using heavily loaded devices to generate or answer pings. On Cisco IOS devices, the task that processes pings runs at low priority. Therefore, it is possible for a busy device to fail to respond to a ping. If a device you are trying to ping is not in the ARP table, the first ping will often time out on Cisco devices. Because of this, most network-management applications using ping will send several pings before announcing a connectivity loss event. For the same reason, you should be cautious about using ping to determine latency or throughput on a network because you may be measuring the ICMP performance of the end points more than the actual network performance.

Traceroute

Traceroute is most commonly used to troubleshoot connectivity issues. If all you know is that you can't get to host D from host A, traceroute will show you whether the connectivity loss exists at one of the intermediate routers—B or C or elsewhere. Note that traceroute works at Layer 3 and is most commonly implemented for IP using UDP.

In the first set of packets sent, the time-to-live (TTL) field is set to 1 and the port number is set to a port that is not likely to be valid, most commonly 33434. The consequence of setting TTL to 1 is that the first node receiving this packet will decrement the TTL, notice that the TTL is now 0, drop the packet, and return an ICMP timeout message. The TTL and port numbers are increased by one for each subsequent set of packets until either the TTL hits a maximum or the desired remote host is reached. Therefore, one link in the path to the destination will be discovered per packet.

Traceroute determines that the destination has been reached when it receives an ICMP destination port unreachable message. Note that you are actually discovering the path that the ICMP timeout messages are taking when they come back. In most cases, this will be the same as the forward path, but not always.

Most traceroute implementations will send several packets with the same TTL and port, and then increment the TTL and port for the next set of packets to assist in the discovery of alternate routes or lossy connections.

An example of using traceroute is to trace the path from one router to another. Figure 8-1 contains an example network. Starting from the router chelliot-isdn and tracing the route to nms-comm1, the results are shown in Example 8-1.

Figure 8-1   *Example Network for Traceroute*

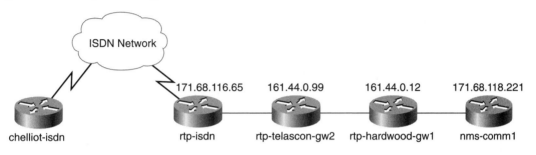

Example 8-1   *Results of a traceroute.*

```
chelliot-isdn#traceroute nms-comm1

Type escape sequence to abort.
Tracing the route to nms-comm1 (171.68.118.221)

  1 rtp-isdn (171.68.116.65) 28 msec 28 msec 28 msec
  2 rtp-telascon-gw2 (161.44.0.99) 32 msec 28 msec 28 msec
  3 rtp-hardwood-gw1 (161.44.0.12) 56 msec 32 msec 28 msec
  4 nms-comm1 (171.68.118.221) 32 msec *  40 msec
chelliot-isdn#
```

By default, Cisco IOS devices repeat the traceroute for each TTL three times, as indicated by the three time measurements on each line of the output. Notice that the last line has an asterisk instead of the middle time measurement. This is because Cisco routers limit the rate of ICMP destination unreachable messages it outputs. Therefore, the second message is dropped before the destination sends it back.

Terminal Emulators

Terminal emulators are used for many purposes in network management, including user access to network devices. Obviously, access is useful for configuring and troubleshooting devices. There are also times when information or operations on network devices are not available through SNMP and scripts must be written to access this information or capability through terminal access.

Telnet is the traditional way of obtaining terminal emulation access to network devices. Cisco IOS devices also support remote shell, or rsh.

Cisco IOS software provides two methods for obtaining terminal emulation access in a secure manner: Secure Shell (SSH) and IP Security (IPSec) with Virtual Private Networks (VPN). SSH, which devices are just starting to support, provides much greater security for the connection than Telnet. Cisco IOS devices started supporting SSH in 12.0(5)S. Cisco Catalyst devices don't support SSH as of software version 5.2.

IPSec with VPN provides a standards-based method to implement security and includes the capability to secure a terminal emulation session. Cisco IOS devices started supporting IPSec with VPN in IOS 12.0(5)T.

If a program or script needs to obtain information through a terminal session, it needs to be able to watch for prompts from the device and enter commands at the right time and speed so that they are recognized by the device and do not overrun any input buffers. Such a capability is commonly known as an Expect script, after the Expect language written over the TK/TCL programming language. Expect-like libraries are available for PERL, Java, C, as well as the original TK/TCL program.

See Example 19-9 in Chapter 19, "Frequently Asked Questions," for an example of an Expect script written in PERL.

Simple Network Management Protocol

The Simple Network Management Protocol (SNMP) is the most commonly used protocol that is specific to network management. Network managers need a good understanding of the capabilities and limitations of SNMP. This section provides an overview of SNMP. If you desire a more complete treatment of SNMP, please see the references at the end of the chapter.

SNMP is a protocol specifically designed to manage devices. It defines management entities, typically your NMS, and agent entities, typically your network devices, or more accurately, processes that run on your NMS and network devices. The information available through SNMP is organized into a Management Information Base (MIB). The structure of this information is defined in the Structure of Management Information (SMI). One or more MIB files define the MIB supported by a given SNMP agent. The bottom line is that SNMP provides management information in a structured manner that is well suited to retrieval and modification via applications. A variety of SNMP command line utilities give you the ability to do SNMP operations yourself, but sometimes the complexity of the operation or the number of operations is so high that it's best to leave the job to an application.

The Remote Monitoring MIB document, RMON, is an important MIB document because it added a new level of complexity to SNMP agents, both in SNMP capabilities and in the ability of the agent to provide information to an NMS. RMON is also an example of an MIB document that is structured so that it is almost a requirement that you use an application that understands the RMON MIB document to be able to use the capabilities defined in the MIB document.

SNMP has been (and continues to be) defined in a series of RFCs. Table 8-2 shows the different RFCs and their relationships. For explanations of the different statuses, see the Best Practice document BCP0009, currently also published as RFC 2026.

Table 8-2   *SNMP RFCs*

SNMP Area	Status	RFC
Standard Gateway Monitoring Program (SGMP)	Historic	1028
SNMPv1	Standard	1067→1098→1157
SNMPv2,SNMPv2p	Historic	1441,1445–1449,1452→1901, 1905–1906,1908
SNMPv2u	Experimental	1909,1910
SNMPv2*	Expired Proposed Draft	Never assigned RFC numbers
SNMPv2c	Experimental	1901
SNMPv3	Draft Standard	2261–2265→2271–2275→2571–2575
MIB-I	Standard	1066→1156
MIB-II	Proposed Standard	2011, 1158→1213, 2012–2013
Interfaces group	Proposed Standard	1229→1573→2233
SMIv1	Standard	1065→1155,1212 (concise MIB format)
SMIv2	Standard	1442–1444→1902–1904→2578–2580
Get-bulk	Experimental	1187
RMON	Draft Standard	1271→1757
RMONv2	Proposed Standard	2021
SMON	Proposed Standard	2613

Arrows indicate RFCs that replace or update earlier RFCs.

The following sections discuss aspects of SNMP and SMI in more detail.

SNMP Versions

SNMP has gone through several revisions so far in its lifespan. The following sections provide details of those revisions.

SNMPv1

SNMPv1 was defined fairly quickly and with little dissension through the standards process. It supported a fairly simple set of operations: get, get-response, get-next, set-request, and trap. (See "SNMP Operations," later in this chapter, for definitions of these operations.)

SNMPv1 included the capability to use different security models, but the only one defined was the community-based security model. Using community-based security, each SNMP packet includes a community string that is used to determine the access level that the originator of the request will have to the MIB in the agent. Agents include the community string in the get-response and notification packets, but most managers do not check or use it. Agents can restrict access that a user of a particular community string has to the objects in its MIB. Commonly, access is given to either read-only objects or to read-write objects. Note that the MIB defines some objects as read-only and these objects can't be written, no matter what community string is used. Cisco Catalyst code includes another level—secret, or read-write-all—which adds the capability to access and change the MIB objects that control the community strings on the device.

SNMPv1 defined a capability called a *view* that enables you to restrict access to the MIB. ("SNMP Views," later in this chapter, describes the view capability in more detail.)

The Cisco Catalyst secret or read-write-all community string can be seen as a community string that has read-write access to, or view of, the whole MIB. The read and read-write community strings in Catalyst software can be seen as strings with a view applied that allow read and read-write access, respectively, to all objects except those that can view and change the community strings.

This security model has been criticized as being insecure, but it is only trivially less secure than Telnet or ftp, both of which pass usernames and passwords in clear text. There are some methods to increase security while still using SNMPv1, including using a dedicated network or VLAN for management and applying access lists to the SNMP community strings (supported in Cisco IOS software, but not in Cisco Catalyst software).

All SNMP MIB objects, including objects defined using SMIv1 or SMIv2, can be used with SNMPv1 (with the exception of objects of the 64-bit integer or derivative types, including Counter64). Cisco IOS and Catalyst software supports SNMPv1 in all releases.

SNMPv1 has the following limitations:

- A primitive security model

- Support for 32-bit integer objects only
- A perceived need for better performance

The next few sections discuss the efforts to solve these issues.

SNMPv2

SNMPv2 was designed to add security and increase performance. It included a party-based security mechanism and added both a get-bulk and an inform operation, as well as support for 64-bit integers, including counters. SNMPv2 also grouped traps and informs into notifications and cleaned up the way SNMP notifications (traps or informs) are identified. SNMPv2 is also known as SNMPv2p, where the p designates support for the party-based security mechanism. Competing versions with different security mechanisms include SNMPv2u, with a user-based security mechanism, and SNMPv2*, with an alternative user-based security mechanism.

The IETF standards committee (including some of the original authors of SNMPv2) could not agree on the security mechanism defined in SNMPv2, so it was never ratified. The disagreement was over concerns that the party-based security mechanism would be too complex to implement.

Cisco IOS devices supported SNMPv2 from early in the version 10 train until 11.2(4)F, when SNMPv2c support replaced SNMPv2. The 11.2F train features were rolled into 11.3, so all 11.2 trains support SNMPv2, whereas 11.3 and above support SNMPv2c instead. 64-bit counters were not supported while SNMPv2 was supported. Cisco Catalyst devices never supported SNMPv2. Neither SNMPv2u nor SNMPv2* have been supported by Cisco devices.

Because SNMPv2 never became a standard, few network management systems supported it. So, SNMPv2 can be and has been ignored by network managers for the most part.

SNMPv2c

Because of the dissension in the standards committee about SNMPv2 security, the committee decided to release RFCs that described the part of SNMPv2 that could be agreed upon. Thus, SNMPv2c was drafted without the troublesome security aspects of SNMPv2. The *c* in SNMPv2c signifies that it supports the same community-based security model of SNMPv1.

As noted previously, Cisco IOS devices first supported SNMPv2c in version 11.2(4)F and support for SNMPv2 was dropped at the same time. Because this feature train's capabilities were rolled into 11.3, SNMPv2c is supported in all 11.3 and above IOS versions. Cisco Catalyst devices added support for SNMPv2c in version 3.1 software, including support for 64-bit counters.

In general, 64-bit counter support didn't become available until Cisco IOS version 12.0(3)T. The Cisco 12000 GSR routers supported an enterprise MIB, CISCO-C12000-IF-HC-COUNTERS-MIB, to add limited support for 64-bit counters. This MIB paired two 32-bit integers together that could be combined at the management station to create a 64-bit counter. It provided support only for the ifInOctets, ifOutOctets, ifInUcastPkts, and ifOutUcastPkts objects. This MIB had a very limited lifespan and was supported only in the 11.2GS train for the 12000 GSR routers.

SNMPv3

The IETF SNMP standards committees were able to hammer out a security scheme that could be agreed upon, and added this capability to SNMPv2c to make SNMPv3.

SNMPv3's security is a user-based security model (USM). It supports secure authorization of the user sending a packet, as well as the privacy or encryption of the packet. SNMPv3 allows you to use SNMPv1-style community strings as well as v3 users.

Authorization of the source of the packet not only increases the security of network management, but may also increase its reliability.

You can still use views (now renamed View-based Access Control Models (VACMs)) to limit what users and community strings can access and modify in the MIB.

Users contemplating using SNMPv3 authorization or privacy will need to implement a key management system that will manage the keys required to authorize and encrypt the packets.

Cisco IOS devices started supporting SNMPv3 in IOS version 12.0(3)T, and 64-bit counter support for SNMPv2c and SNMPv3 were added at the same time. Cisco Catalyst devices support SNMPv3 as of software version 5.4.

Until SNMPv3 security can be used in production networks, there are some methods that can be used to significantly increase the security of your network management transactions. See the section called "Controlling SNMP Access Using Views and Access Lists" in Chapter 18, "Best Practices for Device Configuration," for coverage of some of these methods.

SNMP Packet Formats

This section shows the packet formats for the three versions of SNMP still in use: SNMPv1, SNMPv2c, and SNMPv3.

SNMPv1 Packet Formats

An SNMPv1 packet contains two pieces: a message header and a protocol data unit (PDU). The message header has two fields: the version number and the community name. Figure 8-2 illustrates the basic format of an SNMPv1 packet.

Figure 8-2   *SNMPv1 Packet Format*

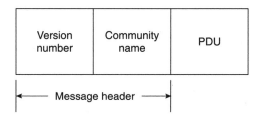

As can be seen from Figure 8-2, SNMPv1 protocol headers contain two fields: version number and community name.

- **Version number**. Specifies the version of SNMP used. SNMPv1 is version 1.

- **Community name**. Defines the community string that determines the access rights of this packet.

SNMPv1 Protocol Data Unit

SNMPv1 PDUs vary in format depending on the PDU type. The following sections will detail these formats.

Get, Get-next, Get-response, and Set-request PDU Format   This PDU format specifies an operation (get, set-request, etc.), a unique ID, error fields, and fields that specify the objects to be operated on with values. SNMPv1 PDU fields are variable in length, as prescribed by Abstract Syntax Notation One (ASN.1). Figure 8-3 illustrates the fields of the SNMPv1 get, get-next, get-response, and set-request PDUs.

Figure 8-3   *SNMPv1 get, get-next, get-response, and set-request PDUs*

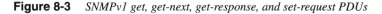

The following describes each of the fields in Figure 8-3:

- **PDU Type**. Specifies the type of PDU (get, get-next, etc.).

- **Request ID**. A unique ID for this request. Responses use the same ID as the request they are satisfying.
- **Error Status**. The status of a get-response. Zero indicates no error.
- **Error Index**. Specifies the variable binding that the error status refers to.
- **Variable Bindings**. Each variable binding specifies an OID and the value of this OID. Each of these values (the OID and its value) are encoded using Basic Encoding Rules (BER) and are represented as a triplicate of the object type, length in bytes, and value. For example, for an OID the type is OID, the length is the encoded length of the OID, and the value is the BER-encoded OID. A 32-bit integer would have a type of integer, and the length would be the encoded length of the integer, which could be from 0 for a 0 or null value and up to 5 for a 32-bit integer with the high-order bit on. The value is the BER-encoded value of the integer.

Trap PDU Format   Figure 8-4 shows the fields of the SNMPv1 Trap PDU.

Figure 8-4   *The SNMPv1 Trap PDU*

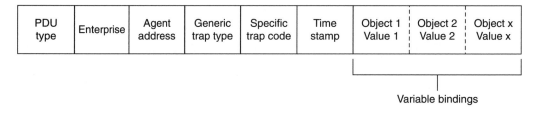

Variable bindings

The following list discusses the various fields in Figure 8-4:

- **PDU Type.** Specifies the type of PDU (trap).
- **Enterprise**. For generic traps, specifies an OID that indicates the type of device generating the trap. For specific traps, this field specifies the trap (SMIv1) or notification (SMIv2) section's OID for the MIB document containing the definition of the specific trap.
- **Agent Address**. Specifies the address of the device generating the trap.
- **Generic Trap Type**. Indicates which SNMPv1 generic trap this trap is or if it is not a generic trap (see Table 8-4).
- **Specific Trap Code**. Indicates a specific trap number. Specific traps are defined in MIB documents. The combination of the enterprise OID and the specific trap specifics a unique trap.
- **Time Stamp**. Provides sysUpTime at the time the trap was generated.
- **Variable Bindings**. As in other SNMP packets, this field consists of one or more variable bindings. Each variable binding consists of an OID and a value for that OID.

SNMPv2c Packet Format

SNMPv2c packets have the same format at this level as SNMPv1 packets. The version number for SNMPv2c is 2.

SNMPv2c Protocol Data Unit

SNMPv2c PDUs vary in format depending upon the PDU type. The following sections detail these formats.

Get, Get-next, inform, Get-response, set-request, and Trap PDU Formats

SNMPv2c get, get-next, inform, get-response, set-request, and trap PDUs all contain the same fields as the SNMPv1 packet format shown in Figure 8-2. Note that this is a change for the trap PDU from SNMPv1. Also, the trap and inform PDUs in SNMPv2c format include two mandatory variable bindings: the trap enterprise OID and the value of sysUpTime at the time the trap was generated, must be the first two variable bindings for these PDU types.

Get-bulk PDU Format   Figure 8-5 shows the fields of the SNMPv2c get-bulk request.

Figure 8-5   *SNMPv2c get-bulk PDU format*

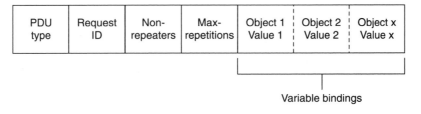

The following descriptions summarize the fields illustrated in Figure 8-5:

- **PDU Type**. Identifies the PDU as a get-bulk operation.
- **Request ID**. Same as for a SNMPv1 PDU.
- **Non-repeaters**. The number of variable bindings that should be retrieved no more than once. This field is non-zero when some of the variable bindings are not objects in a table. All non-repeaters (if any) must appear first in the list of variable bindings.
- **Max-repetitions**. Defines the maximum number of times that the repeating variables should be retrieved.
- **Variable Bindings**. Same as for a SNMPv1 PDU.

SNMPv3 Packet Format

SNMPv3 packets have a different header format from SNMPv1. All PDU formats are identical to SNMPv2c. Figure 8-6 shows this new header format.

Figure 8-6 *SNMPv3 Packet Format*

Message version	Message ID	Message max size	Message flags	Message security model	Message security parameters	Context engine ID	Context name	PDU

Each of the fields in Figure 8-6 is described as follows:

- **Message Version**. Specifies the protocol version. SNMPv3 is 3.

- **Message ID**. Specifies which message stream this packet belongs to.

- **Message Max Size**. The maximum size of an SNMP packet that the sender can receive.

- **Message Flags**. Contains the reportable, priv, and auth flags. The reportable flag indicates that the sender expects a reply, for example, for a get, get-next, get-bulk, set-request, or inform operation. The priv and auth flags indicate whether encryption and authentication are used for this packet.

- **Message Security Model**. Indicates which security model is used. SNMPv1 is 1, SNMPv2c is 2, and the User Security Model (USM), defined with SNMPv3, is 3.

- **Message Security Parameters**. Defined by the particular security model selected.

- **Context Engine ID**. A unique identifier of the sender of the packet.

- **Context Name**. A name associated with the current context.

- **PDU**. All SNMPv3 packets use the same PDUs as defined for SNMPv2c.

SNMP Operations

SNMPv1 defined five protocol operations: get, get-response, get-next, set-request, and trap. SNMPv2 added get-bulk and inform, and redefined the trap operation packet format. All of these operations were carried over to SNMPv2c and SNMPv3. Neither added any new operations. Each of these operations will be discussed briefly in the following sections.

The basic structure of an SNMP packet is a header that includes an authentication structure (a community string, SNMPv2 party information, or SNMPv3 user information), a request-id or sequence number, and an error status and error index. (Get-bulk overlays the error status and error index fields with the non-repeaters and max-repetitions fields. See the section "Get-bulk.") See the previous section for more details.

Get

The get operation is the simplest of the operations. Basically, a get operation is a request for an agent to return one or more objects or specific pieces of information. For each object requested, the agent will return that object's value.

The network management system can request as many objects as will fit into one packet. However, as the length of the objects in the packet are zero (a value of null), the agent may not be able to send a get-response packet back with all the information filled in if doing so would cause the packet to exceed the maximum size that the agent supports for an SNMP packet. Although the standard doesn't mention a maximum size, all agents and managers have a maximum that they can handle. If the agent can't finish filling the packet, it will return an error of tooBig. All agents must be able to handle 484-byte packets.

Cisco IOS devices had a default maximum size of 484 bytes until IOS version 10.3, when the default maximum was increased to 1500. By using the Cisco IOS global configuration command, **snmp-server packetsize** *byte-count*, you can change the maximum size. The command will accept any number up to 8192, but there are other factors in the SNMP implementation that limit the maximum to 3072 until IOS 12.1. Cisco Catalyst devices have a hard-coded maximum of 1500 bytes.

Get-response

The get-response operation is the packet type that SNMP agents send in response to receiving a get, get-next, get-bulk, or set-request packet. Management stations send a get-response operation to acknowledge. A get-response packet is virtually the same format as all of these requests, so it is very easy for the agent to construct. The agent just has to fill in the blanks, change the packet type to get-response, and send it back. Although this is a rather simplistic representation of the operation of an SNMP agent, it is sufficiently accurate for most network managers (with the exception of when the received packet is a get-bulk type. See the "Get-bulk" section for further details).

Get-next

The get-next operation allows a network management system to request the "next" object or objects in the MIB supported by the agent. For each object requested, the agent will return the object that is next in the MIB tree, in lexicographical order. *Lexicographical ordering* means that the next item must always have a greater OID than the last.

This operation allows an NMS to request information from an agent without knowing all the information about the MIB supported by that agent or the instances of all objects. In particular, it is useful for retrieving rows of information from tables without requiring the NMS to know all the indexes for the tables. This is the SNMP operation that is most commonly used to implement a method to retrieve a table or the whole MIB from an agent. This is commonly known as an *SNMP walk*.

There were some changes in how the interface table is structured that first occurred in RFC 1573. These changes were solidified in RFC 2233 and are now considered a best practice for all SNMP tables. Basically, the major change that affects polling tables is the requirement that objects that don't have data for a particular row must not be instantiated. The result is called a *sparse table* because fields that don't make sense don't exist. See section 3.1.4 of RFC 2233 for more details.

For example, consider a Frame Relay connection, consisting of the physical connection and one or more virtual connections. Error counters such as ifInErrors have no meaning for virtual connections; if the packet contains an error, determining which virtual connection the packet was meant for isn't possible. Therefore, standards-compliant implementations of the interfaces table will contain holes or missing data for these instances. In particular, Cisco IOS software started supporting sparse tables in version 11.1. Cisco Catalyst software does not support sparse tables as of version 5.1; however, LANE modules installed in a Catalyst switch and polled through the supervisor module do support sparse tables.

Sparse tables mean that certain assumptions that have been made are no longer true. The assumption that affects get-next is that all columns in the table will have the same number of entries. Consider the sparse interfaces table in Table 8-3. What happens when you query it using get-next?

Table 8-3   *Example of Part of a Sparse Interfaces Table*

ifIndex	ifInOctets	ifInErrors	ifOutOctets
1	20345	123	14325
2	345	n/a	432
4	1311	11	103

Following are a query and results for the first row of the table:

```
>snmpnext <device> ifInOctets ifInErrors ifOutOctets
ifInOctets.1 = INTEGER 20345
ifInErrors.1 = INTEGER 123
ifOutOctets.1 = INTEGER 14325
```

And for the next row:

```
>snmpnext <device> ifIndex.1 ifInOctets.1 ifInErrors.1 ifOutOctets.1
ifInOctets.2 = INTEGER 345
ifInErrors.4 = INTEGER 11
ifOutOctets.2 = INTEGER 432
```

What happened here? The query returned all the content of the second row of the table, but ifInErrors is from the third row with the ifIndex of 4. You need to be careful not to assume you got just objects from row 2.

Continuing with the third row:

```
>snmpnext <device> ifInOctets.2 ifInErrors.4 ifOutOctets.2
```

```
ifInOctets.4 = INTEGER 1311
ifInUnknownProtos.1 = INTEGER 0
ifOutOctets.4 = INTEGER 103
```

This time, ifInErrors is not returned, but rather the next object in the table. This result indicates that all the ifInErrors column has been returned. You should continue to try to get the next row, as follows:

```
>snmpnext <device> ifInOctets.4 ifOutOctets.4
ifInUcastPkts.1 = INTEGER 19871
ifOutUcastPkts.1 = INTEGER 13210
```

This result indicates that all the other rows in the previous get-response have been returned because all the columns have returned data beyond what we are interested in. So you're done.

There are commercially available packages that query sparse tables incorrectly. If you see strange results when polling data through SNMP, an inaccurate package might be the reason. You can test to see if the inability to support sparse tables is the problem by turning off sparse tables in Cisco IOS software with the **no snmp-server sparse-tables** global configuration command. There is no way to turn off sparse tables on a LANE module in a Catalyst switch.

Get-bulk

The get-bulk operation was added by SNMPv2 and improves the performance of retrieving large amounts of SNMP data. This operation allows the agent to pack as many values in each get-response packet as will fit without exceeding the maximum SNMP packet size. This can significantly reduce the management overhead on a network and also can significantly increase the speed of retrieving large amounts of data.

The get-bulk operation allows the agent to maximize the amount of information returned in a packet. You need to give the command some hints about what you want it to do in the form of two arguments. The first argument is the number of objects that are specified exactly, that is, objects that you want just one of, such as sysUpTime.0, sysDescr.0, or ifNumber.0. Such items are referred to as *non-repeaters*. All non-repeaters must be specified before the repeating arguments.

The second argument, for the repeating objects, is the maximum number of repeats you want. The agent will fill the get-response with as many objects as will fit in one packet, up to the maximum number of objects non-repeaters and repeaters you asked for.

There are at least three methods to handle instances when you don't know how many rows exist in a table you want to retrieve:

- Determine how many rows by querying an object, if one exists for the table in question.
- Specify a very high repeaters number and deal with the possibility that you will receive lots of stuff you don't want.

- Specify a relatively small repeaters number and realize that you may have to do more get-bulk requests to get the whole table.

The first method can be used only for tables where there is an object to tell you how many rows there are. The ifTable has such an object, called ifNumber. Using the data from Table 8-3 as an example, here is what querying the object looks like:

```
>snmpget <device> ifNumber.0
ifNumber.0 = INTEGER 3
```

Now, consider how to retrieve the ifTable information in Table 8-3 with the get-bulk operation. There are no non-repeaters to retrieve, so set that argument to 0 and use ifNumber+1 for the number of repeaters you want. The reason for adding 1 to ifNumber is so you get at least one set of objects beyond the end of the table. This will ensure that you get the whole table in cases where rows get added after you queried ifNumber. Example 8-2 shows the query and results.

Example 8-2   *Using the get-bulk operation.*

```
>snmpbulk <device> 0 4 ifInOctets ifInErrors ifOutOctets
ifInOctets.1 = INTEGER 20345
ifInErrors.1 = INTEGER 123
ifOutOctets.1 = INTEGER 14325
ifInOctets.2 = INTEGER 345
ifInErrors.4 = INTEGER 11
ifOutOctets.2 = INTEGER 432
ifInOctets.4 = INTEGER 1311
ifInUnknownProtos.1 = INTEGER 0
ifOutOctets.4 = INTEGER 103
ifInUcastPkts.1 = INTEGER 19871
ifInUnknownProtos.2 = INTEGER 0
ifOutUcastPkts.1 = INTEGER 13210
```

In Example 8-2, only one request was made and the whole table was returned. It is quite possible that you would not receive the whole table in the first packet. In that case, you would have to count the number of rows you did receive, subtract that number from the number of repeaters you requested, and set the objects to be retrieved to the last set of objects received in your next request. You would continue this process until you retrieved the entire table and one set of objects beyond.

Set-request

The set-request operation is virtually identical to the get operation, with the exception that the manager fills in the desired values for the objects and the agent is requested to change the value of these objects. The agent sends back a get-response packet with the new values of the objects set, along with the status of the set-request operation.

Note that the agent will not allow a set-request operation unless the manager has write access through the correct community string or other authorization method, the object(s) are writeable by the agent, and the SNMP view for the security method used allows write access to the object(s).

Just like the other SNMP operations, with set-request it is possible to specify several objects—as many as will fit into one packet. And, just like the get operation, it is possible to specify more objects than the agent can fit in the return packet. In this case, the set-request operation is not done and an error of tooBig is returned in the get-response packet.

All set-requests should succeed on all objects or should fail for all objects. The errIndex in the reply (a get-response operation) should point to the first object that was found to be in error.

Notifications

SNMPv1 defined a method for an SNMP agent to asynchronously deliver event notifications. This operation was called a trap. In SNMPv1, the event notification was also called a trap. SNMPv2 defined a new operation, inform, which added acknowledgment of the receipt of the notification and retransmission in the event that an acknowledgment was not received. SNMPv2 clarified the difference between the operations and the event notifications by redefining event notifications from traps to notifications. Traps and informs are covered in more detail in the following sections.

Traps

Trap operations allow an SNMP agent to send asynchronous notifications that an event has occurred. Traps are sent on a best-effort basis and without any method to verify whether they were received.

Traps have identifiers that specify which trap this operation is for. SNMPv1 defined a fairly awkward method of determining the trap identifier. This method involved using two fields—generic-trap and specific-trap—as well as the enterprise field, which holds an OID. To determine which trap it is, you must first look at the generic-trap field. This field can have the settings listed in Table 8-4.

Table 8-4   *Generic-trap Field Values*

Trap type	Type value
ColdStart	0
WarmStart	1
LinkDown	2
LinkUp	3
AuthenticationFailure	4
EgpNeighborLoss	5
EnterpriseSpecific	6

If generic-trap is anything but enterpriseSpecific(6), the value of generic-trap specifies the trap type. If generic-trap is enterpriseSpecific(6), the value of the specific-trap field specifies which trap this is, relative to the enterprise field. The enterprise field is usually populated with the OID of the trap portion of the MIB that the trap is defined in. Therefore, it is usually possible to look at the enterprise field and determine where the trap is defined. Then, the specific-trap value will specify the trap number within the relevant MIB.

Let's look at an example SNMPv1 trap and see how we would need to determine what trap it is.

Here are the relevant fields from the packet:

- generic-trap = enterpriseSpecific(6)
- specific-trap = 1
- enterprise = 1.3.6.1.4.1.9.9.41.2

So we know that this trap is not a standard trap because generic-trap is marked as enterpriseSpecific. We then need to search for the MIB that contains this trap. Usually, subtracting one field from the enterprise OID will yield the desired result. So, searching for 1.3.6.1.4.1.9.9.41 in the OID directory (http://www.cisco.com/public/mibs/oid) shows that this trap is in the CISCO-SYSLOG-MIB. Because this is an SNMPv1 trap, let's look at the SMIv1 form of the MIB. Searching that MIB (http://www.cisco.com/public/mibs/v1/CISCO-SYSLOG-MIB-V1SMI.my), you see the following line:

```
ciscoSyslogMIBNotificationPrefix OBJECT IDENTIFIER ::= { ciscoSyslogMIB 2 }
```

This is consistent with the .2 at the end of the enterprise OID. There may be multiple traps or notifications defined in this MIB, so we use the specific-trap to determine which one this trap is. Looking further down in the MIB, you see the following:

```
clogMessageGenerated TRAP-TYPE
-- Reverse mappable trap
    ENTERPRISE ciscoSyslogMIBNotificationPrefix
    VARIABLES {
        clogHistFacility, clogHistSeverity, clogHistMsgName,
        clogHistMsgText, clogHistTimestamp }
--  Status
--    mandatory
    DESCRIPTION
        "When a syslog message is generated by the device a
        clogMessageGenerated notification is sent.  The
        sending of these notifications can be enabled/disabled
        via the clogNotificationsEnabled object."
    ::= 1
```

The ::= 1 corresponds to the specific-trap field, so you now know that this trap is a clogMessageGenerated trap.

SNMPv2 redefined the trap PDU, making its format the same as the rest of the SNMP PDU types. It simplified the determination of the trap type by combining the enterprise, generic-trap, and the specific-trap fields into a varbind, snmpTrapOID.0, which contains a single OID that specifies what this trap is.

So, let's take the same SNMP notification delivered as an SNMPv2 trap. Here, we need to look at only one field to determine what trap we are looking at, snmpTrapOID.0, which is always the second varbind in a SNMPv2 trap:

```
snmpTrapOID.0 = 1.3.6.1.4.1.9.9.41.2.0.1
```

Here, you subtract three fields from the OID and search for this OID again. Because you get the same OID as previously (1.3.6.1.4.1.9.9.41), you get the same MIB: CISCO-SYSLOG-MIB. Because this time you are looking at a SNMPv2 format trap, you'll look at the SMIv2 format MIB (http://www.cisco.com/public/mibs/v2/CISCO-SYSLOG-MIB.my). Here, you see the same line as before:

```
ciscoSyslogMIBNotificationPrefix OBJECT IDENTIFIER ::= { ciscoSyslogMIB 2 }
```

This corresponds to the third to the last field in snmpTrapOID. Looking further, you see the following:

```
ciscoSyslogMIBNotifications OBJECT IDENTIFIER
                    ::= { ciscoSyslogMIBNotificationPrefix 0 }
```

This 0 corresponds to the second to last field in snmpTrapOID. Finally, we find the trap or notification definition:

```
clogMessageGenerated NOTIFICATION-TYPE
        OBJECTS    {    clogHistFacility,
                        clogHistSeverity,
                        clogHistMsgName,
                        clogHistMsgText,
                        clogHistTimestamp
                   }
        STATUS     current
        DESCRIPTION
               "When a syslog message is generated by the device a
                clogMessageGenerated notification is sent.  The
                sending of these notifications can be enabled/disabled
                via the clogNotificationsEnabled object."
        ::= { ciscoSyslogMIBNotifications 1 }
```

Here, ciscoSyslogMIBNotifications 1 corresponds to the last field in snmpTrapOID. So, with a SNMPv2 trap, you have to look at only one field, snmpTrapOID, to know exactly what trap you received.

Informs

Informs allow the agent to keep track of the notifications sent to each recipient and receive acknowledgments of the receipt of these notifications. The agent can resend the notifications if an acknowledgement is not received in a reasonable time.

It is important to note several reasons why a particular event notification will not be received by a NMS. These include the following:

- The agent was reinitialized.
- The agent ran out of space to save informs and had to drop one or more.
- The agent suppressed certain notifications.

- The network lost or dropped the packet containing the notification multiple times.
- There is not currently network connectivity between the agent and the NMS.

The agent is not state-full through reinitializations. That is, if the agent is reset, it does not remember any notifications sent before the reset and therefore cannot determine whether they were received.

All agents have finite resources and may have to throw away informs that have not been delivered if those resources are exhausted.

Many agents will suppress notifications if they come at a rate above a certain value. This helps the agent, manager, and network to not be overwhelmed with notifications in the event of very rapid state changes that generate event notifications. Take, for example, the case of a flapping WAN interface, where the operational status is changing several times a second. If a linkDown or linkUp notification were sent for every state change, the agent, manager, and network could be flooded with information, making the problem even worse.

Cisco IOS devices limit traps to two per second to a particular device. Any notifications received over this limit will not be sent. Note that this means that it is possible for an NMS to receive multiple linkDown notifications in a row or for the interface to be up and operational. Yet, the NMS has not received a linkUp notification—it was not sent by the agent because the agent limited the volume of traps.

Decoding a SNMPv2 inform is done in the identical way as a SNMPv2 trap because the second varbind is also snmpTrapOID and is formatted in the same way. See the previous section for an example of determining which trap is received.

Structure of Management Information

The Structure of Management Information (SMI) for SNMP was first defined as part of SNMPv1 in RFC 1065. SMI defines how SNMP objects and the MIBs in which they are defined are structured.

SMI defines that the structure of all objects is a tree, starting at or rooted at iso (see Figure 8-7). All names of objects have corresponding numbers; iso is 1 and is commonly represented as iso(1). All SNMP objects exist under a branch off of iso, org(3), dod(6), and then internet(1). Thus, the pathway to SNMP objects can be represented as iso.org.dod.internet or 1.3.6.1. This designation is known as an Object Identifier (OID). OIDs can be represented as all text, all numeric, or a combination of both. A fully-qualified OID (one starting at iso(1)) is guaranteed to be unique.

Figure 8-7   *High-level MIB Tree*

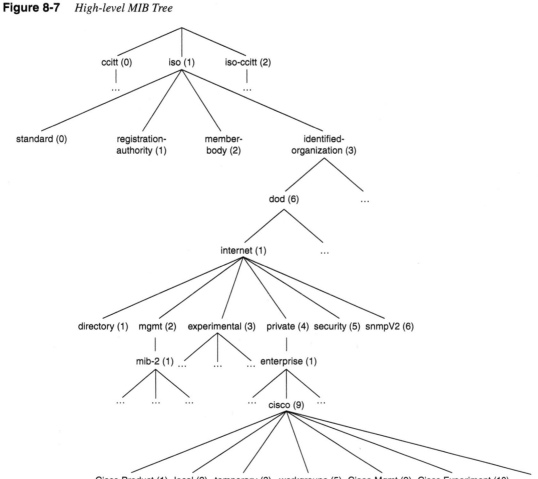

The branch that most of the standard MIBs are defined under is mgmt(2). New MIBs expected to be standardized are defined initially under the experimental(3) branch. MIBs defined by other organizations are defined under the private(4) branch. Security is defined as the security(5) branch, and finally, SNMPv2-related items are defined under the snmpV2(6) branch. Some other interesting points on the tree are mib-2, which is defined as the first branch off of the management branch, and the cisco branch, which is off of enterprise, which in turn is off of the private branch.

So far, there have been two major versions of SMI: v1 and v2. The next two sections discuss these versions. The third section discusses the different SNMP object types.

SMIv1

SMIv1 was first defined in RFC 1065 and re-released as RFC 1155 with no substantial changes. SMIv1 was revised into concise format in RFC 1212, which was compatible with the previous definition, but more rigorous in its definitions. For a good description of the changes, see section 4 of RFC 1212 (because it is interesting mainly for historical purposes, we are not covering it here).

All MIBs that Cisco provides are in either the SMIv1 concise format or in the SMIv2 format. Most SMIv2-format MIBs are also provided in SMIv1 concise format for the use of management stations that don't support the SMIv2 format. For more information on this, see Appendix A, "CCO, MIBs, Traps, and Your NMS."

SMIv2

SMIv2 was defined at the same time as SNMPv2, but SMIv2 format-defined MIB objects can be used by any version of SNMP, with the exception of 64-bit integer objects. 64-bit integers can be used only with SNMP version 2 and higher; SNMPv1 has no method to handle these objects in the protocol.

SNMP Object Types

SNMP is based upon ASN.1 syntax and inherits several object types from it. Additional object types are defined by SNMP as extensions to these base types. A method to add further object types as extensions to any existing type is defined in SNMP.

Some of the more commonly used object types are listed in Table 8-5 using the SMIv1 syntax.

Table 8-5   *SMIv1 Object Types*

Type	Size	Description
INTEGER	4 bytes (32 bits), signed	A 32-bit integer object.
Gauge	4 bytes, unsigned	An integer object that reflects the current value of something.
Counter	4 bytes, unsigned	An integer that counts the amount of something and always increases in size until hitting its maximum value. It then wraps back to 0 and starts ascending again.

Table 8-5   *SMIv1 Object Types (Continued)*

OCTET STRING	0 or more bytes	A string of 8-bit values.
DisplayString	0 to 255 bytes	An octet string in which all values are printable.
ObjectIdentifier	Variable	An OID (for example, 1.3.6.1.4.1.9).
TimeTicks	4 bytes, unsigned	A measure of time, in hundredths of a second, since an event.
IpAddress	4 bytes	A 32-bit IP address.
PhysAddress	Variable	A physical address such as a 6-byte Ethernet MAC address.
NetworkAddress	Variable, but only IP is defined, so should be 4 bytes	A Layer 3 network address. Only IP addresses are defined.
BIT STRING	Variable	An enumerated bit string.

Counters should never be reset or zeroed unless the SNMP agent is reinitialized (and sysUpTime is reset) or a corresponding time value is also reinitialized.

The reason clearing counters should not be allowed on an SNMP agent is that it becomes a problem when an agent is being managed by more than one management application. This is because if an application is monitoring a particular counter, it has no way to tell whether another application clears that counter. So, if the application suddenly sees a counter go to zero, it may assume the counter has wrapped, and calculates an inaccurate (probably huge) delta value for that counter.

See Chapter 12, "Monitoring System Interfaces" for more information on calculating rates from objects with the type of counter.

SMIv2 redefined some of these types, so Table 8-6 lists these new or redefined types.

Table 8-6   *SMIv2 Object Types*

Type	Size	Description
Integer32	4 bytes (32 bits), signed	Same as INTEGER
UInteger32	4 bytes, unsigned	An unsigned 32 bit integer
Gauge32	4 bytes, unsigned	Same as Gauge
Counter32	4 bytes, unsigned	Same as Counter
Counter64	8 bytes, unsigned	A larger Counter

Note that the only 64-bit type defined is Counter. Work is proceeding on defining other 64-bit types.

SNMP Views

Cisco IOS devices allow you to apply a view to an SNMPv1 community string, an SNMPv2 party, or an SNMPv3 user. Views give network managers the capability of limiting what can be accessed through each access method defined. For example, service providers could define a community string that has access only to the statistics for one interface. They could then provide the community string for a particular interface to the customer attached to that interface, therefore allowing that customer to monitor just that interface. The customer could provide the same level of access to the service provider to their external access router.

A common use for SNMP views is to limit access to certain tables. This capability is useful because SNMP can have an impact on the CPU load on the devices polled.

More specifically, Cisco IOS devices store the routing and address resolution protocol (ARP) tables in the most efficient order for routing and ARP lookups. However, the SNMP tables defined by MIB II (RFC 1213) require that these tables be delivered in lexicographical order. Therefore, Cisco IOS devices must sort these tables if they receive a request for these tables via the get-next or get-bulk operations. This can cause the CPU load on these devices to increase significantly. Because the SNMP process runs at low priority in Cisco IOS devices, this added CPU load will usually not affect core services. However, certain services also run at low priority and can be affected by a high CPU load caused by SNMP polling, including X.25 translation services. Starting before IOS 11.1(20)CC, a change was made in the method used to traverse the routing table to improve multitasking that further exacerbated this issue when polling the routing table. This change affected the 11.1CA and CC trains, as well as all 12.0 releases, but not 11.2 or 11.3. A subsequent change was made to allow SNMP to query the CEF table for routing entries if CEF switching is used. This significantly improves the situation.

Network managers sometimes choose to disable access to these tables via an SNMP view. Doing so prevents network management stations from polling these tables and, therefore, placing a high CPU load on network devices. Disabling the polling of the ARP table can cause problems with programs that use the ARP table to convert MAC addresses to IP addresses, such as user tracking applications. Disabling the polling of the routing table may slow down network auto-discovery by an NMS, but will usually not disable it.

Cisco IOS devices started supporting views in IOS version 10.0. Cisco Catalyst devices do not support SNMP views as of software release 5.1.

Evolution of the Interfaces Group

The interfaces group was first defined in the original MIB at the same time SNMPv1 was defined. This MIB was revised in RFC 1158 and then redefined in RFC 1213 to become the MIB-II that network managers know and love. This MIB made certain assumptions and enforced certain limitations based on a static view of the interfaces table. These assumptions and limitations became problematic as networking equipment evolved from devices with a fixed number of interfaces or ports to devices that can have physical interfaces swapped in and out without rebooting the system, and virtual and logical interfaces defined and deleted at any time during their operation.

The problems were first addressed in RFC 1573, which has been superceded with RFC 2233.

One important problem was that the interfaces group defines an object, ifNumber, which is defined as the number of interfaces, and a table of interfaces with an index (ifIndex) of 1 to ifNumber. Now, take an NMS that is collecting information about a particular interface. The objects that this NMS is interested in are indexed with a particular ifIndex. If an interface is removed from the device, the corresponding row in the interfaces table is deleted and ifNumber is decremented by 1, or else the interfaces table ends up cluttered with unused entries, with no standard way to define unused entries. According to the definition of the interfaces table in RFC 1213, if a row is deleted and ifNumber decremented, then all ifIndexes for all interfaces with a higher ifIndex than the one deleted would have to be decremented. There is no standard way to report this event to the NMS, which may blithely continue to collect data using the original ifIndex, despite the change. This can severely impact the accuracy of the collected data.

RFC 1573 separated ifIndex from ifNumber. It also required the agent to use a particular ifIndex for a single interface only. If this interface is deleted, its row should be deleted from the interfaces table and the corresponding ifIndex should not be reused. RFC 1573 suggests using ifName or ifAlias as keys to determining what ifIndex is what when the SNMP agent is reinitialized (sysUpTime is reinitialized).

Cisco Catalyst software will attempt to reuse ifIndexes only if a physical interface is removed and an identical interface is reinserted. RFC 1573 also allows ifIndexes to be renumbered if the SNMP agent is reinitialized. Cisco Catalyst software versions since 3.1 will also attempt to preserve ifIndex numbers through reboots.

Another problem is that no method of associating sub-interfaces with the main interface or virtual interfaces with physical interfaces the way the interface table was defined in RFC 1213. RFC 1573 adds a new table, the ifStackTable, to address this issue.

Remote Monitoring MIB and Related MIBs

RMON is just another SNMP MIB. Yet it was one of the first MIBs to support row creation in tables, thus allowing much more flexibility in designing MIBs. RMONv1 defined a method to manipulate rows, called the EntryStatus or RMON method. RMONv2 was defined after RFC 1903 was released and, therefore, uses that RFC's method to manipulate rows, known as the RowStatus method.

The RMON MIB allows an NMS to request that an agent do many types of things, some of which are usually thought of as the domain of either the NMS itself or network analyzers. The advantage of this capability is that the network can monitor itself in a more autonomous fashion. Conversely, RMON requires more resources from the SNMP agent than the typical MIB. RMON can quite easily exhaust an agent's memory or processing resources if not used with caution.

RMONv1 supports nine groups, as follows:

- statistics—only supported for ethernet (etherStats table)
- history—statistics over time, only ethernet statistics
- alarm—threshold setup
- hosts—MAC-layer tracking of host statistics
- hostTopN—busiest hosts
- matrix—MAC-layer conversation pair statistics
- filter—setup filters on channels to restrict packets seen on that channel
- capture—capture packets—can use filter
- event—what to do when an alarm is triggered

RMONv2 adds nine new groups, mostly concentrated on the higher layers of the protocol stack:

- protocolDir—the protocols supported by the device
- protocolDist—statistics on a per-protocol basis
- addressMap—MAC to higher-layer protocol address mapping
- nlHost—higher-layer host statistics
- nlMatrix—higher-layer conversation pair statistics
- alHost—application-layer host statistics
- alMatrix—application-layer conversation pair statistics
- usrHistory—history statistics for user-defined criteria
- probeConfig—configuration of RMON features

Cisco IOS devices have supported RMONv1 since IOS 11.1. All Cisco IOS devices support two groups: the alarms and the events groups. These two groups allow an agent to trigger RMON events when an integer object crosses a threshold and to have that RMON event trigger an action such as logging that event or sending an SNMP notification. See Chapter 5, "Configuring Events," for more information about these groups. In addition, certain Cisco IOS devices support more groups. Cisco 2500 routers, and AS5200 and AS5300 access servers support all nine groups on ethernet interfaces only. Cisco IOS-based switches such as 29xxXL and 85xx devices support four groups: statistics, history, alarm, and events. This set of four groups is also known as mini-RMON.

Cisco Catalyst devices support the four mini-RMON groups.

Cisco SwitchProbes and Network Analysis Modules (NAMs) support all of RMONv1 as well as RMONv2. Although RMONv1 was very centered on the OSI Layers 1 and 2, RMONv2 can be used to monitor points in the protocol stack all the way to Layer 7.

The HC-RMON MIB (Internet draft draft-ietf-rmonmib-rmonhc-00.txt) adds 64-bit counter support to RMONv1 tables. It is not supported in Cisco IOS software; it is supported starting in Cisco Catalyst software version 5.1.

Syslog

The syslog protocol was first defined as part of the UNIX operating system to log messages within the OS. Syslogs allow a computer or device to deliver messages to another computer. Syslog messages have a particular format that associates a facility, and a severity or priority with a message.

The facility code allows syslog to group messages from different sources and take action based on this facility or group. The facilities are described in Table 8-7 and the priorities supported are described in Table 8-8.

Table 8-7   *Syslog Facilities*

Facility	Description
Auth	Authorization system
Cron	Cron facility
Daemon	System daemon
Kern	Kernel
local0-7	Reserved for locally defined messages
Lpr	Line printer system
Mail	Mail system
News	USENET news
sys9	System use
sys10	System use
sys11	System use
sys12	System use
sys13	System use
sys14	System use
Syslog	System log
User	User process
Uucp	UNIX-to-UNIX copy system

Table 8-8   *Syslog Priority Levels and their Descriptions*

Level Name	Level	Description	Syslog Definition
Emergencies	0	System unusable	LOG_EMERG
Alerts	1	Immediate action needed	LOG_ALERT
Critical	2	Critical conditions	LOG_CRIT
Errors	3	Error conditions	LOG_ERR
Warnings	4	Warning conditions	LOG_WARNING
Notifications	5	Normal but significant condition	LOG_NOTICE
Informational	6	Informational messages only	LOG_INFO
Debugging	7	Debugging messages	LOG_DEBUG

Syslog is usually used to deliver log messages from devices to a central repository. A syslog daemon runs in this central repository, which is most often a UNIX system. What is done with syslog messages is controlled by the configuration of the syslog daemon. On UNIX systems, this configuration is normally kept in the /etc/syslog.conf file. A typical line in a syslog.conf file to direct syslog messages coming in on the local7 facility to a log file would be formatted as follows:

```
local7.info   /var/log/messages
```

Cisco devices can use the syslog protocol to deliver log messages, including messages you would see if you were on the console of the device or typed show log on the device. These messages complement (and sometimes duplicate) SNMP notifications.

Cisco devices normally use the local7 facility, but that can be changed using the **logging facility** *facility-type* global IOS command, or the **set logging level** or **set logging server facility** Catalyst commands. The severity or priority of the syslog message is hardcoded into the message itself, but you can control what severity of messages are delivered via syslog by using the **logging history** *level* global IOS command, or the **set logging level** or **set logging server severity** Catalyst commands. Note that all messages of equal or higher severity are delivered. See Table 8-8 for the order of severities.

Cisco Discovery Protocol

Cisco Discovery Protocol (CDP) is a Layer 2 discovery protocol. Cisco devices send out CDP packets every thirty seconds (they are sent as multicast packets). Cisco devices, including switches, do not forward these packets, so only devices on the segment the packets were sent on see them. Cisco devices record the information in a CDP table that can be queried by the cdpCacheTable in the CISCO-CDP-MIB or shown by the **show cdp neighbors [*detail*]** CLI command. This table includes the following information:

- Each neighbor's Layer 3 address (typically the IP address)
- The type of device the neighbor is
- The port on the neighbor that is directly connected to the reporting device in ifName format
- The duplex of the directly connected port
- The VTP domain in which the neighbor is located
- The VLAN in which the port is located

This information can be used to determine the Layer 2 topology of your network. Knowledge of the Layer 2 topology of your network can be used for many purposes, including Layer 2 fault correlation and determining what information is redundant for performance collection and analysis.

Note, however, that non-Cisco devices do not support CDP and will not be discovered by CDP. If a link between two Cisco devices transits one or more non-Cisco devices, the type of devices transited will determine the result. Non-Cisco routers will block the CDP multicasts. Non-Cisco switches or hubs will transmit or flood the CDP packets and, thus, will be transparent to CDP.

All Cisco IOS devices have supported this protocol since release 10.3. Cisco Catalyst devices have supported CDP since the initial software release.

Name Service

Many network management packages attempt to use name service to resolve the IP addresses of network devices from their names and vice versa. If you choose to define your network devices to name service, the way you set up name service can influence how well your network management software works. Conversely, the way your NMS uses name resolution can be more or less robust.

It really doesn't matter what form of name service you use, as all of them work and our recommendations apply to all of them. The three methods of providing name service in common usage today are the following:

- A hosts file: on UNIX, commonly known as /etc/hosts; and on Windows NT, /WINNT/system32/drivers/etc/lmhosts.sam file
- The Domain Name Service (DNS) protocol
- Sun's Network Information Service Plus (NIS+) protocol

Keep this in mind if you want your NMS to continue to work during network outages. If you have implemented name service so that name resolutions don't happen in a timely fashion during outages, you may find that your NMS is not able to report on the outages while it's waiting for responses to name-resolution queries. Therefore, you should be sure to have a means to access the information locally if you choose to use name resolution.

For DNS, this means that the NMS should be a secondary DNS server with a full copy of the DNS tables—not a caching server. It should not be used to provide DNS services to other hosts because the real-time needs of DNS clients may conflict with the processing needs of your NMS.

The same should be done for NIS+ or other name services.

A common problem that network management systems have that can involve name service is not recognizing that a particular IP address belongs to a particular device. Consider a router that has many interfaces, each with a unique IP address. Cisco routers normally will label a packet with the source IP address of the interface the packet is going out. If the router is sending your management system syslog messages, the source IP address is the only thing that identifies the device the messages came from. So, if this router sends a syslog message to the management station through the interface Ethernet 0, the packet will have a source address of the IP address of Ethernet 0 by default. But suppose there is redundancy in the network and Ethernet 1 appears to be the same cost as Ethernet 0 to get to the management station. The router may choose to send a second syslog message via Ethernet 1, with Ethernet 1's source IP address. Two different IP addresses, but the same device. Your NMS needs to recognize this and attribute both messages to the same device.

We recommend that you ensure that all network devices have a designated address for management purposes, such as a loopback address, and that the address be used in all packets sourced by that device. See the section called "Setting Up a Loopback Interface" in Chapter 18 for more details on how to implement this.

You can also assist your NMS in determining the source device by defining all addresses on each network device and ensuring that reverse lookups (looking up a name from an address) for all addresses for each device resolve to the same name.

Another problem that an NMS that implements polling, either for availability or performance, must solve is determining what tag (name or IP address) to use to communicate with the device. You, as the network administrator, also will want to communicate with your network devices by using a tag that works as reliably as possible. If name service resolves the name of the device to a loopback or other high-availability address on the device, both your NMS and you can use the name of the device reliably. Otherwise, both your NMS and you will need to keep a list of the possible addresses on the device and try all of them until one works (hopefully). Let your dynamic routing protocols do the work for you by defining loopback addresses on your devices, and by using these addresses as the only address or the first address returned by name service.

The way you set up name service also can help when troubleshooting your network. Say you want to ping the IP address on a particular interface on a device to determine whether you have connectivity to that interface. You can either remember all your device's IP addresses and what interfaces they are on or you can have name service remember this for you. Say you have a device called router1. You could set up name service so that for each interface on router1 with an IP address, there is a corresponding alias in name service pointing to that IP address. For example, if this router has an Ethernet 0 interface, you could use the alias router1-eth0.

Summary

This chapter has given you an introduction or refresher to the common protocols used in network management. We covered the following protocols:

- Ping
- Traceroute
- Telnet
- SNMP
- Syslog
- Cisco Discovery Protocol
- Name service

Chapters in Part 2 of this book examine specific MIB and syslog messages, as well as CLI messages, for a variety of network management tasks. Before delving into those specifics, however, one more bit of background is needed. Chapter 9, "Selecting the Tools," discusses how to select tools to manage your network.

References

Books

Internetworking Technologies Handbook, Second Edition. Indianapolis, IN: Macmillan Technical Publishing, 1998.

Perkins, David and Evan McGinnis. *Understanding SNMP MIBs*. Prentice Hall Canada, 1997.

Rose, Marshall T. *The Simple Book: An Introduction to Internet Management*, Revised Second Edition. Upper Saddle River, NJ: Prentice Hall, 1996.

Stallings, William. *SNMP, SNMPv2, SNMPv3, and RMON 1 and 2*, Third Edition. Reading, MA: Addison-Wesley, 1999.

CHAPTER 9

Selecting the Tools

Most network managers will choose to use existing tools to do the majority of their network management tasks. Choosing those tools is a major task, especially considering that there is no single package that provides all desired network management functionality.

This chapter describes tools that provide fault and performance management functionality. The following is discussed for each category of tool:

- Which criteria to use when evaluating this type of tool.
- How Cisco device-specific issues, if any, might influence your choice.
- What the tool will do for you.
- Ideas about how to implement this tool.
- Some tools that you might consider using in each category.

NOTE   Note that the list of tools in this chapter is not comprehensive. Any inclusion or omission does not reflect the authors' opinion of the tool or its publisher. We mention the names of specific tools in this chapter solely to provide starting points when investigating a type of tool.

Also note that how we classify or describe a particular tool in this chapter reflects our understanding and experience with the tool at the time of this writing. Please consult with the application's vendor or refer to the references at the end of this chapter for more detail.

It is important to understand the interrelationships between these categories. Figure 9-1 describes the interrelationships between the categories of network management software that are described in this chapter.

Figure 9-1 *Interrelationships of Network Management Tools*

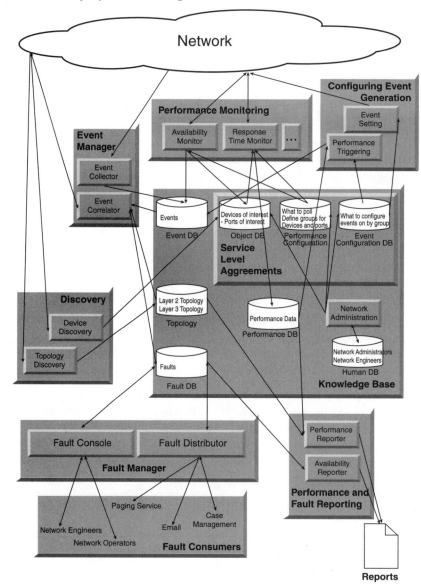

Figure 9-1 will be referenced throughout this chapter to help you understand how the different tools need to integrate.

This chapter covers the following categories of network management tools:

- NMS frameworks
- Knowledge base
- Performance measurement and reporting
- Event and fault management
- Policy management

For each of these categories, this chapter will discuss the criteria you might use to determine which tool to use. Some of these criteria apply across all categories of software. These criteria include the following:

- Capability to integrate with other applications. We list the capability to integrate with other applications first. If you will be able to meld these various tools into a comprehensive network management system (NMS) for your network, it is very important that the tools you select can do tasks such as share data and launch one tool from the other.

- Support for the equipment in your network. Sophisticated network management is not useful if it doesn't support the equipment you have in your network. Checking the supported equipment against your network is an important part of the criteria for choosing your set of tools.

- Application reliability. Nothing is more frustrating than having a tool fail when you are trying to debug a serious problem. Application reliability may be hard to determine, but it is an important criterion in network management tool selection. Because the vendors of network management systems are not likely to advertise the reliability of their tools, you will have to evaluate that for yourself. You can start by getting references for the tool and checking them. It is very important to try the tools out on your network. Try performing all the functions you will need to use and evaluate their reliability for yourself.

- Capability to scale to support the number of network devices in your network. All applications have limits for how much they can support. Check the tools you are evaluating against the number of devices you need to manage. Note that the amount of devices supported by an application probably will vary, depending upon how you use the application. For example, an application that polls your devices will be able to support more devices at a slower polling frequency than at a higher polling frequency.

- Adequate performance. A related criterion is application performance. Although a tool may technically support the number of devices you need to manage and do what you want to do, it may not meet your requirements for speed while doing so. You'll probably also need to determine whether a tool provides adequate performance by evaluating the tools that otherwise meet your requirements.

- Ease of use and maintenance. Obviously, tools that are easy to use and maintain are preferred. Easier-to-use tools will also save on training costs.

- Operating system and platform support. Your company probably has selected a standard computer type and operating system. Tools that run in that environment will be easier for you to support and use. However, tools that have a web-based GUI may allow you to use tools, even if they must run on a non-optimal platform for your company—or even a mix of platforms. You must evaluate the increased support costs against the other criteria for each category of tool.

- The capability to work when the network is under stress. Your network management tools must help you solve problems on your network when your network is not healthy. If you must use the network to access your tools, you may have problems using them under certain conditions. Careful network design, including dedicated management networks or VLANs, and isolating the NMS components from other parts of your network may help your NMS deal with this. If your event and fault management systems are so overwhelmed with processing events during a network crisis that they can't supply you with correlated faults, they won't be of much use to you just when you need them. Stress testing the tools you select is an important part of the selection process.

Now, on to the tool categories.

NMS Frameworks

An *NMS framework* is an application that is designed to be the core network management application and allows integration with other network management applications. NMS frameworks tend to provide more than one of the functions covered in this chapter. Often, network administrators will start with an NMS framework and then enhance it with additional applications that when combined give them a more comprehensive network management solution.

Typically, an NMS framework application provides the following base functionality:

- Integration with other applications
- IP auto-discovery
- Layer 3 map generation
- Device and link status
- SNMP Trap reception and logging

A network management framework may provide some or all of the capabilities shown in Figure 9-1.

The first and most important quality to look for in an NMS framework is the capability to integrate with other applications. With network management, you need the capability to combine best-in-class applications that are appropriate for your particular network. The goal of integration is to tie various applications into a seamless whole and reduce redundant functionality.

Some of the criteria that you will want to use to determine the best NMS framework for your environment include the following (the more important criteria are higher up in the list):

- Capability to integrate with planned and existing applications in your shop
- Support for your particular network equipment
- Capability to scale support for the number of network devices in your network
- Application reliability and performance
- Ease of use and maintenance
- Operating system and platform support

Often, network administrators will also expect the NMS framework to provide many other capabilities such as a knowledge base, network discovery, availability monitoring, and event collection. With a flexible tool, the network administrator can choose to use the capabilities built into the NMS framework and yet be able to choose another tool for a specific area if they determine that a more capable tool is required for their environment.

An issue with integrating products together is that it can be hard to find versions of each tool that all support each other. And once you do find an assemblage of tools that work together, it can be difficult to upgrade to newer versions. Hopefully, newer methods of integrating tools, such as CIM/XML, will allow a more robust integration that won't be as sensitive to software versions.

Some of the available NMS frameworks, spanning a wide range of prices and capabilities include the following (in alphabetical order):

- Aprisma Spectrum
- Bullsoft OpenMaster
- Castle Rock SNMPc Enterprise Edition
- Computer Associates Unicenter TNG
- Fujitsu SystemWalker
- Hewlett-Packard OpenView Network Node Manager
- Ipswitch WhatsUp Gold
- Tivoli NetView

Knowledge Base Tools

You learned in Chapter 3, "Developing the Network Knowledge Base," that a knowledge base helps consolidate the data that you maintain about your network. As shown in Figure 9-1, it is the central piece in your NMS. Although we show one central knowledge base in this figure, the information that makes up your knowledge base can be implemented in many ways, and parts of it may reside in each of your NMS tools.

You will probably use a mixture of tools and techniques to implement a knowledge base. You can use the information stored in several commercially available tools that have a database and tie them together using scripts or tools you develop or buy.

Alternatively, you may choose to implement a central repository for your knowledge base that you can use to feed all of your network management tools. Most NMS frameworks and tools have interfaces or APIs (application programming interfaces) that allow you to integrate these tools into your network-management strategy. You may choose to make use of "glue" programs or scripts to combine the various tools you use into a whole by using your knowledge base as the core.

As mentioned in Chapter 3, developing and using a knowledge base generally requires programming capabilities such as script writing and database design. Various applications provide the capability to collect and maintain some network-related data. Through integration, data exchange, and some programming, you can work toward a common knowledge base.

Some people may feel intimidated by the thought of knowledge bases and custom programming, but if you can clearly formulate and articulate your needs, you can design a system that meets your needs. It may be that no commercial system can do this for you. And programmers can make fine resources to develop well-defined "glue" programs or scripts.

The way you collect the information and the way you store it will depend upon the tool(s) you select to manage your network. For example, you may choose to use a tool that collects information about your network through its auto-discovery feature. You may also use its database as your knowledge base. However, you may find that the tool has limited means for customizing its data for your purposes.

Instead, you can extract the information collected by such a tool and combine it with your knowledge of your network. From the data and knowledge, you can then produce a knowledge base that is tailored to your environment. Automating the task of data collection and coordination tasks can make the tasks more maintainable and easier to update.

The following criteria should be considered when evaluating tools that may contribute to your knowledge base (once again, more important criteria for knowledge base tools are placed higher on the following list):

- The key capability for your knowledge base is data exchange. To be successful in using a common knowledge base, there must be robust ways to share this information across your network management tools.

- It may be important to have your knowledge base accept dynamic updates and be able to push out these changes to all tools that use the updated knowledge. An example of this would be your NMS framework running auto-discovery. It discovers a new network device and adds it to the knowledge base. It would be desirable for your performance management and reporting tools to automatically start collecting data and reporting on this new device.

- You may want to be able to access this information through your choice of tools, whether they are Excel, PERL scripts, or whatever. This will allow you to generate custom reports or ad hoc queries, as well as provide a way to interface tools that don't directly allow data exchange or support different protocols for data exchange.

See Chapter 3 for details on how a knowledge base might be structured. Bear in mind that you want to develop a schema that can accommodate the growth and change in your network.

In addition to flat files, spreadsheets, and databases, some of the following tools are useful, either as a central repository or as contributors to the knowledge base:

- Aprisma Spectrum—either as a contributor or as a repository
- Computer Associates Unicenter TNG—either as a contributor or as a repository
- Cisco CiscoWorks 2000 Resource Manager Essentials Inventory—as a contributor of detailed device inventory knowledge
- Cisco CiscoWorks 2000 Campus Manager User Tracking—as a contributor of end node Layer 2 connectivity information
- Hewlett Packard OpenView Network Node Manager—either as a contributor or as a repository
- SAS Institute, The SAS SYSTEM—as a repository
- Tivoli NetView—either as a contributor or as a repository
- Visionael—as a repository

Here is an example of how to take advantage of the knowledge contained in an application and integrate it with your network knowledge base.

The user-tracking portion of Campus Manager provides a wealth of information about end nodes in a network, including the following:

- MAC address
- IP address

- Host name
- Switch and board and port on the switch it's connected to
- VLAN and the VLAN type the device is in
- VTP Domain the switch is a member of
- Date/time when this node was last seen on the network at this location

This last item is especially useful for tracking hardware utilization of your network equipment, such as tracking the ports on your switches that are currently in use and how many free ports are available. It can also be used to track the usage of IP addresses, so unused ones can be reassigned. Note that the node-related date/times that most NMS frameworks have are not related to the Layer 2 location in the network in which the device is currently located, so the two can be used together to provide a richer set of capabilities.

User tracking also supports the capability to have the user annotate fields with username and notes, which could be used to store custom data of pretty much any type. Unfortunately, there is not an easy method to programmatically insert data into these fields.

User tracking includes facilities for searching and exporting this information from a GUI interface as well as exporting the data from the CLI. You could export this data as a comma-separated file or through XML, and then import it into your knowledge base.

This knowledge then could be used in the following way:

- User tracking will discover not only the MAC addresses, but also the host names of devices if you have name services configured.
- If you have all your servers configured using some sort of name (such as Server1, etc.), your knowledge base will give you the information about what switch ports your servers are connected to.
- Then, you could monitor the usage on these ports by using your event configuration tool to set up thresholds on each of these ports.

Performance Measurement and Reporting Tools

It's important that you be informed of problems before your users start screaming. Monitoring your network is often the first defense for detecting and resolving problems. The main areas you will want to measure or monitor are availability, response time, utilization, and accuracy. These areas are covered in detail in Chapter 4, "Performance Measurement and Reporting."

As Figure 9-1 shows, data about what to monitor is obtained from the knowledge base and is used to drive the collection of this information from the devices in your network. That information then can be used by other tools to trigger events and to generate reports.

The data collected through performance monitoring is useful for both reactive and proactive reporting. In reactive mode, it can be used with your event-management tools to trigger events when set conditions are met. In proactive mode, your performance-reporting tools can use this data to produce reports and graphs to analyze your network's performance and help plan for future capacity needs or identify other issues that will need attention.

There are a couple of issues that will affect your selection of a tool or tools to perform these tasks for you: reducing NMS traffic and tracking interface data. The next two sections cover these issues.

Reducing NMS Traffic

If you selected an NMS framework, it probably includes the capability to auto-discover your network. It may also automatically poll your network devices for availability or other performance measurements. Other tools you select may also auto-discover your network. None of these tools attempts to consolidate their polling together to lessen the load on your network and the devices being polled. So you will want to be aware of the duplication and work to lessen its impact on your network.

For example, a tool may have the capability to monitor your network for availability, but you are using the tool for another purpose. Be sure to turn off the availability function on this tool to lessen the load on the network and the confusion about which tool to use for what function.

Another example is in the case of auto-discovery. You may find that although a tool can discover your network, you have another tool that you prefer to use for discovery. Many tools can support importing devices and sometimes topology information from other products, thus reducing the amount of traffic on your network due to network-discovery processes.

Basically, you should select the best tool for each task and ensure that your other tools don't duplicate that function and add unnecessary traffic to your network or consume additional resources.

Tracking Interface Data

Another issue to pay attention to when evaluating data that collects information on an interface basis is how the tool keeps track of interfaces. The ifIndex of an interface can change due to several events. These may include the following:

- If the device is reset or the SNMP process on the device is reinitialized, all ifIndexes may be renumbered.
- If a board is removed and a new board is inserted to replace it, the ifIndexes of the interfaces on that board may change.

- An interface may go down and you may, in the process of debugging the problem, move the physical connection from one interface to another. Thus, the ifIndex for the physical interface didn't change, but the function of the interface did.

The application should have some mechanism for tracking interfaces that is independent of ifIndex. SNMP provides several alternative variables that can be used. These include ifDescr from the MIB-II interfaces table, ifName and ifAlias from the RFC 1573 update to the interfaces table, and enterprise-specific variables such as portName from the CISCO-STACK-MIB. You need to determine what behavior you prefer and then evaluate tools to determine whether they work as you want them to.

First, you need to determine whether you want to track interfaces based upon function, such as 'WAN link to Kenogami Lake, Ontario'; or upon physical interface, such as 'Board 1, Port 1 on device Switch1.' You may want to handle your WAN links one way and your LAN links another because it is often more important to track performance on WAN links. The configuration of WAN links, including speed, tends to vary more from link to link for WAN links.

For interfaces that you want to track by function, you will need to label the interface in some way. Cisco routers allow you to set ifDescr with the **description** interface config command. Cisco Catalyst switches allow you to set portName through the use of the **set port name** command. Your network management software will need to track the relationship between the object(s) you set and ifIndex.

Tracking interfaces by physical interface doesn't require you to set anything. Your network management software will need to choose an object such as ifName to label each interface with. It will need to track the relationship between this object and ifIndex to ensure that the correct data is associated with the correct interface.

You need a way to specify types of ports and devices that should be included in the polling. Polling every single device and interface found by auto-discovery might be okay in some instances, but in others it may lead to information overload.

To reduce the amount of performance data that is stored, some systems will automatically aggregate data as it ages. This can be a real advantage, allowing you to see trends over a longer period of time and speeding up the time it takes to generate reports because less data has to be processed. Make sure, however, that the aggregation process doesn't hinder the capability to compare recent data to past data.

You may find that it is easier to collect data on all ports and not aggregate data, but throw data away after it gets to a certain age. This strategy is more practical now that disk space has become rather cheap.

Performance Monitoring and Reporting

It's only half of the job to collect data. You will want to do several things with this data. These things fall into two broad categories: performance monitoring and performance reporting.

Performance monitoring is reactive in nature. You will need to set up triggers and thresholds against which events are generated and processed by your event management system. Tools to help you do this are covered in the section called "Event and Fault Management."

Performance reporting is proactive in nature. Here, you are using tools that generate tabular reports, graphs, gauges, and dials; and using this data for planning and troubleshooting. These reports will also help you baseline your network, so you know what is normal and what triggers and thresholds to set for your network.

As more and more users are demanding that reports be available through the Web, your reporting tool should be able to present data through a web interface. You should not be limited to canned reports. You should be able to define new or modify existing reports to give you exactly the information you want, preferably through a web interface.

Most likely, you will need different levels of reports. First, reports that tend to be more ad hoc and specific. Second are general reports that operations and designer folks can use to understand general trends in the network. Third are reports for upper management; reports that demonstrate at a high level how the network is performing and help justify any further expenditures for network growth.

Criteria for Selecting Performance Management and Reporting Tools

The criteria you'll want to consider for performance management and reporting tools, in addition to the general criteria covered in the beginning of this chapter, include the following:

- The tools should work with your other tools, including the capability to use the knowledge base to obtain the list of devices to monitor instead of duplicating the functions (and the network traffic) of other tools. They should also integrate with your event and fault management tools.

- The tools should handle ifIndex changes intelligently and in the way that you prefer to have them handled.

- The monitoring tools should be able to limit polling to those devices and interfaces that you are interested in. Alternatively, they should be able to collect data on all devices and interfaces without your intervention, saving you time at the cost of resources.

- You may want a tool that aggregates data over time to reduce the resources that are required to store the data and speed up generating reports.

Performance Measurement and Reporting Tools

Some of the tools that provide performance measurement and reporting are listed in the following sections.

Availability:

- Aprisma Spectrum
- Castle Rock SNMPc Enterprise Edition
- Computer Associates Unicenter TNG
- Hewlett Packard OpenView Network Node Manager
- Ipswitch WhatsUp Gold
- Tivoli NetView

Response-time monitoring:

- Concord Network Health Suite
- Cisco Internetwork Performance Monitor
- Cisco Traffic Director
- NetScout Manager
- Perform Sage/X

Accuracy:

- Concord Network Health Suite
- Multi Router Traffic Grapher (MRTG)
- Tavve Performance Reporting Monitor (PRM)

Utilization:

- Aprisma Spectrum
- Avesta Trinity
- Castle Rock SNMPc Enterprise Edition
- Cisco Traffic Director
- Computer Associates Unicenter TNG
- Concord Network Health Suite
- Desktalk TREND
- Hewlett Packard OpenView Network Node Manager
- Multi Router Traffic Grapher
- NetOps DSM
- NetScout Manager

- NextPoint S^3 Traffic Manager
- ProactiveNet eBiz.IT
- OnionPeel Network Reporting Depot
- Perform Sage/X
- Smarts InCharge
- Tavve Performance Reporting Monitor
- Tivoli NetView

Performance reporting:

- Aprisma Spectrum
- Avesta Trinity
- Castle Rock SNMPc Enterprise Edition
- Computer Associates Unicenter TNG
- Concord Network Health Suite
- Desktalk TREND
- Hewlett Packard OpenView Network Node Manager
- Ipswitch WhatsUp Gold
- Onion Peel Network Reporting Depot
- Perform Dashboard
- ProactiveNet eBiz.IT
- SAS Institute IT Service Vision
- Tavve Performance Reporting Monitor
- Tivoli NetView

Event and Fault Management Tools

The goal of event and fault management is to determine if there are issues that need attention, to generate faults where they do, and to present these faults to the correct people to ensure they get fixed in priority order. Your network should generate as few faults as possible while still covering all issues that need attention. The steps to do this are as follows:

- Configuring event generation
- Event collection
- Event correlation
- Fault management

Figure 9-1 shows how each of these steps interrelate and how they must interoperate with the rest of your NMS tools.

Configuring Event Generation

Configuring event generation assists with the configuration of thresholds and event generation for network devices.

As shown in Figure 9-1, an event configuration tool should be able to configure thresholds and event generation based on information gathered from performance polling and the knowledge base. This will entail configuring devices to check triggers and thresholds and generate events. In some cases, devices may not be able to monitor themselves, so there needs to be a mechanism for generating events based on performance monitoring.

A tool that can configure event generation needs a combination of the following capabilities:

- Configure RMON alarms and events against any available SNMP object. The tool should help to configure these alarms against the interfaces you want to apply them to. For utilization, the tool should be able to compute what the thresholds should be so you can input a percentage of utilization. Cisco IOS devices allow the configuration RMON either through SNMP or via the command line.

- Cisco devices have several capabilities for generating events. These include the built-in SNMP traps and syslog messages. An event configuration tool should have knowledge of these events to avoid generating duplicate events.

- An event configuration tool could include support to generate events based upon measurements of response time using the CISCO-RTTMON-MIB.

- The EXPRESSION-MIB allows a device to monitor a formula made up of individual objects. A RMON alarm and event could be configured to send an event if the expression exceeds a threshold. A tool in this category could make good use of this capability.

- It is important that this tool be able to configure a large number of devices and interfaces in a unified fashion. You don't want to be configuring each interface on each device. This tool should be able to take your policies and apply them across your network.

Some of the tools that allow you to configure event generation include the following:

- Cisco CiscoWorks2000 Resource Manager Essentials 3.x NetConfig
- Cisco Internetwork Performance Monitor
- Cisco Traffic Director
- NetScout Manager

In addition, most or all of the products listed under the performance management and reporting sections of this chapter should be able to set triggers and thresholds against the collected data, and deliver these events to your event collection system.

Event Collection Tools

Events come in many forms and from many sources, including syslog messages, SNMP traps, and log files as outlined in Chapter 5, "Configuring Events." Your event collection tool should be able to handle many types of events from many devices and many different protocols. It should be able to normalize these events into a common event format so that your events can be easily processed by your event correlation tool. This relationship is shown in Figure 9-1.

Your event collector needs to understand many different types of events and know the format your event correlation tool expects the events in, so that it can normalize them.

Cisco devices use several methods to communicate events. These include SNMP notifications (traps or informs) and syslog messages. Other sources of events come from your availability and performance monitoring tools and may use different protocols for delivery of these events.

As your collection tool receives events, it may receive multiple copies of the same event or a notification through syslog as well as SNMP that a particular event happened. This is a good time to eliminate these duplicate events.

Also, this is a good point for filtering events to eliminate events that you don't have any interest in. This can significantly reduce the resources required to process events.

Some of the criteria to look at for a tool in this category include the following:

- Flexibility in handling many different formats or sources of events, including your availability and performance monitoring tools
- Ease of adding new event sources or protocols
- Production of normalized events in the format your event correlation tool needs them in
- The capability to "de-bounce" or de-duplicate events to reduce the load on the event processor
- The capability to filter messages

Some of the products that have capabilities to be event collectors include the following:

- Aprisma Spectrum
- Castle Rock SNMPc Enterprise Edition
- Cisco InfoCenter

- Cisco Traffic Director
- Computer Associates Unicenter TNG
- Hewlett Packard OpenView Network Node Manager
- Ipswitch WhatsUp Gold
- The Knowledge Group WideAwake
- Micromuse Netcool Suite
- NetScout Manager
- Tivoli NetView

Some of these collectors are specific to one type of event protocol. To generate an enterprise-wide event collector, you may find that you need to combine several of these tools.

Event Correlation Tools

Your event correlation serves one main purpose: to recognize faults among a series of events. Your NMS receives many events, but many of them represent the symptoms, not the problem. Correlation of the events allows the root cause of a problem to be presented, not all the events that were received and had the same problem or fault as the root cause.

As Figure 9-1 shows, this tool is where raw events are processed into fault data. It is central to the process of determining what, if anything, is actually wrong with your network.

An example of correlation is a problem in which a router loses power. Your availability monitor will detect this and report it as an event. However, it also detects that it can't reach any of the other devices behind the router and also reports these as events.

Your event correlation tool needs to have enough knowledge of the topology of the network to determine that the router or the link to the router is the root cause of all these events. It then needs to send this single fault on to the fault manager for processing.

Your correlation tool needs to have detailed information about the devices in your network. For example, the symptoms of buffer issues in Cisco IOS devices vary according to the IOS version, the specific device hardware, and the switching method configured on the interfaces on that device. To be able to correlate interface errors or slow application performance to issues with buffers requires knowledge of all this information.

Correlation tools come in two types: passive and active. A *passive correlation tool* relies on the events it receives to determine the state of your network. An *active correlation tool* actively polls your network devices as it gets events to supplement the information supplied by these events. This can lead to a more complete and timely knowledge of the state of your network at the cost of more network traffic. Through your knowledge of your network, you may develop new correlations that work in your network. Some tools will allow you to add these correlations to the tool.

The criteria to look for in an event correlation tool include the following:

- The intelligence in handling different types of correlations, including Layer 2 and 3 topology issues. The tool should have a good selection of correlations built in.
- A detailed knowledge of the devices in your network to be able to do device-level correlations.
- The capability to actively poll for supplemental data to help determine the root cause.
- The capability to be tailored to accept new correlations that may work in your network.
- The capability to work with your event collector and fault manager.

Correlation tools can be divided into two categories: those that do device-level correlation and those that do network topology-based correlation. The following tools do device-level correlation:

- Avesta Trinity
- Cisco CiscoWorks 2000 Resource Manager Essentials Syslog Collector and Reloads Report
- Cisco Info Center
- Concord Network Health Suite
- Micromuse Netcool Suite
- NetOps Visionary
- Smarts InCharge
- Tavve EventWatch
- Veritas NerveCenter

The following tools do network topology-based correlations:

- Avesta Trinity
- The Knowledge Group WideAwake
- Smarts InCharge
- Tavve EventWatch

Fault Management Tools

Fault managers are simply responsible for receiving faults from your event correlation tool and making sure they are handled correctly. As shown in Figure 9-1, fault managing may include delivering faults on to other systems—such as paging or email systems, case management systems, network health displays and reports, and fault logs—as well as maintaining a fault console.

Your fault management system's main job is delivering faults appropriately. You may want to deliver different priorities of faults differently, as well as delivering different types of faults to different recipients. The tool you select should be able to deliver faults flexibly.

Many network administrators use network health displays to monitor the health of the network. These displays vary from two- and three-dimensional maps of the network with the icon colors reflecting device health, to a simple grid of every device being monitored with color reflecting status, to a list of the top faults. Whatever you choose, be sure that your fault management system can accurately deliver fault status (including when the fault is resolved) to these systems.

A fault console needs to accept faults and display them to interested parties. Some capabilities that you may want in a fault console include the capability to assign faults to a responsible party, log the status of the work being done on the fault, and clear the fault when it is fixed. Many or all of these tasks can be handled by a case management system. In some cases, a full case management system may be overkill. Other network administrators choose to use case management systems for all faults, especially in larger companies or where one is already in use in the company.

Whatever method you choose to use to distribute your faults, you'll want to be able to sort and rank faults differently for different users or purposes. Operators want to look at the faults in a different way from network designers or managers. Operators often want the worst set of faults to always be at the top of a continually refreshing display. On the other hand, network engineers tend to want to look at events in chronological order, with the ability to sort and find based on different criteria. Managers tend to want to see the worst things and their durations over a period of time.

So, some of the criteria you'll need to use in choosing a fault management tool include the following:

- The tool works with the faults delivered by your event correlation tool.
- The tool can flexibly deliver faults to many different systems, including logs, email systems, paging systems, and case management systems.
- The tool includes a fault console for displaying, tracking, and clearing fault conditions.

Some of the products that provide fault management include the following:

- Avesta Trinity
- Smarts InCharge
- Cisco InfoCenter
- The Knowledge Group WideAwake
- Tavve EventWatch

Policy Management Tools

A *policy management* tool helps you manage your SLAs, policies, and rules to ensure that your network is configured properly to best meet these requirements. In addition, it needs to verify that your network is meeting these requirements and alert you when it is not, or when the network can reasonably be expected to not meet your user's needs—in the area of bandwidth, for example.

Policy management tools provide many of the same capabilities that were covered in the earlier sections of this chapter and shown in Figure 9-1. The difference is the focus of the tool. Similar to the shift from the structured programming techniques to object-oriented programming, policy management tools make your agreements with the users of your network and the goals you have for your network the focus, instead of configuring and monitoring individual devices.

Currently, policy-based management tools are highly specific and implement their own forms of policy definition. There are efforts to standardize the specifications of policies. Until such a point of standardization, the policies in one application cannot be combined with those of another. After these standards are in place, you will be able to define policies in your knowledge base and apply them using one set of tools and check for compliance using another set of tools.

So, your tool should be able to take policies and turn them into the configurations required to implement these policies in your network. You also want a tool that can monitor a deployed set of policies and ensure that the intended policies are not being violated.

Policy-based configuration changes are the first set of applications to implement network-wide configuration changes. This means that the submission of a single policy presents the chance to misconfigure many devices in a network and threatens the reliability of the network. Therefore, it is important that the software developer do extensive testing in environments similar to yours. A bug in the policy software has the potential to destroy an entire network.

Because policy-based configuration requires that the software make configuration changes to devices, be sure that the software implement appropriate security measures that are applicable for your shop. Depending on how you run your network operations, different people may have different roles that necessitate varying access levels for devices.

Part of policy-based software is the grouping of devices into logical groups. A policy can then be applied to one or more groups rather than to a list of devices. There must be a way to exchange group membership information among other apps in order to keep the groups from getting out of sync. Your policy software should be able to either use groups of devices defined in your knowledge base or provide the definition of the groups it is used to your knowledge base so that other tools can share these definitions.

The criteria you need to use in choosing a policy management tool include the following:

- Takes policies and configures your network to implement them.
- Monitors compliance to your policies.
- The software is fully tested to ensure that it is low risk to use the tool in your environment.
- Can configure your devices using the security policies you have in place for your network devices.
- Defines and/or uses logical groupings of network devices.

The policy management tools are still evolving. Expect rapid change in these tools. Many of them today are able to do only part of the whole task of policy management. The following is a list of some of the current tools for policy management:

- Cisco Access List Manager
- Cisco QoS Policy Manager
- Cisco Service Level Agreement Manager
- Concord Network Health Modules—Service Level Management
- Ganymede Pegasus
- InfoVista VistaViews
- Intellops ForeSight
- Jyra Service Level Monitor
- NextPoint S^3 Service Level Manager

Summary

This chapter described the various tools that support the technologies discussed in Part 1 of this book. You should use the information in this chapter as a beginning for researching the appropriate fault and performance tools for your network management strategy.

The types of tools covered include the following:

- NMS frameworks
- Knowledge base
- Performance measurements and reporting
- Configuring event generation
- Event management
- Fault management
- Policy management

Because the network management landscape is constantly changing, applications may have changed, disappeared, or added. Please consult the listed references that follow and contact your Cisco representative for up-to-date information.

In the next chapter, you will learn about some statistical methods that can be used to better understand your network's performance.

References

Internet Resources

Aprisma Spectrum

> http://www.aprisma.com/spectrum/

Avesta Trinity

> http://www.avesta.com/documents/products.asp

Bullsoft OpenMaster

> http://www.bullsoft.com/openmaster/index.htm

Castle Rock SNMPc Enterprise Edition

> http://www.castlerock.com/products/products.htm

Cisco Access Control List Manager

> http://www.cisco.com/warp/public/cc/cisco/mkt/enm/caclm/index.shtml

Cisco CiscoWorks 2000 Campus Manager User Tracking

> http://www.cisco.com/warp/public/cc/cisco/mkt/enm/campman/index.shtml

Cisco CiscoWorks 2000 Resource Manager Essentials

> http://www.cisco.com/warp/public/cc/cisco/mkt/enm/rman/index.shtml

Cisco Info Center

> http://www/warp/customer/cc/cisco/mkt/enm/cicen/

Cisco Internetwork Performance Monitor

> http://www.cisco.com/warp/public/cc/cisco/mkt/enm/cw2000/ipm/index.shtml

Cisco QoS Policy Manager

http://www.cisco.com/warp/public/cc/cisco/mkt/enm/caplqospm/index.shtml

Cisco Service-Level Agreement Manager

http://www.cisco.com/warp/public/cc/cisco/mkt/enm/entmgt/esm/index.shtml

Cisco Traffic Director

http://www.cisco.com/warp/public/cc/cisco/mkt/enm/cwsiman/dir/traf/index.shtml

Computer Associates Unicenter TNG

http://www.ca.com/unicenter/prodinfo.htm

Concord Network Health Suite

http://www.concord.com/products/nh/nh.htm

Concord Network Health Modules—Service Level Management

http://www.concord.com/products/nh/mod_slev.htm

Desktalk TREND

http://www.desktalk.com/

Fujitsu SystemWalker

http://www.fujitsu.co.jp/hypertext/globalsoft/SystemWalker/

Ganymede Pegasus

http://www.GanymedeSoftware.com/products/pegasus/index.phtml

Hewlett-Packard OpenView Network Node Manager

http://openview.hp.com:80/products/nnm/

InfoVista VistaViews

http://www.infovista.com/products/frproducts.html

Intellops ForeSight

http://www.intellops.com/services.html

Ipswitch WhatsUp Gold

http://www.ipswitch.com/Products/WhatsUp/index.asp

Jyra Service Level Monitor

http://www.jyra.com/

The Knowledge Group WideAwake

http://www.wideawake.co.uk/productframe.htm

Micromuse Netcool Suite

http://www.micromuse.com/products/overview.html

Multi Router Traffic Grapher (MRTG)

http://ee-staff.ethz.ch/~oetiker/webtools/mrtg/mrtg.html

NetOps DSM/Visionary

http://www.netops.com/

NetScout Manager

http://www.netscout.com/Products/NSM/nsm.html

NextPoint S3 Traffic Manager

http://www.nextpoint.com/products/prod_traffic.htm

NextPoint S3 Service Level Manager

http://www.nextpoint.com/products/prod_servman.htm

OnionPeel Network Reporting Depot

http://www.ops.com/prodinfo2/nerd/nerd.html

Perform Dashboard

http://www.perform.fr/Products/Dashboard/Index.html

Perform Sage/X

> http://www.perform.fr/Products/Sagex/Index.html

ProactiveNet eBiz.IT

> http://www.proactivenet.com/products/prod.html

RiverSoft OpenRiver

> http://www.riversoft.com/product2.html

SAS Institute IT Service Vision

> http://www.sas.com/software/it_vision/

SAS Institute The SAS SYSTEM

> http://www.sas.com/software/sas_system/

Smarts InCharge

> http://www.smarts.com/incharge.html

Tavve EventWatch

> http://www.tavve.com/pages/product/EventWatch.html

Tavve Performance Reporting Monitor

> http://www.tavve.com/pages/product/PRM.html

Tivoli NetView

> http://www.tivoli.com/products/index/netview/

Veritas NerveCenter

> http://www.veritas.com/us/products/nervecenter/

Visionael

> http://www.visionael.com/products/index.html

Managing Devices and Technologies

Part II cuts through the hundreds of Cisco MIBs and thousands of MIB objects to highlight useful data for managing fault and performance in your network. Within Part II you will find selected MIB objects, show commands, syslog messages, and traps useful for fault and performance management of the included technologies.

The information presented in Part II applies to the following Cisco devices:

- All IOS routers

- Catalyst switches, including 1900, 2900xl, 2900, 4000 series, 5000 series, 5500 series, and 6000 series

Part II chapters are broken into three groups:

- Systems   Managing router and LAN switch systems resources such as memory, buffers, and backplane.

- LAN   Managing the LAN technologies implemented on routers and LAN switches such as ethernet, VLANs, and LANE

- WAN   Managing the WAN technologies implemented on routers such as Frame Relay and dial up.

Each of these sections are similarly formatted. First, the technology is introduced. While not exhaustive, the overview should provide you with enough information to understand the rest of the material in a chapter. Then, useful data is presented, split up into a performance section and a fault section. Each chapter presents the most useful MIB variables, SNMP traps, show commands, and syslog messages.

- Chapters 10–12 begin the discussion by providing information about network system hardware, processes, resources, and interfaces. Examples include CPU utilization, buffers, memory, and general interface management

- Chapters 13–17 discuss the recommendations for LAN and WAN technologies. Topics include Ethernet (10BaseT, 100BaseT, and Gigabit), ATM, VLANs, Frame Relay, ISDN, and dial-up.

CHAPTER 10

Managing Hardware and Environmental Characteristics

This chapter is geared toward analyzing the hardware and environmental characteristics of Cisco routers and Cisco Catalyst series LAN switches. Hardware and environmental characteristics typically are more responsive to fault management than to performance management. Environmental factors in particular lend themselves more to error-monitoring, with regard to power and temperature monitoring; this chapter will look at fault management of both environmental and hardware characteristics. In addition, it will look at the performance side with respect to the backplane or chassis in the devices by identifying the type and location of the cards installed in the modularized devices, like 7x00 series routers and 5x00 series Catalyst switches.

The chapter topics are organized as follows:

- Hardware characteristics of routers
- Hardware characteristics of Catalyst LAN switches
- Environmental characteristics of routers and switches
- Performance management data for router hardware
- Performance-management data for switches
- Error/fault data for router hardware
- Error/fault data for switch hardware
- Error/fault data for router environmental characteristics
- Error/fault data for switch environmental characteristics

Hardware Characteristics of Routers

The performance data you can gather for hardware in routers and switches is minimal. But one aspect of hardware that indirectly affects performance is effective backplane utilization versus backplane oversubscription. This is true, especially on the core high-end routers and switches, such as the 7513 router or 5500 switch, respectively. Physical card positioning in these devices is crucial for achieving optimal performance in the network. Because these devices are typically placed in the core portion of the network, it is important to understand the interdependencies between the card positioning and the backplane bus architecture of the device. By understanding the architecture and physical layout of the devices, you also can manage assets more effectively.

We'll first look briefly, as an example, at the 7513 series router backplane bus architecture and the dependencies with the interface processors (IPs) and their respective slot positions. Based on these dependencies, you can reference the appropriate MIBs and show commands, as defined in sections of this chapter, to draw a correlation between the slot position or card type and the relative bus speeds on the backplane of the chassis. We'll then consider some of the specifics of the hardware characteristics, such as hardware buffer carving and IDBs (Interface Descriptor Blocks). Understanding how these specific details apply to the different type of interface cards will assist you in determining the appropriate kind of hardware to place in the appropriate location in the chassis.

Backplane Bus Architecture in the 7x00 Series Routers

The 7513 and 7507 have two buses of 1.066 Gbps each, one on either side of the RSPs (Route Switch Processors).

On the 7513:

CyBus 0 is slots 0–5
CyBus 1 is slots 8–12

On the 7507:

CyBus 0 is slot 0–1
CyBus 1 is slots 4–6

The 7505, of course, has only one 1.066 Gbps bus.

When loading IPs in the 7500 series routers, follow these guidelines:

- Distribute IPs evenly across the two buses.

- Start with high-bandwidth IPs (or Interface Processors) and VIPs (Virtual Interface Processors) if they are being used—namely the CIP (Channel IP), AIP (ATM IP), FEIP (Fast-Ethernet IP), and VIPs. Balance them on the buses by putting one on one side of the RSP(s) and then one on the other.

- Start filling the slots nearest the RSP; then continue out to the sides of the system. This matches the default slot loading process used in manufacturing.

- Add in any other interface processors in any slot, and again balance them on the two sides.

IDBs (Interface Descriptor Blocks)

When deciding what kind of cards (IPs) and how many cards to put in a router, one more characteristic needs to be taken into consideration, namely IDBs, or Interface Descriptor Blocks. Each of the following interface types requires an IDB:

- Virtual (tunneled, emulated LAN, and vLAN)
- Logical
- Sub-interfaces
- Channel groups

Table 10-1 lists the maximum limits for the IDBs across the different IOS releases as they apply to the 7500 series routers. Other router platforms may exhibit different limits, but generally are in the 300-range limit. Please note that the 7000 series router keeps 40 IDBs to itself.

Table 10-1   *IDB Limits*

IOS	IDB Limit
11.0	256
11.1	300
11.1CA	1024
11.2	300
12.0	1000

Hardware Buffers

In addition to IDBs, hardware allocation is a factor in determining what gets configured on the router. Hardware buffers are divided up at boot time. Based on the amount of like interface media and common MTU sizes, the appropriate hardware buffer sizes and quantities are alloted to unique buffer pools. These buffer pools are taken from MEMD or packet memory. Packet memory resides on the RSP and is typically 2 MB in size. The older RSPs and RP/SP combination in the 7000 series have 512 KB of MEMD.

This "buffer carving" takes place only on the high-end routers. Low-end routers (4x00, 3600, 2500 series) use I/O memory or shared memory for their hardware buffer allocation for the interfaces. The more interfaces you have in a router, the smaller your hardware buffer pool will be for each interface. When there is a shortage of hardware buffers, "ignores" are typically incremented on the interface because there is no place to put the incoming packet.

MEMD Buffer Carving Details

MEMD buffer carving is the portion of CBUS initialization in which MEMD buffers or packet buffers are allocated, based upon media interface bandwidths and MTUs. Buffers of a given size share a common free pool to be shared by all interfaces with closely matched MTUs. The buffer-carving algorithm is based on fair share, but it has some built-in low water marks and configurable high-water marks. The algorithm works like this:

1　All of the interfaces' MTUs are consulted, and the interfaces are grouped into similar buffer pools. For example, a system with six Ethernets and two FDDIs would get two buffer pools; the six Ethernets would share a pool of 1500-byte buffers, whereas the two FDDIs would share a pool of 4500-byte buffers.

2　The default receive bandwidths of all interfaces within a buffer pool are summed to form an aggregate receive bandwidth for that pool. Using the previous example, the 1500-byte Ethernet pool would be assigned 60 Mbps of aggregate receive bandwidth (6×10 Mbps), whereas the 4500-byte FDDI pool would get 200 Mbps (2×100 Mbps).

3　MEMD buffer space is then divided based upon proportional aggregate bandwidths. Again using the previous example, the Ethernet pool would get (60 / (60 + 200)), or 23 percent of MEMD, whereas the FDDI pool would get (200 / (60 + 200)), or 77 percent of MEMD.

4　The number of buffers in each pool is then calculated and divided evenly among interfaces within the pool (regardless of relative bandwidth). In this example, the result is 79 Ethernet buffers ((0.23 × 504 KB) / 1500), and 88 FDDI buffers ((0.77 × 504 KB) / 4500). This gives 12 buffers per Ethernet and 44 buffers per FDDI. The per-interface buffer count is referred to as an interface's *receive queue limit* (RQL).

5　Before doing the final carving, the system makes sure that there is a minimum of 16 KB of buffer space in every pool. That minimum configurable burst count worth of buffers is available to every interface within a pool, and therefore a configurable *maximum buffer* limit has not been exceeded for any interface.

6　Finally, the RSP carves out the buffers as specified by the above algorithm. The actual packet memory is not touched at this time, only the buffer headers that point to packet memory.

MEMD Quantities

Two important quantities mentioned in the preceding discussion of buffer carving are maximum buffers and receive queue limit (RQL). Another important quantity is transmit queue limit (TQL). Following are brief explanations of each of these quantities:

- **Maximum buffers**—A 512-KB system has room for 320 Ethernet-sized MEMD buffers or 110 FDDI buffers. With the optional 2 MB MEMD buffers on the SSP or RSP, you can quadruple FDDI buffers to 440. However, you are limited to just 470 Ethernet-sized buffers on a 2 MB MEMD system due to the buffer header limitation.

- **Receive queue limit (RQL)**—Each interface gets configured with an RQL equal to the total buffers in its buffer pool divided by the number of interfaces sharing that pool. If that number results in less than 16 KB of buffer space, then the RQL is overridden with (16384 / MTU). Interfaces are not allowed to allocate receive buffers from their free pools when the count drops to less than one, and they decrement the count each time a buffer is removed. The RSP or SP increments the RQL every time it returns an interface's receive buffer to the free pool after the packet is transmitted, copied, or dropped.

- **Transmit Queue Limit (TQL)**—The transmit queue limit is the maximum number of buffers that the RSP will have outstanding on an interface's transmit queue before transmit packets are dropped. First, find the smallest buffer pool with bandwidth greater than the interface, N. Then, find the number of interfaces in the current interface's receive buffer pool, I. For each interface, TQL is calculated as N divided by the square root of I.

Hardware Characteristics of Catalyst LAN Switches

In the Catalyst series switches, we'll look specifically at the 5513 and 5509 chasses and the dependencies between the line cards and the different buses located on the backplane because this backplane architecture varies, depending on slot position. All other switch platforms have constant bus speeds across all slot positions, either 1.2 Gbps (5x00 series), 24 Gbps (4000 series), or 32 Gbps (6000 series).

The 5500 has three buses (classified as A, B, and C) of 1.2 Gbps each, and 13 slots. Figure 10-1 shows the bus and slot designations for a 5513 switch.

Figure 10-1 *5513 Chassis Bus Designation*

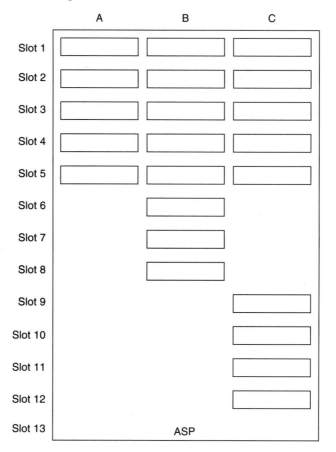

The slots are designated as follows:

- Slot 1 is reserved for the supervisor engine, which provides switching, local and remote management, and multiple uplink interfaces.

- Slot 2 can contain a redundant supervisor engine, which provides a backup function in case the first module fails. A failure of the active supervisor engine is detected by the standby module, which takes control of supervisor engine-switching functions. If a redundant supervisor engine is not required, slot 2 is available for any switching module.

- Slots 3 through 12 are available for any combination of switching modules.

Note   High-speed line cards such as the gigabit Ethernet cards can go only in slots 2 through 5 due to the backplane connection required into all three of the buses.

- Slot 13 is a dedicated slot, which accepts only the ATM switch processor (ASP) module or the Catalyst 8510 CSR (campus switch router) switch route processor (SRP). When using the ASP in slot 13, the Catalyst 5500 switch accepts LightStream 1010 ATM port adapters in slots 9 through 12. When using the Catalyst 8510 CSR SRP in slot 13, the Catalyst 5500 switch accepts Catalyst 8510 CSR modules in slots 9 through 12.

The Catalyst series switches allocate 192 KB of packet buffers to each port on the switch. This is equivalent to the hardware buffers on the router, yet are static in nature. Due to the switching architecture of the Catalyst, dynamic assignments of hardware buffers are irrelevant. This 192 KB resides on the individual line cards and is not controlled or given out by the supervisor card's memory or DRAM. The supervisor's DRAM has nothing active to do with data packets flowing through the switch, except to initially populate the CAM table with the first instance of a frame.

Environmental Characteristics

Environmental characteristics in Cisco devices involve data points such as temperature, voltages, and fan statuses. There is no compelling reason to proactively track any of this kind of data to determine the performance of your Cisco device, so we will focus only on fault management for these environmental characteristics. If you do want to get these data points, you can retrieve them on demand with SNMP queries or show commands. The router can also notify the network management station via SNMP traps of thresholds being exceeded.

Most of the environmental factors that can be monitored reside in the core Cisco devices, such as the 7xxx series routers or the 5xxx series Catalyst switches. Most of the low-end routers and switches do not display or report the environmental characteristics, except for the 3600 series routers. Because of the variable nature and constant fluctuation of environmental data, SNMP traps are the main source of identifying environmental problems. That is, you'll let the device tell the network Management Station (NMS) when a problem occurs. (The ENVMON SNMP trap is discussed later in this chapter.)

In the 7500 series routers, the chassis interface controls the environmental monitoring and reporting functions. The monitoring functions constantly monitor the internal chassis air temperature and DC voltage and currents.

Each power supply monitors its own voltage and temperature, and shuts itself down if it detects a critical condition within the power supply. If conditions reach Shutdown thresholds, the system shuts down to avoid equipment damage from excessive heat. There are also Warning and normal condition thresholds reported prior to Shutdown state. In addition to temperature and voltage monitoring, the router also monitors the fan and blower in the chassis. SNMP trap notifications, console log messages, or syslog messages are reported when certain thresholds are reached and exceeded relating to these characteristics.

For the Catalyst series switches, there are three levels of status conditions relating to environmental characteristics:

- Normal: All monitored parameters are within normal tolerances.

- Alarm: An out-of-tolerance temperature or voltage condition exists. The system may not continue operation. If a voltage measurement reaches this level, the power supply can shut down the system. Immediate action is required. The +24 VDC line remains enabled to allow the fan assembly to continue operation.

- Power supply shutdown: The power supply has detected an out-of-tolerance voltage, current, or temperature condition within the power supply, and has shut down. This status condition is typically caused by one of the following conditions:

    — Loss of AC power (you turned off the system power, or the AC source failed).

    — Power supply detected an overvoltage, overcurrent, undervoltage, or overtemperature condition within the power supply.

When alarm conditions are met on the switch, SNMP traps and log messages, syslog and console, are reported, indicating the threshold-exceeded condition.

Performance Management Data for Router Hardware

Performance monitoring in hardware relates mainly to slot positioning in the chassis; the following MIB variables can help you identify the type of interface processors (IPs) installed. Based on the slot positioning of these cards, you can effectively predict and determine the backplane, hardware buffer, and IDB usage in the chassis—based on the architectural overview discussed at the beginning of this chapter. Because hardware versions and sometimes serial number ranges (due to Cisco Field Notices) on cards and chassis can affect performance, we also look at ways to gather that information through MIBs and through command-line interface (CLI) commands. The polling period for all these performance management-oriented MIBs should be right after a change management window period because that should be the only time these parameters should change.

MIB Variables for Chassis Information

From OLD-CISCO-CHASSIS-MIB cardTable, MIB variables to watch for chassis information include the following:

- chassisType: Identifies the kind of router the device is.
- chassisVersion: Identifies the hardware version of the router.
- chassisID: Shows the serial number of the chassis itself.
- chassisSlots: Represents how many slots are available in the router for Interface Processors (IPs).

These four MIB objects together produce a nice, concise inventory table on the router model and its corresponding attributes. The purpose of these MIB objects is to give you an understanding of the type of routers that exist in the network. Polling these MIB objects after a change management window is ideal to get an up-to-date and accurate inventory of your network. You can also use this data to quickly assess any issues that may arise, based on Cisco Field Notices, regarding major hardware defects. This data can be used in conjunction with performing the network audit, as explained in Chapter 1, "Conducting the Network Audit."

TIP	You can readily access the Cisco Field Notices via the following URL: http:// www.cisco.com/warp/customer/770/.

From ENTITY-MIB (RFC2037), MIB objects related to these four include from the entPhysicalTable:

- entPhysicalVendorType
- entHardwareRevision
- entPhysicalDescr

NOTE	The ENTITY Mib is not supported on the routers until IOS release 11.3(2)NA or greater.

CLI Commands for Chassis Information

Several CLI commands are related to the MIBs just discussed.

show diagbus

The **show diagbus** command is available only on the high-end routers, such as the 7x00 series. The Slot 31 or "virtual" slot in the 7500 chassis is the output where the equivalent MIB values related to chassis information are reported, except for the **chassisSlots**. The 7200 series router reports the chassis information in the output from the command **show c7200**. All other router platforms report the chassis information in the show version output.

Probably the two most useful bits of information you can get from this output, assuming you use SNMP to get the **chassisVersion** and **chassisID**, are the board revision and RMA number. These two values cannot be retrieved from SNMP and can only be gathered from CLI commands. The board revision is like the maintenance release of a major IOS version. From the board revision you can determine data points such as "Is my router a 4700 or 4700M?" Output from the **show version** command is illustrated in Example 10-3, shown later in this chapter.

The RMA number field is used by Cisco's Logistics department to keep a record of the chassis or Interface Processor cards returned to Cisco due to possible customer failure. So, if the value in that field is anything other than 0, the card probably went through the Cisco RMA department. There are no MIB values for the board revision and RMA number.

Example 10-1 shows output from the **show diagbus** command.

Example 10-1 *Obtaining router chassis information with the **show diagbus** command.*

```
Router> show diag
…
…
Slot 31 (virtual):
        EEPROM format version 1
Chassis Interface, HW rev 1.00 A, board revision B0 B
Serial number: 03185411 C Part number: 73-1306-02
        Test history: 0x00        RMA number: 00-00-00 D
        Flags: cisco 7000 board
EEPROM contents (hex):
            0x20: 01 10 01 00 00 30 9B 03 49 05 1A 02 00 00 00 00
            0x30: 58 00 00 00 FF 00 00 00 00 00 00 00 00 00 00 00
```

Pertinent features of the output in Example 10-1 are flagged with letters A, B, C, etc. (This practice will be followed for subsequent Examples as well.) Here are the meanings of the flagged features:

A "HW rev" is the hardware version of the chassis.

B "board revision" is the appropriate iteration of the hardware version.

C "Serial number" is obviously the serial number of the chassis.

D "RMA number" is used by Cisco to track defective, or possibly defective, routers/ cards in the customer base. If the value in this output is equal to 0, the card has not been through Cisco's RMA department, so it has more than likely been in the field since it was first deployed. If the RMA number is not 0, that does not mean the card is bad. It is just a way for Cisco to track the cards that come through the RMA department. Cisco thoroughly tests out the cards prior to redeploying them to the field.

show c7200

The output from **show c7200** is the same type of output as the Slot 31 virtual interface from the 7500 series router, except that it's specific for the 7200 series routers.

As with **show diagbus**, probably the two most useful bits of information you can get from this output are the board revision and RMA number, assuming you use SNMP to get the **chassisVersion** and **chassisID**. The board revision can also be obtained from the **show version** command, as you will see in Example 10-3. In the meantime, Example 10-2 shows sample output from the **show c7200** command.

Example 10-2   *Obtaining router chassis information with the **show c7200** command.*

```
Router#sh c7200
C7200 Network IO Interrupt Throttling:
 throttle count=0, timer count=0
 active=0, configured=0
 netint usec=3999, netint mask usec=200
C7200 Midplane EEPROM:
        Hardware revision 1.3 ᴬ  Board revision M0 ᴮ
        Serial number     8519955 ᶜ       Part number    73-1539-03
        Test history      0x0            RMA number     00-00-00 ᴰ
        MAC=0090.bff4.2800, MAC Size=1024
        EEPROM format version 1, Model=0x6
        EEPROM contents (hex):
          0x20: 01 06 01 03 00 82 01 13 49 06 03 03 00 90 BF F4
          0x30: 28 00 04 00 00 00 00 00 4C 03 90 B0 FF FF 00 FF
C7200 CPU EEPROM:
        Hardware revision 2.1 ᴬ  Board revision A0 ᴮ
        Serial number     4390454 ᶜ       Part number    73-1536-03
        Test history      0x3            RMA number     25-99-30 ᴰ
        EEPROM format version 1
        EEPROM contents (hex):
          0x20: 01 15 02 01 00 42 FE 36 49 06 00 03 03 19 63 1E
          0x30: 50 00 00 00 FF FF FF FF FF FF FF FF FF FF FF FF
```

Here are the meanings of the flagged items in Example 10-2:

A "Hardware revision" is the hardware version of the chassis.

B "Board revision" is the appropriate iteration of the hardware version.

C "Serial number" is obviously the serial number of the chassis.

D "RMA number" is used by Cisco to track defective, or possibly defective, routers/cards in the customer base. If the value in this output is equal to 0, the card has not been through Cisco's RMA department, so it has more than likely been in the field since it was first deployed.

show version

In addition to the IOS version and interface inventory from the **show version** output, the key data points to look at that relate to the chassis are the processor and chassis revisions as well as the processor ID. Memory, flash, and NVRAM total installed are also reported. Probably the most useful chassis bit of information you can get from this output, assuming you use SNMP to get the **chassisVersion** and **chassisID**, is the board revision. There is no MIB variable for board revisions. Example 10-3 shows sample output for **show version**.

Example 10-3 *Obtaining router chassis information with the **show version** command.*

```
Router> show version
Cisco Internetwork Operating System Software
IOS (tm) 4500 Software (C4500-IS56I-M), Experimental Version 11.3(9)
Copyright  1986-1999 by cisco Systems, Inc.
Compiled Tue 30-Mar-99 14:09 by vilhuber
Image text-base: 0x60008930, data-base: 0x608A4000
ROM: System Bootstrap, Version 5.2(7b) [mkamson 7b], RELEASE SOFTWARE (fc1)
BOOTFLASH: 4500 Software (C4500-BOOT-M), Version 11.2(8), RELEASE SOFTWARE (fc1)
Router uptime is 1 week, 2 days, 20 hours, 32 minutes
System restarted by reload at 16:21:04 UTC Thu Apr 8 1999
System image file is "flash:c4500-is56i-mz.jan9", booted via flash
cisco 4500 (R4K) processor (revision B [A]) with 32768K/16384K bytes of memory.
Processor board ID 03770977 [B]
R4700 processor, Implementation 33, Revision 1.0 [C]
G.703/E1 software, Version 1.0.
Bridging software.
X.25 software, Version 3.0.0.
2 Ethernet/IEEE 802.3 interface(s)
2 Token Ring/IEEE 802.5 interface(s)
1 FDDI network interface(s)
128K [D] bytes of non-volatile configuration memory.
16384K [E] bytes of processor board System flash (Read/Write)
4096K [F] bytes of processor board Boot flash (Read/Write)
Configuration register is 0x2102 [G]
```

Here are the meanings of the flagged items in Example 10-2:

A The first "revision" seen in the **show version** output is equivalent to the "board revision" from the **show diag** output. From here, you can determine whether or not your router is a 4500 or 4500-M. In this case, this router is a 4500-M based on the revision of "B." You can search Cisco Connection Online for details on the different revisions, especially under the OpenForum section: http://www.cisco.com/cgi-bin/search-openf.

B   The "Processor board ID" is equivalent to the **chassisID** MIB.

C   The second "revision" seen in this output is the hardware version of the chassis or **chassisVersion**.

D   The "non-volatile configuration memory" line shows you how much NVRAM is installed in the router. Configurations are stored in the NVRAM.

E   The "processor board system flash" line shows how much system flash memory is installed on the router. IOS images are mainly stored in flash. Sometimes, the configuration files can reside here as well. There may also be PCMCIA flash memory as well to help store IOS images or configurations.

F   The "bootflash" line is the amount of bootflash installed in the router. Bootflash is used to store the initial IOS image and is like the "reserve" IOS image, in case the main flash IOS image is not present or working correctly. It is like the ROM on older platform routers.

G   The "configuration register" line shows the bit settings of the router that gives the router its boot characteristics, such as boot from flash or from bootflash, or try to boot so many times from flash and then boot from bootflash.

TIP   It is recommended to keep the configuration register setting at 0x2102. This setting tells the router to boot from system flash and if it fails five times and then boot from bootflash or ROM, and to ignore the BREAK key, which halts the boot process.

MIB Variables for Card Information

From OLD-CISCO-CHASSIS MIB cardTable, MIB variables to watch for card information include the following:

- CardType: The kind of card installed in the router, especially modularized routers.

- CardDescr: A text description of the card.

- CardSerial: The serial number of the card.

- CardHwVersion: The hardware revision of the card.

- CardSwVersion: The firmware or microcode version of the card.

- CardSlotNumber: The slot relative to the location of the card in the chassis. If slot position is irrelevant, a −1 value will be present on low-end routers (4x00 series, etc.), for example.

- CardOperStatus: The operational status of the card. The values are "up" when a card is recognized by the device and is enabled for operation; they are "down" if the card is not recognized by the device, or if it is not enabled for operation; they are "standby" if the card is enabled and acting as a standby slave.

The purpose of these MIB objects is to give you an understanding of the type of cards installed in the network. Polling these MIB objects after a change management window is ideal to get an up-to-date and accurate inventory of your network. You can also use this data to quickly assess any issues that may arise with particular common hardware platforms based on Cisco Field Notices that may come out regarding major hardware defects. From ENTITY-MIB (RFC2037), MIB objects related to these four include the following from the entPhysicalTable:

- EntPhysicalVendorType
- entHardwareRevision
- entPhysicalDescr
- entSerialNumber
- entPhysicalParentRelPos

CLI Commands for Card Information

Several CLI commands are related to the MIBs just discussed.

show controller cbus

This command displays the hardware characteristics of each card in the 7x00 series router. Things such as hardware revisions, microcode levels, card types, and hardware buffer memory allocation are displayed in this output. The main bit of data that can be gathered from this command that cannot be gathered via SNMP is the hardware buffer pool allocation from MEMD. This is where the concept of over-subscription really hits home. If there are no hardware buffers available in the router, or if there are a low amount of hardware buffers, interfaces will fail to perform as designed and "ignores" will increment on the interfaces when congestion occurs. Slot position, card type, hardware version, and microcode version are also available in this output as well.

Example 10-4 *Obtaining router card information with **show controller cbus**.*

```
Router#show controller cbus
MEMD at 40000000, 2097152 bytes (unused 3584, recarves 1, lost 0)
  RawQ 48000100, ReturnQ 48000108, EventQ 48000110
  BufhdrQ 48000128 (2809 items), LovltrQ 48000140 (10 items, 2016 bytes)
  IpcbufQ 48000150 (16 items, 4096 bytes)
  IpcbufQ_classic 48000148 (8 items, 4096 bytes)
  3570 buffer headers (48002000 - 4800FF10)
```

Example 10-4   *Obtaining router card information with **show controller cbus**. (Continued)*

```
pool0: 9 buffers, 256 bytes ᴬ, queue 48000130
pool1: 481 buffers, 1536 bytes ᴬ, queue 48000138
pool2: 233 buffers, 4544 bytes ᴬ, queue 48000158
pool3: 4 buffers, 4576 bytes, ᴬ queue 48000160
slot1 ᴮ: AIP ᶜ, hw 1.3ᴰ, sw 20.18 ᴱ, ccb 5800FF30, cmdq 48000088, vps 8192
  software loaded from system
  ATM1/0, applique is SONET (155Mbps)
    gfreeq 48000158, lfreeq 48000168 (4544 bytes)
    rxlo 4 ᶠ, rxhi 189 ᴳ, rxcurr 0, maxrxcurr 0
    txq 48000170, txacc 48000082 (value 0), txlimit 66 ᴴ
slot4 ᴮ: VIP2 ᶜ, hw 2.4 ᴰ, sw 22.20 ᴱ, ccb 5800FF60, cmdq 480000A0, vps 8192
  software loaded from system
  IOS (tm) VIP Software (SVIP-DW-M), Version 12.0(2)T,  RELEASE SOFTWARE (fc1)
  ROM Monitor version 17.0
  FastEthernet4/0/0, addr 0090.f2d0.e080 (bia 0090.f2d0.e080)
    gfreeq 48000138, lfreeq 48000178 (1536 bytes)
    rxlo 4 ᶠ, rxhi 481 ᴳ, rxcurr 2, maxrxcurr 3
    txq 48001A00, txacc 48001A02 (value 320), txlimit 320 ᴴ
  FastEthernet4/0/1, addr 0090.f2d0.e081 (bia 0090.f2d0.e081)
    gfreeq 48000138, lfreeq 48000180 (1536 bytes)
    rxlo 4, rxhi 481, rxcurr 0, maxrxcurr 0
    txq 48001A08, txacc 48001A0A (value 0), txlimit 320
```

Here are the meanings of the flagged items in Example 10-4:

A Buffer pool assignment based on the MEMD buffer carving algorithm aforementioned in the introduction of this chapter.

B Slot position of the Interface Processor (IP). Equivalent to MIB cardSlotNumber.

C Interface Processor (IP) Type: Equivalent to MIB cardType.

D "hw" is the hardware version of the IP, which is equivalent to MIB cardHwVersion.

E "sw" is the microcode version of the IP, which is typically "bundled" within the IOS and downloaded at boot time. Microcode levels hold true only for the 7x00 series routers. The "bundled" microcode can be overridden by a separate microcode version stored in Flash memory. This is equivalent to the MIB cardSwVersion.

F "rxlo" is the minimum amount of receive hardware buffers allowed on the particular interface. This is based again on the MEMD buffer carving algorithm performed at boot time.

G "rxhi" is the maximum amount of receive hardware buffers allowed on the particular interface. This is based again on the MEMD buffer carving algorithm performed at boot time.

H "txlimit" is the transmit buffer limit for the particular interface. This is the only value that can be changed via the command line (CLI) prompt, via the configuration command tx-queue-limit. This command should *not* be used unless instructed to do so by a Cisco Support Engineer (TAC).

show diagbus

This command shows you the hardware information for the high-end routers. The board revision and insertion time are the two fields displayed in this output that cannot be retrieved from a MIB object. Probably the three most useful bits of information you can get from this output, assuming you use SNMP to get the chassisVersion and chassisID, are the board revision, RMA number, and insertion time.

The *insertion time* is the time at which the Interface Processor card was inserted into the router. If this value is different from the router uptime, you know that the card was probably OIRed (Online Insertion and Removal). You can correlate this time with the OIR syslog messages seen, such as %OIR-6-INSCARD.

Example 10-5 shows sample output from **show diagbus**, with emphasis on card information.

Example 10-5 *Obtaining router card information with **show diagbus**.*

```
Router#sh diagbus
Slot 1:
        Physical slot 1 A, ~physical slot 0xE, logical slot 1, CBus 0
        Microcode Status 0x0
        Master Enable, LED, WCS Loaded
        Board is analyzed
        EEPROM format version 1
        EIP B controller, HW rev 1.07 C, board revision D0 D
        Serial number: 03356234 E Part number: 73-0906-04
        Test history: 0x0E        RMA number: 05-20-19 F
        Flags: cisco 7000 board; 7500 compatible
        EEPROM contents (hex):
          0x20: 01 00 01 07 00 33 36 4A 49 03 8A 04 0E 05 14 13
          0x30: 68 00 00 00 00 00 00 00 00 00 00 00 00 00 00 00
        Slot database information:
        Flags: 0x4        Insertion time: 0x1A38 (4w0d ago) G
Slot 2:
        EEPROM format version 1
        Route/Switch Processor 2 B, HW rev 1.02 C, board revision B0 D
        Serial number: 03719351 E Part number: 73-1324-05
        Test history: 0x0E        RMA number: 00-00-00 F
```

Example 10-5   *Obtaining router card information with **show diagbus**. (Continued)*

```
              Flags: cisco 7000 board; 7500 compatible
              EEPROM contents (hex):
                0x20: 01 0F 01 02 00 38 C0 B7 49 05 2C 05 0E 00 00 00
                0x30: 58 FF FF 00 00 00 00 00 00 00 00 00 00 00 00 00
  Slot 6:
              Physical slot 6 ᴬ, ~physical slot 0x9, logical slot 6 , CBus 0
              Microcode Status 0x4
              Master Enable, LED, WCS Loaded
              Board is analyzed
              Pending I/O Status: None
              EEPROM format version 1
              VIP2 ᴮ controller, HW rev 2.10 ᶜ, board revision B0 ᴰ
              Serial number: 08206403 ᴱ Part number: 73-1684-04
              Test history: 0x00        RMA number: 00-00-00 ᶠ
              Flags: cisco 7000 board; 7500 compatible
  EEPROM contents (hex):
                0x20: 01 15 02 0A 00 7D 38 43 49 06 94 04 00 00 00 00
                0x30: 58 00 00 01 00 00 00 00 00 00 00 00 00 00 00 00
       Slot database information:
              Flags: 0x4      Insertion time: 0x1A38 (4w0d ago) [G}
              Controller Memory Size: 64 MBytes DRAM, 2048 KBytes SRAM
  PA Bay 0 ᴬ Information:
                      Token Ring PA, 4 portsPA-4R ᴮ
                      EEPROM format version 1
                      HW rev 1.10 ᶜ, Board revision A0 ᴰ
                      Serial number: 04948569 ᴱ Part number: 73-1390-05
  --Boot log begin--
  Cisco Internetwork Operating System Software
  IOS (tm) VIP Software (SVIP-DW-M), Version 11.2(17)P,  RELEASE SOFTWARE (fc1)
  Copyright  1986-1999 by cisco Systems, Inc.
  Compiled Tue 12-Jan-99 12:22 by pwade
  Image text-base: 0x600108D0, data-base: 0x6015C000
  --Boot log end--
  Slot 31 (virtual):
              EEPROM format version 1
              Chassis Interface ᴮ, HW rev 1.00 ᶜ, board revision B0 ᴰ
              Serial number: 03185411 ᴱ Part number: 73-1306-02
              Test history: 0x00        RMA number: 00-00-00 ᶠ
              Flags: cisco 7000 board
              EEPROM contents (hex):
                0x20: 01 10 01 00 00 30 9B 03 49 05 1A 02 00 00 00 00
                0x30: 58 00 00 00 FF 00 00 00 00 00 00 00 00 00 00 00
```

Here are the meanings of the flagged items in Example 10-5:

A "Physical slot" is the slot position of the IP card. Equivalent to MIB cardSlotNumber.

B The preceding acronym or word to "controller" is the IP type or MIB cardType.

C "HW rev" is the hardware version of the chassis.

D "board revision" is the appropriate iteration of the hardware version.

E "Serial number" is obviously the serial number of the chassis.

F "RMA number" is used by Cisco to track defective, or possibly defective, routers/cards in the customer base. If the value in this output is equal to 0, then the card has not been through Cisco's RMA department, thus has more than likely been in the field since it was first deployed.

"Insertion time" is the time when the Interface Processor (IP) card was inserted in the chassis.

show controller

This command is useful on the low-end routers such as the 4x00, 3600, 2500, and 2600 series platforms. It produces the same kind of output as show controller cbus for the high-end routers, but in a little different format. If you execute this command as is on the high-end routers, it will produce output specifically for the token ring interfaces if they exist; otherwise, no output will be displayed.

From this output, you can retrieve the NIM (Network Interface Module) chip set based on the cardType, slot position of the NIM, and the hardware version of the NIM. The chipset is probably the most useful out of this output. The output from this command varies due to the different kinds of chip sets and reported output for each kind of card and router type. See Example 10-6 for an illustration of the different reporting styles (for example, LANE versus FDDI).

To get the hardware information on low-end routers, it may be more effective to use SNMP to get the cardType and cardHwVersion than to use the CLI command **show controller** to get the same set of data points.

Example 10-6 *Obtaining router card information with **show controller**.*

```
Router#sh controller
LANCE A unit 0, NIM slot 0 B, NIM type code 9, NIM version 2 C
Media Type is 10BaseT, Link State is Up, Squelch is Normal
idb 0x60CB060C, ds 0x60CB1E88, eim_regs = 0x3C000000
IB at 0x40006F18: mode=0x0000, mcfilter 0000/0002/0100/0080
station address 0060.837b.5850   default station address 0060.837b.5850
buffer size 1524
RX ring with 32 entries at 0x40006F60
Rxhead = 0x40006F60 (0), Rxp = 0x60CB1EA0 (0)
00 pak=0x60CBA3E4 ds=0xA8021D62 status=0x80 max_size=1524 pak_size=0
…

…
LANCE A unit 1, NIM slot 0 B, NIM type code 9, NIM version 2 C
Media Type is 10BaseT, Link State is Down, Squelch is Normal
idb 0x60CBE81C, ds 0x60CC0098, eim_regs = 0x3C000800
IB at 0x4002FBD4: mode=0x0000, mcfilter 0000/0000/0100/0000
```

Example 10-6 *Obtaining router card information with **show controller**. (Continued)*

```
station address 0060.837b.5853  default station address 0060.837b.5853
buffer size 1524
RX ring with 32 entries at 0x4002FC18
Rxhead = 0x4002FC18 (0), Rxp = 0x60CC00B0 (0)
00 pak=0x60CC85F4 ds=0xA804AA1E status=0x80 max_size=1524 pak_size=0
...
...
FDDI A: unit 0, NIM slot 1 B, NIM type code 3, NIM version 3 C
 dual attach, state 4, idb 0x60CCCA2C, ds 0x60CCE290, module_regs 0x3C100000
 Phy-A is multi mode, Phy-B is multi mode
 hardware address: 0060.837b.5851 (wire order 0006.c1de.1a8a)
 default hardware address: 0060.837b.5851
 loopback disabled
 CAM hardware present (Software: Rev 17, Tue Oct 17 08:34:02 PDT 1995)
 Registers: csr = 0x7003
 BSI silicon revision Number 0x0000004C (BSI-2 Rev B)
 Registers: mr 0x10, pcar 0x4A, mbar 0x5, mar 0x0
...
...
```

A On the low-end routers, you'll see the cardType defined here as representative of the chipset typically for the appropriate media type.

B "NIM slot" is the position of the Network Interface Module in the router. The positioning is especially important on the modularized routers such as the 4x00, 3600, and 2600 series routers.

C "NIM version" is the hardware version of the NIM. This is equivalent to the cardHwVersion MIB.

Syslog Messages for Card Information

A number of syslog messages are useful for router chassis performance management, and apply directly to the MIB objects and CLI commands previously discussed. They are collected in Table 10-2.

Table 10-2 *Syslog Messages for Card Information*

Message	Explanation
%OIR-6-INSCARD: Card inserted in slot [dec], subcard [dec], interfaces administratively shutdown	The specified hot-swappable card was inserted in the system. The interface(s) on the card will remain administratively disabled until specifically enabled because they may need to be configured. This is an informational message only. Configure the interface(s) and enable them.

Table 10-2 *Syslog Messages for Card Information (Continued)*

Message	Explanation
`%OIR-6-REMCARD: Card removed from slot [dec], subcard [dec], interfaces disabled`	The specified hot-swappable card was removed from the system. This is an informational message only. No action is required.
`%OIR-4-NOEOIR:[char] [char] version [int].[int] not capable of EOIR`	This card is capable of online insertion and removal (OIR), but is not capable of extended online insertion and removal (EOIR). Even though no damage would occur to the hardware, removal or reinsertion of the card will cause a CBUS complex restart, which would be disruptive to traffic on other cards in the system. Try to restrict removal or reinsertion of this card to instances when a CBUS complex restart will be least disruptive. Or, upgrade the card to the latest revision that supports EOIR.

Chassis and Card Information via the Entity MIB

There are several MIBs to watch for chassis and card information. Those from the ENTITY-MIB (RFC2037) from the entPhysicalTable with the CISCO-ENTITY-VENDORTYPE-OID-MIB and CISCO-ENTITY-ASSET-MIB are as follows:

- entPhysicalVendorType: Equivalent to chassisType and cardType
- entHardwareRevision: Equivalent to chassisVersion
- entPhysicalDescr: Equivalent to cardDescr
- entSerialNumber: Equivalent to cardSerial,
- entPhysicalParentRelPos: Equivalent to cardSwVersion, cardHwVersion, and cardSlotNumber

The MIB describes managed objects used for managing multiple logical and physical entities managed by a single SNMP agent. The hardware is generalized into one of the following types: chassis, backplane, container, powerSupply, fan, sensor, module, or port. This MIB is flexible enough to determine the hardware type based on an MIB definition relating to the ENTITY MIB. In this case, that MIB is called CISCO-ENTITY-VENDORTYPE OID MIB. The purpose of these MIBs is to replace the existing OLD-CISCO-CHASSIS-MIB and make it more of a standard based on the RFC 2037 definition. The only MIB not covered by the ENITITY MIB is the **chassisID** MIB.

Performance Management Data for Switches

This section looks at performance monitoring for switches. Many of the issues are the same as for routers. As with routers, performance monitoring in switch hardware relates mainly to slot positioning. MIBs and CLI commands are again the main ways of collecting information on switch chasses and cards. As with routers, the polling period for switch performance MIBs should be right after a change management window period.

MIB Variables for Chassis Information

From CISCO-STACK-MIB, MIB variables to watch for chassis information include the following:

- chassisBkplType: The chassis backplane type—either fddi, fddiEthernet, Gigabit, or multiples of Gigabit.
- chassisNumSlots: The number of slots available for plug-in modules, such as line cards.
- chassisSlotConfig: An indication of which slots in the chassis have modules inserted. This is an integer value with bits set to indicate configured modules. It can be interpreted as a sum of f(x) as x goes from 1 to the number of slots, where f(x) = 0 for no module inserted and f(x) = exp(2, x–1) for a module inserted.
- chassisModel: The chassis Model number.
- chassisSerialNumberString: The serial number of the chassis, either numeric or alphanumeric.

The purpose of these MIB objects is to give you an understanding of the type of LAN switches you have in the network. Polling these MIB objects after a change management window is ideal to get an up-to-date and accurate inventory of your network. You can also use this data to quickly assess any issues that may arise with particular common hardware platforms based on Cisco Field Notices that may come out regarding major hardware defects.

From ENTITY-MIB (RFC 2037) from the entPhysicalTable, other MIB objects relating to these five are as follows:

- entPhysicalVendorType
- entHardwareRevision
- entPhysicalDescr
- entSerialNumber
- entPhysicalParentRelPos

Chassis Information via show version

The **show version** command can be used to obtain chassis information for performance management of a switch. For the scope of this portion of performance management, the important data reported in this output are the hardware version of the chassis, the chassis model, and the chassis serial number because all other data relates to the supervisor cards or line cards. The total number of slots in the chassis is not visible here, but the total number of configured slots is available indirectly. The **show version** command is useful for displaying all the hardware information for the entire switch in a single CLI output. Example 10-7 focuses on the chassis-specific data.

Example 10-7 *Obtaining switch chassis information with* ***show version****.*

```
Switch> show version
WS-C5500 Software, Version McpSW: 4.5(1) NmpSW: 4.5(1)
Copyright  1995-1999 by Cisco Systems
NMP S/W compiled on Mar 29 1999, 16:09:01
MCP S/W compiled on Mar 29 1999, 16:06:50
System Bootstrap Version: 3.1.2
Hardware Version: 1.2 A Model: WS-C5500 B Serial #: 069002256 C
Mod Port Model      Serial #  Versions
--- ---- ---------- --------- ----------------------------------------
1 D  2    WS-X5530   011437543 Hw : 2.0
                               Fw : 3.1.2
                               Fw1: 4.2(1)
                               Sw : 4.5(1)
2 D  2    WS-X5101   003397731 Hw : 1.1
                               Fw : 1.1
                               Fw1: 1.3
                               Sw : 3.1(1)
6 D  12   WS-X5213   003974709 Hw : 1.0
                               Fw : 1.4
                               Sw : 4.5(1)

        DRAM                   FLASH                  NVRAM
Module Total   Used    Free    Total   Used    Free    Total Used  Free
------ ------- ------- ------- ------- ------- ------- ----- ----- -----
1       32640K  14322K  18318K   8192K   4118K   4074K  512K  109K  403K
Uptime is 11 days, 8 hours, 8 minutes
```

Following is the annotated information from Example 10-7:

A "Hardware Version" is the hardware version of the chassis.

B "Model" is the chassis model type based on Cisco's part number.

C "Serial #" is the chassis serial number associated with the switch.

D The "Mod" column shows the modules installed in the switch. By adding up the amount of cards in the different modules, you can come up with the chassisSlotConfig MIB value.

MIB Variables for Card Information

From CISCO-STACK MIB moduleTable, MIB variables to watch for chassis information include the following:

- moduleModel
- moduleSerialNumberString
- moduleHwVersion
- moduleFwVersion
- moduleSwVersion
- moduleStatus
- moduleNumPorts
- moduleSlotNum

These MIBs report the hardware characteristics of the supervisor and line cards installed in the switch, such as hardware, firmware, and software versions. Typically, the line cards exhibit the same firmware and software version as the supervisor card because the supervisor card controls most line cards. There are some line cards, however, that have their own versions of software running on them, such as the FDDI modules and ATM LANE modules. These two line cards require separate software images stored in flash memory.

As with the MIBs for chassis information, polling these MIB objects after a change management window is a good way to obtain up-to-date and accurate inventory of your network. You can also use this data to quickly assess any hardware defects that you learn about through Cisco Field Notices.

In addition to these MIB objects, the following are comparable MIBs from the ENTITY MIB from the entPhysicalTable:

- entPhysicalVendorType
- entHardwareRevision
- entPhysicalDescr
- entSerialNumber
- entPhysicalParentRelPos

CLI Commands for Line Card Information

In addition to MIB objects that gather hardware information on the switches, there are also a couple of show commands that can get the same bit of information from the MIBs previously discussed.

Line Card Information from show version

For the scope of this portion of performance management, the important data reported in this output are the hardware version, model, and serial number of the supervisor and line cards. The DRAM, flash, and NVRAM memory installed are reported here under module 1 or 2 where the supervisor card resides. The **show version** command is useful for displaying all the hardware information for the entire switch in a single CLI output. Example 10-8 focuses on the supervisor and line card specific data here.

Example 10-8 *Obtaining switch card information with* ***show version***.

```
Switch> show version
WS-C5500 Software, Version McpSW: 4.5(1) NmpSW: 4.5(1)
Copyright  1995-1999 by Cisco Systems
NMP S/W compiled on Mar 29 1999, 16:09:01
MCP S/W compiled on Mar 29 1999, 16:06:50
System Bootstrap Version: 3.1.2
Hardware Version: 1.2  Model: WS-C5500  Serial #: 069002256
Mod Port Model        Serial #      Versions
--- ---- ----------- ----------    -------------------------------------------
1 A   2 B   WS-X5530 C  011437543 D Hw : 2.0 E
                                    Fw : 3.1.2 F
                                    Fw1: 4.2(1)
                                    Sw : 4.5(1) G
2 D   2 B   WS-X5101 C  003397731 D Hw : 1.1 E
                                    Fw : 1.1 F
                                    Fw1: 1.3
                                    Sw : 3.1(1) G
6 A   12 B  WS-X5213 C 003974709 D Hw : 1.0 E
                                    Fw : 1.4 F
                                    Sw : 4.5(1) G
          DRAM                 FLASH                NVRAM
Module  Total   Used   Free   Total  Used   Free   Total Used  Free
------  ------  ------ ------ ------ ------ ------ ----- ----- -----
1 A   32640K H 14322K 18318K  8192K I 4118K  4074K  512K J 109K  403K
Uptime is 11 days, 8 hours, 8 minutes
```

Following is the annotated information from Example 10-8:

A The "Mod" column shows the slot location of the line cards in the chassis.

B The "Port" column shows you how many physical ports are associated with a particular line card or supervisor card.

C The "Model" column is the line card model type based on Cisco's part number.

D The "Serial #" column is the serial number associated with the line card or supervisor card.

E "Hw" is the hardware version of the individual line card or supervisor card.

F "Fw" is the firmware version of the line card or supervisor card. The next column, "Fw1," is really irrelevant and not important enough to look at.

G "Sw" is the software version running on the particular card. Typically, you'll see the same software version as defined on the supervisor card, unless it is a specific feature card that requires its own software, such as the ATM LANE card or FDDI module.

H The "DRAM Total" column displays how much system memory is installed on the switch supervisor card.

I The "FLASH Total" column reports how much flash memory is installed on the supervisor card. This is where the software images reside for both the supervisor card and the feature-specific cards, such as the FDDI module or ATM LANE module.

J The "NVRAM Total" column reports how much NVRAM is available on the supervisor card. This is where the switch configuration file resides, as well as the log for the switch as displayed with the CLI command show log.

NOTE   Please note that the software for these feature cards is stored in flash on the supervisor card, not on the individual cards directly.

TIP   It is good practice to clear the log after upgrading the software on the switch to accurately track the issues seen with the new software release; for example, possible exception errors or other failures that exists on the switch.

Line Card Information from show module

The **show module** command will show you just about the same bits of information as the **show version** command, except for the module description and module status, as displayed in Example 10-9. This command allows you to see what kind of card is installed in the switch chassis and what the status is of the line cards or supervisor cards. You can also get the module, number of ports, card model, serial number, hardware version, firmware version, and software version from this output. You can also see from this output any sub-model types typically installed on the supervisor card, such as the netflow feature card

(NFFC) or the uplink modules. This data is especially prevalent on the newer Supervisor cards (Supervisor III or WS-X5530).

Example 10-9 *Obtaining line card information from* ***show module.***

```
Switch>show module
Mod  Module-Name            Ports  Module-Type            Model      Serial-Num  Status
---  -------------------    -----  --------------------   ---------- ----------  -------
1ᴬ                          2ᴮ     100BaseFX MMF Superviᶜ WS-X5530ᴰ 011437543ᴱ  okᶠ
2ᴬ                          2ᴮ     MM MIC FDDIᶜ                      WS-X5101ᴰ 003397731ᴱ  okᶠ
6ᴬ                          12ᴮ    10/100BaseTX Ethernetᶜ WS-X5213ᴰ 003974709ᴱ  okᶠ
Mod  MAC-Address(es)                           Hw      Fw          Sw
---  ---------------------------------------   ------  ---------   --------------------
1    00-e0-4f-73-8e-00 to 00-e0-4f-73-91-ff    2.0ᴳ    3.1.2ᴴ      4.5(1)ᴵ
2    00-60-3e-cd-55-6c                         1.1ᴳ    1.1ᴴ        3.1(1)ᴵ
6    00-60-83-5d-8a-ec to 00-60-83-5d-8a-f7    1.0ᴳ    1.4ᴴ        4.5(1)ᴵ
Mod  Sub-Type   Sub-Model  Sub-Serial    Sub-Hw
---  --------   ---------  -----------   -----
1ᴬ   NFFCᶜ      WS-F5521ᴰ  0011437958ᴱ   1.1ᴳ
1ᴬ   uplinkᶜ    WS-U5533ᴰ  0008588482ᴱ   1.0ᴳ
Mod  SMT User-Data       T-Notify   CF-St ECM-St      Bypass
---  ----------------    ---------  --------------    ------------
2    WorkGroup Stack     30         c-Wrap-B in       absent
```

A The "Mod" column shows the slot location of the line cards in the chassis.

B The "Ports" column shows you how many physical ports are associated with a particular line card or supervisor card.

C The "Module-Type" column displays the description of the line card or supervisor card installed. We group "Sub-Type" into this description, as well for the daughter card modules installed on the supervisor card, such as the NetFlow feature card (NFFC).

D The "Model" column is the line card model type based on Cisco's part number. The "Sub-Model" is grouped under here as well.

E The "Serial-Num" column is the serial number associated with the line card or supervisor card. The "Sub-serial" number of the daughter card is also grouped here as well.

F The "Status" column shows you the current state of the module. It can be one of the following values: ok, disable, faulty, other, standby, or error. If there is a "faulty" condition on the module, you can issue the **show log** or **show test** [*mod_num*] commands to see why it is faulty.

G "Hw" is the hardware version of the individual line card or supervisor card.

H "Fw" is the firmware version of the line card or supervisor card. The next column, "Fw1," is really irrelevant and not important enough to look at.

I "Sw" is the software version running on the particular card. Typically, you'll see the same software version as defined on the supervisor card unless it is a specific feature card that requires its own software, such as the ATM LANE card or FDDI module. Please note that the software for those kinds of cards is stored in flash on the supervisor card, not on the individual cards directly.

SNMP Traps and Syslog Messages for Chassis and Line Card Information

A number of syslog messages are useful for switch chassis performance management, and apply directly to the MIB objects and CLI commands previously discussed. They are collected in Table 10-3.

Table 10-3 *Syslog Messages for Card Information*

Message	Explanation
`SYS-5-MOD_INSERT: Module [dec] has been Inserted`	This message indicates that module [dec] was inserted; [dec] is the module number. This message is provided for information only. If a module is inserted and the message does not appear, this might indicate a problem. Enter the **show module** or **show port** [*mod_num/port_num*] command to verify that the system has acknowledged the module and brought it online.
`SYS-5-MOD_REMOVE: Module [dec] has been Removed`	This message indicates that module [dec] was removed; [dec] is the module number. This message is provided for information only. If a module is removed and the message does not appear, this might indicate a problem. Enter the **show port** [*mod_num/port_num*] command to query the module. The system should respond as follows: Module n is not installed.
`SYS-5-MOD_RESET: Module [dec] reset from [chars]`	This message indicates that module [dec] was reset from [chars]; [dec] is the module number and [chars] is a console number if the request is from a console session, or an IP address if the request is from a Telnet session or Simple Network Management Protocol (SNMP).
`SYS-5-SYS_RESET: System reset from [chars]`	This message indicates that the system was reset from [chars]; [chars] is a console number if the request is from a console session, or an IP address if the request is from a Telnet session or SNMP.

continues

Table 10-3 *Syslog Messages for Card Information (Continued)*

Message	Explanation
`SYS-5-MOD_OK: Module [dec] is online`	This message indicates that module [dec] passed diagnostic self-test and is online; [dec] is the module number.

Chassis and Card Information via the Entity MIB

From ENTITY-MIB (RFC 2037) with the CISCO-ENTITY-VENDORTYPE-OID-MIB and CISCO-ENTITY-ASSET-MIB, here are some MIBs that are useful for chassis and card information:

- EntPhysicalVendorType: Equivalent to chassisType and modelType

- EntHardwareRevision: Equivalent to moduleHwVersion

- EntPhysicalDescr: Equivalent to chassisBkplType

- EntSerialNumber: Equivalent to chassisSerialNumberString and moduleSerialNumberString

- EntPhysicalParentRelPos: Equivalent to chassisSlotConfig and moduleSlotNum

The purpose of these MIBs is to replace the existing CISCO-STACK MIB and make it more of a standard based on the RFC 2037 definition. The Entity MIBs are still evolving.

Error/Fault Data for Router Hardware

Previous sections looked at the MIB variables that tell what kind of hardware is in the network and how everything is physically allocated in the devices. This section turns to examining the variables you can use for error and fault management for the routers and switches.

For fault management in routers, this discussions focuses mainly on the SNMP traps and syslog messages that tell when hardware issues are arising in the network, versus actively going out and polling MIB objects. However, there are a few MIB variables that should be polled in conjunction with the reception of other events, such as a syslog message or defined MIB threshold being exceeded.

MIB Variables for Router Failure

From OLD-CISCO-SYSTEM MIB and OLD-CISCO-CHASSIS MIB cardTable, MIB variables to watch for router failure are as follows:

- whyReload: The reason for the router's most recent reboot.

- CardOperStatus: The status of the Interface Processor or NIM cards in the chassis.

These two MIB objects will indicate the general health of the router. After the router is up and you verified "whyReload," all you would need to poll for is cardOperStatus to validate the status of the Interface Processor or NIM cards in the chassis. Most of the time, you will not even actively poll any of these objects to test for hardware faults. It is recommended to use SNMP traps and syslog messages to trigger a response to a possible hardware failure in the network. Based on appropriate syslog messages or SNMP traps received on your Network Management console, you can determine when you need to actively go out and poll these MIB objects. Polling these objects after one of those events is where these MIB objects are meaningful and add value.

CLI Commands for Router Failure

The following are comparable show commands that get the same type of resulting data points as the MIB objects described previous for analyzing router health.

Router Health from show version

Note that show version does display the reason why the router reloaded the last time. From this output, you can get more details on a particular reload error, such as a software-forced crash or exception error. This command output, in conjunction with a **show stack** output, can help determine the cause of a router crash.

TIP   If your router reloaded due to a software-forced crash or anything other than "power on" or "reload," take the output from the show stack command and "paste" it into the following URL on Cisco's Connection Online (CCO) to automatically search for known IOS or hardware defects:

http://www.cisco.com/stack/stackdecoder.shtml

If no "hits" are displayed in this search engine, please open a case with the Cisco TAC and provide the engineer with a show tech support output that includes this command.

Example 10-10 emphasizes output from the **show version** command that is related to router health.

Example 10-10   *Obtaining router health information with **show version**.*

```
Router>show version
Cisco Internetwork Operating System Software
IOS (tm) 4000 Software (C4000-JS-M), Version 11.2(17), RELEASE SOFTWARE (fc1)
Copyright  1986-1999 by cisco Systems, Inc.
```

continues

Example 10-10 *Obtaining router health information with **show version**. (Continued)*

```
Compiled Mon 04-Jan-99 18:40 by ashah
Image text-base: 0x00012000, data-base: 0x0077EBC0
ROM: System Bootstrap, Version 4.14(7), SOFTWARE
Router uptime is 16 minutes
System restarted by error - Software forced crash, PC 0xF9128 A
System image file is "c4000-js-mz.112-17.bin", booted via flash
cisco 4000 (68030) processor (revision 0xB0) with 16384K/4096K bytes of memory.
Processor board ID 5026712
G.703/E1 software, Version 1.0.
Bridging software.
SuperLAT software copyright 1990 by Meridian Technology Corp).
X.25 software, Version 2.0, NET2, BFE and GOSIP compliant.
TN3270 Emulation software.
2 Ethernet/IEEE 802.3 interface(s)
2 Serial network interface(s)
128K bytes of non-volatile configuration memory.
4096K bytes of processor board System flash (Read/Write)
Configuration register is 0x2102
```

The "System restarted by" line (A) indicates the reason for the router last reset. In this example, you can tell that the router reloaded due to a software-forced crash of some kind. This data alone does not mean anything to you or to a Cisco Support Engineer in the Technical Assistance Center (TAC). You need to also gather output from the **show stack** command to get an accurate representation of where the failure occurred in the IOS or hardware. You or a TAC engineer can feed the output from the **show stack** command into the stack decoder on CCO to determine whether a defect exists: http://www.cisco.com/stack/stackdecoder.shtml

You also may need to get a "core dump" of the memory in the router if a defect is not accurately identified. A core dump is useful to the Cisco IOS development engineers to help determine the cause of the crash. Please refer to the following URL on CCO for information on creating a core dump:

http://www.cisco.com/warp/customer/68/15.html

CAUTION   Please consult with the Cisco TAC prior to producing a core dump for the TAC.

Router Health from show stack

The output from this command gives you more details on why the router reloaded, especially if it was caused by an error of some kind. You or a TAC engineer can feed the output from the **show stack** command into the stack decoder on CCO to determine whether a defect exists: http://www.cisco.com/stack/stackdecoder.shtml

You may be required to also get a "core dump" of the memory in the router if a defect is not accurately identified. A core dump is useful to the Cisco IOS development engineers to help determine the cause of the crash. Please refer to the following URL on CCO for information on creating a core dump:

http://www.cisco.com/warp/customer/68/15.html

CAUTION   Again, please consult with the Cisco TAC prior to producing a core dump for the TAC.

Example 10-11 provides show stack output, with emphasis on information for router health.

Example 10-11   *Obtaining router health information from **show stack**.*

```
Router>sh stack
 Minimum process stacks:
  Free/Size    Name
  1408/2000    Router Init
  2632/4000    Init
 Interrupt level stacks:
  Level    Called Unused/Size  Name
    3        7810   2540/3000  Network interfaces
    4          0    3000/3000  High IRQ Int Handler
    5        1355   2896/3000  Console Uart
 System was restarted by error - Software forced crash, PC 0xF9128 A
 4000 Software (C4000-JS-M), Version 11.2(17), RELEASE SOFTWARE (fc1)
 Compiled Mon 04-Jan-99 18:40 by ashah (current version)
 Image text-base: 0x00012000, data-base: 0x0077EBC0
 Stack trace from system failure:
 FP: 0x843978, RA: 0xFFC9A
 FP: 0x84399C, RA: 0xE9936
 FP: 0x8439B8, RA: 0xFCC46
```

Starting with the "System restarted by error…" in line (A) and continuing to the end of the command output, these lines provide information relating to the cause of a router crash or reload. Again, this data should be provided to a TAC engineer or should be fed into the stack decoder on CCO, as indicated previously, to search for possible known defects.

Router Health from show diagbus

The **show diagbus** command displays cards in the router that are not recognized for one reason or another. Nuances such as "UNKNOWN," hardware revisions of "255.255," or serial numbers with all zeroes are the key values to pick out of this data. This output can be correlated to syslog messages or SNMP traps relating to failing hardware or incompatible hardware. Boards can show up "UNKNOWN" if the card is not supported by the IOS release running on the router or if there is a hardware problem with the card. Sometimes, if you see valid output in this command for a particular card when an issue of some kind is seen, the output from **show controller cbus** will show no microcode installed on the card (Sw 0.00). This typically indicates an IOS compatibility problem with the Interface Processor (IP).

The example given in Example 10-12 is an extreme one, but it is still feasible. All the highlighted fields indicate a problem with the cards installed. There is no valid data in the appropriate fields, either "UNKNOWN," all zeroes, or "maxed out" to the size of the space, such as "255.255" for hardware revision.

Example 10-12 *Obtaining router health information from show diagbus.*

```
Router#sh diagbus
 Slot 0:
 UNKNOWN ᴬ port adapter
         Port adapter is analyzed
         Port adapter insertion time unknown
         Hardware revision 255.255 ᴬ       Board revision UNKNOWN ᴬ
         Serial number    4294967295    Part number    800-11534335-255
         Test history     0xFF          RMA number     255-255-255 ᴬ
         EEPROM format version 255
         EEPROM contents (hex):
           0x20: FF 77 FF FF FF FF FF FF FF FF FF FF FF FF FF FF
           0x30: FF FF FF FF FF FF FF FF FF FF FF FF FF FF FF FF
 Slot 1:
 UNKNOWN ᴬ port adapter
         Port adapter is analyzed
         Port adapter insertion time unknown
         Hardware revision 255.255 ᴬ       Board revision UNKNOWN ᴬ
         Serial number    4294967295    Part number    800-11534335-255
         Test history     0xFF          RMA number     255-255-255 ᴬ
         EEPROM format version 255
         EEPROM contents (hex):
           0x20: FF 77 FF FF FF FF FF FF FF FF FF FF FF FF FF FF
           0x30: FF FF FF FF FF FF FF FF FF FF FF FF FF FF FF FF ᴬ
 Slot 2:
         Ethernet port adapter, 4 ports
         Port adapter is analyzed
         Port adapter insertion time unknown
         Hardware revision 0.0 ᴬ           Board revision UNKNOWN ᴬ
         Serial number    0 ᴬ           Part number    00-0000-00 ᴬ
         Test history     0x0           RMA number     00-00-00
         EEPROM format version 0
         EEPROM contents (hex):
           0x20: 00 42 00 00 00 00 00 00 00 00 00 00 00 00 00 00
           0x30: 00 00 00 00 00 00 00 00 00 00 00 00 00 00 00 00
 Slot 3:
         Ethernet port adapter, 4 ports
         Port adapter is analyzed
         Port adapter insertion time unknown
```

Example 10-12   *Obtaining router health information from* **show diagbus**. *(Continued)*

```
        Hardware revision 1.1          Board revision A0
        Serial number    5361301       Part number    800-02027-02
        Test history      0x0          RMA number     00-00-00
        EEPROM format version 1
        EEPROM contents (hex):
            0x20: 01 42 01 01 00 51 CE 95 50 07 EB 02 00 00 00 00
     0x30: 50 00 00 00 97 05 30 00 FF FF FF FF FF FF FF FF
```

SNMP Traps for Router Failure [4]

From MIB CISCO-GENERAL-TRAPS, several SNMP traps are relevant to router failure, as follows:

- reload
- coldStart
- linkdown
- linkUp

A *reload trap* signifies that the sending protocol entity is reinitializing itself so that the agent's configuration or the protocol entity implementation can be altered. This trap uses the values from the MIBS sysUptime and whyReload in its packet generation (varbinds).

A *coldStart trap* signifies that the sending protocol entity is reinitializing itself so that the agent's configuration or the protocol entity implementation may be altered. This trap uses the values from the MIBS sysUptime and whyReload in its packet generation (varbinds).

A *linkDown trap* signifies that the sending protocol entity recognizes a failure in one of the communication links represented in the agent's configuration. This trap uses the values from the MIBs ifIndex, ifDescr, ifType, and locIfReason in its packet generation (varbinds).

A *linkUp trap* signifies that the sending protocol entity recognizes that one of the communication links represented in the agent's configuration has come up. This trap uses the values from the MIBS ifIndex, ifDescr, ifType, and locIfReason in its packet generation (varbinds). From the linkup trap timestamp, you can determine how long a particular interface was down relative to the linkDown trap. This is especially useful when calculating network availability.

Syslog Messages for Router Failure

The messages reported in Table 10-4 represent some of the more common syslog messages. This does not mean that all other messages are not important, but they are seen less frequently. You can use the basic methodology defined with these messages to do correlations with SNMP MIB objects or show commands. The same methodology can be applied to other messages seen in the syslog, which are not reported here. Most of the syslog messages reported here are seen on the high-end routers such as the 7x00 series routers.

The syslog messages have different severity levels, as indicated by the number in the message. The lower the number, the more severe the issue in the router. You should act on severities between 0 and 3 and be aware of messages with severities of 4 through 7.

TIP	It is recommended to use timestamps in syslog to determine when an event occurred. Note that if the device and the syslog server have different clock sources, the times may be slightly different.

Table 10-4   *Syslog Messages for Router Health Information*

Message	Explanation
%SYS-5-RELOAD: Reload requested	A reload or restart was requested, typically issued from the CLI command reload. This message is generated prior to the router resetting.
%SYS-5-RESTART: System restarted - [chars]	This message is seen after the router comes back online after booting up. Based on this message, you can poll the MIB object whyReload to get the reason for the reload, especially if it is an unscheduled reload.
%CBUS-3- CMDTIMEOUT: Cmd timed out, CCB [hex], slot [chars], cmd code [chars]-Traceback= [hex]	A command sent from the system to an interface processor failed to complete successfully. The system recovered by generating an error code to the requester. Copy the error message exactly as it appears on the console or in the system log, call your Cisco technical support representative, and provide the representative with the gathered information. Based on receipt of this syslog message, you can poll the MIB cardOperStatus for the particular interface processor to find out if whether is still operational. Also, executing the CLI command **show diag** or **show controller cbus** can give you an understanding of what is going on with the card. This message is sometimes seen with other messages at the same time, such as RSP-3-oriented messages.

Table 10-4 *Syslog Messages for Router Health Information (Continued)*

Message	Explanation
`%CBUS-3-INITERR: Interface [dec], Error ([hex]), idb [hex] [dec] [chars] - cbus_init()`	The switch processor or ciscoBus controller signaled an error while processing a packet or selecting an interface. This indicates a software problem. Copy the error message exactly as it appears on the console or in the system log. Issue the **show tech-support** command to gather data that may provide information to determine the nature of the error. If you cannot determine the nature of the error from the error message text or from the **show tech-support** output, call your Cisco technical support representative and provide the representative with the gathered information. Looking specifically at the output from **show controller cbus** or **show diag** within the **show tech-support** output can assist you in isolating the problem.
`%CBUS-3-OUTHUNG: [chars]: tx[char] output hung ([hex] - [chars]), [chars]`	This message is commonly seen with hex characters of 800E. You may see support personnel refer to these messages as "800E messages." 800E means that the transmit queue was full at the time a request for a transmit buffer was sent by the RP on that particular interface. The 800E error occurs only if the full state is persistent (tql == 0 && output-hold-queue does not equal NULL several consecutive attempts from IOS). A transmission attempt on an interface failed. The interface might not be attached to a cable or there might be a software problem. Check to see that the interfaces are all connected to the proper cables. Monitor the **show controller cbus** for possible isolation of the problem.
`%RSP-2-QAERROR: [chars] error, [chars] at addr [hex] ([chars]) log [hex], data [hex] [hex]`	A software error was detected during packet switching. This means that an interface freed the same queue element twice (reused) or attempted to free a zero queue element. An error was detected in the queueing hardware. Using the command **show controller cbus** or **show diag** should help you pinpoint the location of the problem.
`%DBUS-3 (All messages)`	All DBUS errors usually indicate a hardware problem with the processor card or with an interface processor card. The recommended course of action when seeing these errors is to replace the problematic card, usually based on the "slot" reported in the DBUS error message. Interface Processor cards are typically in bad shape if you see one of these messages.

Error/Fault Data for Switch Hardware

For fault management in switches, you will depend mainly on the SNMP traps and syslog messages to tell you when hardware issues are arising in the network, versus actively going out and polling MIB objects. However, we will look at some MIB objects that you may want to actively poll for or poll for based on some event correlation, such as a syslog message or defined RMON thresholds exceeded, based on SNMP traps.

MIB Variables for Switch Failures

From MIB CISCO-STACK MIB, the following variables are relevant to switch failures:

- chassisMinorAlarm: A minor alarm varbind within an snmp trap message.
- chassisMajorAlarm: A major alarm varbind within an snmp trap message.

From the moduleTable within the CISCO-STACK MIB:

- moduleStatus: The status of a module within the switch chassis.
- moduleTestResult: The result of a power-on self test for a module within the switch chassis.

Only two of these MIB objects are worth polling: moduleStatus and moduleTestTesult. And they need to be actively polled based on only an SNMP trap or syslog message seen. The other two MIB objects, chassisMajorAlarm and chassisMinorAlarm, are varbinds within the SNMP trap chassisAlarmOn and chassisAlarmOff.

Minor and Major Chassis Alarms

When the system LED status turns to red, a chassisMajorAlarm is generated. When the system LED status turns orange, a chassisMinorAlarm is generated. The trap generated will be a chassisAlarmOn trap. Included with the traps are variables that indicate whether the trap is from a chassisTempAlarm, a chassisMinorAlarm, or a chassisMajorAlarm. Decoding the trap indicates what kind of alarm generated the trap.

A chassisMajorAlarm exhibits one of the following conditions:

1 Any voltage failure

2 Simultaneous Temp and Fan failure

3 100 percent power supply failure (2 out of 2 or 1 out of 1)

4 EEPROM failure

5 NVRAM failure

6 MCP communication failure

7 NMP status "unknown"

A chassisMinorAlarm exhibits one of the following conditions:

1 Temp alarm

2 Fan failure

3 Partial power supply failure (1 out of 2)

4 Two power supplies of incompatible types

Based on appropriate syslog messages or SNMP traps received on your Network Management console, you can determine when you need to actively poll these MIB objects.

CLI Commands for Switch Failure

The following are show commands that can be used to get the same type of data points as the MIB objects mentioned previously for switch health.

Switch Health from show system

The **show system** command for this section will "zoom" in on the system status (Sys-Status) as displayed in the output. Other components seen in this output are power supply, fan, and temperature status. The normal system status should have a value of "ok". The only other value seen here is "faulty," which is based on a particular alarm that triggered, either Major or Minor.

Example 10-13 shows ouput from **show system**, with emphasis on information regarding switch health.

Example 10-13 *Obtaining switch health information from **show system**.*

```
Switch>show system
PS1-Status PS2-Status Fan-Status Temp-Alarm Sys-Status Uptime d,h:m:s Logout
---------- ---------- ---------- ---------- ---------- --------------- --------
ok         none       ok         off        ok A           4,23:06:16     20 min
PS1-Type   PS2-Type   Modem      Baud  Traffic Peak Peak-Time
---------- ---------- -------    ----- ------- ---- ------------------------
WS-C5508   none       disable 9600    0%      0% Wed Apr 21 1999, 15:57:24
System Name             System Location          System Contact
------------------     ------------------------  ------------------------
```

"Sys-Status" (A) displays the current state of the switch based on the "health" of the processor. If there are any alarms triggered that are power-, temperature- or fan-related, the Sys-Status would be affected, in addition to the other variables. Think of the Sys-Status as the main reporting mechanism for the switch as a whole.

Switch Health from show module

This command allows you to see what kind of card is installed in the switch chassis and what the status is of the line cards or supervisor cards. You can also get the module, number of ports, card model, serial number, hardware version, firmware version, and software version from this output. You can also see from this output any sub-model types typically installed on the supervisor card, such as the netflow feature card (NFFC) or the uplink modules. This data is especially prevalent on the newer Supervisor cards (Supervisor III or WS-X5530).

The focus for Example 10-14 is on the individual module Status column.

Example 10-14 *Obtaining switch health information from* ***show module***.

```
Switch> sh module
Mod Module-Name        Ports Module-Type           Model     Serial-Num Status
--- ------------------ ----- --------------------- --------- --------- -------
1                      2     100BaseFX MMF Supervi  WS-X5530  011437543 ok A
2                      2     MM MIC FDDI            WS-X5101  003397731 ok A
6                      12    10/100BaseTX Ethernet  WS-X5213  003974709 ok A
Mod MAC-Address(es)                          Hw    Fw        Sw
--- --------------------------------------- ----- --------- -----------------
1   00-e0-4f-73-8e-00 to 00-e0-4f-73-91-ff 2.0   3.1.2     4.5(1)
2   00-60-3e-cd-55-6c                       1.1   1.1       3.1(1)
6   00-60-83-5d-8a-ec to 00-60-83-5d-8a-f7 1.0   1.4       4.5(1)
Mod Sub-Type Sub-Model Sub-Serial Sub-Hw
--- -------- --------- ---------- ------
1   NFFC     WS-F5521  0011437958 1.1
1   uplink   WS-U5533  0008588482 1.0
Mod SMT User-Data                T-Notify CF-St    ECM-St    Bypass
--- ------------------------     -------- -------- --------- -------
2   WorkGroup Stack              30       c-Wrap-B in        absent
```

The "Status" column (A) shows you the current state of the module. It can be one of the following values: ok, disable, faulty, other, standby, or error. If there is a "faulty" condition on the module, you can issue the **show log** or **show test** [*mod_num*] command to see why it is faulty.

SNMP Traps for Switch Failure

From MIBCISCO-STACK-MIB TRAPS, several SNMP traps are relevant to switch failure:

- chassisAlarmOn
- chassisAlarmOff
- moduleDown
- moduleUp

A chassisAlarmOn trap signifies that the agent entity has detected the chassisTempAlarm, chassisMinorAlarm, or chassisMajorAlarm object, and this MIB has transitioned to the on(2) state. The generation of this trap can be controlled by the sysEnableChassisTraps object in this MIB or by using the CLI command **set snmp trap enable chassis**.

A chassisAlarmOff trap signifies that the agent entity has detected the chassisTempAlarm, chassisMinorAlarm, or chassisMajorAlarm object, and this MIB has transitioned to the off(1) state. The generation of this trap can be controlled by the sysEnableChassisTraps object in this MIB or by using the CLI command **set snmp trap enable chassis**.

A moduleDown trap signifies that the agent entity has detected that the moduleStatus object in this MIB has transitioned out of the ok(2) state for one of its modules. The generation of this trap can be controlled by the sysEnableModuleTraps object in this MIB or by using the CLI command **set snmp trap enable module**.

Refer to the Chassis Alarm MIBs previously discussed for an explanation of when a certain trap would be seen.

A moduleUp trap signifies that the agent entity has detected that the moduleStatus object in this MIB has transitioned to the ok(2) state for one of its modules. The generation of this trap can be controlled by the sysEnableModuleTraps object in this MIB or by using the CLI command **set snmp trap enable chassis**.

Syslog Messages for Switch Failure

The syslog functionality was first introduced to the Catalyst series switches in software release 2.4. Table 10-5 summarizes only those messages that apply to hardware and to the variables already discussed in this section.

TIP	It is recommended to turn on timestamps on the log messages so you can correlate events to issues in the network. Using the command **set logging timestamp enable** will turn on the timestamps for the log messages.

Table 10-5 *Syslog Messages for Switch Health Information*

Message	Explanation
SYS-3- MOD_FAILREASO N: Module [dec] failed due to [chars][chars][chars] [chars]	This message indicates that the module [dec] has failed because of [chars]. [dec] is the module number and [chars] is one of the following: CPU Initialization Error, Memory Test Failed, Boot Checksum Verification Failed, SPROM Checksum Verification Failed, EOBC Loopback Test Failed, LTL-A Error, Flash Erase/Write Error, Pinnacle CBL Error, Pinnacle Packet Buffer Error, Pinnacle TLB Error, or Unknown or Undocumented Error. The first [chars] line is Ports disabled if the module is a non-ATM/Route Switch Module (RSM) (non-IOS). The second [chars] line is a description of the module type configured in NVRAM. The third [chars] line is a description of the module type inserted in the slot. Execute the CLI command **show test** [*mod_num*] to see what specifically failed.

Table 10-5 *Syslog Messages for Switch Health Information*

`SYS-3-`
`MOD_MINORFAIL`
`: Minor`
`problem in`
`module [dec]`
	This message indicates that a module [dec] failed the self-test; [dec] is the module number. Execute the CLI command **show test** [*mod_num*] to see what specifically failed.

`SYS-3-`
`MOD_FAIL:`
`Module [dec]`
`failed to`
`come online`
	This message indicates that module [dec] failed to come online; [dec] is the module number. Execute the CLI command **show module** to see the status of the module.

`SYS-5-`
`MOD_INSERT:`
`Module [dec]`
`has been`
`Inserted`
	This message indicates that module [dec] was inserted; [dec] is the module number. This message is provided for information only. If a module is inserted and the message does not appear, this might indicate a problem. Enter the **show module** or **show port** [*mod_num/port_num*] command to verify that the system has acknowledged the module and brought it online.

`SYS-5-`
`MOD_REMOVE:`
`Module [dec]`
`has been`
`Removed`
	This message indicates that module [dec] was removed; [dec] is the module number. This message is provided for information only. If a module is removed and the message does not appear, this might indicate a problem. Enter the **show port** [*mod_num/port_num*] command to query the module. The system should respond as follows: Module n is not installed.

`SYS-5-`
`SYS_RESET:`
`System reset`
`from`
`[chars]`
	This message indicates that the system was reset from [chars]; [chars] is a console number if the request is from a console session or IP address if the request is from a Telnet session or SNMP.

`SYS-5-MOD_OK:`
`Module [dec]`
`is online`
	This message indicates that module [dec] passed diagnostic self-test and is online; [dec] is the module number. Usually seen after the SYS-5-SYS_RESET message occurs if modules are working properly.

Error/Fault Data for Router Environmental Characteristics

We'll specifically look at the high-end routers, such as the 7x00 series, since that is where most, if not all the environmental characteristics are reported. Tables 10-6 through 10-13 summarize the environmental specifications (temperature and voltages) of each router type (7500 series and 7200 series). Subsequent sections look at the MIBs and data points to monitor for those values.

The router also reports fan status messages, but we will not go into those messages specifically because you'll start to see a pattern in the voltages and temperature monitoring. You can apply the same methodology to the fan status.

Table 10-6   *Typical Processor-Monitored Temperature Thresholds (Cisco 7505)*

Parameter	Warning	Normal	Warning	Critical	Shutdown
Inlet Air	< 10° C	10–39° C	39–46° C	46–64° C	> 64° C
Airflow	<10°C	10–70° C	70–77° C	77–88° C	> 88° C

Table 10-7   *Typical Power Supply-Monitored Voltage Thresholds (Cisco 7505)*

Parameter	Critical	Normal	Critical
+5VDC	< 4.74	4.74-5.26	> 5.26
+12VDC	< 10.20	10.20 to 13.8	> 13.80
–12VDC	> –10.20	–10.20 to –13.80	< –13.80
+24VDC	< 20.00	20.00 to 28.00	> 28.00

Table 10-8   *Typical Processor-Monitored Temperature Thresholds (Cisco 7507)*

Parameter	Normal	High Warning	High Critical	Shutdown
Inlet	10–40° C	44° C	50° C	-
Hotpoint	10–40° C	54° C	60° C	-
Exhaust	10–40° C	-	-	-
Processors	-	-	-	70° C
Power Supply	-	-	-	75° C
Restart	40° C	-	-	-

Table 10-9   *Typical Power Supply-Monitored DC-Voltage Thresholds (Cisco 7507)*

Parameter	Normal	Low Critical	Low Warning	High Warning	High Critical
+5VDC	4.74 to 5.26	4.49	4.74	5.25	5.52
+12VDC	10.20 to 13.8	10.90	11.61	12.82	13.38
–12VDC	–10.20 to –13.80	–10.15	–10.76	–13.25	–13.86
+24VDC	20.00 to 28.00	19.06	21.51	26.51	28.87

Table 10-10 *Typical Processor-Monitored Temperature Thresholds (Cisco 7513)*

Parameter	Normal	High Warning	High Critical	Shutdown
Inlet	10–40° C	44° C	50° C	-
Hotpoint	10–40° C	54° C	60° C	-
Exhaust	10–40° C	-	-	-
Processors	-	-	-	70° C
Power Supply	-	-	-	75° C
Restart	40° C	-	-	-

Table 10-11 *Typical Power Supply-Monitored DC-Voltage Thresholds (Cisco 7513)*

Parameter	Normal	Low Critical	Low Warning	High Warning	High Critical
+5VDC	4.74 to 5.26	4.49	4.74	5.25	5.52
+12VDC	10.20 to 13.8	10.76	11.37	12.64	13.24
–12VDC	–10.20 to –13.80	–10.15	–10.76	–13.25	–13.86
+24VDC	20.00 to 28.00	19.06	21.51	26.51	28.87

Table 10-12 *Typical Processor-Monitored Temperature Thresholds (7200 Series: NPE-100, NPE-150, and NPE-200)*

Parameter	High Warning	High Critical	Shutdown
NPE-100 or NPE-200			
Chassis inlet	04° F (40° C)	122° F (50° C)	-
Chassis outlet 1	109° F (43° C)	127° F (53° C)	136° F (58° C)
Chassis outlet 2	167° F (75° C)	167° F (75° C)	-
Chassis outlet 3	122° F (50° C)	140° F (60° C)	149° F (65° C)
NPE-150			
Chassis inlet	04° F (40° C)	122° F (50° C)	-
Chassis outlet 1	109° F (43° C)	127° F (53° C)	136° F (58° C)
Chassis outlet 2	167° F (75° C)	167° F (75° C)	-
Chassis outlet 3	131° F (55° C)	149° F (65° C)	158° F (70° C)

Table 10-13 *Typical Power Supply-Monitored DC-Voltage Thresholds (7200 Series)*

Parameter	Low Critical	Low Warning	High Warning	High Critical
+3.45V	+3.26V	+3.34V	+3.55V	+3.63V
+5.15V	+4.86V	+4.99V	+5.31V	+5.43V
+12.15V	+11.39V	+11.67V	+12.62V	+12.91V
−11.95V	−9.52V	−10.73V	−13.16V	−14.38V

MIB Variables for Voltages (Power Supply)

From CISCO-ENVMON MIB, the following variables are relevant to voltages:

- ciscoEnvMonVoltageStatusDescr: The state of the voltage characteristics in a router.

- ciscoEnvMonVoltageState: Can have one of the following values: normal, Warning, Critical, Shutdown, or notPresent.

- ciscoEnvMonVoltageStatusValue: The actual voltage value.

From these MIB objects, you can identify the state of the voltage settings on the router. It may not be necessary to constantly go poll these MIB objects, but to go poll only the objects when an SNMP trap is received. These three values are used as varbinds in the ciscoEnvMonVoltageNotification Trap message. After the trap is received, you may want to go out and poll the node for awhile, especially if it exceeds a threshold setting defined in Table 10-14.

Table 10-14 summarizes the recommended baseline thresholds for voltage]

Table 10-14 *Voltage Threshold—7x00 Series Routers*

Router Type	Low Voltage Threshold (Volts DC)				High Voltage Threshold (Volts DC)			
	+5 +3.45 (7200)	+12 +5.15 (7200)	−12 +12.15 (7200)	+24 −11.95 (7200)	+5 +3.45 (7200)	+12 +5.15 (7200)	-12 +12.15 (7200)	+24 −11.95 (7200)
7505	< 4.74	< 10.20	> −10.20	< 20.00	> 5.26	> 13.80	< −13.80	> 28.00
7507	< 4.74	< 11.61	> −10.76	< 21.51	> 5.25	> 12.82	< −13.25	> 26.51
7513	< 4.74	< 11.37	> −13.25	< 21.51	> 5.25	> 12.64	< −13.25	> 26.51
7200	< 3.34	< 4.99	< 11.67	> −10.73	> 3.55	> 5.31	> 12.62	< −13.16

Related MIB objects from CISCO-ENVMON MIB are as follows:

- ciscoEnvMonVoltageThresholdLow
- ciscoEnvMonVoltageThresholdHigh
- ciscoEnvMonVoltageLastShutdown

CLI Commands for Voltages

The following are show commands relating to environmental characteristics of a router. These values are comparable to the data points gathered from the MIB variables previously mentioned.

Router Environment from show env all

If you include the keyword "all" at the end of the **show env** command, the output reported is what the voltages are currently measured at. The threshold settings are not displayed in this output. All environmental characteristics are updated every 60 seconds for CLI reporting.

Example 10-15 focuses on the voltage readings from **show env all** output.

Example 10-15 *Obtaining router voltage information with **show env all**.*

```
Router# show env all
Environmental Statistics
  Environmental status as of Wed 5-10-1995 19:10:41
  Data is 31 second(s) old, refresh in 29 second(s)
  WARNING: Fan has reached CRITICAL level
  Power Supply: 1200W AC
  No Intermittent Powerfails
  +12 volts measured at  12.00(V) A
   +5 volts measured at   5.02(V) A
  -12 volts measured at -12.05(V) A
  +24 volts measured at  23.70(V) A
  Airflow temperature measured at 35
  Inlet   temperature measured at 26
Arbiter type 1, backplane type 7513 (id 2)
Power supply #1 is 1200W AC (id 1), power supply #2 is removed (id 7)
Active fault conditions: Blower #3
Fan speed is 50%
Active trip points: none
15 of 15 soft shutdowns remaining before hard shutdown
```

The router reports the current 4 DC voltages (A). The 7200 series uses different voltage data points, as indicated in Table 10-13. These values are updated every minute.

Router Environment from show env table

This command reports the threshold settings for the appropriate router's environmental characteristics. It reports the values seen in Table 10-14. The thresholds are categorized as either Warning or Critical.

Example 10-16 focuses on the voltage readings available from **show env table**.

Example 10-16   *Obtaining router voltage readings with **show env table**.*

```
Router# show env table
Sample Point    LowCritical     LowWarning      HighWarning     HighCritical
RSP(2) Inlet       44C/111F       50C/122F
RSP(2) Hotpoint             54C/129F       60C/140F
RSP(2) Exhaust    101C/213F      101C/213C
RSP(3) Inlet       44C/111F       50C/122F
RSP(3) Hotpoint             54C/129F       60C/140F
RSP(3) Exhaust    101C/213F      101C/213F
+12 Voltage       10.90   11.61      12.82      13.38 A
+5 Voltage         4.49              4.74        5.25           5.52 A
-12 Voltage      -10.15            -10.76      -13.25         -13.86 A
+24 Voltage       19.06             21.51       26.51          28.87 A
Shutdown boards at            101C/213F
Shutdown power supplies at    101C/213F
```

All the threshold settings are reported here, both Warning and Critical. Table 10-14 reports everything that exceeds the Warning level because an SNMP trap will be generated when the Warning threshold is exceeded.

SNMP Traps for Voltages

From CISCO-ENVMON MIB, the ciscoEnvMonVoltageNotification trap is relevant to voltages.

A ciscoEnvMonVoltageNotification is sent if the voltage measured at a given testpoint is outside the normal range for the testpoint (that is, at the Warning, Critical, or Shutdown stage). Because such a notification is usually generated before the Shutdown state is reached, it can convey more data and has a better chance of being sent than does the ciscoEnvMonShutdownNotification. The ciscoEnvMonVoltageStatusDescr, ciscoEnvMonVoltageStatusValue, and ciscoEnvMonVoltageState MIB variables are used as the varbinds or variables within this SNMP trap message.

Syslog Messages for Voltages

Some of the environmental syslog messages may start with "ENV" or "ENVM," depending on the IOS running on the router or router platform. They are summarized in Table 10-15.

Table 10-15   *Syslog Messages for Router Environment Information*

Message	Explanation
%ENV-2-VOLTAGE: [chars] testpoint measured [chars]. Shutdown margin is [chars]	The ENV card indicates the voltage it is measuring (for example, +5, +12, –5, –12), the amount of voltage that it measured, and the voltage at which the processor will shut down the system.
%ENV-1-SHUTDOWN: Environmental Monitor initiated shutdown	One of the environmental measurements reached Shutdown status. The system is about to shut down the processor to prevent damage to the hardware.

MIB Variables for Temperature

From CISCO-ENVMON MIB, the following variables are relevant to temperature:

- ciscoEnvMonTemperatureStatusDescr
- ciscoEnvMonTemperatureStatusValue
- ciscoEnvMonTemperatureState

The latter can have one of the following values: normal, Warning, Critical, Shutdown, or notPresent.

From these MIB objects, you can identify the state of the temperature settings on the router. It may not be necessary to constantly go poll these MIB objects, but to only go poll the objects when an SNMP trap is received. These three values are used in the ciscoEnvMonTemperatureNotification Trap message as varbinds. After the trap is received, you may want to go out and poll the node for awhile, especially if it exceeds a threshold setting defined in Table 10-16.

Table 10-16 summarizes the recommended baseline thresholds for temperature. Table 10-17 summarizes the temperatures that will cause the router to shut down.

Table 10-16   *Temperature Threshold—7x00 Series Routers*

Router Type	Low Temperature Threshold (Celsius - C°)				High Temperature Threshold (Celsius - C°)			
	Inlet	Airflow	Outlet	Hotpoint	Inlet	Airflow	Outlet *	Hotpoint
7505	< 10°	< 10°	-	-	> 39 °	> 70 °	-	-
7507	-	-	-	-	>= 44°	-	-	>= 54°
7513	-	-	-	-	>= 44°	-	-	>= 54°
7200*	-	-	-	-	> 39°	-	> 42° > 49° > 74°	-

* 7200 Series outlet temperature thresholds range from 43 C° to 75 C°, depending on the outlet point 1, 2, or 3.

Table 10-17   *Shutdown Temperature Threshold—7x00 Series Routers*

Router Type	Inlet (in C°)	Airflow (in C°)	Processors (in C°)	Power Supply (in C°)	Outlet * (in C°)
7505	> 64°	> 88°	-	-	-
7507	-	-	70°	75°	-
7513	°	-	70°	75°	-
7200*	-	-	-	-	58° 65° 70°

* 7200 Series outlet shutdown temperature thresholds range from 58 C° to 70 C°, depending on the outlet point 1 or 3 and NPE type (100, 150, or 200).

Related MIB objects fromCISCO-ENVMON are the following:

- ciscoEnvMonTemperatureThreshold
- ciscoEnvMonTemperatureLastShutdown

CLI Commands for Temperature

Two show commands that provide data relating to temperature statistics are **show env all** and **show env table**.

Router Temperature Information from show env all

If you use the keyword "all" at the end of the show env command, the output reported is what the temperatures are currently measured at. The threshold settings are not displayed in this output. All environmental characteristics are updated every 60 seconds for CLI reporting.

Example 10-17 focuses on temperature data supplied by **show env all**.

Example 10-17 *Obtaining router temperature information with **show env all**.*

```
Router# show env all
Environmental Statistics
  Environmental status as of Wed 5-10-1995 19:10:41
  Data is 31 second(s) old, refresh in 29 second(s)
  WARNING: Fan has reached CRITICAL level
  Power Supply: 1200W AC
  No Intermittent Powerfails
  +12 volts measured at  12.00(V)
   +5 volts measured at   5.02(V)
  -12 volts measured at -12.05(V)
  +24 volts measured at  23.70(V)
  Airflow temperature measured at 35 A
  Inlet   temperature measured at 26 A
Arbiter type 1, backplane type 7513 (id 2)
Power supply #1 is 1200W AC (id 1), power supply #2 is removed (id 7)
Active fault conditions: Blower #3
Fan speed is 50%
Active trip points: none
15 of 15 soft shutdowns remaining before hard shutdown
```

The current Inlet and Airflow temperature (A) is reported in this output. If there is a fault in the temperature, you will see the fault here, just as you see a warning for the fan in the beginning of this sample output. Table 10-16 reports everything that exceeds the Warning level because an SNMP trap will be generated when the warning threshold is exceeded. Table 10-17 reports the temperature where the routers will shut down.

Router Temperature Information from show env table

This command reports the threshold settings for the appropriate router's environmental characteristics. It reports the values seen in Table 10-16 and Table 10-17. The thresholds are categorized as Warning, Critical, or Shutdown.

Example 10-18 shows output from **show env table**, with emphasis on temperature values.

Example 10-18   *Obtaining router termperature information with show env table.*

```
Router# show env table
Sample Point        LowCritical     LowWarning        HighWarning       HighCritical
RSP(2) Inlet        44C/111F        50C/122F  A
RSP(2) Hotpoint     54C/129F        60C/140F  A
RSP(2) Exhaust      101C/213F       101C/213C A
RSP(3) Inlet        44C/111F        50C/122F  A
RSP(3) Hotpoint     54C/129F        60C/140F  A
RSP(3) Exhaust      101C/213F       101C/213F A
+12 Voltage         10.90           11.61             12.82             13.38
+5 Voltage          4.49            4.74              5.25              5.52
-12 Voltage         -10.15          -10.76            -13.25            -13.86
+24 Voltage         19.06           21.51             26.51             28.87
Shutdown boards at              101C/213F  B
Shutdown power supplies at      101C/213F  B
```

Following are the annotated highlights of Example 10-18:

A All the temperature threshold settings are reported for each temperature data point on the router. The Fahrenheit values are also reported in addition to the Celsius values. These values match Table 10-16 values.

B The shutdown values are reported for the power supplies, Processor boards, Airflow, or Inlet temperature. These values are the extreme values at which the routers will shut down. The shutdown values in Table 10-17 are the high-end values used so that SNMP trap messages can still be sent to inform of an imminent shutdown. The trap ciscoEnvMonShutdownNotification is sent when the values in Table 10-16 are met.

SNMP Traps for Temperature

From CISCO-ENVMON MIB, the ciscoEnvMonTemperatureNotification trap is relevant to temperature. This trap is sent if the temperature measured at a given testpoint is outside the normal range for the testpoint (that is, it is at the Warning, Critical, or Shutdown stage). Because such a notification is usually generated before the Shutdown state is reached, it can convey more data and has a better chance of being sent than does ciscoEnvMonShutdownNotification. The ciscoEnvMonTemperatureStatusDescr, ciscoEnvMonTemperatureStatusValue, and ciscoEnvMonTemperatureState MIB variables are used as the varbinds or variables within this SNMP trap message.

Syslog Messages for Temperature

Table 10-18 summarizes the syslog messages related to temperature. Some of the environmental syslog messages may start with "ENV" or "ENVM," depending on the IOS running on the router or router platform.

Table 10-18 *Syslog Messages for Router Temperature Information*

Message	Explanation
`%ENV-2-TEMP: Ambient temperature measured [chars]. Shutdown at [chars]`	The ENV card indicates the temperature it measured and the temperature at which it shuts down.
`%ENV-1-SHUTDOWN: Environmental Monitor initiated shutdown`	One of the environmental measurements reached SHUTDOWN status. The system is about to shut down the processor to prevent damage to the hardware.

Error/Fault Data for Switch Environmental Characteristics

The following section looks at the switch environmental characteristics such as power supply statistics, temperature status, and fan status. We'll identify some MIBs as well as some show commands to identify the data points for these variables.

MIB Variables for Voltages (Power Supply) and Fan

From CISCO-STACK MIB, the following variables provide voltage and fan data for switches:

- chassisPs1Type
- chassisPs1Status
- chassisPs1TestResult
- chassisPs2Type
- chassisPs2Status
- chassisPs2TestResult

These MIBs indicate the type of power supplies installed in the chassis as well as their statuses. There are unique MIBs for each power supply installed, either power supply 1 or 2.

The status MIBs report either an ok status, a minorFault status, or a majorFault status. If the status is not ok, the value of TestResult MIBs give more detailed information about the power supply's failure condition(s). Polling these variables is a lot more flexible than actively polling the router's environmental variables. Specifically, if an alarm is triggered, then you can actively poll the TestResult MIBs to get a reason why a failure occurred. If the statuses are flagged as a minor or major fault, it triggers the appropriate chassisMinorAlarm or chassisMajorAlarm, thus triggering the chassisAlarmOn SNMP trap.

Table 10-19 summarizes the recommended baseline thresholds for voltages:

Table 10-19   *Power-Supply-Monitored Voltage Thresholds*

Parameter	Alarm	Normal	Alarm
+5V	< 4.74V	4.74–5.26V	> 5.26V
+12V	< 11.40V	11.40–12.60V	> 12.60V
+24V	< 20.00V	20.00–30.00V	> 30.00V

Related MIB objects from MIB CISCO-STACK are the following:

- chassisMinorAlarm
- chassisMajorAlarm
- chassisFanStatus
- chassisFanTestResult

Voltage and Fan Information via show system

The **show system** command can be used to zoom in on the power supply status (PS1-Status and PS2-Status) and fan status. The normal status of the power supplies is ok or none if no redundant power supply is installed. The failed values are either fan failed or faulty, which triggers either a major or minor alarm. The normal status for the fan is ok—anything else is a fault with the fan. Example 10-19 shows output from a show system command.

Example 10-19   *Obtaining power supply and fan status information with **show system**.*

```
Switch>show system
PS1-Status PS2-Status Fan-Status Temp-Alarm Sys-Status Uptime d,h:m:s Logout
---------- ---------- ---------- ---------- ---------- -------------- --------
okA        none A      ok B       off        ok         4,23:06:16      20 min
PS1-Type   PS2-Type   Modem  Baud  Traffic Peak Peak-Time
---------- ---------- ------- ----- ------- ---- -------------------------
WS-C5508 C none C      disable 9600  0%      0% Wed Apr 21 1999, 15:57:24
System Name           System Location          System Contact
---------------------- ------------------------ -------------------------
```

Following are annotated highlights of Example 10-19:

A The "PS-Status" columns display the current state of the power supplies installed in the switch. The possible values are ok, none, fan failed, or faulty.

B The "Fan-Status" column displays the current state of the fan installed in the switch. The possible values are ok, faulty, or other.

C The "PS-Type" columns display kind of power supplies installed in the switch chassis. If no redundancy is used, one of the types will be "none".

SNMP Traps for Voltage and Fan Information

From CISCO-STACK-MIB TRAPS, two SNMP traps are relevant to voltage and fan information:

- chassisAlarmOn
- chassisAlarmOff

A chassisAlarmOn trap signifies that the agent entity has detected the chassisTempAlarm, chassisMinorAlarm, or chassisMajorAlarm object, and this MIB has transitioned to the on(2) state. The generation of this trap can be controlled by the sysEnableChassisTraps object in this MIB or by using the CLI command set snmp trap enable chassis.

A chassisAlarmOff trap signifies that the agent entity has detected the chassisTempAlarm, chassisMinorAlarm, or chassisMajorAlarm object, and this MIB has transitioned to the off(1) state. The generation of this trap can be controlled by the sysEnableChassisTraps object in this MIB or by using the CLI command set snmp trap enable chassis.

Syslog Messages for Voltage and Fan Information[1]

Table 10-20 summarizes the syslog messages from the switch that relate to the voltage and fan statistics.

Table 10-20 *Syslog Messages for Switch Voltage and Fan Information*

Message	Explanation
`SYS-2-PS_OK: Power supply [dec] okay`	This message indicates that the power supply has been turned on or has returned to a proper state; [dec] is the power supply number.
`SYS-2-PS_FAIL: Power supply [dec] Failed`	This message indicates that the power supply [dec] failed; [dec] is the power supply number. Replace the indicated power supply.
`SYS-2-PS_FANFAIL: Power supply [dec] fan failed`	This message indicates that the power supply [dec] fan failed; [dec] is the power supply number. Replace the indicated power supply fan.

---

[1]. Message and Recovery Procedures; http://www.cisco.com/univercd/cc/td/doc/product/lan/cat5000/rel_4_5/sys_msg/emsg.htm

Table 10-20 *Syslog Messages for Switch Voltage and Fan Information (Continued)*

`SYS-2-PS_NFANFAIL:`
`Power supply [dec]`
`and power supply`
`fan failed`
	This message indicates that the power supply [dec] and power supply fan failed; [dec] is the power supply number. Replace the indicated power supply and fan.

`SYS-2-FAN_OK: Fan` `okay`	This message indicates that the chassis fan tray was plugged back in or returned to a proper state.
`SYS-2-FAN_FAIL: Fan` `failed`	This message indicates that the chassis fan failed. Replace the fan.

MIB Variables for Temperature

From CISCO-STACK MIB, the chassisTempAlarm MIB indicates the temperature alarm status as off, on, or critical. Refer to Table 10-16 for the temperature thresholds.

The temperature alarm status is not an object typically actively polled because the SNMP trap chassisAlarmOn uses this variable as a varbind, unlike the power supply and Fan MIBs. Treat this MIB just like the router environmental MIBs. Use the SNMP trap as the way to determine the temperature status; "only notify me when it is an issue."

Table 10-21 shows the recommended baseline threshold for temperature:

Table 10-21 *Processor-Monitored Temperature Thresholds [2]*

Parameter	Normal	Alarm
Airflow	10–55° C	> 55° C

[2] Catalyst 5000 Series Power Supply Configuration Notes; http://www.cisco.com/univercd/cc/td/doc/product/lan/cat5000/cnfg_nts/hw_cns/2236_01.htm

Temperature Information via show system

Example 10-20 emphasizes the temperature alarm status (Temp-Alarm) as displayed in **show system** output.

Example 10-20 *Obtaining temperature information with **show system**.*

```
Switch>show system
PS1-Status PS2-Status Fan-Status Temp-Alarm Sys-Status Uptime d,h:m:s Logout
---------- ---------- ---------- ---------- ---------- -------------- --------
ok         none       ok         off A       ok         4,23:06:16     20 min
PS1-Type   PS2-Type   Modem  Baud  Traffic Peak Peak-Time
---------- ---------- ------- ----- ------- ---- -------------------------
```

continues

Example 10-20   *Obtaining temperature information with **show system**. (Continued)*

```
WS-C5508    none      disable  9600   0%     0% Wed Apr 21 1999, 15:57:24
System Name               System Location        System Contact
-------------------- ------------------------- -------------------------
```

The "Temp-Alarm" column (A) is either "on" or "off". The normal state is off. If it is on, look for an SNMP trap chassisAlarmOn with a value of contained from chassisTempAlarm, either on or critical.

SNMP Traps for Temperature Information

The chassisAlarmOn and chassisAlarmOff traps can be useful in obtaining temperature information. See the earlier section, "SNMP Traps for Voltage and Fan Information," for a description of these traps.

Syslog Messages for Temperature Information

Table 10-22 summarizes syslog messages that provide temperature information for switches.

Table 10-22   *Syslog Messages for Switch Temperature Information*

Message	Explanation
`SYS-0-TEMP_CRITOK: Temp critical okay`	This message indicates the temperature is under 50° C (122° F); this message applies only to the redundant supervisor engine in the switch.
`SYS-0-TEMP_CRITFAIL: Temp critical Failure`	This message indicates the temperature is above 70° C (158° F). The system automatically powers down after five minutes; this message applies only to the redundant supervisor engine in the switch. The recommended actions are to power down the system and contact your technical support representative.
`SYS-0-TEMP_CRITRECOVER: Temp critical Recovered`	This message indicates the temperature dropped below 70° C (158° F), and the automatic powerdown was canceled; this message applies only to the redundant supervisor engine in the switch.
`SYS-2-TEMP_HIGHOK: Temp high okay`	This message indicates that the temperature returned to a normal state 20° C-40° C (68° F–104° F).
`SYS-2-TEMP_HIGHFAIL: Temp high failure`	This message indicates that the temperature is between 40° C –50° C (104° F–122° F); this message applies only to the redundant supervisor engine in the switch.

Summary

This chapter identified the key hardware and environmental characteristics of the routers and Catalyst switches. We looked at performance management of the hardware by identifying the types of cards and the positioning of the cards in the chassis and related it to the architecture of the device. We looked at specific data points that could affect the hardware performance, such as hardware version and microcode version. Actively updating your inventory through polling the recommended MIBs after a change management window can greatly increase your network's stability and your knowledge of the network.

We looked at how to monitor faults in the network relating to hardware and environmental characteristics. One thing unique about error/fault monitoring of these characteristics is that you depend more on syslog and SNMP trap messages than on actively polling the MIB variables. With so much hardware out there in the network and a low percentage of environmental failures, it makes sense to let the device tell you when an issue arises instead of always asking the device "Are you OK?" just to get a response of "Yes, I'm OK." Relying on syslog and trap messages also reduces the amount of overhead on the network compared to polling these characteristics. The following chapters do not lend themselves to this kind of methodology. Instead, you'll find that most of the chapters in Part 2 of this book concern some kind of active polling.

References

Internet Resources

Catalyst 5000 Series Product Overview

> http://www.cisco.com/univercd/cc/td/doc/product/lan/cat5000/hardware/installg/01intro.htm

Catalyst 5000 Series Power Supply Configuration Notes

> http://www.cisco.com/univercd/cc/td/doc/product/lan/cat5000/cnfg_nts/hw_cns/2236_01.htm

CISCO-GENERAL TRAPS.my

> http://www.cisco.com/public/mibs/v1/CISCO-GENERAL-TRAPS.my

CISCO-STACK-MIB.my

> http://www.cisco.com/public/mibs/v1/CISCO-STACK-MIB-V1SMI.my

Message and Recovery Procedures

> http://www.cisco.com/univercd/cc/td/doc/product/lan/cat5000/rel_4_5/sys_msg/emsg.htm

Preparing for Installation (7500 Series)

http://www.cisco.com/univercd/cc/td/doc/product/core/cis7505/cicg7500/
cicg75pi.htm

CHAPTER 11

Monitoring Network Systems—Processes and Resources

This chapter is geared toward analyzing the processes and resources in the IOS-based router hardware and Catalyst series switches with respect to performance and fault/error management. We first look at performance variables and then identify the fault and error management variables that apply to these systems. This analysis specifically looks at objects and values relating to the following:

- CPU usage
- Backplane utilization
- Memory
- Buffers

We apply and correlate the appropriate MIBs, CLI commands, traps, and syslog messages with these variables. Specific correlations are drawn under each section between the different MIB objects, CLI output, SNMP traps, and syslog messages. There are certain objects and values that can only be collected either by an SNMP MIB or by a CLI command, not both. These data points are identified. After reading this chapter, you should have a good understanding of what to monitor, when to monitor, and how to monitor these different components in Cisco devices.

This chapter includes the following topics:

- An overview of processor characteristics
- Performance data relevant to router processors
- Performance data relevant to switch processors
- Error and fault data relevant to router processors
- Error and fualt data relevant to switch processors

Overview of Processor Characteristics

Before delving into management details, we need to review the basic architecture of a Cisco router and Catalyst switch.

NOTE   Please note that not all platforms are covered in this chapter due to the lack of public information available at the time of this writing. For more details regarding other Cisco platforms, such as the 12000 series routers or the 6000 and 8500 series Catalyst switches, refer to Cisco Connection Online, or CCO, and the product literature. The purpose of this chapter is not to educate you on the architecture, but to give you a general understanding about what is important when looking at performance and fault management.

Router Processors

Because each Cisco router model acts differently, depending on processor speed and features, a useful first step in this overview is to identify what is common to all platforms and pinpoint some of the differences.

The most common variable on the processors is the IOS, or the software running on the router. All Cisco routers run IOS software, except for the 700 series access routers. The majority of the MIBs and CLI (command-line interface) commands for all IOS-based routers give you roughly the same output format across all platforms. There are additional features on certain routers that relate only to that platform. For example, the Netflow feature is supported only on the 7200 and 7500 series routers, whereas only the 2500 series routers support all nine groups of RMON.

The processors on routers contain system DRAM memory, shared (I/O) memory (platform-specific), flash memory, NVRAM, MAC addresses for the interfaces, and environmental monitoring statistics. On high-end routers, such as the 7xxx series, shared (I/O) memory is either broken out from system DRAM memory, SRAM (RSP4), or by a separate card called the SP (or switch processor), as seen in the 7000 series routers. Mid-range and low-end routers, such as the 4xxx, 2500, 2600, 3600, and 1600 series, have separate I/O memory from system memory, either physically on a different DRAM chip or partitioned independently on the system memory DRAM chip. More details regarding memory follow later in the section entitled "Router Memory."

Some interface processors on the high-end routers have their own processor and memory. These cards are called *VIPs*, or *versatile interface processors*, and are supported on the RSP platform routers. A subset of the IOS is loaded on these cards from the main IOS image residing on the main RSP. The memory installed on these cards is allocated to the data packets coming and going from the individual port adapters installed on the VIP. The more detailed statistics for these cards, such as diagnostics, are accessible through a Telnet session via the RSP, using the CLI command **if-con <slot>**. if-con presents the user with an interface similar to that of the CLI prompt. From that prompt, you can execute show commands equivalent to the normal CLI prompt.

NOTE	**if-con** is considered a hidden command and is not supported by Cisco, but it does provide useful information such as VIP CPU usage: **show proc cpu**.

The VIP cards also perform distributed switching, which cannot be done elsewhere on the router.

Catalyst Switch Processors

There are currently three different types of processors, or supervisor engines, for the Catalyst series switches, excluding the 1200 and 8500 series. Each one is basically an enhancement of the other, starting with the Supervisor I (WS-5005, WS-C5006, and WS-C5009), then the Supervisor II (WS-C5505, WS-C5506, and WS-C5509), and then the Supervisor III (WS-C5530). Table 11-1 provides a breakdown comparison of each.

NOTE	Please note that the 6500 series and 8500 series switches are not covered here, but the Supervisor cards for those switches resemble that of the Supervisor III. The purpose of Table 11-1 is to give you an idea of what you're looking for on the Supervisor cards. The same methodology can be applied to the 6500 and 8500 series switches. For more information on the 6500 and 8500 series architecture, refer to CCO.

Table 11-1   *Comparison of Supervisor Cards in the Catalyst 5000 Series*

Supervisor Type	Processor Speed	Default DRAM Memory	Default Flash Memory	Default NVRAM	Maximum Logical Ports [1]	Backplane Interface Speed
Supervisor I	25 MHz Motorola MC68EC040	20 MB	4 MB	256 KB	400	1.2 GB
Supervisor II	25 MHz Motorola MC68EC040	16 MB	8 MB	256 KB	1500	1.2 GB
Supervisor III	150 MHz R4700 RISC	32 MB	8 MB	512 KB	4000	3.6 GB

[1] where the sum of all logical ports = (number of non-ATM trunks on the switch × number of active VLANs on that trunk) + (number of ATM trunks on the switch × number of active VLANs on that trunk × 2) + number of non-trunking ports on the switch. This applies to all ports running spanning tree.

For more details on the logical port calculation and VLANs, see Chapter 15, "Monitoring VLANs."

All the Supervisor versions support up to 16,000 MAC addresses in the CAM table and a maximum of 1024 VLANs. The Supervisor II and III have extra key features, such as redundant Supervisor cards, and the use of the NetFlow Feature Card (NFFC) for Layer 3 switching. The Supervisor IIG and IIIG models include the NFFC on the card and do not require an additional daughter card.

A switch performs most of the packet forwarding without impacting the CPU. As such, measuring the CPU of a switch is of little importance when determining the switch's packet-forwarding performance. Therefore, we do not cover trending or monitoring the switch CPU in the performance and fault/error management sections of this chapter.

Switching decisions are performed on the switch ASICs and, depending on the switch type, the bridging table may be stored on an ASIC as well. Some of the operations performed by the switch's CPU include spanning tree, Telnet services, Cisco Discovery Protocol (CDP), security (such as Terminal Access Controller Access Control System [TACACS]), remote monitoring (RMON), VLAN Trunk Protocol (VTP), port aggregation, dynamic VLANs, and SNMP processing. If anything makes the CPU busy on the switch, it is broadcast and multicast traffic. This is usually caused by the VLAN assignment to the sc0 port on the switch. For more details on best practices regarding the configuration of the switch, see Chapter 18, "Best Practices for Device Configuration."

Router Switching Paths

Depending on the router platform you have, different switching paths are available, especially when you get into the high-end routers such as the 7500s or 7200 series. All router platforms have the capability of performing process switching or fast switching of packets. Through the switching process, the router determines the next hop toward the destination address. Switching moves traffic from an input interface to one or more output interfaces. Switching is optimized and has lower latency than routing because it can move packets, frames, or cells from buffer to buffer with simpler determination of the source and destination of the traffic. It saves resources because it does not involve extra lookups. Reduced latency can be attributed to the following factors:

- Cached Layer 2 header and outbound lookup (reduced code path)
- Fast lookup of cache entry
- Capability to do all the header/checksum rewrite during interrupt time, versus after a context switch to a regularly scheduled process invocation

Figure 11-1 shows the path of a packet through the router.

Figure 11-1 *Path of a Packet Through a Router*

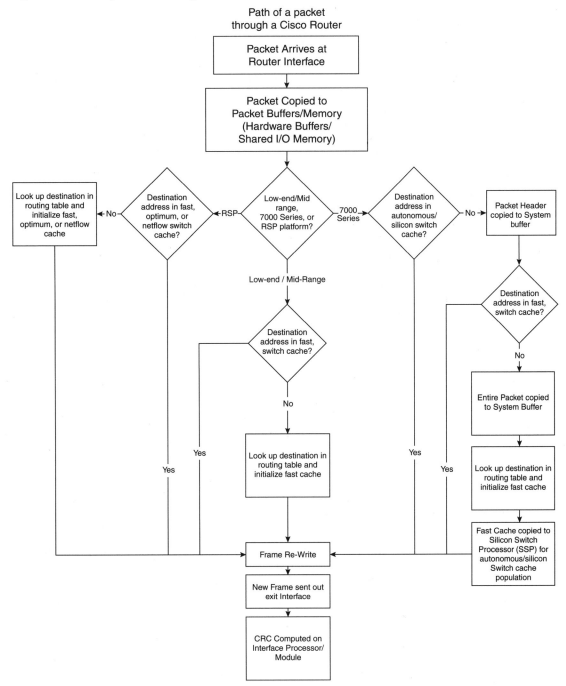

If you want to view the switching path of packets through a router, you can execute the CLI command **show interface switch**.

Process Switching

In *process switching*, the first packet that enters a router's interface is copied to the system buffer. The router looks up the Layer 3 network address in the routing table and initializes the fast-switch cache. The frame is rewritten with the destination address and sent to the exit interface, where the destination resides. Subsequent packets for that destination are sent by the same switching path.

Fast Switching

In *fast switching*, the first packet is process switched. The router then caches some of the IP or other Layer 3 header, the new Layer 2 header, and the internal index of the outbound interface. Subsequent packets can then be compared against the cached Layer 3 information. If a match is found, the Layer 2 header replaces the existing Layer 2 header without moving the packet around in memory, and the outbound interface information is then used to queue the packet for output. Fast switching is enabled by default on all interfaces that support fast switching, except on the 7500 series routers, where optimum switching is the default.

Optimum Switching

Optimum switching is similar to the format of fast switching, but is a bit faster because it utilizes the associative array capabilities of the RISC processor. The cache entry is found a lot faster by the processor due to this array structure. Optimum switching is enabled by default on Cisco 7500 series routers and first appeared in IOS 11.1.

Distributed Switching

In *distributed switching*, the switching process occurs typically on the VIP (Versatile Interface Processor). The VIP card maintains a copy of the routing cache information needed to forward packets. Because the VIP card has the routing information it needs, it performs the switching locally, making the packet forwarding much faster and much more efficient. Router throughput is increased linearly, based on the number of VIP cards installed in the router. Distributed switching is supported on the Cisco 7500 series and 12000 Series routers.

NetFlow Switching

NetFlow switching enables you to collect the data required for flexible and detailed accounting, billing, and chargeback for network and application resource utilization. Accounting data can be collected for both dedicated line and dial-access accounting. NetFlow provides an optimized code path that allows for efficient statistics collection as well as access list processing. NetFlow switching is supported on the Cisco 7200 and 7500 series routers. NetFlow switching is also supported over switched LAN or ATM backbones, allowing scalable inter-VLAN forwarding.

Catalyst Switch Switching Paths

All Catalyst 5xxx and 29xx series switches (excluding the IOS-based 2900XLs) utilize the store-and-forward approach to delivering packets. The store-and-forward switching mode stores complete packets and checks for errors prior to transmission. In store-and-forward mode, latency is measured as last-bit-received to first-bit-transmitted or "Last-In, First-Out" (LIFO). This does not include the time it takes to receive the entire packet, which can vary, according to packet size. The time required to receive a packet at 100 Mbps varies between 51.2 microseconds and 1.2 milliseconds. At 10 Mbps, the time required to receive a packet varies between 5.12 microseconds to 120 microseconds. The cut-through technology as seen on the 3000 series switches is faster, but may introduce the forwarding of bad packets because the packet is not checked for errors when switched.

Figure 11-2 is an illustration of the path of a packet through a switch.

Router Memory

There are different types of memory in routers: System DRAM, I/O memory, Flash, and NVRAM. The following sections briefly describe what each one does and how each one functions in the router.

Figure 11-2 *Path of a Packet through a Switch*

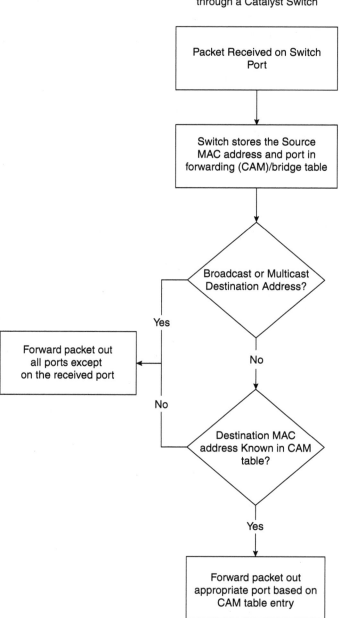

System Memory

When a router initially boots up, the IOS image running on the router must first be loaded into *system memory* prior to any other process gaining access to this memory pool. This holds true for all routers except for some of the 2500 series routers, in which the IOS image is run from flash and is never loaded into main system memory. After the IOS image is decompressed and loaded, all the router's processes can begin to utilize the rest of main system memory.

TIP	The IOS image stored on flash is smaller in size than the image stored in RAM due to the compressed nature of the flash memory file. Make sure you take that into consideration when looking at system memory requirements.

This division of system memory explains why your "Total memory available" on the router never equates to the amount of system memory installed. This difference can be verified by executing the **show memory** command on the router, as shown in Example 11-1.

Example 11-1   *The **show memory** command reveals that total memory available and amount of memory installed are not equivalent.*

```
Router>sh mem
            Head        Total(b)    Used(b)    Free(b)     Lowest(b)    Largest(b)
Processor   60DC38E0    52676384^A  1801772    50874612    50862952     50873820
     Fast   60DA38E0      131072      48184       82888       82888        82844
...
...
Router>show ver
...
cisco RSP2 (R4700) processor with 65536K^B/2072K bytes of memory.
R4700 processor, Implementation 33, Revision 1.0
Last reset from power-on
G.703/E1 software, Version 1.0.
G.703/JT2 software, Version 1.0.
SuperLAT software copyright 1990 by Meridian Technology Corp).
Bridging software.
X.25 software, Version 2.0, NET2, BFE and GOSIP compliant.
TN3270 Emulation software (copyright 1994 by TGV Inc).
...
...
Router>sh flash
-#-  ED --type-- --crc--- -seek-- nlen -length- ---------date/time------ name
1    .. FFFFFFFF 674BED34 11A1B20 24   6994832  Jan 28 1999 rsp-jv-mz.111-18.CA1.bin
```

This image, rsp-jv-mz.111-18.CA1.bin, equals 12859616 bytes uncompressed, or 65536000 bytes(B) minus 52676384 bytes (A).

More details regarding system memory characteristics and monitoring follow in the section "MIB Variables for Memory Utilization on Routers," especially relating to free memory, contiguous free memory, and process memory allocation based on the CISCO-MEMORY-POOL-MIB, **show mem** CLI command, and **show proc mem** CLI command.

I/O Memory

One of the first things the router does after booting up is allocate hardware buffers for the interfaces on the router. The buffers typically are distributed via the Cbus architecture (RSP, SP, or SSP cards) on the high-end routers, such as the 7xxx series; or by the I/O memory on the low-end routers, such as the 4xxx, 3600, and 2500 platforms.

I/O memory is physically separated from the system memory on the low-end routers (4xxx, 3600, 2500 series, etc.) and requires a separate memory SIMM to be installed. The core routers, or high-end 7xxx series routers, use portions of their system memory to allocate hardware buffers. These hardware or MEMD buffers are allocated based upon media interface bandwidths and MTUs. Here's the process:

1 Buffers of a given size share a common free pool to be shared by all interfaces with closely matched MTUs.

2 All the interfaces' MTUs are consulted, and the interfaces are grouped into such as buffer pools.

3 The default receive bandwidths of all interfaces within a buffer pool are summed to form an aggregate receive bandwidth for that pool.

4 The MEMD buffer space is then divided based upon proportional aggregate bandwidths.

5 The number of buffers in each pool is then calculated, and the number of buffers per interface within a pool is divided evenly (regardless of relative bandwidth).

The final resulting values for each interface can be validated by executing the CLI command **show controller**. Refer to annotated item A in Example 11-2 to see where the interface buffers are reported. For more details on hardware buffers, see the section entitled "Hardware Buffers" in Chapter 10, "Managing Hardware and Environmental Characteristics."

Example 11-2 shows the output for both a low-end router and a high-end router.

Example 11-2   *Using the **show controller** command to view the buffers allocated to the interfaces on the router.*

```
Router4500>show controller
AM79970 unit 0 NIM slot 2, NIM type code 22, NIM version 1
Media Type is AUTOSELECT, 10BaseT selected, Half Duplex, Link State is Up, Squelch
is Normal
idb 0x60CADD14, ds 0x60CAF900, eim_regs = 0x3C210000
IB at 0x4003ED50: mode=0x0010, mcfilter 0000/0008/0100/0020
station address 00e0.1e4d.18c2  default station address 00e0.1e4d.18c2
buffer size 1524ᴬ
RX ring with 32 entries at 0x4003E2E8
Rxhead = 0x4003E328 (8), Rxp = 0x60CAF938 (8)
00 pak=0x60CBB11C ds=0xA810AFAA status=0x80 max_size=1524 pak_size=92
01 pak=0x60CB7684 ds=0xA80FE5A2 status=0x80 max_size=1524 pak_size=300
…
…
High-end 7500 series router output is as follows:
Router7500>sh controller cbus
MEMD at 40000000, 2097152 bytes (unused 128, recarves 1, lost 0)
  RawQ 48000100, ReturnQ 48000108, EventQ 48000110
  BufhdrQ 48000120 (2353 items)
  IpcbufQ_classic 48000140 (8 items, 4096 bytes)
  3570 buffer headers (48002000 - 4800FF10)
  pool0: 9 buffers, 256 bytes, queue 48000128
  pool1: 1196 buffers, 1536 bytes, queue 48000130
  pool2: 4 buffers, 1568 bytes, queue 48000138
  slot0: EIP, hw 1.10, sw 20.05, ccb 5800FF20, cmdq 48000080, vps 4096
    software loaded from system
    Ethernet0/0, addr 0090.f2d0.e000 (bia 0090.f2d0.e000)
      gfreeq 48000130, lfreeq 48000148 (1536 bytes)
      rxlo 4, rxhi 1196, rxcurr 0, maxrxcurr 2ᴬ
      txq 48000150, txacc 48000082 (value 797), txlimit 797ᴬ
    Ethernet0/1, addr 0090.f2d0.e001 (bia 0090.f2d0.e001)
      gfreeq 48000130, lfreeq 48000158 (1536 bytes)
      rxlo 4, rxhi 1196, rxcurr 0, maxrxcurr 0
      txq 48000160, txacc 4800008A (value 797), txlimit 797
…
…
High-end 7000 series router output is as follows:
Router7000>sh controller cbus
Switch Processor 5, hardware version 12.0, microcode version 11.15 Altera 0
  Microcode loaded from system
  512 Kbytes of main memory, 128 Kbytes cache memory
  4 256 byte buffers, 4 1024 byte buffers, 312 1520 byte buffersᴬ
  Restarts: 0 line down, 0 hung output, 0 controller error
…
…
```

Flash Memory and NVRAM

Flash memory in the routers is responsible for storing the IOS image, Interface Processor microcode, and sometimes the router's configuration. Flash memory is either on the processor board or on a PCMCIA card that is installed on the router. The newer generation routers have Flash on the PCMCIA flash cards versus directly on the system board. NVRAM typically is where the router configuration file is stored and usually has a size of 256 KB or 512 KB—much smaller than the Flash memory.

Switch Memory

Memory on the Catalyst switches works a bit differently than on the router. The "I/O" equivalent memory is fixed for each port on the switch to a 192 KB buffer. The system memory on the switch Supervisor card is used mainly for the CAM or bridging table and can safely store 16,000 MAC entries. A portion of the system memory is allocated to the buffers and clusters of the switch, called mbufs. Mbufs are discussed next, under "Router Buffers." The flash memory on the switch is used for the software image; the NVRAM is used for the configuration file and logging, both syslog output and show log output.

Router Buffers

We already discussed how hardware buffers are allocated in routers in Chapter 10. This section focuses on how the system buffers work in the routers. System buffers are broken out into six different types, as summarized in Table 11-2.

Table 11-2   *Buffer Sizes*

Buffer Type	Packet Size Range in Bytes
small	60–104 bytes
middle	105–600 bytes
big	601–1524 bytes
verybig	1525–4520 bytes
large	4521–5024 bytes
huge	5025–18024 bytes

These system buffers only affect process switched traffic through the router. Each buffer type is allocated a fixed amount of permanent buffers at boot time. These values can be overwritten based on the presence of the **buffer permanent** command in the configuration of the router. Permanent buffers are the number of buffers the system tries to create and keep, and are normally not trimmed by the system. Any packets hitting these system buffers are process-switched packets, such as routing updates, broadcasts, explorers, etc. Here are some terms and definitions relating to router buffers:

- *Buffer hits* count the number of successful attempts to allocate a buffer when needed.
- *Buffer misses* count the number of buffer allocation attempts that resulted in growing the buffer pool.
- *Buffer trims* are counted when the router gives back buffer space to main memory when they are not needed.
- *Buffer creates* are counted when the router needs to create more buffers based on the need.
- *Fallbacks* are a count of buffer allocation attempts that resulted in the process of resorting to the public buffer pool and choosing a buffer size bigger than the one originally sought.
- *Public buffer pools* are the system buffers stored on the processor.
- *Interface buffer pools* are the buffers allocated to each interface at router boot time.

These variables are analyzed in more depth later in the section called "Performance Data for Router Processors." For more information regarding buffers, refer to the online documentation on CCO.

Switch Buffers

Mbufs are fixed buffers on the switches and are permanently set. They come in two "flavors:" mbuf and clusters. Each mbuf is segmented into 128 bytes (116 data bytes) whereas clusters are packets greater than 1664 bytes (13 mbufs and 1508 data bytes). The only traffic that affects the mbuf and cluster counters is traffic destined to the supervisor engine, such as BPDUs, VTP, or CDP. The critical values that need to be looked at with switch buffers are the "free" and "lowest free" mbufs and clusters because they can help identify possible memory leaks or lack of proper memory resources. These values can be validated by executing the CLI "enable" command **show mbuf**.

Performance Data for Router Processors

You can gather the appropriate performance information for router processors through MIBs or through the command-line interface (CLI) via Telnet or rsh. We will look at both methods, as well as explain what the highlighted variables indicate, why they are useful, and how to manage the resulting factors. We will also identify some starting point thresholds to set and watch for when monitoring performance. But please note that the threshold settings defined in this section reflect only a starting point and nothing more. You must first understand your network traffic flows and network characteristics before making the appropriate threshold setting. Thresholds will constantly need tweaking and re-evaluation to meet the needs of your environment.

MIB Variables for Router CPU Utilization

Process-intensive tasks, such as process switching data packets, routing updates, interface flapping, or broadcasts/multicasts can cause the CPU to increase on the router.

From OLD-CISCO-CPU MIB or OLD-CISCO-SYS MIB, the avgBusy5 value reports the percentage of the processor in use over a running five-minute average.

NOTE   Starting in IOS version 12.0(3)T, the CISCO-PROCESS MIB and the MIB object cpmCPUTotal5min are used to replace the avgBusy5 object from the OLD-CISCO-CPU MIB.

The avgBusy5 MIB provides a more accurate view of your router's performance over time than using the MIBs avgBusy1 and BusyPer, which look at CPU at one minute and five-second intervals, respectively. It is valuable for trend monitoring and capacity planning of the network. Watching the CPU closely when it exceeds the rising threshold value is more important than watching the falling threshold value, especially when you are troubleshooting performance degradation. In other words, a higher CPU might indicate a problem, whereas a lower CPU may not be an issue.

The recommended baseline rising threshold for avgBusy5 is 90 percent.

TIP   Depending on the platform, some routers running at 90 percent, such as 2500s, may exhibit performance degradation versus a high-end router, such as the 7500 series, which may operate fine. Trending of CPU over time is important for developing your baseline.

Related MIB objects from OLD-CISCO-CPU MIB or OLD-CISCO-SYS MIB are as follows:

- avgBusy1: One minute exponentially-decayed moving average of the CPU busy percentage.
- BusyPer: CPU busy percentage in the last five-second period. Not the last five real time seconds, but the last five-second period in the scheduler.

CLI Commands Relating to CPU on the Router

The **show proc cpu** command displays the five-second, one-minute, and five-minute CPU utilization for the router. It also provides a breakdown of the individual processes running on the router and what percentage of the CPU each process takes. This command is very useful when you are troubleshooting, especially when avgBusy5 exceeds the threshold you define. Many valuable data points in the display output can help you identify possible problem areas with the router or in your network. Looking at the individual processes running with high CPU percentages associated with them can help narrow your scope of where a particular problem may lie.

Example 11-3 shows sample output from **show proc cpu**.

Example 11-3   *Using **show proc cpu** to get cpu information.*

```
Router>sh proc cpu
CPU utilization for five seconds:12%A /3%B ;one minute:7%C ;five minutes:10%D
 PID  Runtime(ms)    Invoked   uSecs   5Sec    1Min    5Min    TTY    Process
 1         0             1        0   0.00%   0.00%   0.00%     0    SCOP Input
 2      179548        30793     5830   0.00%   0.00%   0.00%     0    Check heaps
 3         4             9      444   0.00%   0.00%   0.00%     0    Pool Manager
 4         0             2        0   0.00%   0.00%   0.00%     0    Timers
 5       8272        711817      14   0.00%   0.00%   0.00%     0    OIR Handler
 6         0             1        0   0.00%   0.00%   0.00%     0    IPC Zone Manager
 7         0             1        0   0.00%   0.00%  10.00%E    0     IP InputF
 8         0          74520       0   0.00%   0.00%   0.00%     0    IPC Seat Manager
 9       116          26351       4   0.00%   0.00%   0.00%     0    ARP Input
 ...
 ...etc.
```

Important information from Example 11-3 is annotated as follows:

A The CPU utilization over the last five seconds (also available via MIB busyPer).

B The percentage of CPU time at interrupt level (fast-switched packets), over a five-second period. If you take the difference between A and B, you'll get the five-second percentage the router spent at the process level. In this case, the router spent 9 percent at the process level over the last five seconds—processed switched packets. (No MIB available.)

C The CPU utilization over the last minute (also available via MIB avgBusy1).

D The CPU utilization over the last five minutes (also available via MIB avgBusy5).

E The five-minute average of an individual process running on the router. In this example, you see that IP input is taking up 10 percent of the processor over a five-minute time frame.

F The name of the individual process running. You may be able to correlate an individual process that is running high CPU usage with other similar processes. For example, if IP Input is high, you may also want to look and see whether any of the IP routing processes are running high as well to help you narrow down the specific IP process causing the high CPU.

MIB Variables for Router Device Uptime

From MIB RFC 1213, the sysUpTime variable indicates how long the router has been up since the last reboot, caused commonly either by a power-on, reload, or software exception error. It is in units of 1/100 second.

sysUpTime is not that valuable by itself, but it can be useful as a comparison or correlation to other variables. Comparing sysUpTime relative to other routers in the network can help you correlate downtimes and network availability in the network. You should be able to easily correlate sysUpTime on routers to your change management "windows." For example, if you have a scheduled power outage on a weekend in one portion of the network, you should be able to correlate the sysUpTime on all the routers in that area to approximately the same sysUpTime. If you see any routers whose sysUpTime is significantly different from the others, then you know something unexpected happened.

The recommended baseline threshold for sysUpTime is that all the routers in a common region of the network reflect approximately the same sysUpTime value. Change management practices and accurate documentation will provide the evidence on why and when the router reloaded.

A related MIB object from OLD-CISCO-SYS MIB is WhyReload, which returns a printable octet string that contains the reason why the system was last restarted.

CLI Commands Relating to sysUptime

The **show version** command displays the IOS software release running and the hardware inventory of what is installed on the router, as well as the configuration register setting, which can directly affect how the router boots up when it reloads. This output also displays the reason for the last restart.

Example 11-4 shows sample output from **show version**.

Example 11-4   *Using **show version** to obtain uptime information.*

```
Router>sh ver
Cisco Internetwork Operating System Software
IOS (tm) GS Software (RSP-J-M), Version 11.1(18)CA1, EARLY DEPLOYMENT RELEASE
SOFTWARE (fc1)
```

Example 11-4   *Using show version to obtain uptime information.*

```
Synced to mainline version: 11.1(18)
Copyright (c) 1986-1998 by cisco Systems, Inc.
Compiled Tue 21-Apr-98 19:41 by richardd
Image text-base: 0x60010900, data-base: 0x607AE000

ROM: System Bootstrap, Version 11.1(2) [nitin 2], RELEASE SOFTWARE (fc1)
ROM: GS Software (RSP-BOOT-M), Version 11.1(6), RELEASE SOFTWARE (fc1)

GOAL uptime is 2 days, 10 hours, 57 minutes
System restarted by reload at 10:44:07 UTC Thu Jan 28 1999ᴬ
System image file is "slot0:rsp-j-mz.111-18.CA1", booted via slot0

cisco RSP2 (R4700) processor with 65536K/2072K bytes of memory.
R4700 processor, Implementation 33, Revision 1.0
Last reset from power-on
G.703/E1 software, Version 1.0.
G.703/JT2 software, Version 1.0.
SuperLAT software copyright 1990 by Meridian Technology Corp).
Bridging software.
X.25 software, Version 2.0, NET2, BFE and GOSIP compliant.
TN3270 Emulation software (copyright 1994 by TGV Inc).
Chassis Interface.
1 HIP controller (1 HSSI).
1 FIP controller (1 FDDI).
1 HSSI network interface.
1 FDDI network interface.
123K bytes of non-volatile configuration memory.

16384K bytes of Flash PCMCIA card at slot 0 (Sector size 128K).
4096K bytes of Flash internal SIMM (Sector size 256K).
No slave installed in slot 3.
Configuration register is 0x2102
```

The "System restarted by..." line (A) tells you why the router was reloaded. Other values you may see here are "power-on" or "software forced crash."

If the router was restarted by a software error, the **show stack** command output provides details on why the router crashed, mainly in hex code. This information is valuable when you open a case with the Cisco Technical Assistance Center (TAC) because the engineers there have internal tools that can decode the stack trace. Or you can decode it yourself on CCO's (Cisco Connection Online) Stack Decoder Web page: http://www.cisco.com/stack/stackdecoder.shtml.

MIB Variables for Memory Utilization on Routers

An unstable network, such as one with flapping routes, can cause fragmented memory or constant system buffer creates and trims. Actively monitoring the largest contiguous memory block free in a router helps trend and gauge the available contiguous memory. You can have all the free memory you want, but if the contiguous block free is too low, then the router will not function properly. Processes won't be able to run if they cannot get enough free contiguous memory to execute effectively. You'll know you are hitting a critical point here when you start seeing %SYS-2-MALLOCFAIL or %SYS-2-NOMEMORY in syslog, or if you are unable to Telnet into the router due to low memory. Typically, you'll start seeing the syslog messages prior to being kicked out of a Telnet session. Memory leaks or other defects may cause this fragmentation.

The following MIBs are relevant for monitoring memory utilization on routers:

- ciscoMemoryPoolLargestFree (from CISCO-MEMORY-POOL-MIB)
- ciscoMemoryPoolFree (from CISCO-MEMORY-POOL-MIB or OLD-CISCO-MEMORY-MIB)
- freeMem (prior to IOS 11.1; from CISCO-MEMORY-POOL-MIB or OLD-CISCO-MEMORY-MIB)

The ciscoMemoryPoolLargestFree variable indicates the largest number of contiguous bytes from the memory pool that are currently unused on the managed device. This MIB was first introduced in IOS release 11.1. IOS prior to 11.1 requires the execution of the CLI command **show mem** to get the same data. This variable, ciscoMemoryPoolLargestFree, is called fragmented memory.

The recommended baseline threshold for ciscoMemoryPoolLargestFree is 500 KB for the low watermark.

The ciscoMemoryPoolFree and freeMem variables indicate the number of bytes from the memory pool that are currently unused on the managed device. It is still important to trend the amount of memory free on the router for capacity planning, even when monitoring the largest memory block free.

Monitoring total memory free helps mainly in the capacity planning of your network. Changing traffic patterns or the addition of more networks to the infrastructure can cause the free memory in the routers to change. Total memory changes would be even more evident when you upgrade your router to another IOS release. Recall from the previous introduction to system memory that IOS takes up a portion of the total DRAM installed, thus leaving you with the actual amount of free memory you have to play with for other processes. It is wise to baseline your free memory after an IOS upgrade to accurately represent the amount you have for processes in the router. The memory pool is accessed when buffers are needed to process incoming packets or when a router process needs more memory, such as when routing updates are sent out. When buffers free up the memory, you'll see the trim counters increment.

The recommended baseline threshold for ciscoMemoryPoolFree and freeMem is 1 MB for the low watermark.

CLI Commands for Memory Usage

There are several show commands relating to memory utilization on routers. The following two will be discussed here:

- **show mem**
- **show proc mem**

Using the show memory Command

The **show mem** output displays the following:

- Total amount of memory available
- Amount of used memory
- Amount of current free memory
- Lowest amount of free memory since the last restart
- Largest contiguous memory block currently available

Data for the processor memory, fast cache, and I/O memory is seen here. When gathering this data, it is important to leave your terminal length set to 24 because the output of this command can be rather large. The most pertinent data needed from this output is within the first four lines displayed. The output fields are shown in bytes indicated by a (b) (see Example 11-5).

The primary use of **show mem** is for routers that are not running IOS version 11.1 or greater, which has the support for the CISCO-MEMORY-POOL MIB. The "Largest(b)" field is the value you want to trend here because it is equivalent to the MIB ciscoMemoryPoolLargestFree. You can also use this command to trend how low the memory has dropped based on the "Lowest(b)" field since the last time the router restarted. This variable is not available via a MIB.

Example 11-5 shows sample output from **show mem** for both high-end and low-end routers.

Example 11-5   *Using **show mem** to obtain information on memory usage.*

```
High-end routers (7xxx series)
Router>show mem
           Head        Total(b)    Used(b)     Free(b)     Lowest(b)   Largest(b)
Processor  60E6F330    18418896ᴬ   2156560ᴮ    16262336ᶜ   16117456ᴰ   16157784ᴱ
Fast       60E4F330    131072ᴬ     80144ᴮ      50928ᶜ      50928ᴰ      50892ᴱ
--More--
Low-end routers (4xxx,2500,3600,etc.series)
Router>sh mem
           Head        Total(b)    Used(b)     Free(b)     Lowest(b)   Largest(b)
Processor  60947BF0    23823376ᴬ   1890660ᴮ    21932716ᶜ   21783296ᴰ   21801520ᴱ
      I/O  40000000    16777216ᴬ   1390348ᴮ    15386868ᶜ   15384516ᴰ   15386356ᴱ
--More--
```

The following information is highlighted in Example 11-5:

A   "Total(b)" is the total amount of memory, in bytes, available for the processor after the IOS is loaded. If you want to know how much memory the IOS is taking on the router, subtract the Total bytes shown here from the total amount of DRAM or system memory (processorRam) installed on the router. The total I/O memory or Fast memory is based on the physical I/O memory installed on the low-end routers or based on the amount of packet memory allocated on high-end routers from system memory (typically, 2 MB on RSP platforms).

B   "Used(b)" is the total amount of memory, in bytes, currently used (ciscoMemoryPoolUsed) by the router.

C   "Free(b)" is the total amount of memory, in bytes, currently free (ciscoMemoryPoolFree or freeMem) in the router.

D   "Lowest(b)" is the lowest amount of memory that was free at some point in time since the last reload of the router. There is no equivalent MIB for this value.

E   "Largest(b)" is the largest contiguous block of memory free in the router (ciscoMemoryPoolLargestFree). This is the most important field to look at in this output.

Using the show proc memory Command

The command **show proc mem** displays the amount of memory taken by each process running on the router. It shows the following information:

- Amount of allocated memory by each process
- Amount of freed memory by a process
- Number of times the process requested a packet buffer or relinquished a packet buffer
- Total amount of memory allocated to all processes

This output, which is available only via the CLI, provides an understanding of what processes are being used most and least in the router. Typically, all processes running on the router take up a fixed amount of memory, as defined by the process when it starts up, and the amount stays fairly constant over time. But if you see a steady increase in memory "held" (the Holding column) by a process, it could be an indication of a memory leak. A memory leak can occur when there is additional memory allocated for processes and the memory is not released or given back to main memory when not in use.

Example 11-6 shows sample output from **show proc mem**.

Example 11-6   *Using **show proc mem** to obtain memory usage information.*

```
Router# show proc mem

Total: 5611448, Used: 2307548, Free: 3303900
PID   TTY   Allocated      Freed    Holding    Getbufs    Retbufs  Process
  0     0      199592       1236   1907220ᴬ          0          0  *Init*
  0     0         400      76928       400           0          0  *Sched*
  0     0     5431176    3340052    140760      349780          0  *Dead*
  1     0         256        256      1724           0          0  Load Meter
  2     0         264          0      5032           0          0  Exec
  3     0           0          0      2724           0          0  Check heaps
  4     0       97932          0      2852       32760          0  Pool Manager
  5     0         256        256      2724           0          0  Timers
  6     0          92          0      2816           0          0  CXBus hot stall
  7     0           0          0      2724           0          0  IPC Zone Manager
  8     0           0          0      2724           0          0  IPC Realm Manager
  ...
 77     0         116          0      2844           0          0  IPX-EIGRP Hello
                            2307224 ᴮ Total
```

Following is the highlighted information in Example 11-6:

A The only field that needs attention here is the "Holding" column. It is displayed in bytes, and represents how much memory is currently used by each individual process.

B The total amount of memory allocated to processes in the router at a given time. The value should be fairly close to, if not the same as, the MIB ciscoMemoryPoolUsed.

MIB Variables for Buffer Utilization on Routers

From OLD-CISCO-MEMORY-MIB, the following variables are relevant to buffer utilization on routers:

- bufferMdMiss—This MIB is indicative of the middle buffer misses seen. Packets ranging in size of 105 to 600 bytes.
- bufferMdHit—This MIB is indicative of the middle buffer hits seen.

Either one of these MIBS alone doesn't mean much. You need to correlate the two together to develop a percentage of misses to hits using Equation 11-1:

Equation 11-1

$$(\text{bufferMdMiss} / \text{bufferMdHit}) \times 100\%$$

Using the percentage approach puts the number of misses in perspective; thus, routers with the most misses do not necessarily require tuning first. We are focusing on the middle buffer pool because these buffers fall in what we feel is the most common data packet range: 105–600 bytes. Remember that packets that hit these system buffers are process-switched packets, such as IPX RIP/SAP packets. The same principle and correlation can be drawn between the other buffer sizes as well. The amount of traffic hitting each buffer pool determines which pools need more attention than others. If we were to rank the buffers in order of most to least important, the relevant order for most routers would be: Medium, Big, Small, VeryBig, Large, and then Huge.

Tuning buffers is not an easy task. Misunderstanding what actually utilizes buffers is common and results in the incorrect configuration of system buffers. We have developed an understanding that tuning should occur when the total number of misses divided by the total number of hits for a given buffer pool is less than 0.5 of 1 percent. Small buffers are used mainly for broadcast traffic such as explorers, ARPs, GNS requests, etc., and should not necessarily be tuned to perfection. Allowing more broadcast traffic in to further be processed out is not a good practice. In fact, process-oriented packet drops often can be beneficial to the health of the overall network, such as in the case of SNA and NetBIOS broadcast storms.

Our approach on buffer analysis begins with middle buffers. Because most packets hitting this buffer pool control routing stability and session data for process-switched protocols, RIP and SAP updates, and others, it is essential to tune this pool first. Looking at the buffer miss-to-hit analysis gives you a good understanding of buffer stability. In other words, you will have some buffer misses and this is normal because broadcast and bursty traffic exist from time to time in any network.

NOTE This methodology relating to buffers represents the authors' views based on experience, and does not reflect the views of Cisco in general.

The recommended baseline threshold is a miss-to-hit percentage of 0.5 of 1 percent. This initial baseline value holds true for all buffer sizes.

CLI Commands for Buffer Usage

The **show buffers** command displays the statistics for all the different buffer pools on the router. The configured values for permanent, max-free, and min-free buffers for each size are displayed in this output, as well as the hits, misses, and "no memory" values.

The **show buffers** command actually provides you with the same data as from the buffer MIBs, except for one value: the "fallbacks" counter under the interface pools. Buffers, unlike other counters on the router, are cumulative values since the last restart; thus, they cannot be cleared. Because SNMP is cumulative as well, the buffer values you see in this output should be similar to the appropriate MIB values.

Example 11-7 shows sample output from **show buffers**.

Example 11-7   *Using the **show buffers** command to get router buffer information.*

```
Router# show buffers

Buffer elements:
      398 in free list (500 max allowed)
      1266 hits, 0 misses, 0 created

Public buffer pools:
Small buffers, 104 bytes (total 50ᴬ, permanent 50 ᴮ):
      50 in free list (20 min, 150 max allowed)
      551 ᶜhits, 0ᴰ misses, 0 ᴱ trims, 0 ᶠ created
Middle buffers, 600 bytes (total 25, permanent 25):
      25 in free list (10 min, 150 max allowed)
      39 hits, 0 misses, 0 trims, 0 created
Big buffers, 1524 bytes (total 50, permanent 50):
      49 in free list (5 min, 150 max allowed)
      27 hits, 0 misses, 0 trims, 0 created
VeryBig buffers, 4520 bytes (total 10, permanent 10):
      10 in free list (0 min, 100 max allowed)
      0 hits, 0 misses, 0 trims, 0 created
Large buffers, 5024 bytes (total 0, permanent 0):
      0 in free list (0 min, 10 max allowed)
      0 hits, 0 misses, 0 trims, 0 created
Huge buffers, 18024 bytes (total 0, permanent 0):
      0 in free list (0 min, 4 max allowed)
      0 hits, 0 misses, 0 trims, 0 created


Interface buffer pools:
Ethernet0 buffers, 1524 bytes (total 64, permanent 64):
      16 in free list (0 min, 64 max allowed)
      48 hits, 0 ᴳ fallbacks
      16 max cache size, 16 in cache
Ethernet1 buffers, 1524 bytes (total 64, permanent 64):
      16 in free list (0 min, 64 max allowed)
      48 hits, 0 fallbacks
      16 max cache size, 16 in cache
Serial0 buffers, 1524 bytes (total 64, permanent 64):
      16 in free list (0 min, 64 max allowed)
      48 hits, 0 fallbacks
      16 max cache size, 16 in cache
Serial1 buffers, 1524 bytes (total 64, permanent 64):
      16 in free list (0 min, 64 max allowed)
      48 hits, 0 fallbacks
      16 max cache size, 16 in cache
```

Example 11-7   *Using the show buffers command to get router buffer information. (Continued)*

```
TokenRing0 buffers, 4516 bytes (total 48, permanent 48):
    0 in free list (0 min, 48 max allowed)
    48 hits, 0 fallbacks
    16 max cache size, 16 in cache
TokenRing1 buffers, 4516 bytes (total 32, permanent 32):
    32 in free list (0 min, 48 max allowed)
    16 hits, 0 fallbacks
0 ᴴ failures (0 ᴵ no memory)
```

Following are the highlighted values from Example 11-7:

A   "Total" identifies the total number of buffers in the pool, including both used and unused buffers. Also available via MIB buffer<buffer pool size>Total.

B   "permanent" identifies the permanent number of allocated buffers in the pool. These buffers are always in the pool and cannot be trimmed away. Also available via MIB buffer<buffer pool size>Total.

C   "hits" identifies the number of buffers that have been requested from the pool. The "hits" counter provides a mechanism for determining which pool must meet the highest demand for buffers. Also available via MIB buffer<buffer pool size>Hit.

D   "misses" identifies the number of times a buffer has been requested and the processor detected that additional buffers are required (the number of buffers in the free list has dropped below "min"). The "misses" counter represents the number of times the processor has been forced to create additional buffers. Also available via MIB buffer<buffer pool size>Miss.

E   "trims" identifies the number of buffers that have been trimmed from the pool by the route processor when the number of buffers "in free list" exceeds the number of "max-allowed" buffers. Also available via MIB buffer<buffer pool size>Trim.

F   "created" identifies the number of buffers that have been created in the pool by the RP when demand for buffers has increased so that the number of buffers "in free list" is less than "min" buffers and/or a "miss" occurs due to zero buffers "in free list." Also available via MIB buffer<buffer pool size>Create.

G   "fallbacks" are counts of buffer allocation attempts that resulted in falling back to the public buffer pool that is the smallest pool at least as big as the interface buffer pool. No MIB associated with this value.

H   "failures" identifies the number of failures to grant a buffer to a requester, even after attempting to create an additional buffer. The number of "failures" represents the number of packets that have been dropped due to buffer shortage. Also available via MIB bufferFail.

I   "no memory" identifies the number of "failures" due to insufficient memory to create additional buffers. Also available via MIB bufferNoMem.

Correlating Different Router Performance Variables

After you've gathered the MIB or CLI data on router performance, what can you do with it? This section provides some ideas on how to correlate the different data points you gathered for use in performance management. A lot of what you gather in performance management can be applied to fault/error management as well, as noted in the preceding discussion of buffer variables. We'll discuss some options to assist performance based on thresholds being exceeded.

Correlating High CPU Values

Based on a high avgBusy5 value, you can look at the individual processes running on the router by executing the following CLI command: **show proc cpu**. From this output, you can identify what tasks are taking up the majority of the CPU cycles. You may also want to look at the switching paths of the data flowing through the router, such as process, fast, and autonomous switching. By using the CLI commands **show interface stat** or **show interface switch**, you can identify how much traffic is process switched versus the other switching mechanisms (fast, autonomous, distributed, and so on.) per interface. Wherever possible, try to offload some of the process switched traffic to other switching paths. Configuration parameters that involve route-caches on the interfaces can be applied to address these process-switching issues. Buffer misses can also be attributed to process-switched packets, which can be corrected by turning on some faster switching mechanisms.

High CPU can also be caused by broadcasts hitting the router, which cannot be controlled by adjusting the switching paths because broadcasts are always process switched. Broadcasts such as routing updates, IPX SAPs, or IP-UDP broadcasts have been known to cause high CPU usage on routers.

NOTE   For more details on performance numbers relating to broadcasts and CPU, see the case study entitled "Broadcasts in Switched Internetworks" on CCO. See the References at the end of this chapter for specific URL locations.

Here are some general suggestions for controlling the amount of broadcasts in your network. To control routing updates, depending on the protocol, you can use a different routing protocol that utilizes neighbor adjacencies to relay information about routes, such as EIGRP or OSPF. It is also a good idea to have a good network design in place to minimize the amount of broadcasts through your network, such as route summarization. To control IPX SAPs, you can use incremental SAP updates by using a subset of EIGRP for IPX and the rsup option, or you can use SAP access-list filters. For UDP broadcasts, there are several options: UDP turbo flooding or IP Helpering. Refer to the case study regarding UDP broadcast flooding on CCO for more details on setting this up in the router.

NOTE	For more details on controlling broadcasts in networks refer to the following case studies on CCO:
	"Designing Large-Scale IP Internetworks"
	"Reducing SAP Traffic in Novell IPX Networks"
	"UDP Broadcast Flooding"
	See the References at the end of this chapter for specific URL locations.

Correlating High Memory Usage and Fragmentation

High memory utilization can be caused by several things: instability in routing tables (flapping routes), memory leaks, or just not enough memory to handle the software and processes running on the router. Memory fragmentation in routers typically cannot be cleared unless the router is reloaded. Sometimes, you can free up some contiguous memory by turning off some of the unstable processes. However, the majority of the time the router needs to be reloaded. This is why it is important to trend the lowest fragmented memory and the process holding memory so you can proactively determine the process taking up memory and when the router may start experiencing memory fragmentation.

Correlating Buffer Misses

We won't get into the details of buffer-tuning the routers here because it is not advisable to tune them without consulting Cisco first. But we will discuss some general guidelines and hints for tuning buffers. Do a **show memory** to see how much memory is free. Creating buffers uses memory. In the low-end boxes, such as the 4000, 2500, etc., the buffers come out of shared I/O memory. In the high-end boxes, such as the 7xxx series, system memory is used. When you add buffers, you can multiply the number of permanent buffers you create by their size to see how much memory you will start off using. You will often see high-end boxes (and now some of the low-end) with 12 or 13 MB of free memory. Don't be afraid of using it if you have a problem.

Check the no memory field at the bottom of the **show buffers** output. If you see a non-zero number here, it means that you ran out of memory trying to make buffers. Tuning probably won't help. You are most likely to see this in the low-end routers when there is not enough shared I/O memory. You'll need to upgrade the shared memory first and then tune if necessary. In rare cases, a non-zero number in the no memory field could also warn you of a memory leak. A **show memory** could confirm this.

There are no firm rules for buffer tuning, but here are some useful guidelines:

1 Take the number of total buffers in a pool, add about 20 percent (depending on how many misses you are getting and how many buffers you currently have free), and make that your Perms for that buffer pool.

2 Set min to about 20–30 percent of your perms.

3 Set max to something greater than the sum of perms and mins.

Here's an example from a **show buffers** output:

```
Small buffers, 104 bytes (total 356, permanent 120):
    347 in free list (50 min, 350 max allowed)
    7254759 hits, 45947 misses, 45351 trims, 45587 created
```

Here, the router has total of 356 buffers, and it's getting a fair number of misses. Use the following guidelines:

1.2 x 356 = 427

Round up and make the permanent = 430 with the following command (assuming there is enough memory installed):

```
buffers small perm 430
```

You should probably double the mins of 50 to 100, which puts you in the middle of the guideline of 20–30 percent of perms (.25 x 425 = 106), so you would configure the following:

```
buffers small min 100
```

425 + 100 = 525, so you should probably set max to about 600 with the following command:

```
buffers small max 600
```

Some final words regarding buffer tuning:

- Buffer tuning won't cure things such as explorer storms, overutilization of the network, or too-slow serial links.

- If you create lots of buffers and you still get lots of misses, you probably should try to get an understanding of where the traffic is coming from so you can control it through filtering or loop elimination.

- Always try to leave some free memory to allow for changing conditions.

- Buffer tuning is not a substitute for good network design, implementation, or management.

- Buffer tuning is more of an art than a science, so please consult with an experienced Cisco engineer prior to tuning the buffers.

Performance Data for Switch Processors

As with routers, switches have performance variables that need to be monitored. This section identifies some MIB variables, as well as CLI output variables that are important to watch for switches.

MIB Variables for Switch Backplane Utilization

From CISCO-STACK MIB, two variables for monitoring switch backplane utilization are as follows:

- sysTraffic
- sysTrafficMeter

The sysTraffic and sysTrafficMeter MIBs report the percentage of bandwidth utilization for the previous polling interval. sysTrafficMeter is the newer MIB object based on the System Traffic table, whereas sysTraffic is the original MIB object from the CISCO-STACK MIB. With the newer Supervisor III cards, which "touch" all three backplanes in the 5500 series switches, there are three different backplane percentages, one for each. This MIB object is gathered from sysTrafficMeter with sysTrafficMeterType of switchingBusA, B, or C. sysTraffic is equivalent to sysTrafficMeter, where switchTrafficMeterType equals systemSwitchingBus.

These MIB objects are important to assist in monitoring the backplane performance of the switch. All traffic must traverse the backplane of the switch to get to the appropriate destination ports. Typically, the utilization on the backplane is very small, due to the near wire rate speeds. You may find it more beneficial to monitor the sysTrafficPeak and sysTrafficMeterPeak if the utilization of the backplane is consistently low. These peak values are cleared when the system resets or when the port counters are cleared.

The recommended baseline thresholds for backplane utilization are 30 percent for the low threshold and 50 percent for the high threshold.

CLI Commands for Switch Processor Backplane Statistics

The **show system** and **show traffic** commands provide information related to that provided by the sysTraffic and sysTrafficMeter MIBs

Using the show system Command

A **show system** command output displays the current traffic percentage seen on the backplane of the switch, as well as the peak traffic percentage and the time it peaked. Switch hardware status indicators are also reported in this output, along with the system uptime.

The important data in this output are the traffic percentage, the peak backplane percentage, and the peak time. Correlations can be done between like switches in the network regarding the peak time to help determine possible issues. The traffic utilization number here is representative of the backplane speed of 1.2 Gbps. For a look at all three backplanes, as seen on the 5500 series switches with Supervisor III cards, refer to the **show traffic** command.

Example 11-8 shows sample output for **show system**.

Example 11-8   *Using **show system** to obtain information on switch backplane usage.*

```
Console> show system
PS1-Status  PS2-Status  Fan-Status Temp-Alarm  Sys-Status Uptime d,h:m:s  Logout
----------  ----------  ---------- ----------  ---------- --------------  ------
ok          none        ok         off         ok         3,02:08:53      20 min

PS1-Type  PS2-Type Modem    Baud  Traffic  Peak     Peak-Time
--------  -------- -----    ----  -------  -------  -------------------------
WS-C5008A none     disable  9600  0%A      0%B      Wed Oct 22 1997, 14:17:56C

System Name       System Location   System Contact
----------------  ----------------  -------------------------
Catalyst 5000     San Jose, CA      Susan x237
```

The relevant information from Example 11-8 is as follows:

A "Traffic" refers to the current backplane utilization as it relates to the 1.2 Gbps backplane.

B "Peak" refers to the peak backplane utilization seen since the last reboot or the last clearing of the port counters.

C "Peak-Time" is the time at which switch reached its peak backplane utilization. This is important to track in order to compare to possible issues in the network that occur at roughly the same time. The ability to make such comparisons is why it is a good idea to keep all switches synchronized with respect to the time and date.

Using the show traffic Command

This command applies to the Supervisor III card engines only and is representative of all three 1.2 Gbps backplane utilizations in the switch, A, B, and C. The current and peak utilizations and peak time are displayed. The command will show up only in switches that have the Supervisor III card.

The output from this command identifies the usage on each 1.2 Gbps backplane as it applies to the Catalyst 5500 series switches. Typically, the traffic percentages should be the same across all backplanes. The newer line cards, such as gigabit ethernet, use all three backplanes when transmitting and receiving frames, whereas the older line cards, such as the 10/100 ethernet cards, use only one of the backplanes. It is important to note the slot layout in the 5500 chassis to understand what cards can go where. See Chapter 10 for details relating to the slot/bus dependencies.

Example 11-9 shows sample output for **show traffic**.

Example 11-9   *Using the* **show traffic** *command to get information on switch backplane utilization.*

```
Console> sh traffic
Switching-Bus Traffic  Peak     Peak-Time
------------- -------  -------  ------------------------
A             5%ᴬ      10%ᴮ     Thu Jun 18 1998, 22:45:20 ᶜ
B             4%ᴬ      15%ᴮ     Fri Nov 13 1998, 09:59:31ᶜ
C             6%ᴬ      8%ᴮ      Fri Nov 13 1998, 11:30:13 ᶜ
```

The following information is of interest in Example 11-9:

A   "Traffic" refers to the current backplane utilization as it relates to the appropriate 1.2 Gbps backplane.

B   "Peak" refers to the peak backplane utilization seen since the last reboot or the last clearing of the port counters.

C   "Peak-Time" is the time at which the switch reached its peak backplane utilization. This is important to track in order to compare to possible issues in the network that occur at roughly the same time. This is a reason why the use of NTP in the network can assist in this correlation. See the section entitled "Setting Up NTP" in Chapter 18 for more information.

CLI Commands for Monitoring Traffic Utilization on NMP

There are really no MIB objects to look at relating to the processor traffic or the NMP (Network Management Processor) on the switch. You must rely mainly on show commands to get this information— specifically, **show netstat interface** and **show netstat stats**.

The command **show netstat interface**, in conjunction with **show netstat stats**, indicates the amount of traffic hitting the NMP along with the IP traffic destined to the switch, such as SNMP, Telnet sessions, or ICMP pings.

These two commands are useful for baselining the amount of traffic, necessary or unnecessary, hitting the processor on the switch. Ideally, the amount of traffic destined to and from the switch's NMP should be minimal and the majority should be IP. Unnecessary traffic would be frames such as broadcasts from user segments, which indicate that the sc0 port on the switch is in the same VLAN as the user traffic. It is recommended to keep the NMP (sc0) interface off the user segment VLANs to avoid this unwanted traffic; otherwise, the processor can get bogged down processing these frames. Looking at both the IP traffic and total NMP traffic allows you to draw a comparison between the IP and "other" packets. IP traffic is typically the traffic destined to the switch, such as Telnet sessions, SNMP requests, and ICMP pings. Other traffic typically seen on the NMP is BPDUs for all VLANs.

Example 11-10 provides example output for both **show netstat interface** and **show netstat stats**.

Example 11-10   *Using **show netstat interface** and **show netstat stats** to get switch backplane utilization information.*

```
Switch> sh netstat int
Interface          InPackets      InErrors OutPackets OutErrors
sl0                        0            0          0          0
sc0                    50000ᴬ           0      32000 ᴮ        0
Interface Rcv-Octet              Xmit-Octet
......... ....................   ....................
sc0       60000ᶜ                 20000ᴰ
s10       0                      0
Interface Rcv-Unicast            Xmit-Unicast
......... ....................   ....................
sc0       100000ᴱ                20000ᶠ
s10       0                      0

Switch> sh netstat stats
udp:
        0 incomplete headers
        0 bad data length fields
        0 bad checksums
        0 socket overflows
        103 no such ports
tcp:
        161 ᴳ packets sent
                85 data packets (139 bytes)
                0 data packets (0 bytes) retransmitted
                68 ack-only packets (64 delayed)
                0 URG only packets
                0 window probe packets
                4 window update packets
                4 control packets
        122 packets received
                87 acks (for 141 bytes)
                4 duplicate acks
                0 acks for unsent data
                111 packets (6375 bytes) received in-sequence
                0 completely duplicate packets (0 bytes)
                0 packets with some dup. data (0 bytes duped)
                0 out-of-order packets (0 bytes)
                0 packets (0 bytes) of data after window
                0 window probes
                0 window update packets
```

continues

Example 11-10 *Using **show netstat interface** and **show netstat stats** to get switch backplane utilization information. (Continued)*

```
                       0 packets received after close
                       0 discarded for bad checksums
                       0 discarded for bad header offset fields
                       0 discarded because packet too short
             2 connection requests
             0 connection accepts
             2 connections established (including accepts)
             2 connections closed (including 0 drops)
             0 embryonic connections dropped
             87 segments updated rtt (of 89 attempts)
             0 retransmit timeouts
                       0 connections dropped by rexmit timeout
             0 persist timeouts
             2 keepalive timeouts
                   2 keepalive probes sent
                   0 connections dropped by keepalive
   ip:
             293488 ᴴ total packets received
             0 bad header checksums
             0 with size smaller than minimum
             0 with data size < data length
             0 with header length < data size
             0 with data length < header length
             0 fragments received
             0 fragments dropped (dup or out of space)
             0 fragments dropped after timeout
             0 packets forwarded
             0 packets not forwardable
             0 redirects sent
   icmp:
             Redirect enabled
             24 calls to icmp_error
             0 errors not generated 'cuz old message was icmp
             Output histogram:
                   echo reply: 3
                   destination unreachable: 24
             0 messages with bad code fields
             0 messages < minimum length
             0 bad checksums
             0 messages with bad length
             Input histogram:
                   echo reply: 67808
                   destination unreachable: 24
                   echo: 3
             3 ᴵ message responses generated
```

Here are the relevant data from Example 11-10:

A "InPackets" are the total amount of all packets received on the NMP.

B "OutPackets" are the total amount of all packets transmitted from the processor (NMP).

C "Rcv-Octet" is the total amount of bytes received on the NMP. From this value, in conjunction with the "receive packet" count, you can determine the traffic utilization of the NMP, as well as the average packet sizes hitting the NMP. Refer to Chapter 4, "Performance Measurement and Reporting," for utilization formulas.

D "Xmit-Octet" is the total amount of bytes transmitted from the processor. Because the backplane interface from the processor is full-duplex, you can determine the outbound utilization for the NMP as well. Based on the utilization formula defined in Chapter 4, you can use the Outpackets and Xmit-octets to get your result, but typically the NMP won't be sending a lot of information. You really should need to focus only on the inbound packets to get utilization numbers for the processor.

E "Rcv-Unicast" is the total amount of unicast packets received on the processor. From this value, along with "InPackets," you can determine the amount of broadcast and multicasts hitting the NMP by using Equation 11-2:

Equation 11-2

$$(\text{InPackets} - \text{Rcv-unicast}) / \text{InPackets} \times 100\% = \% \text{ broadcasts received/multicasts received}$$

F "Xmit-Unicast" is the total amount of unicast packets sourced from the processor (NMP). There is no need to calculate broadcast utilization on the outbound side of the processor because the switch sources few, if any, broadcast packets.

G TCP "packets sent" is one of two counters you can use to figure out how many IP packets were sourced from the switch because these are the only two counters for transmit. The other counter is ICMP "message response generated."

H IP "total packets received" is the total amount of IP packets destined to the switch processor (NMP).

I ICMP "message response generated" is the total amount of ICMP packets, such as ping, sourced from the processor. Used in conjunction with TCP packets sent, it basically gives you the total amount of IP packets transmitted from the processor.

MIB Variables for Dynamic CAM Entries

From the BRIDGE-MIB, which is extracted from RFC 1493, you can use the dot1dTpFdbAddress from the dot1dTpFdbTable, where the value is equal to 3 or "learned," to determine what MAC addresses are in the forwarding table on the switch. This value is stored as a unicast MAC address for which the bridge has forwarding and/or filtering information. These MAC address values alone don't mean much and can produce a lot of data. Therefore, you need to count the number of entries and store that count value, based on a dot1dTpFdbStatus equal to "learned" (value of 3).

Trending MAC address data is valuable for keeping track of the total number of CAM entries (MAC addresses) learned dynamically by the switch. This monitoring helps keep track of the "flatness" in your network, especially when correlating to the total number of VLANs per switch. For example, if you have one VLAN defined on the switch and you see 8,000 MAC addresses, you know you have 8,000 MAC addresses for one VLAN, which is extensive for one subnet.

Because the CAM aging time, by default, is five minutes, you should gather the CAM table frequently. For example, poll for the data prior to your busy time and then maybe once during your busy time. Because users can turn off their computers when they leave for the day, it is wise to snapshot the CAM table during the day when computers are up and active to find the maximum CAM entries learned. There is more than enough memory to store up to 16,000 MAC address in the bridge (forwarding) table on the Catalyst 5xxx series switches.

The recommended baseline threshold is 8,000 entries or 50 percent of the maximum entries allowed per switch. The numbers should be much smaller per subnet or VLAN. Depending on the type of traffic per VLAN, the number of CAM entries can vary. If there is nothing but TCP/IP traffic, 500 nodes may the limit, whereas on Appletalk segments, 200 may be the limit.

A related MIB object from the BRIDGE MIB (RFC 1493) is dot1dTpFdbStatus. This MIB provides the status of the MAC address entry.

The meanings of the values are as follows:

- **other(1)**: none of the following. This would include the case where some other MIB object (not the corresponding instance of dot1dTpFdbPort, nor an entry in the dot1dStaticTable) is being used to determine if and how frames addressed to the value of the corresponding instance of dot1dTpFdbAddress are being forwarded.

- **invalid(2)**: This entry is no longer valid (for example, it was learned but has since aged out), but has not yet been flushed from the table.

- **learned(3)**: The value of the corresponding instance of dot1dTpFdbPort was learned, and is being used.

- **self(4)**: The value of the corresponding instance of dot1dTpFdbAddress represents one of the bridge's addresses. The corresponding instance of dot1dTpFdbPort indicates which of the bridge's ports has this address.

- **mgmt(5)**: The value of the corresponding instance of dot1dTpFdbAddress is also the value of an existing instance of dot1dStaticAddress.

CLI Commands for CAM Entries

The output from **show cam dynamic** shows the MAC addresses, the VLAN, the port the MAC is learned on, and the total number of dynamically learned CAM entries (MAC addresses) on the Catalyst series switches, excluding the XL series. The **show cam count dynamic** command shows only the total CAM entries learned.

The output from **show cam count dynamic** may be an easier way than using SNMP to get the data you're ultimately looking for, especially if you are concerned about the amount of data flowing over your network. With this command, you don't have to grab the whole forwarding table and then act on it.

Example 11-11 shows sample output from **show cam dynamic**.

Example 11-11   *Using **show cam dynamic** to get CAM entry information.*

```
Switch> sh cam dynamic
VLAN  Destination MAC      Destination Ports or VCs
----  -----------------    ------------------------
5ᴬ    00-60-2f-44-f6-99    2/52ᴮ
5     00-10-0b-c2-bb-fe    4/1
5     00-60-3e-cd-71-ac    2/61
5     00-90-92-b8-63-ff    2/61
Total Matching CAM Entries = 4 ᶜ


Switch> sh cam count dynamic
Total Matching CAM Entries = 4 ᶜ
```

The information highlighted in Example 11-11 is as follows:

A "VLAN" shows what VLAN the appropriate MAC address resides in.

B "Destination Ports or VCs" displays the port or ATM VC (LANE) where the MAC address originates.

C "Total Matching CAM Entries" is the total number of MAC address entries seen by the switch.

MIB Variables for Calculating Logical Ports

Five MIBS need to work together to determine the number of logical ports configured on the switch. From CISCO-STACK-MIB, they are as follows:

- portIndex
- vlanIndex
- vlanPortIslVlansAllowed
- vlanSpantreeEnable
- vlanPortIslOperStatus

PortIndex, vlanIndex, and vlanPortIslVlans are used to enumerate the number of ports and VLANS on the switch. vlanSpantreeEnable is used to determine whether the vlan is running spanning tree, which is required to determine logical ports, and vlanIslOperStatus is used to determine what ports are trunks. For non-ISL-based trunk ports, such as 802.1q and 802.10, the vlanIslOperStatus, in conjunction with the vlanIslAdminStatus, will dictate what ports are trunk ports in those configurations. VLAN indexing is described in detail in the section "MIBs to Monitor for Spanning Tree Topology Changes" in Chapter 15, "Monitoring VLANs."

On your Catalyst 5xxx series switch, ensure that the sum of the logical ports across all instances of spanning tree for different VLANs does not exceed the number allowed for each supervisor engine type and memory configuration. Refer to Equation 11-3 and the following port constraints based on the Supervisor cards to compute this sum. Practical port constraints (not based on the Catalyst Series Release note) are the following:

- 250 for Supervisor Engine I (with 20 MB DRAM)
- 1000 for Supervisor Engine II
- 1000 for Supervisor Engine III (with fiber connections)
- 2500 for Supervisor Engine III

Equation 11-3

The sum of all logical ports = (number of non-ATM trunks on the switch × number of active VLANs on that trunk) + (number of ATM trunks on the switch × number of active VLANs on that trunk × 2) + number of nontrunking ports on the switch.

Equation 11-3 is taken from the "Release Notes for the Catalyst 5000 Series Switches" available on CCO. See the References at the end of this chapter for the specific URL reference.

NOTE

When using Fast EtherChannel, be sure to count each port independently, not as one trunk. In addition, reduce the number of allowed spanning tree instances given in the formula for the number of logical ports when using Fast EtherChannel. This reduction will depend upon your specific topology.

In the formula, an ATM trunk is an ATM interface with a LAN Emulation Client (LEC) or an RFC 1483 PVC.

The recommended baseline threshold for number of logical ports is 50 percent of the total amount allowed, based on supervisor hardware version.

CLI Commands for Calculating Logical Ports

The **show version** command is helpful for getting the total number of physical ports installed on the switch. The **show trunk** command displays the total amount of trunk ports and the total number of VLANs per trunk port on the switch.

From these two commands, you can get the variables or calculate the variables needed to determine the amount of logical ports on the switch, based on the previous formula. You have to use the configuration to indicate which ports have spanning tree enabled and which ones don't. Only ports with spanning tree enabled apply to the formula.

Tracking of the logical ports can also help determine whether VTP, or Virtual Trunking Protocol, pruning needs to be turned on for the trunks, in order to restrict unnecessary VLANs from populating the switch.

TIP

There is no need for a switch to know about a particular VLAN if there are no users in that VLAN hanging directly off that switch or if the switch is acting as a transit switch for other users.

Example 11-12 shows sample output from the **show version** and **show trunk** commands.

Example 11-12   *Using **show version** and **show trunk** to get information on the number of logical ports.*

```
Switch> show version
WS-C5505 Software,Version McpSW:4.1(1)NmpSW:4.1(1)
Copyright (c) 1995-1998 by Cisco Systems
NMP S/W compiled on Jun 19 1998,11:55:01
MCP S/W compiled on Jun 19 1998,11:48:25

System Bootstrap Version:3.1.2

Hardware Version:1.0 Model:WS-C5505 Serial #:066058343

Mod  Port  Model         Serial #          Versions
---  ----  ------------  ---------------   -------------------------
1    2 A   WS-X5530      007472986         Hw : 1.5
                                           Fw : 3.1.2
                                           Fw1: 3.1(2)
                                           Sw : 4.1(1)
3    1     WS-X5302      006809652         Hw : 4.5
                                           Fw : 20.7
                                           Fw1: 2.2(4)
                                           Sw : 11.2(14)P,
4    12    WS-X5213      001906072         Hw : 1.0
                                           Fw : 1.4
                                           Sw : 4.1(1)
```

continues

Example 11-12 *Using **show version** and **show trunk** to get information on the number of logical ports. (Continued)*

```
5     12      WS-X5203      007573748        Hw : 1.1
                                             Fw : 3.1(1)
                                             Sw : 4.1(1)

                ...
                ... etc.


Switch> sh trunk
Port      Mode          Encapsulation  Status        Native vlan
--------  -----------   -------------  ------------  -----------
 5/1ᴬ          on            isl   trunkingᴮ 1


Port      Vlans allowed on trunk
--------  ------------------------------------------------------------
 5/1      1-1005


Port      Vlans allowed and active in management domain
--------  ------------------------------------------------------------
 5/1 ᴬ             1-4,6-10ᶜ


Port      Vlans in spanning tree forwarding state and not pruned
--------  ------------------------------------------------------------
 5/1      1
```

Information of interest in Example 11-12 is as follows:

A "Port" is the total number of ports per module. Summing up these ports for all modules will give you the total number of ports for the switch. Under the **show trunk** output, each unique port number is displayed. Thus, all you need to do is total up the amount of ports shown under the command to get total number of trunk ports associated with the switch.

B "Status" indicates which trunk ports are in the ACTIVE trunking state.

C "Vlans allowed and active..." are the VLANs that are allowed to traverse each trunk port. Summing up all unique instances of VLANs per trunk port will give you the total number of VLANS per trunk port.

Related commands are the following:

- **show port**: Provides the trunking status for the ports, but not for the ATM interfaces.
- **show vlan**: Provides the number of VLANS assigned to the switch.

Error/Fault Data for Router Processors

The format of this section is identical to the performance sections, except that in addition to MIBs and CLI commands, we also will present relevant SNMP traps and syslog messages.

SNMP traps require you have a trapd daemon running on some SNMP server and the router must point to that server configured via the **snmp server-host configuration** command. Syslog messages can be stored on a syslog server or on the router itself, either on the console or in a buffer. If stored in the buffer, executing the command **show logging** will show the same values as seen on a syslog server. This feature is especially important to use in addition to a syslog server when the network is down or when the route to the syslog server is down or unavailable. See "Setting Up SNMP" in Chapter 18 for more information on best practices for SNMP configuration.

MIB Variables for Memory Leaking or Depletion

The bufferNoMem variable, from OLD-CISCO-MEMORY-MIB, is a counter of the number of buffer create failures due to no free memory. If there is not enough system memory to allocate an appropriate size buffer, the buffernoMem counter is incremented. Increments in buffernoMem can also provide you with locations of some of your network issues. If this counter increases at all, then a packet probably is being dropped.

In "Performance Data for Router Processors," we focused on looking at the CPU processes and the memory usage. Here, we look at the way system buffers affect memory. System buffers are dynamic in nature and constantly changing, either by creating or trimming, thus affecting the buffers' interaction with system memory. Ideally, you want to have the trims and creates stay fairly constant. We'll look at the trims and creates in the "show" command output a little later in this section.

The buffernoMem MIB can be used in correlation with the memory MIBs ciscoMemoryPoolFree, freeMem, or ciscoMemoryPoolLargestFree.

The recommended baseline threshold for BufferNoMem is that the value should be relative to sysUptime. But even a value of 1 can be an indication to start looking at where the misses are occurring because misses cause creates, and create failures cause "no memory" conditions.

A related MIB object from OLD-CISCO-MEMORY MIB is bufferFail, which is a count of the number of buffer allocation failures. This MIB is really a superset of bufferNoMem variable, and is typically seen as the same value as bufferNoMem.

CLI Commands for Analyzing Memory Usage

See "CLI Commands for Buffer Usage" for details on the **show buffers** command and output (see Example 11-7). For details on the **show memory** command and output (see Example 11-5), see "Using the **show memory** Command."

Syslog Messages Relating to Memory Issues

A number of syslog messages are useful for memory fault management, and apply directly to the MIB objects and CLI commands previously discussed. They are collected in Table 11-3.

Table 11-3 *Syslog Messages for Memory Information*

Message	Explanation
%SYS-2-MALLOCFAIL: Memory allocation of [dec] bytes failed from [hex], pool [chars], alignment [dec]	The requested memory allocation is not available from the specified memory pool or system buffer. The current system configuration, network environment, or possibly a software error might have exhausted or fragmented the router's memory. If this message is seen in the syslog, you more than likely are experiencing a memory leak of some kind in the router. To assist in isolating where the problem lies, look at the fragmented memory or largest block free from a **show memory** output to get that number, as well as looking at the amount of memory allocated (holding) for each process from the CLI command **show proc mem**. By trending the holding memory for each process and the largest memory block free, you can easily pinpoint where the memory leak is occurring. Record your findings and report it to the Cisco TAC (Technical Assistance Center) or search the Bug Navigator tool on CCO URL to identify possible known defects: http://www.cisco.com/support/bugtools/bugtool.shtml.
%SYS-2-NOMEMORY: No memory available for [chars] [dec]	This syslog message indicates that an operation could not be accomplished because of a low-memory condition. The current system configuration, network environment, or possibly a software error might have exhausted or fragmented the router's memory. This message typically is attributed to fragmented memory. The **show memory** CLI command or ciscoMemoryPoolLargestFree MIB variable values can be directly correlated to these kinds of system messages.

MIB Variables for Identifying Router Reloads

The WhyReload MIB, from OLD-CISCO-SYSTEM MIB, contains a printable octet string that contains the reason why the system was last restarted. Reasons include things such as "power on," user-initiated reload, exception, or some other error.

The whyReload MIB can help you track change management windows, such as scheduled powerdowns and possible IOS defects, when values such as exceptions are seen for reasons. Used in conjunction with the SNMP trap **reload**, whyReload can provide further insight.

For example, based on a reload trap seen on the snmp server-host, you can trigger an SNMP poll of the **whyReload** MIB variable to find the reason why the router reloaded.

The recommended baseline threshold is that any value other than "power-on" or "reload" should be flagged because it can identify possible software or hardware errors.

CLI Commands for Analyzing Reload Crash Conditions

The **show stacks** command is useful for troubleshooting software-forced crashes on the router that caused the reload SNMP trap to initiate. The result of the whyReload MIB can lead you to look at this command output. See Chapter 10 for details on the output from the **show stack** command in the section "Router Health from **show stack**."

SNMP Traps Relating to Reload Conditions

The reload trap, from CISCO-GENERAL-TRAPS, indicates that your router reloaded for some reason. It is sent when the router detects that it is booting because a trap is unlikely to successfully get sent when the router is in the act of rebooting itself. The following section displays the syslog messages relating to reload conditions. When a reload syslog message is reported, the reload trap will follow and correspond to that message. Refer to your network management vendor for details on the format of the reload trap.

Syslog Messages Relating to Reload Conditions

A number of syslog messages are useful for analyzing why routers reload, and apply directly to the MIB objects and CLI commands previously discussed. They are collected in Table 11-4.

Table 11-4   *Syslog Messages for Router Reload Information*

Message	Explanation
%SYS-5-RELOAD: Reload requested	This message indicates that someone or something requested a reload of the router. This can happen if the actual reload command is typed from the command line or if the router reloaded due to a software error.
%SYS-5-RESTART: System restarted --[chars]	This syslog message indicates the router has restarted and is up and operational, or is at least done booting up the IOS.

The two syslog messages in Table 11-4 are good baseline or "threshold" points to monitor, once for when the reload was requested and once for when the router is back online. Also, you can determine how long it takes for the router to boot up from these two syslog messages, from the reload request to the "restarted" message.

Error/Fault Data for Switch Processors

Here, we'll look at switch information relating to fault management. We'll identify some key MIBs and show commands that relate to switch health.

MIB Variables for Switch and Module "Health" Status

From CISCO-STACK-MIB, the ModuleStatus variable provides the operational status of the module. If the status is not ok, the value of moduleTestResult gives more detailed information about the module's failure condition(s). The possible values seen in this MIB object are as follows:

- other(1)—none of the following
- ok(2)—status ok
- minorFault(3)—minor problem
- majorFault(4)—major problem

By polling this MIB, you can keep watch on the modules installed in the switch versus keeping track of every port on a switch. The latter can be excessive, except for the trunk and other "critical" ports that you identify.

A related MIB object from CISCO-STACK MIB is ModuleTestResult, which provides the result of the module's self-test. A zero indicates that the module passed all tests. Bits set in the result indicate error conditions.

CLI Commands for Analyzing Switch and Module Health

The **show module** and **show test** commands are related to the ModuleStatus MIB. For details on the output from the **show module** command, see Chapter 10.

Using the show test Command

The **show test** command shows you the status of the self-tests run against the individual modules. The status of the test results assists you in pinpointing the possible cause for minorFault or majorFault, as indicated by the values in the moduleStatus MIB.

Example 11-13 shows sample output for **show test**.

Example 11-13   *Using **show test** to determine the health of a module.*

```
Switch> sh test 2

Module 2 : 48-port 4 Segment 10BaseT Ethernet
Repeater Port Status:
   Ports 1  2  3  4  5  6  7  8  9  10 11 12 13 14 15 16 17 18 19 20 21 22 23 24
   ---------------------------------------------------------------------------
         .  .  .  .  .  .  .  .  .  .  .  .  .  .  .  .  .  .  .  .  .  .  .  .
   25 26 27 28 29 30 31 32 33 34 35 36 37 38 39 40 41 42 43 44 45 46 47 48
   ---------------------------------------------------------------------------
    .  .  .  .  .  .  .  .  .  .  .  .  .  .  .  .  .  .  .  .  .  .  .  .


LCP Diag Status for Module 2  (. = Pass, F = Fail, N = N/A)
   CPU        : .    Sprom     : .    Bootcsum : .    Archsum  : N
   RAM        : .    LTL       : .    CBL      : N    DPRAM    : N    SAMBA : N
   Saints     : .    Pkt Bufs : .    Repeater : .    FLASH    : N

   SAINT/SAGE Status :
    Saint 1  2  3  4
    ----------------
          .  .  .  .

   Packet Buffer Status :
    Saint 1  2  3  4
    ----------------
          .  .  .  .

   Loopback Status [Reported by Module 1] :
    Saint  1  2  3  4
    ----------------
           .  .  .  .
```

The type of card you have installed in each slot determines what kind of output you see in the **show test** [*mod_num*] output. If the card is working properly, you should see all "." next to the individual tests. If something failed on the card, you'll see an "F."

Using the show log Command

The **show log** command shows you the error log of the system, such as reboot histories, module reset counts, exception errors with corresponding hex dumps, and self-test results for the supervisor modules.

This command is very useful for examining the overall health and stability of your switch. If there are any exceptions to why the Supervisor card reset, the results are stored here.

The **show log** output on a switch is stored in NVRAM, so it is not cleared after a reset of the switch. You have to manually clear the log to take all values back to 0. It is good practice to clear the log every time you upgrade the software on the switch, due to possible exception counters stored under the network management processor. There is no need to store an exception count for a software release other than the current running release.

Output from **show log** also is good for comparing the last reset time and date of the supervisor with that of the other modules in the switch. Drawing that correlation can assist you in determining when module cards were OIRed (online insertion and removal) or reset by other methods without the entire switch resetting.

Example 11-14 shows sample output from **show log**.

Example 11-14   *Using **show log** to determine the health of the switch or module.*

```
Switch> show log

Network Management Processor (ACTIVE NMP) Log:
  Reset count:    3[A]
  Re-boot History:    Feb 18 1998 17:14:18 0 [B], Feb 05 1998 15:16:28 0
                      Feb 05 1998 14:20:33 0
  Bootrom Checksum Failures:      0 [C] UART Failures:                0
  Flash Checksum Failures:        0    Flash Program Failures:       0
  Power Supply 1 Failures:        0    Power Supply 2 Failures:      0
  Swapped to CLKA:                0      Swapped to CLKB:            0
  Swapped to Processor 1:         0    Swapped to Processor 2:       0
  DRAM Failures:                  0
  Exceptions:        9
    Last Exception occurred on Feb 18 1998 17:14:18 [B]
    Software version = 2.4(2) [D]

NVRAM log:


Network Management Processor (STANDBY NMP) Log:
  Reset count:    3 [A]
  Re-boot History:    Feb 18 1998 17:14:18 0 [B], Feb 05 1998 15:16:28 0
                      Feb 05 1998 14:20:33 0


  Bootrom Checksum Failures:      0 [C] UART Failures:                0
  Flash Checksum Failures:        0    Flash Program Failures:       0
  Power Supply 1 Failures:        0    Power Supply 2 Failures:      0
  Swapped to CLKA:                0      Swapped to CLKB:            0
  Swapped to Processor 1:         0    Swapped to Processor 2:       0
  DRAM Failures:                  0
  Exceptions:                     0

NVRAM log:
```

Example 11-14   *Using **show log** to determine the health of the switch or module. (Continued)*

```
Module 3  Log:
  Reset Count:    4 A
  Reset History: Wed Feb 18 1998, 17:14:18 B
  Sun Feb 15 1998, 04:34:12
                  Thu Feb 5 1998, 15:17:38
                  Thu Feb 5 1998, 14:21:43
```

The following items are highlighted in Example 11-14:

  A "Reset count" is the number of times that particular line card resets. Notice the difference between the reset count on the two Network Management Processors (slots 1 and 2) and the slot 3 module. Slot 3 must have been reset manually or by the reset command one extra time.

  B The "Re-boot History" line indicates the time and date of the all the resets the line card exhibited, up to 10. You can compare this to the line "Last Exception occurred..." below it.

  C The failures for the Supervisor cards are highlighted here. These are cumulative counts of failures that occurred on the Network Management Processor or Supervisor card. Typically, you'll see power supply failure increase more than others because every time the switch resets, the power supply failure increments.

  D The "Software version" line, as indicated here, is the software version the exception occurred in. If this is not the current software running, you should clear the log to get an accurate count of the appropriate errors that may occur with the current release of software.

SNMP Traps Relating to Switch Health

The moduleUp and moduleDown traps (CISCO-STACK-MIB.traps) indicate that a module in the switch chassis has either just come online or just gone offline. Here, you can track when cards are inserted into the chassis by OIR, or track when cards are removed or having problems.

The coldStart and whyreload trap (CISCO-GENERAL-TRAPS) indicate that the switch was powered on and restarted. These traps will be sent when the switch is coming up very similar to that of the router or when the switch unexpectedly restarts.

Syslog Messages Relating to Switch Health

A number of syslog messages are useful for analyzing switch health, and apply directly to the MIB objects and CLI commands previously discussed. They are collected in Table 11-5.

Table 11-5 *Syslog Messages for Switch Health Information*

Message	Explanation
SYS-5-SYS_RESET: System reset from [chars]	The switch has been reset, either by a failure or by manual intervention, such as from a change management window.
SYS-3-MOD_MINORFAIL: Minor problem in module [dec] SYS-3-MOD_FAILREASON: Module [dec] failed due to CBL0 error SYS-3-MOD_FAIL: Module [dec] failed to come online	These three syslog messages indicate that some type of failure on a particular line card or Supervisor card has occurred. These can be correlated to the moduleDown trap received or to the moduleStatus MIB object. Based on this result, you should actively poll for the moduleStatus for the given module number as indicated by the [dec] placement in the message.
SYS-5-MOD_INSERT: Module [dec] has been inserted SYS-5-MOD_REMOVE: Module [dec] has been removed SYS-5-MOD_RESET: Module [dec] reset from [chars]	These three syslog messages explain when a module is inserted, removed, or reset—either by a failure as illustrated above, or by manual intervention.
SNMP-5-MODULETRAP: Module [dec] [[chars]] Trap SNMP-5-COLDSTART: Cold Start Trap SNMP-5-WARMSTART: Warm Start Trap	These three SNMP syslog messages are indications that a SNMP trap was sent out based on the message type. The moduleUp/Down trap, coldStart trap, and warmStart trap are indicated here. The warmStart trap is an indication that the switch has supervisor redundancy and the backup Supervisor card is now active. You can correlate these syslog messages to the trapd daemon running on your management station to see whether the appropriate trap was received.

CLI Commands for Analyzing Switch System Resources

The key system resources needing evaluation on switches, such as resource errors and low clusters, cannot be gathered from SNMP MIB objects, so CLI commands are used instead.

Here are several show commands relating to the evaluation of system resources on a switch. This section will cover the following:

- **show inband**
- **show biga**
- **show mbuf**

Using the show inband and show biga Commands

The **show inband** command applies to the Supervisor III engines and the **show biga** command applies to Supervisor I and II engines.

The **show inband** or **show biga** command shows statistics from the SAGE ASIC chip that front-ends the processor for data traffic. The chip resides on the processor card. The output you need to concern yourself with here is the field RsrcErrors. These commands can be executed only from the enable mode.

Resource errors are important to look at over time when you are experiencing performance problems. If this counter is increasing rapidly over a short amount of time, you are "starving" the resources on the switch processor. Thus, it cannot process frames such as BPDUs, VTP, ISL, and CDP. Incrementing resource errors typically means that the switch cannot allocate memory or buffers (mbufs) for frames received on the processor. When the switch cannot process these frames, especially BPDUs, the switch network can become unstable. For example, if the processor does not see BPDUs, ports in blocking mode can go to forwarding mode and thus cause a snowball effect of a bridge loop and disable.

Example 11-15 shows sample output for **show biga** and **show inband**.

Example 11-15   *Using **show biga** and **show inband** to evaluate available system resources on a switch.*

```
Switch (enable) sh biga
BIGA Registers:
    cstat:       00  upad :     FFFF  pctrl :     0000  nist :      0000
    sist :     0098  hica :     0000  hicb  :     0000  hicc :        00
    dctrl:     F5FF  dstat:     0000  dctrl2:       80  npim :      00F8
    thead: 102FC804  ttail: 102FC804  ttmph : 102FC804  tptr : 10497E62
    tdsc : 00000500  tlen :     0000  tqsel :       05
    rhead: 102FA5D0  rtail: 102FA5B4  rtmph : 102FA5EC  rptr : 104E5280
    rdsc : 80000000  rplen: 102FA5E4  rtlen : 00000000  rlen :      1572
    fltr :     00FF  fc   :       00  Rev   :       04  CFG  : 02020202
BIGA Driver:
    Initializd:     TRUE  SpurusIntr: 00000000  NPIMShadow:      00F8

BIGA Receive:
    RxDone      :     FALSE
    First RBD : 102FA534  Last  RBD : 102FC118
    SoftRHead : 102FA5C0  SoftRTail : 102FA5A4
    FramesRcvd: 00202501  BytesRcvd : 21197580
    QueuedRBDs: 00000256  RsrcErrors: 00006520[A]

BIGA Transmit:
    First TBD : 102FC134  Last  TBD : 102FC818
    SoftTHead : 102FC134  SoftTTail : 102FC134
```

continues

Example 11-15 *Using **show biga** and **show inband** to evaluate available system resources on a switch. (Continued)*

```
       Free TBDs : 00000064  No TBDs   : 00000000
       AcknowErrs: 00000000  HardErrors: 00000000
       QueuedPkts: 00000000  XmittedPkt: 01604290
       XmittedByt: 136665648  Panic    : 00000000
       Frag<=4Byt: 00000000

Switch(enable) sh inband

Inband Driver:
DriverPtr:  A067D300   Initializd:   TRUE  SpurusIntr: 00000000
     RxDone:        FALSE  TxDMAWorking:  FALSE  RxRecovPtr: 00000000(-1)
     FPGACntl:      004F  Characteristics:0000  LastISRCause:     04

     Transmit:
      First TBD : A0681B84(0  )  Last  TBD : A0682B64(0  )
      TxHead    : A0681D44(14 )  TxTail    : A0681D44(14 )
      AvailTBDs : 00000128       QueuedPkts: 00000000
      XmittedPkt: 00247610       XmittedByt: 22625836
      PanicEnd  : 00000000       PanicNullP: 00000000
      BufLenErrs: 00000000       Len0Errs  : 00000000
      Frag<=4Byt: 00000665       SpursTxInt: 00000000
      No TBDs   : 00000000       NullMbuf  : 00000000

     Receive:
      First RBD : A067D384(0  )  Last  RBD : A0681B60(511)
      RxHead    : A067E320(111)  RxTail    : A067E2FC(110)
      AvailRBD  : 00000512       RsrcErrors: 00000000ᴬ
      PanicNullP: 00000000       PanicFakeI: 00000000
      FramesRcvd: 03173999       BytesRcvd : 246115897
      RuntsRcvd : 00000000       HugeRcvd  : 00000000

GT64010 IntMask: F00F0000  IntCause: 0330E083
GT64010 TX DMA (CH 1):
     Count: 0000  Src  : 013D5C62   Dst   : 4ff10056   NRP  : 000000
     Cntl :       15C0
GT64010 RX DMA (CH 2):
     Count: 0680  Src  : 4FF20000   Dst   : 01c84d80   NRP  : 0067BC
     Cntl :       55C0

PSI (PCI SAGE/PHOENIX Interface) FPGA:
     Control : 004F  TxCount : 0056
     RxDMACmd: 35C0  RxBufSiz: 0680  MaxPkt  : 0680
     IntCause: 0000  IntMask : 0003
```

Monitoring RsrcErrors (A) is important over time, especially over a short time frame when switch performance problems are occurring. If this counter is incrementing over a long period of time, it is not as crucial.

Using the show mbuf command

The fixed buffers on switches are permanently set and come in two flavors: mbuf and clusters. Each mbuf is segmented into 128 bytes (116 data bytes), whereas clusters are packets greater than 1664 bytes (13 mbufs and 1508 data bytes). The only traffic that affects the mbuf and cluster counters is traffic destined to the supervisor engine, such as BPDUs, VTP, or CDP. The **show mbuf all** output displays the current amount of mbufs free and clusters free, as well as the lowest mbufs and clusters free.

The critical values that need to be looked at with switch buffers are the "free" and "lowest free" mbufs and clusters because they can help identify possible memory leaks or lack of proper memory resources. Free mbufs, lowest free mbufs, clfree, and lowest clfree should be flagged if they go below 100, which is used as an initial baseline threshold.

Example 11-16 shows sample output from **show mbuf**.

Example 11-16 *Using **show mbuf** to determine system resources available on a switch.*

```
Switch(enable) sh mbuf
MBSTATS:
          mbufs                  10224    clusters        3932
          free mbufs             9946ᴬ    clfree          3675 ᴮ
          lowest free mbufs      9935 ᶜ   lowest clfree   3665 ᴰ

MALLOC STATS :
Block Size        Free Blocks
   16                 1
   48                 2
  112                 1
  144                 1
  208                 1
  240                 1
  400                 1
 > 496                4

Largest block available : 7510096
Total Memory available  : 7546400 ᴱ
Total Memory used       :  563952
```

The highlighted information from Example 11-16 is as follows:

A "free mbufs" is the number of current mbufs free for the processor. The amount of DRAM installed in the switch determines the size of the mbufs allocated at boot time, as indicated by the mbufs row.

B "clfree" is the number of current clusters free for the processor. The amount of DRAM installed in the switch determines the size of the clusters allocated at boot time, as indicated by the clusters row.

C "lowest free mbufs" is the field you need to trend and watch for memory resource usage.

D "lowest clfree" needs close attention as well because it also trends memory resource usage.

E "Total Memory available" is the amount of fixed DRAM memory allocated for mbufs.

Summary

This chapter identifies key data points relating to the system processes and resources in IOS routers and Catalyst switches. Highlights include some common best practices, such as buffer tuning, for working with key components needed to manage your network effectively. Buffer utilization, and how it affects the router, is an important component of performance management. Other important performance management issues include identifying CPU on the router and backplane utilization on the switch, and monitoring router memory, such as memory fragmentation and free memory.

Important error/fault management issues include checking resource errors on switches via the **show inband** and **show biga** commands.

The use of SNMP MIBs, along with CLI output, can assist in maintaining high performance and proactive fault/error management in your network. We'll look at the common interface-specific variables in the next chapter, which can be used in conjunction with these system data points for correlation.

References

Internet Resources

"Broadcasts in Switched Internetworks."

> http://www.cisco.com/univercd/cc/td/doc/cisintwk/idg4/nd20e.htm

"Designing Large-Scale IP Internetworks."

> http://www.cisco.com/univercd/cc/td/doc/cisintwk/idg4/nd2003.htm

"Message and Recovery Procedures."

> http://www.cisco.com/univercd/cc/td/doc/product/lan/cat5000/rel_4_4/sys_msg/emsg.htm

"Reducing SAP Traffic in Novell IPX Networks."

> http://www.cisco.com/univercd/cc/td/doc/cisintwk/ics/cs005.htm

"Release Notes for the Catalyst 5000 Series Switches."

> http://www.cisco.com/univercd/cc/td/doc/product/lan/cat5000/c5krn/sw_rns/78_5861.htm

"Troubleshooting Commands."

http://www.cisco.com/univercd/cc/td/doc/product/software/ios120/12cgcr/fun_r/frprt3/frtroubl.htm

"UDP Broadcast Flooding."

http://www.cisco.com/univercd/cc/td/doc/cisintwk/ics/cs006.htm

CHAPTER 12

Monitoring System Interfaces

This chapter covers performance and fault monitoring for device interfaces in general. There are parameters you will want to monitor that are common to all interfaces, regardless of whether they are on a router or a switch, LAN or WAN. We will also cover some characteristics unique to the way Cisco devices manage their interfaces. Use this chapter as a general guideline to monitor your interfaces. Subsequent chapters will cover specifics for a given type of interface.

We will discuss several points on how Cisco implements management information on different types of interfaces:

- Sub-interfaces
- Interface counters
- High-speed interfaces
- Performance data to monitor
- Fault data to monitor

Overview of System Interfaces

Interfaces have several characteristics that affect the way you monitor them. The topology, duplexity, and transmission characteristics all affect how you calculate utilization and what errors you monitor.

One characteristic is the topology: point-to-point or broadcast. A *point-to-point* link connects two interfaces. Generally, all WAN interfaces fall in this category. A *broadcast* topology has more than two interfaces connected. Broadcast topologies are used almost exclusively in LANs. Shared Ethernet is a good example of a broadcast topology. However, with the rise of switched Ethernets, many Ethernet links are now point-to-point.

The duplexity has a great effect on performance measurements and calculations. A link is either full- or half-duplex. Full-duplex interfaces can transmit and receive data simultaneously. Half-duplex interfaces can only either transmit or receive data. Full-duplex interfaces are generally point-to-point; half-duplex interfaces may be multipoint or point-to-point.

Another characteristic is transmission speed or bandwidth of the link. Obviously, you need to know the transmission speed of a link in order to calculate the utilization of the link. For WAN links, the transmission speed is generally determined by a separate clock signal. For LAN links, the transmission speed is predetermined and the clock is embedded in the data itself. There is an object in the ifTable called ifSpeed. Cisco routers use an interface configuration command:

bandwidth *kilobits*

The bandwidth interface command will set the value of ifSpeed, which is useful for calculating the utilization of an interface.

Special Considerations for Sub-interfaces

There are some special types of interfaces that you will need to monitor. Initially, interfaces table (ifTable) from RFC 1213 had an entry for every physical interface on a device. But newer technologies such as Frame Relay, ATM, and VLANs introduced a different type of interface: the virtual interface, or sub-interface. On a Frame Relay interface, for example, you may have several different Permanent Virtual Circuits (PVCs). Several functional aspects, such as split horizon, make it desirable to treat each PVC as a separate virtual interface, although they all reside on the same physical interface. Sub-interfaces allow you to treat each PVC as a separate interface. And although the overall utilization of the physical interface is most important, the amount of traffic on individual sub-interfaces is of great interest as well.

However, from the definitions in RFC 1213, it is difficult to fill all the entries in the ifTable for sub-interfaces. It is quite possible that not all objects in the ifTable apply to a particular sub-interface. For example, how do framing errors apply to a virtual interface? Framing errors are physical errors and therefore apply only to the physical rather than the virtual interface. The concept of sparse tables was introduced in RFC 1573 (later superceded by RFC 2233). This concept means that a row in the ifTable for a sub-interface may not have values in columns where the objects do not apply to the sub-interface.

Cisco IOS implemented support for generic sub-interfaces, starting in IOS version 11.1. Frame Relay and ATM LANE sub-interfaces support was added in IOS 11.1. Support of other ATM sub-interfaces was added in IOS 12.0T. As of this writing, ifTable support for ISL VLAN sub-interfaces is planned for IOS version 12.1(3)T.

With the addition of rows for sub-interfaces to the ifTable, the table becomes sparse. For a sub-interface row, there will be no values for the objects that do not apply to the sub-interface. The device will return a "no such name" error when such an object is accessed. The SNMP **get** and **getNext** operations have no problem dealing with sparse tables. However, there are some NMS applications that may have problems when they try to walk a sparse table. There is a workaround in IOS with the hidden global configuration command:

no snmp-server sparse-table

This workaround causes those objects to return a value of 0 rather than a "no such name" error.

Special Considerations for ifIndex

A further complication introduced with the ifTable support of sub-interfaces is that of ifIndex. When sub-interfaces are added on the fly, they are appended to the end of the ifTable. However when the router re-initializes, the interfaces re-index—with the result that for many interfaces, the ifIndex changes. Because ifIndex can change from re-boot to re-boot, you should not depend on ifIndex to know which interface you are polling. For example, if you poll ifDescr in a router with a Frame Relay connection:

```
%4> snmpwalk 10.29.4.2 ifDescr
interfaces.ifTable.ifEntry.ifDescr.1 : DISPLAY STRING- (ascii):  Ethernet0
interfaces.ifTable.ifEntry.ifDescr.2 : DISPLAY STRING- (ascii):  Serial0
interfaces.ifTable.ifEntry.ifDescr.3 : DISPLAY STRING- (ascii):  Serial1
interfaces.ifTable.ifEntry.ifDescr.4 : DISPLAY STRING- (ascii):  Loopback0
interfaces.ifTable.ifEntry.ifDescr.5 : DISPLAY STRING- (ascii):  Loopback253
interfaces.ifTable.ifEntry.ifDescr.6 : DISPLAY STRING- (ascii):  Serial0.1
interfaces.ifTable.ifEntry.ifDescr.7 : DISPLAY STRING- (ascii):  Serial0.2
interfaces.ifTable.ifEntry.ifDescr.8 : DISPLAY STRING- (ascii):  Serial0.3
interfaces.ifTable.ifEntry.ifDescr.9 : DISPLAY STRING- (ascii):  Serial0.4
interfaces.ifTable.ifEntry.ifDescr.10 : DISPLAY STRING- (ascii):  Serial0.5
interfaces.ifTable.ifEntry.ifDescr.11 : DISPLAY STRING- (ascii):  Serial0.6
interfaces.ifTable.ifEntry.ifDescr.12 : DISPLAY STRING- (ascii):  Serial0.7
interfaces.ifTable.ifEntry.ifDescr.13 : DISPLAY STRING- (ascii):  Serial0.8
interfaces.ifTable.ifEntry.ifDescr.14 : DISPLAY STRING- (ascii):  Serial0.9
interfaces.ifTable.ifEntry.ifDescr.15 : DISPLAY STRING- (ascii):  Serial0.100
interfaces.ifTable.ifEntry.ifDescr.16 : DISPLAY STRING- (ascii):  Async1
```

Now, if a new circuit is added:

```
%5> snmpwalk 10.29.4.2 ifDescr
interfaces.ifTable.ifEntry.ifDescr.1 : DISPLAY STRING- (ascii):  Ethernet0
interfaces.ifTable.ifEntry.ifDescr.2 : DISPLAY STRING- (ascii):  Serial0
interfaces.ifTable.ifEntry.ifDescr.3 : DISPLAY STRING- (ascii):  Serial1
interfaces.ifTable.ifEntry.ifDescr.4 : DISPLAY STRING- (ascii):  Loopback0
interfaces.ifTable.ifEntry.ifDescr.5 : DISPLAY STRING- (ascii):  Loopback253
interfaces.ifTable.ifEntry.ifDescr.6 : DISPLAY STRING- (ascii):  Serial0.1
interfaces.ifTable.ifEntry.ifDescr.7 : DISPLAY STRING- (ascii):  Serial0.2
interfaces.ifTable.ifEntry.ifDescr.8 : DISPLAY STRING- (ascii):  Serial0.3
interfaces.ifTable.ifEntry.ifDescr.9 : DISPLAY STRING- (ascii):  Serial0.4
interfaces.ifTable.ifEntry.ifDescr.10 : DISPLAY STRING- (ascii):  Serial0.5
interfaces.ifTable.ifEntry.ifDescr.11 : DISPLAY STRING- (ascii):  Serial0.6
interfaces.ifTable.ifEntry.ifDescr.12 : DISPLAY STRING- (ascii):  Serial0.7
interfaces.ifTable.ifEntry.ifDescr.13 : DISPLAY STRING- (ascii):  Serial0.8
interfaces.ifTable.ifEntry.ifDescr.14 : DISPLAY STRING- (ascii):  Serial0.9
interfaces.ifTable.ifEntry.ifDescr.15 : DISPLAY STRING- (ascii):  Serial0.100
interfaces.ifTable.ifEntry.ifDescr.16 : DISPLAY STRING- (ascii):  Async1
interfaces.ifTable.ifEntry.ifDescr.17 : DISPLAY STRING- (ascii):  Serial0.200
```

You can see that the new sub-interface is appended to the end of the ifTable. But if the router is reloaded, the interfaces will re-index:

```
%6> snmpwalk 10.29.4.2 ifDescr
interfaces.ifTable.ifEntry.ifDescr.1 : DISPLAY STRING- (ascii):  Ethernet0
interfaces.ifTable.ifEntry.ifDescr.2 : DISPLAY STRING- (ascii):  Serial0
interfaces.ifTable.ifEntry.ifDescr.3 : DISPLAY STRING- (ascii):  Serial1
interfaces.ifTable.ifEntry.ifDescr.4 : DISPLAY STRING- (ascii):  Loopback0
```

```
interfaces.ifTable.ifEntry.ifDescr.5 : DISPLAY STRING- (ascii):  Loopback253
interfaces.ifTable.ifEntry.ifDescr.6 : DISPLAY STRING- (ascii):  Serial0.1
interfaces.ifTable.ifEntry.ifDescr.7 : DISPLAY STRING- (ascii):  Serial0.2
interfaces.ifTable.ifEntry.ifDescr.8 : DISPLAY STRING- (ascii):  Serial0.3
interfaces.ifTable.ifEntry.ifDescr.9 : DISPLAY STRING- (ascii):  Serial0.4
interfaces.ifTable.ifEntry.ifDescr.10 : DISPLAY STRING- (ascii):  Serial0.5
interfaces.ifTable.ifEntry.ifDescr.11 : DISPLAY STRING- (ascii):  Serial0.6
interfaces.ifTable.ifEntry.ifDescr.12 : DISPLAY STRING- (ascii):  Serial0.7
interfaces.ifTable.ifEntry.ifDescr.13 : DISPLAY STRING- (ascii):  Serial0.8
interfaces.ifTable.ifEntry.ifDescr.14 : DISPLAY STRING- (ascii):  Serial0.9
interfaces.ifTable.ifEntry.ifDescr.15 : DISPLAY STRING- (ascii):  Serial0.100
interfaces.ifTable.ifEntry.ifDescr.16 : DISPLAY STRING- (ascii):  Serial0.200
interfaces.ifTable.ifEntry.ifDescr.17 : DISPLAY STRING- (ascii):  Async1
```

The problem is how to know which interface you are actually polling. The preceding example makes it clear that you cannot poll a specific ifIndex and expect to always poll the same interface. The trick is to poll for a handle so you know which entry in the ifTable corresponds to the desired interface. There is an object (ifDescr) that fits the bill to a certain degree. Although ifDescr is descriptive enough to use in routers, in switches it only returns the type of interface: "10/100 utp Ethernet (cat 3/5)," for example. Not a very helpful description if you are looking for slot and port number.

There were several extensions to the ifTable defined in RFC 1573 (later superceded by RFC 2233) in the ifXTable. Two of these new objects can assist you in identifying which interface you are polling. One object is ifName. ifName is a DisplayString that will return the name of an interface such as "Serial0/0.2" for a router and "5/22" for a switch.

You may want your own definable handle to identify an interface. Another object, ifAlias, is a display string that returns whatever handle you assign to it. The alias can be configured either via an **snmp set** or via the interface configuration command:

description "string"

ifAlias takes the place of the deprecated lofIfDesc object from the OLD-CISCO-INTERFACES MIB.

However, ifAlias only applies to Cisco routers. Catalyst switches do not support ifAlias. Catalyst switches have implemented a different object that you may use as an identifying handle. Catalyst switches use the portName object in the portTable in Cisco's proprietary STACK MIB. You may set this alias with the following command:

set port name x/y

where x/y is the slot number/port number.

Special Considerations on Interface Counters

In SNMP, a counter is defined to count occurrences of a particular event such as the transmission of a bit or a packet. In general, an SNMP counter will count events starting at system initialization and keep increasing until the register hits the limit. That would be 2^{32} (or 4,294,967,296) for a 32-bit counter for example. Then, the counter wraps back to 0 and starts over. So an SNMP counter will go to 0 when the counter wraps or if the system reinitializes. When you are sampling counters, it is important to distinguish between when the counter wraps or when the counter is set back to 0 by a reload or reset. Generally, you can monitor the object sysUpTime in the mib-2 systems group to see how long the system has been operational. If your sampling of a counter detects that it went to 0, you can check sysUpTime to see whether the system was also reset during the last sampling period. If the system did not reset, it is reasonable to assume that the counter wrapped.

There are notable exceptions to the previous rule. When using **show** commands to troubleshoot a problem, it is common to use a command called **clear counters** to reset the **show interface** counters to 0. That action sets the counters to more sane levels so you can perceive increments in certain errors, etc. The exception here is a difference between the way the **clear counters** command was implemented on Cisco IOS on routers and on Cisco IOS on Catalyst switches:

- In routers, the **clear counters** command clears only the show interface counters. The SNMP counters remain intact.

- In Catalyst switches, the **clear counters** command clears both the **show** command counters and the SNMP counters. Both the **show** command counters and the SNMP counters are reset to zero.

So, on a Catalyst switch, an SNMP counter may go to 0 because of a wrap, a reset, or the execution of the **clear counters** command. The **clear counters** command on a Catalyst switch clears both port and mac counters for both **show** command and SNMP counters. To determine whether an SNMP counter has been reset to 0 by the **clear counters** command, there are two objects in the CISCO-STACK-MIB. sysClearMacTime and sysClearPortTime are similar to sysUpTime. They will tell you in TimeTicks how long it has been since that command was executed.

Special Considerations on High-Speed Interfaces

The original interface counters defined in mib-2 are 32-bit counters. For a 10 Mbps interface, a 32-bit counter could theoretically wrap in 57 minutes. Avoiding discontinuities is easy with such a long period. But for 100 Mbps, the minimum theoretical wrap time is 5.7 minutes. And for 1 Gbps interfaces, it falls to 34 seconds. Granted these times are for transmission of back-to-back full-sized packets, a theoretical ideal. Even so, the higher the interface speed, the harder it becomes to avoid missing a counter wrap. As a solution to this problem, SNMPv2 SMI defined a new object type—counter64—for 64-bit counters. Therefore, there are several new 64-bit counters defined in the extension interface table (ifxTable) defined in RFC 1573 (later superceded by RFC 2233):

- ifHCInOctets
- ifHCInUcastPkts
- ifHCInMulticastPkts

- ifHCInBroadcastPkts
- ifHCOutOctets
- ifHCOutUcastPkts
- ifHCOutMulticastPkts
- ifHCOutBroadcastPkts

Although basic support for 64-bit counters was written into to router IOS in version 11.3, as of IOS 12.0, only ifHCInOctets and ifHCOutOctets have been implemented for ATM LANE LEC sub-interfaces only. For Catalyst workgroup switches, 64-bit counter support was implemented in version 3.1.

NOTE   You must use SNMPv2c or SNMPv3 protocol to retrieve any counter64 objects.

Performance Monitoring for System Interfaces

Performance management of system interfaces really boils down to monitoring bandwidth utilization, which means counting the octets that flow across a given interface and measuring those counts against the bandwidth of the interface. This way, you can determine whether you are overutilizing a particular link and when you need to increase the capacity of a link. In Chapter 4, "Performance Measurement and Reporting," we discussed the method for calculating link utilization:

1 Calculating the delta (difference) between two collections of ifInOctets and ifOutOctets each.

2 Adding the deltas together.

3 Converting the combined value to bits per seconds ($\times$ 8 / (num of seconds in Δ)).

4 Dividing the bits by ifSpeed (interface speed in bits).

5 Multiplying the result by 100 in order to form a percentage.

Other data that are generally of interest are the total amount of broadcast and multicast traffic as they relate to overall traffic. Originally in the ifTable in RFC 1213 there were counters for unicast packets and non-unicast packets: ifInUcastPkts, ifOutUcastPkts, ifInNUcastPkts, and ifOutNUcastPkts. These counters lumped both multicast and broadcast traffic into one counter. As more and more applications use IP multicast, it is important to have counters that give the resolution to distinguish between multicast and broadcast traffic. RFC 1573 (later superceded by RFC 2233) defines new counters in the interface extension table (ifXTable): ifInMulticastPkts, ifInBroadcastPkts, ifOutMulticastPkts, ifOutBroadcastPkts. These counters are supported starting in Cisco Catalyst switches version 3.1 and Cisco routers IOS version 12.0.

Performance Measurements for Full-Duplex Interfaces

For full-duplex interfaces, you will want to monitor input and output traffic separately. You often hear that the effective bandwidth of a full-duplex link is twice the transmission speed. For example, a 100 Mbps, full-duplex Ethernet link actually has an effective bandwidth of 200 Mbps because if both directions were fully utilized, there would be 200 megabits of data flowing on the link each second. But this bit of common wisdom needs more careful scrutiny.

For example, consider a 100 Mbps, full-duplex interface in which most of the traffic is one-way. It may be in the path to an FTP server. Most of the traffic to the FTP server is relatively light, consisting of requests for a given file. The traffic in the other direction—from the FTP server—consists of the actual files and is much heavier. When is this interface fully utilized? You might be tempted to add the transmitted and received traffic rates and divide by 200 Mbps. But that result would be misleading. For example, if the traffic to the FTP server is running an average of 5 Mbps and the traffic from the server is pegged at 100 Mbps, you might conclude that the interface has just over 50 percent utilization.

But we know that one direction—from the FTP server—is fully loaded at 100 Mbps. There is really no more capacity available on this link. It is 100 percent loaded, not 50 percent loaded.

You must take the maximum traffic rate—either input or output—and divide it by the transmission speed of the interface. See "Measuring Utilization" in Chapter 4 for more information on calculating the utilization.

Performance Measurements for Sub-interfaces

A common question is how to measure utilization of sub-interfaces. However, because utilization is measured against the bandwidth, the question becomes "What is the bandwidth of a sub-interface?" That is a hard question to answer. It does not make sense to measure multiple sub-interfaces against the bandwidth of the same physical interface. The utilization of several sub-interfaces may all appear quite low, which leads one to believe that all is okay. Combined together, however, they might total almost 100%. However, it is of interest to know the amount of traffic flowing through a sub-interface.

The easiest way to measure sub-interface traffic is through the sub-interface table. Depending on the speed of the interface, you can use either ifInoctets and ifOutOctets; for high-speed interfaces (greater than 100 Mbps), you can use ifHCInOctets and ifHCOutOctets.

An alternate way to measure sub-interface traffic is to use the media-specific MIB. For example, using the frCircuitTable from the Frame Relay MIB is a way to measure PVC traffic. However, it is often easier to use the same method for each interface because you can reuse the same scripts to poll the data. Only the indexing changes from interface to interface.

In the next few sections, we go over methods to retrieve performance data, either via the command line or via SNMP from the MIB. For reporting and alarm purposes, the data gathered via SNMP requires less processing and is easier to gather. The **show** commands are better used to troubleshoot a problem on a particular router or switch. They are very useful for drilling down to the cause of a particular problem.

MIB Variables for Interface Traffic

There are several MIB variables to watch for interface traffic.

From MIB rfc2233, the relevant MIBs are as follows:

- ifInOctets, ifOutOctets   The number of octets transmitted or received on a given interface.

- ifHCInOctets, ifHCOutOctets   The number of octets transmitted or received on a given high-speed interface (but support does not start until IOS 12.0 or Catalyst switch OS 3.1).

- ifInUcastPkts, ifOutUcastPkts   The number of unicast packets transmitted or received on a given interface.

- ifInNUcastPkts, ifOutNUcastPkts   The number of broadcast and multicast packets transmitted or received on a given interface.

- ifInMulticastPkts, ifOutMulticastPkts   The number of multicast packets transmitted or received on a given interface (not supported until IOS 12.0 or Catalyst switch OS 3.1).

- ifInBroadcastPkts, ifOutBroadcastPkts   The number of broadcast packets transmitted or received on a given interface (not supported until IOS 12.0 or Catalyst switch OS 3.1).

- ifName   The name of the interface as assigned by the device. It should be—but is not guaranteed to be—unique.

- IfAlias   A name or alias for the interface assigned by the network manager. It can be used as a non-volatile handle used by management applications to identify the interface.

From MIB RFC 1213, the relevant MIB object is sysUpTime, which returns the number of time ticks counted since the device was initialized. This MIB object is needed on each poll to determine whether the interface counters rolled over.

From MIB CISCO-STACK-MIB, the relevant MIB objects are sysClearMacTime and/or sysClearPortTime, which return the number of time ticks since the counters were cleared. These MIB objects are needed on each poll for Catalyst switches to determine whether the counters were cleared.

The Cisco Private Interfaces Table

In Cisco's private MIB branch, there is a another interfaces table—lifTable—defined in the OLD-CISCO-INTERFACES-MIB. This table contains a great deal of data, but most of the data represents a level of resolution far beyond what is required for most performance measurements. For example, there are counts for different kinds of errors. But it is easier to just poll ifInErrors, which is an aggregate of the different errors.

Additionally, all the OLD-CISCO-* MIBs are deprecated. They are all written in SNMPv1 SMI and will not be updated to SNMPv2 SMI. Instead, they will be replaced with newer, more complete MIBs. Currently there is no replacement for the OLD-CISCO-INTERFACES-MIB. We recommend using objects from open standard MIBs wherever possible.

However, there are some useful data objects in the lifTable:

- locIfInBitsSec,locIfOutBitsSec   Gives a 5-minute average of the traffic rate (refer to "Moving Exponential Average for Cisco Routers CPU Calculation" in Chapter 7, "Understanding and Using Basic Network Statistics," for an explanation on the way this average is calculated). With these objects, you do not need to do any extra calculations to determine the traffic rate.

- locIfReason   Gives the reason for the last interface state change. This object is also included as a variable binding in the linkDown trap from Cisco routers.

CLI Commands for Interface Traffic

The **show interface** command gives complete performance data for a given interface. Example 12-1 demonstrates its usage.

Example 12-1 *Using the **show interface** command to obtain interface data.*

```
Router# show interfaces Ethernet 0
Ethernet 0 is up, line protocol is up
      Hardware is MCI Ethernet, address is aa00.0400.0134 (bia 0000.0c00.4369)
            Internet address is 131.108.1.1, subnet mask is 255.255.255.0
            MTU 1500 bytes, BW 10000 Kbit, DLY 1000 usec, rely 255/255, load 1/255
            Encapsulation ARPA, loopback not set, keepalive set (10 sec)
      ARP type: ARPA, PROBE, ARP Timeout 4:00:00
            Last input 0:00:00, output 0:00:00, output hang never
            Last clearing of "show interface" counters never[C]
            Output queue 0/40, 0 drops; input queue 0/75, 2 drops
            Five minute input rate 61000 bits/sec, 4 packets/sec[A]
            Five minute output rate 1000 bits/sec, 2 packets/sec
                        2295197 packets input[B], 305539992 bytes, 0 no buffer
                        Received 1925500 broadcasts, 0 runts, 0 giants
                  3 input errors, 3 CRC, 0 frame, 0 overrun, 0 ignored, 0 abort
            0 input packets with dribble condition detected
                        3594664 packets output, 436549843 bytes, 0 underruns
output errors, 1790 collisions, 10 interface resets, 0 restarts
```

The annotated information in Example 12-1 is as follows:

A A 5-minute input and output rate: a 5-minute moving average of the bit or packet rate.

B The input or output bit or packet count: A total of the number of bits or packets received or transmitted on that interface. The count is since the last time the **clear counters** command was issued.

C Last clearing of **show interface** counters: An important piece of information to check when you last cleared the counters.

Error/Fault Monitoring

Error and fault monitoring on any interface consist of monitoring the operational status and framing, signaling, or other errors that result in the loss of a frame. Each type of interface has its own unique errors. For example, Ethernet links have collisions. T1 links have bipolar violations. But all interfaces do share some basic fault data. The rest of this chapter is devoted to generic fault management of interfaces.

Link Status

The most basic fault management element of an interface is monitoring the link status. ifAdminStatus and ifOperStatus will show whether the interface is operational or not as far as the device is concerned. If ifAdminStatus is disabled, it is because the device administrator configured it that way. A device interface generally can be disabled either through the command line or via SNMP set commands. If ifAdminStatus is down, ifOperStatus is also down.

ifOperStatus indicates the operational state of the interface. The original mib-2 specification in RFC 1213 defined ifOperStatus with three states: up, down, or testing. An operational interface is up. An interface with a serious fault such as a cable break is down. An interface in some testing mode such as a WAN interface in Loopback mode has ifOperStatus set to "testing."

RFC 1573 defined a new state for ifOperStatus— dormant. A dormant interface is not operating but rather is in a pending state. A dial-on-demand interface is dormant. Dialer interfaces in spoofing mode are dormant. Cisco router IOS started support for this new state in IOS 11.1.

You can monitor the operational status of an interface via active polling of ifOperStatus or receiving a link trap. RFC 1157 defined linkUp and linkDown traps. A device will generate a linkUp trap when ifOperStatus transitions from the down state to either the up or dormant state. Similarly, a device will issue a linkDown trap when ifOperStatus enters the down state.

An additional object in the portTable of the CISCO-STACK-MIB for Catalyst workgroup switches is portOperStatus.

portOperStatus can take four values:

- other(1)—any state other than ok, minorFault, or majorFault
- ok(2)—the same as ifOperStatus in up state
- minorFault(3)—a port administratively disabled
- majorFault(4)—the same definition as ifOperStatus in down state.

Most Cisco devices also use the linkUp or linkDown trap, as defined by RFC 1157, to proactively notify a management station of an interface state change for a physical interface. However, link traps are not implemented for any sub-interface types. The rationale is that if a physical interface goes down, a router would generate only one trap rather than a trap for the physical interface and each sub-interface.

Further, it may be troublesome to receive link traps for every port status change. Some interfaces change state as part of the normal course of operation(for example, asynchronous dial up ports or closet switch ports). Routers offer an interface configuration command:

no snmp trap link-status

The corresponding command for Catalyst switches:

set port trap *mod_num/port_num* **enable | disable**

You can use these commands to filter needless traps from clogging up the event logs on your management station.

Standard linkDown and linkUp traps are sent with ifIndex, ifDescr, and ifType as variable bindings. Cisco Routers also add a proprietary object (locIfReason) from the OLD-CISCO-INTERFACES-MIB. locIfReason is just an ASCII string. Some of the possible values you might see for locIfReason include the following:

- Fatal Tx Error
- Keepalive failed
- Lost Carrier
- Late Collision
- Excessive collision
- Open Failure, Lobe
- Ring Beaconing
- Duplicate Address
- Remove MAC
- Keepalive failed

- Wire-fault
- Auto-removal
- Ring Beaconing
- LAPB down
- EIA signal lost

However, the link traps generated by the Catalyst switches only send out ifIndex, ifDescr, and ifType.

In addition to link traps, there are also system error messages that may be logged to a buffer on the device or to a syslog server.

Link Errors

All framing schemes on various types of media contain some type of error check field at the end of the frame. Bad media commonly cause framing errors. Bad media may consist of faulty interfaces, bad cables and connectors, or out-of-spec cables (too long). Most agents will count such errors in relevant fields in the ifInErrors column in the interface table. The ifOutErrors column indicates problems within the device itself, where it could not transmit the frame for some reason.

Each medium has a specified maximum error rate. For example, the IEEE 802.3 specification states that an Ethernet's error rate will not exceed 10^{-8}. To get the received error rate, you want to divide the received errors by the number of received packets—not the number of received octets. A single bit error in a frame will cause the whole frame to be discarded. From Chapter 4, the equation for calculating the input error rate is as follows:

$$\text{Error Rate} = \frac{(\Delta\text{ifInErrors}) \times 100}{(\Delta\text{ifInUcastPkts} + \Delta\text{ifInNUcastPkts})}$$

It is important to note that the output errors generally are related to resource availability (for example, internal buffers) of the router or switch rather than faulty interface or media. Therefore, output errors rates should not necessarily hold to specification.

Acceptable error rates vary between different media types. We will cover specific media types in subsequent chapters.

MIB Variables for Interface Errors

From MIB RFC 2233, the MIBs relevant to interface errors are as follows:

- ifInErrors, ifOutErrors   The number of frames containing some type of error that prevents them from being forwarded

- ifInDiscards, ifOutDiscards   The number of error-free frames the device had to discard, generally because of some resource problem internal to the device such as no free input buffers. Please refer to Chapter 11 for more details.

Summary

Generic interface management basically boils down to monitoring the amount and type of traffic on and error rate of a given interface. Almost all relevant information is available via SNMP from the ifTable or ifXTable. Link status also can be proactively monitored via link traps or syslog messages.

In the next few chapters, we cover different interface types such as Ethernet, Frame Relay, and others in specific detail. Each technology has its own unique characteristics, which require different measurement techniques. Some media tolerate more errors than others. Some media tolerate higher utilization rates than others. The principles covered in this chapter apply to all media types. In the subsequent chapters, you will learn how to fine-tune these principles to manage the media types deployed in your network.

References

Books

Leinwand, A. and K. Fang Conroy. *Network Management: A Practical Perspective*. Reading, MA: Addison-Wesley, 1996.

Rose, M. T. and K. McCloghrie. *How to Manage Your Network via SNMP: The Network Management Practicum*. Upper Saddle River, NJ: Prentice Hall, 1994.

Standard

RFC 2233. "The Interfaces Group MIB Using SMIv2," by K. McCloghrie and F. Kastenholz.

CHAPTER 13

Monitoring Ethernet Interfaces

In this chapter, we will cover how to manage Ethernet interfaces. We will cover what data to monitor and how to retrieve it in the following sections:

- An overview of Ethernet theory and implementation
- Performance data for Ethernet
- Fault/error data for Ethernet

Ethernet Overview

Ethernet is a physical and Data Link layer networking standard defined by the IEEE 802.3 set of protocols. These protocols define frame size, connection rules, cable types and lengths, transmission speeds, and a host of other specifications. This overview of Ethernet is intended for background only. For more detailed information on Ethernet specifications, see References at the end of this chapter.

Architecture and Theory

An Ethernet can be either a bus topology or a star topology. *Bus topologies* have multiple stations connected to a cable or segment. *Star topologies* have stations connected to a central device such as a hub (repeater) or a switch. An Ethernet repeater (or hub) connects Ethernet segments together at the physical layer. A repeater essentially extends a segment. A bridge or switch connects Ethernet segments together at the data link layer. Ethernets on either side of a bridge or switch are separate physical Ethernet segments. Ethernets on either side of a repeater are the same Ethernet. Physical segment refers to a collision domain, the extent of cabling where length and Ethernet collision timing rules apply.

Access Method

Ethernet stations can attempt to transmit any time they need to when the wire is not in use. They use a method known as Carrier Sense Multiple Access Collision Detection (CSMA/CD) to govern access to the media. An Ethernet station listens to make sure that the Ethernet is quiet (no carrier) before transmitting a frame. During transmission, the station listens for a set period to make sure that the frame did not collide with another frame. As long as the Ethernet is built with a precisely defined set of limitations, a station will always hear when a collision occurs. A collision occurs any time two or more stations attempt to transmit at the same time. If a collision occurs, each station involved uses a back off algorithm to determine when to retransmit the frame. The back off algorithm helps to ensure that no stations will try to re-transmit at the same time and thus collide again.

Collision Domain

An important concept is the collision domain. A *collision domain* is a system of Ethernet segments and repeaters (or hubs). A collision domain stops at the Data Link layer. A bridge (or switch) connects two or more collision domains.

Especially in older Ethernet networks, proper management of the collision domain was the most important factor in a properly functioning Ethernet. Making sure that all cable types, lengths, and repeater counts were within specification would go a long way toward keeping your Ethernet running properly. With the declining costs of switches, Ethernet networks that violate these specifications are getting rarer as collision domains shrink. But even in switched Ethernet networks—particularly 100 Mbps or higher—it is very important to follow cable and length restrictions.

An Ethernet repeater (or hub) is used to extend an Ethernet, but there are limitations. An Ethernet frame eventually runs out of either signal or time. Repeaters will reform the signal but they cannot overcome the timing issue. Therefore, there are strict limits to the number of repeaters one can use within a collision domain.

For 10-megabit Ethernets, there is the 5-4-3 rule:

- No more than 5 repeated segments
- No more than 4 repeaters between any two stations
- Only 3 of those segments may be populated with stations (the other two would be just link segments—a segment connecting two repeaters with no other stations)

For 100-megabit Ethernets, there are two types of repeaters: class I or II. Class I repeaters can connect different media types (copper to fiber). Class II can only connect similar media types. Only one class I repeat can be used in a collision domain. Only two class II repeaters may be used in a collision domain. The two classes of repeaters cannot be mixed within a collision domain.

Standards

There are several types of Ethernets that vary in cable types and topology. Here are the most common standards:

- 10Base2, 10Base5   Bus topologies based on coaxial cable with multiple stations on a single segment of cable. The 10Base corresponds to a transmission speed of 10 megabits per second. The 2 and 5 correspond to the maximum segment lengths: 200 and 500 meters. Stations transmit and receive on the same cable. Neither 10Base2 nor 10Base5 is commonly deployed currently. 10Base5 is also known as *thicknet*; 10Base2 is also known as *thinnet*. These names came from the difference in cable sizes.

- 10BaseT, 10BaseFL   Star topologies based on twisted pair or fiber and separate transmit and receive channels. Each station is connected to a central hub (repeater). Although transmission speed is still 10 Mbps, the separate transmit and receive channels make full-duplex operation (receiving and transmitting simultaneously) possible. 10BaseT and 10BaseFL links are either half- or full-duplex. Both stations on either end of the link must be configured the same. Almost all repeater hubs are half-duplex. The maximum length for 10BaseT is 100 meters. The maximum length for 10BaseFL is 2000 meters.

- 100BaseTX, 100BaseFX   Star topologies based on twisted pair and fiber cables. Stations are connected to a central hub (or often to a switch). As in 10BaseT/FL, full-duplex operation is possible. But the transmission speed is increased an order of magnitude to 100 megabits per second. For 100BaseTX, the maximum cable length is the same as for 10Base-T, but the cable must meet Category 5 specifications. In fact, it is not only important that the cable meet category 5; the patch panels, terminations, and wall jacks must also meet category 5. The maximum length for a 100BaseFX segment is 412 meters.

- Gigabit Ethernet   A star-based topology currently supporting only fiber (although copper twisted pair will be available soon). Currently only switches are available—there are no gigabit Ethernet hubs. And as the name implies, the transmission speed is 1 gigabit per second (1000 Mbps).

Switched Ethernet Versus Shared Ethernet

Virtually all Ethernets built today are star topologies based on the 10/100BaseT/F standards. It is the device at the center of the star that causes controversy. In 10 M or 100 M Ethernets, the central device may be either a shared hub or a switch. With the declining price in switches, many designers opt for fully switched Ethernets, which means there are no shared segments in the network.

Concern for collision rates also has been a motivation for migrating to fully-switched networks. In fully-switched, full-duplex Ethernets, collision counts are of no concern and should be 0. However, this motivation is misguided. Although monitoring collision rates in a shared Ethernet is important, collision rates should not be primary indicators of the health of your Ethernet. Ethernet collisions are normal. Collisions provide the access control mechanism. If there were no collisions on a shared segment, it would mean that no one (or perhaps only one) was transmitting.

An often-cited bit of conventional wisdom is that collision counts should total no more that 1 percent of the frames transmitted. However, changing to a fully-switched network to reduce collision rates to 1 percent may actually degrade the performance of your network. Switches introduce more latency than a hub. So, for some applications, a shared hub may perform better than a switch. It is important to choose whatever works best for your needs and to manage it accordingly.

Collision rates of 5 percent or even 10 percent can be fine. It is more important to monitor true Ethernet errors such as CRC errors, late collisions, runts, or jabbers. (These terms are discussed in more detail in "Error/Fault Detection" later in this chapter.) The MAC layer retransmits a frame destroyed by a collision almost instantaneously. In contrast, the MAC layer discards frames corrupted by cable problems or late collisions. For these problems, it is a higher layer's responsibility to request retransmission, and then only after a lengthy timeout. The performance impact of a 10 percent collision rate pales in comparison to even a 0.1 percent CRC error rate.

Some useful guidelines for collision rates for a given utilization are shown in Table 13-1. However, these numbers are only guidelines. More accurate numbers are obtained from baselining collision counts for your network under normal operations.

Table 13-1   *Collision Rates Versus Utilization*

Segment Utilization	Maximum Percent Packets Colliding
0–19%	1%
20–49%	5%
>50%	15%

There are much better reasons to use Ethernet switches. Moving to switches allows full-duplex operation between stations and switches, which effectively doubles the bandwidth. The capabilities of VLANs to partition LANs and facilitate Moves, Adds, and Changes are another reason to migrate to a switched environment.

Performance Data

Monitoring performance on Ethernet interfaces comes down to monitoring bandwidth utilization using the methods described in Chapter 12, "Monitoring System Interfaces."

MIB Variables for Ethernet Traffic

The following MIB objects (from RFC 2233) are the most useful in measuring the amount of traffic flowing across Ethernet interfaces:

- ifInOctets, ifOutOctets   The number of octets transmitted or received on a given interface.

- ifHCInOctets, ifHCOutOctets   The number of octets transmitted or received on a given high-speed interface (but support does not start until OS 12.0 or Catalyst switch OS 3.1).

- ifInUcastPkts, ifOutUcastPkts   The number of unicast packets transmitted or received on a given interface.

- ifInNUcastPkts, ifOutNUcastPkts   The number of broadcast and multicast packets transmitted or received on a given interface.

- ifInMulticastPkts, ifOutMulticastPkts   The number of multicast packets transmitted or received on a given interface (not supported until OS 12.0 or Catalyst switch OS 3.1).

- ifInBroadcastPkts, ifOutBroadcastPkts   The number of broadcast packets transmitted or received on a given interface (not supported until OS 12.0 or Catalyst switch OS 3.1)

- ifName   The name of the interface as assigned by the device. It should be (but is not guaranteed to be) unique.

- ifAlias   A name or alias for the interface assigned by the network manager. It can be used as a non-volatile handle used by management applications to identify the interface.

From RFC 1757, the etherStatsOctets object provides a count of input and output octets summed together.

From MIB RFC 1213, the sysUpTime object provides the number of time ticks counted since the device was initialized. This object must be sampled on each poll to determine whether the interface counters rolled over.

From MIB CISCO-STACK-MIB, the sysClearMacTime and sysClearPortTime objects provide the number of time ticks since the counters were cleared. On Catalyst switches, these objects must be sampled on each poll for Catalyst switches to determine whether the counters were cleared.

The separate input and output counters from the ifTable must be used for full-duplex interfaces. The single counter from the etherStats table is handy for half-duplex interfaces because it already sums the counts together.

The high-capacity counters are necessary to measure traffic on Gigabit Ethernet interfaces. Otherwise, you must poll the device too frequently to make sure you do not miss the counter rolling over.

CLI Commands for Ethernet Traffic

The **show interface Ethernet x/y** command gives complete performance data of a given Ethernet interface. It not only shows the number of octets and frames, but also the interface load, an averaged throughput, and much other data.

Example 13-1 provides sample output for the **show interface Ethernet x/y** command.

Example 13-1   *Using **show interface Ethernet x/y** to evaluate Ethernet traffic.*

```
nms-7010a#sh int fa0/0
FastEthernet0/0 is up, line protocol is up
 Hardware is cyBus FastEthernet Interface, address is 0060.5490.f800 (bia
0060.5490.f800)
 MTU 1500 bytes, BW 100000 KbitᴬA, DLY 100 usec, rely 255/255, load 1/255ᴮ
 Encapsulation ARPA, loopback not set, keepalive set (10 sec), fdxᶜ, 100BaseTX/FX
 ARP type: ARPA, ARP Timeout 04:00:00
 Last input 00:00:01, output 00:00:01, output hang never
Last clearing of "show interface" counters 00:43:40ᴰ
 Queueing strategy: fifo
 Output queue 0/40, 0 drops; input queue 0/75, 0 drops
 5 minute input rate 2376 bits/sec, 27 packets/sec
 5 minute output rate 1000 bits/sec, 7 packets/sec
 3653980 packets input, 269895525 bytesᴱ, 0 no buffer
 Received 3499 broadcasts, 0 runts, 0 giants
 1119 input errors, 1119 CRC, 540 frame, 0 overrun, 0 ignored, 0 abort
 0 watchdog, 744 multicast
 0 input packets with dribble condition detected
 1507771 packets output, 161101301 bytes, 0 underruns
 0 output errors, 0 collisions, 2 interface resets
 0 babbles, 0 late collision, 0 deferred
 0 lost carrier, 0 no carrier
 0 output buffer failures, 0 output buffers swapped out
```

The highlighted information in Example 13-1 is as follows:

A BW is the bandwidth of the interface.

B Load indicates a five-minute sliding average of the traffic load on the interface expressed as a fraction of 255. The average is calculated using the formula for a five-minute sliding average, as explained in Chapter 7, "Understanding and Using Basic Network Statistics."

C FDX indicates that the interface is full-duplex. For interfaces capable of only half-duplex operation, this data is not displayed. You can assume that if the mode is not explicitly stated in the show interface output, it is in half-duplex mode.

D The Last clearing of show interface counters shows the last time the **clear counters** command was executed. It does no good to know that 1000 bytes have been received if you do not know how long it took to receive them.

E The 5-minute bit and packet rates are calculated using a 5-minute sliding averaging algorithm, as explained in "Moving Exponential Average for Cisco Routers CPU Calculation" in Chapter 7. Also present are the total byte or packet counts.

For Catalyst switches, the **show mac** command gives you raw performance data, showing the number of octets and frames as well as the type of frames: unicast, broadcast, or multicast. This command is illustrated in Example 13-2.

Example 13-2   *Using **show mac x/y** to obtain performance data for Ethernet traffic.*

```
nms-5500a> (enable) show mac 4/2
MAC       Rcv-Frms   Xmit-Frms   Rcv-Multi  Xmit-Multi Rcv-Broad  Xmit-Broad
--------  ---------- ----------  ---------- ---------- ---------- ----------
  4/2     124553     623141      11715      464879     22         90320

MAC       Dely-Exced MTU-Exced  In-Discard Lrn-Discrd In-Lost    Out-Lost
--------  ---------- ----------  ---------- ---------- ---------- ----------
  4/2     0          0           0          0          0          0

Port      Rcv-Unicast          Rcv-Multicast        Rcv-Broadcast
--------  -------------------- -------------------- --------------------
  4/2     112816               11715                22

Port      Xmit-Unicast         Xmit-Multicast       Xmit-Broadcast
--------  -------------------- -------------------- --------------------
  4/2     67942                464879               90320

Port      Rcv-Octet            Xmit-Octet
--------  -------------------- --------------------
  4/2     20344641             49348209

Last-Time-Cleared
--------------------------
Fri Jan 22 1999, 15:07:39
```

Note that for switch software versions 2.x, you only can get frame counts with **show mac x/y**. For switch software versions 3.x and higher, you can see both frame and octet counts.

The **show counters x/y** can be a useful command. It generates a complete dump of all the mac and port counters for the switch. Here, you will see the counters from the **show mac** and the **show port** command as well as SNMP counters from RFC 1757 (RMON MIB) and RFC 2358 (dot3 MIB). Please refer to Example 13-3.

Example 13-3   *Using the **show counters** command to obtain all the mac and port counters for the switch.*

```
nms-5505a (enable) sh counters 1/1
64 bit counters
0 ifHCInOctets       =    29477694204
1 ifHCInUcastPkts    =       0
2 ifHCInMulticastPkts  =    120599698
3 ifHCInBroadcastPkts  =       0
```

continues

Example 13-3   *Using the **show counters** command to obtain all the mac and port counters for the switch. (Continued)*

```
 4 ifHCOutOctets       =     26516883506
 5 ifHCOutUcastPkts       =       0
 6 ifHCOutMulticastPkts      =     143919486
 7 ifHCOutBroadcastPkts      =       0

32 bit counters
 0 etherStatsFragments    =   1
 1 dot3StatsInternalMacRxErrs =   1
 2 etherStatsJabbers     =   0
 3 baseX100StatsSymCodeViolates =   0
 4 dot1BasePortDelayExcdAborts =   0
 5 badTxCRC       =   0
 6 dot3StatsLateCollisions   =   0
 7 dot3StatsExcessiveCollisions =   0
 8 dot3StatsSQETestErrors   =   0
 9 dot3StatsCarrierSenseErrors =   0
10 dmaOverflow      =   0
11 linkFail       =   26
12 txJabber       =   0
13 dmaTxLengthErrors     =   0
14 dmaRxLengthErrors     =   0
15 dmaXferLengthErrors    =   0
16 dmaMonitorPkts     = 40960399
17 dot1dTpPortInFrames    = 120599700
18 dot3StatsFCSErrors    =   0
19 dot1dTpPortOutFrames    = 143919491
20 dot3StatsSingleColFrames  =   0
21 dot3StatsMultiColFrames   =   0
22 dot3StatsInternalMacTxErrs =   0
23 dot3StatsDeferredTx    =   0
24 dot3StatsBadPreamble    =   0
25 dot3StatsAbortLateCollision =   0
26 dot3StatsABortExcessiveLen =   0
27 dot1dTpPortInDiscards   =   125
28 rxRuntErrors      =   0
29 dmaMacMismatch     =   10
30 etherStatsRxPkts256to511  = 13384238
31 etherStatsRxPkts512to1023 = 3024640
32 etherStatsRxPkts1024to1518 = 3203146
33 etherStatsOversizePkts   =   0
34 dot3StatsAlignmentErrors  =   0
35 etherStatsRxMulticastPkts = 120599700
36 etherStatsRxBroadcastPkts =   0
37 etherStatsTxPkts64    =   8
38 etherStatsTxPkts65to127   = 50334315
39 etherStatsTxPkts128to255  = 79605022
40 etherStatsTxPkts256to511  = 10598850
41 etherStatsTxPkts512to1023 = 1827874
42 etherStatsTxPkts1024to1518 =   180548
43 dmaLastChance     =   0
44 etherStatsRxPkts65to127   = 35634715
45 etherStatsRxPkts128to255  = 63332105
```

Example 13-3 *Using the **show counters** command to obtain all the mac and port counters for the switch. (Continued)*

```
46 etherStatsTxBroadcastPkts =   0
47 etherStatsTxMulticastPkts = 143919491
48 etherStatsRxOctets    = 3707890908
49 etherStatsTxOctets    = 747080475
50 dmaTxFull     =   0
51 dmaRetry      =   0
52 dmaLevel2Request     =   0
53 etherStatsUndersizePkts  =   0
54 dot3StatsTotalCollisions  =   0
55 etherStatsRxPkts64    =   9
```

Error/Fault Detection

The most fundamental fault detection for Ethernet interfaces is the same as that for any system interface—whether the interface is operational or not. Changes in interface state trigger linkUp or linkDown traps. You may also monitor ifOperStatus. For further details, on this type of fault monitoring, please refer to the section on system interfaces in Chapter 12, "Monitoring System Interfaces." The rest of this section discusses Ethernet-specific fault management.

Ethernet errors come in a variety of flavors, but all represent a framing error of some sort. There is either an FCS error or the frame is too short or too long. Following are the basic Ethernet errors and a brief explanation of each:

- CRC or FCS errors   The Frame Check Sequence (FCS) is a 32-bit cyclic redundancy check (CRC) appended to the end of each Ethernet frame transmitted. If the receiving station detects an error in the FCS, one or more of the bits in the Ethernet frame are in error and the frame is discarded. CRC errors should occur very rarely. Ethernets (according to the IEEE 802.3 specification) should have an error rate no greater that 10^{-8}. On an Ethernet transmitting 1500-byte packets at 100 percent load, that translates to one erred frame out of approximately 82 million frames. Cable problems, poor connections, or faulty interfaces can cause CRC errors. If you detect such errors, it is time to utilize some Layer 1/Layer 2 test equipment, such as a cable tester, to determine whether the cables and connections are up to specification.

- Alignment Errors   The frame does not have an integer number of octets and does have a bad frame check sequence. These errors indicate a faulty transmitter or a cable problem.

- Runts or Fragments   Runts or fragments are frames on the wire that are shorter than 64 bytes and that usually have an invalid FCS. The observance of fragments is normal because they can be the result of collisions.

- Jabbers   A jabber is a frame longer than 1518 bytes and with a bad FCS error. Jabbers are usually due to a malfunctioning interface.

- Collisions   These are not errors; they are normal occurrences on shared Ethernet segments. You do want to monitor them, however, because a higher-than-normal collision count can indicate a congested segment or other problems on the segment.

Collisions Caused by Duplex Configuration Errors

Although collisions are not technically errors, a very common cause of collisions on twisted pair links is a duplex-configuration error. Section 28 of the IEEE 802.3u standard defines Auto-Negotiation, which is the process for two devices to negotiate a common link speed and duplex configuration. However, interoperability between vendors on this process is notoriously poor. For two devices from different vendors to negotiate to different duplex configurations—for one side to be half-duplex and the other full-duplex—is a common occurrence. Such a configuration error will cause abnormally high collision rates and CRC errors. The solution is to manually configure both ends of the link to the proper link speed and duplex.

And just as in monitoring traffic, there can be different sources for very similar data. The next few sections discuss various sources of fault and error data.

MIB Variables for Ethernet Errors

The following list shows the MIB objects you can poll to collect the statistics on Ethernet interface errors:

- ifInErrors from RFC 2233   For an Ethernet interface, this counter is the sum of three error conditions: alignment, giants, and FCS errors.
- dot3StatsAlighnmentErrors, dot3StatsFrameTooLongs, dot3StatsFCSErrors from RFC 2358   These three variables summed together equal ifInErrors.
- etherStatsCRCAlignErrors, etherStatsJabbers from RFC 1757   These variables are only available on the 2500 routers and Catalyst switches. Summed together, they equal ifInErrors.

For Ethernet, any framing error or data corruption is bad because it causes the MAC layer to discard the frame. Any request for retransmission of the lost frame must come after timeouts from the upper-layer protocols. Even very small numbers of framing errors can cause major degradation in performance.

Most framing errors and data corruptions are due to a physical layer problem such as a faulty interface or bad cable. In general, it is best to monitor ifInErrors because it is the sum of the main types of framing errors.

MIB Variables for Ethernet Collisions

The following list shows the MIB objects you can poll to collect the statistics on Ethernet collisions:

- dot3StatsSingleCollisionFrames, dot3StatsMultipleCollisionFrames from RFC 2358   These counters are available on either switches or routers. As their names indicate, they are the number of frames that encountered either a single collision or multiple collisions before transmission was possible.

- etherStatsCollisions from RFC 1757   The total number of collisions (single or multiple) on a given interface.

The RMON collision counter is easier to monitor because it is one object with the complete count of all collisions, but it is available only on 2500 routers and Catalyst switches. However, for the 2500 routers, the lance Ethernet chip used will detect collisions only when transmitting. Do not use this counter on the 2500 router to get collision counts for the whole segment. For other routers, the dot3 MIB objects are the best choice. Remember that collisions are natural on shared Ethernet or half-duplex Ethernet. The presence of collisions does not mean there is a problem. It is important to baseline the collision rate on a given segment and then watch for sudden inexplicable increases.

However, on a full-duplex segment, you should see no collisions. The presence of collision on a full-duplex segment often means that one interface on the link is configured for half-duplex transmission and the other is for full-duplex transmissions.

CLI Commands for Ethernet Errors

For routers, the best show command for examining Ethernet interface errors is the **show interface** command. It gives in details the current state of the interface. Example 13-4 provides sample output for **show interface**.

Example 13-4   *Using **show interface** to get error information on a router's Ethernet interfaces.*

```
nms-7010a#sh int fa0/0
FastEthernet0/0 is up, line protocol is up
 Hardware is cyBus FastEthernet Interface, address is 0060.5490.f800 (bia
0060.5490.f800)
 MTU 1500 bytes, BW 100000 Kbit, DLY 100 usec, rely 255/255, load 1/255
 Encapsulation ARPA, loopback not set, keepalive set (10 sec), fdx, 100BaseTX/FX
 ARP type: ARPA, ARP Timeout 04:00:00
 Last input 00:00:01, output 00:00:01, output hang never
Last clearing of "show interface" counters 00:43:40
 Queueing strategy: fifo
 Output queue 0/40, 0 drops; input queue 0/75, 0 drops
 5 minute input rate 2376 bits/sec, 27 packets/sec
 5 minute output rate 1000 bits/sec, 7 packets/sec
  3653980 packets input, 269895525 bytes, 0 no buffer
  Received 3499 broadcasts, 0 runts,^A 0 giants^B
```

continues

Example 13-4 *Using **show interface** to get error information on a router's Ethernet interfaces. (Continued)*

```
1119 input errors,D 1119 CRC,C 540 frameG, 0 overrun, 0 ignored, 0 abort
0 watchdog, 744 multicast
0 input packets with dribble condition detectedH
1507771 packets output, 161101301 bytes, 0 underruns
0 output errors, 0 collisionsE, 2 interface resetsF
0 babbles, 0 late collisionI, 0 deferredJ
0 lost carrier, 0 no carrier
0 output buffer failures, 0 output buffers swapped out
```

The annotated information in Example 13-4 is as follows:

A runts: The number of input packets discarded because they were less than 64 bytes long.

B giants: Equivalent to jabbers, the number of packets discarded because they were greater that 1518 bytes long.

C CRC: The number of input frames where the checksum calculated by the router does not match the checksum at the end of the frame.

D input error: The total number of errors.

E collisions: The number of frames that had to be retransmitted because of a collision.

F interface resets: The number of times the interface has been reset—either by an internal error condition or through an administrative shutdown.

G frame: The number of frames received with a CRC error and a non-integral number of octets. Could be the result of a collision or a faulty interface.

H dribble condition: The device received a frame that was slightly too long, but the frame is accepted and forwarded. The counter is for information only.

I late collision: An error indicating that something in the Ethernet is out of specification. Either the cable is too long or perhaps there are too many repeaters.

J deferred: A packet has not been transmitted due to excessive number of collisions.

For Catalyst switches, the best command to examine Ethernet interface errors is the **show port counters** command, as illustrated in Example 13-5.

Example 13-5 *Using **show port counters** to get error information for a switch's Ethernet interfaces.*

```
nms-5505a (enable) show port counters 1/1

Port  Align-ErrA  FCS-ErrB    Xmit-ErrC   Rcv-ErrD    UnderSizeE
----- ----------  ----------  ----------  ----------  ---------
1/1   0           0           0           0           0


Port  Single-ColF Multi-CollG Late-CollH Excess-ColI Carri-Sen RuntsJ     GiantsK
----- ----------  ----------  ---------- ----------  --------- ---------- --------
1/1   0           0           0          0           0         0          -
```

Example 13-5 *Using **show port counters** to get error information for a switch's Ethernet interfaces. (Continued)*

```
Last-Time-Cleared
------------------------
Thu Jan 21 1999, 16:55:02
```

A Align-Err: The number of frames that do not have an integer number of octets and have an incorrect frame check sequence.

B FCS-Err: The number of frames with an incorrect frame check sequence.

C Xmit-Err: The internal transmit buffer is full.

D Rcv-Err: The internal receive buffer is full.

E UnderSize: Frames smaller than 64 bytes with a good FCS.

F Single-Col: The number of times the port had a single collision before transmitting the frame.

G Multi-Coll: The number of times the port had more than one collision before transmitting the frame. Note that this counter does not count how many actual collisions occurred trying to transmit the frame—only that it was more than once.

H Late-Coll: An error indicating that the Ethernet is out of specification. A cable is too long or there are too many repeaters.

I Excess-Col: The number of frames that were dropped because the port saw 16 sequential collisions attempting to transmit that one frame.

J Runts: Frames less than 64 bytes long and with a bad FCS.

K Giants: Frames greater than 1518 bytes long and with a bad FCS—the same as a jabber.

Syslog Messages Relating to Ethernet Errors

Table 13-2 outlines several common System Error messages and their general causes. Each message is specific to the chipset used on the Ethernet interface. Please refer to the "Cisco IOS Software System Error Messages" guide for details on each individual message.

Table 13-2 *Ethernet System Error Messages*

Message	Explanation
AMDP2-1-MEMERR	This list of messages usually indicates a problem on the device—such as faulty interface hardware, software problems, or memory problems.
AMDP2_FE-3-SPURIDON	
AMDP2_FE-1-DISCOVER	
AMDP2_FE-1-INITFAIL	
AMDP2_FE-3-UNDERFLO	
DEC21140-1-DISCOVER	
DEC21140-3-ERRINT	
DEC21140-3-ERRINT	
LANCE-4-BABBLE	
LANCE-3-BADCABLE	
LANCE-1-MEMERR	
AMDP2_FE-5-COLL	These types of messages are most likely the result of a duplex mismatch or just general congestion on the line. A sudden flurry of these messages may also indicate cabling problems.
AMDP2_FE-5-LATECOLL	
DEC21140-5-COLL	
ETHERNET-1-TXERR	
LANCE-5-COLL	

Summary

Fundamentally, managing Ethernet interfaces is the same as almost any LAN interface. There are some errors and conditions unique to Ethernet interfaces, as described in this chapter. Basically, however, the interfaces table (ifTable) provides the majority of the information needed for performance and fault management of Ethernet interfaces.

The concepts in this chapter can also be applied to other LAN interfaces, such as Token Ring and FDDI. In the next chapter, we discuss a very different technology: ATM.

References

Books

Rose, Marshall T., and Keith McCloghrie. *How to Manage Your Network Using SNMP: The Networking Management Practicum.* Upper Saddle River, NJ: Prentice Hall, 1994.

Spurgeon, Charles E. *Practical Networking With Ethernet (Practical Networking Series).* Stamford, CT: International Thomson Computer Publishing, 1995

Standards

RFC 2233. "The Interfaces Group MIB using SMIv2," by Keith McCloghrie and F. Kastenholz.

RFC 2358. "Definitions of Managed Objects for the Ethernet-like Interface Types," by J. Flick and J. Johnson.

Paper

Seifert, R. "The Effect of Ethernet Behavior on Networks Using High Performance Workstations and Servers." White paper, 1995. Available at

http://wwwhost.ots.utexas.edu/ethernet/descript-misc.html

Internet Resource

University of New Hampshire Interoperability Lab's tutorial page

http://www.iol.unh.edu/training/index.html

CHAPTER 14

ATM Performance and Fault Management

A complete treatment of ATM technology would fill up an entire book and is beyond the scope of this chapter. Instead, this chapter will focus on how to obtain performance and fault-related data from Cisco ATM devices. It is assumed that the reader is already familiar with ATM. For further details, refer to the References listed at the end of the chapter.

This chapter contains the following topics for managing ATM interfaces:

- A brief general discussion on ATM technology to establish some background and terminology
- Performance management for Cisco router and Catalyst switch ATM interfaces
- Performance management for LS1010 and Catalyst 8500MSR ATM switches
- Fault management for Cisco router and Catalyst switch ATM interfaces
- Fault management for LS1010 and Catalyst 8500MSR switches

Overview of ATM

ATM, or Asynchronous Transfer Mode, is a widely deployed networking technology. ATM has many applications, including both wide area and campus area backbones. It has a lot of flexibility because it is designed for both constant bit rates services such as voice and variable bit rate services such as data.

ATM devices are connected together via point-to-point links. These links can consist of different media and can operate at different transmission speeds. The most common transport for ATM is a SONET (Synchronous Optical Network) or SDH (Synchronous Digital Hierarchy) network. Both network types are very similar. They use OC (Optical Carrier) standards. OC standards specify a range of properties and speeds, starting at OC1 at 51.84 MBps ranging up to OC192 at 9953.28 MBps. The most common are OC3 and OC12.

ATM networks are connection-oriented. They use virtual circuits to transfer the data. The end-to-end virtual connection is made from a Virtual Channel Connection (VCC) and a Virtual Path Connection (VPC). A VCC or VPC is really made up of multiple links between the end points of the connection. The individual links are called Virtual Channel Links (VCL) or Virtual Path Links (VPL). Each VCL or VPL has a unique number assigned: the

Virtual Channel Identifier or Virtual Path Identifier (VCI/VPI). Each link along the path may well have different VCI/VPI numbers. The switches in the path make the end-to-end connection by routing cells between the links that make up the path.

ATM virtual circuits come in two basic flavors:

- Permanent Virtual Circuits (PVC)
- Switched Virtual Circuits (SCV)

PVCs are built by manually configuring each link between each ATM switch in the end-to-end path. SVCs are built using a signaling protocol between the ATM switches.

The data in an ATM circuit rides in 48-byte units. There is a 5-byte header that contains the VPI/VCI and other information. The 48-byte payload and the 5-byte header together are known as a cell. The way data gets from the higher layers down to the ATM cell layer is through an ATM adaptation layer (AAL). There are different adaptation layers for different types of data. AAL1 is used for constant bit rate services such as voice. AAL3/4 and AAL5 are used for data. AAL5 is a simplified version of AAL3/4 and is virtually the only scheme used. This chapter concentrates on data for the ATM and the AAL5 layer.

A data payload is presented to the ATM AAL5 layer for transport on an ATM link. The convergence sub-layer appends some padding and a trailer so the payload is now an integer multiple of 48 bytes. The trailer contains the length of the frame and a CRC. The data, padding, and trailer form the Common Part Convergence Sub-layer (CPCS) protocol data unit (PDU). The CPCS PDU passes through the AAL5 layer to the Segmentation and Reassembly (SAR) sub-layer, where it is segmented into 48-byte units, which are the SAR PDUs. Now, a 5-byte header is placed at the front of each SAR PDU and this unit makes up the 53-byte ATM cell (see Figure 14-1 for details).

Figure 14-1 *AAL5 Cell Preparation*

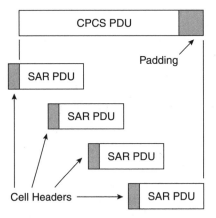

Performance Management

Performance management of ATM includes measuring the traffic on both the physical interface and the individual virtual circuits in the interface. There are many ways to retrieve this data. The method to use depends on the device, the software level on the device, and the configuration of the device.

This performance section is divided into an edge section that covers IOS routers and Catalyst switches, and a switch section covering the ATM switches in the middle. The MIBs and their implementation differ greatly between the two types of devices and therefore must be addressed separately.

Router/Catalyst Switch Interfaces

This section covers how to gather performance data from ATM interfaces on Cisco routers and Catalyst switch interfaces. We will use both SNMP and CLI show commands to gather this data.

ATM Interface Entries in the ifTable

An ATM interface will show up multiple times in the ifTable. Looking at the most common example, an OC3 type interface, you see the following entries:

- The physical layer (in this case, sonet)
- The ATM cell layer
- The AAL5 layer
- Any sub-interfaces supported and configured (depending on the IOS level)

Example 14-1 shows the ifTable entries from a 7500 router running 12.0(5)T IOS code. It illustrates these types of entries:

Example 14-1 *ifTable entries for an ATM interface.*

```
interfaces.ifTable.ifEntry.ifDescr.2 : ATM4/0
interfaces.ifTable.ifEntry.ifDescr.16 : ATM4/0-atm layer
interfaces.ifTable.ifEntry.ifDescr.17 : ATM4/0-aal5 layer
interfaces.ifTable.ifEntry.ifDescr.20 : ATM4/0.1-atm subif
interfaces.ifTable.ifEntry.ifDescr.21 : ATM4/0.1-aal5 layer
interfaces.ifTable.ifEntry.ifDescr.22 : LEC.1.3
interfaces.ifTable.ifEntry.ifDescr.23 : ATM4/0.2-atm subif
interfaces.ifTable.ifEntry.ifDescr.24 : ATM4/0.2-aal5 layer
interfaces.ifTable.ifEntry.ifDescr.25 : LEC.2.3
interfaces.ifTable.ifEntry.ifDescr.26 : ATM4/0.3-atm subif
interfaces.ifTable.ifEntry.ifDescr.27 : ATM4/0.3-aal5 layer
interfaces.ifTable.ifEntry.ifDescr.28 : LEC.3.3
```

continues

Example 14-1 *ifTable entries for an ATM interface. (Continued)*

```
interfaces.ifTable.ifEntry.ifType.2 : sonet
interfaces.ifTable.ifEntry.ifType.16 : atm
interfaces.ifTable.ifEntry.ifType.17 : aal5
interfaces.ifTable.ifEntry.ifType.20 : atmSubInterface
interfaces.ifTable.ifEntry.ifType.21 : aal5
interfaces.ifTable.ifEntry.ifType.22 : aflane8023
interfaces.ifTable.ifEntry.ifType.23 : atmSubInterface
interfaces.ifTable.ifEntry.ifType.24 : aal5
interfaces.ifTable.ifEntry.ifType.25 : aflane8023
interfaces.ifTable.ifEntry.ifType.26 : atmSubInterface
interfaces.ifTable.ifEntry.ifType.27 : aal5
interfaces.ifTable.ifEntry.ifType.28 : aflane8023
```

As stated in Chapter 12, "Monitoring System Interfaces," generic sub-interface support for the interfaces table began in IOS 11.1. However, support for different sub-interface encapsulations differs. LAN Emulation (LANE) sub-interface support began in IOS 11.2. Support for other encapsulations, such as RFC 1483 and RFC 1577, started in IOS 12.0T. In Example 14-1, you see two entries for each LANE sub-interface. The LEC entry has been available since 11.1. But in 12.0(3)T, when ATM sub-interface support began, the other entry pops up.

You must consider how the ATM stack works in order to understand what traffic can be measured, and how it is measured, at each layer. An AAL5 PDU will be padded out to a multiple of 48 bytes. These are the bytes that get counted at the AAL5 layer. The CPCS PDU is then segmented into multiple 48-byte SAR PDUs. The 5-byte cell header is then placed on each SAR PDU to make a 53-byte cell. These are the bytes that get counted at the ATM layer.

The traffic statistics you can get from the ifTable for ATM interfaces is limited because of several factors. The ATM chipsets used in Cisco routers and Catalyst switches do not support cell counts. Therefore, a table entry for a router or catalyst switch will have no traffic counts whatsoever at the ATM cell layer. The ATM cell layer entry for a sub-interface will inherit these limitations.

You can get octet and packet counts at the sonet layer. But non-unicast, broadcast, and multicast counters have no meaning at this layer; they are either not present or set to 0. For example the ifTable and ifXTable entries for the sonet entry from a 7500 router running IOS 12.0(5)T are shown in Example 14-2:

Example 14-2 *Interface table entry for the sonet layer.*

```
ifDescr.2 :  ATM4/0
ifType.2 : sonet
ifMtu.2 : 4470
ifSpeed.2 : 155520000
ifInOctets.2 : 245512134
ifInUcastPkts.2 : 1558340
ifInNUcastPkts.2 : 0
```

Example 14-2   *Interface table entry for the sonet layer. (Continued)*

```
ifOutOctets.2 : 214064371
ifOutUcastPkts.2 : 1385648
ifOutNUcastPkts.2 :  0
ifXEntry.ifName.2 :    AT4/0
ifXEntry.ifHCInOctets.2 :   245490684
ifXEntry.ifHCInUcastPkts.2 :   1558179
ifXEntry.ifHCOutOctets.2 :   214043781
ifXTable.ifXEntry.ifHCOutUcastPkts.2 :   1385491
```

In Example 14-3, a walk of the entire ifTable entry of the ATM layer interface shows no counters of any kind, however. Example 14-3 shows an ATM layer entry in the ifTable and ifXTable for a router running IOS 12.0(5)T:

Example 14-3   *ATM layer entry in the ifTable and ifXTable for a router running IOS 12.0(5)T.*

```
ifIndex.16 :   16
ifDescr.16 : ATM4/0-atm layer
ifType.16 : atm
ifSpeed.16 :155520000
ifPhysAddress.16 :
ifAdminStatus.16 : up
ifOperStatus.16 : up
ifLastChange.16 : (2792) 0:00:27.92
ifName.16 : AT4/0
ifXEntry.ifLinkUpDownTrapEnable.16 : disabled
ifXEntry.ifHighSpeed.16 : 156
ifXEntry.ifPromiscuousMode.16 : false
ifXTable.ifXEntry.ifConnectorPresent.16 : false
```

At the AAL5 layer, you can get both octets and packet counts. The octet counts are the number of octets in the AAL5 CPCS PDUs. The packet counts are the number of AAL5 CPCS PDUs. As with the sonet layer, you can get only unicast packet counts. AAL5 sub-interface entries have the same counters. See Examples 14-4 and 14-5 for details:

Example 14-4   *ATM traffic ifTable counter entries for the AAL5 layer.*

```
ifIndex.17 : 17
ifDescr.17 :   ATM4/0-aal5 layer
ifType.17 : aal5
ifInOctets.17 : 218085
ifInUcastPkts.17 : 20900
ifOutOctets.17 : 224307
ifOutUcastPkts.17 :20779
ifName.17 : AT4/0
ifXEntry.ifInMulticastPkts.17 : 0
ifXEntryifInBroadcastPkts.17 : 0
ifXEntry.ifOutMulticastPkts.17 : 0
ifXEntry.ifOutBroadcastPkts.17 : 0
```

Example 14-5 *ATM traffic ifTable counter entries for the AAL5 sub-interface.*

```
ifIndex.21 : 21
ifDescr.21 :  ATM4/0.1-aal5 layer
ifType.21 : aal5
ifInOctets.21 : 26487249
ifInUcastPkts.21 : 372882
ifOutOctets.21 : 540
ifOutUcastPkts.21 : 3846
ifXEntry.ifName.21 :  AT4/0.1
ifXEntry.ifInMulticastPkts.21 : 0
ifXTable.ifXEntry.ifInBroadcastPkts.21 : 0
ifXTable.ifXEntry.ifOutMulticastPkts.21 : 0
ifXTable.ifXEntry.ifOutBroadcastPkts.21 : 0
```

MIB Variables for ATM Traffic

To get packet and octet counts at the sonet layer, use the interfaces table (ifTable) and the interfaces extension table (ifXTable). To get packet and octet counts at the AAL5 layer, use the interfaces table and the interfaces extension table. But the broadcast and multicast packets counts are set to 0 at this layer, per RFC 2515.

From RFC 2233, the MIB variables relevant to ATM traffic are as follows (subject to limitations as described in the preceding section):

- ifInOctets, ifOutOctets
- ifInUCastPkts, ifOutUCastPkts
- ifHCInOctets, ifHCOutOctets
- ifHCInUcastPkts, ifHCOutUcastPkts

To get packet and octet counts on individual virtual circuits (per VC) use Cisco's extension to the aal5VccTable from RFC 1695 (the AToM MIB). The aal5VccTable contains only error counters. The extensions in the CISCO-AAL5-MIB have packet and octet counts. The entries in the cAal5VccTable are indexed by the interface index of the sonet entry, then the VPI, and then the VCI. If you want to look at the VPI/VCI of 0/16, you would poll cAal5VccInOctets.2.0.16 (refer to Example 14-1). Support for this table began in IOS 11.3.

From CISCO-AAL5-MIB, the relevant variables are as follows:

- cAal5VccInOctets, cAal5VccOutOctets: The number of AAL5 CPCS PDU octets transmitted or received on a given VCC
- cAal5VccInPkts, cAal5VccOutPkts: The number of AAL5 CPCS PDU packets transmitted or received on a given VCC

CLI Commands for ATM Information

You can also use CLI show commands to retrieve traffic data. However, they would be awkward to use to obtain data for trending purposes or to retrieve data on many virtual circuits. Instead, the CLI show commands should be used when your NMS alerts you to an anomaly to drill down to the issue. You can use these commands to get real time data on your interfaces or virtual circuits. We will cover several different commands to get octet and packet counts from both interfaces and virtual circuits.

The **show interface atm** command (see Example 14-6) shows basic traffic statistics for the physical interface.

Example 14-6   *Using **show interface atm** to obtain ATM information for a router or Catalyst switch.*

```
nms-7507a#show int atm4/0
ATM4/0 is up, line protocol is up
  Hardware is cxBus ATM
  MTU 4470 bytes, sub MTU 4470, BW 155520 Kbit, DLY 80 usec,
      reliability 255/255, txload 1/255, rxload 1/255ᴬ
  Encapsulation ATM, loopback not set
  Keepalive not supported
  Encapsulation(s): AAL5, PVC mode
  256 TX buffers, 256 RX buffers,
  2048 maximum active VCs, 1024 VCs per VP, 21 current VCCs
  VC idle disconnect time: 300 seconds
  Signalling vc = 2, vpi = 0, vci = 5
  UNI Version = 4.0, Link Side = user
  Last input 00:00:00, output 00:00:00, output hang never
  Last clearing of "show interface" counters never ᴰ
  Queueing strategy: fifo
  Output queue 0/40, 0 drops; input queue 0/75, 0 drops
  5 minute input rate 8000 bits/sec, 8 packets/sec
  5 minute output rate 8000 bits/sec, 7 packets/secᴮ
      1656932 packets input, 260382286 bytesᶜ, 0 no buffer
      Received 0 broadcasts, 0 runts, 0 giants, 0 throttles
      0 input errors, 0 CRC, 0 frame, 0 overrun, 0 ignored, 0 abort
      1475252 packets output, 227529370 bytesᶜ, 0 underruns
      0 output errors, 0 collisions, 2 interface resets
      0 output buffer failures, 0 output buffers swapped out
```

The annotated lines of output from Example 14-6 are as follows:

A   The txload and rxload represent the traffic load on the interface as a fraction of 255. This fraction is calculated using the 5-minute exponential averaging algorithm discussed in Chapter 7 "Understanding and Using Basic Network Statistics."

B   The 5-minute input/output bit and packet rate. Once again the 5-minute average is calculated using the 5-minute exponential averaging algorithm detailed in Chapter 7.

C The total packet and byte counts since the last clearing of the interface counters. You must check when the counters were cleared in order for these numbers to make any sense.

D The last clearing of "show interface" counters shows how long the counters have been counting packets. Generally, you will clear the counters first in order to get a point of reference with the CLI show commands.

The **show atm traffic** command shown in Example 14-7 gives a quick snapshot of the traffic statistics. Of interest here is the total number of AAL5 packets transmitted or received (A).

Example 14-7 *Obtaining ATM information with the **show atm traffic** command.*

```
nms-7507a#sh atm traff
3255301 Input packets
2156303 Output packetsA
0 Broadcast packets
0 Packets received on non-existent VC
111 Packets attempted to send on non-existent VC
0 OAM cells received
F5 InEndloop: 0, F5 InSegloop: 0, F5 InAIS: 0, F5 InRDI: 0
F4 InEndloop: 0, F4 InSegloop: 0, F4 InAIS: 0, F4 InRDI: 0
0 OAM cells sent
F5 OutEndloop: 0, F5 OutSegloop: 0,    F5 OutRDI: 0
F4 OutEndloop: 0, F4 OutSegloop: 0,    F4 OutRDI: 0
0 OAM cell drops
```

The **show atm vc** command (see Example 14-8) gives a list of all virtual circuits, either PVC or SVC. To get details—including traffic statistics of individual VCs—you can specify the VC of interest (as shown in Example 14-9).

Example 14-8 *Using **show atm vc** to obtain a list of virtual circuits.*

```
nms-7507a#sh atm vc
            VCD /                                    Peak  Avg/Min Burst
Interface   Name    VPI   VCI   Type   Encaps   SC   Kbps  Kbps    Cells  Sts
4/0         2       0     5     PVC    SAAL     UBR  155000               UP
4/0         1       0     16    PVC    ILMI     UBR  155000               UP
4/0.1       7       0     39    SVC    LANE-LEC UBR  155000               UP
4/0.2       8       0     40    SVC    LANE-LEC UBR  155000               UP
4/0.3       9       0     41    SVC    LANE-LEC UBR  155000               UP
4/0.1       10      0     42    MSVC-1 LANE-LEC UBR  155000               UP
4/0.2       11      0     43    MSVC-1 LANE-LEC UBR  155000               UP
4/0.3       12      0     44    MSVC-1 LANE-LEC UBR  155000               UP
4/0.1       13      0     45    SVC    LANE-LEC UBR  155000               UP
```

Example 14-9 *Specifying a VC for more detailed information with the **show atm vc** command.*

```
nms-7507a#show atm vc 8
ATM4/0.2: VCD: 8, VPI: 0, VCI: 40
UBR, PeakRate: 155000
LANE-LEC, etype:0x6, Flags: 0x14C7, VCmode: 0xE000
```

Example 14-9   *Specifying a VC for more detailed information with the **show atm vc** command. (Continued)*

```
OAM frequency: 0 second(s)
InARP DISABLED
InPkts: 3436, OutPkts: 11790, InBytes: 108, OutBytes: 673704
InPRoc: 1, OutPRoc: 6238, Broadcasts: 0
InFast: 0, OutFast: 0, InAS: 3435, OutAS: 5552
OAM cells received: 0
OAM cells sent: 0
Status: UP
TTL: 0
interface = ATM4/0.2, call locally initiated, call reference = 6
vcnum = 8, vpi = 0, vci = 40, state = Active(U10)
 , point-to-point call
Retry count: Current = 0
timer currently inactive, timer value = 00:00:00
Remote Atm Nsap address: 47.00918100000000902B458B01.00902B458751.02
, VC owner: ATM_OWNER_LANE
```

LS1010 and Catalyst 8500MSR Interfaces

This section covers different methods for obtaining traffic statistics from Cisco ATM switches: the LS1010 and the Catalyst 8500MSR. We cover both interface and per VC statistics. In addition to SNMP and show commands, we take a look at ATM accounting and ATM RMON.

The primary data to watch are traffic counts. On ATM switches, we look at counts on the interfaces as well as counts on the individual virtual circuits. Counts at the AAL5 layer do not usually apply on ATM switches, unless an AAL5 entity is configured on the switch. An AAL5 entity can be configured to access internal resources on the switch (such as in-band management of the SNMP agent).

MIB Objects for ATM Switch Interfaces

The traffic you can count on the LS1010 and 8500MSR interfaces includes cell counts and octet counts. For total cell or octet counts, the interfaces table works well. In addition, the 8500MSR supports the High Capacity 64-bit counters in the interfaces extension table. Therefore, the polling interval can be much less on high-speed ATM interfaces.

For traffic counts, use the following MIB objects from RFC 2233:

- ifInOctets, ifOutOctets: The octet counts for all cells, including OAM (Operation And Management) cells on this interface.
- ifInUCastPkts, ifOutUcastPkts: The number of cells received or transmitted over that physical port.
- ifHCInOctets, ifHCOutOctets: The same as ifIn/OutOctets, except counters are 64-bit instead of 32-bit. Only supported on the 8500MSR.

Currently, in order get cell counts in individual virtual circuits, the proprietary ciscoAtmVclTable must be used. Entries in this table are indexed by the interface index, the VPI, and the VCI. This is the same indexing as the cAal5VccTable from the preceding router section.

For cell counts on individual virtual circuits, use the following MIB injects from the CISCO-ATM-CONN-MIB: ciscoAtmVclInCells, ciscoAtmVclInCells.

CLI Commands for ATM Switch Information

As with routers and catalyst switches, the LS1010 and Catalyst 8500MSR ATM switches have a multitude of CLI show commands you can use to obtain real time traffic data. SNMP and the MIB objects described in the preceding section are the best mechanisms for collecting data for trending and other analysis. However, you will at times need to drill down and collect some information in real time. The following CLI show commands should provide you with that information.

The **show interface atm** command gives octet counts for a given interface, as shown in Example 14-10.

Example 14-10 *Obtaining octet counts for a given interface with **show interface atm**.*

```
nms-1010a#show interface atm0/0/0
ATM0/0/0 is up, line protocol is up
  Hardware is oc3suni
  MTU 4470 bytes, sub MTU 4470, BW 155520 Kbit, DLY 0 usec, rely 255/255, load 1/255
  Encapsulation ATM, loopback not set, keepalive not supported
  Last input 00:00:00, output 00:00:00, output hang never
  Last clearing of "show interface" counters 00:00:32 D
  Queueing strategy: fifo
  Output queue 0/40, 0 drops; input queue 0/75, 0 drops
  5 minute input rate 7000 bits/sec, 17 packets/sec
  5 minute output rate 13000 bits/sec, 33 packets/sec A
     1166 packets input, 61798 bytes,B 0 no buffer
     Received 0 broadcasts, 0 runts, 0 giants, 0 throttles
     0 input errors, 0 CRC, 0 frame, 0 overrun, 0 ignored, 0 abort
     1815 packets output, 96195 bytes,C 0 underruns
     0 output errors, 0 collisions, 0 interface resets
     0 output buffer failures, 0 output buffers swapped out
```

Annotated items in Example 14-10 are as follows:

A The input and output cell and bit rate: These rates are a 5-minute average calculated using the 5-minute exponential sliding average, as described in Chapter 7.

B Input cell and octet counts: The packet count is the number of cells received on that interface.

C Output cell and octets counts: The packet count is the number of cells transmitted from that interface.

D The time elapsed since interface counters were cleared: In this example, counters were cleared 32 seconds before the show interface command was executed.

The **show atm traffic** command gives a breakdown of cell counts for each interface, as shown in Example 14-11.

Example 14-11 *Obtaining cell counts per interface with **show atm traffic**.*

```
nms-1010a#sh atm traffic

Interface ATM0/0/0
Rx cells: 151076606
Tx cells: 287452750
5 minute input rate: 7000 bits/sec, 16 cells/sec
5 minute output rate: 15000 bits/sec, 35 cells/sec
```

The **show atm vc traffic** command shows per VC cell counts, as shown in Example 14-12.

Example 14-12 *Obtaining cell counts per VC with **show atm vc traffic**.*

```
nms-1010a#sh atm vc traffic
Interface    VPI    VCI    Type     rx-cell-cnts    tx-cell-cnts
ATM0/0/0     0      5      PVC          38336           38135
ATM0/0/0     0      16     PVC             41             677
ATM0/0/0     0      39     SVC             15               3
ATM0/0/0     0      40     SVC          30957               3
ATM0/0/0     0      41     SVC          24444               3
```

ATM Accounting

ATM accounting, a feature on the LS1010 and Catalyst 8500MSR, provides accounting and billing data for VCs on the switch. The implementation on the LS1010 and Catalyst 8500MSR are defined in the ATM-ACCOUNTING-INFORMATION-MIB and the ACCOUNTING-CONTROL-MIB. As implemented at the time of this writing, these branches are hung off the ciscoExperimental branch. However, these two MIB documents are on a standards track and are officially defined in RFC 2512 and RFC 2513.

The type of data collected is described in the ATM-ACCOUNTING-INFORMATION-MIB. This MIB branch cannot be accessed via SNMP. It only provides the list of objects ATM Accounting can collect data for. The amount of data this mechanism collects is too large for SNMP collection. Instead, you would use SNMP or the CLI to configure ATM Accounting. The control features for SNMP are described in RFC 2513 and the ACCOUNTING-CONTROL-MIB. The CLI mechanism is described in the device-configuration documentation.

The data that can be collected is formally defined in the ATM-ACCOUNTING-INFORMATION-MIB. There is a branch defined with 35 sub-trees hanging from it. Each sub-tree is a particular data point that is sampled and stored into a file. The data collected includes the connection type, interface information, and usage (cell counts). You configure which of the 35 data objects will be sampled and stored into the file either via SNMP or the CLI ATM Accounting commands.

The ATM Accounting data is collected on the switch in a file. The file can be transferred to the NMS via tftp or ftp, or the device can be configured to remotely log the ATM Accounting records via a TCP pipe. The remote logging daemon would reside on the NMS station and listen for a connect request from the ATM switch. After the connection is established, the remote daemon collects the records and writes them to a file. You must configure tftp on the ATM switch to allow a tftp client to issue a read request to retrieve the file. Use the following command:

```
tftp-server {atm-acct-active:acctng_file1 | atm-acct-ready:acctng_file1}
```

Use the atm accounting selection commands to configure which ATM-ACCOUNTING data objects to collect.

Use the atm accounting file commands to configure the accounting file itself.

Then, you want to set a threshold on how full the file must be before an acctngFileNearlyFull or acctngFileFull SNMP trap is sent. After the trap is received, you need to trigger the tftp transfer of the file. Please refer to the ACCOUNTING-CONTROL-MIB for details on these traps.

The file (whether remotely logged or transferred from the switch) is a binary file in ASN.1 format. Currently the name of the file on the switches is fixed as acctng_file1. Please see Appendix B, "ATM Accounting Files," for details on the file format and how to decode it.

Please refer to the "Configuring ATM Accounting and ATM RMON" section of the LS1010 or Catalyst8500MSR documentation for full details on configuring ATM accounting. For further details on the account file and how to decode it, please see Appendix B.

ATM RMON

ATM RMON provides another mechanism to collect traffic statistics and much more information. ATM RMON is very similar to standard RMON. There are four tables, as follows:

- atmStatsTable
- atmHostTable
- atmMatixSDTable
- atmMatrixTopNTable

To start collecting ATM-RMON data, you must define a port select group via the CLI or SNMP. You can define more than one port select group. The port select group allows a group of ports on the device to be configured as an aggregate.

Like standard RMON, ATM RMON generates traffic statistics and host, matrix, and TopN tables for the port select group. The port select group is configured for atmStats, the size of the host and matrix tables. Then, the port select groups are enabled on the desired interfaces. So, a port select group collects the data for a set of desired interfaces for each service class.

Two service classes are defined in ATM RMON:

- cbrAndVbr: Constant and variable bit rate services
- abrAndUbr: Available and unspecified bit rate services

ATM-RMON will collect data on these two service classes separately.

After ATM RMON collection is configured and enabled, data on each port select group is sampled and stored in the ATM RMON tables. Each table provides cell counts, call attempts, calls, and connect time. Cell counters are both 32- and 64-bit counters. If your NMS can use only SNMPv1, the 32-bit counters are your only choice. There is also a rollover counter provided in each table to track how often the 32-bit counter has rolled over. Given the high bandwidth of ATM interfaces, the rollover counter and the 32-bit counter must be sampled. If your NMS supports SNMPv2c, you should use the 64-bit counters.

There are four basic ATM RMON tables:

- atmStatsTable: This table includes a row for each port select group and service class. The table is indexed by portSelGrpIndex and atmStatsClass. In this table are the statistical totals for all ATM addresses discovered in the configure port select groups.

- atmHostTable: This table includes a row for each ATM host and class of service for each port select group configured. The table is indexed by portSelGrpIndex, atmHostAddress, and atmHostSClass. The atmHostAddress is the host's NSAP address. For a given port select group, you can find the traffic generated by each ATM host for a given class of service.

- atmMatixSDTable: This table is a matrix of the source and destination host pairs for a given port select group. The table is indexed by portSelGrpIndex, atmMatrixSDSrcAddress, atmMatrixSDDstAddress, and atmMatrixSDSClass. The type of data collected is the same as the other tables.

- atmMatrixTopNTable: This table shows the top traffic generators from the atmMatrixSDTable.

An example will clarify how the data is collected. If you have a port select group configured on the switch

```
atm rmon portselgrp 7 maxhost 500 maxmatrix 2000 host-prio 1 owner "test"
```

and that port select group is enabled on interface ATM0/0/1

```
nms-1010a#sh atm rmon status
PortSelGrp: 7 Status: Enabled  Hosts:  13/500  Matrix:  58/2000
        ATM0/0/1
```

a walk of the atmStatsTable will look like Example 14-13.

Example 14-13   *A walk of the atmStatsTable.*

```
atmStatsControlDropEvents.7 : 0
atmStatsControlOwner.7 : test
atmStatsControlStatus.7 : Active
atmStatsCreateTime.7.1 : (10828535) 1 day, 6:04:45.35
atmStatsCreateTime.7.2 : (10828535) 1 day, 6:04:45.35
atmStatsCells.1 : 0
atmStatsCells.7.2 : 1571269959
atmStatsCellsRollovers.7.1 : 0
atmStatsCellsRollovers.7.2 : 0
atmStatsNumCallAttempts.7.1 : 0
atmStatsNumCallAttempts.7.2 : 1571269959
atmStatsNumCallAttempts.7.1 : 0
atmStatsNumCallAttempts.7.2 : 16199
atmStatsNumCalls.7.1 : 0
atmStatsNumCalls.7.2 : 15369
atmStatsConnTime.7.1 : 0
atmStatsConnTime.7.2 : 51829224
```

You see in the example that the table is first indexed by 7, the port select group number. The table is then indexed by 1, the CBR/VBR service class; or by 2, the ABR/UBR service class. There is no activity in the CBR/VBR service class; therefore, all traffic is in the ABR/UBR service class.

Fault Management for ATM Interfaces

Fault management for ATM interfaces involves monitoring for errors at the various levels of the ATM stack. There may be bit errors at the ATM level or SAR errors at the AAL5 level. The errors may be due to bad media, interface hardware, or internal resource limitations. This section covers the meaning of different error counters from both the MIB and the CLI.

Some standard errors are as follows:

- HEC errors: The HEC (Header Error Control) in the ATM cell header is an 8-bit CRC code. HEC errors would be similar to FCS errors in Ethernet (see the "Error/Fault Monitoring" section in Chapter 12.

- SAR timeouts: For the AAL5 layer—this error indicates CPCS PDUs that are discarded because they were not reassembled in the required time period.

- SDUs too long: Also for the AAL5 layer—this error means that CPCS PDUs were discarded because they are too long.

This fault section is divided into two sections, one on edge devices (the routers and catalyst switches) and one on ATM switches (the LS1010 and the 8500MSR).

Router/Catalyst Interfaces

For routers, you need to watch for errors at both the ATM layer and at the AAL5 layer because routers are an ATM host. But some Cisco router ATM interfaces have limited support for certain error counters due to chipset limitations. You will not see counts for them in the MIB or the show interface command. The ifTable shows no information for interface errors or discards at any layer for ATM interfaces.

MIB Variables for ATM Interface Errors

Because AAL5 plays a much bigger part on the edge of the ATM cloud, the aal5VccTable from the AToM MIB is particularly useful here.

From RFC 2215, the following MIB variables are useful for detecting ATM interface errors:

- aal5VccCrcErrors: Indicates the number of CPCS PDUs with CRC errors.

- aal5VccSarTimeOuts: Indicates CPCS PDUs that could not get reassembled within the required time period.

- aal5VccOverSizedSDUs: Indicates thatCPCS PDUs were discarded because they are too big.

The preceding three objects are all in the aal5VccTable, which is indexed by ifIndex, VPI, and VCI. These counters are supported only on the Enhanced ATM Port Adapter and on IOS 11.3 or above. They are not supported for the ATM Interface Processor (AIP) or the original ATM Port Adapter.

In addition, you can use the generic error counters from the interfaces table. However, the same object may have different meanings, depending on whether you are looking at the ATM cell layer or the AAL5 layer. From RFC 2233, the following MIB variables are useful:

- ifInDiscards, ifOutDiscards (Available only for the AAL5 layer): The number of AAL5 CPCS PDUs discarded. Could be due to buffer errors.

- ifInErrors: At the AAL5 layer, this object is the sum of the three error counters in the aal5VccTable. At the ATM cell layer, it is the number of cells with HEC errors.

- IfInUnknownProtos: The number of received cells with unrecognized VPI/VCI errors.

CLI Commands for ATM Interface Errors

Use your NMS to monitor for errors via SNMP collections. When errors are detected, you should turn to the CLI show commands to drill down to find the problem. This section covers several show commands that are useful for tracking down problems on your ATM interfaces.

The **show interface** command (see Example 14-14) gives you the most information on the current state of an ATM interface.

Example 14-14 *Obtaining ATM error information with the **show interface** command.*

```
nms-7507a#sh inter atm1/0/0
ATM1/0/0 is up, line protocol is up
  Hardware is cyBus ENHANCED ATM PA
  MTU 4470 bytes, sub MTU 4470, BW 44209 Kbit, DLY 190 usec, rely 255/255, load
1/255
  Encapsulation ATM, loopback not set, keepalive not set
  Encapsulation(s): AAL5 AAL3/4
  4096 maximum active VCs, 1 current VCCs
  VC idle disconnect time: 300 seconds
  Last input never, output 00:03:14, output hang never
  Last clearing of "show interface" counters never
  Queueing strategy: fifo
  Output queue 0/40, 0 drops^G; input queue 0/75, 0 drops
  5 minute input rate 0 bits/sec, 0 packets/sec
  5 minute output rate 0 bits/sec, 0 packets/sec
     8 packets input, 743 bytes, 0 no buffer^F
     Received 0 broadcasts, 0 runts^D, 0 giants^E
     0 input errors, 0 CRC^C, 0 frame, 0 overrun^A, 0 ignored^B, 0 abort
     5 packets output, 560 bytes, 0 underruns
     0 output errors, 0 collisions, 0 interface resets
     Output buffers copied, 0 interrupts, 0 failures
```

The highlighted items in Example 14-14 are as follows:

A overrun: Input stack overflow due to a lack of SAR buffers.

B ignore: A problem processing packets further up the stack after the SAR layer.

C CRC: Either line noise or cell drops due to resource limitations on the ATM adapter.

D runts: Packets smaller than a single cell due to cell corruption.

E giants: Packets larger than the VC MTU.

F no buffer: Internal SAR resource limitations.

G Output queue drop: Packets dropped due to resource limitation on the Virtual Interface Processor or the port adapter itself.

The CRC, runts, and giant errors would be due to faulty media or interface hardware. The remaining errors are related to traffic load, so the amount of traffic is more than the device can process through the ATM stack.

LS1010/8500MSR Interfaces

For ATM switches, we are more concerned with the cell layer statistics than with AAL5 layer statistics. The vast majority of the traffic passing through the switch is transit rather than terminating on the switch itself. Therefore, we are not concerned with AAL5 statistics.

The best indicators of errors on both the LS1010 or Catalyst 8500MSR are in the ifTable. ifInErrors counts HEC-type errors at the ATM cell layer. At the AAL5 layer, ifInErrors is a sum of CSPS CRC errors, SAR timeouts, and SDU Oversize errors.

The CISCO-ATM-IF-PHYS-MIB counts error statistics at the physical layer. The ciscoAtmIfPhysTable is a subset of objects from the sonet and ds3 MIBs.

MIB Variable for Errors on the LS1010/Catalyst8500

As with performance management, for error management of ATM switches in the cloud we are more concerned with the ATM cell layer than the AAL5 layer. For a big picture view, objects from RFC 2233 work fine. If you need to drill down to the physical layer to look at low-level errors, use the CISCO-ATM-IF-PHYS-MIB. The following MIBs are particularly relevant:

- ifInErrors: From the ifTable—a count of HEC errors.
- ifInUnknownPro: From the ifTable—a count of cells with invalid VPI/VCIs.
- ciscoAtmIfPhysTa: From the CISCO-ATM-IF-PHYS-MIB—any entries applicable to the type of interface (sonet or DS3) are of interest.

CLI Commands for Errors on ATM Interfaces

The **show interfaces** command shows several error types, including several counters you can ignore. As shown in Example 14-15, the runt, giant, overrun, ignore, and abort counters are all not applicable to ATM interfaces on the LS1010 or the 8500MSR.

Example 14-15 *Obtaining ATM error information for a switch with the **show interfaces** command.*

```
nms-5500a-asp>sh interface atm12/0/0
ATM12/0/0 is up, line protocol is up
  Hardware is oc3suni
  Description: testit
  MTU 4470 bytes, sub MTU 4470, BW 155520 Kbit, DLY 0 usec, rely 255/255, load 1/255
  Encapsulation ATM, loopback not set, keepalive not supported
  Last input 00:00:00, output 00:00:00, output hang never
  Last clearing of "show interface" counters never
  Queueing strategy: fifo
  Output queue 0/40, 0 drops; input queue 0/75, 0 drops
  5 minute input rate 9000 bits/sec, 47 packets/sec
  5 minute output rate 18000 bits/sec, 63 packets/sec
```

continues

Example 14-15   *Obtaining ATM error information for a switch with the **show interfaces** command. (Continued)*

```
22143052 packets input, 1173581756 bytes, 0 no buffer
Received 0 broadcasts, 0 runts, 0 giants, 0 throttles
0 input errors ᴬ, 0 CRCᴮ, 0 frameᶜ, 0 overrun, 0 ignored, 0 abort
350516665 packets output, 1397514061 bytes, 0 underruns
0 output errors, 0 collisions, 0 interface resets
0 output buffer failures, 0 output buffers swapped out
```

The relevant information from Example 14-15 is as follows:

A The input counter counts damaged cells.

B The CRC counter counts cells with HEC errors.

C The frame counter counts those cells with framing/alignment errors.

The **show controller atm** command (see Example 14-16) gives details on physical and clocking problems. All error counters should be close to zero.

Example 14-16   *Using the **show controller atm** command to obtain information on physical and clocking problems.*

```
nms-5500a-asp>sh cont atm12/0/0
IF Name: ATM12/0/0    Chip Base Address: A8E08000
Port type: OC3    Port rate: 155 Mbps    Port medium: MM Fiber
Port status:Good Signal    Loopback:None    Flags:8308
TX Led: Traffic Pattern    RX Led: Steady Green  TX clock source:  network-derived
Framing mode:  sts-3c
Cell payload scrambling on
Sts-stream scrambling on

OC3 counters:

  Key: txcell - # cells transmitted
       rxcell - # cells received
       b1     - # section BIP-8 errors
       b2     - # line BIP-8 errors
       b3     - # path BIP-8 errors
       ocd    - # out-of-cell delineation errors - not implemented
       g1     - # path FEBE errors
       z2     - # line FEBE errors
       chcs   - # correctable HEC errors
       uhcs   - # uncorrectable HEC errors

txcell:350556951, rxcell:22168814
b1:0, b2:0, b3:0, ocd:0
g1:0, z2:0, chcs:0, uhcs:0

OC3 errored secs:
b1:0, b2:0, b3:0, ocd:0
g1:0, z2:0, chcs:0, uhcs:0

OC3 error-free secs:
```

Example 14-16   *Using the **show controller atm** command to obtain information on physical and clocking problems. (Continued)*

```
b1:446692, b2:446692, b3:446692, ocd:0
g1:446692, z2:446692, chcs:446692, uhcs:446692

Clock reg:8F

  mr 0x30, mcfgr 0x70, misr 0x00, mcmr 0x0F,
  mctlr 0x08, cscsr 0x50, crcsr 0x20, rsop_cier 0x00,
  rsop_sisr 0x00, rsop_bip80r 0x00, rsop_bip81r 0x00, tsop_ctlr 0x80,
  tsop_diagr 0x80, rlop_csr 0x00, rlop_ieisr 0x00, rlop_bip8_240r 0x00,
  rlop_bip8_241r 0x00, rlop_bip8_242r 0x00, rlop_febe0r 0x00, rlop_febe1r 0x00,
  rlop_febe2r 0x00, tlop_ctlr 0x80, tlop_diagr 0x80, rpop_scr 0x00,
  rpop_isr 0x00, rpop_ier 0x00, rpop_pslr 0x13, rpop_pbip80r 0x00,
  rpop_pbip81r 0x00, rpop_pfebe0r 0x00, rpop_pfebe1r 0x00, tpop_cdr 0x80,
  tpop_pcr 0x80, tpop_ap0r 0x00, tpop_ap1r 0x90, tpop_pslr 0x13,
  tpop_psr 0x00, racp_csr 0x04, racp_iesr 0x01, racp_mhpr 0x00,
  racp_mhmr 0x00, racp_checr 0x00, racp_uhecr 0x00, racp_rcc0r 0x04,
  racp_rcc1r 0x00, racp_rcc2r 0x00, racp_cfgr 0xFC, tacp_csr 0x04,
  tacp_iuchpr 0x00, tacp_iucpopr 0x6A, tacp_fctlr 0x00, tacp_tcc0r 0x2A,
  tacp_tcc1r 0x00, tacp_tcc2r 0x00, tacp_cfgr 0x08,
  phy_tx_cnt:350556951, phy_rx_cnt:22168808
```

Monitoring PVC Status

In addition to looking at interface errors, monitoring the status of PVCs is important. It is quite possible to have an error-free link and perfectly functioning interfaces, but if the PVC is down for some reason, traffic will not pass.

As defined in RFC 2515, the ATM Interface VCL Table shows you all the VCs on a given interface. You can monitor atmVclOperStatus in that table for a given VC—indexed by ifIndex, VPI, and VCI—to ensure the PVC is operational.

Or you can go proactive: As of IOS 12.0T, Cisco routers support some extensions to the atmInterfaceConfTable from RFC 2515. These extensions are currently under the ciscoExperiment branch, but will be moved out to a standard branch at future date. For now, the objects are defined in the CISCO-IETF-ATM2-PVCTRAP-MIB. In this document, an SNMP notification (trap) is defined for PVC failures: atmIntfPvcFailuresTrap. This notification must be enabled either via SNMP set on the atmIntfPvcFailuresTrapEnable objects or via the CLI with the following command:

```
snmp-server enable trap atm pvc
```

Summary

This chapter covered a variety of methods to retrieve performance and fault data from ATM interfaces on Cisco devices. As of this writing, this area of management is new and very dynamic. Many efforts currently are underway in the IETF to expand ATM management capabilities. The ATM RMON MIB is an IETF draft. As implemented in Cisco devices, that MIB is under the Cisco branch. After the MIB moves to a standards track, future implementations will likely change to match the standard. You need to keep up with these developments if this area is important for your operations.

References

Books

Pan, Heng. *SNMP-Based ATM Network Management*. Boston, MA: Artech House, 1998.

Standards

RFC 2512, "Accounting Information for ATM Networks," McCloghrie, K., 1999.

RFC 2513, "Managed Objects for Controlling the Collection and Storage of Accounting Information for Connection-Oriented Networks," McCloghrie, K., 1999.

RFC 2515, "Definitions of Managed Objects for ATM Management," Tesink, K., 1999.

Internet Resource

Alles, A. ATM Internetworking, 1995

http://www.cisco.com/warp/customer/614/12.html

CHAPTER 15

Monitoring VLANs

The concept of a "virtual" LAN or VLAN is essentially that of an isolated broadcast domain that exists in LAN-switched environments. Ports sharing the same VLAN can switch packets between them at Layer 2 of the OSI stack. You can also think of a VLAN as an individual IP subnet. Cisco CCO describes the functions of VLANs as follows:

VLANs enable efficient traffic separation, provide better bandwidth utilization, and alleviate scaling issues by logically segmenting the physical local-area network (LAN) infrastructure into different subnets so that packets are switched only between ports within the same VLAN. When combined with central configuration management support, VLANs facilitate workgroups and client/server additions and changes.

This chapter identifies some of the key components of VLANs in Cisco-switched environments that relate to both performance management and fault management. We'll address the following VLAN features and characteristics:

- Logical ports versus physical ports
- VLAN utilization based on broadcast and multicast traffic
- Running spanning tree within VLANs

Most of the discussion in this chapter applies to the Catalyst Series switches, and is basically not pertinent to the routers. Refer to Chapter 12, "Monitoring System Interfaces" for information on monitoring interfaces as it applies to the routers. VLAN interfaces act just like regular interfaces on routers in terms of monitoring.

Overview of VLAN Characteristics

Before diving into the details of performance and fault management for VLANs, we define some of the relevant terms and features of the technology. We'll look specifically at the following:

- Logical ports versus physical ports
- VLAN trunking
- Spanning tree as it applies to VLANs

This is not an exhaustive discussion regarding VLANs, just a brief overview. For more details regarding VLAN architecture, refer to the documentation on CCO or some of the specific references cited at the end of this chapter.

Logical Versus Physical Ports

One of the main reasons for lack of system resources on Catalyst Series switches is the presence of too many logical ports configured or allowed on the switch. Each VLAN instance configured on a trunk port runs its own instance of spanning tree, which can cause extensive CPU resources to be used. Refer to Chapter 11, "Monitoring Network Systems—Processes and Resources," for specifics on the switch resources.

A logical port is a summation of all physical ports installed on a switch plus the amount of VLANs configured on all trunk ports, assuming spanning tree is active for all those VLANs—see Equation 15-1.

Equation 15-1

Sum of all logical ports <= (number of non-ATM trunks on the switch × number of active VLANs on that trunk) + (number of ATM trunks on the switch × number of active VLANs on that trunk × 2) + number of nontrunking ports on the switch

where the sum of all logical ports equals:

400 for Supervisor Engine I (with 20-MB DRAM)

1500 for Supervisor Engine II and III F

4000 for Supervisor Engine III

We'll refer to this formula throughout the chapter when discussing logical ports.

NOTE

Equation 15-1 is taken from the Catalyst Series Software release notes. The Usage Guidelines and Restrictions section includes the following comments:

Ensure that the total number of logical ports across all instances of spanning-tree for different VLANs does not exceed the maximum number supported for each supervisor engine type and memory configuration. Use Equation 15-1 to compute the total number of logical ports on the switch.

If you enable numerous memory-intensive features concurrently (such as VTP pruning, VMPS, EtherChannel, and RMON), or if there is switched data traffic on the management VLAN, the maximum number of supported logical ports is reduced.

TIP

Based on past experiences and field trials, the recommended practical maximum number of logical ports is as follows:

- 250 for Supervisor Engine I (with 20 MB DRAM)

- 1000 for Supervisor Engine II

- 2500 for Supervisor Engine III

VLAN Trunking

Trunking in VLAN environments is a way to send multiple VLANs over one physical port using some kind of encapsulation method such as Cisco's Inter-Switched Link (ISL), ATM LANE, IEEE's 802.10, or IEEE 802.1q. By trunking VLANs, you eliminate the need for multiple ports, one per VLAN, to interconnect two switches. Trunk ports typically connect directly to upstream switches, such as core or distribution switches, from closet switches. VLANs that traverse multiple buildings or campuses more than likely require the use of trunk ports somewhere in the network design. But which trunk encapsulation method is used depends on the network infrastructure put in place.

For example, if you have Fast-Ethernet, Category 5 twisted pair and all Cisco devices in the campus, you probably use Cisco's proprietary ISL or Inter-Switched Link VLAN trunking encapsulation. If you have an FDDI ring connecting campuses together, you probably use 802.10 as the VLAN trunking encapsulation. If your network has an ATM core with switches directly attached to the ATM "cloud," you probably use LANE as your VLAN trunking encapsulation. If you are standardizing on Ethernet trunking and trying to get away from proprietary trunking methods, 802.1q encapsulation is probably going to be used. For more information regarding the different VLAN encapsulation methods, refer to the Cisco documentation available on CCO.

NOTE	The newer switches and port architecture, such as the 6500s and Gigabit Ethernet, utilize the 802.1q trunking protocol. This protocol is not discussed much in this chapter. Instead, a more general discussion of trunking is provided to help calculate logical ports on a switch.

Figure 15-1 illustrates how trunks are applied in VLAN environments. The bold links between Switch E and the rest of the switches are identified as trunk ports. Notice the different VLANs 10 and 20 traversing multiple switches. The trunk ports are used to send data from both of these VLANs over one physical port.

Figure 15-1 *VLAN Trunking*

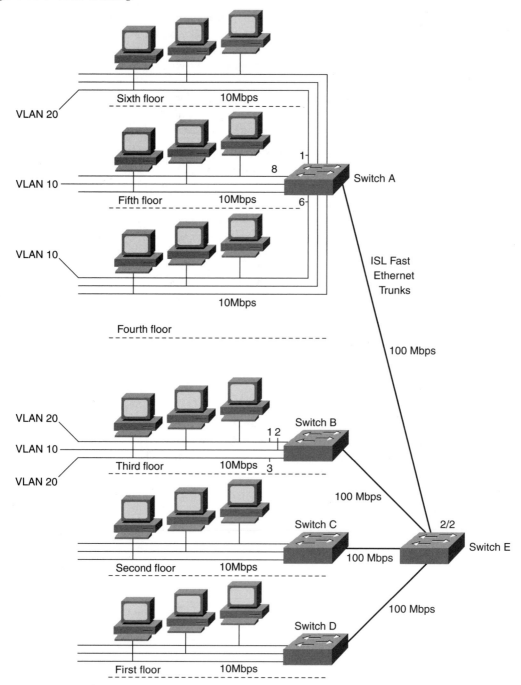

VLAN trunking comes into play with network management when looking at logical ports versus physical ports or when looking at trunk utilization (refer to Chapters 12 and 4 for interface utilization calculations and explanations).

Spanning Tree (802.1d)

When creating fault-tolerant switched internetworks, a loop-free path must exist between all nodes in the network. A spanning tree algorithm is used to calculate the best loop-free path through a Catalyst-switched network. Spanning tree packets or BPDUs (Bridge Protocol Data Units) are sent and received by switches in the network at regular intervals. These packets are not forwarded by the switches participating in the spanning tree, but are instead processed to determine the spanning tree itself. The IEEE 802.1D bridge protocol, sometimes referred to as Spanning Tree Protocol or STP, processes the BPDUs or spanning tree packets for Catalyst Series switches.

The Catalyst Series switches normally do use STP on all VLANs. The STP detects and breaks loops by placing some connections in a blocked state; blocked connections are activated in the event of a primary connection going down. A separate STP runs within each configured VLAN, ensuring valid Layer 2 topologies throughout the network.

The supported STP states are as follows:

- Disabled
- Forwarding
- Learning
- Listening
- Blocking

The state for each port initially is set by the configuration, either forwarding (if the "portfast" or "backbonefast" feature is enabled) or blocking and later modified by the STP process. After the port state is set, the 802.1D bridge specification (RFC 1493) determines whether the port forwards or blocks packets.

If not properly designed, the spanning tree feature can cause more headaches to network managers than any other issue in the network. At a minimum, therefore, we recommend the following configuration:

- Root bridges and backup root bridges statically defined in the Core or Distribution switches when using spanning tree.
- Spanning tree should be activated on all trunk ports for all VLANs.
- Optionally, you can activate spanning tree on end-user switch ports as well, in case a loop is mistakenly created in the network. By default, STP is enabled on all ports, so enabling it typically is not required.

Such small precautions can prevent your network from grinding to a halt when a loop is created.

Spanning tree affects network management in the context of logical ports versus physical ports, as well as fault management of VLANs. We'll look later in this chapter at MIBs from the BRIDGE-MIB as it pertains to spanning tree as well as the SNMP traps associated with STP.

For more detailed information on designing switched networks, refer to the Design guides on CCO relating to Switched Internetworks.

Performance Management Data for VLANs

For performance management of VLANs, we'll look at two major components:

- Logical ports versus physical ports
- Measuring VLAN utilization

Logical Versus Physical Ports

As discussed in the VLAN overview, a logical port is a summation of all physical ports installed on a switch plus the amount of VLANs configured on all trunk ports, assuming spanning tree is active for all those VLANs. We will refer often to the logical port formula (see Equation 15-1) as reference for this section.

NOTE   The ATM trunks are broken out separately in Equation 15-1. The product of the ATM trunks multiplied by the number of VLANs over that trunk needs to be doubled. The ATM trunks are the LANE ports as seen on the ATM LANE modules.

MIBs to Monitor for Logical Ports Versus Physical Ports

From CISCO-STACK MIB, the following two variables pertain to physical versus logical ports:

- ModuleNumPorts: How many physical ports are assigned to each module
- ModuleIndex: How many modules are installed in the switch

To use these MIBs, sum up all of the module ports by adding all moduleNumPorts for each instance of moduleIndex associated with each switch. Then, subtract the trunk ports from this number by referencing the VLANPortOperStatus MIB where it equals "trunking." The resulting value gives you a total physical ports portion of the logical ports formula (see Equation 15-1).

The following MIBs from CISCO-STACK MIB can be used together to obtain the number of VLANs associated with trunk ports based on the MIB VLANOperStatus:

- VLANPortVLAN
- VLANPortModule
- VLANPort
- VLANSpantreeEnable
- VLANPortIslOperStatus
- VLANPortIslAdminStatus

Get the total number of VLANs associated with each trunk port by summing up all unique instances of VLANPortVLAN for each VLANPortModule and VLANPort where VLANSpantreeEnable equals "enabled" and VLANPortIslOperStatus equals "trunking." The VLANIslAdminStatus MIB object is used when 802.1q or 802.10 trunks are utilized, instead of ISL based trunk ports. You'll look for a value of "on" when 802.1q or 802.10 trunking is used.

By calculating the number of VLANs associated with each trunk port, based on the previous algorithm you can determine the rest of logical ports formula by taking the calculated value multiplied by the number of VLANPort where VLANPortIslOperStatus equals "trunking."

Related MIB objects from the CISCO-STACK MIB are

- VLANPortModule
- VLANPort

Related MIB objects from the RFC1213 are

- portIndex
- portModuleIndex
- ifIndex

CLI Commands Relating to the Calculation Of Logical Ports

Because VLANs should be fairly constant and static in networks, the idea of polling the preceding MIB objects and making formulas based on them may seem a little extreme. A better approach is to write a script (for example, in PERL) that gathers output from Telnet data, as described in this portion of the logical ports calculation, to parse out the necessary parts to calculate logical ports.

Using the show port Command

From the **show port** command, you can identify how many physical ports are installed in the switch as well as which ports are trunks and which ones are VLAN ports. The total number of ports for the switch can also be gathered from the command **show module**, but it does not break down the VLANs over the trunk ports.

Summing up the VLAN ports minus the trunk ports gives you the number of nontrunking ports on the switch for use in the logical port formula, stated earlier. The rest of the formula components (see Equation 15-1) can be gathered from the **show trunk** command, which is explained in the next section.

Example 15-1 shows sample output from **show port**.

Example 15-1   *Using **show port** to determine the number of nontrunking ports.*

```
SWITCH# (enable) show port
Port   Name                   Status      Vlan     Level   Duplex Speed Type
-----  -----------------      ----------  -------  ------  ------ ----- ------------
 2/1ᴬ                         notconnect  1ᴮ       normal  half     100 100BaseTX
 2/2                          notconnect  1        normal  half     100 100BaseTX
 5/1                          connected   Trunk    normal  a-full a-100 10/100BaseTX
 5/2                          inactive    2        normal  auto    auto 10/100BaseTX
 5/3                          notconnect  1        normal  auto    auto 10/100BaseTX
 5/4                          notconnect  1        normal  auto    auto 10/100BaseTX
 5/5                          notconnect  1        normal  auto    auto 10/100BaseTX
 5/6                          notconnect  1        normal  auto    auto 10/100BaseTX
 5/7                          notconnect  1        normal  auto    auto 10/100BaseTX
 5/8                          notconnect  1        normal  auto    auto 10/100BaseTX
 5/9                          notconnect  1        normal  auto    auto 10/100BaseTX
 5/10                         notconnect  1        normal  auto    auto 10/100BaseTX
 5/11                         notconnect  1        normal  auto    auto 10/100BaseTX
```

The highlighted information from Example 15-1 is as follows:

A   Summing up all unique instances of the ports from this command minus the trunk ports, as reported as Trunk in the Vlan column, gives you the number of non-trunking ports.

B   The Vlan column shows what VLAN is assigned to what port. The trunk ports are identified as well.

Using the show trunk Command

The **show trunk** command reports which ports are trunk ports, what VLANs are allowed on the each trunk port, and which VLANs are active on each trunk port.

You can get the rest of the components for the logical ports formula through this command:

*   Number of non-ATM trunks on the switch
*   Number of active VLANs on that trunk
*   Number of ATM trunks on the switch
*   Number of active VLANS on ATM trunks

Example 15-2 shows sample output from **show trunk**.

Example 15-2 *Using **show trunk** to obtain values for components of the logical port formula.*

```
SWITCH#  (enable) show trunk
Port      Mode         Encapsulation  Status        Native vlan
--------  -----------  -------------  ------------  -----------
2/1ᴬ      auto         dot1q          trunking      1
4/9ᴬ      auto         isl            trunking      1
4/10ᴬ     desirable    isl            trunking      1
Port      Vlans allowed on trunk
--------  ------------------------------------------------------------
2/1       1-1005ᴮ
4/9       1-1005ᴮ
4/10      1-1005ᴮ
Port      Vlans allowed and active in management domain
--------  ------------------------------------------------------------
2/1       1-5,10,50,152,500,521-524,570
4/9       1,4-5,1003,1005
4/10      1,4-5,1003,1005
Port      Vlans in spanning tree forwarding state and not pruned
--------  ------------------------------------------------------------
2/1       1-5,10,50,152,500,521-524,570
4/9       1005
4/10      1005
```

The highlighted information from Example 15-2 is as follows:

A This output is the physical port that is defined as a trunk port. If the port is an ATM trunk you'd see a port like the following: 5/1-2 (this is why the ATM trunks are doubled in Equation 15-1).

B The VLANs "allowed and active" show what actively configured VLANs are coming across the trunk port. By summing up all unique instances of the VLANs active, you'll define the "number of active VLANs on that trunk" per Equation 15-1. In this example, there are 10 VLANS active on port 5/1.

VLAN Utilization

Due to the nature of switched environments, it is not necessary to measure traffic utilization based on total unicast frames for ports belonging to a particular VLAN. For example, suppose two servers in the same VLAN are exchanging information. This traffic does not affect the performance of two users on different ports and on the same VLAN because switching architecture sends unicast traffic directly to a source or destination port where the MAC address resides. Simply put, the unicast traffic is hidden from the rest of the ports associated with the same VLAN. It may be important, however, to monitor the bandwidth utilization over the trunk ports or critical ports, such as file server ports. Refer to Chapters 12 and 4 for details on monitoring system interfaces and bandwidth utilization, respectively.

A better measurement of VLAN traffic utilization is the measurement of broadcast and/or multicast traffic for a particular VLAN. But how do you get an accurate representation of the broadcast traffic on a VLAN when ports are going up and down due to users turning on and off their host machines, such as PCs. Well, here are a few ways to alleviate that problem:

- Monitor the transmitted broadcast or multicast traffic on file server or application server ports because they are up most of the time.

- In the case of VLANs without file servers, monitor critical ports attached to that VLAN such as ports attaching directly to routers.

- If you don't have router ports, actively poll ports to find the port with the highest transmitted broadcast or multicast traffic for a VLAN, which would indicate that the port has been up the longest in that VLAN on that switch. From that information, you can calculate a broadcast or multicast utilization for the VLAN using the following formula (which uses Broadcasts as an example):

Maximum **XmitBroadcast**/((Sum **XmitFrames** – Sum **XmitBroadcast**) + Maximum **XmitBroadcast**) × 100%

> where **XmitBroadcast** and **XmitFrames** are the transmitted broadcasts and frames for the VLAN based on all the ports associated with that VLAN.

Here's an example:

```
Switch>  show mac
Port     Xmit-Unicast          Xmit-Multicast          Xmit-Broadcast
-------- --------------------- ----------------------- --------------------
 2/1              100000                    0                    20000
 2/2                   0                    0                        0
 5/1             3000000               551828                   310853
```

From this output, you can see that Port 5/1 has the most broadcasts. We'll assume that both of these ports are on the same VLAN for this example. Plugging the numbers into the formula, we get the following results:

310853 / ((100000+20000+3000000+551828+310853) – (20000+310853) + 310853) × 100 %

Simplified:

(310853 / 3962681) × 100 % = 7.845 % broadcasts on this VLAN

For more information on switch traffic characteristics and monitoring best practices, refer to the White Paper on CCO regarding "Cisco Network Monitoring and Event Correlation Guidelines."

MIBs to Monitor for Determining VLAN Utilization

From RFC 1213 (MIB II), the following variables are relevant to VLAN usage:

- ifOutNUcastPkts
- ifOutUcastPkts

The ifOutNUcastPkts MIB combines multicast packets with broadcast packets. This value added to the value of ifOutUcastPkts can allow you to get a percentage of broadcast/multicast traffic per port (interface) relative to total traffic.

By isolating all the ports per VLAN on a switch, you can sum up all traffic, both unicast and non-unicast packets for the whole VLAN, and use the highest ifOutNUcastPkts to calculate the formula denoted in Equation 15-2.

Equation 15-2

VLAN broadcast/multicast utilization = Maximum ifOutNUcastPkts / (ifOutUcastPkts + maximum ifOutNUcastPkts)

You can also compare the VLAN you calculated the utilization on to the VLAN assigned to the sc0 interface on the switch, which is the supervisor card (NMP). Having high broadcasts and multicasts on the NMP or the supervisor can impact switch performance. Please refer to Chapter 11, "Monitoring Network Systems—Processes ad Resources," for more details on system resources.

The recommended baseline threshold for broadcast and multicast traffic on the VLAN is greater than 50 percent, especially if the VLAN is the same as the sc0 interface.

CLI Commands Relating to the Determination Of VLAN Utilization

The **show mac** command displays the number of packets transmitted:

- unicast
- multicast
- broadcast

This command, in conjunction with the **show port** command and the VLAN assignment displayed there, can allow you to calculate the broadcast or multicast traffic utilization for each VLAN. Determine which ports are associated with each VLAN, based on **show port** output (see Example 15-1 for more details on this output) and use the **show mac** command to get the transmitted packets per VLAN.

Example 15-3 shows sample output for **show mac**.

Example 15-3 *Using **show mac** to obtain the number of transmitted packets per VLAN.*

```
Switch>show mac
Port      Rcv-Unicast           Rcv-Multicast         Rcv-Broadcast
--------  --------------------  --------------------  --------------------
2/1                         0                     0                     0
2/2                         0                     0                     0
5/1                         0                551828                310853
5/2                         0                     0                     0
5/3                         0                     0                     0
5/4                         0                633399                     0
5/5                         0                     0                     0
5/6                         0                     0                     0
5/7                         0                     0                     0
5/8                         0                     0                     0
5/9                         0                     0                     0
5/10                        0                     0                     0
5/11                        0                     0                     0
5/12                        0                     0                     0

Port      Xmit-Unicast          Xmit-Multicast        Xmit-Broadcast
--------  --------------------  --------------------  --------------------
2/1                         0               32000A                 50000B
2/2                         0                     0                     0
5/1                         0                     0                     0
5/2                         0                     0                     0
5/3                         0                     0                     0
5/4                         0                95431A                     0
5/5                         0                     0                     0
5/6                         0                     0                     0
5/7                         0                     0                     0
5/8                         0                     0                     0
5/9                         0                     0                     0
5/10                        0                     0                     0
5/11                        0                     0                     0
5/12                        0                     0                     0
Port      Rcv-Octet             Xmit-Octet
--------  --------------------  --------------------
2/1                         0               8000000
2/2                         0                     0
5/1                  58178441                     0
5/2                         0                     0
5/3                         0                     0
5/4                  46271071               9926256
5/5                         0                     0
5/6                         0                     0
5/7                         0                     0
5/8                         0                     0
5/9                         0                     0
5/10                        0                     0
5/11                        0                     0
5/12                        0                     0
```

Example 15-3   *Using **show mac** to obtain the number of transmitted packets per VLAN. (Continued)*

```
MAC      Dely-Exced  MTU-Exced  In-Discard  Lrn-Discrd  In-Lost   Out-Lost
-------- ----------  ---------- ----------  ----------  --------- ----------
2/1           0          0          0           0           0          0
2/2           0          0          0           0           0          0
5/1           0          0          0           0           0          0
5/2           0          0          0           0           0          0
5/3           0          0          0           0           0          0
5/4           0          0        107           0           1          0
5/5           0          0          0           0           0          0
5/6           0          0          0           0           0          0
5/7           0          0          0           0           0          0
5/8           0          0          0           0           0          0
5/9           0          0          0           0           0          0
5/10          0          0          0           0           0          0
5/11          0          0          0           0           0          0
5/12          0          0          0           0           0          0
```

Highlighted information from Example 15-3 is as follows:

A   The Xmit-multicast column shows the number of multicast packets per port. Identify the port with the highest number of transmitted multicast traffic for each VLAN, and divide that number by the total number of (Xmit-unicast + the total number of Xmit-Broadcast) minus the total number of Xmit-Multicast plus the HIGHEST number of Xmit-Multicast. See Equation 15-2 for further clarification of its components.

B   The Xmit-Broadcast column shows the number of broadcast packets per port. Identify the port with the highest broadcast traffic for each VLAN, and divide that number by the total number of (Xmit-unicast + the total number of Xmit-Multicast) minus the total number of Xmit-Broadcast plus the HIGHEST number of Xmit-Broadcast. See Equation 15-2 for further clarification.

Error/Fault Data for VLANs

When troubleshooting VLANs, the most common and most difficult issue to deal with is the constant changing of the spanning tree topology for each VLAN. Each VLAN has its own instance of spanning tree running. In this section, we'll identify how to monitor and keep track of the spanning tree topology changes in each VLAN.

MIBs to Monitor for Spanning Tree Topology Changes

The following MIBs, from BRIDGE-MIB, keep track of the spanning tree topology in the network:

- dot1dStpTimeSinceTopologyChange
- dot1dStpTopChanges
- dot1dStpDesignatedRoot
- dot1dStpPortState

A unique aspect of VLANs is that each one has its own instance of spanning tree. So, how can you tell which VLAN is changing spanning tree topology? Well, this is where VLAN and community string indexing come into play. For example, the Catalyst switch includes one instance of the standard BRIDGE-MIB for each VLAN in the switch. If the read-only community string is "public" and the read-write community string is "private," you could use **public@25** to read the BRIDGE-MIB for VLAN 25 and use **private@33** to read and write the BRIDGE-MIB for VLAN 33. Only using the community string **public** or **private** will result in always accessing the BRIDGE-MIB for VLAN 1 (default behavior).

A trap sent from a MIB that is indexed by a community string also indicates the instance of the MIB to which it corresponds by using community string indexing. For example, an STP newRoot trap from the BRIDGE-MIB for VLAN 25 would have a community string of **public@25** in the trap community field, assuming the read-only community string is **public**.

For fault management, you will rely more on the SNMP trap messages than on these particular MIBs. But based on the receipt of an SNMP spanning tree trap, you can actively poll for these objects to determine where the difference lies.

CLI Commands Relating to the Spanning Tree

Several CLI commands are associated with the MIBs just discussed. We will cover **show spantree** and **show spantree summary** in the following sections.

Using the show spantree Command

The **show spantree** command shows details of the spanning tree characteristics associated with each VLAN. By default, without the VLAN number at the end of the command, VLAN 1 spanning tree characteristics will be seen. You'd have to execute this command for every VLAN defined on the switch that has spanning tree enabled.

The key components of this output are the designated root bridge address, the ports assigned to the VLAN, the port state, and whether or not the fast start feature is enabled on the port.

Ideally, when spanning tree is enabled, you'll want to statically configure the root bridge up in the distribution portion of the network, versus letting it be dynamically elected somewhere in the access switches, so you can control the data path for certain VLANs.

With respect to the fast start feature or portfast feature, it is recommended that you enable portfast on file server ports and on end user ports so spanning tree does not inadvertently change state based on a user port or "end host" port going down. When portfast is enabled, when the port comes up, the port goes right to forwarding state until it hears a BPDU packet on that port; if it does, it goes to the listening, learning states. Portfast allows for users to come online faster.

Example 15-4 shows a sample output from **show spantree**.

Example 15-4   *Using **show spantree** to determine spanning tree topology for the VLAN.*

```
Switch> show spantree 1005
VLAN 1005
Spanning tree enabled A
Designated Root            00-40-0b-8f-8b-ec B
Designated Root Priority  32768
Designated Root Cost      0
Designated Root Port      1/0
Root Max Age  6 sec    Hello Time 2 sec   Forward Delay 4 sec

Bridge ID MAC ADDR         00-40-0b-8f-8b-ec
Bridge ID Priority         32768
Bridge Max Age 6 sec   Hello Time 2 sec   Forward Delay 4 sec
Port,Vlan Vlan Port-State     Cost  Priority Fast-Start Group-method
--------- ---- -------------- ----- -------- ---------- -----------
  3/1 C    1005 forwarding D    80       32  disabled E
```

Highlighted information from Example 15-4 is as follows:

A First displayed is the spanning tree state for the VLAN, either enabled or disabled.

B Designated root is the MAC address of the root bridge in the VLAN. Ideally, you want the root somewhere in the distribution portion of the network versus in the access layer or in the closets. The root bridge should also be statically defined.

C The port,Vlan column displays the ports associated with the VLAN.

D The port stat column shows the spanning tree state of the port, either disabled, inactive, not-connected, blocking, listening, learning, or forwarding.

E The Fast-Start column shows whether or not the portfast feature has been enabled for a particular port.

Using the show spantree summary Command

The output from **show spantree summary** is a consolidated spanning tree status of all VLANs as it relates to the port states for each VLAN.

From this one command, you can get a summary of how many ports are in which state for each VLAN. This information is especially important when trying to load share VLANs over distribution switches or over the core switches in the network.

Example 15-5 shows sample output for **show spantree summary**.

Example 15-5 *Using **show spantree summary** to get a summary of number of ports in each state for each VLAN.*

```
Switch> show spantree summary
Summary of connected spanning tree ports by vlan
Uplinkfast disabled for bridge.
Backbonefast enabled for bridge.
Vlan  Blocking Listening Learning Forwarding STP Active
----- -------- --------- -------- ---------- ----------
   1 A    0 B       0 B       0 B        1 B         1 C
Vlan          Blocking  Listening Learning  Forwarding   STP Active
-----         --------  --------- --------  ----------   ----------
Total         0 D       0 D       0 D       1 D          1 D
BackboneFast statistics
-----------------------
Number of inferior BPDUs received (all VLANs) : 0
Number of RLQ req PDUs received (all VLANs)  : 0
Number of RLQ res PDUs received (all VLANs)  : 0
Number of RLQ req PDUs transmitted (all VLANs) : 0
Number of RLQ res PDUs transmitted (all VLANs) : 0
```

The highlighted information from Example 15-5 is as follows:

A The Vlan column identifies the VLAN to which the spanning tree information in the following columns pertains.

B The next four columns relate to the port states per VLAN. It is basically the sum of all the port states related to each VLAN.

C The STP Active column reports how many ports are actively participating in spanning tree per VLAN.

D The Total row totals up all the port states across all VLANs for the switch. From this data, you can determine how busy a switch is, relative to other parallel or redundant switches in the network.

SNMP Traps Relating to Spanning Tree

Two SNMP traps from the BRIDGE MIB relate to spanning tree:

- newRoot: The newRoot trap indicates that the sending agent has become the new root of the spanning tree; the trap is sent by a bridge soon after its election as the new root (for example, upon expiration of the Topology Change Timer immediately subsequent to its election).

- topologyChange: A topologyChange trap is sent by a bridge when any of its configured ports transitions from the Learning state to the Forwarding state or from the Forwarding state to the Blocking state. The trap is not sent if a newRoot trap is sent for the same transition.

syslog Messages Relating to Spanning Tree

A number of syslog messages are useful for spanning tree and apply directly to the MIB objects and CLI commands previously discussed. They are collected in Table 15-2. These syslog messages will be displayed if spanning tree topology changes for ports on the switch. Upon receipt of these messages, a network manager can address the problem by polling for certain spanning tree MIB objects from the Bridge MIB, or by Telnetting to the device. This troubleshooting technique, however, is beyond the scope of this book.

Table 15-1   *syslog Messages for spanning tree Information*

Message	Explanation
SPANTREE-6-PORTBLK: port [dec]/ [chars] state in vlan [dec] changed to blocking	The identified port has changed to a blocking state. No data traverses the port in this state.
SPANTREE-6-PORTFWD: port [dec]/ [chars] state in vlan [dec] changed to forwarding	The identified port has changed to a forwarding state.
SPANTREE-6-PORTLISTEN: port [dec]/[chars] state in vlan [dec] changed to Listening	The identified port has changed to a listening state, indicating that a spanning tree topology change just took place. No data is traversing the port in this state.
SPANTREE-6-PORTLEARN: port [dec]/[chars] state in vlan [dec] changed to Learning	The identified port has just changed to a learning state, meaning that no data is traversing the port in this state.

Summary

Several key areas relating to the performance and fault monitoring of VLANs are as follows:

- Logical ports versus physical ports
- VLAN Utilization based on broadcast and multicast traffic
- Running spanning tree within VLANs

The logical ports calculation addresses the hardware limitation of the supervisor cards installed in the switches. The formula is documented in the Catalyst Series release notes available on CCO and is reiterated here:

sum of all logical ports <=
 (number of non-ATM trunks on the switch × number of active VLANs on that trunk)
 + (number of ATM trunks on the switch × number of active VLANs on that trunk × 2)
 + number of nontrunking ports on the switch.

Monitoring broadcasts and multicasts to determine the VLAN utilization versus monitoring unicast traffic through the switches is important. Because the purpose of VLANs is to isolate your broadcast domain, it makes sense to monitor the broadcast traffic to get an understanding about how the VLAN is performing. Here is the formula we came up with for calculating VLAN utilization:

VLAN broadcast/multicast utilization = Maximum ifOutNUcastPkts / (ifOutUcastPkts + maximum ifOutNUcastPkts)

Keeping track of spanning tree changes in multiple VLAN environments is tough to do in switched networks. Rely mainly on the SNMP bridge traps to point out your next step in managing the VLAN properly and assist in identifying the changes.

References

Internet Resources

"Cisco Network Monitoring and Event Correlation Guidelines." Cisco Connection Online

http://www.cisco.com/warp/partner/synchronicd/cc/cisco/mkt/enm/cw2000/tech/cnm_rg.htm

"Release Notes for Catalyst 5000 Family Software Release 4.x." Cisco Connection Online

http://www.cisco.com/univercd/cc/td/doc/product/lan/cat5000/c5krn/sw_rns/78_5861.htm#xtocid652213

"VLAN Standardization via IEEE 802.10." Cisco Connection Online

http://www.cisco.com/warp/customer/537/6.html

CHAPTER 16

Managing WAN Technologies— Frame Relay

Frame Relay is a Wide Area Network (WAN) service enterprise that customers can purchase from service providers to provide connectivity between LANs in geographically different locations. There are two ways to look at Frame Relay:

- From a provider perspective—a Frame Relay network is a network of Frame Relay switches providing connectivity between many points.

- From a user perspective—a Frame Relay network is just a cloud whose inner workings are transparent. The Frame Relay cloud provides connectivity between the customer's various LANs.

This chapter will look at Frame Relay from a user perspective. It will cover how you can monitor the performance and fault information of your Frame Relay cloud through the devices (routers) connected to the edge of the cloud at your various locations. One of the objectives of Frame Relay management should be to confirm that your Frame Relay service is delivering the level of service you purchased. Another should be to confirm that the service you purchased meets your needs. Consider the Frame Relay cloud as a network device you cannot monitor directly, much like a piece of network cable.

The following topics are covered in this chapter:

- An overview of Frame Relay
- Identifying the Frame Relay interfaces
- Performance data for Frame Relay
- Error/fault data for Frame Relay

Overview of Frame Relay

Frame Relay is a WAN service optimized for modern data applications. It has higher throughput than X.25, and it makes more efficient use of network resources than individual leased lines running basic HDLC.

Frame Relay more efficiently utilizes bandwidth of a physical link by allowing connectivity to multiple sites through a single physical connection. LAN traffic is bursty by nature, and Frame Relay takes advantage of that burstiness by layering multiple logical connections on a single physical circuit. The individual connections within the physical connection are known as *virtual circuits* (see Figure 16-1).

Frame Relay performance management consists of monitoring the utilization of a single physical link and the throughput and latency of the individual virtual circuits. Frame Relay fault management consists of monitoring for dropped or errored frames across the Frame Relay cloud.

Figure 16-1 *Typical Frame Relay Network*

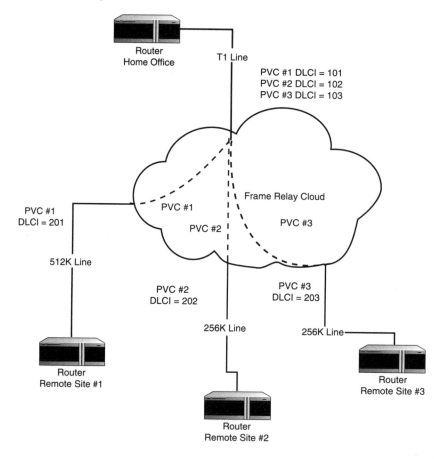

Network managers have discovered that there are many Frame Relay vendors, and each has its own implementations and naming conventions. The terms discussed are described as they should work, but your actual performance may vary according to the service provider selected. However, the generic description of the following terms should make some sense out of what can be chaos:

- *PVC (Permanent Virtual Circuit)* is a Frame Relay logical connection. The PVC is defined by its end points and class of service. It is identified at each end point by a Data Link Connection Identifier.

- *DLCI (Data Link Connection Identifier)* is a unique number assigned to a PVC at one of its end points. It is a Layer 2 network address that is analogous to a MAC address on a LAN. As seen in Figure 16-1, DLCIs are locally significant, meaning that they are unique only on a particular physical link.

- *CIR (Committed Information Rate)* is the rate—in bits per second—a service provider agrees to transfer across a given PVC. This rate is averaged over the Committed Rate Measurement interval (T_c). B_c (*Committed Burst*) is the maximum number of bits that the switch has been programmed to transfer during any Committed Rate Measurement Interval (T_c) without any policing. B_e (*Excess Burst*) is the maximum number of uncommitted bits that the switch will attempt to transfer beyond the CIR.

- *DE (Discard Eligible)* is a bit in the Frame Relay header. When set, it indicates that the frame is eligible for discard in the event of network congestion. The bit is set when a frame entering the switch is determined to be in excess of the CIR.

- *FECN (Forward Explicit Congestion Notification)* is a bit in the Frame Relay header. It is set by the network Frame Relay switch to notify the end station receiving the frame that the frame has been delivered through a congested path of the network.

- *BECN (Backward Explicit Congestion Notification)* is a bit in the Frame Relay header. It is set by the network Frame Relay switch to notify the source (sending) station that congestion exists in the path it is transmitting into.

To put some of these terms into perspective, consider the following. When data is transmitted across the physical link into the Frame Relay switch, it is transferred at the link access rate. The switch counts the incoming bits on a per-VC basis as B_c bits within time interval T_c. Any bits arriving in excess of the B_c limit are counted as B_e bits, and the frame containing these bits will have the DE bit set. Frames with the DE bit set are forwarded if there is no congestion detected in the network. After you go beyond the B_e limit, the switch discards new incoming frames.

Identifying Frame Relay Interfaces

Before going into either performance or fault management for Frame Relay, you need to be able to associate the physical interface, sub-interface, and PVC. This section discusses steps for finding out whether Frame Relay is set up on a serial port. The process discussed should reveal the following information for a Cisco router:

- Number of interfaces
- Types of interfaces
- Whether Frame Relay is configured

- Sub-interface and DLCI numbers using the cfrExtCircuitTable
- Statistics from the frCircuitTable (RFC 1315)

The variables used to gather this data are not covered in detail here, but are shown as examples of what you would need to gather to effectively map the router interfaces to the appropriate DLCIs. (The ifTable objects shown in the next example were covered in more detail in Chapter 12, "Monitoring System Interfaces.")

Identifing Frame Relay Interfaces

To examine the serial ports to find if any are configured for Frame Relay, use the ifName and ifType variables from the ifTable:

```
> snmpwalk 10.29.4.2 ifName
ifName.1 : Et0
ifName.2 : Se0
ifName.3 : Se1
ifName.4 : Nu0
ifName.5 : Lo0
ifName.6 : Lo253
ifName.7 : Se0.1
ifName.8 : Se0.2
ifName.9 : Se0.3
ifName.10 : Se0.4
> snmpwalk 10.29.4.2 ifType
ifType.1 : ethernetCsmacd
ifType.2 : frameRelay
ifType.3 : propPointToPointSerial
ifType.4 : other
ifType.5 : softwareLoopback
ifType.6 : softwareLoopback
ifType.7 : frameRelay
ifType.8 : frameRelay
ifType.9 : frameRelay
ifType.10 : frameRelay
```

Now you know that the first serial port 0 and its sub-interfaces are Frame Relay.

Using the Cisco Frame-Relay MIB to Identify the Sub-interface

Identifying the sub-interface and associated DLCIs is essential for starting the data collection for either performance or fault management. At this point, you will need to use the Cisco Frame-Relay MIB's cfrExtCircuitTable; specifically, the following variables:

- cfrExtCircuitIfName DisplayString: The text name of the interface or sub-interface with the associated DLCI. This is the same name string of an interface used in the configuration and all console displays, such as 'serial 0', 'serial 3/0.3', for instance: ciscoMgmt.49.1.2.2.1.1.5.20 = Serial1.3, where the OID 49.1.2.2.1.1 is the cfrExtCircuitIfName.

- cfrExtCircuitIfType INTEGER: The type of the sub-interface this DLCI is associated with, if configured—mainInterface(1), pointToPoint(2), multipoint(3). For instance, ciscoMgmt.49.1.2.2.1.2.5.20 = 3 would indicate 49.1.2.2.1.2 as the cfrExtCircuitIfType, 5 is the main interface from the frCircuitIfIndex, 20 is the DLCI, and this sub-interface is configured for multipoint.

- cfrExtCircuitSubifIndex InterfaceIndex: For a value greater than 0, this variable indicates the network management interface index for the sub-interface associated with this DLCI. Value 0 means the DLCI is not associated with any sub-interface. For example, ciscoMgmt.cfrExtCircuitSubifIndex.2.201 = 7 would indicate that the ifIndex for this sub-interface is 7.

The cfrExtCircuitTable is indexed by frCircuitIfIndex, frCircuitDlci. It provides the ifIndex value of the ifEntry this virtual circuit is layered onto and the DLCI for this virtual circuit. In the following example, the indexed number is 2, with the DLCI number following:

```
> snmpwalk 10.29.4.2 cfrExtCircuitIfName
cfrExtCircuitIfName.2.101 : Serial0.1
cfrExtCircuitIfName.2.201 : Serial0.2
cfrExtCircuitIfName.2.301 : Serial0.3
cfrExtCircuitIfName.2.401 : Serial0.4
> snmpwalk 10.29.4.2 cfrExtCircuitIfType
cfrExtCircuitIfType.2.101 : pointToPoint
cfrExtCircuitIfType.2.201 : multipoint
cfrExtCircuitIfType.2.301 : multipoint
cfrExtCircuitIfType.2.401 : multipoint
```

From the data gathered in this example, you can build a table such as Table 16-1.

Table 16-1 *Correlating Interfaces, Sub-interfaces, and Virtual Circuits*

ifIndex	Namestring	Subiftype	DLCIs
7	Serial0.1	PointToPoint	101
8	Serial0.2	Multipoint	201
9	Serial0.3	Multipoint	301
10	Serial0.4	Multipoint	401

This gives you the basic information needed to correlate the performance and fault data in the chapter to the interface or sub-interface and the virtual circuits.

Performance Data for Frame Relay

You can gather Frame Relay performance information either through MIBs or through the command-line interface (CLI) via Telnet or RSH. We will look at both methods, including what the highlighted variables indicate, why they are useful, and how to manage the resulting factors. Where appropriate, we also will identify some starting point thresholds to set and watch for when monitoring performance. But please note that the threshold settings defined in this section reflect only a starting point and nothing more. You must understand your network traffic flows and network characteristics before making the appropriate threshold setting. Thresholds constantly need re-evaluation and adjustment to meet the needs of your environment.

We will consider the following performance issues for Frame Relay:

- Measuring utilization on virtual circuits
- Congestion monitoring

Measuring Utilization On Frame Relay Virtual Circuits

To accomplish this task, you must be able to associate the collected data with the appropriate DLCI and interface. The data in Table 16-1 will be used in this section for example purposes. The standard ifTable variables are important to gather as well (refer to Chapter 12 for more information).

MIBs to Monitor for Utilization

As in any circuit, the variables that you want to monitor are the packets (frames, in this case) and octets transmitted and received. The relevant variables from RFC 1315 are as follows:

- frCircuitSentFrames: The number of frames sent from this virtual circuit since it was created
- frCircuitSentOctets: The number of octets sent from this virtual circuit since it was created
- frCircuitReceivedFrames: The number of frames received over this virtual circuit since it was created
- frCircuitReceivedOctets: The number of octets received over this virtual circuit since it was created

The preceding variables provide you with the base utilization statistics for the specified virtual circuit. The variable frCircuitThroughput appears to be useful, but the variables that are used in the calculation frCircuitCommittedBurst and frCircuitExcessBurst are set to 0 unless Frame Relay traffic shaping is configured. Even then, the variables are manually configured by you (see "Traffic Shaping for Frame Relay" later in this chapter).

There is no threshold recommended. The CLI command **show frame-relay pvc** is covered in subsequent sections for each of the performance variables. Also, an example of an SNMP collection that extends the earlier table of virtual circuits and interfaces will be covered.

CLI Commands for Utilization

The **show frame-relay pvc** command (or **show frame pvc**, for short) displays the number of frames sent, octets sent, frames received, and octets received; as well as frames from the network indicating forward or backward congestion since the virtual circuit counters were cleared. It also provides the local DLCI number, creation time, and discard eligible packets.

The **show frame pvc** command is useful when you are troubleshooting the Frame Relay circuit. It contains several valuable data points in the display output that can help you identify possible problem areas with the router or in your network. Example 16-1 shows output from the **show frame pvc** command.

Example 16-1 *Using the* **show frame pvc** *command to obtain utilization information.*

```
router#sh frame pvc

PVC Statistics for interface Serial2/0 (Frame Relay DTE)

CI = 460, DLCI USAGE = LOCAL, PVC STATUS = ACTIVE, INTERFACE = Serial2/0

  input pkts 183521960ᴬ      output pkts 186990758ᴮ   in bytes 3108846619ꟲ
  out bytes 3787418196ᴰ      dropped pkts 4           in FECNᴱ pkts 49912
  in BECN pkts 227072        out FECNꟳ pkts 0         out BECN pkts 0
  in DEᴳ pkts 7488798        out DEᴴ pkts 0
  pvc create time 33w0d, last time pvc status changed 00:15:48
```

Here are the meanings of the annotated features in Example 16-1:

A The input packets(related to SNMP variable frCircuitReceivedFrames)

B The output packets (related to SNMP variable frCircuitSentFrames)

C The input bytes (related to SNMP variable frCircuitReceiveOctets)

D The output bytes (related to SNMP variable frCircuitSentOctets)

E The input FECN packets (related to SNMP variable frCircuitReceivedFECNs—see "MIBs to Monitor for Forward/Backward Explicit Congestion Notification")

F The output FECN packets that will remain at 0 unless Frame Relay traffic shaping has been configured (see "MIBs to Monitor for Forward/Backward Explicit Congestion Notification")

G The number of incoming DE (Discard Eligible) marked packets (see "MIBs to Monitor for Discard Eligible Packets")

H The number of output DE marked packets—normally 0 unless configured on the router (see "MIBs to Monitor for Discard Eligible Packets")

SNMP Example for Utilization

Using the frCircuitTable and the ifIndex information you already gathered, you can loop through all the PVCs in the frCircuitTable to gather the following information:

```
KEY=2.101
frCircuitIfIndex=7
frCircuitDlci=101
frCircuitState=active
frCircuitReceivedFECNs=14
frCircuitReceivedBECNs=23
frCircuitSentFrames=576
frCircuitSentOctets=345987
frCircuitReceivedFrames=464
frCircuitReceivedOctets=238971
frCircuitCreationTime=42:30:07.48
frCircuitLastTimeChange=8:00:10.11
frCircuitCommittedBurst=0
frCircuitExcessBurst=0
frCircuitThroughput=0
```

After this information has been collected for each ifIndex and DLCI, you can extend Table 16-1, as shown in Table 16-2.

Table 16-2 *Frame Relay Utilization and Performance Information*

if Index	Name String	SubIf Type	DLCI	Sent Frames	Sent Octets	Rcvd Frames	Rcvd Octets	FECN	BECN
7	Serial0.1	PointTo Point	101	342	105467	258	100568	0	0
8	Serial0.2	Multipoint	201	576	345987	464	238971	14	23
9	Serial0.3	Multipoint	301	322	193416	288	172993	0	0
10	Serial0.4	Multipoint	401	221	100396	204	94044	0	0

Congestion Monitoring

Congestion management in Frame Relay networks is a challenge for network managers. Although Frame Relay technology has congestion-notification mechanisms built into the specifications and switch vendors have implemented them, the notifications primarily have been intended for end systems, which are usually the source of the congestion.

MIBs to Monitor for Forward/Backward Explicit Congestion Notification

Congestion is a network problem that can result in severe degradation of the network in both response time and throughput. One of the essential elements in preventing congestion is through flow control. The two mechanisms that Frame Relay uses to notify users, routers, and Frame Relay switches about congestion are the BECN and FECN bits.

Two relevant variables, from RFC 1315, are the following:

- frCircuitReceivedFECNs: Reports the number of frames received from the network, indicating forward congestion since the virtual circuit was created
- frCircuitReceivedBECNs: Reports the number of frames received from the network, indicating backward congestion since the virtual circuit was created

These are good MIB variables to collect because they indicate that the Frame Relay circuit is receiving congestion. The variables are valuable for trending and capacity planning of the network. When a Frame Relay switch begins to experience congestion due to its queues becoming full or a problem with memory management, the switch usually will inform its upstream and downstream nodes through the setting of the FECN, BECN, and DE bits. Therefore, this data provides you and your circuit provider with information to use when making decisions on circuit sizing. Cisco routers currently record only the congestion variable numbers. Unless Frame Relay traffic shaping is configured for the Frame Relay interface, the router does not support any congestion control using the FECN, BECN, or DE bits.

The recommended baseline values to watch for are delta values greater than 100.

The **show frame-relay pvc** command (refer to Example 16-1) displays the number of frames received from the network, indicating forward or backward congestion since the virtual circuit counters were cleared. Looking at the packets that are marked for DE and the number of FECN and BECN packets received can provide an insight into the level of congestion on the Frame Relay circuit.

MIBs to Monitor for Discard Eligible Packets

The following variables, from CISCO-FRAME-RELAY-MIB, indicate the number of discard eligible packets that have been received or transmitted since the PVC was established:

- cfrCircuitDEins
- cfrCircuitDEouts

cfrCircuitDEins is an important variable because it indicates that the committed information rate (CIR) for the VC is being exceeded. This variable indicates that the DE bit in the Frame Relay header has been set. The setting of this bit indicates that the frame is eligible for discard in the event of network congestion. The bit is set when a frame entering the switch is determined to be in excess of the Committed Information Rate (CIR), but less than the excess burst limit. If the B_e (excess burst) limit is exceeded, the frame should be dropped during normal operation.

The option to not enforce the use of the DE bit is available in some Frame Relay switches and may be useful where Ingress and Egress access speeds are equal and where full bandwidth could be used when available. All access being equal would allow full bandwidth to be used if needed. This type of scenario would usually apply to private Frame Relay networks, such as an internal stratacom network.

The cfrCircuitDEouts indicate that the DE bit has been set before entering the Frame Relay switch cloud by DTE equipment, such as a router. Cisco IOS allows the setting of DE bit for packets classified through standard access lists.

The recommended baseline threshold values are delta greater than 100.

As shown in Example 16-1, the CLI command **show frame-relay pvc** also provides information on the number of DE-marked packets, both incoming and outgoing.

MIBs to Monitor for Packet Discards

Actively monitoring the Frame Relay dropped packets provides you with an immediate insight into the circuit congestion. The relevant variable, from CISCO-FRAME-RELAY-MIB, is cfrCircuitDropPktsOuts, which indicates the number of drops on a virtual circuit.

The recommended baseline threshold is a delta value greater than 100.

Related MIB objects from OLD-CISCO-INTERFACE are as follows:

- locIfInputQueueDrops: Indicates the number of packets dropped because the input queue was full

- locIfOutputQueueDrops: Indicates the number of packets dropped because the output queue was full

Related MIB objects from RFC-1213-MIB/IF-MIB are as follows:

- ifInDiscards: Indicates the number of inbound packets that were discarded even though no errors had been detected to prevent their being deliverable to a higher-layer

- ifOutDiscards: Indicates the number of outbound packets that were chosen to be discarded even though no errors had been detected to prevent their being transmitted

The **show frame-relay pvc** command (refer to Example 16-1) also provides packet discard information. In this case, you would look specifically at the amount of output drops, input drops, and no buffer values.

Committed Burst and Excess Burst Rates

The routers that connect the end stations to the Frame Relay network have largely played a passive role in Frame Relay congestion management. Many protocols do not have a mechanism to provide for congestion notification; that is, the protocol header contains no congestion indication bit. This has driven the need for more control and led to the development of a Frame Relay traffic shaping congestion-management feature that can also prioritize the data going into a Frame Relay network.

Traffic Shaping for Frame Relay

Before looking at MIBs and CLI commands for committed burst and excess burst information, you need to understand more about traffic shaping for Frame Relay. This feature, available in IOS release 11.2, allows the router to regulate and prioritize the transmission of frames on a per-VC basis to the network as well as react to congestion notification from the Frame Relay network. Traffic shaping for Frame Relay can be broken down into three main components:

1 Rate Enforcement on a per-VC basis: Define and enforce a rate on the VC at which the router will send traffic into the network.

2 Generalized BECN support on a per-VC basis: Enable router to dynamically fluctuate the rate at which it sends packets, depending on the BECNs it receives. For example, if the router begins receiving numerous BECNs, it will reduce the frame transmission rate. As BECNs become more intermittent, the router will increase the frame transmission rate.

3 Virtual Circuit Queuing (Custom, Priority, and FIFO): For circuits carrying more than one protocol, queuing can now be applied on a per-VC basis. This can be accomplished by configuring queuing as in earlier releases and then applying either the keywords **queue-list** (for custom queuing) or **priority-group** (for priority queuing) to the **map-class** command used in traffic shaping. (See Example 16-2 for a sample traffic shaping configuration for Frame Relay.) It is essential for performance that queuing be defined the same when sending and receiving routers for proper operation.

The functions just described apply to both PVCs and SVCs. Additional overall feedback is provided to the traffic shaping algorithm by monitoring the queue depth of the physical interface. This means that you can populate the variables. Based on the accuracy of your input, this capability can assist you in managing your Frame Relay network.

The rate enforcement algorithm used incorporates a two-stage queuing process. The first stage is where the queuing on a VC basis is implemented, using Custom, Priority, or the default First Come, First Served mechanism. These first-stage queues output into a single interface-level queue. Traffic is then metered at the output of the per-VC queues, based on the traffic-shaping configuration parameters specified for each of these queues. It is important to note that Weighted Fair Queuing and Traffic Shaping over Frame Relay are mutually exclusive.

Configurable Parameters

For each Frame Relay virtual circuit, the user may configure the following router parameters:

- CIR—Committed information rate

- B_c—Committed burst size
- B_e—Excess burst size
- Q—Queuing algorithm to be used within the VC

These variables are used to ensure that the router paces traffic to match the service level agreement with the service provider. They pace traffic going out, but do not alter the settings on the connected FR switch.

Facilities are provided so that a user may configure a default profile for all VCs at the interface or sub-interface level that can be overridden at the individual VC level, if required. See the configuration Example 16-2 of Frame Relay traffic shaping.

End User Interface

The end user interface on the router is configured using the following command:

```
frame-relay traffic-shaping
```

The following interface level command turns on traffic shaping and per-VC queuing:

```
frame-relay traffic-rate average [peak]
```

where *average* is the average rate equivalent to CIR in bps and *peak* is the peak rate equivalent to CIR + Be/t = CIR(1+Be/Bc). If peak is omitted, the default value used is derived from the BW (interface bandwidth) parameter.

The following command marks the section where the traffic shaping parameters are defined:

```
map-class frame-relay
```

Some other related Frame Relay traffic shaping commands are as follows:

- **frame-relay custom-queue-list** *list-number*—Uses custom queuing to apply against the **map-class** command.

- **frame-relay priority-group** *list-number*—Uses priority queuing to apply against the **map-class** command.

- **frame-relay becn-response-enable**—Enables the use of congestion reduction when BECN bits are received.

- **frame-relay class** *map-class-name*—Enables the use of setting up the *map-class* name.

Example 16-2 shows output from the sample traffic-shaping configuration for Frame Relay. Note that comment lines are provided to highlight the purpose of specific command lines. The routers used in Example 16-2 are named FR-Hub and FR-spoke router.

Example 16-2 *Sample traffic-shaping configuration for Frame Relay.*

```
FR-Hub router configuration
Current configuration:
!
version 11.2
!
```

Example 16-2 *Sample traffic-shaping configuration for Frame Relay. (Continued)*

```
hostname FR-Hub
!
!
interface Ethernet0
ip address 10.100.1.1 255.255.255.0
media-type 10BaseT
!
!
interface Serial0
no ip address
encapsulation frame-relay
no fair-queue
!
!Enable Traffic Shaping on physical interface
!
frame-relay traffic-shaping
!
interface Serial0.1 point-to-point
ip address 10.20.1.113 255.255.255.240
ipx network AB449D80
!
!the map-class defined below is assigned to this subinterface
frame-relay class 32cir
frame-relay interface-dlci 101 broadcast
!
interface Serial0.2 point-to-point
ip address 10.20.1.129 255.255.255.240
!
!the map-class defined below is assigned to this subinterface
frame-relay class 16cir
frame-relay interface-dlci 102 broadcast
!
interface Serial0.3 point-to-point
ip address 10.20.1.145 255.255.255.240
!
!the map-class defined below is assigned to subinterface
frame-relay class bc64
frame-relay interface-dlci 103 broadcast
!
!
router eigrp 100
network 10.20.0.0
!
map-class frame-relay 32cir
!
!the average & peak rates are set to the VC's CIR, and Excess Burst
frame-relay traffic-rate 32000 64000

!
!a custom queue list is also assigned to this map class
frame-relay custom-queue-list 1
```

continues

Example 16-2 *Sample traffic-shaping configuration for Frame Relay. (Continued)*

```
!
map-class frame-relay 16cir
!
!the average & peak rates are set to the VC's CIR, and Excess Burst
frame-relay traffic-rate 16000 64000

!
map-class frame-relay bc64
frame-relay cir in 32000
!
!Here, specific control of parameters is possible on a bi-directional basis
frame-relay cir out 32000
frame-relay bc in 32000
frame-relay bc out 64000
frame-relay be in 64000
frame-relay be out 64000
!
queue-list 1 protocol ip 1
queue-list 1 protocol ipx 2
queue-list 1 queue 1 byte-count 4200
queue-list 1 queue 2 byte-count 1400
!
!
end

FR-Spoke Configuration
Current configuration:
!
version 11.2
!
hostname FR-Spoke
!
enable password cisco
!
ipx routing 0000.0c18.d70c
!
interface Ethernet0
ip address 10.21.1.1 255.255.255.0
ipx network ABC001
!
!
interface Serial0
ip address 10.20.1.146 255.255.255.240
encapsulation frame-relay
ipx network ABC010
frame-relay traffic-shaping
!
!the map-class defined below is assigned to interface
frame-relay class 32cir

!
```

Example 16-2 *Sample traffic-shaping configuration for Frame Relay. (Continued)*

```
router eigrp 100
network 10.20.0.0
!
!
no ip classless
!
map-class frame-relay 32cir
!
!the average & peak rates match those in the Hub router
frame-relay traffic-rate 32000 64000

frame-relay custom-queue-list 1
!the custom queue list matches that in the Hub router
!
queue-list 1 protocol ip 1
queue-list 1 protocol ipx 2
queue-list 1 queue 1 byte-count 4200
queue-list 1 queue 2 byte-count 1400
!
!
end
```

Benefits of Frame Relay Traffic Shaping

Traffic shaping allows you to prioritize packets on a per-VC basis, which is important when multiple protocols are configured on the same DLCI.

Frame Relay traffic entering a Frame Relay network does so at the link access rate, regardless of any parameters set on the switch such as CIR, Excess Burst, or Committed Burst. Of course, the rate and volume of traffic entering the switch will be monitored at the input, and decisions will be made on what to do with the traffic based on these parameters. The Frame Relay traffic shaping provides control over how much data is sent into the network. It enables you to ensure, for example, that packets enter the Frame Relay network within CIR and thus have a guarantee of being propagated through. You can further ensure that traffic enters the network within the Excess Burst limit so that immediate drops do not occur.

By working with your service provider, understanding your network traffic patterns, and experimenting with the different levels, you can find the correct rate-enforcement parameters for your particular environment. Finding these parameters can result in maximizing the available resources while minimizing the amount of dropped frames.

In the event of congestion within the Frame Relay network where Backward Explicit Congestion Notification (BECN) is provided to the source (in this case, the router), a further throttling of data that is network-bound will occur. The congestion in the Frame Relay network then has a much better chance of dissipating quickly, with the result that fewer DE packets are dropped.

The throttling occurs if a router receives any BECNs during the current time interval (Interval = B_c/CIR, with the maximum size being 125ms). Whether the router receives 1 or 1000 BECNs in this time interval, it decreases the transmit rate by 25 percent. The rate will continue to drop with each BECN (the limit is one drop per time interval) until the traffic rate gets to mincir, where it stops. The mincir is the minimum amount of data to be sent during periods of congestion. By default, this is half of CIR.

After the traffic rate has decreased, it takes 16 time intervals of receiving no BECNs to start to increase traffic again. The amount that traffic increases by is (B_e+B_c)/16, or (more accurately) the byte limit that shows up in **show traffic** and **sh frame pvc x** divided by 16. Therefore, it takes much longer to get back to CIR than it does to drop to mincir. This is similar to the slow start in TCP/IP. One way of making this length of time much shorter would be to set B_e to 7 times the value of B_c, which would ensure that the traffic rate gets back to CIR immediately after going through 16 time intervals without a BECN.

It is important to note two issues. First, this throttling occurs only when traffic shaping is configured. If traffic shaping is not configured, the transmit increment will stay the same whether BECNs are being received or not. Second, traffic shaping of your circuits within the presence of congestion from other customers who are not traffic shaping can lead to limiting the traffic on your circuits while another's traffic saturates the trunk.

MIBs to Monitor for Committed Burst and Excess Burst Information

From RFC 1315-MIB, the variables to monitor for B_c and B_e are as follows:

- frCircuitCommittedBurst: This variable indicates the maximum amount of data, in bits, that the network agrees to transfer under normal conditions, during the measurement interval.

- frCircuitExcessBurst: This variable indicates the maximum amount of uncommitted data bits that the network will attempt to deliver over the measurement interval. By default, if not configured when creating the entry, the Excess Information Burst Size is set to the value of ifSpeed.

Neither of these MIB variables means anything without the configuration of Frame Relay traffic shaping.

Again, you can use the CLI command **show frame-relay pvc** to obtain similar information to these MIB variables (refer to Example 16-1).

Correlating Performance Variables

The MIB variables for FECN, BECN, DE, and dropped packets all are correlated statistically with respect to performance management. Also, much of what you gather in performance management can be applied to fault/error management.

Specifically, you should look for a high number of FECNs or BECNs, combined with a high number of received packets with DE bit set. This correlation is the only indication, other than calls from the users, that you are experiencing congestion on the Frame Relay circuit. When a Frame Relay switch begins to experience congestion due to its queues becoming full or problems with memory management, the switch sets the FECN, BECN, and DE bits to inform its upstream and downstream nodes. Therefore, you can use this data in conjunction with your Frame Relay provider to make decisions on circuit sizing or in the use of features such as Frame Relay traffic shaping.

Using the performance variables in the frCircuitTable, detailed previously, with the cfrExtCircuitTable variables detailed in the section "Identifying the Frame Relay Interface," you can build a table that correlates ifIndex, interface type, and virtual circuit with the utilization and congestion data. This is essential to both understanding and managing your Frame Relay network.

Error/Fault Data for Frame Relay

The means to monitor errors and faults for Frame Relay are essentially the same as those covered in Chapter 12. The problem is being able to manage virtual circuit utilization and end-to-end delay measurements, which is mandatory for assessing the impact of network queuing. Beyond the statistics that we have covered under the performance section, decodes and traces of Layer 3 protocols are required for the complete isolation of virtual path problems. Packet capture and decodes are used to verify the integrity of application traffic.

This section covers the following:

- Monitoring Frame Relay Circuit Flapping
- Monitoring Frame Relay Errored Frames

Monitoring Frame Relay Circuit Flapping

From RFC 1315-MIB, several MIB variables are useful for monitoring circuit flapping:

- frCircuitState: Indicates whether the particular virtual circuit is operational.
- frCircuitCreationTime: Indicates the value of sysUpTime when the virtual circuit was created, whether by the Data Link Connection Management Interface or by a SetRequest.
- frCircuitLastTimeChange: Indicates the value of sysUpTime when last there was a change in the state of the virtual circuit.
- frTrapState: Indicates whether the system produces the frDLCIStatusChange trap.

In the absence of a Data Link Connection Management Interface, virtual circuit entries (rows) may be created by setting the virtual circuit state to active (frCircuitState in the previous performance SNMP example) or deleted by changing circuit state to invalid. Whether or not the row actually disappears is an implementation issue, so the frCircuitState object may actually read as invalid for some arbitrary length of time. It is also legal to set the state of a virtual circuit to inactive to temporarily disable a given circuit.

Changes in the circuit state and the creation time of the circuit can provide you with indications of circuit problems with your Frame Relay provider. They also provide a way to check the frDLCIStatusChange trap on your network management station. If the FrCircuitCreationTime is not changing, but you are receiving the frDLCIStatusChange trap, then your circuit may not be fluctuating. Therefore, looking at the FrCircuitCreationTime caching, comparing to the last value, and reporting if there is a change will help to correlate with the frDLCIStatusChange traps that are received.

The recommended baseline threshold values are related to each other. If frCircuitState changes, other variables should experience a corresponding change.

See the output from **show frame-relay pvc** in the performance section (refer to Example 16-1) for CLI command information that corresponds to these MIBs.

From CISCO-FRAME-RELAY-TRAP, a related SNMP trap message is frDLCIStatusChange. This reload trap indicates that the Frame Relay PVC specified by the DLCI has changed.

A number of syslog messages are useful for Frame Relay circuit fault management and apply directly to the MIB objects and CLI commands previously discussed.

Specifically, %FR-5-DLCICHANGE indicates that the state of the Frame Relay PVC specified by the DLCI has changed.

Monitoring Frame-Relay Errored Frames

From RFC 1315-MIB, the following MIB variables can provide data on the number and types of Frame Relay-specific errors that the circuits are receiving:

- frErrType: Indicates the type of error that was last seen on this interface. This variable does not contain a printable octet string, but contains a numerical value that indicates the reason for the error. This would include the following: unknownError(1), receiveShort(2), receiveLong(3), illegalDLCI(4), unknownDLCI(5), dlcmiProtoErr(6), dlcmiUnknownIE(7), dlcmiSequenceErr(8), dlcmiUnknownRpt(9), noErrorSinceReset(10).

- frErrData: An octet string containing as much of the error packet as possible. At a minimum, it must contain the Q.922 address or as much as was delivered. It is desirable to include all information up to the PDU.

- frErrTime: The value of sysUpTime at which the error was detected.

These variables are valuable because they can assist you in identifying errors and help you in working with your Frame Relay service provider.

There are no corresponding CLI show commands to get the Frame Relay error types.

Summary

Within this chapter, the tools to correlate sub-interfaces and virtual circuits with various other performance and fault variables have been covered. Probably the capability to use the cfrExtCircuitTable to accomplish this correlation is one of the more useful skills when it comes to supporting Frame Relay circuits.

However, as stated earlier, the variables needed to identify application or user traffic at a lower level are not available through SNMP. One method that could be used is some form of accounting—netflow, MAC accounting, IP accounting or IPX accounting—to gather this information. For instance, information about MAC accounting, the ARP cache, and a BGP routing table can be correlated and used to identify BGP neighbor changes. The tradeoff is that router performance will be degraded with the addition of an accounting method.

The next chapter continues the discussion of wide area networking and network management by examining ISDN and dial networks.

References

Books

Black, Uyless D. *Frame Relay Networks: Specifications and Implementations*. New York, NY: McGraw-Hill, 1996.

Cavanagh, James P. *Frame Relay Applications: Business and Technical Case Studies*. San Francisco, CA: Morgan Kaufmann Publishers, Inc, 1997.

Smith, Philip. *Frame Relay: Principles and Applications*. Reading, MA: Addison-Wesley, 1993.

Papers

Fournier, Adrien. "Design Implementation Guide: Frame Relay." 1996.

Swanson, David. "Frame Relay PVC Scalability Project." (ENG-17443).

Standards

RFC 1315, "Management Information Base for Frame Relay DTEs," C. Brown, F. Baker, C. Carvalho, April 1992.

RFC 1604, "Definitions of Managed Objects for Frame Relay Service," T. Brown, March 1994.

RFC 2115, "Management Information Base for Frame Relay DTEs Using SMIv2," C. Brown, F. Baker, September 1997.

CHAPTER 17

Monitoring WAN Technologies— ISDN and Dial

The use of network access servers (NAS) transcends the division between service providers and enterprise networks. *Service providers* tend to supply public and private dial-in services for businesses or individual home users. *Enterprises* tend to provide private dial-in access for employees dialing in from remote LANs (a remote office) or individual remote nodes (a telecommuter). Additionally, there are hybrid forms of dial access—virtual private dial networks (VPDNs)—that are jointly owned, operated, and set up by service providers and enterprises.

Both service providers and enterprise network managers have to find ways to manage the modems, lines, and calls that are being made through the remote access part of the network. Often, the user's perception of the network is driven by their ability to have "remote" access. If your remote access users have consistently poor connectivity to the network, they will perceive that the entire network is poor. Therefore, the success of your remote access strategy becomes a key customer-satisfaction issue.

Now for some bad news: Very few organizations can manage their network access solely through SNMP. There appear to be a few reasons for this:

- Not all information needed is accessible through MIBs.
- There are few commercial access management applications.
- The polling of modem variables can have an adverse effect on the router CPU.

There are no definitive performance guidelines relating a level of SNMP polling to the respective level of CPU utilization. Polling the modem variables is analogous to polling hundreds of interfaces on a router. Therefore, if another CPU-intensive process such as OSPF recalculation occurs at the same time as the SNMP polls, the CPU utilization can increase to nearly 100 percent and the router might even start dropping packets.

Therefore, most customers are using a combination of SNMP, Cisco IOS show commands, and logs (syslog and AAA) to gather the data needed to manage remote access.

This chapter covers the following topics:

- An overview of dial networking
- Performance data for ISDN and dial
- Correlating different variables and performance issues
- Error/fault data for dial and ISDN

Overview of Dial Networking

Remote access or dial networking refers to setting up one or more network access servers (NAS) to allow on-demand service connectivity. Dial networking is often used for connection to the small office/home office (SOHO), remote office/branch office (ROBO), and individual remote users. In the United States, many companies regard telecommuting (SOHO and ROBO) as a way to solve problems with space and save on rental, office furniture, and parking costs. Telecommuting also can help attract new employees, particularly if it saves them hours of commuting or provides flex hours. It can assist an organization in conforming to the Clean Air Act and make employees more productive.

In Europe, companies are looking for solutions that allow central offices to connect to remote sites. Dial-on-Demand Routing (DDR) allows you to quickly enable a WAN connection through the use of analog telephone lines (POTS). Also, DDR can save money because the line is used on an as-needed basis, whereas a leased line is paid for even when the line is not in use.

Analog modems have been (and still are) widely used to enable users to gain remote access to the network. As users needed additional bandwidth, they started looking at ISDN. ISDN provides additional bandwidth (up to 128 KB) without requiring a leased line. Today, with the advent of higher-speed analog modems (33.6 KB and higher), analog modems once again can provide the necessary connectivity over serial lines needed by business executives, salespeople, and technical support engineers, depending on their application use and needs.

This chapter addresses network management with respect to the needs of the remote access network manager/administrator. For managing events, the administrator needs information about the following:

- Modems—errors and status (faulty modems)
- Equipment—T1/E1 controller status and signaling
- Lines—errors, signaling, and status

For performance management, the administrator needs information about the following:

- Modem utilization
- Line utilization
- Data transferred by user
- Most-frequently-accessed locations

Also, this chapter will look at the two basic types of calls in dial networking: sent and received, as follows:

- Circuit-Switched Digital Calls Circuit—usually ISDN 56 Kbps or 64 Kbps data calls that use the point-to-point protocol (PPP). An ISDN router that functions as an access server or a terminal adapter connected to a client workstation initiates these calls.

Individual synchronous serial DS0s (B channels) are used to transport circuit switched digital calls across WANs. These calls do not transmit across standard plain old telephone service (POTS) lines.

- Analog Modem Calls Analog—modem calls that travel through traditional telephone lines and ISDN lines. Regardless of the media used, these calls are initiated by a modem and terminate on another modem at the remote end.

Access Through Virtual Terminal (VTY) Lines

A third type of call is the asynchronous character stream call, which enters the router or access server through VTY lines and virtual asynchronous interfaces (VTY-async). These virtual lines and interfaces terminate incoming character streams that do not have a physical connection to the access server or router (such as a physical serial interface).

For example, if you begin a PPP session over an asynchronous character stream, a VTY-async interface is created to support the call. Generally, you autocommand on the presence of characters, usually a Telnet, possibly to a paired async port on another terminal server; or use a tunnel and then protocol translate back.

The following types of calls are terminated on a virtual asynchronous interface: Telnet, LAT, V.120, TN3270, and PAD calls. I have not found a way to manage these calls for either fault or performance. You can get a TTY trap on termination of a character-triggered Telnet and the traps could let you manage repeated failures, but not one failure and then the inability to re-establish Telnet.

An overall dial example may be an AS5300 that receives and routes both incoming digital and analog calls that come in through E1/T1 PRI interfaces. Analog calls originated by modem users pass through to the asynchronous interfaces, lines, and modems. Digital calls originated by remote ISDN users pass through to the E1/T1 controllers, ISDN dialer interface, loopback interface, and D-channel serial interfaces.

In later sections, both MIB variables and Cisco IOS show commands are described or illustrated for data gathering. Syslog and AAA logs generally will not be discussed.

Access Physical Resources

To connect to the NAS, some type of connection at the server must be configured. A channelized T1 (CT1) or E1 (CE1) is an analog line that was originally intended to support analog voice calls, but has evolved to support analog data. Digital calls (ISDN or ADSL) do not transmit over CT1 or CE1 lines. One of the key differences between the CT1/CE1 and non-channelized lines is that the channelized lines do not have D-channel signaling.

The T1 and E1 controller that is provided on the Cisco NAS can have its available channels allocated in several ways:

- All channels can be configured to support ISDN PRI (T1-PRI (23B+D) or E1-PRI (30B+D)).

- All channels can be configured to support robbed-bit signaling on a T1, if you are not running ISDN PRI. This enables a Cisco AS5x00 modem to receive and transmit analog calls using in-band signaling.

- All channels can be configured to support channel-associated signaling (CAS) on an E1, if you are not running ISDN PRI. This enables a Cisco AS5x00 modem to receive and transmit analog calls using out-of-band (OOB) signaling.

- All channels can be configured in a single channel group.

- Channels can be mixed and matched to support ISDN PRI and channel grouping.

- Channels can be mixed and matched to support ISDN PRI, robbed-bit signaling, and channel grouping across the same T1 line.

Other physical access resources are to use the ISDN BRI (2B+D), physical terminal (TTY) lines for asynchronous interfaces or modems, synchronous serial ports for point-to-point leased-line, or dial-up communications.

The different configuration options above are covered in the Cisco documentation online (www.cisco.com). Also, the Cisco Press book *Cisco IOS Dial Solutions* contains different configuration examples.

Access Logical Resources: Logical Constructs and Logical Interfaces

A *logical construct* is an intangible device in an NAS that stores data or configuration information for physical interfaces. Therefore, you could say that a logical construct stores the core protocol characteristics to assign to physical interfaces. It is important to note that no data packets are forwarded to a logical construct. This means that there is no actual network management available for the logical construct. Cisco uses two types of logical constructs in its access servers and routers:

- **Group Asynchronous Interface**—Stores and projects specific protocol characteristics to a specified range of asynchronous interfaces (see Example 17-1).

- **Virtual Template Interfaces**—Stores and projects protocol configuration information for temporary virtual access interfaces (triggered by multilink or virtual private dial-up network (VPDN) session events) and protocol translation sessions (see Example 17-2).

Example 17-1 *Sample IOS configuration for a group-asynchronous interface.*

```
interface Group-Async1
 ip unnumbered Loopback0 <- loopback for IP Address
 encapsulation ppp <- encapsulation type
 async mode interactive <- setting the interactive mode
 peer default ip address pool dialin_pool
 no cdp enable <- turning off Cisco Discovery Protocol
 ppp authentication chap pap dialin <-setting authentication
 group-range 1 48 <- assigning the channels to the group
```

Example 17-2 *Sample IOS configuration for a virtual template interface.*

```
 ip unnumbered Loopback0 <- loopback for IP Address
 no ip mroute-cache <- turn off multicast route cache
 peer default ip address pool dialin_pool
 ppp authentication chap pap dialin <- setting authentication
 ppp multilink <-enable multilink PPP (MPPP)
```

A logical interface is a device on an NAS that does receive and transmit data packets. Also, the logical interface controls physical interfaces. Cisco IOS provides three logical interfaces used for dial access:

- Dialer interfaces
- Virtual access interfaces
- Virtual asynchronous interfaces (VTY-async)

A *dialer interface* is a parent interface that stores and projects protocol configuration information that is common to all D-channel members of a dialer rotary group. Data packets pass through dialer interfaces, which in turn initiate dialing for inbound calls. Without a dialer interface configuration, each D channel would have to be configured separately. If a dialer interface engages in a multilink session, a dialer interface is in control of a virtual access interface, which in turn controls the D channel for a PRI (for example, s0:23).

A *virtual access interface* is a temporary interface created to terminate incoming PPP streams that do not have physical connections. Virtual access interfaces are cloned from virtual interface templates and are not directly configurable by a user. After the tunnels or multilink sessions are ended, the dynamically created virtual access interface disappears. Thus, you would not see this type of interface through an SNMP query and would not be able to get the interface utilization statistics.

A VTY-async is created on demand to support calls that enter the router through a non-physical interface. They are not user-configurable. For example, asynchronous character stream calls terminate on non-physical interfaces. These types of calls include inbound Telnet, LAT, and PPP over character-oriented protocols (such as V.120 or X.25), and Packet Assembler Disassembler (PAD) calls. A virtual asynchronous interface is also used to terminate L2F/L2TP (Layer 2 Forwarding/Layer 2 Tunneling) tunnels, which are often travelling companions with multilink sessions. A virtual asynchronous line is used to access a virtual asynchronous interface.

Key-Managed Modem Benefits

There are two important capabilities that managed modems provide the network administrator. First, they give the network administrator the ability to remotely control a modem; being physically located near the access servers is not necessary. Second, managed modems provide access to everything that is happening in the modem.

Through the management features available with managed modems, a network administrator can access the modem to capture statistics. This type of support enables the administrator to understand and solve problems that might take days with unmanaged modems.

Another advantage involves the management of the NAS versus the remote devices. Gathering the data that is locally aggregated on the NAS is better than polling all the remote devices. In other words, in a hub and spoke environment, collect from the hub and not from all the spokes. This fact probably seems obvious for remote access users who are dialing in with a modem over a POTS line—there really is no other way to manage the access.

However, it is also true in the case of ISDN used for either SOHO or direct user connectivity. Again, the NAS is an aggregation point for data and can help reduce the amount of network management overhead by polling it rather than a remote device. It is still important to enable traps on the remote devices, and possibly include the use of RMON events and alarms to threshold data from remote devices.

In the preceding sections, you saw various types of interfaces for Cisco devices, the intended use of each kind of interface, and whether packets flow through the interface. This information affects whether or not you can obtain data and manage the interface.

Performance Data for ISDN and Dial

This section looks in detail at the following performance issues:

- Monitoring modem status
- Monitoring connection statistics
- Error-monitoring of modems
- Measuring utilization of modems

MIB Variables for Modem Status Monitoring

The Modem Management MIB, from CISCO-MODEM-MGMT-MIB, is arranged into three groups:

- **cmSystemInfo Group**: For system configuration and status information
- **cmGroupInfo Group**: For modem-grouping configuration
- **cmLineInfo Group**: For individual modem configuration, statistics, and status information

  Under the cmLineInfo group are the variables that provide the data needed for modem status, both performance and fault. This line-status data provides the basic information needed to begin managing the NAS utilization. As you will see, the other data points within this MIB provide data and statistics that increase your ability to effectively manage the modems, server, calls, and lines. With this data, you can monitor for server, modem, and line congestion, which can result in a severe degradation of the network in both response time and throughput.

However, from the cmGroupInfo group, the variables cmSlotIndex and cmPortIndex are the modem feature card slot and port number, respectively, in the group.

Each of the following variables is a counter. They are correlated with the CLI **show modem** command in Example 17-3. These are some of the most significant variables for monitoring the status of your modems. These objects exist only for modems that have cmManageable to be true.

- **cmLineInfo.cmLineStatisticsTable.cmRingNoAnswers**: Records the number of the calls for which ringing was detected, but the call was not answered at this modem.
- **cmLineInfo.cmLineStatisticsTable.cmIncomingConnectionFailures**: Similar to cmRingNoAnswers in that it is a record of the number of incoming connection requests that this modem answered, in which it could not train with the other DCE.
- **cmLineInfo.cmLineStatisticsTable.cmIncomingConnectionCompletions**: Records the number of incoming connection requests that this modem answered and successfully trained with the other DCE.
- **cmLineInfo.cmLineStatisticsTable.cmOutgoingConnectionFailures**: Records the number of outgoing calls from this modem that successfully went off-hook and dialed, in which it could not train with the other DCE. This variable may not be needed if you do not allow outgoing calls.
- **cmLineInfo.cmLineStatisticsTable.cmOutgoingConnectionCompletions**: Records the number of outgoing calls from this modem that resulted in successfully training with the other DCE. This variable may not be needed if you do not allow outgoing calls.

- **cmLineInfo.cmLineStatisticsTable.cmFailedDialAttempts**: Records the number of call attempts that failed because the modem didn't go off-hook or there was no dial tone. This variable may not be needed if you do not allow outgoing calls.

- **cmLineInfo.cmLineStatisticsTable.cmNoDialTones**: Records the number of times the dial tone was expected but not received. This variable may not be needed if you do not allow outgoing calls.

- **cmLineInfo.cmLineStatisticsTable.cmDialTimeouts**: Counts the number of times the dial time-out occurred. This variable may not be needed if you do not allow outgoing calls.

The recommended threshold value for success is => 95 percent. The incoming and outgoing calls need to be observed and measured for your environment. At that point, you should be able to come up with threshold values for your network. In the preceding cmLineInfo group variables, the one variable not defined is the percentage of success or failure. It would not be difficult to write a script to calculate a percentage of in-or-out success and fail values that could be used to set a threshold in your Network Management platform. The same threshold value of => 95 percent would be appropriate.

CLI Commands for Modem Status Monitoring

The CLI command related to the MIBs just discussed is the **show modem** command. This command displays the number of calls received by each modem in the NAS.

The **show modem** command is useful for both fault and performance management, as well as when troubleshooting the NAS. It contains several valuable data points in the display output that can help you identify possible problem areas with the modems or in the network itself. Looking at the number of failed modem connections can assist in determining the number of calls that the NAS is receiving and attempting to process. If all the modems show similar failure characteristics over time, the number of calls being received probably exceeds the NAS' capability to handle them. The modem data also can help you to diagnose modems that need to be replaced due to hardware failure.

Example 17-3 shows output from the **show modem** command.

Example 17-3 *Obtaining modem status information with the **show modem** command.*

```
AS5300# show modem

                Inc calls    Out calls    Busied  Failed  No        Succ
  Mdm[A] Usage[B] Succ[C] Fail[D] Succ[E] Fail[F] Out[G]  Dial[H]  Answer[I]  Pct.[J]
* 1 / 0   17%     74     3      0      0      0      0      0       96%
b 1 / 1   15%     80     4      0      0      0      1      1       95%
* 1 / 2   15%     82     0      0      0      0      0      0       100%
  1 / 3   21%     62     1      0      0      0      0      0       98%
B 1 / 4   21%     49     25     0      0      0      0      0       50%
* 1 / 5   18%     65     3      0      0      0      0      0       95%
d 1 / 6   19%     58     2      0      0      0      0      0       96%
```

Example 17-3   *Obtaining modem status information with the **show modem** command. (Continued)*

* 1/7	17%	67	5	0	0	0	1	1	93%
* 1/8	20%	68	3	0	0	0	0	0	95%
1/9	16%	67	2	0	0	0	0	0	97%
1/10	18%	56	2	0	0	0	1	1	96%
* 1/11	15%	76	3	0	0	0	0	0	96%
* 1/12	16%	62	1	0	0	0	0	0	98%
1/13	17%	51	4	0	0	0	0	0	92%
D1/14	16%	51	5	0	0	0	0	0	91%
1/15	17%	65	0	0	0	0	0	0	100%
1/16	15%	73	3	0	0	0	0	0	96%
T 1/17	17%	67	2	0	0	0	0	0	97%
T 1/18	17%	61	2	0	0	0	0	0	96%
* 1/19	17%	74	2	0	0	0	0	0	97%
1/20	16%	65	1	0	0	0	0	0	98%
* 1/21	16%	58	3	0	0	0	0	0	95%
* 1/22	18%	56	4	0	0	0	0	0	93%
* 1/23	20%	60	4	0	0	0	0	0	93%

See Table 17-1 for a description of the modem states under the "Mdm" column of Example 17-3. These states are important in understanding what is occuring with your modems. For instance, the "b" and "B" are important in telling whether a modem is operational or not, and can be gathered through either the CLI or SNMP.

The annotated items from Example 17-3 are as follows:

A "Mdm"—Slot and modem port number. Also, modem states can appear to the left of a slot/modem port number; see Table 17-1 for a listing of the states. The same data is available through the MIB variables cmSlotIndex and cmPortIndex.

B "Usage"—Percentage of the total system uptime that all modems are in use.

C "Inc calls Succ"—Number of incoming calls that have successfully connected to a modem. The same data is available through the MIB variable cmIncomingConnectionCompletions.

D "Inc calls Fail"—Number of incoming calls that have not successfully connected to a modem. In other words, this is just the opposite of the previous item. The same data is available through the MIB variable cmIncomingConnectionFailures.

E "Out calls Succ"—Number of outgoing calls that successfully dialed out from an available modem. The same data is available through the MIB variable cmOutgoingConnectionCompletions. This field is not useful if outgoing calls are not allowed in your environment.

F "Out calls Fail"—Number of outgoing calls that have not successfully dialed out from an available modem. The same data is available through the MIB variable cmOutgoingConnectionFailures. As with item E, this may not be of use in your environment.

G "Busied Out"—Number of times the modem has been manually removed from service.

H "Failed Dial"—Number of modems that attempted to dial into the network, but failed to make a connection. The same data is available through the MIB variable cmFailedDialAttempts.

I "No Answer"—Number of modems that detected an incoming ring but failed to answer the call. The same data is available through the MIB variable CmRingNoAnswers.

J "Succ Pct."—Successful connection percentage of total available modems.

Table 17-1   *Modem States*

Modem State	Description	Corresponding MIB Variable
b	Modem was removed from service with the **modem shutdown** command or the **modem busyout** command.	cmState busiedOut(5)
B	Modem is suspected to be inoperable or bad. No calls can be made with this modem. Can also mean that a modem firmware download failed for the specified modem. In this case, try unmarking the modem as bad with the **no modem bad** command and upgrading the modem firmware again.	cmBad and cmState bad(7)
d	The RAM-based DSP code, which supports K56flex, is not configured. The modem will revert to transmitting at 33.6.	None
D	Modem is currently downloading firmware.	cmState Download Firmware(9)
R	Modem is held and isolated in a suspended state by the **modem hold-reset** command.	None
T	Modem is conducting a back-to-back test with another modem.	CmState loopback(8)
*	Modem is connected or dialing	CmState connected(4)

Some of the data from **show modem** can be very useful. First, the number of modems that are bad should be tabulated (cmBad and cmState). It may be that the entire bank of modems cannot be replaced for a single or even multiple bad modems, but keeping track of the ones that are bad can help with troubleshooting, capacity, and performance management. In an environment where the NAS only has incoming calls, then all of the "out" data can be discarded. The incoming data, both success and fail (cmIncomingConnectionCompletions and cmIncomingConnectionfailures), can help you identify problem areas before a complete failure occurs. The same is true of dial-out connections, if your environment allows them.

You can produce a useful table by collecting and summarizing information from **show modem** commands from each of the servers (see Table 17-2). This information could also be collected through SNMP with the following variables:

- cmIncomingConnectionCompletion
- cmIncomingConnectionFailures
- cmState
- cmOutgoingConnectionCompletion
- cmOutgoingConnectionFailures
- cmFailedDialAttempts

However, an easier way to gather the data is through the use of the **show modem summary** command. Example 17-4 shows sample output from **show modem summary**.

Example 17-4   *Obtaining aggregated data on modem status with* **show modem summary***.*

```
NASPPP011#sh mod sum
              Incoming calls    Outgoing calls  Busied   Failed  No    Succ
Usage  Succ   Fail  Avail   Succ   Fail  Avail   Out      Dial    Ans   Pct.
  0%  39887   1843   48      0      0     48      2        0       65    95%


NASDU04#sh mod sum
              Incoming calls    Outgoing calls  Busied   Failed  No    Succ
Usage  Succ   Fail  Avail   Succ   Fail  Avail   Out      Dial    Ans   Pct.
  0%  40109   1745   48      0      0     48      0        0       52    96%
```

The data in Example 17-4 corresponds to that of Tables 17-2 and 17-3, but is obtained through the use of a single command rather than summing the data from all of the modems.

Table 17-2   *Aggregation of Modem Calls by NAS*

Network Access Server Name	Up Time Days	Total Calls Good Bad 48 Ports	Inc. Calls Succ	Inc. Calls Fail	Out Calls Succ	Out Calls Fail	Busied Out	Failed Dial
NASPPP01	25.9	41795	39887	1843	0	0	2	0
NASPPP02	25.9	41854	40109	1745	0	0	3	0
NASPPP03	25.9	41531	39682	1885	0	0	1	0
NASPPP04	4.2	8904	6625	2262	0	0	0	0

Table 17-2   *Aggregation of Modem Calls by NAS (Continued)*

Network Access Server Name	Up Time Days	Total Calls Good Bad 48 Ports	Inc. Calls Succ	Inc. Calls Fail	Out Calls Succ	Out Calls Fail	Busied Out	Failed Dial
NASPPP05	4.7	6203	6016	177	0	0	1	0
NASPPP06	4.25	5913	5733	171	0	0	3	0
NASPPP07	8.3	36769	29689	6935	0	0	0	0
NASPPP08	5.1	6912	6712	194	0	0	0	0
NASPPP09	5.2	7331	7132	191	0	0	0	0

From Table 17-2, you can see (Out Calls Succ, Out Calls Fail, and Failed Dial) that this environment does not allow for dial-out from the NAS. Therefore, we can do a little improvement on the chart by removing those columns and adding others.

Table 17-3   *Improved Aggregation of Modem Calls by NAS*

Network Access Server Name	Up Time Days	Total Calls Good /Bad 48 ports	Inc. Calls Succ	Inc. Calls Fail	Busied Out	No Answer	Succ %	Av. Calls Per Port Per Hour	Av. Calls Per Box Per Day
NASPPP01	25.9	41795	39887	1843	2	65	95	1.400786	1613.706
NASPPP02	25.9	41854	40109	1745	3	52	96	1.402764	1615.984
NASPPP03	25.9	41531	39682	1885	1	63	95	1.391938	1603.513
NASPPP04	4.2	8904	6625	2262	0	17	74	1.840277	2120
NASPPP05	4.7	6203	6016	177	1	9	97	1.145648	1319.787
NASPPP06	4.25	5913	5733	171	3	6	95	1.207720	1391.294
NASPPP07	8.3	36769	29689	6935	0	145	81	3.845486	4430
NASPPP08	5.1	6912	6712	194	0	6	97	1.176470	1355.294
NASPPP09	5.2	7331	7132	191	0	8	95	1.223791	1409.807

By removing the dial-out information that was not important in this particular scenario, adding the data on "no answer" and "success percentage," and using "time" to look at the number of calls by hour and day, the information becomes much more useful. Here, the No Answer column is bold because of its importance to the analysis. In rows 4 and 7 of Table

17-3, the number of failed calls (2262 and 6935, respectively) is quite a bit higher than for the other servers. In those same rows, the success percentages (74 and 81) also indicate that there is some problem with these two servers.

Two other potential problems are indicated in the table. First, NASPPP04 (row 4) has a relatively low number of "no answer" calls (17) and a moderately high number of "average calls per day" (2120) when compared to the other servers. NASPPP04 should be investigated for possible modem problems—hardware or firmware.

Second, NASPPP07's data of 145 "no answer," 3.85 "average calls per day," and 4430 "average calls per box per day" would seem to indicate that this server cannot handle the call volumne that it's receiving. Therefore, you would want to investigate capacity issues. A threshold value of 95 percent for "success %" is recommended. Experience has shown that once this threshold is exceeded, the "success %" often falls rapidly. Table 17-4 may not help isolate the cause, but it is the starting place to look at standard NAS health and may even indicate that some standard router health checking might help isolate the problem.

MIB Variables for Monitoring of Connection Statistics

From CISCO-MODEM-MGMT-MIB, the cmLineStatisticsTable is the table that contains the variables to poll for most of the connection statistics data. The entries in cmLineStatisticsTable indicate the number of connection completions, failures, and other important statistical data needed to monitor the modem performance.

From the cmLineStatusTable, the cmDisconnectReason is one of the most important variables. It indicates the reason that the last connection or call attempt disconnected. Because this variable is considered essential to monitoring performance of the NAS, the meaning of each "error type" is explained in Table 17-4. The 15 most common error types have been highlighted. Also, the fields from the CLI **show modem statistics** command have been mapped into the last column as appropriate.

Table 17-4 *cmDisconnectReason Table*

Error Type	#	Description	Show Modem Stat Fields
Unknown	1	The failure reason is unknown or there has been no previous call.	
LostCarrier	2	The call was disconnected because the loss of carrier.	LostCarr
NoCarrier	3	The dial-out attempt failed because the modem detects no carrier.	NoCarr

continues

Table 17-4 *cmDisconnectReason Table (Continued)*

Error Type	#	Description	Show Modem Stat Fields
NoDialTone	4	The dial-out attempt failed because the modem failed to detect a dial tone.	NoDitone
Busy	5	The call attempt failed because the modem detected a busy signal.	Busy
ModemWatchdog Timeout	6	The modem internal watchdog timer expired.	WdogTimr
DtrDrop	7	DTR has been turned off while the modem is to disconnect on DTR drop.	Dtrdrop
UserHangup	8	Normal disconnect where the user hangs up call.	UserHgup
CompressionProblem	9	The call is disconnected due to a problem detected during compression in the modem.	Compress
RetrainFailure	10	The modem did not successfully train and reach data mode on the previous connections.	Retrain
RemoteLink Disconnect	11	The remote link disconnected the connection.	RmtLink
Abort	12	The call was aborted.	Abort
InactivityTimeout	13	The modem automatically hangs up because data is not sent or received within the inactivity time-out.	InacTout
DialStringError	14	The dialed phone number is invalid.	DialStrg
LinkFailure	15	The modem detects a link failure.	LinkFail
ModulationError	16	The modem detects a modulation error.	ModuFail
DialTimeout	17	The modem times out while attempting to dial.	DialTout
RemoteHangup	18	The remote side hangs up the connection.	RmtHgup
mnp10ProtocolError	19	MNP10 Protocol Error.	MnpProt

Table 17-4   *cmDisconnectReason Table (Continued)*

Error Type	#	Description	Show Modem Stat Fields
LapmProtocolError	20	LAPM Protocol Error.	LapmProt
FaxClass2Error	21	Fax Class 2 Error.	FaxClasz
TrainupFailure	22	Failure to trainup with a remote peer.	Retrain
FallbackTerminate	23	User has EC fallback set to disconnect.	
ExcessiveEC	24	Link loss due to excessive EC retransmissions. EC packet-transmit-limit exceeded.	
HostDrop	25	Host initiated link drop.	
Terminate	26	Lost Carrier Microcom HDMS product relating to password-security issues.	Terminate
AutoLogonError	27	An autologon sequence did not complete successfully.	AutoLgon
CcpNotSeen	28	The Credit Card Prompt was not detected.	
CallbackFailed	29	Applies to leased line connection. If after a switched line dialback due to a leased line connection failure, the switched line connection also fails and a connection can still not be made on the leased line, a disconnect occurs with this reason set.	CallBkfa
Blacklist	30	In countries that support blacklisting, an attempt was made to go off-hook with a null dial string (ATD).	Blacklst
LapmTimeout	31	Timed-out while waiting for a reply from remote.	
ReliableLinkTxTimeout	32	Has not received the link acknowledgment in the first 30 seconds of the connection.	
DspAccessFailure	33	Timed-out while trying to access the DSP chip.	

continues

Table 17-4 *cmDisconnectReason Table (Continued)*

Error Type	#	Description	Show Modem Stat Fields
CdOffTimeout	34	Timed-out while waiting for carrier to return after a retrain or rate renegotiations.	
CodewordSizeMismatch	35	The codeword sizes are mismatched.	
DspDownloadFailure	36	Error during the DSP code download.	

The cmDisconnectReason variable should be mapped using a table like Table 17-4 and into each of the different error types. Then, the cmDisconnectReason or the data from the CLI **show modem statistics** command could be used to correlate the SNMP result (column 2) with the error type. This correlated data could then be graphed for each modem or aggregated for each NAS against the different types of reasons for disconnection. Finally, the use of another column in the mapping that contained the summation of the reason that a disconnect type occurred among all the modems in the NAS would provide excellent data on the modem health of the NAS.

The next section maps the variable cmDisconnectReason and the entries from the cmLineStatisticsTable to the show modem call-stat data.

CLI Commands for Monitoring of Connection Statistics

Use the command **show modem call-stat** to get modem statistical data (see Example 17-5). Specifically, look for the category of disconnect reasons that can happen in either a dial-in or dial-out scenario. This command is used to find out why a modem ended its connection or why a modem is not operating at peak performance..

Example 17-5 *Sample output from the **show modem call-stat** command.*

```
tanr#sh modem call-stat
  dial-in/dial-out call statistics


          lostCarr  rmtLink wdogTimr compress  retrain inacTout linkFail moduFail
     Mdm   #   %    #   %    #   %    #   %     #   %    #   %    #   %    #   %
   * 2/0    1  20   13   3    0   0    0   0     0   0    0   0    0   0    0   0
   * 2/1    0   0   14   4    0   0    0   0     0   0    0   0    0   0    0   0
   * 2/2    0   0   15   4    0   0    0   0     0   0    0   0    0   0    0   0
           .
           .
           .

   * 2/29   0   0   15   4    0   0    0   0     0   0    0   0    0   0    0   0
```

Example 17-5 *Sample output from the **show modem call-stat** command. (Continued)*

```
   Total   5      338        0        0        0        0        0        0
      dial-out call statistics


              noCarr      abort noDitone       busy dialStrg autoLgon dialTout   rmtHgup
     Mdm      #   %      #   %    #   %      #   %    #   %    #   %    #   %     #   %
   * 2/0      0   0      6   1    0   0      0   0    0   0    0   0    0   0     0   0
   * 2/1      0   0      0   0    0   0      0   0    0   0    0   0    0   0     0   0
   * 2/2      0   0      0   0    0   0      0   0    0   0    0   0    0   0     0   0
   * 2/3      0   0      0   0    0   0      0   0    0   0    0   0    0   0     0   0



          .
          .
          .
   Total    0   0      0   0    0   0      0   0    0   0    0   0    0   0     0   0
      dial-out call statistics
```

The description of fields from **show modem call-stat** is in the last column of Table 17-4. It is included there to provide you with the correlation between the SNMP variable and the show command fields.

The lostCarr, rmtLink, and inacTout errors all result from errors external to the router. The wdogTimr errors are a result of errors within the router. Finally, compress, retrain, linkFail, and moduFail errors need further investigation to determine which side has the problem.

In Example 17-5, the number of times an error occurred on a specific modem is displayed (see the # column). The % column (which does not have an SNMP variable equivalent) shows the percentage of occurences of a specific disconnect reason charged to a specific modem, compared with all the modems. For example, out of all the times the lostCarr error occurred on all the modems in the system, the lostCarr error occurred 20 percent of the time on modem 2/8.

As you can see in Table 17-4, there is a good deal of overlap between the cmDisconnectReason and the **show modem call-stat** command. Again, this data should be looked at in a tabular form and possibly graphed to provide information that can be used for trending and fault analysis. After the data has been collected in the user environment for a time, the use of RMON events and alarms for specific variables could provide a proactive approach to the problems seen. For instance, suppose you found that only when the access server was experiencing particularly heavy traffic volumes did users receive autologin errors. Using RMON, you could trigger a trap on this particular variable. See the section "Remote Monitoring MIB and Related MIBs" in Chapter 8, "Understanding Network Management Protocols," for more information on how to use RMON for thresholding and proactive fault management.

MIB Variables for Monitoring Modem Connection Speeds

As noted earlier, the entries in cmLineStatisticsTable are the primary set of variables that indicate the number of connection completions, failures, and other important statistical data needed to monitor the modem performance. This table also contains variables to assist you in monitoring the connection speed of your modems. This data is very useful in troubleshooting the modem connections. The following are the connection speed variables:

- cm2400OrLessConnections
- cm2400To14400Connections
- cmGreaterThan14400Connections

If connections are consistently being made at 2400 or less, or even between 2400 and 14000, you can be pretty sure that there is some type of problem in the system. It could be with the line or with the "training" between the client and NAS modem.

One problem with using SNMP rather than a script that gathers the information through the CLI command is the granularity involved. The CLI commands allow an administrator to gather data on the transmit and receive speed counters in the following range: 75, 300, 600, 1200, 2400, 4800, 7200, 9600, 12000, 14400, 16800, 19200, 21600, 24000, 26400, 28800, 31200, 33600, 32000, 34000, 36000, 38000, 40000, 42000, 44000, 46000, 48000, 50000, 52000, 54000, and 56000 bps. The SNMP variables do not provide that level of detail. Although this much detail may not be necessary in every environment, it has come into use in troubleshooting a particularly difficult issue with modems that would not synch except at 300–2400. In this particular scenario, there were users that still had 2400 bps modems and the additional granularity down to 300 was needed. Later, as the users were upgraded to 56 KB modems, the administrator wanted to see and report to the executive level exactly the speeds at which the users were connecting to the servers.

In the following secions on the CLI commands, several tables and a graph are provided as examples of how to use this data. The variables cm2400OrLessConnections, cm2400To14400Connections, and cmGreaterThan14400Connections could also be used in a similar manner. Again, the greatest difference is the amount of granularity that you get using the CLI command versus the SNMP variables. If this is not an issue in your environment, these might meet your needs.

CLI Commands for Monitoring Modem-Connection Speeds

The **show modem connect-speeds** command displays a log of connection speed statistics, starting from the last time the access server or router was power cycled or the clear modem counters command was issued.

Because most terminal screens are not wide enough to display the entire range of connection speeds at one time (for example, 75 to 56000 bps), the max-speed variable is used. This variable specifies the contents of a shifting baud-rate window, which provides you with a snapshot of modem connection speeds for your system.

To display a complete picture of all the connection speeds and counters on the system, you must enter a series of commands. Each time you issue the **show modem connect-speeds** max-speed command, only 9 bps rate columns can be displayed at the same time.

To gather all the data for connection speeds up to 56,000, the following four commands would have to be used:

```
show modem connect-speeds 56000
show modem connect-speeds 38000
show modem connect-speeds 21600
show modem connect-speeds 12000
```

Example 17-6 shows output from the **show modem connect-speeds 56000** command. For brevity, the other show commands are not shown.

Example 17-6   *Obtaining modem connection speed information with the **show modem connect-speeds** command.*

```
as5800-as5300#show modem connect-speeds 56000

  transmit connect speeds

      Mdm^A  48000^B 49333 50000 50667 52000 53333 54000 54667 56000 TotCnt^C
      1/3/00    0     1     0     0     0     0     0     0     0     1
      1/3/01    0     0     0     1     0     0     0     0     0     1
      1/3/02    0     0     0     1     0     0     0     0     0     1



  B   1/5/13    0     0     0     0     0     0     0     0     0     0
  B   1/5/14    0     0     0     0     0     0     0     0     0     0
  B   1/5/15    0     0     0     0     0     0     0     0     0     0
      Tot^D     0     1     0     8     0     0     0     0     0    13
      Tot %^E   0     7     0    61     0     0     0     0     0

  receive connect speeds

      Mdm   48000 49333 50000 50667 52000 53333 54000 54667 56000 TotCnt
      1/3/00    0     0     0     0     0     0     0     0     0     1
      1/3/01    0     0     0     0     0     0     0     0     0     1
      1/3/02    0     0     0     0     0     0     0     0     0     1
      1/3/03    0     0     0     0     0     0     0     0     0     1



  B   1/5/13    0     0     0     0     0     0     0     0     0     0
  B   1/5/14    0     0     0     0     0     0     0     0     0     0
  B   1/5/15    0     0     0     0     0     0     0     0     0     0
      Tot       0     0     0     0     0     0     0     0     0    13
      Tot %     0     0     0     0     0     0     0     0     0
```

A The "transmit connect speeds" is the connection speeds for calls initiated by the system. The "receive connect speeds" is the connection speed for incoming calls. A graph of each range will be produced of the total # of calls (Tot) at each speed across all modems.

B Mdm slot/port—Specified slot and port number assigned transmit connect speeds to the modem (cmSlotIndex and cmPortIndex).

C speed counters—The transmit and receive speed counters are 75, 300, 600, 1200, 2400, 4800, 7200, 9600, 12000, 14400, 16800, 19200, 21600, 24000, 26400, 28800, 31200, 33600, 32000, 34000, 36000, 38000, 40000, 42000, 44000, 46000, 48000, 50000, 52000, 54000,and 56000 bps.

D "TotCnt"—For the specified modem, the sum of the number of times a connection was initiated or received at one of the specified connection rates (75 to 56,000 bps).

E "Tot"—For all modems loaded in the system, the total number of times a call was initiated or received at the specified speed.

F "Tot %"—Percentage of the total number of calls that were initiated or received at the specified speed.

The data (speed counter/modems) can be gathered and reported on a daily, weekly, monthly, and quarterly basis. The data is usually summarized on the weekly, monthly, and quarterly reports for the entire NAS, as shown in Tables 17-5, 17-6, and 17-7. This type of report can help the remote access administrator foresee and prevent problems with user connectivity.

MIB Variables for Measuring Modem Utilization of the NAS

The same variables discussed in the section "MIB Variables for Modem Status Monitoring" in the CISCO-MODEM-MGMT-MIB, cmLineInfoGroup, provide the variables for modem utilization.

The line status data provides the basic information needed to begin managing both modem and NAS utilization. As you've seen, the other variables within this MIB provide data and statistics that increase your ability to effectively manage the modems, server, calls, and lines. Through this information, you can monitor for server, modem, and line congestion— which can result in a severe degradation of the network in both response time and throughput.

CLI Commands for Measuring Utilization of the NAS

The three show commands that can provide the data needed to manage the NAS utilization are **show modem** (see Example 17-3), **show modem connect-speeds** (see Example 17-5), and **show modem summary**.

By summarizing the data gathered from the **show modem connect-speeds** commands into tables, you will have something like Tables 17-5, 17-6, and 17-7.

Table 17-5   *40000–56000 Modem Transmit and Receive Connect Speeds*

Router	40000	42000	44000	46000	48000	50000	52000	54000	56000
as5200-a	0	34	66	24	2	0	0	0	0
as5200-b	0	12	33	12	1	0	0	0	0
Total	0	46	99	36	3	0	0	0	0

Table 17-6   *24000–38000 Modem Transmit and Receive Connect Speeds*

Router	24000	26400	28800	31200	33600	32000	34000	36000	38000
as5200-a	0	44	74	24	2	0	0	0	0
as5200-b	0	22	40	12	1	0	0	0	0
Total	0	66	114	36	3	0	0	0	0

Table 17-7   *2400–21600 Modem Transmit and Receive Connect Speeds*

Router	2400	4800	7200	9600	12000	14400	16800	19200	21600
as5200-a	0	24	74	24	2	0	0	0	0
as5200-b	0	2	40	12	1	0	0	0	0
Total	0	26	114	36	3	0	0	0	0

By using a relatively simple bar chart to graph the data from all three tables (see Figure 17-1), you have the connection speeds for the NAS (over some specified period of time). This type of data can help you represent the different connection speeds and their frequency. One interesting item to note here is the connections at 4800 bps. This particular environment has deployed 33.6 KB and 56 KB modems. In this sample network, all of the lower-speed modems at all of the remote sites have been eliminated.

In addition to the preceding data, the aggregated data in Tables 17-2 and 17-3, collected from the **show modem summary** command, are useful in looking at the total number of successful and failed calls over time. As in Table 17-3, the data can then be used to come up with the number of calls per port per hour or the average calls per server per day. Both of these go directly to the question of utilization.

Figure 17-1 *NAS Connection Speeds*

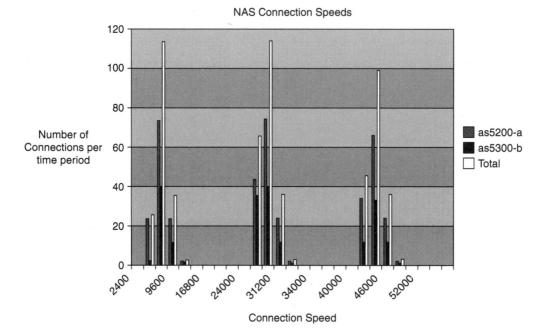

Figure 17-1 is a graphical representaion of the data in the previous tables. It shows at a glance that the users are grouped into three basic connection speeds: 4800 to 9600, 26.4 KB to 33.6 KB, and 42 KB to 48 KB. As stated earlier, this user environment only has 33.6 to 56 KB modems. However, the figure shows an interesting grouping in the 4.8 KB to 9.6 KB range. At this point, the RADIUS log could be used to find the telephone numbers of all users that have connected at this speed. With this list of phone numbers, the network administrator can identify the user locations that have been having the slowest connectivity to the network and begin the process of finding out the reasons for this slowness.

MIB Variables for Measuring ISDN Utilization

From CISCO-CALL-HISTORY-MIB, ciscoCallHistoryTable is the table that provides much of the data needed for call status and utilization. Specifically, the following variables can be of value. The explanation of each variable is taken from the CISCO-CALL-HISTORY-MIB; comments are from the authors.

- ciscoCallHistoryIndex—Index variable to access the CallHistoryEntry of the ciscoCallHistoryTable.

- ciscoCallHistoryCallingNumber—The calling number for this call. If the number is not available, it will have a length of zero. The variable is instantiated if this is an incoming call.

- ciscoCallHistoryCalledNumber—The number this call is connected to. This variable is instantiated if this is an outgoing call. This variable can be of some use in Dial-on-Demand Routing (DDR) scenarios. If you are using multiple servers to dial to, depending on your "interesting traffic," this could provide the data on the number being called and correlate with ciscoCallHistoryDialReason.

- ciscoCallHistoryInterfaceNumber—This is the ifIndex value of the highest number of through which the call was made.

- ciscoCallHistoryDestinationAddress—The address of the host this call is connected to, if it is available. Most devices/routers connected to an interface have an address and this object will store it. The variable is not instantiated if it is not available. This is almost always available and can provide useful data.

- ciscoCallHistoryDestinationHostName—The name of the host this call is connected to. Most devices/routers connected to an interface have a name and this object will store that name.

- ciscoCallHistoryCallDisconnectCause—The reason for the call termination: other(1), normalDisconnectSent(2), normalDisconnectReceived(3), networkOutOfOrder(4), callRejected(5), userBusy(6), noCircuitChannelAvailable(7), and interworkingError(8). This variable is similar to cmDisconnectReason in Table 17-4, but thankfully with a much smaller number of reasons.

- ciscoCallHistoryCallConnectionTime—The value of sysUpTime when the call was connected.

- ciscoCallHistoryCallDisconnectTime—The value of sysUpTime when the call got disconnected last.

- ciscoCallHistoryDialReason—The reason for initiating this call. It may include the destination address of the interesting packet that forced us to dial. This variable is instantiated for an outgoing call.

- ciscoCallHistoryConnectTimeOfDay—The time of day at the time of call connect. Because the connection time is the value of the sysUpTime when the call was connected, this variable helps you to actually correlate time of day with the calls.

- ciscoCallHistoryDisconnectTimeOfDay—The time of day when the call disconnected. Again, this variable can help you to correlate actual time of day with the calls.

- ciscoCallHistoryTransmitPackets—The number of packets transmitted when this call was up.

- ciscoCallHistoryTransmitBytes—The number of bytes transmitted when this call was up.

- ciscoCallHistoryReceivePackets—The number of packets received when this call was up.

- ciscoCallHistoryReceiveBytes—The number of bytes received when this call was up.

In Table 17-8, the variables that were non-zero values for an example environment are placed in a simple format. From this type of table, the network administrator is now able to begin looking at the total number of calls that an interface receives, the number of packets/bytes transmitted and received, and the amount of time the circuits are being utilized.

Table 17-8   *ISDN Line Utilization*

NAS	Call Calling Number	Call Interface Number	Call Dest Address	Call Call Disconnect Cause	Call Connect Time Of Day	Call Disconnect Time Of Day	Call Transmit Packets	Call Transmit Bytes	Call Receive Packets	Call Receive Bytes
NASP PP01	919 472 0052	2:13	10.0.0.1	Normal Disconnect Received	09:01:22	09:12:47	5742	3135132	1123	141498
NASP PP01	919 472 0052	2:10	10.0.0.1	Normal Disconnect Received	10:03:50	10:22:31	11317	5918791	2487	542166

The call history table provides the basic data needed to begin managing ISDN call utilization. As you can see, the variables within this MIB do provide some useful data. There are several cost variables that normally do not: ciscoCallHistoryRecordedUnits, ciscoCallHistoryCurrency, ciscoCallHistoryCurrencyAmount, and ciscoCallHistoryMultiplier.

Another repository for this type of data is the AAA server log. Through the Call History Table and the AAA logs, an administrator is able to monitor for number of calls, the number that the calls are made to (or in the case of the AAA logs, the IP addresses) and begin looking at ISDN utilization on the NAS. The use of an AAA server should be considered a best practice for dial access networks. In particular, the AAA server provides a logging function each time a call is authenticated. This log can be used to gather much the same information as the Call History MIB and provides an excellent source for data validation.

Just as with modem management, using the MIB or the show commands to collect data on the number of calls, duration of calls, errors, and type of traffic passed enables you to understand the performance of your server, make decisions on capacity, and actively manage users' perceptions of the network.

CLI Commands for Measuring ISDN Utilization

The **show isdn history** command displays historic and current call information, including the called number, the time until the call is disconnected, AOC (Advice of Charge) charging time units used during the call, and whether the AOC information is provided during calls or at the end of calls. Example 17-7 shows sample output from show isdn history.

Example 17-7 *Obtaining ISDN utilization information with **show isdn history**.*

```
rtp-isdn>show isdn history
- - - - - - - - - - - - - - - - - - - - - - - - - - - - - - - - - - - - - - - - - - - - -
                          ISDN CALL HISTORY
- - - - - - - - - - - - - - - - - - - - - - - - - - - - - - - - - - - - - - - - - - - - - -
History table has a maximum of 100 entries.A
History table data is retained for a maximum of 15 Minutes.B
- - - - - - - - - - - - - - - - - - - - - - - - - - - - - - - - - - - - - - - - - - - - - -
Call      Calling or Called    Remote     Seconds Seconds Seconds   Recorded Charges
TypeC     Phone numberD        Node NameE UsedF    Left   Idle      Units/Currency
- - - - - - - - - - - - - - - - - - - - - - - - - - - - - - - - - - - - - - - - - - - - - -
In            9194670812 +uller-isdn   242138            0
Out              3625083 +lansk-isdn   184062            0          0
In            9197725168 +riend-isdn   158229            0
In            9198515120 +rinho-isdn   104170            0
In            9195622974 +ltman-isdn    74795            0
In            9198722308 +nkins-isdn    70787            0
In            9198722309 +nkins-isdn    68906            0
In            9195574922 +moore-isdn    36556            0
Out              3626757 +gugan-isdn    28826            0          0
In            9193621042 +odwin-isdn    28435            0
In            9193628901 +hanco-isdn    26133            0
In            9193628902 +hanco-isdn    26127            0
In            9192864873 +lliot-isdn    25767    294     5
In            9194685397 +aylor-isdn    25432            0
Out              4683721 +iralt-isdn    24634            0          0
In            9193872921 +alton-isdn    20892            0
In            9194672574 +brown-isdn    14240            0
In            9197852332  ruthm-isdn    14075            0
In            9198549851 +lland-isdn     8133            0
In            9193045178  jamng-isdn     8066            0
In            9199687239 +aniel-isdn     6964    292     7
In            9197723502 +spain-isdn     6679            0
```

A History Table MaxLength—Maximum number of entries that can be retained in the Call History table.

B History Retain Timer—Maximum number of seconds any entry can be retained in Call History table. This can be changed through the following configuration command available in IOS 11.2(5)F and later releases:

```
NASPPP01(config)#call-history-mib retain-timer ?
  <0-500>  Time (in minutes) for removing an entry
```

C "Call Type"—Has two values incoming or outgoing (In or Out).

D "Calling or Called Phone number"—For incoming calls, this is the number from which the call was received. For outgoing calls, this is the number to which the call was placed. The same data is available through the MIB variables ciscoCallHistoryCallingNumber and ciscoCallHistoryCalledNumber.

E "Remote Node Name"—Name of the host placing the call or the host called. If the name is preceded by a plus sign (+), it has been truncated in the display. The same data is available through the MIB variable ciscoCallHistoryDestinationHostName or ciscoCallHistoryDestinationAddress.

F "Seconds Used"—Number of seconds the call lasted. Indicates whether the call is still active and how many seconds it has lasted so far. This data is not directly available through the MIB. However, through the use of the variables ciscoCallHistoryCallConnectionTime and ciscoCallHistoryCallDisconnectTime, or the variables ciscoCallHistoryConnectTimeOfDay and ciscoCallHistoryDisconnectTimeOfDay, you can subtract to come up with the same value. Also, the seconds used is recorded in the AAA log.

One of the most important new items in Example 17-7 is the addition of Calling or Called Phone number. By knowing the numbers for business-critical applications and significant users, and times when activity is at its highest, you can begin to build thresholds using these numbers. Another approach would be to identify the numbers that have the most consistently low connection rates and then focus on solving their problem (if there is one). After this has been accomplished, use this group as a "threshold" by having an alert sent if another number is added to the set. This would take some relatively sophisticated scripting, but would be worth the time and effort.

Correlating Variables and Performance Issues

In the case of dial, the MIB variables for cmLineStatisticsTable or the data gathered through the CLI show commands can and should be looked at and trended statistically. By looking at these variables over time, you can find trends, such as modems, that are connecting only at low speeds or that have more of a particular type of error. This type of analysis and correlation can help to diagnose performance problems within call groups, signaling levels, and even the lines. As you can see, a lot of what you gather in performance management can be applied to fault/error management.

The data gathered by **show modem conn 56000** can be correlated with the data gathered from the RADIUS or AAA log. The use of the RADIUS or AAA log requires the use of several scripts and someone with a flair for programming. It initially is a great deal of work, requiring parsing of the RADIUS logs text fields, parsing the **show modem conn** fields, and populating a database with the results. At this point, you have a database against which the data can begin to be correlated with time and then reported on. This type of correlation between the two data sources can help validate the reports. In addition, the data from the RADIUS server can also provide a correlation point between the phone number and connection speed. The effort to build this type of correlation database can result in the ability to manage the dial modems and users for both performance and capacity planning.

Error/Fault Data for Dial and ISDN

Like the discussion of performance management, this section on error and fault management looks at MIBs and CLI commands. In addition, as mentioned in previous chapters, the use of syslog is an important part of any fault management plan. In the case of remote access servers, the use of both syslog and the radius logs can add an important aspect to the data that is gathered and analyzed for remote access. In this section, the following will be discussed:

- MIB Variables for Monitoring Connection Errors
- CLI Commands for Monitoring of Connection Statistics
- CLI Commands for Monitoring Modem Firmware
- MIB Variables for Measuring ISDN/PRI Service
- MIB Variables for Monitoring ISDN and Modem Connections
- CLI Commands for Monitoring ISDN/PRI Service
- MIB Variables for Monitoring Modem and ISDN Trap States
- Syslog Messages for Modem and ISDN Trap Information

MIB Variables for Monitoring Connection Errors

The cmLineStatisticsTable provides essential data on modem connection errors. As explained earlier in the section "MIBS for Modem Status Monitoring," cmDisconnectReason is one of the most important variables (see Table 17-4 for the different results). In fault management, these variables help you identify the exact type of disconnect.

For fault management, the cmDisconnectReason variable would be mapped against the different result categories just as in performance management. The table and scripts used for performance can be reused here.

In addition, the entries in cmLineStatisticsTable could indicate the number of connection completions, failures, and other data needed to monitor the modem faults. As mentioned earlier, this data is very useful for troubleshooting the modem connections.

CLI Commands for Monitoring Connection Statistics

See the output from **show modem call-stat** (see Example 17-2). For fault management, you'd use the command **show modem call-stat** to look specifically for disconnect reasons.

CLI Commands for Monitoring Modem Firmware

As mentioned in the first section of this chapter, one of the fundamental parts of provisioning a Network Access Server (NAS) is inspecting and upgrading modem firmware; the modem firmware is not accessible through SNMP.

Although keeping track of the firmware is not usually considered part of fault management with remote access networks, it is an essential part. During the fault identification process, the type of firmware is one of the first things that is checked. Finally, because faults are isolated on servers, the need for understanding the modem firmware becomes essential. Often, the upgrade of modem firmware is one of the first requirements.

Example 17-8 shows output from the **show modem version** command from from the as5800. Examples from other platforms are not included because of their similarity.

Example 17-8 *Using **show modem version** on an as5800 platform.*

```
as5800#show mod ver
 Modem Range            Module   Firmware Rev
    1/3/00 1/3/11         0       2.4.1.0
    1/3/12 1/3/23         1       2.6.1.0


 .
 .
 .

    1/5/12 1/5/23         1       Unknown
    1/5/24 1/5/35         2       2.6.1.0
    1/5/36 1/5/47         3       Unknown
    1/5/48 1/5/59         4       2.6.1.0

       -         -        11         -

Modem board HW version info:

Modem Range:    1/3/00 1/3/11        Modem Module:  0
 Manufacture Cookie Info:
  EEPROM Type 0x0101, EEPROM Version 0x01, Board ID 0xDC,
  Board Hardware Version 1.0, Item Number 73-2988-2,
  Board Revision A48, Serial Number 09820408,
  PLD/ISP Version 255.255, Manufacture Date 3-Aug-1998.
```

Example 17-9 displays information for modem firmware. This information includes modem firmware version, boot code version, controller and DSP code version (56 KB modem modules only), modem board hardware version, and carrier card information. This particular example displays information for 56 KB modem cards installed in a Cisco AS5xoo.

If the version number is displayed as 0.0.0, verify that out-of-band status polling is functioning.

Example 17-9   *Using* **show modem version** *to obtain firmware information.*

```
router# show modem version
            Modem module   Firmware   Boot           DSP
   Mdm^A      Number^B        Rev^C      Rev^D          Rev^E
   0/0            0          3.1(21)  3.0(4)   1.1(0)/1.1(0)
    .
    .
    .
   0/12           1          2.2(8)   1.0(5)
    .
    .
    .
   0/23           1          2.2(8)   1.0(5)
   2/0            0          3.1(21)  3.0(4)   1.1(0)/1.1(0)
                       .
                       .
                       .
   2/23           1          3.1(21)  3.0(4)   1.1(0)/1.1(0)
 Modem board HW version info:
 Slot 0:
   Carrier card:
     hw version= 8, number_of_ports= 24, max_modules= 2, max_oob_ports= 2
   Modem Module 0:
     number_of_modems= 12, option_bits= 1,
     rev_num= 02.00, vendor_model_number= 02,
     vendor_banner= Microcom MNP10 K56 Modem
   Modem Module 1:
     number_of_modems= 12, option_bits= 1,
     rev_num= 03.00, vendor_model_number= 01,
     vendor_banner= Microcom MNP10 V34 Modem
```

Example 17-10 displays modem version information for V.110 modem cards for unmanaged modems.

Example 17-10   *Obtaining modem version information with* **show modem version.**

```
router# show modem version
            Modem module   Firmware   Boot
   Mdm ^A     Number^B        Rev^C      Rev^D
   0/0            0         Unmanaged  Unmanaged

         .
```

continues

Example 17-10 *Obtaining modem version information with **show modem version**. (Continued)*

```
   2/23              1              Unmanaged    Unmanaged

 Modem board HW version info:

 Slot 0: F
   Carrier card: G
     hw version= 3 H, number_of_ports= 12I, max_modules= 1J, max_oob_ports= 1 K
   Modem Module 0: L
     number_of_modems= 12M, option_bits= 1N,
     rev_num= 03.01O, vendor_model_number= 01P,
     vendor_banner= V.110 Terminal AdaptorQ
```

Highlighted field descriptions from Examples 17-9 and 17-10 are as follows:

A "Mdm"—Slot and port number for the specified modem.

B "Modem module Number"—Card number associated with the carrier card.

C "Firmware Rev"—Modem firmware version, or one of the following:

— Unknown—Indicates that the retrieved version is 0.0.0.

— Unknown (F)—Indicates that the modem's out-of-band feature has failed.

— Unknown (NP)—Indicates that the user has disabled the status polling for this modem using the no modem status-polling command.

All firmware on all modems in the same router should be at the same level. If not, the abnormal firmware rev is highlighted yellow. If the firmware rev is Unmanaged, it means that the software to communicate with the modem is not present. This is highlighted yellow.

D "Boot Rev"—Modem boot version, or one of the following:

— Unknown—Indicates that the retrieved version is 0.0.0.

— Unknown (F)—Indicates that the modem's out-of-band feature has failed.

— Unknown (NP)—Indicates that the user has disabled the status polling for this modem using the no modem status-polling command.

E "DSP Rev"—Controller and DSP version, which is displayed for the 56 KB modems only. The first column of numbers correspond to the controller version. The second column of numbers, which begins with a forward slash (/), correspond to the DSP version.

Modem board HW version info:

F "Slot"—Slot number used for the carrier card.

G "Carrier card"—Modem carrier card.

H "hw version"—Modem carrier card hardware version.

I "number_of_ports"—Maximum number of modem ports that can be installed in the carrier card.

J "max_modules"—Maximum number of modem cards that can be installed in a carrier card.

K "max_oob_ports"—Maximum out-of-band ports used in the carrier card.

L "Modem Module"—Modem card.

M "number_of_modems"—Number of modems installed in the modem card.

N "option_bits"—Signal level of the modem A-law and the U-law.

O "rev_num"—Modem card version number.

P "vendor_model_number"—Vendor modem model number.

Q "vendor_banner"—Type of banner displayed by the modem vendor.

The CLI command **show modem version** provides you with the data necessary to begin troubleshooting a firmware problem. It is the first place that you can look to when the Cisco Technical Assistance Center (TAC) asks for the firmware version on the NAS or more particularly on the modem with which you are having a problem.

Table 17-9 summarizes the information collected from the **show modem ver, show version**, and **show CPU** CLI commands. It is intended as an example of how an administrator could organize the information for use. The table's software inventory enables you to look at the access server's IOS version and the different modem versions as well.

Table 17-9 *Summary of Modem Information from show Commands*

Network Access Server	IOS VERSION	Modem Version			Processor CPU
		Firmware	Boot	DSP	
NASPPP01	c5200-i-l_113-4_T.bin	5.1(20)	3.0(4)	22.0/ 47.0	Five seconds: 93%/6%; one minute: 46%; five minutes: 36%
NASPPP02	c5200-i-l_113-4_T.bin	5.1(20)	3.0(4)	22.0/ 47.0	Five seconds: 13%/4%; one minute: 37%; five minutes: 34%

Table 17-9 *Summary of Modem Information from show Commands (Continued)*

NASPPP03	c5200-i-l_113-4_T.bin	5.1(20)	3.0(4)	22.0/47.0	Five seconds: 19%/9%; one minute: 37%; five minutes: 35%
NASPPP04	c5200-i-l_113-4_T.bin	5.1(20)	3.0(4)	22.0/47.0	Five seconds: 19%/8%; one minute: 24%; five minutes: 26%

MIB Variables for Measuring ISDN/PRI Service

From CISCO-POP-MGMT-MIB, cpmDS0UsageTable is the table that provides some of the data needed to monitor the ISDN/PRI Service. This MIB is implemented only on the AS5200/5300/5800/c3620/c7200 images for 11.3(5)T and greater releases.

The primary variables that are useful from the CISCO-POP-MGMT-MIB for ISDN/PRI monitoring are listed as follows with the descriptions from that MIB:

- **cpmDS1SlotIndex**—The slot index indicates the slot number on the device where the DS1 card resides.

- **cpmDS1PortIndex**—The port index indicates the port number of a specific DS1 on the DS1 card in the slot

- **cpmChannelIndex**—The channel index that distinguishes the DS0 timeslot of the DS1 port. The range of the channel index is based on the number of T1/E1 channels: 1–24(T1) and 1–31(E1).

- **cpmConfiguredType**—The configured technology for the channel: ISDN(2), Channelized T1 (3), or Channelized E1 (4).

- **cpmCallCount**—The number of calls that have occupied this DS0.

- **cpmTimeInUse**—The amount of time that this DS0 has been in use. This is computed by summing up the call duration of all past calls that have occupied this DS0.

- **cpmInOctets**—The total number of octets received on this DS0, including framing characters. This object is needed because the IOS provide octet counters only for interfaces, several of which may utilize the same timeslot to carry calls at different times. This object enables the tracking of received octets from these calls over the different interfaces.

- **cpmOutOctets**—The total number of octets transmitted on this DS0, including framing characters. This object is needed because the IOS provides octet counters only for interfaces, several of which may utilize the same timeslot to carry calls at different times. This object enables the tracking of transmitted octets from these calls over the different interfaces.

- **cpmInPackets**—The total number of data packets received on this DS0. This object is needed because the IOS provides packet counters only for interfaces, several of which may utilize the same timeslot to carry calls at different times. This object enables the tracking of received packets from these calls over the different interfaces.

- **cpmOutPackets**—The total number of data packets transmitted on this DS0. This object is needed because the IOS provides packet counters only for interfaces, several of which may utilize the same timeslot to carry calls at different times. This object enables the tracking of transmitted packets from these calls over the different interfaces.

- **cpmAssociatedInterface**—This is the value of ifIndex when the specific channel has an active call with a corresponding interface in the ifTable. For example, a digital ISDN call has a value pointing to the B-Channel entry in the ifTable. A modem call over ISDN or CT1/CE1 has a value pointing to the async interface of the modem assigned to this call. If the channel is idle, this value is 0.

- **cpmISDNCfgBChanInUseForAnalog**—The number of configured ISDN B-Channels that are currently occupied by analog calls.

- **cpmISDNCfgBChannelsInUse**—The number of configured ISDN B-Channels that are currently occupied by both Digital and Analog calls.

- **cpmActiveDS0s**—The number of DS0s that are currently in use.

The preceding variables provide the basis for managing the PRI for the NAS. These variables enable you to measure the usage of the PRI and can be helpful for troubleshooting problems. One cautionary note on the use of this table is that it is not populated for all Cisco devices and is available only in later releases of IOS.

MIB Variables for Monitoring ISDN and Modem Connections

Looking at the CISCO-POP-MGMT-MIB, the cpmCallFailure provides objects that are optimizations so as not to retrieve and count tables. The variables in this section supplement the existing call-termination conditions from the CISCO-CALL-HISTORY-MIB. These variables address the both ISDN and Modem terminations. Again, this MIB is only implemented on a few of the Cisco platform (AS5200/5300/5800/c3620/c7200) images. Also, it is only available in the later IOS images (11.3(5)T and greater releases).

The primary variables that are useful from the CISCO-POP-MGMT-MIB for ISDN and modem monitoring are listed as follows with the descriptions from that MIB:

- **cpmISDNCallsRejected**—The number of rejected ISDN calls in this managed device.

- **cpmModemCallsRejected**—The number of rejected modem calls in this managed device.

- **cpmISDNCallsClearedAbnormally**—The number of connected ISDN calls that have been abnormally cleared, that is, they were cleared by some event other than the following:

  The transmission of a normal disconnect message by the local end.

  The reception of a normal disconnect message from the remote end.

- **cpmModemCallsClearedAbnormally**—The number of connected modem calls that have been abnormally cleared; that is, they were not cleared with the proper modem protocol handshakes.

- **cpmISDNNoResource**—The number of ISDN calls that have been rejected because there is no B-Channel available to handle the call.

- **cpmModemNoResource**—The number of modem calls that have been rejected because there is no modem available to handle the call.

The information from the preceding variables can be organized into a table such as Table 17-10. The table provides a starting point for identifying and isolating problems with resources on an NAS.

Table 17-10 *NAS Resource Monitoring*

NAS	ISDN Calls Rejected	Modem Calls Rejected	ISDN Calls Cleared Abnormally	Modem Calls Cleared Abnormally	ISDN No Resource	Modem No Resource
NASPPP01	0	2	0	26	0	65
NASPPP02	0	3	0	34	0	52
NASPPP03	3	0	16	4	0	63

CLI Commands for ISDN/PRI Service

The **show isdn service** command is used for PRI interfaces only. Also, if the channel were 0, then the state would be valid; in all other cases, the state is ignored. This command provides different information from the cpmDS0UsageTable discussed in the section "MIB Variables for Monitoring ISDN/PRI Service." Although gathering data through the show command is usually preferred because of the reduction of CPU overhead, in this case the cpmDS0UsageTable variables provide a good deal of additional information that is not available through the CLI. Example 17-11 shows sample output from **show isdn service**.

Example 17-11 *Obtaining ISDN/PRI service information with* **show isdn service.**

```
as5800#show isdn service
PRI Channel Statistics:
ISDN Se1/0/0:15, Channel (1-31)ᴬ
  Activated dsl 0
  State (0=Idle 1=Propose 2=Busy 3=Reserved 4=Restart 5=Maint)ᴮ
  0 0 0 0 0 0 0 0 0 0 0 0 0 0 0 0 0 0 0 0 0 0 0 0 0 0 0 0 0 0 3
  Channel (1-31) Service (0=Inservice 1=Maint 2=Outofservice)ᶜ
  0 0 0 0 0 0 0 0 0 2 2 2 2 2 2 2 0 0 0 0 0 0 0 0 0 0 0 0 0 0 2

rtp-isdn>show isdn service
PRI Channel Statistics:
ISDN Se1/0:23, Channel (1-31)ᴬ
  Activated dsl 0
  State (0=Idle 1=Propose 2=Busy 3=Reserved 4=Restart 5=Maint)ᴮ
  2 2 2 2 2 2 2 2 2 2 0 2 2 2 2 2 2 2 2 2 2 3 3 3 3 3 3 3 3
  Channel (1-31) Service (0=Inservice 1=Maint 2=Outofservice)ᶜ
  0 0 0 0 0 0 0 0 0 0 0 0 0 0 0 0 0 0 0 0 0 0 2 2 2 2 2 2 2
```

The highlighted items in Example 17-11 are as follows:

A "ISDN Interface"—ISDN PRI interface corresponding to serial interface 1/0:23 (that is, Se1/0:23).

B "State"—Current state of each channel. Channels 24 through 31 are marked as reserved when the output is from T1. (0=Idle, 1=Propose, 2=Busy, 3=Reserved, 4=Restart, 5=Maint). Channel range 1-31 is a standard format for both T1 and E1 outputs, but the state value shown identifies whether the channel is used.

C "Channel Service"—Service state assigned to each channel. (0=Inservice, 1=Maint, 2=Outofservice). In the previous example, Channel 24 is marked as out of service. If channel 24 is configured as the NFAS primary D channel, NFAS will roll over to the backup D channel if one is configured. If channel 24 is a B channel, calls will not be accepted to it.

The numbers given in state and channel provide an excellent way to look at the status of the PRI interface. For instance, in Example 17-11, you can readily see which are busy and that the "reserve" states are actually out of service. Knowing that this is output from a T1 rather than an E1 makes this piece of information important. Once again, mapping these to a table format and possibly graphing the states/channels over the servers can be a valuable source of information of the fault status of the PRI lines.

MIB Variables for Monitoring Modem and ISDN Trap States

From CISCO-ISDN-MIB, DemandNbrCallInformation is a trap/inform sent to the manager whenever a successful call clears, or a failed call attempt is determined to have ultimately failed.

Syslog Messages for Modem and ISDN Trap Information

A number of syslog messages are useful for Dial and ISDN fault management and apply directly to the MIB objects and CLI commands previously discussed. They are collected in Table 17-11.

Table 17-11 *Syslog Messages for Dial and ISDN Trap Information*

Message	Explanation
DIALER-6-BIND	This message indicates that a dialer interface has been bound to a dialer profile
DIALER-6-UNBIND	This message indicates that a dialer interface has been unbound to a dialer profile
ISDN-6-CONNECT	This informational message is sent when a call is connected.
ISDN-6-DISCONNECT	This informational message is sent when a call is disconnected.
ISDN-6-LAYER2UP	This informational message is sent when the ISDN Layer 2 protocol is up (not spoofing).
ISDN-6-LAYER2DOWN	This informational message is sent when the ISDN Layer 2 protocol is down.

Summary

As discussed in this chapter, any administrator using Network Access Servers to provide users or sites remote access to a network has to find ways to manage the modems, lines, and calls that are being made through these servers and this part of the network. The primary method of doing so is to monitor the number of calls, call duration, call failure reasons, and traffic passed during calls. This data can be gathered through CLI show commands, SNMP, and log data.

CLI commands are recommended over the use of SNMP variables because not all information needed is accessible through MIBs and because the polling of modem variables can have an adverse affect on the router CPU.

Because a customer's perception of a network is often driven by its "remote" access performance, the area of monitoring performance and fault becomes increasingly important. After you have personally explored the variables, captured them, and trended them for your environment, you may wish to look at the use of RMON events and alarms for proactive fault management.

References

Book

Cisco Systems, Inc. *Cisco IOS Dial Solutions*, Indianapolis, IN: Cisco Press, 1998.

Internet Resources

Access Technology—Software Center. (As stated in the first section, this is the location of the modem firmware needed to upgrade the modem software.)

http://www.cisco.com/kobayashi/sw-center/sw-access.shtml

Basic Modem Cabling and Configuration. (This is a starting point for understanding not just the configuration and cabling of modems, but also what is needed to manage this environment.)

http://cio.cisco.com/warp/customer/701/21.html

Dial Solutions Command Reference. (This document provides additional examples of the show commands, as well as information on other commands that can be used for troubleshooting problems.)

http://www.cisco.com/univercd/cc/td/doc/product/software/ios120/12cgcr/dial_c/dcmodmgt.htm

Modem AT Commands for the Cisco 26/36xx. (An excellent listing of the AT commands used for configuration, testing, and troubleshooting of modems on Cisco-supported platforms.)

http://www.cisco.com/univercd/cc/td/doc/product/access/acs_mod/cis3600/analogfw/analogat.htm

Modem Management Commands, Release 12.0. (Provides a complete list of commands used for modem management. All of the examples as well as many more are covered in here.)

http://www.cisco.com/univercd/cc/td/doc/product/software/ios120/12cgcr/dial_r/drprt1/drmodmgt.htm

PART III

Optimal Management

Part III pulls together the techniques and information discussed in Parts I and II and presents them in the form of frequently asked questions for performance and fault management and best practices for enabling network management on Cisco devices.

- Chapter 18 explains how to enable network management capabilities in Cisco devices through the configuration of telnet access, loopback interfaces, NTP, SNMP, RMON, syslog logging. For each of these technologies, configuration examples are given as well as explanations on how the techniques will help you manage your Cisco devices more effectively.

- Chapter 19 provides a list of questions and answers to the most commonly asked performance and fault management questions that are addressed by this book. All question/answer pairs refer back to the chapter and section which provides more details on the topic.

CHAPTER 18

Best Practices for Device Configuration

Having covered the details of what to look for in Cisco devices relating to MIB objects and show commands, we need to address a fundamental issue of network management: configuration. This chapter focuses on the recommended best practices as they apply to setting up Cisco devices for network management, such as SNMP, RMON, and syslogging. By "best practices," we mean recommended ways to configure and maintain Cisco devices.

This chapter covers all the steps that are required and recommended to prepare your Cisco devices for the management strategies discussed in this book. We will identify eight best-practice configuration strategies in this chapter:

- Setting up Telnet access characteristics
- Setting up a Loopback interface
- Setting up NTP
- Setting up SNMP
- Setting up RMON
- Setting up logging
- Setting up CDP
- Setting up SPAN

Setting Up Telnet Access Characteristics

Many network operations folks probably spend most of their time Telnetted into their Cisco devices when they are troubleshooting issues or even looking at statistics, rather than looking at an NMS station's GUI representation of the data. Some folks even use Telnet as their method of managing the network by using scripts written in Spy, Expect, or even Perl. If this is how you manage your network, consider the steps outlined in the following sections.

Set the Terminal Length to 0 When Using Scripts to Gather the Data

When there are multiple "screen dumps" associated with a particular **show** command, it is not efficient to always insert a <space> when the next screen needs to be displayed, as seen from a Telnet session. Use the following CLI command to set the terminal length within a VTY (Telnet) session: In a router, **term length 0** and in a Catalyst switch, **set length 0**.

If scripting around Telnet, be sure and set the terminal length back to 24 when exiting the device.

Use TACACS+ or RADIUS On the Devices for Access

Setting up TACACS+ or RADIUS type of device access does three things:

- Eliminates the need for shared passwords.
- Logs activities, such as configuration changes or who and when someone was Telnetted into the device.
- Restricts who can use what commands in the device, either per command or per privilege level (enable mode versus non-enable mode).

Scripting is a lot easier and more secure when you only have to use one username and password to log in to a router or switch, instead of multiple passwords as defined on the devices themselves.

Setting Up a Loopback Interface

One of the best-kept secrets at Cisco is the use of the Loopback0 interface on a router. The Loopback interface does not apply to Cisco Catalyst switches. The sc0 port on the Catalyst switch acts like a Loopback interface because it is the only IP address assigned to the whole switch. The configuring of the Loopback interface on a router is the recommended use in many IOS features, such as RSRB, DLSW, logging, NTP, and SNMP.

The Loopback interface is a virtual interface on the router that acts as a logical system interface that is, in essence, assigned to the router as one node instead of a multiple interface router. It stays up as long as the router is operational. It has no relationship to any physical interfaces on the router, yet acts as its own logical subnet. The Loopback interface is useful for creating a common source IP address for SNMP trap messages, syslog messages, and as the primary IP address in name resolution or DNS.

Probably the only drawback of using a Loopback interface is that it requires its own IP subnet. But you can use a host mask (255.255.255.255 or /32) for this interface because no other device uses that subnet. If you have available IP address space or can allocate a range of IP subnets for the Loopback interface, it will be easier for you to manage your network, utilizing some of the configuration techniques described in this chapter.

NOTE	Be aware that some network management platforms may not operate properly when a /32 subnet mask is used. It may require you to configure the Loopback interface with a /30 (255.255.255.252) mask.

To configure a Loopback interface on the router, use the following CLI configuration commands:

```
interface loopback0
ip address 10.1.2.3 255.255.255.255
```

If you are short on IP addresses, the Loopback interface is probably not a viable option. In that case, consider "key" physical interfaces, such as backbone-oriented interfaces, for use as source IP addresses for SNMP traps or syslog messages because those interfaces should be up most of the time.

Setting Up NTP

Because most Cisco networks of any size span the globe, it is important to synchronize the times on the devices so that all messages and events are logged based on a common time source, especially if they are managed from a central or regional location.

In order to accomplish this feat, NTP (Network Time Protocol) should be configured on the devices. The Network Time Protocol (NTP) is a protocol designed to time-synchronize a network of machines. NTP runs over UDP and is documented in RFC 1305.

Configuring NTP makes management of your network easier with respect to the consistent timestamps on syslog messages. In conjunction with timestamping the log messages on the router, you can use NTP to synchronize the times for easier event correlation. For example, if a LAN interface goes down on a router and users start complaining about poor performance or lack of connectivity, you can correlate the syslog system timestamp in the log to the first trouble ticket reported by the user to a central network operations center or NOC. If there are local support personnel, they can correlate the local timestamps in the router log to that of the user complaint or the syslog server.

An NTP network usually gets its time from an authoritative time source, such as a radio clock or an atomic clock attached to a timeserver, typically located somewhere on the Internet. NTP then distributes this time across the network.

NTP uses the concept of a stratum to describe how many NTP "hops" away a machine is from an authoritative time source. A stratum 1 timeserver has a radio or atomic clock directly attached, a stratum 2 timeserver receives its time via NTP from a stratum 1 timeserver, and so on. A machine running NTP will automatically choose as its time source the machine with the lowest stratum number that it is configured to communicate with via NTP.

The communications between machines running NTP, known as associations, are usually statically configured; each machine is given the IP address of all machines with which it should form associations. Accurate timekeeping is made possible by exchanging NTP messages between each pair of machines with an association.

Cisco's implementation of NTP does not support stratum 1 service; in other words, it is not possible to connect to a radio or atomic clock via a Cisco device. It is recommended that time service for your network be derived from public NTP servers available in the IP Internet.

If the network is isolated from the Internet, Cisco's implementation of NTP allows a machine to be configured so that it acts as if it is synchronized via NTP, when in fact it has determined the time using other means. Other machines then synchronize to that machine via NTP.

The following are recommended steps to configure NTP in a network that is isolated from the Internet (Use either step 1 or 2, but not both):

1 Identify the source of the higher stratum clock time-server that the master NTP clock router points to, such as a workstation running NTP server software either internal to the network or an external time-server source.

2 Identify a centralized or core router(s) that can act as the NTP master clock server. Ideally, this router(s) should have connectivity to the access portions of your network within two router hops.

Configuring NTP on a Router

Here are the steps to configure NTP on the router if option 2 is used:

1 Set the clock on the identified NTP master router(s) using the following CLI commands:

```
clock set hh:mm:ss dd mmm yyyy
clock update-calendar
```

2 Set up NTP on the NTP master router(s) using the following configuration commands:

```
clock calendar-valid
ntp master 1
ntp source Loopback0
```

3 Point the other routers in the network to the NTP master clock router by executing the following CLI configuration command: **ntp update-calendar**

```
ntp peer ip-address
ntp source Loopback0
```

4 Point all Catalyst Series switches to the master NTP server (router) by using the following CLI **set** commands:

```
set ntp broadcastclient disable
set ntp broadcastdelay 3000
set ntp client enable
set ntp server ip_address
clear timezone
set summertime disable
```

For more information regarding NTP configurations, please refer to the following CCO Web pages (see the references at the end of this chapter for the appropriate URLs):

"Performing the Basic System Management" (Router)

"Configuring NTP" (Catalyst Switches)

For details regarding the different time-serving methodologies that may be implemented in a network refer to the following Web page, Time WWW server: http://www.eecis.udel.edu/~ntp/.

Setting Up SNMP

Configuring SNMP on Cisco devices is the basic method used by most network managers for maintaining and monitoring their network. Network management platforms and applications utilize SNMP heavily for data collection and event correlation of network devices. We'll focus here on the preferred way to set up Cisco devices for SNMP management using SNMPv1 examples. For more information on SNMP and community strings, refer to "Simple Network Management Protocol" in Chapter 8, "Understanding Network Management Protocols."

NOTE   Due to the ever-evolving SNMP technology (especially SNMPv3, currently), there is no discussion on the SNMPv3 set up in the Cisco devices. If you require up-to-date information regarding SNMPv3, please refer to CCO.

Essentially, there are four steps for setting up SNMP:

1 Enable SNMP on the Cisco devices.

2 Control SNMP trap messages.

3 Set the SNMP packet size to the maximum.

4 Control SNMP access using views and access lists.

Following subsections discuss these steps in more detail.

Enabling SNMP on Cisco Devices

By configuring SNMP, you define the Network Management Station's (NMS) IP address where you want the SNMP traps to go to as well as the read-only and read-write community strings for servicing SNMP requests.

On routers, use the following configuration:

```
snmp-server host host
snmp-server community host [ro¦rw]
```

This is the basic configuration. Subsequent sections include a look at views and access-lists in conjunction with the snmp-server community command.

On Catalyst switches, use the following configuration:

```
set snmp trap enable
set snmp trap revr_address revr_community
set snmp community [read-only¦read-write] string
```

Please note that by default, routers have no RW community string configured, and the Catalyst switches do. You should reconfigure these strings before deploying the devices initially into the field. You also can define multiple trap destinations as well as multiple community strings if you don't only manage from a centralized location.

Controlling SNMP Trap Messages

There are several "knobs" you can turn to control how SNMP traps are generated. We'll identify three of those methods as they apply specifically to the routers. Catalyst switches currently don't have these knobs.

Use the snmp-server enable traps configuration command to control what traps are generated. You can override the traps sent from the command **snmp-server host** with this configuration command. With the **snmp-server host** command, you can control what traps go to which host. By default, all traps are sent when this command is executed. You can control the type of SNMP traps sent by defining the specific trap or traps at the end of the **snmp-server enable traps** command. On Catalyst switches, all traps are enabled by default when you enable the SNMP traps.

Source the traps from the Loopback0 interface using the configuration command **snmp-server trap-source Loopback0**. By doing this, you can control where traps are sourced from versus having multiple IP address sourcing the traps. By default, all traps are sourced from the outgoing physical interface's IP address. It's easier to track one IP address or hostname than multiple IP addresses or hostnames from a common host (Cisco device).

Control the flow of linkup/linkdown traps by using the interface configuration command **no snmp trap link-status**. Use this command under interfaces that are highly transient in nature, such as ISDN BRI/PRI interfaces. You may not need to track every time an ISDN interface goes up or down, so turning off the link-status traps on those interfaces is recommended.

Setting the SNMP Packet Size to the Maximum

By default, the router sets the SNMP packet size to either 484 bytes (prior to IOS 11.2) or 1500 bytes (11.2 IOS or higher). Sometimes, multiple varbinds are embedded within an SNMP get request that exceeds the PDU (Protocol Data Unit) size of the configured SNMP packet size. This situation places a high CPU demand on the router during the IP-SNMP process because of the IP fragmentation that needs to take place at the processor level. The Catalyst switches have a fixed SNMP packet size of 1500 bytes and won't be discussed further in this section.

If the MTU size or PDU size is set to the maximum, the router can throw the SNMP response into one packet, place it in the huge system buffer pool for delivery, and perform the IP fragmentation when sending the packet out the interface (based on the MTU size of the media). The maximum configurable allowed packet size prior to 12.0 IOS is 8192 bytes, 12.0 IOS and above 17940 bytes. The practical limit and current implementation for SNMP packet size is 3072 bytes, as discussed in Chapter 8. To set up the SNMP packet size use the following configuration command:

```
snmp-server packetsize 3072
```

Controlling SNMP Access Using Views and Access Lists

Looking at the percentage of unknown community strings relative to total number of SNMP packets received identifies unauthorized network management stations trying to access the router via SNMP gets or sets. For example, it is important to control who can and cannot access the router via SNMP, especially with read-write access (RW), if you want to protect against rogue auto-discovery routines and limit what different users can see via SNMP. One way to police this is with IP standard access lists defined at the end of the **snmp-server community** configuration command or with SNMP views. Following are examples of both.

To set up access lists with SNMP you'd configure the following:

```
snmp-server community string ro 1
access-list 1 permit 10.1.2.3
```

where **1** is the standard IP access list number permitting the appropriate host who can access the router with the Read-Only (ro) community string.

SNMP views are a way to restrict what MIB objects can be gathered by an SNMP host based on the community string. We'll use an example from a common issue seen by customers, dealing with SNMP-gets of routing tables or ARP tables.

The issue is that the routing and arp tables are not in lexicographical order, so the IP SNMP process has to reorder the routing or ARP table. If you have a few thousand routes, IP SNMP will churn on the processor, driving the router CPU through the roof. The way to deal with this is to restrict access to the ipRouteTable and ipNetToMediaTable MIBs, so NMS stations cannot poll those objects. To mask the routing table and ARP table from SNMP getRequests you'd have to configure the following:

```
snmp-server view noarproute internet included
snmp-server view noarproute ipRouteTable excluded
snmp-server view noarproute ipNetToMediaTable excluded
snmp-server view noarproute at excluded
snmp-server community public view noarproute RO
```

where noarproute is the name you give the view. The actual MIB object name can also be substituted with the actual MIB OID.

Setting Up Logging

Setting up logging is probably one of the least-implemented and least-appreciated best practices, yet it is very important. Logging on Cisco devices is probably one of the most valuable tools for managing a network aside from SNMP (perhaps). Logging is synonymous with syslog messaging. Log messages on Cisco devices originate from the processor when some event happens on the device, such as an interface going down or a configuration changing. The only external requirement for logging and tracking these messages is a syslog server running somewhere in the network so the router can send the messages to it.

NOTE	Some Network managers may prefer to use the syslog delivery mechanism to send SNMP traps as well instead of a separate utility. This requires the option syslog at the end of the **snmp-server host** command.

We'll start with the basics of setting up logging on the Cisco devices and then fine-tune its functionality by identifying three configuration best practices that make this message-logging a lot easier to manage.

Essentially, the basic steps and best practices are as follows:

1 Enable logging on the Cisco device.

2 Timestamp the log messages.

3 Source all messages from the loopback0 interface's IP address.

4 Buffer the log messages on the Cisco device.

Enable Logging on the Cisco device

Enable logging on the Cisco device by directing the messages to a syslog server IP address—ideally, one server and not multiple servers:

On a router, use the following configuration:

```
logging host
```

On a Catalyst switch:

```
set logging enable
set logging server ip_address
```

Now it's time to fine-tune.

Timestamp the Log Messages

If you've already set up NTP, all devices should have their times and dates synchronized. Now, by applying timestamps to the log messages, correlation between events throughout the network becomes a lot easier.

To set up timestamps on log messages you need to configure the following on a router:

```
service timestamps debug datetime
service timestamps log datetime
```

On a Catalyst switch, the configuration is:

```
set logging timestamp enable
```

Source All Messages from the Loopback0 Interface's IP Address

This step applies only to routers. Catalyst switches have only one IP address associated to the whole switch versus multiple IP addresses to multiple interfaces. By default, syslog messages use the outgoing physical interface's IP address for the source of the log messages. Tracking only one IP address source is easier than tracking many IP addresses from a common host. Network management software can sometimes make mistakes when trying to correlate the source IP address with other database information and may not be smart enough to realize that one router has multiple IP addresses assigned to it. To set up the logging source, configure the following on the router:

```
logging source-interface Loopback0
```

Buffer the Log Messages on the Cisco Device

Depending on how much memory is available on a Cisco device, you can log a lot of syslog messages to the buffer or memory of the device, viewable from executing the CLI command **show logging**. By logging messages in the memory buffer, you can view what went on in a device if connectivity is lost to the device or to the syslog server.

Logging messages to the console port of the router or switch is not advised due to the 9600-baud interface. For each character outputted to the console port basically performs an interrupt on the processor. By having console logging enabled, it produces unnecessary processing cycles on the device to send out the messages on that port. To disable console logging, execute the following CLI configuration command: on a router, **no logging console** and on a Catalyst switch, **set logging console disable**. You can always view the log messages when on the console port by typing the command **show logging** or executing the commands **term monitor**.

The router can store anywhere from 4096 bytes to 4 GB. The default buffer size varies depending on the router platform. The Catalyst switch can store anywhere from 1 to 500 messages, with the default being 500. If you want to limit the type of messages that are stored in the log, you can restrict the logging to a particular logging level, which will display only messages with the defined severity or higher. For example, if you set the logging level to debugging you will get all messages with a priority of 7 or higher, with 1 being the highest. If you set the logging level to warnings, you'll get only messages with a priority of 4 or higher. The logging level is defined with the **logging** command. Refer to the documentation for more details on the logging levels.

To set up buffer logging, use the following CLI configuration command on the router:

```
logging buffered [size]
```

And on the Catalyst switch, use the following:

```
set logging buffer [number_of_messages]
```

If you want to view the real-time log messages being reported in the Cisco device while you are Telnetted to the device, you can execute the following CLI commands: For a router, **terminal monitor** and for a Catalyst switch, **set logging session enable**. By default, the messages go only to the console port of the device. If you want the messages to be seen from a vty session, these commands need to be executed. These commands affect only the vty session you are actively in. By timestamping the log messages, viewing them in the log makes it easier to correlate outages or events because the log will show the timestamp as well.

Setting Up RMON

Remote monitoring, or RMON, is another method similar to SNMP to track statistics on interfaces or ports on network devices. The RMON feature typically is utilized in a LAN switch environment but is available on the access routers (for example, 2x00 Series) in IOS 11.1 or higher. It may only be required to set up RMON on remote routers when you cannot get access to the LAN equipment, such as hubs, to view the traffic. RMON does not require you to actively poll for SNMP variables on a regular basis. The devices store the information needed, and then it is dumped periodically to an RMON network management station. Please refer to "Remote Monitoring MIB and related MIBS" in Chapter 8 for more details on the RMON functionality. For the purpose of this "best practice," we'll focus on the switch configuration, assuming a switch is at a remote access site in addition to the router, sharing a common LAN segment.

RMON is easily enabled on a switch by using the CLI command **set snmp rmon enable**. When RMON is enabled, the supported RMON groups for Ethernet ports, as specified in RFC 1757 are

- Statistics
- History
- Alarms
- Events

When RMON is enabled, the supported RMON groups for Token Ring ports, as specified in RFC 1513 and RFC 1757, are

- Mac-Layer Statistics
- Promiscuous Statistics
- Mac-Layer History
- Promiscuous History
- Ring Station Order Table
- Alarms
- Events

RMON gets more interesting when you define the rising and falling alarm thresholds for the Alarm and Event groups, as well as turning on Statistics and Histories. Granted, the raw data collected is still valuable, but thresholding allows you to watch things a bit more closely. These threshold settings normally are configured by a remote monitoring application via SNMP and not from the command-line prompt. Cisco and other vendors provide applications to perform these functions. We'll first go through the methodology on when to do what task, and then we'll look briefly at the MIBs needed to enable the appropriate RMON group.

There are several steps that should take place prior to actually implementing thresholds using the Alarm and Event groups. The first step of baselining the traffic flows in your network to understand the patterns, for example, is the traffic local, cross-campus, or campus-to-Internet. Using SNMP or even RMON probes and applications, gather statistics about the environment, such as EtherStats from the Statistics RMON group or the Histories. After a baseline is performed, you should identify critical ports on the switches, like switch trunk ports (ISL or 802.10 based) or file server ports. You should then analyze the normal characteristics associated with those ports by trending the data. Given the normal characteristics, you can start to define alarm thresholds.

After the alarms have been defined and refined, you no longer need to actively poll for traffic statistics as frequently because the device can monitor itself through the use of RMON events and alarms. The purpose for polling now would be solely for historical or availability reasons and not for fault monitoring.

You can continue to use RMON Histories for the whole switch to gather statistics for the RMON application if you don't want to use up network bandwidth for constant SNMP polling. An RMON probe for critical ports such as trunks also can continue to poll the EtherStats over time to see what is happening in the switch.

The MIBs needed to set RMON Alarms and Events as well as define the History characteristics originate from RFC 1757. Refer to this RFC for the MIB specifics or "Remote Monitoring MIB and Related MIBs" in Chapter 8 for more RFCs relating to RMON.

Setting Up CDP

Using CDP, the Cisco Discovery Protocol, is a good method of Cisco network management if you have VTY (Telnet) sessions open on the devices when troubleshooting (or "Telnetting around the network"). From CDP, you can get an idea of the network topology and feature characteristics of other devices that are directly connected around that local device, such as what kind of device is its neighbor or what kind of features are turned on in the neighboring devices. CDP is a useful tool when troubleshooting because most of a network operational engineer's time is spent at the command prompt of a Cisco device. The CLI for viewing CDP information on Cisco devices is **show cdp neighbor detail**. There are tools out there, such as Ciscoworks for Switched Internetworks or CWSI, which use CDP for autodiscovery.

CDP does produce a small amount of overhead on the network by using multicast data-link packets to exchange information between devices. It uses the destination multicast MAC address of 01-00-0c-cc-cc-cc. This minimal traffic is easily justified when uptime and network availability are so crucial. CDP is a quick method for troubleshooters to get a quick understanding of what's in the network around them, from where they are troubleshooting.

CDP is enabled by default on all Cisco devices and on all interfaces (**cdp enable**) except for ATM interfaces and other Non-Broadcast Media (NBMA), where CDP is not supported at all due the nature of the multicast traffic over ATM.

Here are the default characteristics of CDP:

- CDP holds on to learned CDP information for three minutes (Time-to-Live).
- CDP sends out updates every 60 seconds.

Using the default settings for CDP is recommended. The only exception is if you want to disable CDP on interfaces where you are certain that Cisco devices do not exist and you know you have full control of what goes in and out of your network.

Setting Up SPAN on a Switch

On the Catalyst Series switches, there is a feature called SPAN, which is basically a way to monitor transmitted and received traffic on different ports or VLANs on the local switch. (SPAN stands for Switched Port Analyzer.)

TIP   When doing capacity planning, it is recommended to physically allocate one 10 Megabit or 100 Megabit Ethernet port on the switch specifically for the use of the SPAN feature. Doing so eases the pain of troubleshooting traffic through a switch by giving one dedicated port for a network analyzer or RMON probe.

The SPAN feature allows network troubleshooters to have one physical network analyzer or probe per switch and to locate it on only one port instead of having to physically move the analyzer from one segment to another to monitor the network. SPAN is definitely a fault management tool like CDP.

To set up SPAN on the switch use the following CLI **set** command:

```
set span {src_mod/src_vlan} [rx¦tx¦both] enable
```

For more information on configuring the SPAN feature, refer to the documentation on CCO. (See the references at the end of this chapter for specific URLs.)

Summary

In this chapter, we looked at some best-practice techniques for configuring Cisco routers and switches for network management by providing concrete configuration examples. Specifically, we addressed recommendations for the following:

- Setting up Telnet access to the devices
- Configuring the Loopback interface on the router
- Configuring NTP
- Configuring SNMP on the devices for handling SNMP requests as well as SNMP traps
- Setting up logging
- Setting up RMON on the switches
- Setting up CDP
- Setting up SPAN on the switches

We feel that if you use these configuration steps as guidelines for your network, maintaining and supporting the network will be much easier.

References

Internet Resources

"Cisco Network Monitoring and Event Correlation Guidelines"

http://www.cisco.com/warp/partner/synchronicd/cc/cisco/mkt/enm/cw2000/tech/cnm_rg.htm

"Configuring NTP"; (Catalyst Switches)

http://www.cisco.com/univercd/cc/td/doc/product/lan/cat5000/rel_5_1/config/ntp.htm

"Configuring SPAN"

http://www.cisco.com/univercd/cc/td/doc/product/lan/cat5000/rel_5_1/config/span.htm

"Performing the Basic System Management"; (Router)

http://www.cisco.com/univercd/cc/td/doc/product/software/ios120/12cgcr/fun_c/fcprt3/fcgenral.htm

Time WWW server Web page, which describes in detail the different time-serving methodologies that may be implemented in a network

http://www.eecis.udel.edu/~ntp/

CHAPTER 19

Frequently Asked Questions

In this chapter, you will find the answers to frequently asked questions concerning performance and fault management of Cisco devices. The purpose of this chapter is to pull together information from earlier in this book that pertains to commonly asked questions. All question-and-answer pairs in this chapter include specific references to the relevant chapters where you can turn for more details.

The topics are grouped into the following sections:

- General network management
- General interface management
- VLAN/spanning tree
- Frame Relay
- ATM
- Dial/modem/ISDN

Conventions

This chapter follows a number of conventions you should keep in mind as follows:

The term *IOS devices* in this chapter means all routers running IOS as well as switches or any other devices that implement Cisco's IOS. Any exceptions are noted in each question/answer pair.

References to Catalyst switches encompass Catalyst 2900/5000, 4000, 5500, 6000 and 6500 series switches. They do not encompass Catalyst 1800, 1900, 2600, 2800, 2900XL, 3500, and 3900 switches. The distinction is important because Cat 2900/5000, etc. switches run code different then the other switches and routers. Because Catalyst 2900XL and 3500XL switches run IOS, answers involving IOS apply to these switches. Please also note that some of the switches that were not current IOS at the time this book was written may be updated to run IOS code.

To assist you in locating FAQs of particular interest to you, Table 19-1 lists all the FAQs covered in this chapter, along with their page references.

Table 19-1   *Frequently Asked Questions*

FAQ
General Network Management
How do I configure logging to a syslog server?
How do I configure a RMON threshold?
What threshold values should I use?
How can I track whether a router or switch disappears from the network?
How do I graph data that requires a calculation?
How can I enable or disable certain kinds of traps?
How can I collect information that is available in a show command but not through SNMP?
How can I force a router to consistently provide the same source IP address for any traps or syslog messages?
Why can't I collect RMON statistics from a switch?
General Interface Management
How do I collect CPU utilization?
Why is IP SNMP causing high CPU utilization?
How do I collect free and largest block of contiguous memory?
How do I collect Catalyst switch backplane utilization?
How can I measure router or switch health?
How do I measure the ratio of Buffer Hits to Misses?
How do I measure the ratio of process-switched packets to total packets?
How can I avoid a device appearing to be down if a single managed interface goes down?
How can I track when a power supply dies or a redundant supply changes state?
How do I track when a Cisco device reloads and determine the reload reason?
Can MIB II ifTable variables (such as ifInOctets) be collected from sub-interfaces?
How can I collect interface utilization and monitor it over time?
How can I measure utilization for IOS sub-interfaces?
How do I collect interface utilization from high-speed interfaces such as ATM and gigabit Ethernet?
How do I disable/enable traps for specific router or switch ports?
Why is my interface utilization greater than 100%?
How can I measure interface health?
How can I detect if an interface goes down?

Table 19-1   *Frequently Asked Questions (Continued)*

FAQ
How can I determine the bandwidth of an interface or sub-interface?
How do I track the number of broadcasts received on a particular interface?
How do I clear device SNMP counters?
How can I collect interface information when the ifIndex always change for interfaces?

VLAN/Spanning Tree
How do I collect VLAN utilization?
How can I track spanning tree topology changes?
Why do I see the spanning tree for only one VLAN with SNMP?

Frame Relay
How can I measure the number of Frame Relay drops that occur?
How do I measure Frame Relay circuit utilization?
How can I detect whether a Frame Relay PVC changes state?

ATM
How do I get ATM sub-interface traffic statistics?

Dial/Modem/ISDN
How can I track rejected modem and ISDN calls?
How can I track calls that are rejected due to lack of B channels or available modems?
How can I gather the equivalent of a show dialer command using SNMP?

General Network Management

This section covers general network-management issues such as the following:

- Configuring SNMP on devices
- Capturing SNMP and Telnet output through scripting
- Using syslog
- Using RMON

How Do I Configure Logging to a syslog Server?

Aside from traps, Cisco devices provide useful device state information by using the UNIX syslog facility. Whereas SNMP traps are well-defined and tend to reflect stateful changes, logging messages from Cisco devices are free-form text with well-defined names that reflect a wide range of conditions. The types of messages can range from debugging information such as when you enable debugging, to so-called "emergency" level messages, which reflect a catastrophic event such as a failing interface.

You can configure your routers and switches to forward their console messages onto a common syslog server so that you can capture and store all messages from all devices for later use. Enabling syslog messaging helps when troubleshooting and eliminates having to Telnet to different devices in order to view their individual logs.

To enable syslog message forwarding for IOS devices:

```
logging host
```

To enable syslog message forwarding for Catalyst IOS devices:

```
set logging server enable
set logging server ip_addr
```

where *ip_addr* is the IP address of the server running syslogd. You can define more than one destination syslog server if you desire.

You can specify which messages are forwarded to the syslog server based on message severity with the following command on IOS devices:

```
logging trap level
```

where *level* is one of the seven syslog severity descriptions. By specifying a severity level, all messages with that severity level and above (more critical) will be forwarded to the syslog server.

TIP   Setting a logging level of "warnings" should suffice under normal conditions in order to catch all pertinent messages.

For example, with the following command

```
logging trap warnings
```

all syslog messages of severity warnings, errors, critical, alerts, and emergency will be forwarded.

The same mechanism exists for Catalyst IOS switches, but it is more granular in that you can specify severity levels for each family of services on the switch. Please refer to switch configuration documents for the different message types and how to set the severity for message forwarding.

Please see "Setting up Logging" in Chapter 18, "Best Practices for Device Configuration," for more information.

How Do I Configure an RMON Threshold?

RMON thresholds are set by configuring RMON events and alarms. A threshold consists of at least one and usually two components: an alarm (required) and an associated event (optional). The alarm defines the variable to monitor and the rising and falling thresholds to watch for. An event is associated with a particular alarm and defines the action that should occur if a particular threshold has been exceeded. An event action can consist of logging the event, sending a trap, or both.

RMON specifies that you create the thresholds using SNMP. This is the preferred method when creating thresholds using scripts or commercial software. Because the RMON protocols and methods are IETF standards, you can use any vendor's RMON configuration software that supports RFC 1757.

Cisco also provides a method to define thresholds on IOS devices by using the command-line interface. Some Cisco customers find the command line method easier when deploying the same RMON configuration to many devices.

Example 19-1 shows the IOS commands necessary to define a threshold that generates an SNMP trap if a router's CPU utilization exceeds 90 percent (rising threshold) or falls below 50 percent (falling threshold).

Example 19-1   *Using the CLI to define a threshold and alarm.*

```
RMON event 100 log trap public description "CPU avgBusy5 exceeded 90%" owner pdellama
RMON event 101 log trap public description "CPU avgBusy5 no longer excessive" owner
pdellama
RMON alarm 100 lsystem.58.0 60 absolute rising-threshold 90 100 falling-threshold
50 101 owner pdellama
```

Please see Chapter 5, "Configuring Events," and Chapter 6, "Event and Fault Management," for more information concerning events and thresholding. Please see "Remote Monitoring MIB and Related MIBs" in Chapter 8, "Understanding Network Management Protocols," for more details on RMON. See Chapter 9, "Selecting the Tools," for more about the types of tools available for configuring RMON.

What Threshold Values Should I Use?

Throughout Part II of this book, we provide some starting threshold value recommendations, but avoid providing definitive values for you to use.

The reason why most engineers cannot provide a consistent answer to the question of what threshold values to use is that each network is different. No default threshold value can exist for most measurable attributes on a device that is consistent across all implementations.

Threshold values should be based on the current behavior of your network, and related to theoretical maximum capacity or capability of the data you are measuring. Thesholds should also be set at a level that alerts you to a problem before it seriously affects the network's capabilities and performance, but doesn't alert you so infrequently to cause the alarms to be ignored.

Setting thresholds that accurately reflect a particular network's behavior comes from a combination of learning your network and experience. Use the recommended thresholds in Part II as starting values. In addition, Chapter 2, "Policy-Based Network Management," provides tips on how to learn the current network behavior and Chapter 5 provides more information on selecting and defining thresholds.

How Can I Track if a Router or Switch Disappears from the Network?

Using ping (or ICMP) remains the best method to determine the presence of a device. Whether you build your own tool or use the status-monitoring capabilities provided with most network management software, ping/ICMP provides the easiest method for determine whether a device is reachable.

If a device becomes unreachable, it has either died, rebooted, or been turned off; or the network path between the network management station and the device has become unreachable. Either way, using ICMP is the quickest and simplest way to learn of a network fault. Commercial network management software generally displays the presence of a device in terms of availability through color-coded maps or tabular reports.

For more information, please see "Availability" in Chapter 4, "Performance Measurement and Reporting," and refer to "Availability Monitoring" in Chapter 9.

How Do I Graph Data that Require a Calculation?

Sometimes, you need to collect multiple variables in order to analyze the performance of a device or its interfaces.

For instance, to determine the utilization of a given network interface, you must collect the inbound and outbound traffic counts, and compare them to the theoretical maximum capacity of the interface. This analysis also may require the conversion of data to common data types (such as converting everything to bits-per-second).

For more information concerning the calculation of performance related data, see Chapter 4.

How Can I Enable or Disable Certain Types of Traps?

There are two types of traps to enable on Cisco devices: system-related traps and interface-related traps. System traps are those traps that apply to the system as a whole, whereas interface-related traps apply to a specific interface.

Configuring Traps on IOS Devices

As described in Chapter 18, you must use the **snmp-server enable trap** command in conjunction with the **snmp-server host** command to define which trap types will be generated to which trap receivers. By default, no trap receivers are defined.

In short, the **snmp-server enable trap** command defines which traps are available to be sent to trap receivers. The **snmp-server host** command defines trap receivers and the trap types that will be sent to a specific receiver. Thus, you can send different sets of traps to each defined trap receiver.

Because the relationship between these two commands varies for trap types based on IOS version, please refer to the IOS documentation for details related to your version of code.

The configuration in Example 19-2 enables two trap types for the router—config and frame-relay—and specifies two network management trap receivers.

Example 19-2   *Configuring traps and trap receivers on an IOS device.*

```
snmp-server enable traps config
snmp-server enable traps frame-relay
snmp-server host 172.26.10.254 public
snmp-server host 172.26.35.118 public config
```

In Example 19-2, the first trap receiver (172.26.10.254) will receive all traps enabled for this router. The second trap receiver (172.26.35.118) will receive only config-related traps. Note the **snmp-server enable** line. You can enable all available traps by typing the **snmp-server enable traps** command with no argument. Also, note that if **snmp-server enable traps config** were not enabled, config traps would not be sent to the 172.26.35.118 destination.

NOTE   You must specify the trap community string to be used when sending a trap. Like a community string with SNMP gets or sets, the trap community string is intended to provide a simple method to authenticate the source of the trap. Because the community string is sent over the network in clear text, it is not a very secure method for authentication. By default, most network management trap reception software ignores the community string included with a trap. If this form of authentication is inadequate for your SNMP needs, consider using SNMP informs, which are covered in Chapter 8.

Configuring Traps on Catalyst IOS Switches

Suppose you want to configure the following:

- Define a trap receiver of 172.26.10.254 with community string public
- Enable the bridge and chassis traps

Example 19-3 demonstrates how to do so.

Example 19-3   *Sample session of enabling trap receiver on a Catalyst 5000 switch.*

```
Console-outburst> (enable) set snmp trap 172.26.10.254 public
SNMP trap receiver added.
Console-outburst> (enable) set snmp trap enable bridge
SNMP bridge traps enabled.
Console-outburst> (enable) set snmp trap enable chassis
SNMP chassis alarm traps enabled.
```

By default, specific interface linkUp/linkDown traps are enabled. To disable the traps for specific ports, use the **set port trap** command. Also, keep in mind that you must specify a trap receiver with the **set snmp trap** command; otherwise, the port traps will have nowhere to go and will never reach a network management workstation.

In Example 19-4, we have enabled port traps for ports 2/1–2/12. Notice that the **show port** output for port 2/1 now reflects that the port trap is enabled.

Example 19-4   *A sample port trap configuration on a Catalyst 5000.*

```
Console-outburst> (enable) set port trap 2/1-12 enable
Ports 2/1-12 up/down trap enabled.
Console-outburst> (enable) sho port 2/1
Port  Name               Status     Vlan       Level  Duplex Speed Type
----- ------------------ ---------- ---------- ------ ------ ----- -----------
 2/1                     connected  1          normal a-half a-10  10/100BaseTX

Port  Security Secure-Src-Addr   Last-Src-Addr      Shutdown Trap
----- -------- ----------------- ----------------   -------- --------
 2/1  disabled                                      No       enabled  <<<<<<
```

For more information on configuring traps, please refer to "Enabling SNMP on Cisco Devices" and "Controlling SNMP Trap messages" in Chapter 18.

How Can I Collect Information that Is Available in a show Command, but Not Through SNMP?

Unfortunately, not all device information is available via SNMP. In such cases, you must determine whether the information you need is reported in any other form by a device. Sometimes, useful information is available only from a command-line show command or perhaps a console message.

Before resorting to using show commands, keep in mind that Cisco has more than 200 MIB documents published on Cisco Connection Online (CCO), which represent the supported MIB objects in Cisco devices. You should verify that a particular piece of information is not available via SNMP by following the guidelines in Appendix A, "CCO, MIBs, Traps, and Your NMS."

If you decide you must collect information that is only available in a command-line show command, there are multiple methods to do so. The most commonly used method is using the Expect language, which was originally part of the Tcl language, but has since been ported into other languages. The original version of Expect for Tcl was written by Don Libes, and the Tcl Expect homepage can be found at http://expect.nist.gov/.

Expect provides a method to feed input and collect output from a terminal session using a script. Austin Schutz has written a PERL module that performs the same functionality as Tcl Expect. The module can be downloaded from http://www.perl.com/CPAN/modules/by-module/Expect/.

The chapters in Part II of this book contain the most widely used show commands and syslog messages that do not have SNMP equivalents. Please see Appendix B, "ATM Accounting Files," for an sample Expect script written using the Perl Expect module.

How Can I Force a Router to Consistently Provide the Same Source IP Address for Any Traps or syslog Messages?

Because syslog messages and SNMP traps are encapsulated in IP packets, they are subject to IP routing rules. Thus, if there are multiple routes from a Cisco device to a network management workstation, the source IP address of the syslog message or trap can vary, based on which port the packet is sourced from. Figure 19-1 illustrates how traps and syslog messages can contain different source IP addresses when arriving from the same device.

Figure 19-1 *Traps and syslog Messages Have Different Source IP Addresses, Depending on the Interface from Which They Are Sourced*

When traps come in from the same device with different source IP addresses, some network management software may not be able to discern that the messages are from the same device when trying to do a DNS name lookup. In addition, different IP addresses from the same device can make reading an event log difficult.

NOTE   With switches, the source IP address of an event is not an issue because there is only one IP address to manage a switch by. The same IP address will be used when a trap or syslog message is generated.

To alleviate this issue, IOS routers can be configured to use a consistent IP address on syslog messages and traps by implementing a loopback interface.

Example 19-5 illustrates how to implement a consistent source IP address for syslog messages and traps using a loopback interface. (Note that this is a partial configuration.)

Example 19-5   *Configuring a loopback interface for consistent source IP address in traps and syslog messages.*

```
interface Loopback0
 ip address 10.10.100.50 255.255.255.255
!
logging source-interface Loopback0
snmp-server trap-source Loopback0
```

In Example 19-5, a virtual interface called loopback0 is created, which has an IP address of 10.10.100.50 associated with it. Notice that a host subnet mask of 255.255.255.255 can be used to minimize the use of whole subnets. The use of a host subnet mask may cause problems for some network management. If this is the case for you, consider using variable length subnets of /30 instead.

The **logging source-interface** and **snmp-server trap-source** commands specify that any syslog message or trap generated by this box use the source IP address of loopback 0, or 10.10.100.50 in this example.

For more information on using a common source IP address for traps and syslog messages, please see "Setting Up a Loopback Interface" in Chapter 18.

Why Can't I Collect RMON Statistics from a Switch?

By default, RMON is not enabled on Catalyst 4000, 5000, and 6000 switches. This can cause problems when you try to configure any of the RMON groups on a device. For example, when trying to collect etherstats from a Catalyst 6500, you may get an error saying they don't exist.

Most likely, RMON has not been enabled on the switch. Run the following command to enable RMON on a switch:

```
Console-outburst> (enable) set SNMP RMON enable
SNMP RMON support enabled.
```

To verify that RMON is enabled, type the **show snmp** command. Example 19-6 shows sample output from doing so.

Example 19-6   *Run the **show snmp** command to verify that RMON is enabled.*

```
Console-outburst> (enable) sho snmp
RMON: Enabled
Traps Enabled: Port,Chassis,Bridge
Port Traps Enabled: 2/1-12

Community-Access        Community-String
```

Example 19-6   *Run the **show snmp** command to verify that RMON is enabled. (Continued)*

```
...............     ...................
read-only           public
read-write          private
read-write-all      secret

Trap-Rec-Address                        Trap-Rec-Community
......................................  ...................
public
```

System-Related Questions

The questions in this section relate to system characteristics of Cisco devices, such as the following:

- CPU
- memory
- buffers
- environmental

How Do I Collect CPU Utilization?

CPU utilization is a good indicator for determining the health of a network device. The following sections detail how to collect and interpret CPU-related information.

Collecting CPU Utilization on IOS Devices

Critical router functions, such as routing protocol processing and process packet switching, are handled in memory and share the CPU. Thus, if the CPU utilization is very high, it is possible that a routing update cannot be handled or a process-switched packet is dropped.

For routers, collect avgBusy5 from the OLD-CISCO-CPU MIB.

The avgBusy5 variable reflects an exponentially decaying five-minute moving average. By using the avgBusy5, as opposed to busyPer, which reflects CPU utilization in the last 5 seconds, you avoid catching CPU spikes that can inaccurately reflect the longer-term impact of traffic on the CPU.

TIP　　Keep in mind that the polling of CPU utilization variables (and any other SNMP variables) affects the actual CPU utilization. Some customers have reported seeing utilization of 99 percent returned when continuously polling the variable at 1 second intervals. While polling so frequently is overkill, take into consideration the impact to CPU when determining how frequently you want to poll the variable.

If you discover a high CPU utilization, you may want to determine which process or processes are causing it. Output from the IOS **show proc cpu** command (see Example 19-7) will help you identify the offending processes.

Example 19-7　　*A partial **show proc cpu** listing.*

```
CPU utilization for five seconds: 42%/16%; one minute: 47%; five minutes: 50%
  PID  Runtime(ms)  Invoked  uSecs   5Sec   1Min   5Min TTY Process
    1        2364     23730      99  0.00%  0.00%  0.00%   0 Load Meter
    2       64576     41029    1573  0.16%  0.07%  0.06%   0 PPP auth
    3      368608      3950   93318  0.00%  0.19%  0.26%   0 Check heaps
    4          72       259     277  0.00%  0.00%  0.00%   0 Pool Manager
    5           0         2       0  0.00%  0.00%  0.00%   0 Timers
    6           0         2       0  0.00%  0.00%  0.00%   0 Serial Background
    7          88      3962      22  0.00%  0.00%  0.00%   0 Environmental monitor
    8       15676     13224    1185  0.08%  0.02%  0.00%   0 ARP Input
    9       16384     49080     333  0.00%  0.01%  0.00%   0 DDR Timers
   10           0         1       0  0.00%  0.00%  0.00%   0 SERIAL A'detect
   11        5924    191457      30  0.08%  0.02%  0.00%   0 Call Management
   12       20192    464930      43  0.00%  0.00%  0.00%   0 Framer background
   13    15470284   7925310    1952 20.69% 21.83% 23.88%   0 IP Input
   14        3544     13902     254  0.00%  0.00%  0.00%   0 CDP Protocol
   15           0         1       0  0.00%  0.00%  0.00%   0 Asy FS Helper
   16        2084     35167      59  0.00%  0.00%  0.00%   0 PERUSER aux
   17       17904     46273     386  0.08%  0.06%  0.04%   0 PPP IP Add Route
   18          28       200     140  0.00%  0.00%  0.00%   0 MOP Protocols
   19           0         1       0  0.00%  0.00%  0.00%   0 X.25 Encaps Manage
   20       37164    183448     202  0.16%  0.17%  0.17%   0 IP Background
   68     1626176   3415015     476  2.29%  2.48%  2.23%   0 CCP manager
```

The output in Example 19-7 shows that the busiest process is the IP input process, which is responsible for process-switching IP traffic.

Collecting CPU Utilization on Catalyst 4000, 5000, and 6000 Series Switches

For switches, at the time of this writing there is no CPU utilization variable to watch with SNMP. There are alternative methods to collecting CPU utilization from switches, but first we will discuss the importance of CPU utilization for switches.

Unlike routers, for switches, CPU utilization is not as vital an indicator of device health. Switches make packet-forwarding decisions in ASICs, and thus do not need processor time. In fact, we've seen faulty software crash on a switch, yet the switch continues to pass packets.

The switch's processor handles some vital functions such as the processing of bridge BPDUs for spanning tree calculation, but problems tend to manifest themselves in different areas first. Switch CPU utilization issues are discussed in more detail in "Catalyst Switch Processors" in Chapter 11, "Monitoring Network Systems—Processes and Resources."

To collect CPU utilization from a switch, you can use the command line **show pro cpu** (older versions of Catalyst IOS software use the less reliable **ps –c** command). The output contains individual process utilization as well as overall process utilization.

NOTE   Please note that the output of the **ps –c** command is not always accurate due to the priorities of the switch. The results of the command should be used only as a rough approximation of actual process utilization.

Because the switching of traffic is done without involving the switch's CPU, individual key interface utilization and backplane utilization tend to be better measures of device capacity.

For more information on measuring switch and router characteristics, please see "Performance Data for Switch Processors" in Chapter 11.

Why Is IP SNMP Causing High CPU Utilization?

If an IOS device has high CPU utilization caused by the IP SNMP process, there are several possible underlying causes:

- You are polling the device too much. A common culprit is a network management autodiscovery.
- You have the process priority for the IP SNMP process set too high. Set the process priority to low with the following command: **snmp-server priority low**. With the exception of a few 10.x versions of IOS, the priority should be set to low by default.

For more information, please see "Controlling SNMP Access Using Views and Access Lists" in Chapter 18.

How Do I Collect Free and Largest Block of Contiguous Memory?

Memory leaks and abnormal network events are the main reason for monitoring memory consumption and fragmentation. A memory leak occurs when a process requests memory blocks and does not release the block when it is finished with it. Eventually, the process will gobble up all of the available memory. This is considered a bug, and it will eventually cause a router to crash.

Collecting Memory Statistics from IOS Devices

Not having enough memory prohibits the router from, among other things, creating more buffers. The lack of memory can also affect the router's capability to grow data structures such as a routing table.

Monitoring free memory and the largest free block of memory on IOS devices can be good indicators of router health. The variables to watch are ciscoMemoryPoolFree and ciscoMemoryPoolLargestFree from CISCO-MEMORY-POOL-MIB.

Collecting Memory Statistics from Catalyst IOS Switches

With switches, the **show mbuf** command provides output such as that shown in Example 19-8.

Example 19-8   *Abridged output from switch **show mbuf** command.*

```
Largest block available : 3825456
Total Memory available  : 3827728
Total Memory used        : 405840
Total Malloc count       : 99395
```

For more information, please see "Using the **show mbuf** Command" in Chapter 11.

How Do I Collect Catalyst Switch Backplane Utilization?

For traditional Cisco switches that have a single backplane such as the Catalyst 5000 series, sysTraffic from the CISCO-STACK-MIB MIB provides the system backplane utilization. The sysTraffic measurement equates roughly to the meter of the same name on the supervisor card.

For switches that contain multiple backplanes, such as the Catalyst 5500, use the sysTrafficMeterTable from the CISCO-STACK-MIB.

For more information on measuring switch backplane utilization, see "Performance Data for Switch Processors" in Chapter 11.

How Can I Measure Router or Switch Health?

As with any computer, measuring the resources that make a router and switch pass packets allows you to gauge the relative health of the device. Like a workstation or mainframe, routers and switches contain one or more CPUs, RAM, storage, and network interfaces. If a resource becomes busy or faulty, it affects the overall operation of the device.

System resources reflect the capability of the device to pass packets. Ultimately, this is why you should be concerned with device health: anything that prevents the router from operating at peak capacity will affect its capability to pass packets. Monitoring device health allows you to detect events and conditions that may affect the processing of traffic.

Five essential areas can be used to gauge the healthiness of a router. Each of these is covered in detail in Chapter 10, "Managing Hardware and Environmental Characteristics," and elsewhere in this chapter:

- Device availability
- CPU utilization
- Ratio of buffer hits to misses
- Largest block of contiguous memory and free memory
- Ratio of process-switched traffic to other switching paths

For switches, there are fewer overall health indicators:

- Device availability
- Backplane utilization
- Trunk and server port utilization and error rates

Aside from the preceding, switch health should be determined on an interface by interface basis.

Please see Chapters 4, 10, and 11 for more details on router and switch health.

How Do I Measure the Ratio of Buffer Hits to Misses?

When a packet is received by a router and must be process-switched, it is temporarily stored in system buffers.

Buffer misses and failures are good indications of the following:

- Abnormal network events
- Heavy amounts of broadcast traffic
- Lack of available and/or contiguous memory
- High amounts of process switched traffic
- A software bug

The variables in OLD-CISCO-MEMORY-MIB provide most of the desired information to monitor the ratio of buffer hits to misses. Buffer failures are not available via SNMP, but the hit-to-miss ratio should be an adequate indicator of memory resource problems and should allow you to avoid having to process a show command.

Several factors need to be considered when collecting the hit-to-miss ratio. The first is the fact that a high ratio may not indicate a fault. For example, a buffer pool that is seldom used and has few buffers can reflect a high ratio despite the number of hits and misses being extremely low.

The second factor to consider is that you don't want to measure buffers that are bigger than the largest MTU on a router. For instance, if a router has only ethernet and fast ethernet interfaces, the largest MTU will be 1500 bytes; thus, you only need collect information from the small, middle, and big buffers.

For more information, please refer to "MIB Variables for Buffer Utilization on Routers" in Chapter 11.

How Do I Measure the Ratio of Process-switched Packets to Total Packets?

A packet can be forwarded through a router on different switching paths. The slowest, most processor-intensive path is called process switching. Although process switching is not inherently bad, it adds considerable overhead compared to the other switching paths. For example, each time a packet needs to be process switched, it generates a CPU interrupt and must be temporarily stored in a shared system buffer. Thus, it is desirable to have as much traffic as possible switched through paths other than process switching in order to maximize the packet throughput of the router.

Measuring the ratio of process-switched traffic to other switched traffic can be useful when determining network resource utilization. Depending on the type of router, a high amount of process-switched traffic can indicate many different things, including the following:

- Non-standard traffic patterns
- High rate of broadcasts
- Routing protocol problems
- Misconfiguration
- A software bug

High amounts of process-switched traffic can substantially limit the number of packets a router can forward.

For more information, please see "Correlating High CPU Values" in Chapter 11.

How Can I Avoid a Device Appearing to Be Down if a Single Managed Interface Goes Down?

When managing a network device, you must refer to the device by a resolvable name (such as router.your-company.com) or an IP address. If the interface associated with the managed IP address goes down, the entire device will appear to be down because the IP address is unreachable, despite the fact that the rest of the router's interfaces are forwarding packets.

To work around this problem, you should implement a loopback interface on the router. A loopback interface is a Cisco proprietary mechanism that creates a virtual interface that can be reached via any physical interface. Thus, if there are multiple paths to a device from a management workstation, if a path goes down, the device IP address for the loopback address is still reachable. In essence, the loopback interface only goes down if the device itself dies.

Keep in mind that the router must advertise the loopback address so that the rest of the network knows how to reach the device. Also, be sure to have the DNS name of the device resolve to the loopback IP address.

For more information, please see "Setting Up a Loopback Interface" in Chapter 18.

How Can I Track When a Power Supply Dies or a Redundant Supply Changes State?

When devices contain redundant power supplies, you can choose to have the device generate traps when a power supply dies or changes state. Traps exist on both routers and switches that notify of a state change or failure, and point to further information as to the nature of the change.

For routers, watch for the ciscoEnvMonRedundantSupplyNotification trap from the CISCO-ENVMON-MIB document. The variables ciscoEnvMonSupplyStatusDescr and ciscoEnvMonSupplyState provide details on the nature of the change. You must configure the **snmp-server enable traps envmon** command in order to enable the traps.

For switches, watch for the SNMP trap chassisAlarmOn. The variables chassisTempAlarm, chassisMinorAlarm, and chassisMajorAlarm are included with the trap and are necessary for determining the specific chassis alarm in progress.

Several sections in Chapter 10 contain more details: See "MIB Variables for Switch Failure," "Error/Fault Data for Router Environmental Characteristics," and "Error/Fault Data for Switch Environmental Characteristics."

How Do I Track When a Cisco Device Reloads and Determine the Reload Reason?

Sometimes, devices reload. They can crash, be turned off, have a power cable knocked loose, or be issued a reload command. When monitoring for device availability, you should be concerned about two aspects of reloads:

- When did the reload occur
- Why did the reload occur?

There are two methods to determine whether a reload has occurred. The first involves having your network management trap receiver watch for traps, indicating that a device has rebooted.

The second involves polling the sysUpTime value from MIB II (RFC 1213). This value contains the number of seconds since the device became active. Because the number constantly rises, a decrease between polling cycles indicates that either the device rebooted or the counter rolled over back to zero.

Once you determine that a reload has occurred, you can check whyReload from the OLD-CISCO-SYSTEM-MIB to determine the reload reason. This variable contains the same text as can be seen from show version.

For more information, refer to "MIB Variables for Router Failure" and "CLI Commands for Router Failure" in Chapter 10.

General Interface Management

The questions in this section relate to general interface management issues for Cisco devices, such as the following:

- Measuring utilization
- Detecting whether an interface is operational
- Measuring errors

Can MIB II ifTable Variables (such as ifInOctets) Be Collected from Sub-interfaces?

When RFC 1213 (MIB II) was originally drafted, the interface table variables were designed to reflect information about physical interfaces. Since then, the need has arisen to measure certain interface-related characteristics of logical connections that exist over physical lines. For example, a single physical serial interface may carry multiple Frame Relay DLCIs over it.

Starting with IOS version 11.1, Cisco implemented the concept of sub-interfaces to represent multiple logical interfaces over a single physical interface. Consequently, certain sub-interface types are now represented in portions of the ifTable.

Implementation of particular sub-interface types varies, based on technology, platform, and version of IOS. For more details, please see "Special Considerations for Sub-interfaces" in Chapter 12, "Monitoring System Interfaces."

How Can I Collect Interface Utilization and Monitor It Over Time?

In order to track interface utilization, you need to know two aspects of the interface:

- What is the speed/clockrate of the interface?
- Is the interface half- or full-duplex?

If the interface is full-duplex, it does not make sense to report utilization as a single number. This is because a full-duplex interface can have a maximum capacity of twice its bandwidth.

Some network managers choose to report full-duplex utilization as a single number. They do this by using an equation that calculates utilization by taking the maximum of the two values for the differences of in and out bits. Although this approach allows you to report a single utilization number for an interface, it does not provide a very useful picture of what is happening in both directions. Instead, you should calculate two utilization measures: in and out. For more details, please refer to Chapter 4.

How Can I Measure Utilization for IOS Sub-interfaces?

The answer to this question depends on what type of sub-interface you are trying to measure. Different sub-interface types received SNMP support in different levels of IOS.

When interface information is not available for a particular type of sub-interface, there are usually alternative means for collecting the traffic information. For instance, RFC 1315 provides per-circuit octet counts with the frCircuitSentOctets and frCircuitReceivedOctets.

For more information, please refer to "Performance Monitoring for Sub-interfaces" in Chapter 12.

How Do I Collect Interface Utilization from High-Speed Interfaces such as ATM and Gigabit Ethernet?

Although the utilization equations described in "Measuring Utilization" in Chapter 4 apply to high-speed interfaces, you must look at variables other than ifInOctets and ifOutOctets because they can roll over quickly with fast interfaces. With the advent of RFC 1573 (which superceded RFC 1213), high-speed counters were introduced to alleviate problems of high-speed interface counters rolling over too quickly to be useful.

ifHCInOctets and ifHCOutOctets are 64-bit counters (as opposed to 32-bit) and should be used on the high-speed interfaces that support them. Please note that you must use version 2c or version 3 of the SNMP protocol in order to recognize 64-bit counters.

For more information on high-speed counters and the versions of router and switch code on which they are supported, please see ion "Special Considerations for High-Speed Interfaces," in Chapter 12.

How Do I Disable/Enable Traps for Specific Router or Switch Ports?

You may want to disable traps for specific router or switch ports to avoid getting a trap every time someone turns off his or her computer. On a router, issue the **snmp trap link-status** command. On a switch, issue the **set port trap** *mod_num/port_num* {**enable|disable**} command.

If you want to enable or disable interface traps with SNMP, you can set the ifLinkUpDownTrapEnable variable found in RFC 2233. By default, the traps are enabled for router ports and disabled for switch ports.

For more information, please see "Controlling SNMP Trap Messages" in Chapter 18.

Why Does My Interface Utilization Appear to Be Greater than 100 Percent?

This can occur under several circumstances:

- You are measuring utilization of a full-duplex interface using a half-duplex formula.

- You are using an incorrect value for the interface bandwidth and have most likely set the IOS interface bandwidth incorrectly. By default, the setting of bandwidth is the line speed of a physical interface.

- You have an error in the way you calculate utilization.

- You are using a commercial network-management product that incorrectly uses the half-duplex formula on full-duplex media.

For more information, please see "Utilization" in Chapter 4.

How Can I Measure Interface Health?

Like system health, interface health is an essential indicator of network efficiency. The following characteristics should be used for assessing interface health:

- Interface utilization

- Interface errors

- Interface status

Determine which ports to monitor. Generally, you should only manage ports that are critical to the operation of the network or servers. This includes all trunk ports, large router ports, and local WAN connections. Chapter 1, "Conducting a Network Audit," has more detail on how to select critical ports to manage.

For port status, configure port traps to be collected in a trap log. This allows you to report a fault as quickly as the device sends the trap and the network management station can process it. When the trap is received, the network management station displays the trap in its event log and can launch a script in response.

Monitor interface error rates can provide an error percent, or compare the error rate to total traffic to understand the accuracy of transmission.

In your knowledge base, store the device, interface name, speed, and duplexity. These serve as the seed information for polling. Keeping this information current can be a pain, but helps in more accurate data collection.

See "Accuracy" in Chapter 4 for details on measuring interface errors, and see Chapter 3, "Developing the Network Knowledge Base," for information concerning a knowledge base.

How Can I Detect When an Interface Goes Down?

There are three primary methods, all using RFC 2233 variables:

- Watch for linkDown traps from a device.
- Watch for interface status change messages in syslog.
- Poll the ifOperStatus and ifAdminStatus. If ifAdminStatus is up and ifOperStatus is down, the interface is intended to be up, but for some reason is down. There are exceptions to this method with some WAN interfaces. See "Link Status" in Chapter 12 for more details.
- Poll ifLastChange and watch for a change in value. IfLastChange contains the sysUpTime of the last interface state change. If, while polling ifLastChange the value changes, that indicates that the interface state changed since the last poll cycle.

For more information, see "Error/Fault Monitoring" in Chapter 12.

How Can I Determine the Bandwidth of an Interface or Sub-interface?

For LAN interfaces such as ethernet, Token Ring, and FDDI, you must check two things: the interface type and whether the interface is passing traffic full-duplex or half-duplex. So, for instance, a fast ethernet interface set to full-duplex indicates that the interface can simultaneously transfer traffic at 100 MBps in both directions. An SNMP set against ifSpeed for a fast ethernet interface would look like the following:

```
~% snmpget bikini-atoll ifSpeed.3
interfaces.ifTable.ifEntry.ifSpeed.3 : Gauge32: 100000000
```

NOTE	Remember that ifSpeed is based on the IOS bandwidth setting for each interface, and may not reflect the actual speed the interface is using.

For WAN interfaces, determining bandwidth becomes trickier because the interface bandwidth reflects the fastest possible rate for a physical interface rather than the actual service you may be receiving from your service provider. For instance, with Frame Relay, the actual throughput you receive is dependent on multiple characteristics, including the Committed Information Rate you purchased and congestion in the service provider network. In such a case, you should calculate the bandwidth based on the optimal service you expect from your service provider.

For more information, please see Chapter 12.

How do I Track the Number of Broadcasts Received on a Particular Interface?

From RFC 2233, use the ifInBroadcast and ifOutBroadcast variables. Typically, using these variables and comparing them to the total amount of traffic will give you a ratio to determine how broadcast traffic rates may increase or decrease over time, compared to total traffic. These variables are first supported in IOS 12.0.

If you are running IOS prior to version 12.0, please use the RFC 1213 ifInNUcastPkts and ifOutNUcastPkts variables. The disadvantage of these variables is that there is no way to separate multicast counts from broadcast.

For more information, please see "Performance Monitoring for System Interfaces" in Chapter 12.

How Do I Clear Device SNMP Counters?

With Cisco routers, there is no way to reset SNMP counters (such as ifInOctets) without rebooting the device. Doing a **clear counters** command on the console only resets the counters viewed with **show** commands; the equivalent SNMP counters remain untouched. The SNMP counters cannot be reset other than by rebooting or re-initializing the agent (cold and warm restart).

However, with Cisco Catalyst IOS switches, the SNMP counters are reset, along with the **show mac** and **show port** counters, when you do a **clear counters** command.

For more information, please see "Special Considerations on Interface Counters" in Chapter 12.

How Can I Collect Interface Information when the Ifindex Always Changes for Interfaces?

The nature of SNMP is that you cannot depend on the ifIndex always being assigned to the same interface. Each time a box reboots, or each time a card is hot-swapped in or out of a box, the ifIndex can legally change for interfaces. This can create problems for network management software that might look at specific interfaces by using ifIndex.

The RFC 2233 MIB variables ifDescr, ifAlias, and ifName resolve this problem by allowing you to correlate a human readable name with the ifIndex for routers.

For more information, please see "Special Considerations for ifIndex" in chapter 12.

VLAN/Spanning Tree

This section answers questions concerning VLANs and spanning tree on Cisco Catalyst IOS devices.

How Do I Collect VLAN Utilization?

There is no good way to collect VLAN utilization, for the following reasons:

- Not all switch ports in a VLAN see all traffic in the VLAN.
- Not all traffic for a VLAN traverses trunk ports.
- Not all traffic for a VLAN hits a switch backplane.

Therefore, there is no single point at which you can measure traffic to accurately reflect the aggregate bandwidth consumed for a VLAN.

There are more useful methods for measuring capacity consumption. For instance, measuring broadcast and multicast traffic from a specific port can provide a benchmark for rising capacity needs. For a VLAN, this method is useful because all broadcast and multicast traffic is flooded to all ports in a VLAN.

For more information, please see "VLAN Utilization" in Chapter 15, "Monitoring VLANs."

How Can I Track Spanning Tree Topology Changes?

Watch for the topologyChange trap from RFC 1493. You will receive this trap from a switch whenever it detects a topology change.

For more information, please see "Error/Fault Data for VLANs" in Chapter 15.

Why Do I See the Spanning Tree for Only One VLAN with SNMP?

Catalyst 4000, 5000, and 6000 switches run one unique instance of spanning tree for each VLAN configured. Representing these multiple instances of spanning tree with SNMP can be difficult using normal SNMP structural mechanisms such as tables.

In order to view the spanning tree information for different VLANs, you must use a method called community string indexing. To specify which VLAN to view a table for, use a modified community string that contains the following format: *community@vlan number*. The use of this community string is shown in Example 19-9.

Example 19-9 *Collecting spanning tree variables from VLAN 1 and VLAN 10 using community string indexing.*

```
~% snmpwalk -c public bikini-atoll dot1dStpDesignatedRoot
dot1dBridge.dot1dStp.dot1dStpDesignatedRoot.0 : OCTET STRING-   (hex): length =80:
00 09 00 90 92 e9 70 00 -- -- -- -- -- -- -- --      ......p.........

~% snmpwalk -c public@10 bikini-atoll dot1dStpDesignatedRoot
dot1dBridge.dot1dStp.dot1dStpDesignatedRoot.0 : OCTET STRING-   (hex): length =80:
00 09 00 90 92 e9 70 09 -- -- -- -- -- -- -- --      ......p.........
```

In Example 19-9, notice in the first snmpwalk that the community string without VLAN has been specified. By default, VLAN 1 is assumed. In the second snmpwalk, VLAN 10 was specified (public@10), and notice that the mac address for the root bridge is different.

For more information, please see "Error/Fault Data for VLANs" in Chapter 15.

Frame Relay

This section discusses issues surrounding the management of Frame Relay on Cisco routers.

How Can I Measure the Number of Frame Relay Drops that Occur?

Tracking Frame Relay drops allows you to monitor speed mismatch congestion on the router DTE output queue. Keep in mind that there is no way to track drops in the service provider network.

From CISCO-FRAME-RELAY-MIB, CfrCircuitDropPktsOuts indicates the number of drops on a given Frame Relay circuit.

For more information, please see "MIBs to Monitor for Packet Discards" in Chapter 16, "Monitoring WAN Technologies—Frame Relay."

How Do I Measure Frame Relay Circuit Utilization?

Tracking Frame Relay DLCI utilization is similar to tracking the utilization for other types of interfaces in that you track traffic transmitted and received by an interface and compare it with a maximum amount capable.

However, unlike other interfaces, other factors affect the throughput for a particular Frame Relay circuit. For example, CIR, burst rate, and service provider network congestion can affect your ability to accurately calculate utilization.

There are two methods for calculating Frame Relay circuit utilization. The first involves using the frCircuitSentOctets and frCircuitReceivedOctets from RFC 1315. This method measures the in and out octets for each circuit (DLCI). As long as you are not using compression over the circuit, the counters are accurate.

However, you can also gather ifInOctets and ifOutOctets from RFC 2233 for each Frame Relay sub-interface. The advantage of this method is that these counters take into consideration the compressed data statistics rather than the uncompressed.

For more information, please see the following sections:

- "Measuring Utilization on Virtual Circuits" in Chapter 16
- "Performance Monitoring for System Interfaces" in Chapter 12
- "Utilization" in Chapter 4

How Can I Detect if a Frame Relay PVC Changes State?

Have your router generate the frDLCIStatusChange trap from RFC 1315. The trap is generated whenever a PVC changes state. The three possible states are the following:

- Invalid
- Active
- Inactive

You can also get the current state via SNMP by polling the frCircuitState variable from RFC 1315.

Keep in mind that in most service providers' networks, Frame Relay LMI is not end-to-end and that the service provider's switch may not accurately report the loss of a PVC.

For more information, please see "Error/Fault Data for Frame Relay" in Chapter 16.

ATM, ISDN, and Dial

This section addresses common questions involving the management of ATM, ISDN, and dial interfaces.

How Do I Get ATM Sub-interface Traffic Statistics?

Depending on the version of IOS you are running, you can gather per VC statistics based on the ifTable from RFC 2233—provided that each VC is on a separate sub-interface.

SNMP ifTable subinterface support for ATM LANE clients became available in IOS 11.2. Support for all other ATM encapsulations became available in 12.0T.

For more information, please see "Performance Management" in Chapter 14, "ATM Performance and Fault Management."

How Can I Track Rejected Modem and ISDN Calls?

From the CISCO-POP-MGMT-MIB, use the cpmISDNCallsRejected MIB object for ISDN and cpmModemCallsRejected for modems.

"MIB Variables for Monitoring ISGN and Modem Connections" and "CLI Commands for Modem Status Monitoring" in Chapter 17, "Monitoring LAN Technologies—ISDN and Dial," provide some additional information on rejected modem and ISDN calls.

How Can I Track Calls that Are Rejected Due to Lack of B Channels or Modem Available?

From the CISCO-POP-MGMT-MIB, use the cpmISDNNoResource mib object.

For more information, please see Chapter 17.

Summary

This book began with the important general aspects of network performance and fault management, such as conducting a network audit and establishing a knowledge base. It concludes with this chapter on some of the more specific concerns, particularly questions that frequently arise regarding performance and fault management. All answers refer back to the book section for which more details can be found.

PART IV

Appendixes

CCO, MIBs, Traps, and Your NMS

In this appendix, we will discuss different aspects of how to best utilize Cisco management information. The primary items we discuss are as follows:

- The structure of the Cisco MIB branch
- How to find a specific MIB object
- How to find a specific Cisco MIB
- How to access and download Cisco MIBs
- How to compile Cisco MIBs
- How to best ascertain whether a given MIB object is supported on a given device or IOS level

Cisco MIB Evolution

During earlier years, all the objects under the "Cisco MIB" branch were documented in one monolithic document. This document was updated with each new version of IOS. Therefore, there was a 9.0 "Cisco MIB" and a 10.0 "Cisco MIB." In those days, the product line was exclusively routers.

However, as IOS matured and the product line, grew this monolithic MIB model quickly broke down. Within one revision level of IOS, there were different versions, such as the IP only image and the IBM feature set version. The product line also included other devices such as LAN switches running completely different IOS.

Starting with IOS 10.2, the monolithic "Cisco MIB" was broken into component MIB documents, each focusing on a specific feature, technology, or device type. This structure allows quicker implementation of new features. It also allows users to compile only the parts they need into their NMS.

Cisco MIB Structure

Previous to IOS 10.2 the base structure of the Cisco MIB branch is shown in Figure A-1.

Figure A-1   *Cisco MIB Branch, Pre-IOS 10.2*

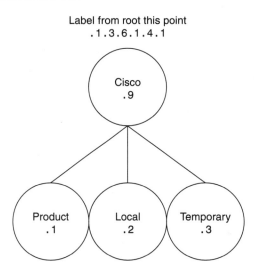

The following list describes the various component branches of the Cisco MIB branch:

- **Product branch**—The product branch holds the sysObjectIDs for most Cisco products. This object identifies the type of productsuch as a 4700 or a 7507 router. Most NMS applications use the sysObjectID to identify the network devices in their database and on the topology map.

- **Local branch**—The local branch originally was the branch where most management objects were located. However, much of the local branch is defined in the OLD-CISCO-* MIB files on CCO. These objects are now deprecated and will be rendered obsolete in some future version of IOS. Much of the same data is available from newer, more powerful objects in the new CiscoMgmt branch.

NOTE   The term deprecated has a specific meaning when referring to MIB objects. It was first introduced in RFC 1158 (the first definition of MIB II). A deprecated object must still be supported but it may be replaced in some future MIB document by a new object of similar or superior functionality. It is important to note which objects are deprecated because you may want to limit their use or at least be prepared to migrate if they become obsolete.

- **Temporary branch**—The temporary branch was the original experimental branch. Any new MIB work was done under this branch until it was ready to migrate to one of the production branches.

With the move away from a monolithic MIB file to component MIB files, new branches were defined, as shown in Figure A-2. Only the branches commonly used are shown in this figure.

Figure A-2   *Cisco MIB Branch, Post-IOS 10.2*

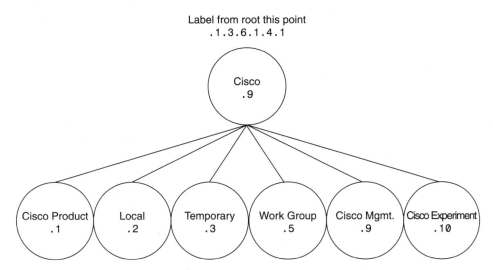

The new MIB structure still has the CiscoProducts branch where the sysObjectID of most Cisco devices are stored. The local and temporary branches are still there. Most local objects are still supported, even though they have been deprecated.

The transition to the new MIB structure marks the support of SNMPv2 SMI (Structure of Management Information). Virtually, all MIB objects for the local branch are SNMPv1 SMI. The branches currently used are as follows:

- **Cisco management branch**—The new structure adds the CiscoMgmt branch, under which most new Cisco MIB objects are defined. Most of the older branches from the local branch also have equivalent branches here. For example, the lflash branch under the local branch has been replaced by the CiscoFlashMIB under the CiscoMgmt branch.

- **Workgroup branch**—The workgroup branch contains objects supported on the workgroup Catalyst switches, such as the Catalyst 4000, 5000, and 6000 families. The commonly used CiscoStackMIB branch is located here. The sysObjectID objects for the Catalyst 4000,5000, and 6000 families of devices are also defined here rather than the CiscoProduct branch.

- **Experimental branch**—The CiscoExperiment branch is now where all new MIB work is based. These may be either IETF or Cisco work-in-progress MIBs. For example, objects defined by IETF-draft MIBs may be implemented first under this branch. However, support for such objects under the CiscoExperiment branch will be deleted when a permanent place is assigned.

There are other branches defined, but the preceding branches are the ones currently used.

How to Navigate MIBs on Cisco's Web Site

All Cisco MIB files are located in the public MIBs area on the Cisco Connection Online (CCO) Web site. The MIB files are all under this URL:

http://www.cisco.com/public/mibs/

The MIBs and many support items are located under various directories at this location. Here, we give descriptions on the contents of each directory.

Under the mibs directory, you find these entries:

- **app-notes**—In this directory are several application notes from wide-ranging areas. Some are dated, but even those can still provide good information. We recommend reading through all the application notes so you are familiar with the material available there.

- **archive**—In this directory, the older monolithic MIB files are kept. The archive directory is something of a mirror of the mibs area. Here, you will find the MIB files, OID files, and schema files for IOS 10.0 and earlier.

- **contrib**—A collection of contributed non-supported scripts or files. Like the app-notes directory, a good place to check out to see what is available.

- **oid**—A useful directory if you have SunNet Manager, which requires the OID strings of each object rather than ASN.1 format MIB files. It is also the best place to find the OIDs of most Cisco-supported MIB objects.

- **schema**—Like the OID directory, these files are provided if you have SunNet Manager that requires MIB files in this format.

- **traps**—Also like the OID and schema directory. These files were made available for SunNet manager.

- **routers**—The support list file for all routers.

- **supportlists**—A listing by device of supported MIB files. The next section of the appendix covers this directory in detail.

- **v1**—A collection of SNMPv1 SMI MIB files. Included are the older MIB files that were implemented in SNMPv1 SMI and also newer SNMPv2 SMI MIB files converted to SNMPv1 SMI.

- **v2**—The newer MIB files, all in SNMPv2 SMI.

- **v2-to-v1**—Obsolete. Originally where converted MIB files were kept, but now it is a symbolic link to the v1 directory.

Researching Support for New Devices and Versions of Code

As mentioned in the previous section, the supportlists and traps directories contain a listing by device of supported MIB files and traps. However, these listings are guidelines only. There is tremendous variation between different versions of a particular device, between release levels of IOS, and even within a single release level between point releases and between image versions and feature sets. The supportlists provide a good starting point for determining whether a particular device supports a given MIB file. However, it is good to confirm further the support on your particular software release, version, and feature set.

Routers are listed by different models, but all entries here actually point to the file under the routers directory. Basically, the IOS release and version determine support rather than device type. There are, of course, some limitations to the precision of these entries. For example, if you drill down through the 2511 entry, you will find the ATM-MIB listed as of IOS 11.2. However, the 2511 has no ATM interfaces, so obviously does not support this MIB. Exceptions such as these are why we emphasize that these listings are guidelines only.

After you have narrowed down the support information, there is a useful undocumented hidden enable-level IOS command for the routers that shows all MIBs supported by the IOS currently running on that router:

```
show snmp mib
```

This command will list all implemented MIB objects for that router. It is a very useful command for verifying support of a certain MIB object on a given router.

Compiling MIBs

Now that there is no longer a single monolithic MIB file, it can be tricky to get all desired MIB objects compiled into your NMS.

Getting MIB files to compile or load into your NMS is usually a matter of getting the order correct. First, the basic tree structure and textual conventions need to be loaded. Those may be found in the following two MIB files:

SNMPv2-SMI.my
SNMPv2-TC.my

Both of these files should already be loaded into most popular NMS applications like HPOV. These two files should allow you to load other open standard MIBs (rfc1213 for example). Now you have the basics, but you have not yet defined any Cisco branch. To load any of the Cisco-specific MIB files, you need to define the private Cisco branch and Cisco-specific textual conventions by loading these files:

CISCO-SMI.my
CISCO-TC.my

After that most Cisco-specific MIB files should load. If there are any errors complaining about undefined nodes, please check the imports sections of the MIB file you are attempting to load to make sure you have all the prerequisites already loaded.

There are many other issues you may run into. An excellent application note on mib compilers is

http://www.cisco.com/public/mibs/app_notes/mib-compilers

This paper covers many common issues you might encounter while trying to load any MIBs into your NMS.

Getting Trap Definitions for OV and NV

The most recent version of the more popular NMS applications will load traps in the event management portion when you load those MIBs. This method is by far the easiest. But you can also only load the traps directly into the NMS. In the contrib directory, there are some useful files for loading trap definitions into the more popular NMS platforms. For example, http://www.cisco.com/public/mibs/contrib/trapd.41x

is an HP OpenView Network Node Manager trapd.conf format file that will integrate the definitions of approximately 100 Cisco enterprise traps into Node Manager. A script that does the same thing for NetView 6000 can be found at

http://www.cisco.com/public/mibs/contrib/traps.script

It is important to note that these utilities are from the /contrib directory, which means they are provided as is with no guarantees. They may have the majority of Cisco enterprise traps, but not all, particularly the traps from the most recent MIBs.

Identifying Unknown Traps

On occasion, you may encounter some unformatted trap in your log. You may find some cryptic entry such as the following:

```
A Minor Tue Dec 02 19:14:02 nms-5505a NO TRAPD.CONF FMT FOR .1.3.6.1.2.1.17.0.1
ARGS(0):
```

The OID of the trap needs to be identified. A handy way to identify such unknowns is to download the entire public/mibs directory to a local server. You may then use standard utilities to match up the above OID.

To determine what trap that is, download the entire public/mibs directory structure—files and all—to a local server for you. Then you can use the following steps to determine what kind of traps you are receiving:

1 Change directories to your local OID directory and use **grep** to find which MIB file contains the trap OID:

```
% cd oid
/home/mibs/oid
% grep 1.3.6.1.2.1.17 *
BRIDGE-MIB.oid:"dot1dBridge"      "1.3.6.1.2.1.17"
.
.
.
```

> You can also use the Windows find utility (advanced tab) to perform a
> similar search on a Windows95 system.

2 Then, change directories to the v1 directory to check out the traps in the BRIDGE-MIB:

```
% cd ../v1
/home/mibs/v1
% grep TRAP-TYPE BRIDGE-MIB.my
        TRAP-TYPE
  newRoot TRAP-TYPE
  topologyChange TRAP-TYPE
```

3 Take a look at the definitions for these traps:

```
newRoot TRAP-TYPE
        ENTERPRISE dot1dBridge
        DESCRIPTION
            "The newRoot trap indicates that the sending agent
            has become the new root of the Spanning Tree; the
            trap is sent by a bridge soon after its election
            as the new root, e.g., upon expiration of the
            Topology Change Timer immediately subsequent to
            its election. Implementation of this trap is
            optional."
        ::= 1

    topologyChange TRAP-TYPE
        ENTERPRISE dot1dBridge
        DESCRIPTION
            "A topologyChange trap is sent by a bridge when
            any of its configured ports transitions from the
            Learning state to the Forwarding state, or from
            the Forwarding state to the Blocking state. The
            trap is not sent if a newRoot trap is sent for the
            same transition. Implementation of this trap is
            optional."
        ::= 2
```

4 The entry from the trap.log file was .1.3.6.1.2.1.17.0.1, where .1.3.6.1.2.1.17 represented the dot1dBridge enterprise and the last digit .1 shows this trap is a newRoot trap. Therefore, to properly format this trap, you should load the BRIDGE-MIB file into your NMS.

With the mibs directories and files on a local server, you can use variations on the previous techniques to identify variable bindings in unformatted traps, find the OIDs of objects you need to poll, and many other handy tricks.

In this appendix, we have covered the structure of the Cisco MIB. We told you where to get the Cisco MIB files and how to load them into your NMS once you got them. We also discussed formatting traps in your NMS and how to use some tricks to identify those unformatted traps your NMS is bound to log at some point. Armed with this knowledge, you should be able to make better use of Cisco MIBs and the public online MIBs area.

ATM Accounting Files

This appendix shows you how to decode the ATM Accounting files you log on your LS1010 or 8500MSR ATM switches. As discussed in the ATM chapter, an LS1010 or 8500MSR ATM switch can be configured to collect data of many different traffic parameters on the virtual circuits the switch is processing. This data can be used to measure the use of each virtual circuit, so it is a useful billing mechanism. The data is collecting in files that reside on the switch. After you retrieve the file from the switch, you must decode it. This appendix discusses the details of decoding these files.

You configure your ATM switches to log values on one or more of the following variables:

```
atmAcctngConnectionType
atmAcctngCastType
atmAcctngIfName
atmAcctngIfAlias
atmAcctngVpi
atmAcctngVci
atmAcctngCallingParty
atmAcctngCalledParty
atmAcctngCallReference
atmAcctngStartTime
atmAcctngCollectionTime
atmAcctngCollectMode
atmAcctngReleaseCause
atmAcctngServiceCategory
atmAcctngTransmittedCells
atmAcctngTransmittedClp0Cells
atmAcctngReceivedCells
atmAcctngReceivedClp0Cells
atmAcctngTransmitTrafficDescriptorType
atmAcctngTransmitTrafficDescriptorParam1
atmAcctngTransmitTrafficDescriptorParam2
atmAcctngTransmitTrafficDescriptorParam3
atmAcctngTransmitTrafficDescriptorParam4
atmAcctngTransmitTrafficDescriptorParam5
atmAcctngReceiveTrafficDescriptorType
atmAcctngReceiveTrafficDescriptorParam1
atmAcctngReceiveTrafficDescriptorParam2
atmAcctngReceiveTrafficDescriptorParam3
atmAcctngReceiveTrafficDescriptorParam4
atmAcctngReceiveTrafficDescriptorParam5
atmAcctngCallingPartySubAddress
atmAcctngCalledPartySubAddress
atmAcctngRecordCrc16
atmAcctngTransmittedPeakCells
atmAcctngReceivedPeakCells
```

Please refer to the ATM-ACCOUNTING-INFORMATION-MIB for details on each of these MIB objects.

The ATM accounting file is a binary file that must be decoded into human readable data. The binary data is in ASN.1 format. At the beginning of the file is a header consisting of the following:

- The system name (sysName)
- A description of the collection (as set in the switch's configuration)
- The start time of the collection
- A list of the objects for which data was collected

The rest of the file is a series of data records that contain the values of the objects in the list.

RFC 2513 formally defines the format of the ATM account file as follows:

```
File ::=
    [1]
        IMPLICIT SEQUENCE {
                            -- header information
            sysName             -- name of the switch
                DisplayString,

            description         -- textual description of the collection
                DisplayString,

            startTime           -- start time of the collection

            DateAndTime,

            SEQUENCE OF {       -- sequence of (subtree, list) tuples
                SEQUENCE {
                    subtree
                        OBJECT IDENTIFIER,
                    list
                        OCTET STRING
                }
            }
                            -- sequence of connection records
            SEQUENCE OF {
                                -- each record containing a sequence
                SEQUENCE OF {   -- per identified tuple

                    SEQUENCE OF {   -- each per-tuple sequence containing
                        value       -- a sequence of object values
                            ObjectSyntax
                    }
                }
            }
        }
```

There is a sample C program to decode the binary file into hex located on Cisco's ftp-eng server:

ftp://ftp-eng.cisco.com/kzm/pub/

The C program acct_decode4 was used to decode a sample binary ATM accounting file, and Example B-1 shows the hex output from that program. Then, you use the definitions in the ATM-ACCOUNTING-INFORMATION-MIB, ATM-MIB and the ISO signaling specification Q.2931 to decode the output shown in Example B-1 into legible data, as shown in Example B-2.

Example B-1 *Hex decode of sample binary ATM accounting file output.*

```
% acct_decode acctng_file1
Read 4 bytes from file acctng_file1
Offset   Tag-Len Data
00000000 a1 80  SEQUENCE IMPLICIT { --- Start of Accounting Data File ----
00000002 04 0b  73 77 69 74 63 68 2d 31 32
00000015 04 13  41 63 63 6f 75 6e 74 69 6e 67
00000036 04 08  07 cc 07 14 10 05 00 00
00000046 30 82  SEQUENCE OF { SelectionEntry
00000048 30 82    SEQUENCE {Read Selection Entry of 18 bytes

00000052 06 16      subtree    2b 06 01 04 01 09 0a 12 01 01
00000063 04 16      list       {1, 2, 3, 4, 5, 6, 7, 8, 9, 10, 11, 12, 13, 14, 15,
17, 19, 20, 21, 22, 23, 24, 25, 26, 27, 28, 29, 30,}
00000069 30 80    SEQUENCE OF { Start of Records

00000073 30 82    SEQUENCE OF {  ------Record #0 ------------
00000079 30 82      SEQUENCE {  Read Record tuple of 146 bytes
00000084 02 01        INTEGER    3
00000087 02 01        INTEGER    1
00000089 04 01        STRING     41 54 30 2f 30 2f 31
00000091 04 01        STRING
00000094 02 01        INTEGER    0
00000097 02 01        INTEGER    78
00000099 04 01        STRING
00000101 04 01        STRING     47 00 91 81 00 00 00 00 60 83 c4 2c 01 00 60 70 fa
38 23 00
00000107 02 01        INTEGER    8389197
00000109 04 01        STRING     07 cc 07 14 10 2e 04 01
00000111 04 01        STRING     07 cc 07 14 10 2e 04 01
00000114 02 01        INTEGER    1
00000117 02 01        INTEGER    16
00000120 02 01        INTEGER    6
00000123 06 01        COUNTER64  0 0
00000126 06 01        COUNTER64  0 0
00000128 06 01        OBJ ID     2b 06 01 02 01 25 01 01 02
00000134 02 01        INTEGER    16777215
00000137 02 01        INTEGER    -1
00000140 02 01        INTEGER    -1
00000143 02 01        INTEGER    0
00000146 02 01        INTEGER    0
00000148 06 01        OBJ ID     2b 06 01 02 01 25 01 01 02
00000154 02 01        INTEGER    16777215
00000157 02 01        INTEGER    -1
00000160 02 01        INTEGER    -1
00000163 02 01        INTEGER    0
00000166 02 01        INTEGER    0
00000168 30 82      SEQUENCE OF {  ------Record #1 ------------
 .
 .
 .
```

The records then repeat, each record being a subsequent sample of the list of objects from the ATM-ACCOUNTING-MIB. A plain-English decode of the hex decode from Example B-1 is shown in Example B-2:

Example B-2 *English translation of sample hex decode shown in Example B-1.*

```
SysName = switch-12
Description = Accounting
Start time = 1996 July 20 16:05:00

Sub tree = 1.3.6.1.4.1.9.10.18.1.1 (atmAcctngDataObjects)

List:

1          atmAcctngConnectionType
2          atmAcctngCastType
3          atmAcctngIfName
4          atmAcctngIfAlias
5          atmAcctngVpi
6          atmAcctngVci
7          atmAcctngCallingParty
8          atmAcctngCalledParty
9          atmAcctngCallReference
10         atmAcctngStartTime
11         atmAcctngCollectionTime
12         atmAcctngCollectMode
13         atmAcctngReleaseCause
14         atmAcctngServiceCategory
15         atmAcctngTransmittedCells
17         atmAcctngReceivedCells
19         atmAcctngTransmitTrafficDescriptorType
20         atmAcctngTransmitTrafficDescriptorParam1
21         atmAcctngTransmitTrafficDescriptorParam2
22         atmAcctngTransmitTrafficDescriptorParam3
23         atmAcctngTransmitTrafficDescriptorParam4
24         atmAcctngTransmitTrafficDescriptorParam5
25         atmAcctngReceiveTrafficDescriptorType
26         atmAcctngReceiveTrafficDescriptorParam1
27         atmAcctngReceiveTrafficDescriptorParam2
28         atmAcctngReceiveTrafficDescriptorParam3
29         atmAcctngReceiveTrafficDescriptorParam4
atmAcctngReceiveTrafficDescriptorParam5

Record #0

svcIncoming(3)
point-to-point(1)
ifName = AT0/0/1
ifAlias =
VPI = 0
VCI = 78
Calling Party =
```

Example B-2 *English translation of sample hex decode shown in Example B-1.*

```
Called Party = 47.0091.8100.0000.0060.83c4.2c01.0060.70fa.3823
Call Reference = 8389197
Start Time = 1996 May 15 10:26:04.1
Collection Time = 1996 May 15 10:26:04.1
Collect Mode = onRelease
Release Cause = 16
Service Category = ubr
Transmitted Cells = 00
Received Cells = 00
Transmitted Traffic Descriptor Type = No CLP, No Sustained Cell Rate (atmNoClpNoScr)
Parameter 1 = 16777215 (CLP=0+1 peak cell rate in cells per second)
Parameter 2 = not used
Parameter 3 = not used
Parameter 4 = not used
Parameter 5 = not used
Received Traffic Descriptor Type = No CLP, No Sustained Cell Rate (atmNoClpNoScr)
Parameter 1 = 16777215 (CLP=0+1 peak cell rate in cells per second)
Parameter 2 = not used
Parameter 3 = not used
Parameter 4 = not used
Parameter 5 = not used
```

The rest of the records can be decoded, as shown in Examples B-2, using the same method as the first record.

As you see, it is not a simple task to turn the ATM accounting files into useful data. But the amount of data generated requires mechanisms different than simple SNMP polling. If you need billing information, however, ATM Accounting is a good mechanism to gather that data.

INDEX

Numerics

5-4-3 rule, 354
10Base2 Ethernet, 355
10Base5 Ethernet, 355
10BaseFL Ethernet, 355
10BaseFX Ethernet, 355
10BaseT Ethernet, 355
10BaseTX Ethernet, 355
64-bit counters
    SNMPv2c, 176
    wrap time, 344
64-bit object types, 192
800E messages, 263
802.1q trunking protocol, 393
7x00 series routers, backplane bus architecture, 230
7200 series routers, temperature thresholds, 270
75xx series routers, thresholds
    temperature, 269–270
    voltage, 269
8500MSR (ATM switch), decoding ATM accounting
    files, 529–533

A

AAL (ATM Adaptation Layer), 370
AAL5, octet counts, 373
ABR (available bit rate), ATM RMON
    collection, 381
absolute continuous thresholds, 93
    configuring on enumerated variables, 103
    discrete data sources, 93
abstraction, policy-based management, 33
access lists (SNMP), configuring, 479
access method, Ethernet, 353
accounting, ATM, 379–380
accuracy
    measuring, 81–82
    monitoring, 55
acknowledgements, SNMP informs, 114
active correlation, 124
    utilities, 216

active polling, 348
    comparing to passive polling, 67
    disadvantages, 66
active VLANs, displaying, 399
addressing
    name services, 197–198
    standardization, 21
administrative states, dormant interfaces, 348
agent-based thresholds, 101
agents (SNMP)
    clearing counters, 191
    informs, 188
    SNMPv1, 174
aggregation, 67–68, 149
    data reduction, 148
    interface data, 210
agreements, SLAs, 40–42
Alarm status (Catalyst switches), 236
alarms
    configuring, 103
    RMON, 115
        thresholds, configuring, 483
    switch chassis, 264–265
aliases, 198
    returning on interfaces, 346
Alignment Errors, 361
"all" keyword, 276
analog modem calls, 434
analyzing
    collected data, correlated predictive reports,
        71–72
    events, 91
    reload crashes, 327
    response time
        case study, 162
        performance, 158–161
    snapshots, 38–39
    switch health
        CLI commands, 328, 330–331
        SNMP traps, 331
        syslog messages, 332
        system resources, 332–333
applications
    availability, 138
    CDP discovery, 23
    event monitoring, 105

D

E

F

Q

R

T

U

CCIE Professional Development

Cisco LAN Switching
Kennedy Clark, CCIE; Kevin Hamilton, CCIE

1-57870-094-9 • AVAILABLE NOW

This volume provides an in-depth analysis of Cisco LAN switching technologies, architectures, and deployments, including unique coverage of Catalyst network design essentials. Network designs and configuration examples are incorporated throughout to demonstrate the principles and enable easy translation of the material into practice in production networks.

Advanced IP Network Design
Alvaro Retana, CCIE; Don Slice, CCIE; and Russ White, CCIE

1-57870-097-3 • AVAILABLE NOW

Network engineers and managers can use these case studies, which highlight various network design goals, to explore issues including protocol choice, network stability, and growth. This book also includes theoretical discussion on advanced design topics.

Large-Scale IP Network Solutions
Khalid Raza, CCIE; and Mark Turner

1-57870-084-1 • AVAILABLE NOW

Network engineers can find solutions as their IP networks grow in size and complexity. Examine all the major IP protocols in-depth and learn about scalability, migration planning, network management, and security for large-scale networks.

Routing TCP/IP, Volume I
Jeff Doyle, CCIE

1-57870-041-8 • AVAILABLE NOW

This book takes the reader from a basic understanding of routers and routing protocols through a detailed examination of each of the IP interior routing protocols. Learn techniques for designing networks that maximize the efficiency of the protocol being used. Exercises and review questions provide core study for the CCIE Routing and Switching exam.

www.ciscopress.com

Cisco Career Certifications

Cisco CCNA Exam #640-507 Certification Guide
Wendell Odom, CCIE

0-7357-0971-8 • AVAILABLE NOW

Although it's only the first step in Cisco Career Certification, the Cisco Certified Network Associate (CCNA) exam is a difficult test. Your first attempt at becoming Cisco certified requires a lot of study and confidence in your networking knowledge. When you're ready to test your skills, complete your knowledge of the exam topics, and prepare for exam day, you need the preparation tools found in *Cisco CCNA Exam #640-507 Certification Guide* from Cisco Press.

CCDA Exam Certification Guide
Anthony Bruno, CCIE & Jacqueline Kim

0-7357-0074-5 • AVAILABLE NOW

CCDA Exam Certification Guide is a comprehensive study tool for DCN Exam #640-441. Written by a CCIE and a CCDA, and reviewed by Cisco technical experts, *CCDA Exam Certification Guide* will help you understand and master the exam objectives. In this solid review on the design areas of the DCN exam, you'll learn to design a network that meets a customer's requirements for performance, security, capacity, and scalability.

Interconnecting Cisco Network Devices
Edited by Steve McQuerry

1-57870-111-2 • AVAILABLE NOW

Based on the Cisco course taught worldwide, *Interconnecting Cisco Network Devices* teaches you how to configure Cisco switches and routers in multi-protocol internetworks. ICND is the primary course recommended by Cisco Systems for CCNA #640-507 preparation. If you are pursuing CCNA certification, this book is an excellent starting point for your study.

Designing Cisco Networks
Edited by Diane Teare

1-57870-105-8 • AVAILABLE NOW

Based on the Cisco Systems instructor-led and self-study course available worldwide, *Designing Cisco Networks* will help you understand how to analyze and solve existing network problems while building a framework that supports the functionality, performance, and scalability required from any given environment. Self-assessment through exercises and chapter-ending tests starts you down the path for attaining your CCDA certification.

CISCO SYSTEMS

CISCO PRESS

Cisco Press Solutions

Enhanced IP Services for Cisco Networks
Donald C. Lee, CCIE

1-57870-106-6 • AVAILABLE NOW

This is a guide to improving your network's capabilities by understanding
the new enabling and advanced Cisco IOS services that build more scalable,
intelligent, and secure networks. Learn the technical details necessary to deploy
Quality of Service, VPN technologies, IPsec, the IOS firewall and IOS Intrusion
Detection. These services will allow you to extend the network to new frontiers
securely, protect your network from attacks, and increase the sophistication of
network services.

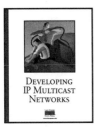

Developing IP Multicast Networks, Volume I
Beau Williamson, CCIE

1-57870-077-9 • AVAILABLE NOW

This book provides a solid foundation of IP multicast concepts and explains
how to design and deploy the networks that will support appplications such as
audio and video conferencing, distance-learning, and data replication. Includes
an in-depth discussion of the PIM protocol used in Cisco routers and detailed
coverage of the rules that control the creation and maintenance of Cisco mroute
state entries.

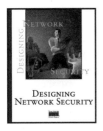

Designing Network Security
Merike Kaeo

1-57870-043-4 • AVAILABLE NOW

Designing Network Security is a practical guide designed to help you
understand the fundamentals of securing your corporate infrastructure. This
book takes a comprehensive look at underlying security technologies, the
process of creating a security policy, and the practical requirements necessary to
implement a corporate security policy.

www.ciscopress.com

Cisco Press Solutions

EIGRP Network Design Solutions
Ivan Pepelnjak, CCIE

1-57870-165-1 • AVAILABLE NOW

EIGRP Network Design Solutions uses case studies and real-world configuration examples to help you gain an in-depth understanding of the issues involved in designing, deploying, and managing EIGRP-based networks. This book details proper designs that can be used to build large and scalable EIGRP-based networks and documents possible ways each EIGRP feature can be used in network design, implmentation, troubleshooting, and monitoring.

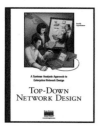

Top-Down Network Design
Priscilla Oppenheimer

1-57870-069-8 • AVAILABLE NOW

Building reliable, secure, and manageable networks is every network professional's goal. This practical guide teaches you a systematic method for network design that can be applied to campus LANs, remote-access networks, WAN links, and large-scale internetworks. Learn how to analyze business and technical requirements, examine traffic flow and Quality of Service requirements, and select protocols and technologies based on performance goals.

Cisco IOS Releases: The Complete Reference
Mack M. Coulibaly

1-57870-179-1 • AVAILABLE NOW

Cisco IOS Releases: The Complete Reference is the first comprehensive guide to the more than three dozen types of Cisco IOS releases being used today on enterprise and service provider networks. It details the release process and its numbering and naming conventions, as well as when, where, and how to use the various releases. A complete map of Cisco IOS software releases and their relationships to one another, in addition to insights into decoding information contained within the software, make this book an indispensable resource for any network professional.

CISCO SYSTEMS

CISCO PRESS

www.ciscopress.com

Cisco Press Solutions

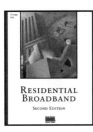

Residential Broadband, Second Edition

George Abe

1-57870-177-5 • **AVAILABLE NOW**

This book will answer basic questions of residential broadband networks such as: Why do we need high speed networks at home? How will high speed residential services be delivered to the home? How do regulatory or commercial factors affect this technology? Explore such networking topics as xDSL, cable, and wireless.

Internetworking Technologies Handbook, Second Edition

Kevin Downes, CCIE, Merilee Ford, H. Kim Lew, Steve Spanier, Tim Stevenson

1-57870-102-3 • **AVAILABLE NOW**

This comprehensive reference provides a foundation for understanding and implementing contemporary internetworking technologies, providing you with the necessary information needed to make rational networking decisions. Master terms, concepts, technologies, and devices that are used in the internetworking industry today. You also learn how to incorporate networking technologies into a LAN/WAN environment, as well as how to apply the OSI reference model to categorize protocols, technologies, and devices.

OpenCable Architecture

Michael Adams

1-57870-135-X • **AVAILABLE NOW**

Whether you're a television, data communications, or telecommunications professional, or simply an interested business person, this book will help you understand the technical and business issues surrounding interactive television services. It will also provide you with an inside look at the combined efforts of the cable, data, and consumer electronics industries' efforts to develop those new services.

Cisco Press Fundamentals

IP Routing Primer

Robert Wright, CCIE

1-57870-108-2 • **AVAILABLE NOW**

Learn how IP routing behaves in a Cisco router environment. In addition to teaching the core fundamentals, this book enhances your ability to troubleshoot IP routing problems yourself, often eliminating the need to call for additional technical support. The information is presented in an approachable, workbook-type format with dozens of detailed illustrations and real-life scenarios integrated throughout.

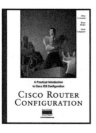

Cisco Router Configuration

Allan Leinwand, Bruce Pinsky, Mark Culpepper

1-57870-022-1 • **AVAILABLE NOW**

An example-oriented and chronological approach helps you implement and administer your internetworking devices. Starting with the configuration devices "out of the box;" this book moves to configuring Cisco IOS for the three most popular networking protocols today: TCP/IP, AppleTalk, and Novell Interwork Packet Exchange (IPX). You also learn basic administrative and management configuration, including access control with TACACS+ and RADIUS, network management with SNMP, logging of messages, and time control with NTP.

IP Routing Fundamentals

Mark A. Sportack

1-57870-071-x • **AVAILABLE NOW**

This comprehensive guide provides essential background information on routing in IP networks for network professionals who are deploying and maintaining LANs and WANs daily. Explore the mechanics of routers, routing protocols, network interfaces, and operating systems.

Cisco Press Fundamentals

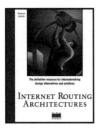